The Papers of
George Washington

The Papers of
George Washington

Dorothy Twohig, *Editor*

Philander D. Chase, *Senior Associate Editor*

Beverly H. Runge, *Associate Editor*

Frank E. Grizzard, Jr., Edward G. Lengel, and
Mark A. Mastromarino, *Assistant Editors*

W. W. Abbot, *Editor Emeritus*

Retirement Series

4

April–December 1799

W. W. Abbot, *Editor*

UNIVERSITY PRESS OF VIRGINIA

CHARLOTTESVILLE AND LONDON

This edition has been prepared by the staff of
The Papers of George Washington
sponsored by
The Mount Vernon Ladies' Association of the Union
and the University of Virginia
with the support of
the National Endowment for the Humanities,
and the National Historical Publications and
Records Commission.
The preparation of this volume has been made possible by a grant from the
Norman and Lyn Lear Foundation and the National Trust
for the Humanities.
The publication of this volume has been supported by a grant from
the National Historical Publications and Records Commission.

THE UNIVERSITY PRESS OF VIRGINIA

First published 1999

Library of Congress Cataloging-in-Publication Data
Washington, George 1732–1799.
    The papers of George Washington. Retirement series / Dorothy
Twohig, editor ; Philander D. Chase, senior associate editor ;
Beverly H. Runge, associate editor ; Frank E. Grizzard, Jr. . . . [et
al.], assistant editors.
        p.   cm.
    Includes index.
    Contents: 1. March–December 1797. . . . 4. April–December 1799.
    1. Washington, George, 1732–1799—Archives.   2. Presidents—United
States—Archives.   3. United States—Politics and
government—1797–1801—Sources.   I. Twohig, Dorothy.   II. Title.
E312.72 1998
973.3'092—dc21
ISBN 0-8139-1737-9 (v. 1 : alk. paper)   97-6770
ISBN 0-8139-1855-3 (v. 4 : alk. paper)   CIP

Contents

NOTE: Volume numbers refer to the *Retirement Series*.

Contents

Illustrations

Editorial Apparatus

Transcription of the documents in the volumes of *The Papers of George Washington* has remained as close to a literal reproduction of the manuscript as possible. Punctuation, capitalization, paragraphing, and spelling of all words are retained as they appear in the original document. Dashes used as punctuation have been retained except when a period and a dash appear together at the end of a sentence. The appropriate marks of punctuation have always been added at the end of a paragraph. Errors in spelling of proper names and geographic locations have been corrected in brackets or in annotation only if the spelling in the text makes the word incomprehensible. When a tilde is used in the manuscript to indicate a double letter, the letter has been silently doubled. Washington and some of his correspondents occasionally used a tilde above an incorrectly spelled word to indicate an error in orthography. When this device is used the editors have silently corrected the word. In cases where a tilde has been inserted above an abbreviation or contraction, usually in letter-book copies, the word has been expanded. Otherwise, contractions and abbreviations have been retained as written and a period has been inserted after an abbreviation. When an apostrophe has been used in a contraction it is retained. Superscripts have been lowered and if the word is an abbreviation a period has been added. If the meaning of an abbreviation or contraction is not obvious, it has been expanded in square brackets: "H[is] M[ajest]y." Editorial insertions or corrections in the text also appear in square brackets. Angle brackets ⟨ ⟩ are used to indicate illegible or mutilated material. A space left blank in a manuscript by the writer is indicated by a square-bracketed gap in the text [ ]. Deletions from manuscripts are not indicated. If a deletion contains substantive material, it appears in a footnote. If the intended location of marginal notations is clear from the text, they are inserted without comment; otherwise they are recorded in the footnotes. The ampersand has been retained and the thorn transcribed as "th." The symbol for per (⅌) is used when it appears in the manuscript. The dateline has been placed at the head of a document regardless of where it occurred in the manuscript.

Since GW read no language other than English, incoming letters written to him in foreign languages were generally translated for his information. Where this contemporary translation has survived, it has been used as the text of the document, and the original version has been included in the CD-ROM edition of the Washington Papers. If there is no contemporary translation, the document in its original language has been used as the text. All of the documents printed in this volume, as well as the routine documents omitted from it and various ancillary materials, may be found in the CD-ROM edition of the papers.

Symbols Designating Documents

AD	Autograph Document
ADS	Autograph Document Signed
ADf	Autograph Draft
ADfS	Autograph Draft Signed
AL	Autograph Letter
ALS	Autograph Letter Signed
D	Document
DS	Document Signed
Df	Draft
DfS	Draft Signed
L	Letter
LS	Letter Signed
LB	Letter-Book Copy
[S]	Used with other symbols to indicate that the signature on the document has been cropped or clipped.

Repository Symbols and Abbreviations

CD-ROM:GW	*see* Editorial Apparatus
CSmH	Henry E. Huntington Library, San Marino, Calif.
CSt	Stanford University, Palo Alto, Calif.
CtHi	Connecticut Historical Society, Hartford
CtWetCD	National Society of the Colonial Dames of America of Connecticut, Wethersfield
CtY	Yale University, New Haven
DGU	Georgetown University, Washington, D.C.
DLC	Library of Congress
DLC:GW	George Washington Papers, Library of Congress
DNA	National Archives
DSoCi	Society of the Cincinnati, Washington, D.C.
Ia-HA	Iowa State Department of History and Archives, Des Moines
ICHi	Chicago Historical Society
KEL	Dwight D. Eisenhower Library, Abilene, Kansas
MBOS	Old South Association, Boston
MdAA	Maryland State Archives, Annapolis

MHi	Massachusetts Historical Society, Boston
MiU-C	William L. Clements Library, University of Michigan, Ann Arbor
MoSM	Mercantile Library Association, St. Louis
MoSW	Washington University, St. Louis
MWA	American Antiquarian Society, Worcester, Mass.
NAlI	Albany Institute of History and Art
NhD	Dartmouth College, Hanover, N.H.
NHi	New-York Historical Society, New York
NIC	Cornell University, Ithaca, N.Y.
NjMoNP	Washington Headquarters Library, Morristown, N.J.
NjP	Princeton University, Princeton, N.J.
NjSu	Free Public Library, Summit, N.J.
NN	New York Public Library, New York
NNGL	Gilder Lehrman Collection at the Pierpont Morgan Library, New York
NNPM	Pierpont Morgan Library, New York
NNS	New York Society Library, New York
PHi	Historical Society of Pennsylvania, Philadelphia
PPOCC	Old Christ Church Preservation Trust, Philadelphia
PPRF	Rosenbach Foundation, Philadelphia
PU	University of Pennsylvania, Philadelphia
PWacD	David Library of the American Revolution, Washington Crossing, Pa.
RG	Record Group (designating the location of documents in the National Archives)
RPJCB	John Carter Brown Library, Providence
ScU	University of South Carolina, Columbia
Vi	Library of Virginia, Richmond
ViAlL	Alexandria-Washington Lodge no. 22 A.F. & A.M, Alexandria, Va.
ViFaCt	Fairfax County Courthouse, Fairfax, Va.
ViHi	Virginia Historical Society, Richmond
ViMtV	Mount Vernon Ladies' Association of the Union
ViU	University of Virginia, Charlottesville
Wv-Ar	West Virginia Department of Archives and History, Charleston

Short Title List

Adams, *Works of John Adams.*   Charles Francis Adams, ed. *The Works of John Adams, Second President of the United States: With a Life of the Author, Notes, and Illustrations.* 10 vols. Boston, 1850–56.

ASP. Walter Lowrie et al., eds. *American State Papers: Documents, Legislative and Executive, of the Congress of the United States.* 38 vols. Washington, D.C., 1832–61.

Brighton, *Checkered Career of Tobias Lear.* Ray Brighton. *The Checkered Career of Tobias Lear.* Portsmouth, N.H., 1985.

Brown, *Dismal Swamp Canal.* Alexander C. Brown. *The Dismal Swamp Canal.* Hilton Village, Va., 1946.

Calendar of Virginia State Papers. William P. Palmer et al., eds. *Calendar of Virginia State Papers and Other Manuscripts.* 11 vols. Richmond, 1875–93.

Carroll, *Library at Mount Vernon.* Frances L. Carroll and Mary Meacham. *The Library at Mount Vernon.* Pittsburgh, 1977.

Chernow, *Robert Morris.* Barbara Ann Chernow. *Robert Morris: Land Speculator, 1790–1801.* New York, 1978.

Columbia Hist. Soc. Recs. *Records of the Columbia Historical Society*, Washington, D.C.

Cook, *Washington's Western Lands.* Roy Bird Cook. *Washington's Western Lands.* Strasburg, Va., 1930.

Crozier, *Virginia County Records.* William Armstrong Crozier, ed. *Virginia County Records: Spotsylvania County, 1721–1800.* Vol. 1. New York, 1905.

Cullen, *Marshall Papers.* Charles T. Cullen et al., eds. *The Papers of John Marshall.* Vol. 4. Chapel Hill, N.C., 1984.

Custis, *Recollections.* George Washington Parke Custis. *Recollections and Private Memoirs of Washington.* New York, 1860.

Day Book. Manuscript Cash Memorandum Book, 1 Sept. 1797–20 Feb. 1799, in John Carter Brown Library, Providence, R.I.

Diaries. Donald Jackson and Dorothy Twohig, eds. *The Diaries of George Washington.* 6 vols. Charlottesville, Va., 1976–79.

Fields, *Papers of Martha Washington.* Joseph E. Fields, comp. *"Worthy Partner": The Papers of Martha Washington.* Westport, Conn., 1994.

Fitzpatrick, *Last Will and Testament of George Washington.* John C. Fitzpatrick, ed. *The Last Will and Testament of George Washington and Schedule of His Property.* N.p., 1960.

Fitzpatrick, *Writings.* John C. Fitzpatrick, ed. *The Writings of George Washington from the Original Manuscript Sources, 1745–1799.* 39 vols. Washington, D.C., 1931–44.

Ford, "Murray-Adams Letters." Worthington Chauncey Ford, ed. "Letters of William Vans Murray to John Quincy Adams, 1797–1803." *Annual Report of the American Historical Association for the Year 1912* (Washington, D.C., 1914): 341–708.

Ford, *Writings of Washington.* Worthington Chauncey Ford, ed. *The Writings of George Washington.* 14 vols. New York, 1889–93.

Fothergill, *Wills of Westmoreland County.* Augusta B. Fothergill. *Wills of*

Westmoreland County, Virginia, 1654–1800. Richmond, 1925. Reprint ed. Baltimore, 1973.

Griffin, *Boston Athenæum Washington Collection*.   Appleton P. C. Griffin, comp. *A Catalogue of the Washington Collection in the Boston Athenæum*. Cambridge, Mass., 1897.

Harris, *Thornton Papers*.   C. M. Harris, ed. *Papers of William Thornton*. 1 vol. to date. Charlottesville, Va., 1995—.

Haw, *John and Edward Rutledge*.   James Haw. *John and Edward Rutledge of South Carolina*. Athens, Ga., 1997.

Hening.   William Waller Hening, ed. *The Statutes at Large: Being a Collection of All the Laws of Virginia from the First Session of the Legislature in the Year 1619*. 13 vols. 1819–23. Reprint. Charlottesville, Va., 1969.

Henry, *Patrick Henry*.   William Wirt Henry, ed. *Patrick Henry: Life, Correspondence, and Speeches*. 3 vols. New York, 1891.

Hill, *William Vans Murray*.   Peter P. Hill. *William Vans Murray, Federalist Diplomat: The Shaping of Peace with France, 1797–1801*. Syracuse, N.Y., 1971.

Holcomb, *Norfolk Naval Hospital*.   Richard C. Holcomb. *A Century with Norfolk Naval Hospital, 1830–1930*. Portsmouth, Va., 1930.

King, *Fairfax Wills and Inventories*.   J. Estelle Stewart King. *Abstracts of Wills and Inventories, Fairfax County, Virginia, 1742–1801*. Baltimore, 1978.

King, *Life and Correspondence of King*.   Charles R. King, ed. *The Life and Correspondence of Rufus King*. 6 vols. New York, 1894–1900.

Laws of Maryland.   *Laws of Maryland: Made and Passed at a Session of Assembly, Begun and Held at the City of Annapolis, on Monday, the Fifth of November, in the Year of Our Lord One Thousand Seven Hundred and Ninety-Eight*. Annapolis, 1799.

Ledger A.   Manuscript ledger in the George Washington Papers, Library of Congress.

Ledger B.   Manuscript ledger in the George Washington Papers, Library of Congress.

Ledger C.   Manuscript ledger in Morristown National Historical Park, Morristown, N.J.

Mattern, *Madison Papers*.   David B. Mattern et al., eds. *The Papers of James Madison*. Vol. 17. Charlottesville, Va., and London, 1991.

Mitchell, *Fairfax County Patents and Grants*.   Beth Mitchell. *Beginning at a White Oak: Patents and Northern Neck Grants of Fairfax County Virginia*. Fairfax, Va., 1977.

Mount Vernon Ledger, 1797–98.   Manuscript ledger owned by Morristown National Historical Park, Morristown, N.J.

Mount Vernon Ledger, 1799–1800.   Manuscript ledger owned by Mount Vernon Ladies' Association of the Union.

Munson, *Alexandria Hustings Court Deeds, 1797–1801*.   James D.

Munson, comp. *Alexandria Virginia: Alexandria Hustings Court Deeds, 1797–1801.* Bowie, Md., 1991.

Pa. Mag. *Pennsylvania Magazine of History and Biography.*

Papers, Colonial Series. W. W. Abbot et al., eds. *The Papers of George Washington, Colonial Series.* 10 vols. Charlottesville, Va., 1983–95.

Papers, Confederation Series. W. W. Abbot et al., eds. *The Papers of George Washington, Confederation Series.* 6 vols. Charlottesville, Va., 1992–97.

Papers, Presidential Series. W. W. Abbot et al., eds. *The Papers of George Washington, Presidential Series.* 8 vols. to date. Charlottesville, Va., 1987—.

Papers, Retirement Series. W. W. Abbot et al., eds. *The Papers of George Washington, Retirement Series.* 4 vols. Charlottesville, Va., 1998–99.

Pinkney, *Christopher Gore.* Helen R. Pinkney. *Christopher Gore: Federalist of Massachusetts, 1758–1827.* Waltham, Mass., 1969.

Powell, *Old Alexandria.* Mary G. Powell. *The History of Old Alexandria, Virginia.* Richmond, 1928.

Prussing, *Estate of George Washington.* Eugene E. Prussing. *The Estate of George Washington, Deceased.* Boston, 1927.

Seilhamer, *American Theatre.* George O. Seilhamer. *History of the American Theatre.* 3 vols. Philadelphia, 1888–91.

Smith, *Freedom's Fetters.* James Morton Smith. *Freedom's Fetters: The Alien and Sedition Laws and American Civil Liberties.* Ithaca, N.Y., 1956.

Sparks, *Writings of Washington.* Jared Sparks, ed. *The Writings of George Washington.* 12 vols. Boston, 1834–37.

Stinchcombe and Cullen, *Marshall Papers.* William C. Stinchcombe, Charles T. Cullen et al., eds. *The Papers of John Marshall.* Vol. 3. Chapel Hill, N.C., 1979.

Syrett, *Hamilton Papers.* Harold C. Syrett et al., eds. *The Papers of Alexander Hamilton.* 27 vols. New York, 1961–87.

Tansill, *U.S. and Santo Domingo.* Charles C. Tansill. *The United States and Santo Domingo, 1798–1873.* Baltimore, 1938.

Tinkcom, *Republicans and Federalists in Pennsylvania.* Harry Marlin Tinkcom. *The Republicans and Federalists in Pennsylvania, 1790–1801.* Harrisburg, Pa., 1950.

Zahniser, *Pinckney.* Marvin R. Zahniser. *Charles Cotesworth Pinckney, Founding Father.* Chapel Hill, N.C., 1967.

The Papers of George Washington
Retirement Series
Volume 4
April–December 1799

From Charles Cotesworth Pinckney

Mulberry Grove on Savannah River [Ga.]
april 20th 1799

Many thanks my dear Sr for your favour of the 31st ultimo, the excellent advice it contains relative to the enforcement of discipline, I shall most assiduously attend to; every word of it shall be engraved on my Memory & it shall be the rule of my conduct.

I am much obliged to you for complying with my request in pointing out an Aid, and I very chearfully accede to the conditions on which you have mentioned Captn Presley Thornton. I shall always feel pleasure in the advancement of every Gentleman of my Family deserving of it. I will trespass on you as I do not know his address to forward the enclosed Letter to him after perusal.[1]

I am happy to find you will give me leave to lay before you from time to time the situation of our military affairs under my care, and with that view I enclose you copies of my three last letters to the Secretary at War, and I shall in future as I transmitt the originals to him, furnish you with copies, without they should be of a trivial nature[2]—The copy of the arrangement for North Carolina I cannot transmitt till I return to Charleston; the one for South Carolina cannot be completed till this State is arranged, and that cannot be done till we are in the upper Country, for we can receive no information of Characters here that we can satisfactorily rely upon. Tomorrow we proceed to the Oconoee, and of our transactions there you shall be duly informed.[3]

To the many obligations you have already conferred upon me, let me request you to add another which is to inform me when you think I have committed, or am about to committ an error, I request this favour with more confidence, as I am assured you are interested in the reputation of your old pupil.

Pray present my best respects to Mrs Washington. I enclose a few more water melon seed they may still be in time for a late Crop. My sincere congratulations attend Mr & Mrs Lewis, may their union be long & their happiness unclouded. But—I do not like this resignation of the army Commission; Matrimony must be a great alterer of sentiment, for I am confident Miss Custis loved a Soldier.

With respectful Compliments to Coll Lear & Mr Custis, I remain with the most grateful regard & esteem Your affectionate & devoted friend & sert

Charles Cotesworth Pinckney

I will immediately forward your Letter to my Brother relative to the Jacks.[4]

ALS, DLC:GW.

1. It was in his second letter to Pinckney of 31 Mar. that GW gave his advice about discipline and also recommended Presly Thornton as an aide-de-camp for Pinckney. Pinckney's letter to Thornton has not been found, but on 5 June GW wrote Pinckney that he had delivered it "with my own hands." On 25 June Pinckney wrote that he had put Thornton "in orders" but "would not have him move Southwardly at present." In September Thornton was still in Fredericksburg, Va., recruiting troops, with little success (see Thornton to GW, 16 Sept. 1799).

2. Pinckney's enclosures in this letter included copies of his letters to Secretary of War James McHenry of 19 and 20 April from Mulberry Grove near Savannah, reporting on his inspection of the coast and its defenses from Charleston to St. Mary's River between Georgia and Florida. Pinckney also sent an extract of his letter of 12 Mar. to McHenry and copies of various orders that he had recently issued.

3. Pinckney wrote GW on 4 June enclosing his letter to McHenry of 19 May reporting from Augusta on his inspection of Fort Wilkinson on the Oconee River on the Georgia frontier.

4. For reference to GW's letter to Thomas Pinckney, see GW to Charles Cotesworth Pinckney, 31 Mar. 1799 (first letter), and GW to William Washington, 31 Mar. 1799, n.2.

Martha Washington to Mary Stead Pinckney

My dear Madam,   Mount Vernon 20th April 1799

I have received with grateful sensibility, your obliging favours of the 16th & 28th of last month; and thank you for the Mellon seeds which you had the goodness to send me & which came safe, & very oppertunely.

It gave me, and all our family much pleasure to hear of your safe arrival, & happy meeting with your friends, in Charleston, after so long & tiresome a journey as you performed in the depth of Winter. In the weather, however, except the few first days of January, you were much favoured; as it was remarkably fine for the Season here. We had only to regret the shortness of your stay at Mount Vernon, a place at which we shall always be gratified in seeing General Pinckney yourself or any of the family; to which let me add a hope, if his Military duties should call him to the State of Virginia, that you will always consider[1] as your head quarters during your abidance in it.

Long 'ere this, I hope the General is safely returned from his

Military Excursion to Georgia, and no one can unite more heartily with you than I do in wishing that the newly proposed Negociation may arrest more serious movements; but from a faithless Nation, whose injustice & ambition know no bounds short of its power to accomplish them little is expected from this Negociation (if the proposi[ti]on should be acceded to ⟨at all⟩ by Tr⟨eaty⟩ by those who wish for a permanent Treaty—Arrogance, or deception, as is best calculated to promote the views of the Directory seem to be the only Rule of the French Government at present—of course nothing ⟨is⟩ to be expected from their domineering spirit when uncontrouled by events—as too many unhappy Nations of Europe and recently, the poor Italians have experienced to the entire annihilation of their Government.

By the first fit conveyance, I will with pleasure send you the Profiles of the General & myself, & feel the compliment of their being asked. They could not go by the Post without folding, & consequent injury or they would have accompanied this letter—a small one however, of his, is herewith enclosed requesting your acceptance of it.[2]

The General's birth day (22d of Feby) united the fortunes of Mr Lewis (who you saw here) and Nelly Custis. They are at present, & have been for sometime, at her Mothers or she would most cordially have united with the General & me in reciprocating all the good wishes of yourself & Miss[3] Eliza, & would rejoice to hear of the happiness of her friend Mrs Harriot Rutledge. With sentiments of perfect esteem & regard I am, my dear Madam, Your Most Obedient Hble Ser.

M: W——n.

Df, in GW's hand, DLC:GW.

1. GW or someone else inadvertently crossed out the words "this place" here.

2. The silhouettes may have been cut by Nelly Custis Lewis. The Mount Vernon Ladies' Association owns a silhouette of Martha Washington cut by Nelly Custis in 1796 which was presented to Gov. and Mrs. Thomas Johnson of Maryland.

3. GW wrote "Mrs" above "Miss" but did not strike out "Miss."

To Clement Biddle

Dear Sir,   Mount Vernon 21st April 1799

Your letters of the 21st of March and 11th instant are both before me.

By the first, it appears that you had shipped by Captn Hand for Alexandria, on my a/c, 12 lbs. of white Clover Seed and the like quantity of Lucerne; but none has been delivered by him at the Custom house, or elsewhere that I can discover, which is a considerable disappointment to me; for depending thereon I enquired for no other; and now, the season for sowing them is too far advanced to go in pursuit of any, elsewhere.

I am obliged to you for Shipping, by Ellwood, the Packages deposited at the Custom Ho. in Phila. for me. I presume they were recd there from the George Barclay from the East Indies, if so, they contain Seeds & exotics from that Country—and ought now, to be in the ground.[1] With esteem & regard—I am Dr Sir Your Obedt

Go: Washington

What are the present prices of Flour and Wheat in Philadelphia?

ALS, PHi: Washington-Biddle Correspondence; ALS (letterpress copy), DLC:GW.
  1. See Thomas Law to GW, c.25 April, and notes.

From Caleb Gibbs

Dear Sir   Boston 21th April 1799

Having observed a List of appointments in which my name was not inserted has filled me with disquiting apprehensions lest for some reason or other it may be entirely omitted.

Although it was the opinion of some of my friends that I might have rested securely on the honorable testimonials of services during the late war from yourself and other respectable characters which were transmitted [to] the Secretary of War, yet in a matter of so much moment I Judged it expedient to repair to Philadelphia for the purpose of renewing my respects to yourself and Major General Hamilton personally and to endeavour to obtain if not possitive assurances, yet some evidence which would prevent or remove, all uneasiness as to the certainty of an appointment. And in fact such was the sort of approbation I received both from yourself and General Hamilton that all my doubts were removed and I returned to this place impressed with the belief that I should not be neglected. But with the chagrin of having performed an unpleasant and expensive Journey I find that my hopes deceived me.

The state of my mind in consequence of an unsuccessful application supported by the documents of yourself and other officers of rank may be immagined and therefore is unnecessary to be further explained. It is not for me to arraign the policy which has dictated a different choice, a comparison of myself with others is a circumstance too delicate to be made.[1]

The Regimental engagements having now been compleated in this quarter leave no hope for me to succeed in my wished for expectation. It is therefore my desire if possible to be arranged in the staff. The Deputy Quarter Master General is a place I flatter myself I could discharge with propriety as activity, arrangement and œconomy are the criterion of that department.[2]

I did myself the honor to visit the President of the United States a few days since, and after recapitulating my disappointment in the Line of the Army, I mentioned to him my ideas respecting this appointment on the staff. he observed to me, that with you Sir as Commander in Chief would orriginate those nominations and advised me without delay to write you on this subject, he expressed a wish to render me every service observing at the same time, that whatever your nominations were he should chearfully coincide in.

Under the circumstance of the case I flatter myself that I may be permitted without offence to appeal to your friendship in Order to obtain the appointment I now solicit[3]—With the greatest regard respect and esteem I have the honor to be Dear Sir Your most Obedient humble servant

Caleb Gibbs

ALS, DLC:GW. An extract of Gibbs's letter is in DLC: Hamilton Papers.

1. Before receiving this letter from Gibbs on 4 May, GW had twice strongly objected to the rejection of the recommendation made by himself, Alexander Hamilton, and Charles Cotesworth Pinckney in Philadelphia in December 1798 that Gibbs be made commander of one of the Massachusetts regiments in the New Army with the rank of lieutenant colonel (GW to McHenry, 25 Mar., 23 April). For the reasons advanced for Gibbs's rejection, see note 1 of GW's letter to McHenry of 25 March.

2. For the names of the Massachusetts officers who were given recruiting assignments in April 1799, see the enclosure in Nathan Rice to Hamilton, 28 April 1799 (Syrett, *Hamilton Papers*, 23:81–84).

3. GW replied on 5 May: "Dear Sir, By yesterday's Mail I received your letter of the 21st Ulto.

"It is with others (if they are disposed to do it) and not for me, to account for the disappointment of your Military expectation. Your name was in the arrangement handed to the Department of War; beyond this, you, probably, can obtain better information than it is in my power to give. But it would be uncandid after saying thus much, not to add that, it would comport neither with propriety, nor with my practice, to bring you forward again.

"If the President is disposed to serve you, in addition to the Letters of recommendation with which you appeared at Phila., he has the evidence of my opinion of your Services, in the arrangement above mentioned. With esteem—I am Dear Sir Your Obedient Hble Servt Go: Washington" (letterpress copy, DLC:GW). Gibbs also wrote Hamilton on 25 April, enclosing two copies of an extract that he had made from this letter to GW.

To William Thornton

Dear Sir,   Mount Vernon 21st April 1799

Your favor of the 19th is before me, and for the details it contains respecting my buildings in the City, I thank you. As I do for directing the exterior door Cills thereof to be made of Stone. I never attended so closely to the specification of the work, as to know they were, originally, intended to be of Wood; On the contrary, as the Frontispiece was to be of Stone I took it for granted that the Cills were to be of Stone also.

By the first Vessel from Boston, I expect the Glass for those houses, which is promised to be good, and of the sizes given in by Mr Blagden.[1]

We hear with much regret, of the death of Miss Dalton. Mr Lear not having returned according to his expectation, & having heard nothing from him since he left this place, we were apprehensive he was sick—and are in the dark yet, respecting it. With esteem & regd I am—Dear Sir—Your Obedt Servt

Go: Washington

P.S. Since writing this letter Mr Lear has popped in having been sick at his own Farm.

ALS, DSoCi; ALS (letterpress copy), DLC:GW.

1. See GW to Thornton, 15 Feb., n.1; see also Benjamin Lincoln to GW, 3 April, and note 1 of that document.

To Jesse Simms

Sir   Mount Vernon 22d April 1799

Until I see General Lee (which according to his promise may be expected early in next month), I shall give no definitive answer to your letter of the 19th instant.[1]

It may not be improper, however, in the meantime to add, that your deceptious treatment of me, has not impressed me with the most favorable sentiments of your candour; and if a report which I hear has been propagated by you, or some person in your behalf, that I have been speculating in your notes, be true; such injurious insinuations place you on worse ground than before, in my estimation; for I am sure you were not to learn that I was to allow General Lee the full nominal amount of your Note; and I am moreover sure, that you could have had no reason to believe, because the fact is known to be notoriously otherwise; that I ever speculated in notes, or certificates, to the amount of a farthing in my life. Such a report then must have been conceived in malice, & propagated for the worst of purposes. I am Sir—Yr Hble Servt

Go: Washington

ALS (letterpress copy), DLC:GW.

1. Letter not found. For what is afoot in GW's dealings with Simms through Henry Lee and William B. Harrison, see Lee to GW, 28 Feb., and GW to Harrison, 5 March.

To James McHenry

Private
My dear Sir,   Mount Vernon 23d April 1799

Six days do I labour, or, in other words, take exercise and devote my time to various occupations in Husbandry, and about my Mansion. On the seventh, now called the first day, for want of a place of Worship (within less than nine miles) such letters as do not require immediate acknowledgment I give answers to (Mr Lear being sick & absent). But it hath so happened, that on the two last Sundays—call them the first or seventh day as you please, I have been unable to perform the latter duty, on account of visits from Strangers, with whom I could not use the freedom to leave alone, or recommend to the care of each other, for their amusement.[1]

This short history of the manner in which I employ my time is given by way of an apology for suffering your letters of the 30th & 31st Ulto to remain so long unanswered—acknowledged they were—and two points which related most immediately to yourself, personally, were dwelt upon in my last. Were it not for this, I should have appropriated sooner, one of the six days I am now about to borrow, for the following communications.

I have perused with attention your Instructions to General Hamilton, and can readily conceive from the purport of them what the tenor of those are which you have issued to General Pinckney. These Instructions appear to me to be well digested; and are appropriate to the ends contemplated.

I once thought, it being more regular, that the old Troops under the command of General Wilkinson, had better have remained subordinate to the Orders of Genl Hamilton—to whom, through the Department of War (for the reasons alledged in the Instructions) all Reports and returns ought to be made. But on more mature consideration of the multiplied—extensive—& chequered position of those Troops, I am disposed to believe that your plan is preferable.[2]

In my last, I gave what I conceiv'd to be the reason why you were uninformed of the intentions of so many of the appointed Officers, and took the liberty of suggesting a mode by which their acceptance, or refusal, might speedily be ascertained[3]—This suggestion, and your Circular (which now appears in all the Gazettes) renders it unnecessary for me to say any thing more on that head.[4]

And if the obstacles which were opposed to the preparatory measures for Recruiting, were such as not to be overcome, like many other things—most desirable—but unattainable, we may regret the loss, though we submit to the disappointment.

Until your Circular appeared, I do not believe that it was the expectation of the newly appointed Officers (who had not received their Commissions[)], that they were to draw pay from the date of their Acceptances; and to this uncertainty, after having thrown themselves out of other business, was their discontents to be ascribed. Your circular communication, and a just arrangement of Rank hereafter, will, no doubt put all matters to rights. But if these Officers are not speedily employed in the Recruiting Service, a clamour will soon arise in another quarter, for it will be asked why are they in actual pay & unemployed.

Care will be taken, I presume, in settling relative Rank not to be governed by the date of the acceptances, for that would give to the Officers of those States who are most contiguous to the Seat of Government, advantages which would be as unjust as they are great.

I do not recollect with precision the circumstance you allude to, as having taken place in the year 1792 under the auspices of one of your Predecesors. But however anxious Officers are to be possessed of their Commissions, I have no hesitation in declaring it as my opinion, that I see no cause they would have to complain at their being withheld, for the reasons you have mentioned, when the matter is explained to them, & they are in the receipt of the emolumts.[5]

With respect to Connecticut, and the States South of Virginia, I was at no loss to account for the delays which had taken place in them, not only as it respected the Recruiting Service, but as it related to the appointment of the Officers also.

General Hamilton having communicated to me his arrangement of the State of Virginia into districts—& sub-divisions—with the places of rendezvous in each, I have suggested a few (unimportant) alterations in the sub-districts, with which I am best acquainted.[6]

In the revised printed Instructions for Recruiting, which you have been pleased to send me, there are several blanks which I presume will be filled up before they are finally issued—These are to be found in the 2d 5th & 28th Articles.[7]

The quotation of the answer given to your representation, respecting the suspension of the arrangement, & consequent delay in Recruiting; betrays a manifest want of knowledge of the Subject. There is a "tide, it is said, in all things" and there was a combination of circumstances at the passing of the Act—among which resentment was not the least—which produced an uncommon enthusiasm; & which, until it began to slacken & ebb, might have been improved to great advantage. But taking the matter up, upon the *principle* of the answer, could there have been a stronger reason assigned agt delay than the *difficulty* of obtaining Men? If the enumerated obstacles were such as would retard the Recruiting Service, it ought to have commenced with redoubled ardour. The voice of the People, as expressed by their representatives adjudged this Force necessary. The Law was positive, where then lay a Power to dispense with, or suspend it? I will go no farther however on this point; perhaps I have gone too far already; but as you have not only authorised, but requested that I would communicate my Sentiments to you with freedom and candour, I could not restrain this effusion while I acknowledge, & have declared upon all *proper* occasions, that you were not responsible for the delay in organizing the army; as you have been informed in my last letter.

In the case of Major Gibbs, I shall make but two short remarks—
1st that it was not from any prediliction to the man that he was
brought forward by the Board of Genl Officers—and 2d that
I should have thought, that the testimony of Generals Lincoln,
Knox, Brooks⟨,⟩ Jackson & others, added to the weight of that
board, would have been a counterpoise to the objectioners; unless
something injurious to his character was adduced.[8] But with respect to young Mercer's promotion, I cannot but express my re-
grets; notwithstanding the high opinion I have of his merit, and
the sincere regard I entertained for his deceased father. This promotion, you may rely on it, is radically wrong; & will be felt sorely.
Although no one is less disposed than I am to call in question the
right of the President to make appointments (with the participation of the Senate) yet I must be permitted to add, that if there is
not a good deal of circumspection observed in the exercise of it,
as it respects the regulation of the army, he will find it much easier
to plunge into, than to extricate himself from, embarrassments occasioned by injudicious arrangements; of this, I can speak from
the experience I have had.

In the arrangement of Mr Mercer at Philadelphia, his comparative pretensions were duly considered, & a Lieutenancy was
conceived to be a handsome appointment for him. Many applications for Captaincies of Dragoons, from meritorious characters,
who had had Commands in the horse on the Western Expedition
in 1794 could not, from the smallness of that Corps be accomodated; & on that acct *only* turned over to the Infantry. Among
these a Captn Thos Turner, highly spoken of as a horse Officer, &
a very respectable character, is numbered. How then must this
Gentleman; how must Captn Randolph—so highly recommended
by Genl Morgan for past services; how must others, who served
through a Winter's Campaign on that occasion with eclat; and
how must the Senior Lieutenants of equal pretensions with those
of Mr Mercer, feel on the appointment of a Student just from College, in preference to them? The question is easily answered; but,
as there is no remedy for it *now*, my only motive for dwelling on
the case, is to shew you how necessary precaution is, in your Military Movemts; & to prove moreover, that after five weeks diligent
application of the three first Officers of your Army, their work
ought not to be battered down by sinester, or local considerations,
unless impeachments, or discoveries unknown, while they were
about it, are of sufficient weight to effect this measure.[9]

Having now gone through all the points of your last letters, I have only to declare that the observations I have made on the several parts of them, and the opinions delivered thereon proceed from the purest motives; and from an earnest desire that the Military system may be well composed; may harmonise in all its parts; may perfectly answer the end of its Institution, and that the President & Secretary of War may find no difficulty, but be quite easy & happy in their government of it. As it respects myself, I have no object seperated from the general welfare, to promote—I have no predelictions—no prejudices to gratify; No friends whose interests or views I wish to advance at the expence of propriety— and I may add in the sincerity of my heart, that there is no wish of it equal to that of their being no exigency in our Affrs which may call me from retirement to take the direction of our forces. With sincere esteem & regard—I am—My dear Sir Your Most Obedt & very Hble Servt

Go: Washington

In the hands of an English Gentleman lately at this place, I have seen a Map of the United States on a large Scale, Edited by Arrowsmith London—It is very necessary the Commander in Chief should be possessed of such an one. If the Public will not furnish it (in a travelling case) I would wish to have one sent to me at my own expence, if to be procured in Philadelphia.[10]

ALS (photocopy), PU: Armstrong Photostats; ALS (letterpress copy), DLC:GW.

1. GW lists in his diary no visitors on Sunday, 14 April, and he lists on Sunday, 21 April, only John Francis Buller Hippisley Coxe of Somerset, England.

2. McHenry enclosed in his letter to GW of 30 Mar. a copy of his instructions to Alexander Hamilton, as set out in his letter to Hamilton of 4 Feb. 1799 (Syrett, *Hamilton Papers*, 22:455–65), for constituting the New Army in the states to the north of Virginia, of which Hamilton was to have immediate command.

3. GW is referring to his first letter of 7 April to McHenry.

4. McHenry's circular, dated 1 April, "*to the officers appointed during the last session of Congress to the additional army*" appeared in the 13 April edition of the *Providence Gazette* (Rhode Island). The notice reads in part: "The materials for the appointment of officers to be drawn from North-Carolina, South-Carolina and Georgia, being yet incomplete, no final arrangements can be made respecting relative rank; it has therefore been thought adviseable to postpone any partial issue of commissions, until the officers from those states shall be appointed. Your pay and emoluments will commence from the date of your letter of acceptance."

5. See McHenry to GW, 31 Mar. and 29 April.

6. See Alexander Hamilton to GW, 27 Mar., n.2, and GW to Hamilton, 10 April.

7. The original edition of the War Department pamphlet *Rules and Regulations*

Respecting the Recruiting Service was published sometime before 28 July 1798. Alexander Hamilton suggested several revisions to McHenry, most of which were included in a new edition of March 1799. When on 21 Mar. McHenry sent Hamilton copies of the new edition of the regulations, he authorized him to fill in the blanks in sections two and five (Syrett, *Hamilton Papers*, 22:560–66). A copy of what is undoubtedly the 1798 edition of the pamphlet is in DLC:GW. For more on the preparation of the pamphlet and a discussion of the different editions, see Alexander Hamilton to Jonathan Dayton, 6 Aug. 1798, and note 6 of that document, Hamilton to McHenry, 10, 15 Mar. 1799, all in Syrett, *Hamilton Papers*.

8. For reference to the rejection of the recommendation of Caleb Gibbs's appointment in the New Army, see Gibbs to GW, 21 April 1799, n.1.

9. See GW to McHenry, 25 Mar., n.2, and Bushrod Washington to GW, 10 April, n.3.

10. Aaron Arrowsmith (1750–1823) published the *Map of the United States of North America* on four sheets in London in 1796.

From Roger West

Sir   W. Grove 23 April [17]99

From the delicate state of my health and the extreme debility I am at present laboring under I am unable to wait upon you personally as I otherwise would do, from these causes I hope to find an apology for troubling you by letter—I have this moment received a paper from Alexa. of this date exhibiting some attempts to prove that in my late application for a Commission in the army contemplated to be raised I have acted with duplicity—with you Sir I had a conversation upon this subject, and if it is my misfortune to differ from you on some political opinions in regard to our Common Country, I rely with entire confidence upon your doing me on all occasions strict and compleat justice—I will therefore proceed to ask the favor of you to state what was the Conclusion in your Mind in regard to my application to you for a recommendation, and beg leave to state as well as I can recollect the prominent parts of our conference—Did you not after reading Colo. Hooe's Letter which I was the bea⟨r⟩er of ask me whether I wanted a Commission in the Army of ten thousand men or whether it was in the provisional Army? and did I not answer that my object was to go into the provisional Army? that the ten thousand men which I calld a standg army would be disagreeable to me while there was no active employment for them? and that it was my determination to unite in repelling any Enemy who might Invade our Country? and were you not pleased to say you were glad to find such a disposition? Did you not add that if I wanted a recommendation for a Commission in the Army of ten thousand men that you would take the matter into consideration, or that you would always be glad to ⟨*illegible*⟩ when you could [do] so consistently? The first question is the most important to my feelings and I beg you Sir to say whether from the whole of the Conversation which passed you were not then and have not been ever since under an impression that ⟨my⟩ application upon that subject was not ⟨*mutilated*⟩ind to the Provisional Army[1]—My ⟨ne⟩rves have been so greatly affected for three or four days past that I can scarcely write legibly I hope to be excused therefor for not copying this letter—permit me to subscribe myself with all possible respect Your mt obt Huble Servt

R: West

ALS, DLC:GW.

Roger West of Fairfax County was the Republican candidate for Congress in the election to be held the next day, in which he lost to Leven Powell. In an address on 13 April, it was reported, West directed his opposition "principally . . . against the army of ten thousand men to be raised, which he very improperly calls a standing army, the increase of the navy, and the alien and sedition laws" (*Columbian Mirror and Alexandria Gazette*, 20 April 1799). The letter in the newspaper from which the quotation is taken, dated 17 April and signed "*A Number of Freeholders*," runs on for several columns spelling out the terms of West's opposition to governmental policy and offering a rebuttal. In the *Mirror* of 23 April Lemuel Bent inserted a letter to the editor, dated 22 April, followed by letters to himself from Henry Piercy, Charles Simms, John Fitzgerald, Robert Townsend Hooe, and Philip Marsteller, all supporting the claim that West had sought an army commission and had not limited it to the Provisional Army. On 1 Aug. 1798 GW had forwarded letters from John Fitzgerald and Charles Simms to Secretary of War James McHenry recommending Bent and Piercy for commissions, which both received in January 1799. Piercy wrote that he and Bent had made it clear to West that they had no intention of going into the Provisional Army but rather into the additional regiments of the regular army, the New Army, and that West "more than once remarked that he hoped we should procure commissions, as he should be much pleased at entering into military service with us as we were neighbors, and . . . [would] pass our time very happily together." In his letter to Bent, Hooe alludes to his own letter of 12 July 1798 to GW recommending West and refers to Marsteller for confirmation of its contents. See Hooe to GW, 12 July 1798, n.1; see also GW's reply to West later this day, 23 April 1799.

When GW, Alexander Hamilton, and Charles Cotesworth Pinckney were in Philadelphia in November and December 1798 to lay the groundwork for the creation of the New Army, they made lists of the men in the various states who had been recommended as officers and often summarized opposite the candidates' names what had been said or written about them (see Editorial Note to Candidates for Army Appointments from Virginia, November 1798, printed above). Opposite West's name is written: "Coll [John] Fitzgerald—Mr Ludlow [Ludwell] Lee—Man of Fortune—Father of a Family—Major of Militia—Coll Sims differed from him in political sentiments, but recommends him—Unblemished Character—strong Military ardour. Wishes to command a regiment *in the provisional army*—Mr [Charles] Lee the Atty Genl says he is in prime of Life & well qualified to command a Regt." At a meeting of Alexandria citizens on 10 May 1798, Roger West opposed the resolution drawn up by David Stuart and John Carlyle Herbert in support of the Adams administration; Charles Simms, a strong Federalist, was one of the supporters of the resolution (see GW to Alexander Hamilton, 27 May 1798, n.4).

1. See GW's reply, this day.

To Roger West

Sir,   Mount Vernon 23d Aprl 1799

I will answer the queries contained in your letter of this date, to the best of my recollection.

In the morning visit you did me the honor to make, sometime last Autumn, at which you delivered me a letter from Colo. Hooe, intimating your desire to engage in the Military Service of our Country,[1] I understood, from the conversation that passed on that occasion, that your object was to enter into the Provisional Army; because it would not comport with your convenience, or inclination, I am not sure wch (for not expecting to be called upon to relate them, My mind was but little impressed with particular expressions) to engage in this line, unless the Country should be Invaded.

I am not impressed with the idea that you objected to an appointment in the twelve Regiments because it might come under the denomination of a *standing* Army, but I clearly understood that your object was the Provisional, for the reason I have assigned. You spoke of a force of which I had never heard; and a good deal of conversation ensued on that, & the situation into which we were thrown; but I am unable to give a precise account of it. Nor have I leisure *now* to recollect myself, as I have strangers in the house, and am besides much hurried in preparing some important dispatches for the Mail of tomorrow. I have heard of your illness with

concern and wish you a perfect restoration of health. being Sir
Your Most Obedt Hble Servt

Go: Washington

I wish you may be able to understand the meaning of this scrawl,
as I am compelled to write it in much haste.[2]

ALS (letterpress copy), DLC:GW.

   1. Robert Townsend Hooe's letter to GW about Roger West's interest in serving
in the army is dated 12 July 1798. GW does not note in his diaries a visit from
Roger West in 1798. In 1775 GW had agreed to become West's guardian should
Col. John West die before his son came of age. In 1791 GW engaged West as a
clerk.

   2. GW seldom crossed out and inserted as many words in a letter as he did in
this one.

From William B. Harrison

Dr Sir   Wednesday Evening April 24th [17]99
   I have Recevd yours of the 10th Instant & Return my Sincear
thanks for your spontanious favours to me & will do my Self the
Honor to take a bed with you & accept the Services of your Clerk
to Survey my Lands[.] on the 14th of may I shall be down for that
perpose I Expect & have no doubt but I can get Chain carriers
amongst my tenants it is out of my power to be down sooner if that
Time will suit you if not I will put it off untill it will[.] if I do not
hear from you to the Contrary between this & that I shall expect
the time fixed as above & will be down accordingly. I have the pleasure to Enclose to you A narration of the Elections of this County
& faquire[.] that of this County I will vouch for I think that of
faquire may be relyd on for I have it from Capt. Crain who this
moment gave it me you will discover Ellzey has but one vote in this
County which was the vote of ⟨Genl⟩ S⟨t⟩. Mason[1] I am with all the
Respect A mortal can ⟨*illegible*⟩ yours &c.

Wm B. Harrison

please Excuse wrote in haste Wm B. H.

ALS, DLC:GW.

   1. U.S. Senator Stevens Thomson Mason, whose role in opposing Jay's Treaty
had made him an anathema to the Federalists, lived at Raspberry Plain in Loudoun County. William Ellzey, Jr., a county surveyor, at this time was one of the
members of the Virginia house of delegates for Loudoun County. Militia captain

Joseph Crane of Berkeley County was recommended for a commission in the Provisional Army by Gen. Daniel Morgan and Col. Thomas Parker (see Morgan to GW, 12 June, n.1).

Enclosure
Election Returns

[24 April 1799]

Faquire County
for government

for Senat of State	Colo. Peyton[1]	447
for Congress	Genl Blackwell[2]	422
for State assembly[3]	Wm Clarkson	386
dto	Elias Edmonds	376
		1631

Against Government

offerd for Congress	Nicholas[4]	196
dto Senat of State	Elzey[5]	159
dto State Legislatr	Gust. Genings[6]	241
⟨dto dto⟩ "	Docr Horner[7]	237
		833

Loudoun County
Federal Party

for Congress	Colo. Powell[8]	548
for Senat of the Stat	Colo. Peyton	620
for the Assembly	Joseph Lewis[9]	504
of the Stat	William Noland[10]	500
		1846[11]

against the government

for senat of State	Wm Elzey	1
for Congress	Roger West	81
for the Assembly	Charles Bins Jones[12]	153
of this state	Abner Osburn[13]	92
		327

AD, DLC:GW. Harrison wrote this on the back of his letter to GW of 24 April, the day that the elections were held. For references to GW's other correspondence respecting the Virginia elections of 24 April 1799, see John Marshall to GW, 1 May, n.3.

1. Except for brief intervals during the Revolution, from 1769 until 1787 Col. Francis Peyton (c.1748–1808) represented Loudoun County first in the co-

lonial house of burgesses and subsequently in the state house of delegates; from 1792 to 1811 he served as senator for Loudoun and Fauquier counties (*The General Assembly of Virginia, July 30, 1619–January 11, 1928: a Bicentennial Register of Members* [Richmond, 1978] 98 et seq.). Francis Peyton, Jr. (d. 1836), the mayor of Alexandria, was an unsuccessful candidate for one of the seats in the house of delegates from Fairfax County.

2. John Blackwell (1755–1808) of Fauquier County, general of the state militia, was in the house of delegates in 1789.

3. William Clarkson (1773–1818) served the term for which he was elected at this time, 1799–1800, and was elected again in Fauquier in 1809. Elias Edmonds (1756–1800) was first elected to the house of delegates from Fauquier in 1786 and was twice reelected; after a brief hiatus he was again elected in 1791 (ibid., 160, 164, 168, 183, 215, 256).

4. John Nicholas (c.1756–1819), son of Robert Carter Nicholas, was first elected to Congress in 1793 and was reelected three times as a Republican.

5. William Ellzey, Jr., represented Loudoun County in the house of delegates from 1795 to 1799. He was again elected in 1828 (ibid., 200, 204, 208, 344).

6. Augustine Jennings represented Fauquier in the house of delegates from 1794 until 1805 except for the one term, 1799–1800. He served one other term, in 1810–11 (ibid., 195, 199, 203, 207, 211, 219, 223, 227, 235, 260).

7. Dr. Gustavus B. Horner was a delegate for Fauquier in 1794 and 1795, 1798-99, and 1800–1801 (ibid., 195, 199, 211, 219).

8. Leven Powell (1737–1810), for many years a leading citizen of Loudoun County, and with whom GW had frequent dealings, was elected to Congress in 1799, replacing Richard Brent (1757–1814) who had served for two terms and was elected again in 1800.

9. Joseph Lewis, Jr., represented Loudoun County in the Virginia legislature from 1799 to 1803. He was elected again in 1817 (ibid., 216, 220, 224, 228, 290).

10. William Noland represented his county in the legislature with occasional interruptions until 1815 (ibid., 216 et seq.).

11. Harrison either recorded the number of votes received by one or more of the candidates incorrectly, or failed to add the correct figures properly.

12. Charles Binns Jones went to the house of delegates for Brunswick County in 1791–92.

13. Abner Osborne, son of Nicholas Osborne (died c.1787), was a leading member of the Society of Friends in Loudoun County.

From William Thornton

Dear Sir   City of Washington April 24th 1799
    I had the honor of your Letter of the 21st, and am afraid that I have not expressed sufficiently clearly my Direction to have the Cills of the exterior Doors of the Basement of Stone. The Cills of the Ground Floor or Entrance are to be, by Specification, as you

supposed, of Stone, as well as the Frontispieces. I meant the Cills of the exterior Doors opening from the Areas into the passages leading to the Kitchens, as they would be constantly subject to the Damp. I should not have troubled you merely with this Explannation, but Mr Blagdin applied to me yesterday for the remaining five hundred Dollars, and will receive from me a check for the same this Day. I enquired when he would want another Supply, he said not till the first of June next: so that there will be no occasion for another Deposit for at least a month or five weeks to come.[1]

We lament exceedingly the relapse of our Friend Colonel Lear, and wish he could have staid a little longer with us; but I must own he is in some respects not a very patient Patient. He was in a great hurry to leave us. We request our sincerest good wishes to your Lady & Family. I am dear Sir with the highest respect your affectionate Friend

William Thornton

Mr Blagdin is glad that the Glass is expected soon, that the Sashes may be finished & weighed, to determine the Sash-weights, & have them cast, if not to be found of the proper poize.

ALS, DLC:GW.

1. On 10 Jan. 1799 GW drew a check on his account in the bank in Alexandria for $1,000 to provide Thornton with the funds to pay the builder George Blagdin, and he probably gave it to Thornton on 11 Jan. when he dined with him in Washington. See Day Book and *Diaries*, 6:330.

From Edward Carrington

Dear Sir   Richmond Apl 25. 1799
  Knowing the anxiety of your mind on the subject of General Marshalls election I can not omit, for a moment, after being ascertained of the State of the polls, to communicate to you the satisfactory intelligence of its having issued fortunately by a majority of 108 Votes.[1] So small a majority after so long and so active a canvas, is an evidence of the deep root which jacobinism had taken in the district; but as that channel of misrepresentation through which we had been deluged with circular letters, is now cut off, we are to hope that a general change of popular opinion in the district will be the consequence, which with the addition of like consequences in some other districts, may pervade the State—It is to be hoped

indeed that we are arriving at a new era of Virginia politics. I am Dear Sir with the Greatest respect Your Most Ob. St

Ed. Carrington

ALS, DLC:GW.

1. The Philadelphia newspapers *Gazette of the United States* and *Porcupine's Gazette* reported John Marshall's margin of victory in the thirteenth congressional district in Virginia as 114 votes over the Republican incumbent John Clopton (1756–1801), a New Kent County lawyer ("Congressional Election Campaign" in Stinchcombe and Cullen, *Marshall Papers*, 3:501).

To Doddridge Pitt Chichester and Daniel McCarty Chichester

Gentlemen,   Mount Vernon 25th April 1799

I shall be obliged to you, or either of you, who may be in the practice of hunting, or driving Deer on my land, for desisting from that practice.

My Lands have been Posted, according to Law, many years; and never has, nor while I possess them, will be revoked. Besides this, in order to have the notification better understood by those who bordered on me, I had (as you will perceive by the enclosed copy thereof) a number of hand bills struck and put up at my Mill & other places, to prevent the plea of want of information, that such trespasses were disagreeable to me.

I have been at much expence, and was at a good deal of trouble, to procure Deer; both of the Country & English kind; and have never yet killed one for my own table, altho' they come into my yard & Gardens, while they are hunted & destroyed by others; and often driven, wounded & maimed into the river by me, and have been found drifted on the shores.

I had them once in a Paddock, but during my absence the fencing was neglected, and getting out, they have run at large ever since. The old ones are now partly wild, and partly tame; their descendants are more wild, but associate with them; and seldom go beyond the limits of my own woodland. But admitting they exceed these, the English deer, more especially, are very distinguishable by the darkness of their colour, and their horns; and I should have hoped, that upon the principle of doing as one would be done by, they would not have been injured by my Neighbours.

You must be sensible that at the stand where I receive the most injury, you can have no right to hunt; for between Mr Chichester's fence (which is close to my line) and the tenement of the Widow Gray, there is no woodland but what belongs to Mr Fairfax or myself; and unless that Gentleman has changed his sentiments very materially of late, he, equally with myself, is averse to having his Lands of Belvoir driven for Deer.[1]

I should not have supposed then, had there not been strong evidence to the contrary, that any Gentleman would poach upon the grounds, & on the rights of another, contrary to Law, and to repeated admonition.

After this notice, as it respects my own Land, and request that you will desist from further injury to my Game, I persuade myself that I shall not, in future, have cause to complain; nor be under the disagreeable necessity of resorting to other means for the preservation of it. I am—Gentleman Your very Hble Servant

                                        Go: Washington

ALS (letterpress copy), DLC:GW.

Doddridge Pitt Chichester and Daniel McCarty Chichester were sons of GW's neighbors Sarah McCarty Chichester and her late husband, Richard Chichester, who had died in 1796. GW was the godfather of Daniel McCarty Chichester and had attended his christening in June 1769 (see *Diaries*, 2:158).

1. Ann Gray was one of GW's tenants at Mount Vernon.

From Thomas Law

Dr Sir   [c.25 April 1799]

The Accompg note will be explanatory[.][1] the Boxes came in the George Berkely by Capn Corfeild who has forwarded my Lre. I am now in the Office writing a building Contract your Corner Stone is to be laid to day & I am to attend[2]—my Garden is preparing & I am planting Poplars—My Square is to day sown with Clover—I am filling in a Wharf.[3] I hope therefore to be excused for this hasty scrawl With affe. regards to Mrs Washington I remain Dear Sir With unfeigned esteem & affn yrs mt Oby

                                        T. Law

I wrote to more persons than one & hope to receive in other Ships.[4]

ALS, DLC:GW. Law's letter is undated, but GW docketed it "Thomas Law ⟨Esqr.⟩ no date recd 5th April 1799." The contents of the letter, however, make it clear that Law wrote it after writing his letter to GW dated 9 April and postmarked at Georgetown 10 April, and so GW could not have received it on "5th April." Furthermore, GW's letter to Clement Biddle of 21 April reveals that at that time GW had not yet gotten the information contained in this letter from Law. It would appear, then, that GW received Law's letter sometime after 20 April and before the end of the month: the assumption has been made that GW intended to write "25th April" instead of "5th April."

1. The enclosed note reads: "Extract 'The present Season is unfavorable for collecting seeds but in three or four months hence Mr Fleming hopes he will be able to furnish a more ample supply. mean while he considers himself as much obliged for the opportunity of offering this small token of his veneration for the illustrious Cincinnatus of America['] — Cal[cutta]: 14 Sept. 1798." For "the Boxes" of seed and plants sent from India by John Fleming (d. 1815), a doctor who was trained at Edinburgh and became president of the Bengal Medical Services, see Law to GW, 9 April, n.4. See also GW to Clement Biddle, 21 April.

2. See William Thornton's report to GW in his letter of 19 April on the progress being made in the construction of GW's houses to the north of the new Capitol.

3. In 1798 and 1799 Law erected three buildings on his Federal City lots in square no. 689, at the corner of New Jersey Avenue and C Street, S.E., including the large house in which he lived with his wife, Martha Washington's granddaughter Elizabeth Parke Custis Law (Harris, *Thornton Papers*, 1:586–88).

4. This makes it appear that Law requested Fleming to send the seed and plants from India.

From Samuel Washington

Dear Uncle   Chas Town April 25th 1799

I received your Letter only four days ago owing to the neglect of the post takeing it to Shepherds Town and from thence to Winchester, and Mr Fairfax sending for Letters found that of yours he keept it for several days so that I have never had it in my power to answer it untill this post.[1] Your Goodness I shall ever Greatfully remember — As the means of saveing me from ruin[.] Mr Brown a Merchant from this place will be a going to Alexandria in about two Weeks and I will get him to wait on you for the Draught.[2] I am setting all my Affairs in Order to leave this County in the Winter, I am fearful I shall find it a difficult thing to settle the Accounts of my Uncle Saml Washington Estate as it all falls on me to do, as my Father and Uncle John both keept bad Accompt's, and I cant with all the Insisting in my power get Bushrod Washington to attend to the business though he is equally Interested,[3] business of that nature the Longer let alone, the harder it is to settle I have mentioned this to you in order to get you to speak to Bushrod should he be at Mountvernon this Summer As a word from you will have a better affect than any thing I can say to him. I dont believe that there ever was any yong Man that has had the difficulties and Misfortunes to Encounter that I have had. This will make the fourth Crop of Wheat I have Lost. I am very sure that I shant reap as much wheat as I sowed. I Mean If I can sell my Land this Summer and can save from the Sale of it Three Thousand pound to purchase One Thousand Acres of Land in Culpepper County about Three Miles of Mr Chas Carters I think it the Greatest Bargain in Land I ever heard of I have been to see it and I think it equal to Land in this County that sells for Three times as much I am in Great hopes that it will not be sold before I sell mine, my Father has recovered his health in a great measure since I wrote you Last. My Wife joines me in our best Wishes for your health, And I remain Dear Uncle your Affectionate Nephew

Saml Washington

ALS, ViMtV.

1. GW wrote to his nephew on 2 April. Mr. Fairfax was probably Ferdinando Fairfax (1769–1820), who lived at Shannondale, his estate in Berkeley County.

2. Mr. Brown has not been identified, but see Samuel Washington to GW, 1 May.

3. Bushrod Washington was the son of GW's brother John Augustine Washington and thus, like Samuel, was a nephew of the late Samuel Washington.

From James Welch

His Excl. Genrl Washashington   Stantown Apr 25th 1799

Sir I Re[ceive]d yours of the 7th instant and Take notes to the contents; it gives me much uneseness To think that I am to Suffer by the Miss Respresentathon To you (by I know not hwo) you Say you have herd To much of my character Lately not To Expect Sundry disapointments; hwo it is that is desposed To inger me I know not nor am I abl to prevent pepel from asarting things that is falce; I know my one Feelings and that my intentiones is not To Trifel with you or Eney other parson (Time will Try all things) Bad as I stand with you at present I am detarmned To prove to you that I am not the man you now think me to be; as to my decleretion of haveing purched your Land I do deny I never in my Life menched the transaction To Eney parson but have been frequently asked if I had purched you Land and have answered yese if Further inqirey was made.

I told the parseon or parseons that the purches depended on the payment of a Large Sum of money at a futer day; as to my indevering To obtain credet in concequence of haveing Transacked Bisenes with you; I do deny I am not a man that inqires into Other peppels Bisenes nor do I make it my Bisenes To tell my Bisenes to Eney parseon; as to my contraction other Debts I do ashure you Sir that the onely Debt I have contracked Since you and I had Dealings was the purches of Two thousand pounds worth of Goods at 18 Monthes credet; these Goods was aplied to The Starting of ireon works and to be paid out of the produc of the Same the works is now agowing; this transaction Toke plac Last winter and was dun in order to inable me To make payments to you if other Recorces Should fail; I do ashure you that in all my tranactions I have made it my Sudy To fix my prorperty in Such a way as To make me abel to pay you; as to my proposeing to purch Lands on credet or for cash since I delt with you I do deny Sundry aplications has Been made To me but my answer was that my present curcumstaince wold not admit of me purching I have Exchanged a considerabl quanty of my Lands for other Lands this was also dun in order that I may be abel to pay you I had no more at present you may be Sure of Seeing me at your plac in the corce of Next Month. I am Sir your Very Hbl. Sarvent

James Welch

ALS, DLC:GW.

To Ludwell Lee

Dear Sir,   Mount Vernon 26th April 1799

Your occupation on Wednesday last, put it out of my power to speak to you without giving interruption to more important business than I am now about to communicate.[1]

Having good information that some land which I hold on four mile run was much depredated on, I went up some short time ago to run round the Lines, and found the fact to be as reported; but not being able to ascertain all the Corners—and those holding the adjacent Lands not being present, I forbore to re-mark any of the lines; but being desirous of doing this, & meeting with all the parties at the Election, monday next is fixed upon for this purpose; who have engaged to meet me at the beginning Corner of Adams's Patent (under which I hold) by nine o'clock on that morning; where, & when, being informed that you have Land adjoining mine, I should be glad to meet you. As you may not know where this Corner is, I shall pass a little house at the junction of the Leesburgh Road (a widows) half an hour before nine on my way.[2] With great esteem & respect—I am Dear Sir Yrs

Go: Washington

ALS (letterpress copy), DLC:GW.

1. On Wednesday, 24 April, GW "went up to Alexa. to an Election of a Representative from the District to Congress & from the County to the State Legisla[tur]e" (*Diaries*, 6:344). Ludwell Lee's cousin Henry Lee was elected to Congress, and Henry Lee's brother Richard Bland Lee was one of the two men elected to the Virginia house of delegates from Fairfax County.

2. In 1774 GW bought from the brothers George and James Mercer for £900 a tract of 1,224 acres on Four Mile Run in Fairfax County, about four miles from Alexandria. See George Mason to GW, 21 Dec. 1773, nn.3 and 6, GW to James Mercer, 12 Dec. 1774, n.3, and 19 Nov. 1786, n.1. See also GW to Alexander Spotswood, 15 July 1799. As early as 1792 GW had expressed concern that his tract on Four Mile Run had "had the wood thereon dealt pretty freely with by unauthorised persons in its vicinity" (GW to Bushrod Washington, 8 Jan. 1792; see also GW to William Pearce, 13 April, 7 Dec. 1794, and GW to George Minor, 13 April 1794). Earlier in this month, on 7 April 1799, GW wrote James McHenry that he had been "on a Survey of some land I hold in the vicinity of Alexandria; on which, as I was informed, & as the fact proved, considerable trespass had been committed." He surveyed the tract on 3 and 4 April, spending both nights at William Fitzhugh's house in Alexandria. On 3 April he "Got on the grd. about 10 Oclock and in Company with Captn. [William Henry] Terret [Jr.] and Mr. [John] Luke commenced the Survey on 4 mile run & ran agreeably to the Notes taken." The next day he "Recommenced the Survey at the upper end where we left off in Company with Colo. Little—Captn. Terret and Mr. Willm. Adams & contd. it agreeably to the Notes until we came to 4 Mile run again which employed us until dark" (*Diaries*, 6:340). To his memorandum drawn from his notes on the survey of 3–4 April GW gives the date 15 April and includes much of the same information quoted here from his diary (ADS, ViMtV). On 29 April GW "Went up to run round my land on 4 Mile run" and spent the night at Col. Charles Little's. The next day he "Engaged in the same business as yesterday & returned home in the afternoon" (*Diaries*, 6:345). It is not known whether Ludwell Lee and any or all of the other owners of adjacent land were present on 29 and 30 April.

From Bushrod Washington

My dear Uncle   Walnut farm April 26 [17]99.

Yesterday Evening we recieved a list of votes from the different Counties of this District, & I have now the pleasure of announcing to you the triumph of federalism in this Corner of the State. Genl Lee is elected by a majority of 32 votes. Had the election been postponed a week longer, it is generally believed that he would have divided even Doctr Jones's County.[1] He had not time completely to do away the illfounded & unceasing calumies which were dayly propagated against him. The people in this District are attached to the government, but until the present contest, not an effort has been made in the two lower Counties to undeceive them upon the grossest misrepresentations which have [been] made to them by a few designing men. I have endeavoured to impress upon all the friends of the government with whom I have had conversation, that so far from permitting our late success to plunge them into their former State of Supineness, that their exertions should be constant and ardent in order not only to maintain, but to improve the ground we have gained. I wish that similar efforts may be made in other parts of the State. We send two federal men from this County; the former member was lost by a considerable majority, & for the honor of Westmoreland he was deserted by his warmest friends upon the single principle of his politics. Lancaster & Richmond are divided, instead of having four votes against the Government as their Situation was in the late Assembly.[2]

Nothing can equal my anxiety to hear from the other Districts & Counties. I hope to be agreably relieved from this State of suspence in a few days. Nancy Joins me in love to my Aunt & yourself—Believe me to be My dear Uncle Most sincerely yr affect. Nephew

                                             Bushrod Washington

ALS, ViMtV.

1. Dr. Walter Jones, a Republican from Northumberland County, was elected to Congress in 1797 in Virginia's nineteenth district. Lee served only the one term. For GW's correspondence regarding the 1799 election in Virginia, and references to the sources for biographical data, see John Marshall to GW, 1 May, n.3, and John Tayloe to GW, 29 April, n.3.

2. Henry Smith Turner and George Garner, both Federalists, were elected to the Virginia house of delegates from Westmoreland County. John P. Hungerford

(1761–1833), who was later a member of the Virginia senate and of the U.S. Congress, was the defeated incumbent; the other incumbent was Henry Lee. In Lancaster County, the Federalist James Ball, Jr. (1755–1825), replaced the Republican Martin Shearman and the Republican Joseph Carter, Jr., was reelected; but in Richmond County the Republican Richard Barnes retained his seat, and the Republican George Glasscock was replaced by William McCarty, who consistently voted with the Republicans.

From Charles Buxton

respected Sir,   Perth Amboy [N.J.] April 27th 1799

In assuming the liberty of troubling you with the enclosed I hope you will attribute the freedom, to the motives that has influenced the action, and of which you will the more readily form an estimate, by perusing the *Intended personal* introductory letter of my (late) highly esteemed friend Doctor John Bard, who cheerfully favoured me (on request) about twelve months past, with the accompanying letter, at which time I contemplated the pleasure of a Journey to the Southward:[1] this desire however, having been unable to accomplish, after repeated procrastinations, and now doubtful if ever it will be realized, Induces me to embrace the present opportunity of Genl Bloomfield's visit to Philadelphia,[2] who very politely takes charge of the package containing two Proof prints, Engraved from a picture composed as mentioned by my (late) friend—It's publication was not originally intended, but the flattering encomiums of a Book-seller, after repeated application, obtained the temporary use of the Drawing for that purpose, & by whom I was presented with a small number of the first Impressions; Your acceptance of those forwarded will prove an ample gratification To, Sir One who feels *all* that gratitude which Ought to warm the heart of *every* American, & Ardently Inspire him with the most lively wishes for the continuation of your life & happiness.[3] With these sentiments Yours in sincerity

Chas Buxton

P.S. My friend Dr Bard Died about 14 days ago.

ALS, DLC:GW.

Charles Buxton (1768–1833), after studying medicine at the University of Edinburgh and at Columbia College in New York, received his medical degree from Rutgers in 1793.

1. The undated letter from Dr. John Bard, Sr. (1716–1799), the distinguished medical scientist, practitioner, and administrator who died on 30 Mar. at Hyde Park, reads: "I have been requested by Doctor Charles Buxton a gentleman I much respect and esteem, who has employed himself during a Season of Bodily indisposition to design and finish an emblematical picture with a view to perpetuate the idea of the american revolution, of which those persons among us of Judgment and taste in these things speak very well. Doctor Buxton is desirous of presenting you with a copy of this Picture as a proper acknowledgment of the just Sense he has of the Share you had in accomplishing this great event. As he is a Stranger, Sir, to you, and is informed I am known to you, he has requested me to mention him to you. . . ."

2. Joseph Bloomfield (1753–1823), who had commanded a brigade of New Jersey militia in the suppression of the Whiskey Rebellion in Pennsylvania, was at this time mayor of Burlington. From 1801 to 1812 he served as governor of New Jersey.

3. GW replied on 30 May: "Sir, The last Post *only*, brought me (through the medium of the War Departmt) your polite & obliging favor of the 27th Ulto accompanied with two proof Prints elegantly executed (one on Sattin) engraved from your emblematical Picture, designed to perpetuate the idea of the American Revolution.

"For this instance of your kind attention to me, I pray you to accept my grateful acknowledgements. And was not the late President of the United States a conspicuous character in the Piece I might say more than would now become me of the fruitfulness of the Design.

"If business, or inclination should ever induce you to make a tour to the Southward, I shall hope to see you at this seat of my retirement. I regret, as you do, the death of our mutual friend Doc⟨tr⟩ Bard. And am Sir Your Most Obedt & obliged Hble Servant Go: Washington" (letterpress copy, DLC:GW).

From Henry Lee, Jr.

Dear Sir   Stratford 27th April [1799]

On my way to North[umberlan]d election I recd yr favor of the ⟨*illegible*⟩ instant.[1]

In the course of the last ⟨month⟩ I rented out my distillery to a Mr ⟨*illegible*⟩ of Frederic, now residing in this county & sold to him all my corn.

Had your application preceded the sale I would most chearfully have given you the preference.

I will try to purchase 100 or 200 ⟨bls⟩ for you on the terms you mention & if I succeed you will know from me personally, as in a few days I shall set out for Alexa. & Loudon. Your most respely

                             H. Lee

ALS, DLC:GW. The letter is misdated 1795 in DLC:GW.

1. For the election in Northumberland County, see Bushrod Washington to GW, 26 April, and John Tayloe to GW, 29 April, n.3. GW's letter to Lee is dated 18 April.

From David Stuart

Dear Sir,   Alexa[ndria] 27th Apl 1799
I found that the letter you had recieved, had been printed a month ago—and had been commented on very properly by Coll Simms—Of this I had no recollection, and I Suppose it had escaped you—It seems, great quantities of them were brought down by the members on their return from Congress—It is therefore clear, it was a fabrication for the express purpose of promoting their interest in the elections—As it had been published, and commented on, I thought it unnecessary to have it published again, with any comments[1]—The money I expected from Baltimore has not yet come, but from the character of the person on whom the draft is, I think there can be [no] doubt of it, in the course of a day or two[2]—You have, I suppose—heard that Marshall is certainly elected—There is a report that Lee is allso elected, tho' it wants confirmation—I fear it is too true that Nicholas is elected.[3] I am Dr Sir with great respect Your affecte Servt
                                            Dd Stuart

ALS, DLC:GW.

1. The letter has not been identified. Colonel Simms is Charles Simms of Alexandria.

2. Stuart wrote GW again on 2 May about this payment due from the estate of John Parke Custis for the rent of Martha Washington's dower lands. See note 1 of that document.

3. Edward Carrington wrote to GW from Richmond on 25 April to report John Marshall's election, and Bushrod Washington wrote from Westmoreland County on 26 April confirming that Henry Lee had won.

To Clement Biddle

Dear Sir,   Mount Vernon 28th Apl 1799
Since my last I have receiv'd the Seeds which you sent me by Captn Hand—after several fruitless enquiries after them.[1]
There was a Manufactury of Machines for raking Meadows, and

Harvest fields after they are cut, at Kensington while I resided in Philadelphia—These are worked by a horse, and were, in my opinion useful impliments on a Farm, for expeditiously gleaning the fields of the scattered grain, or Hay. I would (if now to be had) thank you for sending me one by the first Vessel bound to Alexandria.[2]

What would well cured Shad and Herrings sell for by the Barrel in the Philadelphia Market? I have put up some this Season, and if the price would encourage it, would send you a few barrels of each, to sell on Commission. Be so good as to inform me what price Wheat & Flour bear in your Market—I am—Dr Sir Your Obedient Hble Servant

Go: Washington

ALS (photocopy), Samuel T. Freeman & Co. catalog, 23–24 Feb. 1978; ALS (letterpress copy), DLC:GW.

1. GW wrote Biddle on 21 April.

2. Biddle had difficulty finding the maker of the raking machine, who had moved from Kensington, but he learned from the owner of one of these that the machine moved only on "Ground that was perfectly level & free from Stones" (Biddle to GW, 18 May, n.1). GW wrote on 6 June that he in any case would like to have one of the rakes. None of the letters that GW and his agent Biddle exchanged between 7 June and 13 Nov. 1799 has been found, but there is no indication in GW's surviving accounts that he ever acquired one of the raking machines from Pennsylvania.

From Bryan Fairfax

Dear Sir   London April the 28th 1799.

I was much pleased last week in receiving Your Favor of the 20th January by the Hands of Mr Dandridge. And tho' I am thinking now of my Return, and with anxious expectation of being able to set off in a few weeks yet I could not omit acknowledging the Receipt of it, so sensible am I of the Favor you continue to do me.

I am very glad to find that some of the Letters I mustered up resolution eno. to write on my Arrival have got safe to hand, especially those to you, for I was then very weak indeed, but at present am very well and have continued so for a Week past which is I think a longer space of uninterrupted Health than I have had Since Christmas, having been afflicted most of the winter at York with my old complaint. I thank God for my present good State and the Prospect of it's continuance. At York I heard that you were very ill last Summer, but had the Pleasure of hearing at the same time that you were quite recovered in October.

With respect to your having acceded to the wishes of your Country in taking the Command of the Army I was persuaded it proceeded from a Desire of serving it at a time when it was earnestly required, and this when I heard it wondered why you would accept of an inferior command after having filled the highest Station so long. In my opinion it was one Instance among many of your preferring the public good to every other consideration. Yet still I hope that You will have no Occasion for any further operations than the present preparations, for with you I trust in a kind providence, and several times have hoped that as America had so lately undergone a long course of Affliction that she wo'd not for many years experience any of the great troubles of War, especially as She felt of late the Scourge of Pestilence, or something like it.

I thank you sincerely for your Prayers & good wishes with respect to my restoration to Health & to my Family and Friends, which would now prove a great Blessing even in the decline of Life. My Brother when he was the first time with his Family in England I heard should say that he felt like a Fish out of Water, which I have often thought of since my Arrival.

When I was in England before I compared myself to an Indian who longed for his native Woods—But that strong desire did not come upon me 'till I had been some months here—But now in a measure I had it from my first arrival—Yet this seems to be a desireable country to live in, but a Man must be born here to relish it much, because of that natural Attachment to one's native Land.

With respect to the other Objects of my voyage for which you are pleased to express also your good wishes, particularly the matter of Estates to which I may be entituled, I have been often told from time by Friends that I should finish one thing first—one thing at a time—And this has kept me more in the dark than I need have been—And I have at last got more insight by having recourse to the Study of the Law myself than I had otherwise thro' these delays been able to obtain. And I have also had the Caution of Friends—that tho' the object may be great—the Uncertainty of the Law is such that a man should be very wary in engaging in it. These things have hitherto kept me from going further than the Outlines of Enquiry and that too superficially to avail much.

One Friend indeed in a Letter mentions some in Possession being alarmed at hearing of my Arrival—Yet think it very hard that those who have long been in Possession should now be disturbed.

I am very sorry to find that the Spirit which had been observed before I left home seems rather to increase, but I hope it will not continue, and that it may please God to restore a Spirit of Concord & Unanimity, and this for the same Reason as has been already mentioned, because America has lately undergone a long scene of troubles. As a Man of Peace it is very irksome to me to see such growing Dissentions, being convinced that they originate from an evil Spirit, who can influence & blind the minds of men whenever permitted so to do—So that we must always look ultimately to the supreme disposer of all things.

The Winter here has been very severe, & continued long—& every Body speaks of the present Spring as uncommonly disagreeable from the much Rain & much cold damp Air. The Drougth you had last Fall perhaps might have aided the destructive Fever at Phila. which I find raged with violence—But the Fly is an alarming circumstance to the Farmer. Lord Hawke is a great Farmer in Yorkshire[1]—I forget many particulars—one thing I remember—He makes or has made 2800 Bushels of Oats in a year. His being much engaged in this Line caused us to have much conversation about You, and I was sorry that I was not better qualified than I was to give him more particular Information than I did— He was surprised however to find that your Wheat Fields scarcely produced ten Bushels to the Acre, as their Lands yeild a short Crop when they produce but twenty. He seemed to dwell much upon the practice they have of studying the nature of the Soil, and the successive as well as the kind of successive Crops they intend to raise from it. He did not begin with wheat after a Fallow as I always thought was the Custom here according to what I have read from the old Books, but with some other Sort, such as Turneps— Clover—& something else—making the Process very different from what I had been accustomed to understand it—Such as wheat first after being well manured, then Oats & Barley—then clover for two or three years—Lord Hawke was exceedingly kind to me in instances that shewed a friendly temper.

This of Farming reminds me to inform you that I have not had the Pleasure of seeing Sir John Sinclair—and it has happened unexpectedly—Before I went the last time to York I called at the

House then with an Intention of leaving my Address as usual but after the Coachman had knocked long & no one appearing I returned—And this since my ⟨Return⟩ I called again—& found the House seemingly empty.[2]

And now I cannot but repeat how very friendly Lord Buchan has been by Letter⟨s⟩ from him & also introductory to others—His Brother & his Sister also, Lady Ann Erskine who succeeds the Countess of Huntingdon in her extensive Concerns—for in this Lady I find another Sister as well as Relation—We became soon acquainted and have continued to be very friendly—I am going this moment to see her at 5 o'Clock and expect the Satisfaction of drinking tea with her, & then hearing the Organ & a good Sermon at the Chapel which adjoins the House. Going to her House has afforded me the best Entertainment I have had in England, For my Time has been mostly an unhappy time since I left Home, and some part of it distressing, such as I have passed at home under Spells of the Cholic.[3]

I have Reason to be very thankful to You for the Attention You have been pleased to pay to my Wife & Family—& was much pleased to hear that you & Mrs Washn had dined lately at Mt Eagle. I now conclude with my best Compliments to Mrs Washington, Miss Custis if still so & all the Family at Mt Vernon, & beg you to accept of Assurances of the greatest Regard & unabated Affection from Dr Sir Yr most obliged & Obedt St

Fairfax[4]

I have seen lately in a Book Mr King lent me, two Views, one of Mt Vernon Ho. & the Hill before it, & the other of the River from thence, both as unlike the true Prospects as they could well be. The Author, a late Traveller, who like most other travellers seems to have received the 1st Information—Yet not many mistakes as I expected.[5]

ALS, DLC:GW. Fairfax sent the letter "By the New York Packet."

1. Martin Bladen Hawke, second Baron Hawke, was the son of Admiral Edward Hawke (1705–1781), the victor in the Battle of Quiberon Bay in December 1759. The younger Hawke was a leading figure on Britain's board of agriculture (see GW to John Sinclair, 15 July 1797, n.1).

2. GW wrote a letter of introduction for Fairfax to John Sinclair on 15 May 1798.

3. GW's letter of introduction to Lord Buchan is dated 15 May 1798. GW corresponded with Buchan's brother Thomas Erskine in 1797 (Erskine to GW,

15 Mar. 1797; GW to Erskine, 7 July 1797, printed in note 1 of Erskine to GW, 15 Mar.; see also Bryan Fairfax's references to Erskine and to Selena Hastings, countess of Huntingdon, in his letter to GW of 21–23 Aug. 1798). Lady Anne Agnes Erskine (1739–1804), Buchan's older sister, never married.

4. Bryan Fairfax assumed the title only after arriving in England; he was now eighth Baron Fairfax of Cameron.

5. The book was undoubtedly Isaac Weld's *Travels through the States of North America, and the Provinces of Upper and Lower Canada, during the Years 1795, 1796, and 1797*, published in London in 1799. Weld's account of his visit to Mount Vernon includes the following description of the house: "The rooms in the house are very small, excepting one. . . . All of these are very plainly furnished, and in many of them the furniture is dropping to pieces. . . . The house and offices, with every other part of the place, are out of repair, and the old part of the building is in such a perishable state, that I have been told he wishes he had pulled it entirely down at first, and built a new house, instead of making any addition to the old one" (53–54). Mr. King was Rufus King, U.S. minister to Great Britain.

From James McHenry

Private
My dear Sir.   Philad[elphia] 29th April 1799.

I received, this morning, your letter of the 23d inst. for which I am much obliged to you. I did not in my own mind consider you dilatory in your answer, aware of the nature of your employments, and the incessant interruptions, by company to which you are subject.

There are one or two points you mention which I shall say a few words to.

The officers of the additional Regiments were put upon pay from the date of their acceptances, because such has been the uniform practice of this office; because the obligation of the U.S. to pay is complete from the date of the acceptance; and because the law has left no discretion with the President to withhold their pay. It is true there are instances, where the President has said to certain General Officers, that it was expected they would not consider themselves intitled to pay till called into actual service: But even in such cases the consent of the officer was deemed necessary to give to the United States any right to withhold it.[1]

Some of these officers are now, and all will be speedily employed. Major General Hamilton has completed his arrangements for the recruiting districts in New York Connecticut, New Jersey

Pennsylvania and Delaware, and nearly for Maryland and Virginia; and I have taken all the measures dependent upon me, to give immediate activity to the commencement and vigorous prosecution of the recruiting service. If it should languish at any time it will be on account of some deficiency of cloathing. Mr Francis is exerting himself in this branch of supply.[2]

The President desired me to send him a plan for settling the rank of the field officers of the additional regiments. Inclosed is the plan that appeared to me the best, and which I flatter myself he will approve.[3]

Mr Mercer has declined his second appointment. But altho' the office is once more vacant I apprehend great endeavours will be used to have it filled either from this State or Massachusetts.

Inclosed is the arrangement for the distribution of the artillery, made in conformity with the ideas contained in your letter of Decmbr ulto and my instructions to the Major Generals. I add also a copy of my letter to General Pinckney respecting it.[4]

If I can procure one of Arrowsmith's maps of the U.S. I shall send it to you. I am my dear Sir Yours truely & always

James McHenry

The dollar came safe.[5]

ALS, DLC:GW; ADf, MdAA.

1. For GW's comments on this and McHenry's explanation, see GW to McHenry, 5 May (second letter), and note 1 of that document.

2. In February 1795 the U.S. Senate confirmed GW's nomination of the Philadelphia merchant Tench Francis as purveyor of public supplies.

3. McHenry enclosed a copy of his letter to John Adams of this date (DLC: GW), in which he proposed that, all else being equal, previous military service would determine seniority among the field officers of the New Army. He also proposed that promotion in the army would follow the rule suggested by GW in his second report to McHenry of 13 Dec. 1798, printed as a note to GW's first letter to McHenry of 13 Dec. 1798. See also GW to McHenry, 5 May (second letter), and note 1 of that document.

4. The enclosed "Arrangement of the Artillery," which is printed in Syrett, *Hamilton Papers*, 23:74–77, is composed of seven separate lists, including those for the western army; for Georgia and South Carolina; for New England; for Delaware, Pennsylvania, New Jersey, and New York; for North Carolina, Virginia, and Maryland; and two "For the Field." McHenry's enclosed letter to Charles Cotesworth Pinckney of 29 April provides this explanation: "The inclosed arrangement and distribution of the Artillery and association of its Company Officers has been prepared by Major General [Alexander] Hamilton and is approved of by this department. . . . I have directed Major General Hamilton to cause this

arrangement and distribution, so far as relates to his command, to be carried into immediate effect. You will also be pleased to take prompt order to give efficacy to the same so far as it relates to your command. You will perceive that the right on the sea board, is given to the first Regiment, and the left to the second: that a battalion of the first Regiment is left to the Western Army, that another battalion of the same Regiment is assigned to the posts in Georgia and South Carolina, and a third to the posts in North Carolina Virginia and Maryland As for the fourth it will remain for the troops in the field and may be annexed to the part of the army under your command" (DLC:GW).

5. On 30 June GW wrote McHenry that he "preferred sending a Columbia Bank note for a dollar, to one of Silver (in a letter)." It has not been determined when or for what reason GW sent the "dollar" to which McHenry refers here.

From John Tayloe

Dear Sir   Mount Airy 29th April 1799

I find I shall be detained in Virginia much longer than I expected—& when I set my face north shall pursue the nearest route by Hooes ferry to Annapolis—This being the case—I am compelled to ask the favor of you to forward the letters you promised me for Phi[ladelphi]a under cover to me in Annapolis[1]—as I shall go immediately on to Phia from thence—I have peculiar satisfaction in informing you of the Election of Generals Marshall & Lee—the former by a majority of 111 votes—the latter by a majority of 33[2]—The representation to our Assembly in this District is altered for the better—tho' not up to our wishes[3]—I beg to be very particularly presented to Mrs Washington. In haste—I am very respectfully Your Obliged & Obedt Se⟨rvt⟩

John Tayloe

ALS, DLC:GW.

1. In his letter of 5 May GW reported to Tayloe that he was forwarding to him at Annapolis the letter that he had written to the secretary of war on his behalf. GW's letter to James McHenry, dated 5 May, is printed in note 1 of the letter to Tayloe. See also Tayloe to GW, 14 June.

2. On 25 April Edward Carrington reported to GW from Richmond that John Marshall had won his seat in Congress by 108 votes. See note 1 to that document. The next day Bushrod Washington wrote that Henry Lee had won by 32 votes.

3. Tayloe himself was reelected to the Virginia senate from the district comprising Lancaster, Richmond, and Northumberland counties. For the delegates elected to the house from Lancaster and Richmond counties, see note 2 to Bushrod Washington's letter of 26 April. In the third county, Northumberland, William Ball replaced Thomas Hurst, both of whom voted consistently with the

Republicans in the legislature, and the Republican William Claughton was re-elected. For sources of data about the 1799 elections in Virginia and for correspondence regarding the elections, see John Marshall to GW, 1 May, n.3.

From Alexandria Poor Relief Committee

Sir,   Alexandria 30th April 1799.

We received some time ago from your Manager Mr Anderson, One hundred Dollars to be used for the benefit of the poor in this place.[1] There were many poor among us whom the severity of last winter greatly increased. We sought out the most needy upon whom we bestowed your Charity. Widows with a number of Children, Industrious persons prevented by sickness from earning their daily bread, were preferred. A number of such objects your Charity has relieved. Their names and circumstances we would have inclosed, but we thought it unnecessary as they must altogether be unknown to you. Be assured that every exertion in our power was used to render your Charity as useful as possible. Accept of our expressions of gratitude in being distinguished by you as Instruments of doing good to our fellow Citizens, and receive through us, the acknowledgments of those needy Persons whom you have relieved, and their prayers that the father of Mercies may abundently repay your kindness. Beleive us to be with the greatest respect Sir, Your obt humble Servts

John Dundas
James Muir
Andw Jamieson
Wm Herbert

LS, DLC:GW.

1. The year before, on 8 Jan. 1798, GW gave the Alexandria poor relief committee one hundred dollars, which the committee distributed to twenty-six women (Alexandria Poor Relief Committee to GW, 24 Jan. 1798, n.1). The committee members in 1799 were the same as in 1798, except Andrew Jamieson, a successful baker on Water Street in Alexandria, had replaced Samuel Craig.

From John Marshall

Dear Sir   Richmond May 1st [17]99

You may possibly have seen a paragraph in a late publication, stating that several important offices in the gift of the Executive,

& among others that of secretary of State, had been attainable by me. Few of the unpleasant occurrences produc'd by my declaration as a candidate for congress (& they have been very abundant) have given me more real chagrin than this. To make a parade of profferd offices is a vanity which I trust I do not possess, but to boast of one never in my power woud argue a littleness of mind at which I ought to blush.

I know not how the author may have acquird his information, but I beg leave to assure you that he never receivd it directly nor indirectly from me. I had no previous knowledge that such a publication was designd, or I woud certainly have suppressd so much of it as relates to this subject. The writer was unquestionably actuated by a wish to serve me & by resentment at the various malignant calumnies which have been so profusely bestowd on me. One of these was that I only wish'd a seat in Congress for the purpose of obtaining some office which my devotion to the administration might procure. To repel this was obviously the motive of the indiscreet publication I so much regret.[1]

A wish to rescue myself in your opinion from the imputation of an idle vanity which forms, if I know myself, no part of my character, will I trust apologize for the trouble this explanation may give you.

Messrs Goode & Gray who are the successors of Messrs Claiborne & Harrison arc both fœderalists. Mr Hancock who opposd Mr Trig will, to our general disappointment not succeed. At least such is our present information. Shoud Haymond or Preston be elected the Virginia delegation will stand ten in opposition to the government—nine in support of it.[2] Parties, I fear will not be so nearly balancd in our state legislature.[3] With the most respectful attachment I remain Sir your obedt Servt

J: Marshall

ALS, DLC:GW.

1. The letter to which Marshall is referring appeared in the Richmond newspaper *Virginia Gazette and General Advertiser* on 19 April. See GW's response to Marshall of 5 May.

2. In Virginia's eighth congressional district, the Federalist Samuel Goode (1756–1822) of Chesterfield County defeated Thomas Claiborne of Brunswick County, who had held the seat since 1793 and regained it in 1801. Carter Bassett Harrison of Charles City and Prince George counties, who had also been a member of Congress since 1793, lost in the tenth district to Edwin Gray (b. 1743) of Southampton County. The Federalist Gray remained in Congress until 1813. John Johns Trigg (1748–1804), a Republican from Bedford County, was re-

elected in the fifth congressional district, defeating Federalist George Hancock (1754-1820) of Botetourt County. His brother Abram Trigg (1750–1809) of Montgomery County defeated Francis Preston (1765–1836) to retain his seat for the fourth district. James Machir (d. 1827), one of the three Federalists elected to Congress from Virginia in 1797, stepped aside in 1799 to allow the Federalist John Haymond to face the challenge of the Republican George Jackson (1757–1831), whom Machir had replaced. Jackson won (see Machir to James McHenry, 28 April, quoted in McHenry to GW, 11 May, n.1).

3. In the spring of 1799 several of GW's correspondents wrote him about the elections to the state legislature and to Congress held in Virginia on 24 April. David Stuart wrote on 27 April and 2 May; John Tayloe, on 10 Feb. and 29 April; Bushrod Washington, on 10 and 26 April; Edward Carrington, on 25 April and 10 May; and John Marshall, again on 16 May. See also the returns for Loudoun and Fauquier counties which William B. Harrison sent GW on 24 April. Biographical and other data on the 1799 elections is drawn from *Biographical Directory of the United States Congress, 1774–1989,* (Washington, D.C., 1989), *The General Assembly of Virginia, July 30, 1619–January 11, 1928: A Bicentennial Register of Members* (Richmond, 1978), and Stanley B. Parsons et al., *United States Congressional Districts, 1788–1841* (Westport, Conn., 1978).

From Samuel Washington

Dear Uncle   Cha[rle]s Town May 1st 1799
    Mr Brown the Gentleman who I mentioned in my Last Letter would wait on you, is Obliged to Alexandria sooner than he expected, but he being so good an opportunity—I have got him to ride to mount vernon to see you,[1] And should it be convenient for you to Let him have the Draughft it will be doing me a Great kindness as I know of no person going from this place that I could get to do it, he is a relation of Mr Hammonds[2] therefore will put himself to some trouble to Oblige me I would have waited on you myself, but the Ill health of my Father Lately obliges me to be constantly with him for should any thing happen to him in my absence the Family would be at a great Loss for me. I Remain Dear Uncle your Affectionate Nepthew

                                        Saml Washington

ALS, CSmH. The letter was "F[avore]d by Mr Brown."
    1. GW does not indicate in his diary that he had a visit from a Mr. Brown at this time, but he does note in his Day Book that he issued on 6 May "a Check on the Bank at Alexa[ndri]a in favr of Saml Washington" for $1,000, which, as he indicates in his cash accounts, he had "lent him" (see Ledger C, 52). Samuel Washington's most recent letter was dated 25 April.
    2. Thomas Hammond was Samuel Washington's brother-in-law.

From James McHenry

private
Dear Sir.   War Dept [Philadelphia] 2 May 1799.

As it is by no means improbable those events may take place, which will render it indispensible and proper to raise the eventual army, in part or in whole, it has been thought expedient that measures should be taken, for selecting the best qualified among those who would be willing to serve to fill its different regimental grades, with a view of being prepared to proceed instantly, on the event occurring, to raise the men.

The course of reference to the Senators, has been pursued for the States of New Hampshire, Massachusetts, Rhode Island, Connecticut, Vermont, New York, Pennsylvania, Delaware & Maryland. For Virginia, I have thought it best to refer the subject to yourself; and the States of South Carolina and Georgia to Gen. Pinckney. With respect to North Carolina, I have not yet been happy enough to fix upon proper characters to address, having some reason for overlooking the Governor. I mean, I do not think he is sufficiently impressed with the propriety of selecting real federal men.

The inclosed letter was written some time ago, and purposely detained, till the elections should be over in Virginia.[1]

Inclosed is the act giving eventual authority to the President of the United States to augment the army, in pursuance of which the present measure has been adopted.[2] I am Dr Sir sincerely and Affly your ob. St

James McHenry

ALS, DLC:GW; ADf, MdAA.

1. By one of the acts passed in May 1798 after the publication of the XYZ dispatches, Congress authorized the president when faced with imminent or actual invasion by a foreign foe to create a Provisional Army of 10,000 men. It followed this legislation with an act in July authorizing the addition of twelve regiments to the regular army of the United States (the "New Army"). See McHenry to GW, 3 July 1798, n.1. GW and major generals Alexander Hamilton and Charles Cotesworth Pinckney went to work in November 1798 to identify the men who could serve as the officers of these regiments, and by this time in May 1799 most of the officers had been commissioned and the recruiting of soldiers had begun.

No action was taken under the terms of the Provisional Army act of May 1798, which remained in force only until the end of the year, but on 2 Mar. 1799 Congress enacted a bill that in effect extended the life of the 1798 act while somewhat expanding its scope. Secretary of War McHenry on 10 April wrote this letter to

GW reporting President Adams's decision to take preliminary action under the terms of the new Provisional Army act, but he delayed sending the letter until this time, 2 May: "The President thinks it highly expedient that no time should be lost in selecting proper characters to officer the twenty four regiments of Infantry, the regiment and Battalion of riflemen, the Battalion of artillerists and Engineers, and the three regiments of Cavalry, which may be raised in pursuance of an act giving eventual authority to the President of the United States to augment the army, passed the second of march, last, and contemplates, as soon as the selection shall be closed, to make the appointments. The selection of officers for the eventual army appears to be an object of primary importance, requiring all imaginary circumspection and care; their characters ought, if possible, to be such as to inspire a general and well grounded confidence that the fate of their country may be safely entrusted to them. I have, therefore, to request you will accord your full attention to the subject and furnish me as soon as practicable with a list of the names of such characters in your state, to fill the annexed military grades, as in your opinion, are best qualified, and willing to serve in case of an actual war, which will render it indispensable to recruit men for the most extended army. You will, doubtless, find a facility in forming the list from consulting and co:operating with proper persons in different parts of your State who may be calculated to give information of the requisite particulars, and upon whose patriotism and judgment a full confidence may be placed. Every cautionary measure is necessary to guard against errors in appointments which too frequently result from the case with which recommendations are generally obtained, the partialities of friends, and a delusive hope that men of bad habits, by being transplanted into the army, will become good men, and good officers.

"The officers proposed to be drawn from the State of Virginia are (viz.)

Four Colonels	one Colonel
Eight Majors	Two Majors
Forty Captains	Eleven Captains and
and Eighty Subalterns of Infantry	Twenty two Subalterns of Cavalry

"In making the selection, it will be proper to allow, if fit characters present themselves for a choice, a due proportion of Captains and Subalterns to the several counties, according to their respective population, as well with a view to facilitate the recruiting service as to give general satisfaction; this rule, however, is not meant to be so invariably observed as to exclude great superiority of talents, by too strict an adherence to it. As circumstances may exist at the time of the President's making the appointment's which may render it proper to make some changes in the list with which I may be furnished, you are requested not to give the parties recommended, such positive assurances as will render a change impracticable without wounding, too sensibly, their feelings" (DLC:GW).

As by this letter McHenry makes GW personally responsible for putting together a list of Virginians who were both willing and able to serve as the officers in the four regiments of infantry and one regiment of cavalry that Virginia would be called on to raise if the new Provisional Army became necessary, GW had to abandon the practice that he had been following in the creation of the new regiments of the regular army of forwarding to McHenry whatever applications or recommendations for commissions that happened to be sent to him. Instead, GW himself now began both to seek and to deal with applications and recommendations for commissions in the Provisional Army.

GW wrote McHenry on 13 May saying that because his "acquaintance with the People of *this State*" had become so limited he was turning to generals Henry Lee and John Marshall, and to colonels Daniel Morgan, William Heth, and Edward Carrington for aid in identifying Virginians who might serve as officers in the "eventual army," as the Provisional Army was often called. GW wrote Morgan about this on 10 May, and Morgan provided him with the names of a number of men from the upper part of the state (see Morgan to GW, 12 and 26 June). Henry Lee proved to be less helpful (see Lee to GW, 22 May). On 12 May GW wrote a joint letter to Marshall, Carrington, and Heth, enclosing a copy of McHenry's letter of 10 April (printed here), and asking their aid in compiling a list of potential officers in Virginia, but to little effect (see GW to Marshall, 6, 16 June, and note 2 of the latter document, and Marshall to GW, 16 May, 12 June).

In early June GW decided that in order to identify Virginians who might serve as officers in the Provisional Army, he would "follow the four grand Divisions of the State, as laid off by the Inspector General [Alexander Hamilton] in his arrangements for recruiting" Virginians for the new regular army regiments. In each of these divisions—(1) the Eastern Shore division which also included the tidewater counties to the north of the James River and a part of the Northern Neck; (2) the area of the state on the south side of the James; (3) the portion of the state to the west of the Eastern Shore division, to the north of the James, and east of the Blue Ridge; and (4) the transmontane region of the state—he would choose someone "for the command of a Regiment" and "request him to furnish me with the names of such persons, in his division, as are fit and willing to fill other grades" (GW to Marshall, 6 June; see also Alexander Hamilton to GW, 27 March). In July GW succeeded in securing John Cropper's consent to serve as commanding officer of the Eastern Shore regiment if called upon to do so, and the names of possible commanders for the regiments in other divisions are mentioned in the correspondence, but as far as can be determined no steps were taken to designate any other regimental commanders.

Throughout the summer GW himself continued to seek suggestions, but only rarely and seemingly in passing. As early as 25 May GW sought advice from Burgess Ball, and in July and August he asked for, and received, suggestions from Alexander Spotswood and Richard Kidder Meade. See Ball to GW, 25 May, GW to Spotswood, 15 July, and GW to Meade, 12 August. For the most part, however, GW seems to have been content simply to receive and acknowledge the applications and recommendations that came to him unsolicited. On 26 and 27 June, and again on 4 Sept., GW's friend Leven Powell, who had recently been elected to Congress, supplied GW with the names of men in Loudoun County and its environs who wished to serve as officers in the Provisional Army, and James McHenry forwarded to GW applications received from Virginians by the War Department (see McHenry to GW, 11 May, and notes).

A few unsolicited applications and recommendations for appointments in the regiments of the Provisional Army came in during July. On the thirteenth of that month several men from Fauquier County, Charles Marshall, Joseph Blackwell, Francis Brooke, George Steptoe Washington, and Martin Pickett, wrote a joint letter to GW recommending George Pickett, Jr., "who at present commands a company of militia in Fauquier has expressed a wish of entering into the provisi[o]nal army, We therefore take the liberty of recommending him as a young Gentleman a native of Fauquier whose character and deportment as an officer and private man has deservedly met with our approbation, that should he be promoted in the army of the united States we have not a doubt but he will acquit himself in a manner becoming his rank, He is and has always been friendly to the Government under which he lives and professes himself to be induced only by a wish to serve his County on a more active theatre than that presented in the militia, for offering himself a candidate in the military line" (DLC:GW). On 20 July Benjamin Bullitt wrote from Millfield saying "I hope, whin you send on the list of those who have made application to you for Commissions in the provisional arm⟨e⟩ you will think of me, prohaps as there is a grate number of applacations for Captainces there is a better chance for the Maj's. apointment, how ever should I be honoured with any appointment, I shall be very thank full and shall endevour to do my duty. and do my self Credet in it" (DLC:GW). Four days later, on 24 July, William B. Wallace of Stafford County wrote to apply for the command of a company in the Provisional Army and said about himself: "Not having the honour of a personal acquaintance with your Excellency I ho⟨pe⟩ it is not Ostentatious (for me in support of my pretentions) on this occation to call to mind my services last War which commensed in the year 1775 in the second Virga Regt then commanded by Col. [William] Woodford when after one years service as a private & N. Com. officer I was appointed to a Lieutenancy in one of the 16 additional Regts commanded by Col. [William] Grayson & continued in this till the Regt was broke, when an aversion to leave the army till the end of the war induced me (contrary to a General Military Maxim) to prefer a 2d Lieutenancy in [Charles] Harrisons Regt of Artilly to a Supernumerary Captaincy in Graysons & in this I served to the end of the War, tho. not without experiencing a long and painfull Captivity with the Enemy in South Carolina, whence I again lost rank & came out of an army when promotion had necessarily been so rapid in many instances from the Number of vacancies that occurred with nearly the same grade I commenci[n]g with six or seven years before" (DLC:GW). GW replied on 29 July: "Sir, I have received your letter of the 24th instant, wherein you offer yourself as a Candidate for an appointment in the Provisional Army.

"Measures are now taking to select proper Characters for Officers in this Army, and as it is desireable to obtain those who have had experience in military affairs, and are otherwise qualified, your application will meet with due attention whenever the appointments take place.

"And in the mean time I will thank you to suggest to me the names of such persons, within your knowledge, as are fit & willing to serve in Regimental or Company Offices in case they should be appointed thereto: for my personal knowledge of Characters in this State is too confined to enable me, from that alone, to select proper Characte[r]s for the officers of four Regiments, which is the proportion aloted to Virginia; I must therefore obtain information from every source in my power of those who are qualified and willing to serve without giving any assurance of appointment as that must depend on the will of the President & Senate of the United States. With esteem & regard I am Sir Yr Most Ob. St G. Wn" (Df, DLC:GW).

On 12 Aug. GW wrote McHenry that he saw "no prospect of completing the selection of Officers from this State, for the Provisional Army, within any reasonable time." In the fall of 1799 GW's correspondence regarding the Provisional Army is minimal and intermittent. Most of these letters are quoted in GW to McHenry, 12 Aug., n.1, and GW to Richard Kidder Meade, 12 Aug., n.3.

2. "An Act giving eventual authority to the President of the United States to augment the Army" was approved on 2 Mar. 1799.

From David Stuart

Dear Sir,   Alexa[ndria] 2nd May 1799

I was in town yesterday, and have come again today for no other purpose that to see if the note sent by the Bank of this place to Baltimore had been paid—'tho' the note has been sent near a fortnight, they have not it seems ever heard from their correspendent of its being recieved—This appears to be very strange—I can have no doubt of its being eventually paid when presented; as I gave the person on whom the draft was, notice of it, and recieved a fiew lines informing me, it should be punctually paid—The delay appears to proceed from the negligence of their Correspondent in Baltimore—Expecting it will be here tomorrow evening, I have left a check in the Bank for you amounting to £753.12 which if I am right, is the ballance now due—You will therefore be pleased to send up on saturday.[1] By a gentleman who arrived in the stage last Evening from Richmond, intelligence is recieved that Parker and Evans are reelected, and that Mr Gray Mr Clark and Mr Goode are elected in the places of Harrison, Clayborn⟨e⟩, and Clay—It is allso said that Hancock is certainly elected.[2] I am Dr Sir with great respect Your Affecte Servt

                                                         Dd Stuart

ALS, DLC:GW.

1. Stuart wrote to GW earlier, on 27 April, about the payment of this current balance due from the John Parke Custis estate for the rent of Martha Washington's dower lands in tidewater Virginia. On this day, 2 May, GW noted in his cash account that he had received $2,512, or £753.12, "from Doctr Stuart on acct of my annuity" (Ledger C, 52). On 4 May William Herbert, the president of the Bank of Alexandria, wrote GW: "Doctr Stuart Lodged a Note of a Gentleman in Baltimore In Bank, some time ago, which the Cashier sent forward to the Bank

of Baltimore, I expect to receive an account this Evening of its being paid, in this Event, the Doctor has directed 2512 Dollars to Be Carried to your Credit, of which I will Advise you" (DLC:GW). Herbert wrote again on 6 May: "I Have the pleasure of Informing you that the Money Expected by Doctr Stuart from Baltimore, is paid, & in Consequence thereof, that the Sum of twenty five Hundred & twelve Dollars Stands now at your Credit, in the Books of this Bank, by his order, & Waits your Disposal" (DLC:GW).

2. GW received confirmation from John Marshall in a letter written 1 May in Richmond of the election to Congress of Samuel Goode and Edwin Gray in the place of Thomas Claiborne and Carter Bassett Harrison. Marshall also reported, correctly, that George Hancock had lost his election. Stuart's informant was mistaken as well about the defeat of Republican Matthew Clay (1754–1815) of Pittsylvania County: Clay kept his seat in Congress. Mr. Clark is probably William Clarke of Pittsylvania County who had served in the Virginia house of delegates from 1796 to 1798, first as a Republican and later as a Federalist. For references to the elections, see John Marshall to GW, 1 May, nn.2 and 3.

From William Augustine Washington

My Dr Sir   Haywood May 2d 1799

The Vessel I ingaged to take my Corn up to you, never returned from Baltimore untill the 23 Ulto after repairing her Sealing she came down on friday last to Load, but the rainy and Windy weather ever since has retarded us—she will I hope get ⟨on⟩ her Load in a day or two & will deliver you Two Hundred Barrels, and return immediately for the Ballance; the freight you will be pleased to settle with the Bearer Capt. Bowcock & charge me with the half; you can settle wth me for the Corn after the Ballance is delivered.[1]

If you have any Whiskey of fine quality made intirely of Rye, you would oblige me by sending me a Barrel, it is the only Spirit I make use of, when I can get it good agreeing better with my Complaint, than any other.[2]

I suppose you generally put up a good many Herrings; If you have any to part with, shou⟨ld⟩ be glad to get a Barrel of well cured for my own use.[3]

It give me pleasure to tell you of my improvement in health, & that I leave home tomorrow, with a hope and prospect of making myself as happy as Man [can] be in this World of Woe.[4]

I congratulate you on Genl Lee's & Genl Marshals Election to Congress; I hope it will half retrieve the Honor of the State. with my best respects to Mrs Washington I conclude My Dr Sir Your ever Affectionate Neph⟨ew⟩

Wm A. Washington

P.S. I have directed Bowcocks rect to be inclosed & left my Letter open for that purpose.

ALS, ViMtV. The letter was sent "By Capt. [Henry] Bowcock."

1. For GW's arrangements with his nephew William Augustine Washington to supply him each year with corn for his distillery at Mount Vernon, see GW to W.A. Washington, 26 June, 3 Oct. 1798, and W.A. Washington to GW, 24 July 1798. There was a good deal of confusion at this time about the shipment of corn up from Haywood to Mount Vernon and the sending of fish and whiskey down to Haywood, resulting in the exchange of a number of letters (see GW to W.A. Washington, 20, 24 May, 10 June 1799, and W.A. Washington to GW, 20 May, 1 June, 13 July 1799). In the corrected account with William Augustine Washington in the Mount Vernon distillery and fishery accounts (Mount Vernon Ledger, 1799–1800, 14), William Augustine Washington is credited on 11 May with the delivery of 187½ barrels of "Indian Corn" valued at $500 and 166 barrels valued at $456.50 on 25 May.

2. On 25 May William Augustine Washington was charged $27.50 for "30 Gallons Rectified Whiskie 4th proof 5/6" and $16.95 for "30½ Gallons" common whiskey (Mount Vernon Ledger, 1799–1800, 14; see also the references in note 1).

3. GW presented William Augustine Washington with a barrel of "fine Herrings" (ibid.; see also GW to W.A. Washington, 20, 24 May, and W.A. Washington to GW, 1 June).

4. William Augustine Washington was married on 11 May to his third wife, Sarah Tayloe, sister of John Tayloe of Mount Airy.

From Alexander Hamilton

Private
Dr Sir   New York May 3d 1799

At length the recruiting for the additional regiments has begun in *Connecticut New York New Jersey Pensylvania* and *Delaware*. The enclosed return of cloathing will sufficiently explain to you that it has commenced at least as soon as the preparations by the Department of War would permit—It might now also proceed in Maryland and Massachusettes, and the next post will I trust enable me to add Virginia—but that I do not think it expedient to outgo our supply of Cloathing. It will have the worst possible effect—if the recruits are to wait a length of time for their cloathing.[1]

I anticipate your mortification at such a state of things—various causes are supposed to contribute to it.

It is said that the President has heretofore not thought it of importance to accelerate the raising of the army—and it is well understood that the Secretary of the Treasury is not convinced of its utility—Yet he affirms that for a long time past he has been ready & willing to give every aid depending on his department.[2]

The Secretary of War imputes the deficiency in the article of Cloathing to a failure of a contract which he had made and to the difficulty of suddenly finding a substitute by purchases in the market. It is however obvious that the means which have been since pursued have not been the best calculated for dispatch. The materials procured at distant places have been brought to Philadelphia to be made up—They are stated to be adequate in quantity.

You will observe that 6[oo suits][3] are numbered 1—This applies to a Regiment in the Western Country. I proposed to the Secretary to change the buttons. It has not been done.

Yet if the Secretary's energies for execution were equal to his good dispositions, the public service under his care would prosper as much as could be desired. It is only to be regretted that good dispositions will not alone suffice, and that in the nature of things there can be no reliance that the future progress will be more satisfactory than the past.

Means, I trust sufficient, have been taken to procure from Europe a supply of Cloathing for the next year—And the Secy has assured me that he would immediately take measures for procuring a supply for the succeeding year.

As to other supplies I believe things are in tolerable train— and that there is a certainty of the most essential articles in due abundance.

The officers for North Carolina have been appointed[4]—No nomination has yet come forward from South Carolina.

Not a single field Officer has yet been appointed for the Regiment to be raised in New Hampshire Vermont & Rhode Island— It seems the members of Congress dissuaded from the nomination of those who were proposed by the General Officers and promised to recommend preferable characters—but this promise has not yet been performed. This want of organisation is an obstacle to the progress of the affairs of this Regiment.

It is understood that the President has resolved to appoint

the Officers to the provisional army and that the Secretary has thought fit to charge the *Senators* of each State with the designation of characters.[5] With the truest respect & attachment I have the honor to be Dr Sir Your Obed. ser.

A. Hamilton

ALS, DLC:GW; copy, DLC: Hamilton Papers; copy, DLC: Hamilton Papers.

1. For reference to the return of clothing for the army in Philadelphia, dated 1 May 1799, see Hamilton to James McHenry, 2 May (second letter), n.6, in Syrett, *Hamilton Papers*, 23:91–92.

2. See the comments of John Adams and Oliver Wolcott, Jr., regarding recruiting soldiers for the New Army quoted in notes 2 and 3 to this letter of 3 May from Hamilton to GW, ibid., 98–101.

3. In the ALS there is a blank space following "6"; the material in brackets is taken from one of the DLC copies printed in Syrett, *Hamilton Papers* (ibid., 101).

4. James McHenry sent Hamilton the approved list of North Carolina officers on 10 April (DLC: Hamilton Papers).

5. See McHenry to GW, 2 May, n.1. GW did not respond to Hamilton until 6 June, at which time he wrote a letter marked "Private": "Dear Sir, I have duly received your letter of the 3d of May, and am glad to find that the recruiting service is likely to progress without further delay. To facilitate this, nothing will contribute more than Cl[o]athing.

"It is certainly necessary to push on this business with proper energy, and to be provided with an ample and timely supply of every article wanted, if it is expected that such Troops as we have, should be, in any degree, respectable. This, I trust, will be done. And I should hope, 'ere this, that the field Officers for the Regiment to be raised in New Hampshire &c. have been appointed.

"It is very desireable that the selection of Characters to officer the Regiments, eventually to be raised, should be such as will do credit to the service, if they should be called into the field. The Secretary of War has requested me to furnish him with a list of names for the quota from Virginia, which I am taking measures to do; but, owing to my long absence from this State, I have so little personal knowledge of Characters, that I must rely very much on the information of others in whom I can confide. With very sincere regard I am, Dear Sir, Your Affecte Hbe Servt Go: Washington" (LS, DLC: Hamilton Papers; Df, DLC:GW).

To James McHenry

Private
My dear Sir,   Mount Vernon 5th May 1799
Your private letter of the 29th Ulto was received yesterday, and requires but a short reply.

From an observation of yours, in answer to my letter of the 23d Ulto, I perceive my meaning with respect to the settlement of *rela-*

tive Rank, has been misunderstood, or, if taken properly, I must adhere to the opinion I gave of the injustice which would be inflicted upon the Officers of States remote from the Seat of Government; if those in the vicinity of it are to *Rank* before them, because they were on the spot to announce the acceptance of their appointments at an earlier day.

Rank & Pay are distinct things; the Officer who may have received the latter to *day*, sustains no injury from him who received it yesterday; but if the commencement of *Rank* in the same grades, is to be regulated (under the circumstances I have mentioned) from the dates of their acceptances it will have injustice stamped on the face of it: for in that case those who are most remote— not by any act avoidable in themselves, but from the nature of things—become in almost every instance juniors; when perhaps many of them, in consideration of former Services, or other weighty pretensions might, justly, be entitled to Seniority.[1]

The mode which you have suggested to the President for settling the Rank of the field Officers, is, certainly the best that could be offered to his consideration; and I trust will be approved by him.[2]

Let the vacancy, occasioned by the non-acceptance of Mr Mercer be filled by whomsoever it may, I am glad he has refused it. But, in the name of common modesty, what did this young Gentleman expect? the command of the Regimt? Upon the principle wch governed the Board of General Officers in assigning the *present* addition to it, I think it would be injudicious to fill the Vacancy from a quarter that did not occasion it; Nor can it be better filled, I believe, than with the appointment of Turner, or Randolph—the first of whom is spoken of as possessing talents peculiarly adapted to this Service.

What is the determination of Watts?[3] With very great esteem and regard I am—My dear Sir Your Most Obedient and Affectionate Hble Servt

Go: Washington

ALS, NNGL; ALS (letterpress copy), DLC:GW.

1. McHenry responded on 9 May: "I consider with you that the date of the acceptance of an officer ought to have no part in determining his relative rank with any other officer of the same grade. This is not intended to have the least influence" (DLC:GW).

2. See McHenry to GW, 29 April, n.3.

3. In the List of Officers for Virginia Regiments in the New Army which McHenry enclosed in his letter to GW of 21 May, John Watts, who had been offered the command of a regiment of cavalry, had "not [been] heard from." GW had recommended Watts to McHenry in October 1798. See the Enclosure, GW to McHenry, 15 Oct. 1798; see also GW to John Tayloe, 23 Jan. 1799.

To John Marshall

Dear Sir,   Mount Vernon 5th May 1799

With infinite pleasure I receiv'd the news of your Election. For the honor of the District, I wish the Majority had been greater; but let us be content; and hope, as the tide is turning, the current will soon run strong ⟨in our⟩ favor.

I am sorry to find that the publication you allude to, should have given you a moments disquietud⟨e⟩. I can assure you, it made no impression on my mind, of the tendency apprehended by you.[1]

The doubt you have expressed of Mr Hancock's Election, is as unexpected as it is painful. In these parts, we had set it down as certain; and our calculations went to eleven instead of nine. A few days now, will give us the result of *all* the Elections, to Congress & the Legislature of the State; and as you are at the fountain of information respecting the politics of the members, give me, I pray you, the amount of the parties on each side, if you have leisure & can ascertain them.[2] With very sincere esteem & regard I am— Dear Sir—Yr Obedt & Hble Ser⟨vt⟩

Go: Washington

ALS (letterpress copy), DLC:GW.

1. Marshall's letter to GW is dated 1 May.

2. For Marshall's final, and accurate, reckoning, see his letter to GW of 16 May. See also Edward Carrington to GW, 10 May, n.1.

To Thomas Peter

Dear Sir,   Mount Vernon 5th May 1799

I have had the enclosed Tobacco note by me sometime. Too long perhaps for the best Market.[1]

If Mr Peter (your father) whom I presume is a good judge of these matters, should be of opinion that it had better be sold *now* than wait longer, for a rise in the price of that article, I pray you to sell it for what it will fetch. I give you this trouble because the Tobacco is in the Warehouse at George Town.

Be so good as to let me know by the return of Washington Custis, if there has been any a/c received of the Sales of my Tobacco in London—and inform me at the sametime what the Stock in the Bank of Columbia divided the last half year, that I may know what to draw for.[2] Best wishes attend you all—& I am—Dr Sir—Yr Affecte Servt

Go: Washington

ALS (letterpress copy), DLC:GW.

1. The tobacco note was for tobacco from GW's Montgomery County tenant Priscilla Beall, stored in the Georgetown "Centre" warehouse. It weighed 1,011 lbs. gross and 912 lbs. net, as GW indicated below his signature.

2. For the dividend paid by the Bank of Columbia, see Thomas Peter's reply of 6 May.

To John Tayloe

Dear Sir,   Mount Vernon 5th May 1799

I received, yesterday, your favour of the 29th Ult.; and by tomorrow's Post for Baltimore, the enclosed will be dispatched, to meet you at Annapolis.

I hope the contents of it will meet your ideas—I have given these, as nearly as I could recollect them, in my communication to the Secretary of War.[1]

With sincere pleasure I received the information of Generals Lee & Marshall's Elections. Had the Majorities in their favor been greater, it would have added gout[2] to the result. But they are Elected, and that alone is pleasing. With Mrs Washington's compliments united with mine to Mrs Tayloe—and with my best respects to Govr Ogle—I am—Dear Sir—with esteem & regard Your Obedient Hble Servt

Go: Washington

ALS (letterpress copy), DLC:GW.

1. GW's letter of 5 May to McHenry reads: "Sir, This letter will be presented to you by John Tayloe Esqr. whom the President of the United States was pleased to nominate and appoint to a Majority in the Regiment of Light Dragoons.

"Mr Tayloe waits upon you to explain his motives for declining that honor, *at present*; the propriety of which, I persuade myself you will not only acquiesce in, but applaud, as the result of laudable and Patriotic principles.

"This Gentleman is a Senator in the Legislature of this State. The Politics of which you are not to be informed of—a part however of which is, to suffer no person to remain in either house thereof—nor to enjoy any office under Its government, who holds any Commission, or appointment of whatsoever nature or kind, under that of the General Government. The consequence then of his accepting the Military appointment would be, the vacating of his Senatorial office, and as he informs me, the probable introduction of an opposition Member in his place.

"Mr Tayloe's patriotism leads him to serve his country in any capacity wherein he can be most useful; either in the Civil or Military line; and having been pleased to ask my advice on this occasion, I have frankly given it as my opinion, that under his statement, and in the present aspect of our public affairs, I thought his services in the first—that is—in the Senate—were more immediately necessary and important than they would be in the latter—because they are *now* actively employed in the one case, and may lye dormant in the other, unless hostilities on *Land* should be the result of French politics.

"To this opinion he has yielded, or seems inclined to yield; with a hope however (as there may be an impropriety in keeping the vacancy open) that if the exigency of the times should render it expedient to raise more Cavalry—the service to which he is most attached—that his motives for declining his *present* appointment may not be forgotten—but aid his pretensions to, and solicitude to obtain a new one. Having requested me to relate these circumstances, it was but just I should do so; and to add, that with great respect I am Sir Your Most Obedt Hble Servt Go: Washington" (ALS [photocopy], DLC: James McHenry Papers; letterpress copy, DLC:GW). The ALS was offered for sale by Parke-Bernet Galleries, 30–31 Oct. 1944, as item 342 in catalog 596. See John Tayloe to GW, 10 Feb., 29 April, and GW to Tayloe, 12 Feb. 1799.

2. GW probably means goût, a flavor, or zest.

To Bushrod Washington

My dear Sir   Mount Vernon 5th May 1799
Your letter of the 26th Ulto—as also that of the 10th, have been duly received.

The Elections of Generals Lee and Marshall are grateful to my feelings. I wish however both of them had been Elected by greater majorities; but they *are Elected*, and that alone is pleasing. As the tide is turned, I hope it will come in with a full flow; but this will not happen if there is any relaxation on the part of the Federalists. We are sure there will be none on that of the Republicans, as they have very erroneously called themselves. It is apprehended, *latterly*, that Mr Hancock will not carry his Election; and that in numbers we shall not exceed nine. In point of abilities, I think the majority will be greatly on the side of Federalism.

I have mentioned Mr T. Turners name to the Secretary of War with the respect that it has been handed to me; but in a letter I received from him last night, he thinks the President has given, or will give, the vacant Troop to a Gentleman in another State.[1] Our loves to Mrs Washington. I am Yr Most Affecte Uncle

G. Washington.

ALS, NNS; ALS (letterpress copy), DLC:GW.

1. GW wrote James McHenry on 23 April about Thomas Turner, whom Bushrod Washington had recommended for a commission in the New Army. On 29 April McHenry wrote GW that the captaincy of dragoons for which GW had Turner in mind was likely to go instead to someone from either Massachusetts or Pennsylvania. For Thomas Turner's identity and references to his army appointment, see Bushrod Washington to GW, 21 Sept. 1798, n.1; see also GW to McHenry, 5 May 1799, printed in note 1 of GW to Tayloe, this date.

Letter not found: to William Booker, 6 May 1799. On 15 May Booker wrote GW: "Your letter of the 6 Inst. I duly receivd."

To James McHenry

Sir   Mount Vernon 6th May 1799

It is a point from which I have not deviated, to forward all recommendations, & applications, which have been made to me for Military appointments, to the Department of War.

In confirmation of what is said in the enclosed letters from General Morgan, and the Colonels Meade and Parker,[1] I may add that, the same good report of the merits of Major Lawe Butler has, verbally, been made to me by others. Although he served through the War, his person is unknown to me. This, however, is no evidence of his unfitness to fill the vacancy his friends solicit for him; because, the Virginia line of the Army, to which he belonged, was but a short time under my immediate Command.[2]

With respect to the application of Rowland Cotton, through the medium of Mr Cooper, I have only to add that, the Applicant & Recommender (if it is the Cooper who was in Congress) are as well known to you,[3] as they are to Sir—Your Most Obedient Hble Servant

Go: Washington

ALS (letterpress copy), DLC:GW.

1. The letter from Daniel Morgan may have been that of 3 April, a copy of which from the Hamilton Papers is printed in GW to Morgan, 10 April, n.1. The

letters from Richard Kidder Meade and Thomas Parker have not been identified, but see GW to Meade, 12 Aug. 1799, and Parker to GW, 23, 26 July; the latter two are printed in GW to Alexander Hamilton, 14 Aug., nn.2 and 4.

2. Lawrence Butler was a captain in the 11th Virginia Regiment when he was taken prisoner at Charleston on 12 May 1780. He was appointed major in the 8th Infantry Regiment of the New Army on 24 April 1799.

3. The letter from William Cooper (1754–1809) of Cooperstown, N.Y., the father of James Fenimore Cooper, recommending Rowland Cotton for a commission in the New Army has not been found. Cooper was elected to Congress in 1795 and again in 1799. GW wrote Cooper on 5 May: "Sir, I have been duly favoured with your letter dated the 22d of May (April, I presume was intended) and, as in all applications of a similar nature, I have forwarded it to the Department of War, for the Consideration of the President; to whom alone nominations and appointments belong. I am Sir Yr most Obedt Servant Go: Washington" (ALS [photocopy], ViMtV; letterpress copy, DLC:GW).

From Thomas Peter

Dear Sir,   City of Washington 6th May 1799

I received yours of the 5th by the Hands of Washington Custis, enclosing a Note of Tobacco, nett weight 912 lb. which I disposed off this Morning at Six dollars ⅌ Hd & a dollar for the cask, there was but one person in Town that would give more than 5¾, it being under a thousand; a Mr Williams sold this day ⟨5⟩o Hhds all weighing upwards of 1000 at a Credit of 60 dy for Six & a half dollars. The price falling here & in Europe, induced me to sell yours at the above price.

I called on Mr Carleton the last Eveng respecting the Tobacco you shipt to his House, & find your Tobacco is not yet disposed off, it went in the Hamilton that Sail'd about the 4th of October, the Ampheaton saild in September & as he was informed by a few lines from his Friends they had made sale of a considerable Quantity of Tobacco at 7⟨5⁄7⟩ Stg pr Hd he was hopeing the Hamiltons Cargo was included in the Sale, but Mr Wood of Baltimore (who is an other Partner) informed him on Saturday the Hs. Cargo when he last had advices was on hand, but was expecting daily to hear of the Sale.[1]

Mr Carlton sais if you wish to Draw in favor of any Person in Europe for the Proceeds of the Tobacco when disposed off, that your Bills will be duly Honourd. Enclosed you have two Notes One for 50 & an other for 5 dollars, change 75 Cents.[2] Mrs Stuarts Family are here under inoculation, but not yet Broke out, we are

all well, our best regards attend you & Mrs Washington & I am Dr
Sir—Your Affece Servt

Thomas Peter

P.S. The Bank of Columbia divided 8 p. Ct or $160/100 Cents pr
Share.[3] T.P.

ALS, DLC:GW.

1. In September 1798 GW arranged with Thomas Peter to have some of the
tobacco that he had received in payment from his Maryland tenants shipped to
England on consignment with that of Joseph Carleton, a Georgetown merchant.
See GW to Peter, 1, 4 Sept. 1798, and Peter to GW, 3, 10 Sept. 1798.

2. The payment of $55.75 was what Peter had got in the sale of the tobacco
note that GW sent him on 5 May. See Day Book, 7 May.

3. The dividend of $272 from the Bank of Columbia made up a part of the
$1,000 that GW sent to William Thornton on 31 May for George Blagdin. See
Day Book, 31 May.

From Lafayette

My dear general,   Vianen 9 Mai 1799

your kind and Welcome letter of the 25 december is safely arrived and as my friend Bureau de Puzy has not yet sailed, he will,
along with some introductory lines, Carry these my affectionate
and filial thanks[1]—no, my dear general, it never Entered my Head
to attribute your Silence to any neglect of yours, and I would have
Suspected European piracies, or things much more incredible,
Rather than any abatement in that friendship I have been so long
used to experience, and Conscious, as far as heart Can go, to deserve—I find a greater proportion of my scribling has reached you
than I had thought, and while I regret the sanguine forwardness
that has deprived me of your answers, you will, I know, Readily
apologize for it, as it denotes, how ardently, in spite of difficulties,
I long to be in america.[2]

yet On hearing of the interior divisions which to me appear
more unnatural than to those who have witnessed their progress,
on finding how much in the differences betwenn the united States
and france, the later had been to blame, and how far I am, not
only to influence, but Even to ascertain the dispositions of her
government, I had some times, within myself, Revolved the arguments Contained in your Candid and affectionate letter—a hint
from Hamilton had made me think on it[3]—and among the tender

Motives to wish for a line from you; I had also an Expectation of
your friendly advices—my own objections, However, have been
hitherto Removed by the determination I have formed, & the
right I may claim, not to Embroil my long Earned tranquillity with
party politics—I have from my youth, head, heart, & hand been
devoted to american independance and freedom—I have in Europe Served the Cause & the friends of liberty, and on the extensive & tempestuous stage of the french revolution, impressed
with your letters, My dear general, and those of our friends, I have
with some boldness proclaimed, and not without public approbation for three years supported the principles for which you
have so gloriously fought, and so succesfully led us—and the
Moment, I could not, Consistent with those principles of natural
Right and public justice, hold the high station, which the Con-
quering ⟨fac⟩tion offered to Raise Still higher, I left to others to
Reap the field of military glory I had sown—five years have I in
the imperial & royal fangs, which unluckily Seized me, Expiated
my services to liberty & legal order—Nor thought I, although I
was rescued by the french government, and altho' my fortune (not
the three fifths spent in the cause of the people, but the remainder
of the two fifths Confiscated in his name) Might depend on it, that
I could any how condescend to approve arbitrariness, or caress
immorality—now could not I expect that after I have heartily embraced on the american shore my old Brothers & companions, my
happy visits at Mount-Vernon, my retirement on a small farm, I am
too Utterly ruined to approach the Cities, will not be invaded by
party stimulations?

Your opinion however My dear G[ener]al has with me, as it ever
had, an immence weight—I know you long to fold me to your
paternal heart, yet you advise me against your own satisfaction &
mine—you are better informed, & to your judgement I am used
to submit—your worthy friend Mr Murray to whom I have confidentially imparted it confesses his opinion coincides with yours,[4]
& I must confess, perhaps as a Weackness, that I am not without
some distant hopes, that, altho' an objet of proscription, I may
become not quite useless to the purpose of an american negociation—I am nevertheless narrowly circumstanced as to the conve-
niency of an azilum—The renewal of the War, renders the right
side of the Rhine, to the Eastern end of Europe, Either unsafe, or
improper for me—in france, it little avails to enjoy the esteem &

benevolence of the nation, and altho' the Batavian govt go with
the people in their favour to me, it may become a matter of delicacy, which however I dont believe, to avoid comitting them with
an imperious ally—hitherto I am here, on every account perfectly
well, I owe not only to the conviction you have produced in me,
but to an advice whatever, coming from you, to differ my intended
voyage untill you have answered this letter, & I am sure you will
have the Kindness to obviate the inconveniencess which these
delays, perhaps by some friends misunderstood might have with
respect to them, or the people at large—but in the improbable
case where I would suddenly pop upon you, be certain, my dear
g[ener]al that my motives should be such as to convince you of
their urgency, & then I hope individual independance would be
left to an harassed old friend by american parties—be pleased
therefore, My dear g[ener]al to continue directing your letters
to me in Europe, & to inclose them to Mr Pitcairn, the american
consul in hambourg, or to Mr Murray in holland as opportunity
offers.[5]

The account you give me of internal politics, pains me great
deal, the more so as knowing the superiority of your station, & the
uprightness of your judgement, I am not allowed those defalca-
tions which in party-matters are generally warranted permit me to
take this opportunity, as I dont remember whether a former account made part of the received letters, to state a fact respecting
Doctor logan—I happened to be in hamburg, with my wife then
going to paris, when that gentleman, whom my son remembered
to have seen at your house, called upon me, he was on his way to
france, & having letters of recommendation to some influencing
people, he told me, What, he intended, in private conversation,
to represent to them respecting the injustice & impolicy of the
french govt by the united states, it was indeed the very things I had
lately written, & you would have expressed—it was at that time
difficult for americans to have a french pass, & as the Chargé
d'affaires came the same day to take leave of the family, I requested him to give one to the Doctor, since which I had from
him a letter expressing hopes that came also to me from well informed friends, who added the remonstrances of an american
called Logan, had had a good effect—that I would think useless
to repeat, had I not seen in a paper, that the Doctor had been

blamed, & it is incumbent on me to let you know what I have to say in his favour.[6]

While I have written to you My Dear g[ener]al that I thought the french Directory to be sincerely wishing for a reconciliation with the united states, I was impelled not by any partiality for, neither by an overrated confidence in them, but by the evidence of their interest as french Citizens, as members of govt as ennemies to great Britain, & by every information I could gather, & now, I again say that I firmly believe they wish for a reconciliation, which I know to be the warm, friendly desire, of the nation at large, so that I hope, the two Republics will come to a good understanding.

As to general politics Mr Murray will acquaint you with them— honest Men in all parties cannot but execrate the assassination of the french plenipotentiaries at Radstat, if the horrid news, we have got but yesterday is unhappily confirmed—one of them, Roberjot, who was spoken of for a Director, I particularly regret he was a sensible man, on whose good intention I could depend.[7]

George had on his return from America acquainted me with the melancholy news that my Dear aid de Camp, your worthy nephew was no more—I heartily feel the affectionate attention he had to call after me his eldest Boy—my tenderest wishes shall ever attend what remains of that excellent Man.[8]

What you tell me of practices which after the 10th of august were carried within the united states by agents of the Jacobine faction, I had already heard, lamented, & abhorred, such were with an immense deal of money, & too much success poured upon my enfranchissed country by the British govt that is the old doctrine of Machiavelism—how repugnant to the noble doctrine of liberty, who knows better than you, my dear G[ener]al, I have a right to say, who knows better than me.

Georges is still in paris—the late defeats have encreased his disposition, warm enough already, to serve in the army, & my friends agree in that opinion, not his mother, Georges has got a good head, & a good heart, nothing will he do but what behoves an honest friend of liberty, my advice will not go before I weigh the matter, & then I think that much confidence may be had in his own judgement.

My wife, my daughters, and Son in law, join in presenting their affectionate respects to Mrs Washington & to you my dear g[ener]al the former is recovered & sets out for france on monday next with Virginia—our little grand Daughter is well, will your charming one accept our tender regard? With filial love & respect I am my Dear general Yours

La Fayette

Mr Frestel is now at Paris, & in good health; I need not adding the meeting made Georges, & both indeed very happy.[9]

ALS, NIC.

1. GW does not record in his diary a visit from Jean-Xavier Bureaux de Pusy, Lafayette's friend who shared his exile and imprisonment. Lafayette's "introductory lines" may be the following paragraph, a copy of which, dated "19th April" and without heading or closing, is in NIC: "Mr Murray whom I have had the pleasure to see, and whose appointement as a plenipotentiary to france, makes me particularly happy, will no doubt give a full account of european politics, the coalition are improving the opportunities unfortunatly given them by the Bad conduct of the french govt & certain it is, that instead of having on the popular Side, the majority of each allied people, & of the hostile nations, as it should have been, had good sistems been poursued, the acts of tiranny & pillage within & without, have disgusted many in france, & many abroad, whom nothing but the return of liberty, and that with difficulty, can again reconcile to the new order of things—however there are in popular institution, in legal equality so many advantages over the various aristocraties we had overthrown, the concils of the royal & imperial cabinets, Mr Pitt excepted, are So very absurd, the counter-revolutionary Chiefs are so mad, & the french army so substantial, well disci-plined, & brave, that I am convinced the contest which is now renewed shall again end favorably to france, provided however the returns to the principles of liberty & justice upon which the revolution was begun for it Seems to me there is, not only honestly, but politically no other way to close it. but however averse govt have been to that description of men called *Constitutional*, they have been lately so affraid of the anarchist that their influence in the actual elections has been anti Jacobine, which has produced a pretty good proportion of good Representa-tives—so far as, with the method of *transporting* & *annulling* it may be called a representation the Civil and military events of this summer will probably be interesting."

2. In his letter to Lafayette of 25 Dec. 1798, GW acknowledged the receipt of Lafayette's letters of 6 Oct. and 20 Dec. 1797, and of 26 April, 20 May, 20 Aug., and 5 Sept. 1798.

3. Alexander Hamilton wrote Lafayette on 28 April 1798 advising him not to come to the United States (Syrett, *Hamilton Papers*, 21:450–52).

4. William Vans Murray wrote John Quincy Adams in Berlin on 19 Mar. 1799 that he had returned the day before to The Hague from Utrecht where he had seen Lafayette and his family. "La F[ayette] is young in look and healthy," he wrote, "but what I did least expect he is cheerful. He uninvited announces his attachment 'to Liberty,' as it is called, but what exceeded even the pictures of imaginary perseverance is, that he still, I believe, wishes to be instrumental in

curing political evils—ameliorating mankind!! Lord have mercy upon me!! . . .
He is more in frame of mind like an ingenuous Virginian of little experience and
much metaphysical reading than any European I ever saw. . . . I stated various
things to disincline him from going to the United States, but he is fixed; he will
go in June" (Ford, "Murray-Adams Letters," 528–29). After visiting Lafayette
again in mid-August, Murray wrote GW on 17 Aug. 1799 of Lafayette's continued
desire to go to the United States. Lafayette did not return to America until 1824.

    5. GW had not answered this letter at the time of his death. Joseph Pitcairn of
New York succeeded Samuel Williams as U.S. consul at Hamburg in 1798.

    6. For GW's strongly negative feelings about George Logan's mission to France,
see especially Notes on an Interview with George Logan and Robert Blackwell,
13 Nov. 1798, printed above.

    7. Claude Roberjot (1752–1799) and Ange-Elisabeth-Louis-Antoine Bonnier
d'Alco (1750–1799) were assassinated shortly after the close of the Congress of
Rastadt.

    8. Both the first and second sons of George Augustine Washington and his
wife Frances Bassett Washington were named George Fayette Washington. The
first, born 10 April 1787, lived for only two weeks; the second, born in 1790, lived
until 1867.

    9. Felix Frestel accompanied George Washington Motier Lafayette to America
in 1795 and returned with him to France in the fall of 1797.

From George Lewis

Dr Sir   Marmion, King George County 9th May 1799

    Being anxious to get a Command in the immediate Army, I
wrote to a friend in Congress at an early day on the subject, expressing my desire to be with the Army, and requested him to signify the same to the Secretary of War, or so arrange the business
as I might be considered a candidate for a Command—to this letter I have never received a reply, and am now inform'd by a friend,
that my name is not known at the War office, among those gentlemen who have applied for appointments, how to account for this
inattention I am at a loss.

    Still desierous of an appointment and hearing that the Gentle-
man appointed to the Command of the Cavalry had declin'd his
acceptance—I take the liberty of offering my Services to that
Command. having a Personal acquaintance with most of the Gentlemen belonging to that Regiment, and strongly urged by some
of them to make this application—if this appointment cannot be
had, I am informed that Congress have it in contemplation to raise
another Regiment of Cavalry (if so) I should be thankful Sir (thro.
you) to be considered as a candidate for that Command, having

served the greater Part of my time whilst in the Revolutionary War in the Cavalry, and again as Commander of the Virginia Cavalry on the Western expedition (I feel a Partiallity for that service) Any attention or Service that you can render me in this business will be gratfully acknowledg'd by[1]—Yr Affectionate Nephew

G. Lewis

Copy, in George Lewis's hand, ICHi.

1. On 6 June GW wrote James McHenry and explained why George Lewis was not on the list of the officers that in December GW, Alexander Hamilton, and Charles Cotesworth Pinckney proposed should be named for the New Army. He reviewed his nephew's military experience and strongly recommended him to the secretary of war. Lewis did not receive a commission in the new cavalry unit.

From Gouverneur Morris

My dear Sir,   Newark 9 May 1799

I take the Liberty to enclose a Letter long since transmitted to me for Monsieur de la fayette. It was in London with my Papers when I saw him last at Altona but (if in my Possession) I should perhaps have withheld it as having no probable Relation to any Matter within his present Competency—I should have delivered it into your own Hands at Mount Vernon if Business which demands my Attendance had not compelled me to return from Philadelphia Northward—But I assure you my dear Sir the Pleasure of passing a few Hours with you is among the greatest which I promised myself in returning to my native Country.[1] Render I beseech you my Respect acceptable to Mrs Washington and beleive me as ever yours

Gouv. Morris

ALS, DLC:GW; LB, in Morris's hand, DLC: Gouverneur Morris Papers.

1. Morris saw Lafayette at Altona, the fishing port of Hamburg on the North Sea, on 24 July 1798, before Morris sailed for New York in October. The identity of the letter intended for Lafayette has not been determined. Morris left the letter in London when he departed for the Continent in June 1796, which indicates that the unidentified letter was written before that time. GW acknowledged the receipt of Morris's letter on 26 May: "My dear Sir, Your favor of the 9th Instant from Newark, came duly to hand.

"I offer you my sincere congratulations on your safe return to the United States: It is unnecessary I hope to add, that if either business or inclination should induce you to look towds the South, that I shall be very happy to see you at this Seat of my retirement; where I rather hope, than expect, to spend the remnant of my life in tranquillity; if one may judge from the appearance of both external, & internal causes, which present themselves to our present view.

"Mrs Washington is thankful for your kind remembrance of her, and unites in best wishes for you, with Your ever Affecte Hble Servant Go: Washington" (letter-press copy, DLC:GW).

From Edward Carrington

Dear Sir,   Richmond May 10 1799

I have been honored by the receipt of your letter of the 30th Ult. and take pleasure in complying with your request as far as my information enables me.

In our Congressional Representation we have eight Federal Members towit, Genl Marshall, Evans, Lee, Powell, Robt Page, Goode, Gray, Parker—the first six are certainly in real disposition firm supporters of our Government and the administration of it—Mr Gray is a Young Gentleman of Southampton County who is said to have been antifederal formerly, but is now to be relied upon as federal—it is certain that the election was warmly contested upon the two principles, and that he has been elected as the federal Candidate. As to Colo. Parker you are well acquainted with his political conduct—he is now considered as federal, and as such was Supported against an antifederalist.[1] The remaining eleven Members are undoubtedly violent opponents of Government, mostly old ones reelected. Accounts from the district formerly represented by Mr Machir, which came here somewhat before the election, encouraged a belief that Mr Haymond a federalist, would get in there, but we hear that Jackson, a very opposite Character, has succeeded.[2]

We have gained ground considerably,[3] and as the weight of ability and character, is on the federal side of the Representation, we may hope to keep and add to it. This circumstance will also greatly ensure the preservation of the ground gained in the North Carolina Representation in the last election.

I am not as yet sufficiently informed as to the elections to the State Legislature to enable me to give any useful intelligence on them. Mr Henry is elected, but was too much indisposed to be at the election; and I fear he is not likely to be in health to take his ground when the Session comes on. We had a report a few days ago of his death, but it is contradicted indubitably—his death, or even inability to attend, would be truly deplorable. I have the honor to be Dear Sir Yr affectionate H[umbl]e St

Ed. Carrington

ALS, DLC:GW.

1. Carrington was accurate in reporting that these eight men who were elected could be termed Federalist. Robert Page (1765–1840) of Frederick County served only one term in the U.S. House of Representatives. Josiah Parker (1751–1810) of Isle of Wight County was a member of Congress from 1789 to 1801 and generally voted with the Federalists after 1795. For references to the election, see particularly John Marshall to GW, 1 May, nn.2 and 3.

2. The Republican George Jackson did take the third Virginia district seat, defeating John Haymond's bid to succeed James Machir. See John Marshall to GW, 1 May, n.2.

3. Only three avowed Federalists had been elected to Congress from Virginia in 1797: Daniel Morgan, James Machir, and Thomas Evans of the Eastern Shore.

To Daniel Morgan

Dear Sir   Mount Vernon 10th May 1799

I have just received a letter from the Secretary of War, in which, after giving it as the opinion of the President of the United States, that Officers for the twenty four additional Regiments ought to be had in contemplation; that, in case the exigency of our Affairs should require them, greater dispatch might be used in the formation, is the Extract which follows.[1]

Having given these Extracts, so fully, but little remains for me to add, further than to request your aid in carrying the Secretary's views into effect, conformably to the principles he has laid down; and that you will consider my application to you, as an evidence of my confidence in your knowledge of characters (especially of the old & meritorious Officers of the Virginia line)—of your patriotism, and willingness to form a respectable Corps of Officers for our native State.

I have no objection to your conversing with Colo. Parker; or others on whom you can place reliance; on this occasion. Letting it be clearly understood, however, that the enquiry, and Selection here proposed, is eventual only, not as a thing actual resolved on, but preparatory, in case the President in the recess of Congress should, from the aspect of things, deem it expedient to carry the Law for raising twenty four Regiments into effect.

That you may be enabled, better to understand that part of the Secretary's letter, wch relates to the distribution of Officers to counties, I enclose you the Inspector Generals allotmt of the State into divisions & subdivisions, for the convenience of recruiting & rendesvousing in each.[2] Hoping that you continue to improve in your health, I remain with very sincere esteem & regard, Dear Sir, Your most Obedient and Very Humble Servant

Go: Washington

ALS, NN: Myers Collection; ALS (letterpress copy), DLC:GW.

1. The letter from James McHenry from which the "Extract" that followed here was taken is dated 10 April 1799; McHenry's letter is printed in McHenry to GW, 2 May, n.1. In quoting the letter here, GW omitted only the first sentence and the sentence beginning: "You will, doubtless, find a facility in forming the list. . . ."

2. For Alexander Hamilton's plan for dividing Virginia into four recruiting districts, see Hamilton to GW, 27 Mar., n.2.

From James McHenry

Sir   War Department [Philadelphia] 11th May 1799

I enclose you three letters, one from Mr Posey recommending Mr Thomas Hord to a Majority in the provisional army; another from James Machir Esqr. recommending Mr William Bullett for the same grade; and one from Alexander Spotswood offering his services.[1] You will please to return these letters with the list you have been requested to furnish, when it shall be completed.[2] I have the honor to be, with the greatest respe[c]t, Sir, your most Obt Hle St

James McHenry

LS, DLC:GW.

1. For the role GW played in the compilation of a list of Virginians who might serve as officers if the Provisional Army authorized by Congress on 2 Mar. 1799 were called into being, see McHenry to GW, 2 May, n.1. The letter of 2 May to McHenry from Gen. Thomas Posey (1750–1818), who lived in Kentucky but wrote from Fredericksburg, Va., reads: "I take the liberty of recommending Majr Thomas Hord of Caroline county to your notice in the appointments to be made for officering the provisional Army. I observe by the papers that the President has thought it necessary to organize the provisional Regiments—Should this be the case you may rely in full confidance with respect to the virtue patriotism and abillities of Majr Thomas Hord. He was a valuable Officer in our late revolution— was very much wounded and cut to pieces in Bufords defeat—is a warm friend

to our Genl Government—is a steady Opposer of John Taylor to whome he is a neighbour—and is independant in his circumstances. Majr Hord did not solicit me to write to you for an appointment, but from my knowledge of the man I think he will be a great acquisition to the Army agreeable to the rank he may hold. I asked him if he would accept of a commission in the provisional army, he said if his country needed his services—that is if his country was in danger of an insurection or invasion he was ready and willing to serve in the rank of a field officer should the President think proper to confer such an appointment upon. I think his rank at the end of the war was a captain" (DLC:GW).

Thomas Hord served as an officer in the Virginia forces during the Revolution and had risen to the rank of captain lieutenant in the 6th Virginia Regiment when in May 1780 he was wounded and taken prisoner in Charleston, South Carolina.

Former congressman James Machir wrote to McHenry from Moorefield in Hardy County on 28 April: "Seing a paragraph in a news paper which mentions the presidents determination to rease the provisional army. I am requested to name for an appointment Major William Bullitt of Hardy county whose character & conduct Justifies the recommendation—Major Bullitt commanded a Batalion against the Insurgents in 1793 and was much respected as a good Officer—he is respected in his Neighbourhood as a good member of Society and well qualified should the president think proper to confer a majority on him I have [n]o doubt of Major Bullitts doing honor to the rank in which he may be placed. on my return Home from congress and from a view of our district I was induced to decline taking a poll again—there being a Federal candidate who could not be prevailed upon to give way, and a division of that Interest would have given a greater certainty of success to the democratic candidate—the 24th was the important day in virginia and I am fearful our district has not effected our wish on the occasion⟨.⟩ my friends were displeased at my declining and were sanguine as to my chance of being elected against both Candidates. however I was affraid to risk the matter at this important moment and should the *mock republican* gain the victory it is more to be imputed to Federal imprudence than Jacobinic influence, altho. the exertions of the Latter have been very great th[r]ough the State—and every electioneering trick that could be invented was excercised by them. . . . P.S. our District is extensive and the exact state of the poll unknown" (DLC:GW). John Haymond, who replaced Machir as the Federalist candidate from Virginia's third district, lost to George Jackson in the election held on 24 April (see John Marshall to GW, 1 May, n.2).

GW's friend Alexander Spotswood wrote McHenry from his house New Post on 3 May: "Through you, I beg leave to Tender my Services, to his Excellency the president of the United States, as an officer in the provisional Army. I shall only observe, That I am well acquainted with the wants and detail of an Army; and for my General Tactical Knowledge, and other Requisites Necessary for a man to possess to entitle him to a Command in the American Army; I beg leave to refer to Lieutenant General Washington" (DLC:GW).

2. On 19 July McHenry sent GW: "recommendations of Jesse Bennet, Allyn Pryor, John Allen, Andrew Donnelly, Henry Skyles & Arthur Owens. These recommendations, you will please to return, when a list of the applicants for the

State of Virginia is complete" (DLC:GW). And on 7 Aug. McHenry sent GW "Recommendations in favour of Mr James Glenn for a Captaincy in the Provisional Army" (DLC:GW). See also GW to McHenry, 12 Aug., n.1.

From William Russell

Sir   New York 11th May 1799

The fatality which has so long attended my endeavors to forward the Sheep seems still to attact, for the poor fellow when embark'd in the first Vessell we have had this Spring for New York has met an unusually long passage and by a subsequent detention here is very much reduced in his appearance, however as upon my arrival here I learn that a Sloop is now up for Alexandria I have desird my friend to embark him therein & I expect he will proceed in a day or two in the Sloop Lark Capt. Leaman bound for Alexanda where Mr Thos Porter is to attend to him, unless the Wind is favorable for Landing him at Mount Vernon, which Capt. Leaman has then promis'd to effect—The Sheep will, I know, be very much reduc'd, but a Summers good grass will I doubt not effectually restore him, & Show him a good Sheep, tho not equal to what I wish, & still hope to present you with—By Captn Leaman I also Send the Chaff engine, with another Small Box, which contains the Ground Borer, and an Hoe, made at Middletown, under the direction of an English Gentleman who has found Hoes in that form, preferrable to all others, both for dispatch & effect, and as this Gentleman, has more to do with practice, than theory, I am induced by his opinion, to ask your acceptance of it, with the Borer—This Hoe is of a breadth which he finds best adapted, to general use, but he varies the breadth, according to the purpose for which it is wanted, either in the Farm, or the Garden—I am sorry my Servant omitted to procure a wooden handle for the Borer, but there will be no difficulty in supplying this deficiency— It will be proper, that the Person who fixes the knife of the Chaff Engine in its place, should observe a direction tied round one of the screws appurtaining to it[1]—I take leave to add, that I have just receivd from England, a pair of young Swine, of a celebrated Breed, from which I hope to obtain a family, & if successfull, shall be happy to ask your acceptance of a Pair of them, in the interim I remain with the highest respect Sir Yor Sincere & Obedt

Willm Russell

By an accidental oversight originating in the particular situation of a traveller, this Letter had been detaind in my Port Folio instead of being at the Post Office as I expected.

ALS, DLC:GW.

1. William Russell first wrote GW on 8 Sept. 1798 about sending to Mount Vernon a ram and a chaff machine. GW acknowledged on 26 May the receipt of Russell's gifts.

From Henry Lee, Jr.

dear Sir   Ab. 10 a.[m.] Sunday mor[nin]g [12 May 1799]

I found yr letter by Mr Anderson last evening at my lodgings & took the earliest opportunity of conversing with Mr Page on its contents[1] Mr Page says that on his first conversation with Mr Harrison he rated his property at five pounds pr acre, but that on a subsequent meeting he fell to 50/ pr acre, for which price he could have purchased the land.

He offered 45/ & proposed renewing the negotiation whenever he should again see Mr H.

Mr P. is of opinion that he can now obtain the land for 50/ & if you defer acting in the business when Mr H. comes down, I will thro Mr Page renew the negotiation without any recurrence to you—of the propriety of yr avoiding any bargain with Mr H. you will yrself judge: my own opinion is favorable to such avoidance[2]— I will wait on you in a few days & remain most respy & most affy yr ob: Svt

                                                      H. Lee

ALS, DLC:GW.

1. GW's letter has not been found.

2. On 16 May William Byrd Page wrote his brother-in-law Henry Lee from Alexandria: "you desire to know of me, certainly, what Mr Harrisons Land adjoining to some of Genl Washingtons may be had for. In reply thereto I can only say that for these six Months past, I have been endeavoring to purchase it, and coud once have had it @ 50/ ⅌ Acre, but from a conversation with that Gentleman to day, he tels me I was mistaken and that 60/ was the lowest price he had ever offer'd it for, and he now says (in consequence of a late review of the Property,) he will not take less than 12 Dollars pr Acre. I presume it may be had for 12 Dollars on easy payments" (DLC:GW). Lee sent the letter to GW, who docketed it. For earlier references to the negotiations of Lee and Page with William B. Harrison on behalf of GW, see Lee to GW, 28 Feb. 1799, n.2.

To James McAlpin

Sir   Mount Vernon 12th May 1799
Having heard nothing from you since my last request (now more than two Months ago) that you would complete, and send on my Uniform Suit so soon as the gold thread, which you informed me was expected in the Spring shipping, should have arrived; I give you the trouble of receiving this letter on the Subject: and to request that no unnecessary delay may prevent the accomplishment of it.[1]

Send the cloaths in such a Portmanteau as I described in my former letter, & by some Person (if you can) who may be coming *through*, to Alexandria; to be lodged at the Post Office, or Stage Office in that Town; with the Bill of cost &ca.[2] I am Sir Your Hble Servant

                                        Go: Washington

ALS, ViMtV.

1. GW's letter to McAlpin of 18 Mar. is printed in note 2, GW to McAlpin, 10 Feb. 1799.

2. See GW to McAlpin, 27 Jan. 1799. McAlpin responded from Philadelphia on 16 May: "Your two obliging favours of the 18th March and the 12th inst: I duly received. The Spring Ships not being arrived, I thought it unnecessary to trouble you with an answer to the first. I am much concerned, only to be able to repeat the same unpleasant story—but I beg leave to assure you, that so soon as they do arrive *not an instant* shall be lost in executing your commands. I feel myself too much indebted for past favours, to Neglect, for a moment, any thing that is in my power to perform—My inclination & Interest are equally concerned" (DLC:GW).

To John Marshall, Edward Carrington, and William Heth

Gentlemen   Mount Vernon May 12th 1799
Although the letter, of which the enclosed is a copy, is of old date, it has but just been received from the Secretary of War.[1]

Without aid, it will be impossible for me to carry his views into effect; which, & the confidence I place in you, is the best apology I can make for asking you to assist me, in the business required.

I have, with the exception of short intervals, been so many years absent from this State; & so little from my own home while in it,

that, I am as little acquainted with present characters—a few excepted—as almost any man in it; and, alone, as incompetent to a
judicious selection of Officers to the force contemplated.

The object, and principles, being sufficiently developed in the
letter. Indeed being all the information I have on the subject,
renders it unnecessary for me to add any sentiment of my own
thereto—further than that your aid in making the selection,
would be beneficial in a public view, and obliging me as an
individual.

No reason, that I can perceive, is opposed to the measure's being known, as a cautionary preparative for an exigency, which,
eventually, may happen; and would, should it happen, save much
time in the Organization, when very little could be afforded under
the pressure of the occasion.

That you may want no light I can afford, I enclose also, the Inspector General's division, & Subdivision of the State into Recruiting, & Rendezvousing districts; in order that, the Secretary's idea
respecting the distribution (as near as may be) of Officers to the
population thereof, may have its due consideration.[2] I forward
likewise, a list of the Virginia quota of Officers for the 12 Regiments, as arranged at Philadelphia in November last; but it is not
in my power to discriminate between those who have, & those who
have not accepted their Appointments.[3] With great & sincere esteem & regd—I am always—Your Obedt Servt

Go: Washington

ALS (letterpress copy), DLC:GW; copy, on deposit at ViU.

1. For the text of James McHenry's letter of 10 April, see McHenry to GW,
2 May, n.1. See also GW to Daniel Morgan, 10 May. An asterisk indicates that at
the end of this paragraph should be added: "a reason has been assigned for it."

2. For the plan drawn up by Alexander Hamilton for recruiting soldiers in
Virginia, see Hamilton to GW, 27 Mar., n.2. For the identifying of men who might
serve as officers in the proposed Provisional Army, see McHenry to GW, 2 May, n.1.

3. For the list of Virginia officers recommended to James McHenry for appointment in the New Army, see List of Officers for Virginia Regiments in the
New Army, c.21 May 1799, printed below.

From Ralph Wormeley, Jr.

Dear sir,   Rosegill 12 May 1799
I am about to ask a favour of you, which I think it probable you
may refuse, the frequency of applications of this sort having in-

duced a resolution, on your part, never to comply with any; I mean, "Letters of recommendation"—in June I propose to embark at Norfolk for New York in my way to Boston; my business is to settle my second son as a student at Harvard College Cambridge.[1]

I am not acquainted either with Governor Jay or General Hamilton, both of whom to be introduced to by a medium so respectable as your letter, would do me honour; and, certainly highly gratify me, as it would give me an opportunity of enjoying their company, and their conversation.

At Boston I wish to know Generals Knox & Lincoln, and solicit also Letters to them: you will be so good as to send them by post at your leisure, direct to me Rosegill near Urbanna; Mr Tayloe will not return by Mount Vernon or he would afford a good opportunity of conveying them to me.[2]

Report (too well founded I fear) announces the death of Mr Patrick Henry; he died 'tis said the day after he was elected a delegate to the Assembly: alarmed and indignant at the measures of the majority of the late assembly he offered himself and was elected, and intended to exert all the force of his eloquence to endeavour to change the Temper of the Delegates should that of the present members be similar to that of their predecessors. he is surely a great loss; at *this crisis* and with *this* disposition, what mighty good, would not such a man, with his great powers of Oratory and his known character of integrity, have wrought! but alas! he is gone, leaving behind him few who excel him as an Orator, or, as a Patriot.[3]

you will excuse this digression; nothing but it's being of so interesting a cast would have lead me into it—do me the favour to make my most respectful Compliments to your worthy Lady, and assure yourself that I am with the highest consideration of Esteem & respect, Dear sir Your most obt & most Humble servant

Ralph Wormeley

ALS, DLC:GW.

Ralph Wormeley, Jr. (1744–1806), of Rosegill in Middlesex County, was educated at Eton and at Cambridge University. During the Revolution he was suspected of Loyalist tendencies. Although he was elected to the Virginia house of delegates several times in the late 1780s, he took little part in politics.

1. Wormeley had three sons. The second son, John Tayloe Wormeley (1780–1801), was a student at Rhode Island College (Brown University) in Providence from 1797 until he was lost at sea when sailing for home in 1801. At this time the eldest son, Ralph Wormeley (b. 1777), was already an adult and the youngest,

Warner Lewis Wormeley (1785–1814) was no more than 14 years old; he was later educated at Cambridge not at Harvard.

2. A letter introducing Wormeley written by GW to Henry Knox on 22 May reads: "Dear Sir, Ralph Wormeley Esqr. (who will present this letter to you) carries one of his Sons to Harvard College, to be fixed there as a Student. Being a Stranger in the New England States, I beg leave to introduce him to your Acquaintance & civilities.

"He is a Gentleman of respectability in his own State; a friend to the Constitution & Government of the Union; and a person of Information; qualifications which, I persuade myself, will insure him a ready reception with you.

"Present Mrs Washington's best regards along with mine, to Mrs & Miss Knox; and be assured of the sincere & Affectionate esteem of Yours always Go: Washington" (ALS, CSmH). For the only other known letter of introduction written by GW for Wormeley, see GW to Benjamin Lincoln, 22 May.

3. Patrick Henry was gravely ill at this time, but he did not die until 6 June.

To James McHenry

Sir   Mount Vernon May 13th 1799

Your favour of the 2d Instt, covering your dispatches of the 10th Ultimo, was brought to me by the Messenger who carried my letters *to you* (of the 5 & 6th) to the Post Office in Alexandria.

That no time might be lost in carrying the Presidents Plan, and the request contained in your letter of the 10th Ult., into effect, I have solicited the aid of Generals Morgan, Lee, & Marshall; & the Colonels Heath & Carrington; if other fit & confidential characters should occur, as worthy of employment in the proposed Selection, I will speak, or write to them also; for it is on others I must rely.[1] An absence, with short intervals only, of near twenty five years with the consequent changes, has, in a great measure, obliterated my former acquaintance with the People of *this State*; and my knowledge of the rising generation in it (scarcely ever going from home) is very limited indeed. The task I am imposing upon others is delicate, and not of the pleasantest kind: because, except in a few Instances, it will be very difficult in such an extensive State as Virginia, to ascertain who would, or would not, accept appointments in the Provisional Army without previous enquiry; and to make this enquiry on the hazardous ground of rejection, involves a *round* of delicacy. namely—to the selected, who may have given his consent; to the selector, who may have asked it; and to the Department that is to approve, or disapprove the measure.

Viewing the matter in this light, Let me ask if there would be any impropriety in a notification from the War Office to the effect that as events may render it exped[ien]t to raise the 24 Regiments; and it having been found from experience that much time (when probably it could be least spared) would be required to Select and organise the Officers therefor; it is requested that all those who are desirous of serving their Country on the terms Specified in that act, would, without delay signify the same (producing such recommendations as would bring them forward under favourable auspices) with the grades, to wch reasonable pretensions would entitle them to G. W——n[2] or whomsoever, in this (the same in other States if the measure is approved) as you might be pleased to appoint, for the purpose of receiving the Applications: which ought *all* of them to be in writing, accompanied with the testimonials of merit, as above.

In a State, spreading over so much ground as Virginia does, it would require much time, & be scarely possible even then, to make the object of Government known, & to carry your plan of apportionment to the parts into effect, by any means much short of the one I have suggested: and if the notice is not *general*, the selection must, of consequence, be *partial*.

After allowing sufficient time for the applications to come in, one might then be able with the aid of such characters as could be confided in, to select, & form from the materials thus amassed, Officers agreeably to your list, & apportionment to the State; & without, I do not see how it can be accomplished in any reasonable time—much less efficiently.

There may be objections to this mode which do not occur to me; but sure I am, it would be found the most likely mean of producing characters from all parts of the State, or failing therein, of obviating any charge of partiality; for if men will not come forward when invited, it is their own fault, and not that of the Government.[3]

Under any circumstances, I consider this preparatory measure of the President's, to be eligible; but I am led to believe from his having adopted it, at *this time*, without any previous intimation thereof (that has come to my knowledge) before he left the Seat of Government, that stronger indications of hostility have been received, than appeared when he went away to have occasioned it; if so, I think it ought to be communicated to me in confidence;

for it must not be expected that like a Mercenary, I can quit my family & private concerns at a moments warning. There are many matters necessary for me to settle before I could leave home with any tolerable convenience, and many things, the providing of which would run me to an unnecessary expence, if I am not called to the Field.

And this conjecture, leads me to the consideration of another matter, of very serious importance. It is well known that the great advantage which the Armies of France have over those they contend with, lyes in the Superiority with which their Artillery is served, and in the skill of their Engineers. Let me entreat, therefore, that the most prompt & pointed attention be given to the procuring—and instructing—men in these Sciences. Lamentable indeed must be our case, if we shall have to acquire the knowledge of these arts in the face of an enemy, when *that* enemy ought to experience our Skill in the exercise of them. I do not mean to *recommend* characters as instructors in these branches; but I will mention the names of some who have passed through my mind, & have been recalled to it. Du Portail, Lamoy, Senf, Rivardi, and Latrobe. The last of whom I know nothing of, but have been told that he has knowledge *in*, & professes to be well acquainted with, the *principles* of Engineering. I notice these as persons within your reach, in case nothing better can be done—It is necessary to be provident. Let us not have things to prepare, when they should be in use.[4]

To enable me to carry your request into execution, I ought to be informed, who of the Virginia arrangement have accepted their appointments; who have refused; and from whom you have received no answer.[5] Many whose expectations were not answered in the last organization, & on that account declined, might be gratified on the present occasion with propriety—possibly fr[o]m necessity. With respect, I have the honor to be Sir Your Most Obedt Servt

Go: Washington

ALS, NNGL; ALS (letterpress copy), DLC:GW. The ALS was owned by Christies in 1992.

1. GW's letter to John Marshall, Edward Carrington, and William Heth is dated 12 May; that to Daniel Morgan is dated 10 May. See also, particularly, McHenry to GW, 2 May, n.1.

2. GW drew a line here and inserted above it "G. W——n."

3. GW's role in identifying men who might serve in the Provisional Army authorized by Congress on 2 Mar. 1799 is summarized in McHenry to GW, 2 May, n.1. On 19 May McHenry rejected GW's suggestion that the secretary of war invite men to express a willingness to serve as officers should the Provisional Army be constituted.

4. Louis Le Bègue de Presle Duportail (1743–1802), a Frenchman whom Congress during the Revolution made brigadier-general commandant of engineers for the Continental army, fled from France to America in 1793. Jean-Baptiste-Joseph, comte de Laumoy (1750–1832), a French engineer who served with the American army during the Revolutionary War, left France with Lafayette in 1792 and returned to America. John Jacob Ulrich Rivardi, a Swiss native, was a major in the 1st U.S. Artillery and Engineers and had built fortifications at Alexandria, Baltimore, and New York. See GW to Hamilton, 25 Feb. (first letter), n.2. Benjamin Henry Latrobe (1764–1820) came to Virginia from England in 1796, where, among other things, he completed the exterior of the capitol in Richmond. Since January 1799 he had been in Philadelphia building the Bank of Pennsylvania, which he had designed. Jean Christian Senf, a native of Sweden, had served as an engineer for South Carolina and Virginia. In the late 1780s he was chief engineer for the Santee Canal Company in South Carolina.

5. McHenry enclosed in his letter to GW of 21 May a list of the men who had been offered commissions in the Virginia regiments, indicating who had accepted, who had refused, and from whom no reply had been received.

From William Booker

Sir   Richmond 15 May 1799

Your letter of the 6 Inst. I duly receivd, and agreably to promise I Expect to be at Mount Vernon in the Early part of June.[1]

I Should have answerd you respecting Mr Roberts before this, but Waited to Get the best Information. I hear he resides in the town of petersburg and has for some time Quit the Milling Buiseness and has become Such a Sott that he is by No Means fit for buisiness. Instead of his being reclaimd I am told he is much worse.[2]

I Expect to go to petersburg in a few days, and will be Very particular in Inquiring about his Conduct, and will relate the particulars to you as soon as I return, although I believe the Information I have had to be Correct.

Should you wish any Inquiry to be made about any one Else, or Indeed about any thing that I can be of any Service to you, I will with pleasure Execute it. I am your Obt Sert

Wm Booker

ALS, DLC:GW.

1. This letter has not been found, but for Booker's purpose in coming to Mount Vernon, see GW to Booker, 3 Mar. 1799. See also Booker to GW, 6 June.

2. GW hired William Roberts, a Pennsylvania miller, in 1770 to operate his new gristmill at Mount Vernon. Roberts proved to be a superb miller, but in April 1785 GW reluctantly discharged him because Roberts had become "such an intolerable sot" (GW to Robert Lewis & Sons, 1 Feb. 1785, in *Papers, Confederation Series*, 2:317–18). Despite the fact that Booker on 6 June gave GW an even worse report on Roberts's present conduct, GW a few days later offered Roberts his old job back, which Roberts eagerly accepted (GW to Roberts, 17 June; Roberts to GW, 21 June). When Roberts arrived at Mount Vernon at the end of the summer, however, he apparently was so ill as to be incapacitated. On 16 Nov. 1799 Anderson paid Roberts $35.58 in "full" (Mount Vernon Ledger, 1799–1800). See also GW to Roberts, 8, 17 July, 29 Aug., Roberts to GW, 12, 22 July, and GW to James Anderson, 8 Sept. 1799.

To William B. Harrison

Sir   Mount Vernon 16th May 1799

I have given the proposition you have made me, respecting your part of Chapel land, all the consideration that is necessary; the result of which is.[1]

That I will give, as a Rent, thirty dollars for every hundred acres within the bounds you shall establish; and in that proportion for the overplus, or add[itional] acres, according to measurement: Provided I receive a Lease for the whole quantity, for the term & time of fifteen years; and provided also, that at any time within Seven years after the first rent becomes due, I shall have the priviledge of purchasing the Land in fee simple, on paying Eight dollars for each & every acre that said tract shall contain.

Conscious as I am, that this is a generous offer for your land, and that I do not want to possess it either in fee simple or on Lease for one iota below its real value; conscious also, that in the ordinary course of things (there being nothing within itself) to support & keep it up, that it must grow worse and wor⟨se⟩ every year; and persuaded moreover, that you, and every other discerning mind, must view it in this light, it is unnecessary—especially after the conversation which has passed between us—to assign my reasons for this opinion in full detail.

The Rent I offer is equal to any that is paid for such Lands in the neighbourhood, as you would have learnt from Mr Mason;

and might learn from my Tenant Mrs Gray (on the same Land);[2] and was it not that I make no Tobacco, probably never shall, and of course, for the uncertainty of knowing what sum to provide (from the fluctuating price of that article) I wd as soon give the Rents you receive at present, as what I offer, on a thorough conviction that in *point of Interest*, I should gain by it. And sure I am no man who is a judge of Land and will view the condition of and what is *on* yours, will say, that to obtain it in fee, I have not offered the value of it. With respect to the vague, speculating, and unmeaning offers of men who have not wherewithal to fulfil an engagement, and do not mean (more than probable) to do it—at the time such engagement is entered into, I pay no sort of regard. You, probably, would get into embarrassments with such men by an *ideal* instead of a *real* price for your property, & I get it thereafter on betr term. If you think this proposition of mine worth your attention, I shall be ready at any time to enter on the detail⟨s⟩ and to carry it into effect—being Sir Your most Obedt Servant

Go: Washington

ALS (letterpress copy), DLC:GW.

1. For GW's negotiations with Harrison to acquire control of Harrison's land adjoining Mount Vernon, see GW to Harrison, 4 Nov. 1798, and note 1 of that document. See also Henry Lee to GW, 12 May, and note 2 of that document. Harrison must have made his "proposition" regarding the land while at Mount Vernon on 14 and 15 May when he, GW, and Thomson Mason surveyed Harrison's tract (*Diaries*, 6:347–48; see also GW to Harrison, 10 April, and Harrison to GW, 24 April 1799).

2. On 27 Nov. 1798 Ann (Mrs. William) Gray paid GW $3.00, the "Ballance of last Years Rent" (Mount Vernon Ledger, 1797–98, 189). See also the rental account with Mrs. Gray, 1797–1800, in the Mount Vernon Ledger, 1799–1800, 27.

From John Marshall

Dear Sir   Richmond May 16th [17]99

Neither Colo. Carrington nor Colo. Heth are now in town. So soon as they arrive your letter of the 12th inst. with its inclosures, will be communicated to them. I wish it may be in our power to furnish any useful information on the subjects inquired into.

Returns of all the elections have been receivd. The failure of Colo. Hancock & of Major Haymond was unexpected & has reducd us to eight in the legislature of the Union. In the state elections very considerable changes have been made. There are from fifty to sixty new members.[1] Unfortunately the strength of parties is not materially varied. The opposition maintains its majority in the house of Delegates. The consequence must be an antifœderal Senator & Governor.[2] In addition to this the baneful influence of a legislature hostile perhaps to the Union—or if not so—to all its measures, will yet be kept up.

If it be true that France has declard war against Austria, it will be now apparent that it woud have been wise to have attempted the releif of Ehrenbreightstein & the preservation of Naples & Sardinia.[3] Even this instructive lesson will probably make no impression on the nations of Europe or the people of America. With the utmost respect & attachment I am Sir your Obedt servt

J. Marshall

ALS, DLC:GW.

1. For the Virginia elections of 24 April, see Marshall to GW, 1 May, and notes 2 and 3 of that document.

2. Sen. Henry Tazewell, a Republican, had died in January 1799. The newly elected Virginia legislature chose the Republican Wilson Cary Nicholas to replace him. It also elected James Monroe governor, by a vote of 116 to 66 for his opponent, James Breckenridge (1763–1833).

3. Ehrenbreitstein was a fortress at Coblenz on the Rhine.

From James Welch

Sir   Fredrecksburrg May 16th 1799

I find it out of my power To Rise the money in this place that I am at this time in debted to you; money is Verry Scarce among the marchanes of this place; the[y] cannot be temped to advance money for paper that has Longer then 60 dayes To Run; the paper that I have will be Due on the 25th day of Novembr Next it is Well Securd and will be Puntuelly paid that you Shall have I Start this day for Green brere and will procede on to Kentuckey or Send my Brother in order to Rise money for you; this you may depend apon that I will Exart my Self To Rise the money Due you and will make Every a Ringement in my power To be more puntul with you for the future; at Eney Time you wold think proper To Wright me dereck your Leter to Stantown from that it will be sent to me.[1] I am with Due Respt your Hm. Sarvent

James Welch

P.S. if you dont find it consistant with your ⟨*illegible*⟩ to Giv me a Litel indulgance Let me knaw and I will cum down and Giv up the Bargeon and Sacrafise as much of my Property as will Rise a Sum of money as may be thougt Reseanable for disapointment; the Exposeing of my property to the publick will a meduately prevent the Setelment of the Land from gowing on of corce that wold prevent me from holdin the Bargeon; for my one credet and the Good of that country I prefer cuming to Eney tarmes you may lay down that is Resenable I have no dout that Eney you will shall be. J.W.

ALS, DLC:GW.

1. GW wrote Welch on 7 April to complain bitterly about Welch's failure to make any payment on his purchase of GW's Kanawha lands; on 25 April Welch wrote GW that he could "be Sure of Seeing me at your plac in the corce of Next Month." See GW's response of 26 May.

From Clement Biddle

Dear sir   Philadelphia May 18. 1799

I cannot find the person who made the Machines for raking Meadows—he has removed from Kensington and I can learn no more of him or his machines.[1]

The sellers of Shad & herrings tell me they are very dull sale & a worse prospect at this Market—they ask 4 Drs ℔ bbl for Herrings but nobody to buy them & shad are merely retailed by the single barrel—Flour is 9 to 9½ Ds. for Super fine, common in proportion rather dull, wheat 13/—but the market depends on the Opening the market to Hispaniola—reports of this Day say the British have declared that Island independant but we hear nothing from Dr Stevens our Consul General & Commissioner who was Authorised to treat for Opening the Trade.[2] I am very respectfully Yr mo. Obed. & very humle serv.

                                              Clement Biddle

ALS, DLC:GW.

1. GW wrote Biddle about the raking machine on 28 April. Biddle followed up this letter of 18 May with another one on 21 May: "Since I wrote you on the subject of the Machine for raking Meadows & harvest fields I have seen Jonathan Williams Esqr. who gives me Information where to find the Maker, but, he says he tried One on his farm—that it did not answer—the Teeth broke & it got out of order & would only answer for Ground that was perfectly level & free from Stones—the one he tried was thrown aside on the Canal near his place—No

Change in prices of Wheat or flour since my last nor Appearance of Demand for shad or herrings at this market—Our Exports are remarkably dull" (DLC: GW).

2. For references to developments in Saint Domingue, see Biddle to GW, 5 Feb. 1799, and note 4 of that document.

From James McHenry

My dear Sir   War Dept. [Philadelphia] 19th May 1799
I received your letter of the 13th inst.

Before I concluded to request you to take upon yourself a task which involves the delicacies you have suggested, I had foreseen them, and reflected in what manner they might be avoided, and at the same time, the object in view obtained, without subjecting the government to difficulties or inconveniences which might be more sensibly felt by the Country. To have solicited, in any form, by a public official advertisement, men to offer themselves for offices, would have conveyed to the nations of Europe, that a war with France, or the military service itself, was unpopular, seeing the Executive was obliged to resort to extraordinary means to procure even officers for the army. It was also imagined, that an invitation of this nature, would have brought forward men of different and adverse political principles as competitors, one description of which would have endeavoured to have procured recommendations calculated to deceive, a circumstance, which at least, would have rendered a selection more tedious riskful and difficult.

As the business is now to be conducted, it is only necessary to mark off the State into districts or Counties, to ascertain the number of Captains or[1] Subalterns to be drawn from each district or County, and to request some well known and prominent character in the several districts or Counties, to give in as many names, *as there are offices allotted to their districts*, of those they think would serve, with a short sketch of their qualities. Your own and the general knowledge of the gentlemen, which I expected you would call to your aid, I conceived would be fully adequate to make the best selection of field officers.

With respect to a charge of partiality, on account of the business being conducted without a news-paper notification, I do not think it can be brought forward with even a shadow of propriety. The act authorising the President of the U. States to raise a Provisional army, was passed the 28th of May 1798, to which the act of the last session can be considered as a supplement only, extending the period wherein appointments may be made, by the President, and providing for an increase of the number of Regiments. This act has been sufficiently promulgated.[2] Those who have not or will not come forward, with a tender of their services, and recommendations, it is reasonable to conclude, are detered, by motives of delicacy, which no invitation would obviate, or from an expectation that their merits being known, they will be appointed without any solicitation upon their part.

These and such like reasons induced me to relinquish the idea of a news-paper official invitation for candidates.

I shall send you the list of acceptances and refusals, and also all the names of candidates and their recommendations for appointments in the Provisional army from the State of Virginia.[3]

We have no recent news from Europe since the Presidents leaving the seat of Government of any importance, or indication of the intentions of the Directory of France other than the kind of declaration of war against the U.S. by Desforneaux, the particular agent of the Executive Directory at Guadauloupe.[4]

I am very sensible of our situation as it respects skilful artillerists & Engineers. Of those you have named, not in service, Senf strikes me as the least exceptionable. We have no *rank* for Du Portail, were it perfectly prudent to engage him. Lamoy, I have understood has particular reasons which would prevent him from entering into our service at this moment, were there no objections to him as a French man. Latrobe is said to be more of a civil than military engineer, and besides is fully occupied.[5] Senf, therefore, it will be proper to think seriously about, and learn whether he would relinquish his civil employments in S. Carolina for the pay, and emoluments of a Lt Colonel.

This is sunday. If I have omitted to speak to any point as fully as I ought you will lay it to the charge of the day and my being obliged to prepare myself to go to Church. I am my Dear Sir most affectionately and truely yours

James McHenry

ALS, DLC:GW; ALS (letter-book copy), DLC: James McHenry Papers; ADf, MiU-C.

1. McHenry wrote "&," not "or," in the draft of the letter.

2. This was the act of 2 Mar. 1799 providing for the calling forth under certain circumstances of a Provisional Army.

3. See McHenry to GW, 21 May, and its enclosure.

4. Edme-Etienne Borne Desfourneaux (1767–1849), a French general, was made governor of Guadeloupe in 1798.

5. See GW to McHenry, 13 May.

Letter not found: from Charles Cotesworth Pinckney, 20 May 1799. On 5 June GW wrote Pinckney: "Your favor of the 20th Ulto from Mulberry Grove, came duly to hand."

To William Augustine Washington

My dear Sir,   Mount Vernon 20th May 1799

Your letter of the 2d instant by Captn Bowcock came safe, as the Corn did, in good order; and I should have written to you by his return but the Vessel went from the Landing at which she delivered the Corn unknown to me. But not without the Whiskey and Fish; as I had, previously, directed these to be shipped.[1]

The first I hope you will find good, if no pranks are played with it; Mr Anderson (my Manager) having assured me that he could vouch for it. The latter was among the quantity I had put up for my own use, and hope is not bad.

The money for the Corn shall be ready at your call, be that when it may; but if you have no immediate use for it, it wd be an accomodation to me to suffer it to remain in my hands until there is— for I have been disappointed in *every* sum I expected to receive, and am obliged to borrow, at the Bank of Alexandria (on disadvantageous terms) to fulfil my engagements; and will do the same to answer your call, whenever it is made; Only requesting a postponement so long as it comports *perfectly* with your own convenience.[2]

We had heard of your intended Nuptials, and congratulate you on the consumma⟨tion⟩ of them; and with your lady and family, shall always be happy to see you at this place—The Election of Generals Lee & Marshall to Congress are pleasing Events. The Representation from this State will be much strengthened thereby. The regret is, that there was not more of their politic's sent. The reflection however, that we are gaining ⟨strength⟩ must console us for the present, and stimulate Federal men to greater exertions in future. With much sincerity, I am your affectionate friend and Uncle

Go: Washington

ALS (letterpress copy), DLC:GW. The sale of the ALS by Sotheby Parke-Bernet was reported in the *New York Times* on 18 Oct. 1972.

1. For the shipment of the corn from William Augustine Washington by Captain Henry Bowcock (Bocock), see W.A. Washington to GW, 2 May, n.1. On 24 May GW wrote that he had been mistaken when he said the whiskey and fish had been shipped but that Bowcock had now taken the items aboard. William Augustine Washington on 1 June acknowledged receipt of them. See also W.A. Washington to GW, 2 May, and notes.

2. William Augustine Washington wrote to GW on 1 June about his need to draw immediately on GW for payment for the corn that he had shipped to Mount Vernon. On 10 June GW assured his nephew that he would pay when called upon to do so, and William Augustine Washington drew on GW for the first payment of $500 on 15 June (see W.A. Washington to GW, 13 July, n.1).

From William Augustine Washington

My Dr sir   Haywood May 20th 1799
This will be delivered to you by Capt. Bowcock, who carries up the Ballence of what corn I could spare 166 Barrels—the first Load was 187½ Barrels, he was to have taken 200 but I left home before he had finished the Load, I mentioned that quantity in my Letter but the wind coming on to blow fresh he chose rather to go with that quantity, than to remain longer[1]—I have sent my Steward to day to Mr Wm Floods, who has the disposing of the Corn of Mr Thacker Washingtons Estate and expect an answer this Evening, whether he will let the Estates Corn go to you, under my contract with you—the wind being favorable Capt. Bowcock has called on me to dispatch him, so that I shall not see my Steward, before his Vessel Sails but as he has ordered his skipper to call at Roziers Creek, & he intends to ride up there he will see him, & will be able to inform you whether I am to have the Corn or not, and the probable quantity[2]—I have recd the Barrel of fish, and Capt. Bowcock says he is to get the Whiskey when he goes up⟨,⟩ one Barl of the first quality and another of the second.[3]

I only returned last Night from Mansfield, blest with a charming agreeable Wife, who desires to be most respectfully remembered to you and Mrs Washington. I am My Dr sir with the sincerest respect, your Affectionate Nephew

                                    Willm Augt. Washington

ALS, ViMtV.
1. For William Augustine Washington's shipments of corn to Mount Vernon in May 1799, see W.A. Washington's letter to GW of 2 May, n.1.

2. Thacker Washington, who died in 1798, was the father-in-law of William Pinckard Flood, the son of Dr. William Flood of Westmoreland County. Thacker Washington was the son of GW's first cousin Henry Washington and the nephew of Warner Washington, Senior. Rosiers Creek, just below Thacker Washington's land, was part of the dividing line between Westmoreland and King George counties. For William Pinckard Flood's shipment of corn by Bowcock to Mount Vernon, see W.A. Washington to GW, 1 June, and note 1 of that document.

3. For references to the whiskey and fish, see W.A. Washington to GW, 2 May, nn.2 and 3.

From James McHenry

Dear Sir.　　　　　　War Department [Philadelphia] 21 May 1799
Inclosed is a list of the names of the persons appointed from Virginia, for the Cavalry and Infantry. It distinguishes, 1st Those who have accepted. 2. Those who have declined & 3d Those who have not been heard from.[1]

I sent your letter to McAlpin. But as the Spring vessels have not yet arrived by which the gold thread is expected, of course your uniform is not yet finished. I intended sending the Stars for the Epaulets with the uniform coat. If you have given any orders respecting them which will render this improper I beg you to inform me.[2] I am Dear Sir truely and Affectionately yours

James McHenry

ALS, DLC:GW; ADf, MdAA.
　1. See enclosure.
　2. See GW to James McAlpin, 12 May, and note 2 of that document.

Enclosure
List of Officers for Virginia Regiments in the New Army
[c.21 May 1799]
Seventh Regiment of Infantry.

+　Accepted.
°　Declined.
Blanks, not heard from.

		Field Officers.	
+		William Bentley	Lieut: Colo.	Powhatan
+	1	Robert Beale	Major	Maddison
+	2	James Baytop	Major	Gloucester County
			Companies	

Field Officers (*continued*).

+	1	Daniel Ball	Captain	near Richmond
+	6	Van Bennet	Lieutenant	Shepherds Town
+	8	Andrew M. Lusk	Ensign	Fredericksburg
	9	Edmund Clark	Captain	
+	8	John Brahan	Lieutenant	Winchester
+	9	James Brown	Ensign	Staunton
+	4	John Davidson	Captain	Richmond
○	1	Robert Carrington	Lieutenant	
+	7	John Heiskel	Ensign	Woodstock
+	2	Archibald Randolph	Captain	Goochland Ct House
+	10	Brewer Goodwin Junr	Lieutenant	Isle of Wight near Smithfield
+	4	William Potts	Ensign	Petersburg
	3	Bartholomew Dandridge	Captain	ditto
+	2	Felix Wilton	Lieutenant	Hardy County
+	2	Marcus Combs	Ensign	Winchester
○	5	Thomas Turner	Captain	
+	5	Jesse Ewell Junr	Lieutenant	Dumfries
+	3	George Armistead	Ensign	near Alexandria
+	6	William Campbell	Captain	Lee County
+	7	Joseph Grigsby	Lieutenant	Rockbridge Co: Lexington
○	10	William Deane	Ensign	
+	7	Thomas Greene	Captain	Fredericksburg
+	4	Addison Armistead	Lieutenant	Alexandria
+	5	Horatio Stark	Ensign	Stephensburg
+	8	Robert King	Captain	Hanover
	9	Samuel J. Winston	Lieutenant	
+	6	Peter Lamkin	Ensign	Colchester
+	10	James Caldwell	Captain	Wheeling
+	3	Calvin Morgan	Lieutenant	Staunton
+	1	Jesse Dold	Ensign	Staunton

Cavalry Officers belonging to Virginia
Lieutenant Colonel.

John Watts   not heard from

Major

John Tayloe   under consideration

Captains

John B. Armistead		near Alexandria	accepted
Charles F. Mercer			will not accept

First Lieutenants

George Washington Craik		Alexandria	accepted
Laurence Washington		King George	accepted

Second Lieutenants

Charles Tutt		Culpepper	accepted
George W. P. Custis		Mount Vernon	accepted
Carter B. Fontaine		Dumfries	accepted

Eighth Regiment
Field Officers

+	Thomas Parker	Lieut: Colo.	Frederick
	Simon Morgan	Major	Fauquier
+	William Campbell	Major	Orange

Companies

+	1	Presley Thornton	Captain	Northumberland
+	1	Francis Fouchee	Lieutenant	Ditto
	10	Charles MCallister	Ensign	Spotsylvania
+	2	Robert Gregg	Captain	Culpepper
+	7	James Duncanson	Lieutenant	Ditto
+	1	James Tutt Junr	Ensign	Ditto
+	3	Henry Pearcy	Captain	Fairfax
+	2	Lemuel Bent	Lieutenant	Ditto
+	8	Obadiah Clifford	Ensign	Ditto
+	4	Nathaniel Henry	Captain	Berkley
+	8	Robert Gustin	Lieutenant	Ditto
+	2	Simon Owens	Ensign	Ditto
+	8	George S. Washington	Captain	Ditto
+	3	George Tate	Lieutenant	Ditto
+	6	George W. Humphreys	Ensign	Ditto
+	7	Richard Chinn	Captain	Loudoun
+	4	Charles ⟨ J.⟩ Love	Lieutenant	Ditto
+	3	John Crane Junr	Ensign	Ditto
+	8	Garnet Peyton	Captain	Stafford
+	10	John G. Brown	Lieutenant	Green Brier
°	9	Strother Settle	Ensign	Frederick
+	9	Daniel C. Lane	Captain	Loudoun
+	9	John William⟨s⟩	Lieutenant	Ditto
	7	John C. Williams	Ensign	Prince William

Companies (*continued*).

+	10	Philip Lightfoot	Captain	Culpepper
+	5	Thomas Jameson	Lieutenant	Ditto
	4	Charles Shackleford	Ensign	Ditto

+	5	Edmund Taylor	Captain	Frederick
+	6	John Campbell	Lieutenant	Ditto
	5	Willis Wills	Ensign	Loudoun

Those with this mark + have accepted.
    with this mark ° have declined.
    without any   have not been heard of.

D, DLC:GW. The numbers to the left of the men's names indicate their relative position within their respective ranks in each regiment. The manuscript has a column on the far right in the listing of the officers of the 7th and 8th regiments which simply provides the information that every man was from Virginia. This column has been omitted here.

An earlier version of this list in Charles Cotesworth Pinckney's hand, dating probably from the conclusion of the meeting of GW, Alexander Hamilton, and Pinckney in Philadelphia in December 1798, is in DLC:GW placed at the end of December 1798. A comparison of the two lists indicates that between December 1798 and May 1799 seven changes had been made. In the 7th Regiment, Van Bennet, John Heiskel, Felix Wilton, and Marcus Combs had been entered in place of, respectively, Thomas Opie, Gerard Roberts, Robert Temple, and Alexander Henderson. In the 8th Regiment, Charles MCallister, Nathaniel Henry, and Willis Wills replaced Reuben Thornton, William K. Blue, and a Mr. Fitzhugh. See the Editorial Note to the list of Candidates for Army Appointments from Virginia, November 1798, printed above.

From Henry Lee, Jr.

dear General   Alexa[andria] 22d may [1799]

I have waited here two weeks cheifly to try to finish my engagement with you—But all my endeavors are vain—I shall never recede from my exertions till I do accomplish the end, for no event of my life has given me more anguish.

I would if you consider yr sale injurious rather relinquish the contract & give up the payments made, than to be the instrument of damage to you—The loss of money I am used to, the loss of mental quietude I cannot bear, & pained as I am, I wish to regain tranquility.

Every conversation I hold with you on the subject furnishes additional matter of regret to me—Till then I can close the contract I must avoid their repetition—this I am sure notwithstanding the present & general distress, I shall be able to do in the Course of the summer.[1]

In June I return here for that purpose.

Respecting the military appointment which you did me the honor to consult me upon I have not been able to do any thing satisfactory.

I beleive Byrd, Baytop and Campbell (the two last are Majors in the ten Regts) will best fill the commissions of Colonels. Thos Turner & Archd Randolph are well calculated for the cavalry & ought to command troops. Aylette Lee would make an excellent Captain if reformed; rejected as he was by the senate he had become melancholy & melancholy brought him to the bottle—I beleive he may be considered as restored now.[2]

I mentioned to Captain Thornton the report which reached yr ears with a hope of arresting his progress in a course which must lead to his ruin—His respect for you will I hope ⟨*illegible*⟩ the tendency which has been attached to his character by rumour.[3] with the highest respect & regard I remain yr sincere friend & ob. st

H. Lee

ALS, DLC:GW.

1. The "conversation" was held when Lee was at Mount Vernon on 9 May; its subject was Lee's inability to make his payments on the Dismal Swamp land that he had bought from GW (*Diaries*, 6:346; see also Lee to GW, 28 Feb. 1799, n.2).

2. Byrd is probably Col. Francis Otway Byrd (1756–1800), collector of the port of Norfolk who had been a lieutenant colonel of dragoons during the Revolution. In the list of Virginia officers that James McHenry sent to GW on 21 May, James Baytop of Gloucester County is listed as a major in the 7th and William Campbell as a major in the 8th Infantry Regiment. For reference to the appointment for Thomas Turner, see GW to Bushrod Washington, 5 May 1799, n.1. For Archibald C. Randolph, see GW to James McHenry, 7 April (second letter), 23 April, and to Daniel Morgan, 10 April. Lee wrote GW from Richmond on 11 July to make another recommendation: "Mr Wm Randolph [born c.1769] of Cumberland son to the late Colo. Thomas M[ann] Randolph & son in law to the late governor [Beverley] Randolph [1739–1797] is desirous of being accepted as Captain of Cavalry in the eventual army. His capacity to discharge the dutys of that office I beleive will be universally acknowledged his attachment to govt has been manifested on every occasion which has presented an opportunity & especially in the late elections, & his personal courage is indubitable" (DLC:GW). Capt. William Aylett Lee was the son of Thomas Ludwell Lee and Mary Aylett Lee. Lee did not receive an appointment at this time. For Lee's court-martial several years earlier, see GW to Henry Knox, 14 July 1794 (DLC:GW).

3. When writing on 12 Aug. 1799 to Presly Thornton, whom at GW's request Charles Cotesworth Pinckney had made an aide-de-camp, GW betrays no awareness of Thornton's having problems.

Letter not found: to Benjamin Lincoln, 22 May 1799. *American Book-Prices Current* (1964), 70:884, records that this letter "introducing a Mr. Ralph Wormeley" was sold by Christie, Manson & Woods on 19 Dec. 1963, item no. 241.

To Thomson Mason

Sir,   Mount Vernon 24th May [17]99

I mean to renew the outer fence, on the line between you and me, & in a manner more substantial than usual.

Mr Anderson will explain the method by wch I propose to accomplish this, to you; and ask your leave to profit by your Ditch, & present fence: which can be attended with no temporary inconvenience to yourself—and may, ultimately, be of singular advantage to you, as well as myself; as my fence may subserve your purposes as well as my own.[1] With esteem & regard I am—Sir Your Most Obedt Hble Servt

Go: Washington

ALS, PHi: Washington Manuscripts.

1. Mason replied later in the day from Hollin Hall: "Mr [James] Anderson has delivered me yours of this Date and has explained to me the Method by which you propose to renew the Fence between you & me; I am very glad to find you are about to adopt this plan, and you are perfectly at Liberty to make use of my Fence & Ditch for the purpose, I have no Doubt but we shall both find our advantage in it" (DLC:GW).

To William Augustine Washington

My dear Sir,   Mount Vernon 24th May 1799

The enclosed was written (as you will perceive by the Superscription) to go by General Lee;[1] who, four days ago appointed to be here on his return to Westmoreland, but is not yet arrived. In the meantime; your second letter by Captn Bowcock (dated the 20th instant) has been received.

When the enclosed was written I thot the Whiskey had been sent; but Captn Bowcock postponed taking it on board it seems, until he made his second trip. Now, he has two barrels according to your desire; and if you should want *more*, or any of your neighbours want *any*, it would be convenient, & always in my power, to supply you—and for grain, wheat, Rye or Indian Corn in exchange.[2]

If you are in the habit of laying in Fish, as provision for your black people, as I do, and do not catch them at your own landings, I could supply you every year, and on as good terms as you could get them elsewhere; and for these also, from you, or others, I would receive grain in payment.

Captn Bowcock has delivered more Corn than he received from you; of which Mr Anderson, my Manager, will give you the a/c; as he will also do of the Whiskey; the Barrel of Fish you will please to accept.[3] My best respects & congratulations, in which My Wife joins, are offered to Mrs Washington & yourself on your Marriage. We shall always be glad to see you at this place. With sincere regard and Affection, I remain Your friend

Go: Washington

ALS, PPRF; ALS (letterpress copy), DLC:GW.

1. GW enclosed his letter of 20 May to William Augustine Washington.
2. See W.A. Washington to GW, 2 May, n.2.
3. See W.A. Washington to GW, 2 May, nn.2 and 3, and 1 June.

From Burgess Ball

Dear Sir,   Alexand[ri]a 25th May 1799

The Gentlemen whom I wish to recommend as Officers (and yesterday mention'd to you) are Mr Arther Lee in the County of Northumberland, and Mr Reuben Beale of Richmond County. They are Gent. of Family, and I think will be actuated by proper principles. Those Gentlemen aspire to nothing higher than to commence with an Ensigncy or Cornetcy, provided, Officers of the Cavalry are furnish'd with Horses & accoutraments, if not, Ensigns wou'd be their Object.[1] I wou'd recommend Presley Sanders of Lancaster County as a Capt. in the Provisional Army, in which Rank I think he wd be clever; and as I expect a no. of Old Officers will be applying I've no doubt but he will be satisfy'd, 'tho he wish'd a majority.[2] I will endeavour to find out some men of respectability & Family, for the Provisional Army, takg care to observe your Information & directions respecting them, at the same time not mentiong I had them from you, wch in me might appear Vain. I am with the highest Esteem Yr mo: Obt Servt

B: Ball

ALS, DLC:GW.

1. Arthur Lee, son of Kendall and Betty Heale Lee of Northumberland County, was a student at the College of William and Mary in 1798. Reuben Beale was the son of Thomas Beale of Richmond County who died in December 1799. In July 1807 Reuben Beale was one of a large group of men who pledged to form the "Northern Neck Volunteer Corps of Light Dragoons" (*Calendar of Virginia State Papers*, 9:607).

2. Presley Saunders had by July 1807 become the first major of the "92nd Regiment of Lancaster" County militia (ibid., 9:540).

Letter not found: to Wilson Allen, 26 May. On 29 May Allen wrote GW that he had received "Your letter of date the 26th inst."

To Jedidiah Morse

Revd Sir,   Mount Vernon 26th May 1799
I thank you for your Sermon "Exhibiting the present dangers, and consequent duties of the Citizens of the United States of America" which came to hand by the last Post:[1] and which I am persuaded I shall read with approbating pleasure, as soon as some matters in which I am engaged at present, are dispatch'd. With esteem and regard I am, Revd Sir, Your Obedt & obliged Humble Servant

Go: Washington

ALS, owned (1973) by Mr. Peter Brady, Afton, Va.; ALS (letterpress copy), DLC: GW.

1. GW's copy of Morse's sermon, delivered at Charlestown, Mass., on 25 April 1799 and printed "at the Request of the Hearers," has inscribed on the title page: "Genl Washington from his respectful & obdt Servt The Author" (Griffin, *Boston Athenæum Washington Collection*, 146–47).

To William Russell

Sir,   Mount Vernon 26th May 1799
Your favor of the 11th instant from New York, has been received; and the articles therein alluded to got safe to hand yesterday; for which I pray you to accept my grateful thanks. The Ram, though poor, seems to be in good health, and being turned into as good Pasture as the backwardness of the Season would admit, will, I have no doubt, soon recover his flesh. His wool, and other appearances bespeak him a valuable animal. The other articles shall be applied to the uses they are designed; and will, I have no

doubt, be found to answer. All have come to hand in good Season. For your further kind intention respecting the imported Swine, I feel much obliged; & if you should be so successful as to get into a *full Stock*, would thank you for a pair; as I have a Distillery at which I rear many Hogs. But how, my good Sir, am I to repay all this kindness? In any thing, you may freely Command—Yr Most Obedt & Obliged Hble Servt

Go: Washington

ALS, PWacD; ALS (letterpress copy), DLC:GW.

To James Welch

Sir, Mount Vernon 26th May 1799

I was not disappointed in the contents of your letter of the 16th instant, because I had formed no hope from the proposed application at Fredericksburgh.

Inconvenient, and indeed distressing as it is to me to lay out of the money you were obligated to pay me the first of the present year, and to receive which was the *only* inducement that led to the Bargain which exists between us for my Lands on the Great Kanhawa, yet, rather than resort to the means by which I could do myself justice, at the present moment, I will wait with patience & confidence, for the payment you have promised to make in November ensuing. After which, do not expect further indulgence from—Sir Yr Very Hble Servt

Go: Washington

P.S. I request to be informed with precision, of the number, and names of the Tenants you have placed on the Land; the quantity each is to hold, and what Rent they are to pay; I request also to know what others you have engaged—and what prospect you have of more.

ALS (letterpress copy), DLC:GW.

From Wilson Allen

Sir Richmond May 29th 1799.

Your letter of date the 26th inst. covering a deed to Genl Lee, for lands lying in Kentucky, I recd last evening.[1]

I rather think that when Mr B. Washington requested the deed to be sent to me to be *recorded*, he must have forgot that the lands thereby conveyed lay in Kentucky—for it appears very evident, that all that cou'd *legally* be done with it by any *Court in this state*, has already been done by the Court of Fairfax County. The Clerk of that Court perhaps had better comply with the act of Congress for authenticating records &c. before the deed is sent where it ought properly to be recorded—but nothing farther appears to me now necessary. However Sir you or Mr B. W. may wish it spread on the records of this Court for some particular reason—if so I will with infinite pleasure present it to the Judges at the next term for their directions relative to it.[2] Please to excuse the liberty I have taken, and beleive me to be sir with the greatest esteem & respect, Yr very Humble Servt

Wilson Allen

ALS, DLC:GW.

1. Letter not found.

2. For GW's decision, on Bushrod Washington's advice, to convey his Kentucky lands on Rough Creek back to Henry Lee so that Lee could reconvey the tract to him by a new deed, see Bushrod Washington to GW, 10 April, and the references in note 1 of that document. See also GW's answer of 17 June.

To William White

Revd & Dear Sir,   Mount Vernon 30th May 1799

The Sermon on the duty of Civil obedience as required in Scripture, which you had the goodness to send me, came safe a Post or two ago; and for which I pray you to accept my grateful acknowledgments.[1]

The hurry in which it found me engaged, in a matter that pressed, has not allowed me time to give it a perusal yet: but I anticipate the pleasure & edification I shall find when it is in my power to do it. With every respectful wish, in which Mrs Washington unites, for yourself & the young ladies of your family, I am with great esteem & regard, Dear Sir Your Most Obedt & Very Hble Servt

Go: Washington

ALS, PPOCC; ALS (letterpress copy), DLC:GW.

1. Bishop White's *Sermon on the Duty of Civil Obedience* was delivered at Christ Church and St. Peter's in Philadelphia on 25 April (Griffin, *Boston Athenæum Washington Collection*, 226).

From William Thornton

Sir   City of Washington 31st May 1799

Finding that the Board of Commissrs were exceedingly urged, by Mr George Walker, to lay off and divide certain small portions of Ground, within the lines of his property, between the intersection of various Avenues & Streets, which do not appear in the general plan of the City to have ever been designed for private Occupancy; and perceiving the Board were disposed to adopt the proposal, I declared the measure expressly contrary to the intention of the late President of the United States, and accordingly wrote a formal protest, setting forth the injury that the City would sustain, by admitting a principle which would induce every proprietor to make similar Claims, and requested that the Board would not sanction the Divisions by Signature, until the Opinion of the late president should be fully known, if any hesitation remained on the Minds of my Colleagues after the perusal of your Letters of the 26th of Decr 96, and the 27th of Feby 97.[1] Those Letters explain clearly in my Opinion the Sentiments I have repeatedly heard you express; but, lest your meaning may be misconstrued, in a point so essential to the future Benefit of the City, I request you will pardon me for making so free as to solicit a further Declaration of your former Opinions, if they can be more explicit. There is perhaps one point that may be considered as omitted; I mean the Declaration of these portions as Appropriations; for although many of them are very small, not containing a Standard Lot, and if occupied by Individuals might justly be considered as nuisances, yet if appropriated to public Use, they would be, not only highly useful but also ornamental, as they would serve for Churches, Temples, Infirmaries, Public Academies, Dispensaries, Markets, Public walks, fountains, Statues, Obelisks &c.; and if the whole were to be paid for, as Appropriations, they amount to only 381,683 Square feet, or eight acres, at £25=£200. The only Doubt remaining on the minds of the Commissioners relative to these portions of Ground, was the power of non-insertion; but, it appears to me that their not having been inserted leaves them exactly in the same predicament as the other Portions of the city intended for Appropriation, but neither yet expressly designated as Appropriations nor even as reservations. They may be considered as reservations because the points of Squares have been cut off and these latter therefore are rendered, by your Declaration of

26th Decr 96, subject to payment, and consequently to public Appropriation. If no objection can be made to this, which indeed is warranted by the Deeds of Trust, surely less validity must be given to objections against the adoption of Areas heretofore considered only as streets, which by adoption will be paid for, and rendered highly useful and ornamental. If any objection can arise it has justly been observed in your Letter last quoted, that they might with equal propriety ask payment for the Streets; for these spaces differ in nothing from the Avenues but in extent, and every Avenue might by a parity of claim be reduced to a Street, or be charged to the Public. No Individual has ever contended for the insertion of these irregular portions, except Mr George Walker, but the principle being admitted the right will be universally claimed. Many have sold Lots, fronting on these open Spaces— The Map of the City has been published without them, and complaints of injustice will certainly be made by persons who have already purchased if these Spaces be filled up by private Lots; beside, these Insertions not accompanying the Maps now dispersed, Strangers might be liable to continual Impositions, by purchasing Lots apparently on open Areas in the Map, but in reality only fronting Stables or greater Nuisances; for these Lots are too small to admit of Houses all round and Conveniences within: so that it appears not only against the plan of the City to insert them, (unless for public appropriation which I should advocate) but it would be highly unjust to Individuals, as well those who may purchase as those who have become proprietors, and it would materially injure the convenience of the City, by occupying for private purposes, those places so easy of access, and so necessary for the Public.[2] I have the honor to be Sir with the highest esteem your very respectful Friend &c.

William Thornton

ALS, DLC:GW; copy, DLC: William Thornton Papers; copy, DNA: RG 42, General Records, Letters Received, 1791–1867.

1. By an agreement of 30 Mar. 1791 the landholders within the new Federal District, of whom George Walker (d. 1802) was one of the largest, conveyed their land in the district to the public with the understanding that after it was laid off the land would be divided equally between themselves and the public. The proprietors, who retained their homesteads, would be paid £25 per acre for the land taken by the public except for what was to be used for streets and avenues (see copy, DNA: RG 42, Records of the Commissioners for the District of Columbia, Proceedings, 1791–1802). In his letter to the District of Columbia commissioners of 26 Dec. 1796, a little more than two months before he left office, GW wrote,

among other things: "With respect to the claims of individual proprietors, to be compensated for the spaces occasioned by the intersection of Streets and avenues, I should conceive that they might, with equal propriety, ask payment for the Streets themselves; but the terms of the original contract, or cession, if a dispute on this point should arise, must be recurred to, for I presume the opinion of the President, in such a case, would avail nothing. But, if angles are taken off, at these spaces, the case is materially altered; and, without designing it, you make a square where none was contemplated, and thereby not only lay the foundation of claim for *those angles* but for the space also which is made a square by that act." And on 27 Feb. 1797, a week before his departure, he wrote: "With regard to the open areas in the City, occasioned by the intersection of the Streets and avenues . . . the Proprietors are entitled to no allowance for the spaces which are occasioned—simply—by the width of those Streets and avenues; but, where the areas have been enlarged by taking off the angles, in order to encrease the size of the squares, or to throw them into a circular form, it appears reasonable and just, that they should receive payment for the proportion secured to them by contract, for all such additions; but without any encroachment thereon, or change in the plan."

2. GW wrote Thornton on 1 June supporting Thornton's position, at least to the extent of reaffirming his strong opposition to any unnecessary "Departure from the engraved plan" of the city. George Walker wrote GW on 5 Aug. to rebut what Thornton had written in his letter to GW. Two days later GW forwarded Walker's letter to the District of Columbia commissioners, and on 19 Aug. two of the commissioners, Gustavus Scott and Alexander White, overrode the objections of Thornton as the third commissioner and approved the divisions proposed by Walker. See the editor's notes in Harris, *Thornton Papers*, 1:495.

To William Thornton

Sir,   Federal City June 1st 1799

In replying to your favor of yesterday's date, I must beg leave to premise that, when I left the Chair of Government it was with a determination not to intermeddle in any public matter which did not immediately concern me; and that I have felt no Disposition since to alter this Determination.

But as you have requested that I would give you my Ideas on a certain point, which seems to have occupied the attention of the Board of Commissioners, and on which I presume my Letters to that Body (whilst I had the honor to administer the Government) have not been so clear and explicit as it was my Intention to be, I have no hesitation in declaring (unless I have entirely forgotten all recollection of the fact) that it has always been my invariable opinion—and remains still to be so—that no departure from the

Engraved plan of the City ought to be allowed, unless *imperious* necessity should require it, or some great public good is to be promoted thereby.[1]

Minor Considerations contribute to this opinion; but the primary, and to my mind an unanswerable one, is, that after the original plan (with some Alterations) had been adopted; ordered to be engraved and published; and was transmitted to *several*, if not to *all* our public Agents abroad, for the purpose of inviting purchasers; that it would, for reasons too obvious and cogent to require illustration, be deceptious to lay off Lots for *private purposes*, where none appeared in a plan, which was intended to inform—aid— and direct the Judgment of Foreigners, & others who could not, on the premises, make a choice.

It is not difficult to form an opinion of the ways of thinking, and views of others, by ones own, under similar Circumstances; I shall declare then without reserve, that if I had made choice of a Site for a House on an open Area in the published map, occasioned by the intersection of Avenues, and an Angle thereof should afterwards be filled up, in a manner I might not approve, I should not scruple to complain of both the deception and injury.

But I am straying from my purpose, which was no more than simply to say (if I am not, as beforementioned, greatly forgetful) that I have never had but one opinion of this Subject, and that is, that nothing ought to justify a Departure from the engraved plan, but the probability of some great public Benefit, or unavoidable necessity. With great esteem & regard I am Sir your most obdt Servt

Go. Washington

Copy, in William Thornton's hand, MiU-C: Schoff Collection. GW's docket, "To Willm Thornton Esqr. 1st June 1799," is on the copy. See the editor's note to the letter in Harris, *Thornton Papers*, 1:497.

1. The "*Engraved* plan" was the engraving of Pierre L'Enfant's manuscript plan for the Federal City made by Benjamin and Andrew Ellicott and published in 1792 in Philadelphia.

From William Augustine Washington

My Dr Sir   Haywood June 1st 1799

Your two favors of the 20th & 24th by Capt. Bowcock I have recd with two Barrels of Whiskey & a Barrel of Fish; the first I have not tryed, but have no doubt of its being good, the latter are very fine & I have to return you my thanks for the present.

Mr Wm Flood the Excr of Mr Thacker Washington has consented to let the Estates Corn go in my Contract with you; Capt. Bowcock carried up 39 Barrels the last load which was the reason of the Corn holding out that much more than the rect, that Corn being delivered after the Rect was given—Capt. Bowcock is to call on Mr Flood to fill him up, and expects to receive 100 Barrels or perhaps a little more, so that I expect the whole quantaty sent to you will be about 493 Barrels—I wish it was in my power to accomodate you with the use of the Money for the Corn as long as you might want it; but really my Dr Sir I never was more pushed and distressed for Money in my life to fullfill my contracts, & I really fear with all my exertions I shall fail in doing so, owing to the miserable Crops I made last year.[1]

You will be pleased to let me know at what price the Corn is to be settled at, and I will endeavour to draw on you at—as long time as possable, say 30—60—or 90 days—perheps Mr Flood may want his Money at the shortest period mentioned.[2]

I shall take an opportunity of letting my Neighbours know that you will exchange Whiskey & Fish for Grain; and have no doubt but many will be fond of doing it. Mr Park now sends by Capt. Bowcock, (as he tells me) 169 Bar[rel]s of Corn to exchange for Whiskey[3]—I shall in future get all my Whiskey & Fish from you.

Mrs Washington Unites with me in our most respectful compliments to you & Mrs Washington. I am my Dr Sir with much sincerity Your Affectionate Nephew

Wm Augt. Washington

P.S. If Mr Flood should write for Whiskey, Flower or Fish you will be pleased to furnish him.[4]

ALS, KEL.

1. In William Augustine Washington's account in the distillery ledger (Mount Vernon Ledger, 1799–1800, 14), farm manager James Anderson credits William Pinckard Flood with the delivery of 39 barrels of corn at a cost of $107.25 on 25 May and 91 barrels at $257.84 on 7 June. He charges Flood $60.10 for "Sundries delivered Him," which included seventeen gallons of whiskey on 25 May, and thirty gallons of whiskey and one barrel of flour on 12 June.

2. For GW's payments to William Augustine Washington for the corn that his nephew had shipped to him, see W.A. Washington to GW, 13 July, n.1. For his payment to Flood, see GW to W.A. Washington, 10 June, n.3.

3. On 7 June GW's distillery received 595 bushels of corn at a price of $347.08 from James Park, and on 12 June Park was provided with 557 gallons of whiskey valued at $324.92, potatoes valued at $5, and tierces and barrels valued at $17.17 (Mount Vernon Ledger, 1799–1800, 17).

4. See note 1.

From Charles Cotesworth Pinckney

Dear Sr   Charleston [S.C.] June 4th 1799

I wrote to you from Mulbury Grove the seat of our deceased friend Genl Greene in Georgia, & enclosed you my letter to the Secretary of War giving an account of the progress of Brigr Genl Washington, Major Rutledge & myself on the sea Coast[1]—I now enclose you two other letters to the Secretary, one from Augusta & the other from this place.[2]

The Arrangement for North Carolina, South Carolina & Georgia have been transmitted to the War Department, & copies of them shall be forwarded to you by Brigr Genl Washington, who will set out this day week[3]—He will also carry two plumes for you, one for Coll Lear, & another for Captn Thornton if he does me the honour to accept his appointment—I enclosed a Letter for him from Mulberry Grove[4]— On My return I found Mrs Pinckney had been very ill; she was then better, but has had two relapses since I arrived, & today has been attacked with a vomiting of green black bile; this she trusts will be an excuse to Mrs Washington for not yet answering her last letter[5]—She & my Daughters unite with me in affectionate respects to you both; & I remain with the utmost esteem & veneration Your affectionate & devoted hble Sert

                              Charles Cotesworth Pinckney

ALS, CSmH; Sprague transcript, DLC:GW.

1. When Pinckney wrote to GW from "Mulberry Grove on Savannah River" on 20 April 1799, he enclosed, among other things, copies of his letters to James McHenry of 19 and 20 April.

2. The enclosed copy of Pinckney's letter of 19 May from Augusta, Ga., to James McHenry reads: "Brigr Genl [William] Washington, Major [Henry M.] Rutledge, & myself, arrived yesterday at this place from Fort Wilkinson on the Oconee. Lieutt Coll [Henry] Gaither has doubtless, transmitted you a plan of that Fort; if he has not, I will forward you one. It is beautifully situated on a hill on the South Side of the River. The defences are calculated only against an Indian foe; and if attacked only by such, it is not of so great importance, that is commanded by two heights, one in the front and the other on the right of the

Fort. We think a block house should be constructed on each—I was glad to see an extensive & excellent garden, between the Fort & the River. This peice of internal œconomy should never be omitted, in a garrison, where practicable, as it greatly conduces to the health & comfort of the Soldiers. Both Officers & Soldiers here, enjoy a great share of health, & I think you will find from the inspection of the Returns that the Soldiers in the Garrison & at St Mary's are as healthy as Soldiers are in any part of the U. States. This Fort has been built with great industry by the Soldiers at very little expence to the Government, & they have been kept so closely at this business, that tho a body of fine active young fellows, we did not find them so adroit in handling their arms, & in their marching and manœvering, as we could have wished. This however will be immediately remedied as the Colonel assures me, he will now attend so unremittingly to the training them, that it shall be no easy matter for the new Regiments to equal them. We found that insubordination, of which you were apprehensive, among the Officers, actually to exist, & we were under the necessity of very severely censoring their conduct. It appears to us that it had been produced originally by too much familiarity on the part of the Commandant with his officers, & when he ⟨wished⟩ to restore that respect, which should always be paid by inferior Officers to their Superior, it was too late, & their want of Subordination, broke forth in those unprecedented & unmilitary proceedings of the Courts martial, alike disgraceful to the Courts which permitted, & to the Defendants who utterd the libels—I trust you will not hear again of any such licentious behavior, in these Officers, or in any in the Southern Department, as I am determind to have a strict discipline observed in every part of the command entrusted to my care, & in doing this, I have a firm reliance, on the support, & countenance of the Executive—We entered into an investigation of the various complaints against Coll Gaither, the particulars of which, & the opinions of Brigr Genl Washington & myself thereon, shall be transmitted you from Charleston; they are too long to be transcribed here. In this enclosure you will see a Copy of my Instructions to Capt. [James] Taylor of the Federal Dragoons, whom I have detached with his troop to dislodge, some persons, who are attempting to make settlements, on the Indian territory, beyond the ⟨Ocunna⟩ mountain, & which if not immediately broke up will probably bring on an Indian war. Please to let me know the President's pleasure, with regard to the Old Settlers to whom the Indians, do not object; the distinction I have made between them & the late Intruders, seems to have given great satisfaction . . ." (DLC:GW). In a postscript Pinckney refers to earlier correspondence with McHenry. The copy of Pinckney's second enclosed letter to McHenry, from Charleston, S.C., dated 29 May, is in DLC:GW. Pinckney also enclosed a copy of his instructions of 14 May 1799 to Capt. Taylor and a copy of his letter of 18 May from Capt. Abimeal Nicoll (both copies also in DLC:GW).

3. William Washington did not arrive at Mount Vernon until 7 Sept. (see *Diaries*, 6:364). The lists of officers for North and South Carolina and Georgia have not been found. Gov. William Richardson Davie sent GW a list of candidates for commissions in North Carolina.

4. See Pinckney to GW, 20 April, n.1. GW wrote Presly Thornton about the plume on 12 Aug. (see GW to Pinckney, 10 August).

5. On 20 April GW drafted a letter to Mary Stead Pinckney from Martha Washington, which is printed above.

To William Thornton

Dear Sir   Mount Vernon 4th June 1799

You will perceive by the enclosed letter, and my order, consequent thereof; that the Glass from Boston is arrived at Alexandria, and in good condition. Be so good as to send the order to
Mr Blagden, that he may use his own time & mode of getting it to
the City.[1]

I hope Mr Blagden will be careful of the overplus, as more glass
was written for than the houses will require without loss. With
great esteem & regard I am—Dear Sir Your Obedt Hble Servt

Go: Washington

ALS, CtWetCD.

1. For GW's correspondence with Benjamin Lincoln about securing window
glass for his houses in the Federal City, see Lincoln to GW, 3 April, n.1. The
enclosed letter has not been identified. For GW's payment for the glass, see GW
to Lincoln, 1 July, n.1.

To Charles Cotesworth Pinckney

My dear Sir,   Mount Vernon 5th June 1799

Your favor of the 20th Ulto[1] from Mulberry Grove, came duly
to hand, and would have received an earlier acknowledgment had
I not allowed time for the completion of your visit to the Frontier
Posts, in the State of Georgia.

I thank you for the interesting details you took the trouble of
communicating in that letter, and its enclosures; but it was not,
nor is it, my wish to inflict such burthensome Communications
upon you. To give me a general view of the state of Military matters, and of the temper of our Neighbours on your borders; and
the arrangement of the Southern Corps and prospect of filling
them; Of the disposition of the Troops, and general Politicks of
the three Southern (Atlantic) States, and of Tennessee (as far as
you could ascertain them), is all I had in view by the request contained in my former letter; and all I mean to ask of you at present.

I am fully persuaded, my dear Sir, that your own judgment and
experience in Military matters would be but little assisted by any
advice that is in my power to give you; I feel, nevertheless, the compliment which your asking of it conveys.

Your letter to Captn Presley Thornton I delivered with my own hands. He is grateful for the honor you have conferred, and ⟨holds⟩ himself (as I presume he has, or will inform you, by letter) of his readiness to obey your orders at any time, or in any manner, you may find it expedient to communicate them to him. You will, I trust, find him an honorable man; none was ever more so than his father; and those who are better acquainted with his conduct than I am, say, the son inherits the fathers virtues.

Of those matters which you have communicated to the Secretary of War, I shall say nothing. It rests with him to decide on them; to do which, you have furnished him with clear & ample details, as appears by the copies thereof sent me.

Mrs Washington is thankful to you for the Melon seeds you had the kindness to send her, and unites with me in best wishes for you, Mrs Pinckney and the young ladies; and with sincere esteem & regard I am, My dear Sir, Your Affecte Hble Servant

Go: Washington

ALS (letterpress copy), DLC:GW.

1. As the contents of his letter make clear, GW is referring to Pinckney's letter of 20 April. Pinckney was in Augusta, far up the Savannah River from Mulberry Grove, by 20 May (see Pinckney to GW, 4 June, n.2).

From William Thornton

Dear Sir— City of Washington June 5[–6]th 1799

According to the Desire you signified of knowing how soon Mr Blagdin would require a further Advance of Money, I requested him, the Day after your Departure, to state the Sum and time. He told me that he should shortly have to remit Money to Mr Littleton Dennis, on the Eastern Shore, for Materials, & should want a thousand Dollars by the 15th Instant. I told him that such rapid payments were neither generally expected nor demanded, and that although I knew you would answer his call for money at any time, yet I thought it might appear urgent to make an Application so soon, and desired him to reconsider his Wants. I proposed a thousand Dollars on the first of next month—to which he agreed, and would so arrange his Engagements as to be put to no Inconvenience.[1] With the most respectful Complimts of my Family to your excellent Lady I am dear Sir your sincere & obedt Friend

William Thornton

P.S. June 6th—This morning I had the honor of your Favour of the 4th Inst: with its enclosures, which I shall not fail to deliver to Mr Blagdin, as soon as the Board rises, with a request that he will preserve, as much as possible, the surplus of the Glass.

ALS, DLC:GW.

1. GW spent the weekend in Georgetown and Washington, staying with the Thomas Peters on Friday night, 31 May, and with the Thomas Laws on Saturday. He attended church in Alexandria on Sunday before returning home (*Diaries*, 6: 350). GW wrote Thornton on 16 June that he would send the money for the builder George Blagdin by 1 July. GW noted in his Day Book on 2 July that he had drawn a check for $1,000 payable to Thornton "for the purpose of carrying on my buildings in the City of Washington."

To Clement Biddle

Dear Sir   Mount Vernon 6th June 1799

Your letters of the 18th & 21st Ulto have been duly received.

In reply to them, so far as it respects the raking machines, I agree perfectly with Mr J. Williams, that they will not answr on Stoney, stumpy, or rough land of any kind, for the reason he has assigned; but I am equally well persuaded, that on level & smooth land (which for the most part my fields are) they would be found useful impliments on a Farm. If then, the Inventor and maker of them has removed from Philadelphia, and Mr Williams, or any other Gentleman who has suffered the one he possesses, to be dis-used; will part with it; and it is susceptible of complete repairs; I would buy it; provided I could have it (in the usual course of passages) at this place by the 10th of next month; without which it would render me no service this, and might be unnecessary another year.[1]

Having what little flour I made still on hand; Perceiving by the Gazettes, and an Arrette of Roume & Touissant that the Trade to St Domingo is encouraged; and that Dispatches have been received from Mr Stevens our Consul;[2] permit me to ask what effect this event has had, or is likely to have, on the price of that article. Two motives lead to the enquiry, at the present moment; first, the approaching heats will render it ineligable to keep flour on hand much if any longer; and secondly, because the Merchants in this quarter either do, or affect to, believe, that the Ports of that Island will not be opened, or that we shall derive no benefit from the above mentioned Arrette—I will decide nothing untill I hear from you. With great esteem & regard—I always am Your Most Obedt Servant

Go: Washington

ALS (letterpress copy), DLC:GW. Following GW's letter to Biddle of 7 June, which he enclosed in his letter of that date to James McHenry, none of the letters that GW and his agent exchanged prior to 13 Nov. 1799 has been found.

    1. See GW to Biddle, 18 May, n.1.

    2. For references to the mission of Dr. Edward Stevens to the Haitian general Toussaint L'Ouverture, see GW to James McHenry, 11 Aug. 1799, n.2.

From William Booker

Sir   Richmond 6 June 1799

Since my last letter to you, I have been at Petersburg, where Mr Roberts now lives[1]—I there made particular Inquiry respecting his conduct, and from what I can Learn, I am Sure he Cannot be depended on, I am told he is very fond of strong drink, and when Intoxicated, is very troublesome, Since he Left you he Lost his wife, and married a second time, he has also Lost her, but while merried, was very often put in prison on account of being so Quarrelsome, and his wife was often thought to be in danger of her Life, while he was in those frolicks—I have not seen him (or rather not spoken to him) nor was it my Intention that he should have Known of my Inquiry, but by some means he heard of it, and I am told has been Looking out in that town for me, and Indeed has went up to a Canal about five miles above town he there expressed a Great desire to see me as he had understood you had written for him, I am told he seemd well pleasd with the Expectation of Coming to Live for you.

Altho when drunk he is so troublesome I am told when sober is Tolerable agreable—he has no family nor is he in any business Should you wish a further Inquiry I will with pleasure Obey your Commands.

When I wrote you Last, and for some time before, I expected to have Come to Mount Vernon about this time, the appointment was in Consequence of my having to go to King George County, to Set to work two machines it was Expected that the wheat would have been ripe by the first of June. I have Recd a Letter from one of the Gent. who wishes Me to defer Comeing until about the middle of this Month, as the wheat is much Later than was Expected, and suppose it to be Later with you I hope a Little Longer will make no difference, as the whole of the work to the Mill can be done in 4 or 5 days after I get to Mount Vernon.[2] I am your most Obet Sert

Wm Booker

ALS, DLC:GW.

    1. See Booker's letter of 15 May.

    2. Booker arrived at Mount Vernon on 7 July to build a horse-driven gristmill and remained until 12 July (*Diaries*, 6:356). On 12 July GW paid Booker $80 "for Materials, and his own Services, in putting up a horse grist mill" (Day Book).

To James McHenry

Dear Sir,   Mount Vernon, June 6th 1799

I have been duly favoured with your letters of the 11th, 19th and 21st of last month, with their inclosures.

Referring to my letter of the 13th ultimo for the reasons which prevented my having a personal knowledge of such Characters in Virginia, as may be proper to be selected for Officers in the eventual or provisional Army—and having shewn therein the difficulties which would arise from the extent of this state—and that, in order to obtain the necessary information, I must solicit the aid of others in whom confidence could be placed, I enclose an extract from a letter I have received from General Marshall, and of one from General Lee, in answer to letters I had written to them on this Subject.[1] From these you will see that I have but little hope of aid from those quarters. And as in your letter of the 19th ultimo, you have stated the objections to a public Official Advertisement for bringing forward such Characters as might wish to obtain Commissions, I shall still pursue the object in such a manner as I conceive best calculated to answer the purpose, notwithstanding the delicacy of the task which, as I hinted to you in my letter abovementioned, I should be obliged to impose on others, as well as the unpleasant situation into which I may myself be brought, by raising expectations which may not be realized.

When I mentioned in my last the names of several persons acquainted with Engineering &ca I did not mean, as I then observed, to *recommend* them; but spoke of them merely as passing through my mind.[2] At any rate I should think it improper to employ a Frenchman in that important station at *this* time.

By a letter which I lately received from General Pinckney, I have reason to believe that Colo. Senf would accept the appointment you mention;[3] but whether he possesses all the requisites and qualifications necessary for a person at the head of the Corps of Engineers, would be first proper to be ascertained: And would it not be well also to know if Major Rivardi, who is now in the service, and who is said to have been educated particularly for this branch, is not as well qualified as Senf? And if so, should he not have a preference as being already in the service? I know nothing of the comparative merits or qualifications of these Gentlemen, and have no particular partiality for the one or the other. I merely suggest these things for your consideration, knowing how highly important it is to have the best qualified men we can get in that line.

The enclosed letters, containing Applications for appointments to fill such Offices as may become vacant, in the present establishment, from non-acceptance or resignation, I have thought proper to transmit to you.[4] Such as may come to my hands for appointments in the provisional Army I shall retain until the selection of Officers for that Army shall be made from this State.[5]

The letter from Major George Lewis shews his disappointment in not having had his name brought forward at an earlier day. He did not apply to me at that time; because he knew that I had always felt a delicacy in bringing into public Office any of my own relations. I confess, however, that I regretted not seeing his name on the list which was laid before the General Officers in Philadelphia; because I knew him to be a valuable Officer, and believed that he had a predeliction for the service. In justice to his application I must say, that I think he deserves attention. He served with reputation in the Revolutionary War, and commenced the oldest Captain in Colo. Baylor's Regiment of Cavalry; but marrying, resigned before the close of it. On the Western Expedition he commanded the Virginia Cavalry, with the Rank of Major, and acquited himself with honor. His age and standing in Society qualify him for the appointment which he asks. He makes no claims on the score of preeminent or superior abilities; but he is known to possess a soundness of judgment, qualifications and acquirements at least equal to the place which he wishes; and no man stands higher than he does in the esteem of those who know him, or as a firm & steady friend to Government.[6]

Doctor Wellford ranks high in his profession, and his Character as a friend to the Government, and as a man of integrity, is, I beleive, unimpeachable. He acted as Director of the medical Department on the Western Expedition, and gave great satisfaction. It may be proper to state, that he is a native of Great Britain, and came to this Country with the Army during the Revolutionary war. That service he quitted and ⟨settled⟩ in Fredericksburg, where he married into one of the most respectable families in that quarter, and has resided there ever since.[7]

I perceive, by the list which you sent me of the Officers in this State who had accepted or declined their appointments, that the name of Captn Thomas Turner was among the latter. I have lately seen that Gentleman, who informs me, that, having a strong predeliction for the Cavalry, he had applied for an appointmt in that Corps, and that he had declined his appointment in the Infantry, because he was not acquainted with its duties, and had no turn for that kind of service.[8] I see also, by the aforesaid list, that there was one of the Captaincies in Cavalry vacant. If this is not yet filled, I think, from the Character I have heard of Capt. Turner, he would supply that place with credit. At any rate, I presume it will be filled with an Officer from this State, as the Troop is to be raised here. With due respect and consideration, I have the honor to be, Sir, Your most obedt Servant

Go: Washington

LS (photocopy), in Tobias Lear's hand, DLC: James McHenry Papers; Df, in Lear's hand, DLC:GW. The LS was offered for sale in Parke-Bernet Galleries catalog no. 596 (30–31 Oct. 1944), item 343.

1. See John Marshall to GW, 16 May, and Henry Lee, Jr., to GW, 22 May, presumably the two letters that were abstracted.

2. See GW to McHenry, 13 May.

3. Charles Cotesworth Pinckney does not refer to Christian Senf in his letters to GW of 8 March and 20 April.

4. The forwarded letters of application for appointments in the "present establishment," or the New Army as it was often called, probably included, in addition to George Lewis's letter of 9 May, one from John Carney: on 7 June Tobias Lear wrote Carney that GW had forwarded Carney's letter of 20 Mar. applying to the secretary of war for a commission. GW next forwarded letters of this sort to McHenry on 17 June.

5. For GW's correspondence regarding the identification of men who might

serve as officers in the Provisional Army, see particularly McHenry to GW, 2 May, n.1.

6. See George Lewis to GW, 9 May 1799. In this paragraph GW inserted in the Lear draft the following words and phrases: "commenced," "but marrying resigned before the close of it," "with the Rank of Major," and "or as a firm & steady frd to Government."

7. Dr. Robert Wellford (1753–1823), who was a visitor at Mount Vernon as recently as 26 May (*Diaries*, 6:349), was married to Catherine Yates Thornton Wellford, daughter of the Rev. Robert Yates and widow of John Thornton (d. 1789) of Stafford County. GW inserted "That service."

8. Capt. Thomas Turner of the 7th Infantry Regiment in the New Army visited Mount Vernon with his wife and daughter on 21–22 May (*Diaries*, 6:349). For other correspondence regarding Turner, see GW to Bushrod Washington, 5 May 1799, and note 1 of that document.

To John Marshall

Dear Sir,   Mount Vernon June 6th 1799

Your favour of the 16th ultimo has been duly received, and I sincerely hope it will be in the power of yourself and the other Gentlemen, whom I addressed on the subject, to aid me in making a selection of proper Characters to fill the Offices in the Regiments alotted to Virginia; for, from the causes which I mentioned in my former letter, I find I must rely, for information, on others who are better acquainted with the people of this State than I am. And as there are many desireable points to be combined in those who may be selected, particularly for the higher grades, I can apply only to those in whom I place the highest confidence.

In contemplating the subject I have thought it best to follow the four grand Divisions of the State, as laid off by the Inspector General in his arrangements for recruiting. From each of these to select a proper Character for the command of a Regiment, and to request him to furnish me with the names of such persons, in his division, as are fit and willing to fill other grades.

Enclosed is a letter which I have written, to this effect, to Colo. Cropper of the Eastern Shore, who, I am told, is a person every way qualified to command a Regiment, and who would do credit to the service by his acceptance. I leave it open for the perusal of yourself, Colo. Carrington and Colo. Heth. If you should see no objection, I pray you to seal, direct and forward it; for I do not know the particular part of the Country in which Colo. Cropper lives.[1]

Although these divisions are marked out for a Regiment each; yet I should not feel myself confined particularly to those limits for the Officers of each Regiment, if more suitable Characters offer themselves in others.

Major or Colo. Menice[2] has been recommended to me as a person well qualified to command one of the Regiments, as well from his former services as from his present Character. I must beg the favour of yourself, Colo. Carrington and Colo. Heth (for whom also this letter is intended) to let me know his place of residence, and your opinions of his Eligibility.[3] Should Colo. Cropper and this Gentleman be selected and willing to serve, two of the Districts will be provided with Colonels, vizt—the Eastern Shore District, and that on the south side of James River. For the other two, vizt the Middle Country from Rappahannock to James River, and from the Blue Ridge to the Ohio, provision must yet be made; and I shall be much obliged by your furnishing me with the names of such Characters from these Districts as are suitable for the higher Grades, and any others that you may be able to point out. The Colonels giving in the names of those who are fit and willing to serve in their respective Regiments, will assist much in the detail. I should wish, notwithstanding, to get all the information I can from other sources also.

You will oblige me by letting me hear from you on this subject as soon as is convenient. With great esteem & sincere regard, I am Dear Sir, Your most Obedt Servt

Go: Washington

P.S. I will thank you to give me the Character of General Porterfield of Augusta, as to his fitness to command a Regiment, his politics &c. Should he be considered a qualified person and willing to accept the command of a Regiment, it will provide for another Division.[4]

LS, in Tobias Lear's hand, MoSW; Df, in Lear's hand, DLC:GW. Lear's endorsement on the draft reads: "intended also for Colo. Carrington & Colo. Heth."

1. In his response of 12 June, Marshall raised some questions about GW's letter of 6 June to John Cropper, which he had delayed forwarding until he had received further instructions from GW. On 16 June GW wrote Marshall and asked that he return to him the letter to Cropper. The next day he sent Marshall a new letter for Cropper, which he dated 17 June. For the text of GW's unsent letter to Cropper, see GW to Cropper, 17 June, n.1.

2. Lear inserted an asterisk here and at the bottom of the page wrote: "I spell this name as it is pronounced, I do not know whether it is correct or not. It is the

Gentleman who was on the Grand Jury when Mr Cabell's letter was noticed by them, and who afterwards published a piece in answer to Mr Cabell on that subject." See note 3.

3. See Marshall's comments on the character and qualifications for command of Callohill Mennis in his reply of 12 June.

4. Robert Porterfield (1752–1843), who represented Augusta County in the Virginia house of delegates from 3 Dec. 1798 to 26 Jan. 1799, served in the Virginia Line throughout the Revolutionary War, rising from second lieutenant in 1776 to captain in 1779. He was brigadier general of the Virginia militia during the War of 1812.

To William Hayward Foote

Sir,   Mount Vernon 7th June 1799

In searching old Memos., I found notes of which the enclosed is a Copy. I was uncertain at the time of running the meanders of the run, on which side the body of the water went, of course, as the Run is the boundary, it was then, and still may be, uncertain, to whom the Island belongs. But if my memory serves me, I think it was claimed by George Ashford; and the courses will, I believe, comprehend it. That Survey however, being a private one, made for my own satisfaction, can have no binding effect on the adjacent owner.[1]

It will, of course, be recollected, that as my Survey of the Meanders of the Run was made near 30 years ago, that a considerable variation (perhaps two degrees) have taken place since.[2] I am Sir Your Very Hble Servt

                                        Go: Washington

ALS (letterpress copy), DLC:GW.

1. William Hayward Foote was the nephew and farm manager of Elizabeth Foote Washington, the widow of Lund Washington. After Elizabeth and Lund Washington left Mount Vernon in 1784, GW in 1785 conveyed to Lund 450 acres taken from the three parcels of land to the west of Dogue Run which GW had purchased between 1761 and 1763 from John and George Ashford and Simon Pearson. For the location of the tract and the details of the transaction, see *Diaries*, 1:240, 293, and 4:80–81.

2. Although it does not appear to have a direct connection with the question raised by Foote, it may be noted that on 29 June GW appended this notation to a survey that he made: "not being able to make Mr [Albin] Rawlins's Survey of some of the Fields at Dogue-Run close, I went out with my Compass this day & surveyed the following fields in the following man[ne]r—viz." GW's survey is in DLC:GW.

From Alexander Hamilton

Dr Sir   New York June 7 1799

I did myself the honor to write to you at some length on the 3 of May. I hope the letter got safe to hand.[1]

The recruiting service is now in motion, in Maryland, Delaware Pensylvania New Jersey, New York Connecticut and Massachusettes—I might perhaps add Virginia, from the assurances which I have received as to the transmission of supplies—But I am not as yet informed of its actual commencement in that State. This cannot be much longer delayed.

The field Officers for the Regiment which embraces New Hampshire Vermont and Rhode Island have been lately appointed. They are Rufus Graves Lt Col. Comdt Timothy Darling and Cornelius Lynde Majors.[2] The moment money and cloathing shall arrive the recruiting will begin there and in North Carolina. But I do not view this as *very* near.

I do not understand that the Officers for South Carolina and Georgia have yet been recommended.[3]

The information I receive as to the progress and prospects of the recruiting service are sufficiently encouraging. Colonel Taylor, Commandant of the Regiment raising in Connecticut assures me that he is persuaded if no obstacle arises from supplies, that in two Months his Regiment will be filled by native Americans.[4] From other quarters the intelligence is very well. I permit myself to hope that in this summer and fall the army will be at its complement.

I send you a copy of the arrangement which has been made of the two Regiments of Artillerists—Measures are taking to carry it into execution.[5] The distribution of the Officers with the Western army is referred to Col. Burbeck.[6]

There is nothing further in the military line worthy of your attention to communicate. When I shall have obtained more assistance I shall write more frequently.

A letter from *Mr King* contains this unpleasant intelligence. The publication of the Treaty of *Campo Formio* by the Directory will injure the affairs of the Emperor. It will increase the jealousy of the King of Prussia and of the Empire; whose safety and interests were too little in view in that Treaty. There is no end to the folly of the Potentates who are arrayed against France. We impatiently expect further accounts of the operations of the Arch Duke and entertain a strong hope that his genius and energy will turn to good account the advantage he has gained.[7] Most respectfully & Affecty I have the honour to be Dr S. Yr very obed. Svt

A. Hamilton

ALS, DLC:GW; copy, DLC: Hamilton Papers; copy, DLC: Hamilton Papers.

1. GW's response to Hamilton's letter of 3 May is dated 6 June and is printed as a note to the letter of 3 May.

2. The three men were appointed officers in the 16th Infantry Regiment in the New Army on 14 May 1799 (Syrett, *Hamilton Papers*, 23:178).

3. Charles Cotesworth Pinckney wrote GW on 4 June: "The Arrangement for North Carolina, South Carolina & Georgia have been transmitted to the War Department." See note 3 to that document.

4. Timothy Taylor's letter of 27 May to Hamilton is listed in ibid., 623.

5. Copies of the "arrangement" of the first and second regiments of "Artillerists & Engineers" are in DLC: Hamilton Papers. See Hamilton to GW, 7 June, n.4, in Syrett, *Hamilton Papers*, 23:177–78. See also Hamilton to James McHenry, 26 April 1799, and note 1 of that document (ibid., 72–77).

6. Henry Burbeck on 7 May 1798 was named lieutenant colonel commandant of the artillery and engineering forces of the western army (ibid., 74).

7. See Rufus King to Hamilton, 22 Mar. 1799, n.7, ibid., 22:576–77.

To James McHenry

Private

My dear Sir,   Mount Vernon 7th June 1799

When I began the enclosed letter (left open for your perusal) I intended to address it to Colo. Biddle; who transacts all matters of that sort for me in Philadelphia; but as I wrote on, it occurred that, possibly, the Quarter Master might be a more appropriate character to accomplish my order: for this reason, I have left the letter without a Superscription, in order that you might direct it to the one, or the other, as you shall deem best. and I give you this trouble for the reason which is assigned in it; and for which, & troubling you with such trifles, I pray your excuse.[1]

I had thoughts once, of asking Genl [William] McPherson to execute this Commission for me; (believing, thereby, that it would be well done) but never having been in the habit of corresponding with him, I declined it, on reflection; and of course the Stars for my Epaulets have stood suspended, & I would thank you for sending them to me;[2] and, if it is not heaping too many trifles upon you, also for requesting Mr McAlpin (if he has been able to obtain the gold thread) for letting me have my Uniform Cloaths by the Anniversary of our Independence—forwarded in the manner he has heretofore been directed.[3] I am always and very Affectionately—Yours

Go: Washington

Is the Trade with Hispaniola likely to be opened, or not?

ALS, NhD; ALS (letterpress copy), DLC:GW.

1. The text of the letter of 7 June, the letterpress copy of which is identified as intended for Clement Biddle, reads: "Sir, My Ward, Mr Custis, having entered into the Service of his Country as a (subaltern) Officer of Dragoons, I wish to equip him with every thing suitable thereto; in a handsome, but not an expensive style.

"Let me pray you therefore to provide, and send by one of the first Packets bound to Alexandria, the following articles viz.

A pair of Pistols & Horseman's Sword—Silver mounted

A Saddle—best kind—& proper Halter. A handsome bridle he already has

Holsters, & caps, to suit the Pistols

A proper Horseman's Cap—or Helmet

A horsemans Cloak—suitable to the Unifm

If any other necessary article, is omitted, it may be added to the above list. Let the cost accompany the Invoice, and the amount shall be paid so soon as it is made known.

"I could get these articles in Alexandria, but prefer sending to Philadelphia for them; because the tradesmen of the latter are more in the habit of accomodating Officers in a proper manner; but more especially, because there may have been some direction from the Department of War with respect to some of the Articles, which is better understood there than in the Country Towns: for which reason (wishing to avoid mistakes) I have taken the liberty of passing this letter through the hands of the Secretary of War, open; that, if he shall be pleased to take the trouble of communicating them, his sentiments may be known on any part thereof by you. I am Sir Your most obedt Hble Servant Go: Washington" (letterpress copy, DLC:GW). In his letter to GW of 18 June, McHenry reports that he had engaged Tench Francis, the purveyor of public supplies, to secure these articles for George Washington Parke Custis. McHenry does not indicate that he forwarded GW's letter to Francis, but clearly he did not send it to Biddle. On 14 July GW wrote McHenry that young Custis was making "Daily, fruitless enquiries" about when his "Military equipments" would arrive. On 29 July McHenry wrote that Francis had in hand the sword for the "young warrior" and would soon have the rest, but it was not until 24 Aug. that McHenry reported that "the articles for my young friend" were "now waiting for conveyance." And that was not the end of it (see McHenry to GW, 24 Aug., n.1).

2. See McHenry to GW, 24 June, and note 3 of that document.

3. James McAlpin wrote GW from Philadelphia on 24 June: "This morning—

and not before—I had the pleasure of procuring gold thread sufficient to accomplish your Cloaths. They are already in the hands of an embroiderer, who assures me, that not a moment shall be lost, on his part, to finish the work in time. I have great reason to believe that I shall be able to send the whole by the Mail to Alexandria on Monday morning next. I beg leave to assure you that nothing on my part has been Neglected—And I trust they will give you sattisffaction when received" (DLC:GW). McAlpin soon discovered that he had been too sanguine in his predictions (see McAlpin to GW, 27 June).

To Samuel Mickle Fox

Sir,   Mount Vernon 10th June 1799

Two Bonds due to me, the one from Matthew Richie Esqr., deceased, the other from Colo. Israel Shreve, have been deposited in the Bank of Pennsylvania for Collection.

On each an Instalment was due, and to have been paid into that Bank, on the first day of June 1798; and another on the first day of the present month.

From the Executors of Colo. Ritchie I did, in the course of last sum[mer], receive $1700—and this is all I have received on both Bonds.[1]

Let me pray you to inform me, if any more has been paid into the Bank? and if not, whether any intimation has been given to it, that it will be done?[2] I am unwilling to put the Bonds in suit, if the money could be obtained without: But my want of it is such, that I must have recourse to this expedient soon, if the end cannot be accomplished without—With esteem, I am—Sir Your Most Obedt Hble Servant

Go: Washington

ALS, NAlI. GW addressed this letter to "The President of the Bank of Pennsylvania."

Samuel Mickle Fox (1763–1808) was president of the Bank of Pennsylvania in Philadelphia from 1796 until his death.

1. Matthew Ritchie in 1796 bought GW's 2,813-acre Millers Run tract in Washington County, Pa., for $12,000; the year before Israel Shreve bought GW's 1,664-acre tract in Fayette County, Pa., called Washington's Bottom, for £3,200 (£4,000 Pennsylvania currency). For Ritchie's purchase of the Millers Run tract, see Oliver Wolcott, Jr., to GW, 31 May 1797, n.2, in *Papers, Retirement Series*, 1: 165; for Shreve's purchase of the Washington's Bottom tract, see Shreve to GW, 22 June 1785, source note, in *Papers, Confederation Series*, 3:74. With this letter to Fox, GW initiated in June 1799 a final effort to secure payment of what remained due him for these properties. Fox promptly informed GW that no new

payments on either had been made to GW's account at the Bank of Pennsylvania (see note 2). In early July GW learned from Judge Alexander Addison that Addison from the beginning had been a silent partner of Matthew Ritchie in the purchase of the Millers Run tract, and he at the same time received from Addison the rest of what was due for Addison's half share of the property (see Addison to GW, 6 July). Matthew Ritchie died in February or March 1798. As no payments had been made by Ritchie's estate, both Fox and Addison, as well as James Ross, who had acted as GW's agent in the sale of both the Millers Run and Washington's Bottom tracts, now encouraged Ritchie's widow and Ritchie's brother John to pay GW what he was owed (see Fox to GW, 2 July, Addison to GW, 6 July, 8 Nov., and Ross to GW, 24 July). GW, however, reported to Addison on 24 Nov., shortly before his own death, that he had received nothing from the Ritchies. As for Shreve, GW on 10 Jan. 1799 had put him on notice that unless by the following April he had made the payments due in June 1798 on the purchase of the Washington's Bottom tract, the sheriff would execute an outstanding writ to seize his property in payment. GW wrote James Ross on 26 June 1799 about this, and on 24 July Ross wrote that he had just returned to Philadelphia and would instruct the sheriff to proceed with the seizure. He also reported that Shreve was very ill. Shreve died shortly thereafter, and there is no further reference to him or to his debt in GW's correspondence and no record of any payments has been found in GW's accounts. Among other letters at this time relating to the payments due from Ritchie and Shreve are those from GW to Fox of 26 June and 14 July and from Fox to GW of 20 July. GW indicates in his Ledger C, 12, that he received a total of $10,032.70 in payments for the Millers Run tract and $7,064.63 for the Washington's Bottom tract. See also Ledger C, 22, 24, 25, 27, 40, 48, and 53.

2. Writing from Philadelphia on 13 June, Fox acknowledged the receipt of GW's letter and then reported: "No payments have been made into this Bank upon the bonds of M. Ritchie or I. Shreve deposited here for collection; neither has any intimation been given of an intention to pay the instalments due upon them. On the 12th of April last a deposit of two hundred & fifty dollars was made to the credit of James Ross Esqr. as your Agent by a person who said that he was directed so to do by Mr Ross. If this Institution can be any ways serviceable to you in enforcing the collection of these debts permit me to assure you that such measures as you may be pleased to direct shall be immediately taken" (DLC:GW). See also GW to Fox, 26 June.

To William Augustine Washington

My dear Sir,   Mount Vernon 10th June 1799

Your letter of the 1st instant, and the Corn also in good order, has been received; the a/c of which Mr Anderson, my Manager, will render you; with a certificate from respectable Merchants in Alexa. of the Cash prices of that article at the times of delivery.

It never was, nor is it my intention, to delay payment a moment longer than might suit your own convenience; of course you may draw upon me for the amount of the Corn, so as to answer your own purposes, as to time.[1] My disappointments in the receipts of money, have been such, as to leave little hope of obtaining it through any other medium than by borrowing from the Bank of Alexandria.

For two tracts of Land which I held in the Counties of Washington & Fayette in the State of Pennsylvania, and sold on judgment Bonds payable by Instalments; whereof $6000 was to have been paid the first day of June 1798—and the like sum the first day of the present month, I have received (about eight months ago) only 1700$.[2] Besides these Sums, I ought, by Contract, to have received on or before the first of Jany last upwards of $10,000 for other Lands disposed of; but have not yet got a farthing of the money; and that is not the worst of it, for I see little prospect thereof; in any reasonable time, when I view the conduct of those from whom this latter sum is expected. The first nam'd Sums I did, most assuredly, expect to have received 'ere this; as I had only to present the Bonds of the purchasers to the Courts of the Counties in which the Land lay, to obtain Executions.

I do not mention these things with a view to induce you to postpone your draught a moment longer than you find perfectly convenient to yourself; and with respect to Mr Flood (for the Corn from Mr T: W[ashingto]n's Est.) the money will be ready whenever it is called for.[3] The advantage of a long day, to me—or even a short one, consists in the chance of receiving the money due on the Judgment Bonds, and rendering it unnecessary for me to borrow at the Bank, on disadvantageous terms. All I require is—that you would not draw at sight, that I may be allowed a little time to arrange matters at the Bank. Mrs Washington unites with me in best wishes for you, Mrs Washington and the family, and I am, my dear Sir, Your sincere friend, and affectionate Uncle,

Go: Washington

ALS, PPRF; ALS (letterpress copy), DLC:GW.

1. For William Augustine Washington's drafts drawn on GW for payment for the corn that he shipped to GW's distillery at Mount Vernon in May 1799 and for GW's payments, see W.A. Washington to GW, 13 July 1799, n.1.

2. See GW to Samuel M. Fox, this date.

3. William Pinckard Flood did not draw on GW for payment until fall, and on 25 Oct. GW paid Flood's draft for $200 (Ledger C, 55).

From Francis Deakins

Sir   George Town June 12th 1799
   I now enclose you Mr H. Veatches a/c for rents recd of Mrs P. Beall to the 7th May last Since which he has lodged in my Hands two Hogsheads PB 1080 1005–102–903[;] 1082 1003–97–906— 1809 lbs. & there remains 99 lbs. & Some Cost to Close that a/c— which was very doubtfull[1] & I find with McDades has gave him more Trouble to Accomplish & Secure then the frugal Salary of 20/ pr Tenant I fixed on them 12 or 15 years ago will recompence—I know him corrict & Honist—& the only one convenient to be relied on in the care of that property—was you to permit him to with hold 20 or 30 Dolls. of the Bond he has to Collect from Reed on McDades a/c it may be advisable—tho he has not applied for it—yet he has observed to me the Extra. Trouble—he has now fixed Tenants of his own procuring who I hope will give but Little Trouble[2]—The two Hogsheads Tobo & 26 Dolls. in my Hands Shall be pd to your order on Sight—Tobo now Commands at this place 40/ our money.[3] I am Sir Your Obedt St
                                              Francis Deakins

ALS, DLC:GW.

   1. The account of Mrs. Priscilla Beale, a tenant on GW's land in Montgomery County, Md., covers the interval from 1794, when she became his tenant, until 7 May 1799. It is in DLC:GW following the letter from Deakins. The annual rent was 1,500 lbs. of tobacco. The money value of the payments made before the last two hogsheads were received came to £14.7.5½ Maryland currency; PB 1080 and PB 1082 were the marks or labels of the hogsheads, 1,005 lbs. and 1,003 lbs. were the gross weights of each; 102 and 97 lbs. the weight of the containers; 903 and 906 lbs., the net weight of the tobacco; and 1,809, the total weight of the tobacco.

   2. GW replied on 16 June: "Dear Sir, Your letter of the 12th instant enclosing one of the 11th of March from Mr Veatch to you, and his settlement with Mrs Priscilla Beall (or rather his a/c with her) has been duly received by me.

   "I am willing that Mr Veatch should withhold any part of the Bond he has to collect from Reed on McDades a/c, that you shall think reasonable & just, as compensation for the extra: trouble he has been put to in securing the Rents due from the abovenamed persons, and request that you would be so good as to direct him accordingly, to do so.

   "If it would not be giving you two much trouble, I would ask the favor of you to sell the Tobacco recd on a/c of Mrs Beall's rent, for what it will fetch; and when the Cash is in your hands and I am advised thereof, I will *then* draw upon you for the amount, and the 26 dollars which are already there. With very great esteem & regard I am—Dear Sir Your obedt Hble Servt Go: Washington" (letterpress copy, DLC:GW). "The widow McDaid" (Mrs. Patrick McDaid) and "the widow Beall" were two of the three tenants on the 519-acre tract in Montgomery County, Md., at the time that GW took it over from John Francis Mercer in April 1794 (Deakins to GW, 12 June 1794). See also John Francis Mercer to GW, 13 April 1794, Priscilla Beale to GW, 2 April 1797, source note, and Deakins to GW, 21 June 1799. The letter of 11 Mar. 1799 from Hezekiah Veatch to Deakins is in DLC:GW.

3. GW wrote Deakins on 26 June: "Dear Sir, Below, is a receipt for the Cash arising from the Sale of the Tobo recd from Mrs Beall on a/c of Rent—and for $26 bale paid you by Mr Veatch. What you have done with that Gentleman is perfectly agreeable to—Dr Sir Your Obedt Hble Servant G. Washington" (letter-press copy, DLC:GW).

The attached receipt reads: "Mount Vernon 26th June 1799 Then received from Colo. Frans Deakins Twenty six dollars—bale of cash paid him by Mr H. Veatch on my a/c for Rent; and One hundred & one dollars & 59 Cents for sales of Tobo recd from Mrs Priscilla Beall on same a/c as below. Go: Washington.

PB	1080	1005	102	903
	1082	1003	97	906

1809 @ 5½⟨c.⟩ $99.59

2 Casks   2.
                                                      101.59

From John Marshall

Dear Sir   Richmond June 12th [17]99

Your letter of the 6th inst. which came by the last mail was communicated to Colo. Carrington & woud have been shown also to Colo. Heth had he been within our immediate reach.

Colo. Cropper is a man of fair character correct politics & unquestionable courage. No doubt can be entertaind of his fitness for the command of a regiment nor shoud I have hesitated to transmit him immediately your letter, but for one consideration produc'd by his former military station. He was in our late army a lieut. Colo. & he performd the duties of that office with reputation. It is probable that he may feel wounded at being offerd the same grade under others whom he then commanded & who are perhaps in nothing his superiors. It is presumd that officers in the actual army will command those of the same grade in the eventual army. If we are correct in this then Colonels Bentley & Parker who were both subalterns when Colo. Cropper was a field officer, & who are not supposd to have manifested any superiority over him, will now take rank of him. The former relative rank of officers ought certainly not to be the rule which shoud positively decide their present rank. But among gentlemen in other respects equal it is difficult entirely to lose sight of it. It is suggested by Colo. Carrington that if the eventual army shall be calld into actual service—Brigadiers General will necessarily be appointed from Virginia & he has supposd that Genl Clarke & Colo. Cropper, to whom I will take the liberty of adding Genl Posey, woud be proper persons to contemplate for that station.

For this single reason Colo. Carrington & myself have deemd it advisable to detain your letter to Colo. Cropper until your further directions can be receivd. Shoud you still incline to transmit it to him, we trust the delay will produce no inconvenience.[1]

Colo. Callohil Mennis who resides in the county of Bedford, was in the late war brigade major to Genl Muhlenberg. He is a man of considerable energy of character. His activity & courage recommend him as a military man, but those who know him best suppose him better fitted for the command of a battalion than of a regiment. It is probable that he woud accept a majority under a man he coud respect sufficiently to serve under without mortification. Colo. James Breckenridge of Botetourt, altho never heretofore in service, is beleivd to possess many excellent qualities as a soldier, to which he adds a weight of character which woud I think induce Colo. Mennis to be content with a majority in his regiment. To the appointment of Colo. Breckenridge there woud be this ob jection. It woud take him out of the State legislature where he is a valuable & influential member.[2]

Genl Porterfield of Augusta is in every respect proper for the command of a regiment.

Genl Blackwell of Fauquier was a captain in the late army & in my opinion one of our most valuable officers. He is a cool steady sensible & brave man whose conduct is always correct & who woud in my opinion command a regiment with reputation to himself & advantage to his country.[3]

Colo. Swearingan of Berkeley was also a captain in the late army & maintains a very high reputation. I am not personally acquainted with him but Colos. Carrington & Heth are & they speak highly of him.[4]

I do not immediately recollect any others among the old officers whom I coud name for so high an office as the command of a regiment. I am aware that those I have mentiond cannot, shoud you on further enquiry approve of them, be all appointed, but I have namd them because it is possible that those first applied to may be disinclind to enter into the army.

Virginia has sustaind a very serious loss which all good men will long lament, in the death of Mr Henry. He is said to have expird on thursday last. The intelligence is not absolutely certain but scarcely a hope is entertaind of its untruth. With the most respectful attachment I remain Sir your obedt Servt

J. Marshall

ALS, DLC:GW.

1. See GW to Marshall, 16 June, and notes, and GW to John Cropper, 17 June.

2. Callohill Mennis, who during the Revolution rose to the rank of captain in the 1st Virginia Regiment, was brigade major to Gen. John Peter Gabriel Muhlenberg when he was captured at Charleston in May 1780. Two years before this, on 2 June 1797, Mennis wrote to GW recommending a young friend for military service.

3. Capt. John Blackwell of the 3d Virginia Regiment was wounded at Brandywine in September 1777 and was taken prisoner at Charleston in May 1780. He was made brevet major in September 1783. In April 1799 Blackwell polled 422 votes in Fauquier County as a Republican candidate for the seat in Congress won by the Federalist Leven Powell.

4. Joseph Swearingen of the 12th Virginia Regiment was taken prisoner at Charleston in May 1780.

From Daniel Morgan

Dear Sir   Soldiers Rest June 12th 1799

I was honored with your Letter of the 10th Ultimo. have consulted Colo. Parker on the occasion: inclosed is a list of such characters as I thought would fit the Army, and who offered their services. most of those characters that are inserted in the list of recommendation are in my opinion good men and may be depended on; they are mostly young men of good family and education, who are determined to continue in the Army while their services may be wanting; they enter the service purely from principle, Their attachment to Government are unquestionable.[1]

I should have answered your letter sooner, but wished to inform myself of such characters as would best fit the Army—I find but few of the old Officers that are altogether fit for the Service, from different causes (Vizt) some too old and infirm; others incumbered with large families, and some too much in the habit of drinking which I always view as a very great misfortune to man-kind, should any in future offer of superior talents, I will transmit you a list of their names.

Major James Stephenson who you will find placed on the list of recommendations would command a Regiment with as much pro-priety perhaps, as any officer in the service. he commanded a Company, (in the Army commanded by Genl St Clair in the year 1791) with great propriety and at the defeat of that officer on the 4th of November he rendered very singular service, in addition to what has already been said he is a great disciplinarian and of course will be a great acquisition to a new raised Army; he is also a man of good Character and education, and firmly attached to Government.[2]

I have mentioned Capt. Archd C. Randolph to you some time since I must again repeat it, that I think he will make a great offi-cer, he has not seen so much service as some, but he has seen a good deal, and were I to have my choice of a Cavalry officer I would take him in preference perhaps to most men within my knowledge.[3] I have the Honor to be sir Your Hle Sert

Danl Morgan

LS, DLC:GW.

1. Morgan enclosed the following list of potential officers for the Provisional Army: "James Stephenson Berkeley County, at this time Major and Inspector to Genl [William] Darkes Brigade, he thinks from the Services he has seen he is intitled to the Command of a Regiment.

Samuel Washington, Berkeley County Captain of Cavalry.

Joseph Crane, Berkeley County Recommended by Colo. Joseph Swearingen, as Capt. of Infantry perhaps a first Lieutenancy will do.

Thomas Hammond, Berkeley County Lieutenant to Saml Washington in the Cavalry.

William Eskridge, Frederick County was a Lieutenant in the late War, has been in the Habit of drinking, but has left it off, and says he is determined to do so.

William Baylis, Frederick County—was also a lieutenant in the late war: has been in the habit of drinking too much—and has also left it off and is deter-mined to do so.

William Monroe, Frederick County was a Lieutenant in the late war: a sober man of Good Character.

Samuel Turner Frederick County a man of Good Character has Seen Some Service, and wishes the Command of a Company; which I think him Equal to.

Ferguson Bell Frederick County he now Commands a troop of Cavalry; and wishes to Continue to do so.

John Morgan, Frederick County has Seen Som Service, and wishes the ap-pointment of a Subaltern in the Cavalry.

Samuel Bell, Frederick County has Seen Some Service and wishes a first Lieutenan[c]y.

Tarlton F. Webb—Fredk County first Lieutenant.

George Barnett, Frederick County first Lieutenant.

Benjamin Barnett, Frederick County Second Lieutenant.

Robert Bell Frederick County Second Lieutenant.

Elias Edmonds, Fauquier County, Subaltern.

Matthew Whiting Brooke Fauquier County Subaltern.

Whiting Diggs, Fauqueir County Subaltern.

Joshua Tenneson Fauquier County Subaltern.

these young men from Fauquier County will make as Elegant a set of officers as any in the Army, of their Grade.

John Hilton, Bath Berkeley County Subaltern has Good Education and Talents." Morgan wrote GW again on 26 June and enclosed a second list of nominees for commissions.

2. In his letter of 10 June to Morgan, which Morgan enclosed, Col. Thomas Parker has this to say of James Stephenson: "I saw majr Stephenson a few days ago on his way to Alexandria. he is willing to enter into the Service of his Country if the provisional army is Raised. I think he woud make a Verry Valuable officer & woud do honor to any Rank that may be given him. I think there are few men in this Country who woud Command a Regiment with greater propriety. . . . Majr Stephenson Intends to Call on you as soon as he Returns from Alexandria where he is Called on business of Importance" (DLC:GW). In his letter Parker also recommended Joseph Crain for a captaincy in the Provisional Army, as did Joseph Swearingen in a letter to Morgan of 30 May 1799. Swearingen identified Crane "as a Captain in the 55th Regiment of Virginia Militia" for some years, who wished a commission in the Provisional Army—"Or if any Vacancies Should Happen in the Regiments now Raising, which he could be ⟨calld⟩ upon with propriety to fill, Immediate Service will be most pleasing to him."

On 26 June Morgan sent GW Andrew Waggener's letter of 14 June recommending James Stephenson for colonel of a regiment, in which Waggener called Stephenson "a staunch friend to the Government" and pointed out that Stephenson had been "ever since he left the Western Army Inspector to the 16 Brigade of [Virginia] Militia." Both of the enclosed letters are in DLC:GW.

3. Morgan's letter of 3 April recommending Archibald C. Randolph has not been found. For other references to Randolph, see GW to Morgan, 10 April, n.1; see also GW to McHenry, 7 April (second letter), and note 1 of that document, 23 April, and 5 May 1799.

From John Tayloe

Dear Sir   Mount Airy 14th June 1799

    T'was my intention to have written you from Annapolis—on my return from Phi[ladelphi]a but my time would not allow me that pleasure—I therefore take this opportunity of returning you my warmest thanks for your letter to the Secretary of War—Which I delivered him[1]—He seemed much averse to my declining at this time the acceptance of the Majority in the Regiment of Light Dragoons—saying he did not know twould be necessary immediately to fill the vacancy—as there was not a probability of this Regiment being quickly raised—Under this idea—I consented to remain—as I had stood before—intending instantly to accept—provided the Service of the Regiment is required—else to decline the acceptance any time before the meeting of our next Assembly—provided a vacancy could be left for me—(of equal rank) in the Cavalry to be hereafter raised—This Mr McHenry could see no impropriety in—& promised me to write you—at the same time on the subject—& requested me to do the same[2]—I trust no inconvenience to the service will arise from this arrangement—& that it will meet your *full approbation*. I pray you to present me very respectfully to Mrs Washington—& believe me with esteem your obliged & Obedt Servt

John Tayloe

ALS, DLC:GW.

1. See GW to Tayloe, 5 May, and the references in note 1 of that document.

2. Tayloe never did take up his commission as major in the cavalry. See Return of Officers, 1800, in *ASP: Military Affairs*, 1:147.

From Alexander Hamilton

Private
Dear Sir New York June 15. 1799

I wrote to you a few days since chiefly to inform you of the progress of the measures respecting the recruiting service & that the symptoms with regard to it were sufficiently promising.[1] The accounts continue favourable.

I have just received a letter from General Wilkinson dated the 13 of April, in which he assures me that he will set out in the ensuing month for the seat of Government. The interview with him will be useful.[2]

It strikes me forcibly that it will be both right and expedient to advance this Gentleman to the grade of Major General—He has been long steadily in service and long a Brigadier. This in a so considerable an extension of the military establishment gives him a pretension to promotion.

I am aware that some doubts have been entertained of him, and that his character on certain sides gives room for doubts. Yet he is at present in the service—is a man of more than ordinary talent—of courage and enterprise—has discovered upon various occasions a good zeal—has embraced military pursuits as a profession and will naturally find his interest as an ambitious man in deserving the favour of the Government; while he will be apt to become disgusted, if neglected, and through disgust may be rendered really what he is now only suspected to be—Under such circumstances, it seems to me good policy to avoid all just ground of discontent and to make it the interest of the individual to pursue his duty.[3]

If you should be also of this opinion, I submit to your consideration whether it would not be adviseable for you to express it in a private letter to the Secretary of War.[4] With great respect & Affection I have the honor to be Dr Sir Your obed. servt

A. Hamilton

ALS, DLC:GW; copy, DLC: Hamilton Papers.

1. See Hamilton to GW, 7 June.

2. Hamilton is referring to James Wilkinson's letter of 15 April, not 13 April. For Wilkinson's letter, see Syrett, *Hamilton Papers*, 23:45–49.

3. Wilkinson's commercial ventures and land speculations in the West in the years following the Revolution met with little success but gave him a reputation for tricky dealings. He returned to the army in 1792 and feuded with his superior, Anthony Wayne. He became the senior officer of the army at Wayne's death late in 1796.

4. GW wrote Hamilton on 25 June agreeing that "policy dictates the expediency of promoting Brigadier Wilkinson to the Rank of Majr General." On the same day GW sent the secretary of war copies of both this letter from Hamilton regarding Wilkinson and his reply to it of 25 June.

To John Marshall

Dear Sir,   Mount Vernon June 16th 1799

By the last mail I was favoured with your letter of the 12 instant, and feel much obliged by the attention of Colo. Carrington and yourself to the subject mentioned in my last letters to you.

I am very glad that you did not forward my letter to Colo. Cropper.[1] At the time of writing that letter I was aware of the circumstances which you mention, with respect to the relative rank of

Officers in the actual and eventual Army, and was apprehensive that it might have an effect in the minds of some persons, who otherwise would have no objection to the appointments proposed. Yet I conceived, that, if any event should make it necessary to raise the Troops provisionally authorized, every friend to our Country and its Government would hold himself in readiness to step forward with his personal services, and that those who did not mean to continue in the service beyond the pressure of the exigency which might call them forth, would not hesitate to hold any station where their talents and influence could be made useful to their Country.

Upon further consideration, I have, however, thought it best to write to Colo. Cropper in a way that will lead him to make a tender of his services, if he should be inclined so to do. And, at the same time, draw from him information respecting Characters for other grades. This letter shall be forwarded for your inspecti[o]n & transmission—In the mean time I will thank [you] to return that which is in your hands.[2]

Altho' all the persons you have mentioned cannot be appointed to the Command of Regiments within the number alotted to Virginia; yet a choice of Characters is desireable on every account, and if any others occur I will thank you to forward their names, marking their relative qualifications as they stand in the estimation of yourself and the other Gentlemen applied to on this subject.

In the Death of Mr Henry (of which I fear there is little doubt) not only Virginia, but our Country at large has sustained a very serious loss. I sincerely lament his death as a friend; and the loss of his eminent talents as a Patriot I consider as peculiarly unfortunate at this critical juncture of our affairs. With very great esteem & sincere regard I am Dear Sir Yr most Obedt Servt

P.S. Colo. Cropper would have been brought forward among the late appointments; but as he had never made any application, and it not being known whether he would be willing to serve or not, his name was omitted.

Df, in Tobias Lear's hand, DLC:GW.

1. GW's initial letter to John Cropper, dated 6 June, is quoted in GW to Cropper, 17 June, n.1.

2. GW wrote Marshall the next day, 17 June: "Dear Sir, Enclosed is the letter

for Colo. Cropper which I informed you I should take the liberty of forwarding to your care—It is left unsealed for the inspection of yourself, Colo. Carrington and Colo. Heath [Heth], or either of them, if they should be in Richmond. If there appears no objection to its being transmitted to Colo. Cropper, I will thank you to close and forward it without delay. With very sincere regard, I am Dear Sir, Your most Obedt Servt Go: Washington" (LS, CSmH; Df, DLC:GW). Marshall replied from Richmond on 21 June: "An accidental absence from town prevented my returning by the last mail the inclosd letter. I am extremely happy that the liberty we have taken to suspend its transmission to Colo. Cropper has not displeased you. Your second letter [of 17 June] to that gentleman is just receiv'd & will be immediately put in the post office with a proper direction" (DLC:GW). On 1 July GW wrote: "Dear Sir, Whilst I acknowledge the receipt of your favor of the 21st ultimo, returning the first letter which I wrote to Colo. Cropper, I pray you will accept my thanks for your attention in forwarding the second, and believe me to be, With very sincere regard, Dear Sir, Your most obedt Servt" (Df, DLC:GW).

To William Thornton

Dear Sir,   Mount Vernon 16th June 1799
    Your favor of the 5th instant came duly to hand.
    Mr Blagdens last call for $1000 is, I must acknowledge, sooner than I had contemplated; but I will make arrangements with the Bank of Alexandria to meet it by the first of next month. If his progress in the buildings, & faithful execution of the work, keep pace with his demands (and this is all I require) he shall have no cause to complain of my payments.[1]
    It would seem by a letter I have lately received from a Gentleman in Baltimore, to which place the Glass from Boston had (in the first instance) been sent, that a wrong box from the former, had been sent to Alexan[dri]a; and that the right one would follow by the first conveyance; requesting a return of the mistaken one. If it should have got into Mr Blagdens hands—pray request him to forwd it to Colo. Gilpin[2]—Yrs Obediently

                                                   Go: Washington

ALS, DLC: Thornton Papers; ALS (letterpress copy), DLC:GW.
    1. See Thornton to GW, 5–6 June, and note 1 of that document, and GW to Thornton, 2 July.
    2. Benjamin Lincoln's letter to GW about the glass is dated 4 June and is printed in Lincoln to GW, 3 April 1799, n.1.

To Wilson Allen

Sir,   Mount Vernon 17th June 1799
Your favor of the 29th ulto has been duly received, and would have been earlier acknowledged had I not been in daily expectation of seeing Mr Bushrod Washington on his Circuit.

Fearing he may have taken another route, or passed by without calling, I delay no longer to declare; that I think as you do, that his advice was given on mistaken ground; and in *that case*, a Deed from General Lee to me for the *same land* which he inform'd me, he had sent to your Office sometime ago for the purpose of recording, has taken a wrong course also.

Under this view of the matter I would pray you to withhold the recording of *both* (unless some evil may result from the delay) until I can know his sentimts on the subject, after he is possessed of a complete knowledge of the circumstances; or you yourself should be thoroughly satisfied of the right course for me to take, to give these Conveyances legal, & unequivocal effect.[1] I thank you for your former sentiments on this point, as I shall do for any further information respecting it, being Sir, Your most Obedt & Very Hble Ser⟨vt⟩

Go: Washington

ALS (letterpress copy), DLC:GW.
    1. See Allen's response of 28 June.

To John Cropper, Jr.

Sir,   Mount Vernon, June 17th 1799
Was I not well assured of your Patriotism and firm attachment to the Government of our Country, I should think it necessary to apologize for the trouble I am about to give you.

The Secretary of War has signified to me that the President of the United States thinks it highly expedient that no time should be lost in selecting proper Characters to Officer the twenty four Regiments of Infantry authorized to be *eventually* raised by a law of the last Congress; and has requested me to furnish him with a list of the names of such persons as are best qualified and willing to serve in the respective Grades of four of these Regiments, which is the proportion alotted to Virginia.

Having been absent from home for almost twenty five years, with short intervals only, and in these intervals a necessary attention to my private concerns confining me almost entirely to my own Estate, I find my acquaintance with the Citizens of this State, particularly with the rising generation, very limited indeed. And, therefore, ready as I always am to do anything in my power to promote the public weal, I find it impossible to perform this task without the assistance of others on whom I can place a reliance.

As these troops are authorized to be raised only in case of an actual War with a foriegn power, or of imminent danger of Invasion of our Territory by such power, it is to be presumed that, in such an event, every good Citizen would hold himself in readiness to take the field, if necessary, whether belonging to the eventual Army or not. I therefore flatter myself that when the President's intention of appointing the Officers for this Army shall be fully known, we shall find many of the valuable Officers who served with reputation in the Revolutionary War, as well as others, step forward and *offer* their services in grades which they would not accept, if their object was to pursue a military career for life, or to continue in the service beyond the exigency which might call them forth. This leads me to hope, that, instead of *seeking* for those who are willing to receive appointments, we shall find the best Spirits of our Country *offering* their services in those grades where their talents and influence can be useful, without feeling themselves bound by the scrupulous punctilios of Rank which Officers observe when Arms are assumed as a profession.[1]

But, in order to place the matter upon certain ground, and to pursue it with system, it becomes necessary to make the selection before mentioned. And, as the propriety of drawing the Officers from different parts of the State, observing, as nearly as may be, a due proportion to the respective population, is obvious; I must, of course, obtain my information from various sources, and combine the result in the best manner I can.

I therefore, Sir, take the liberty to ask if you will be so good as to furnish me with the names of such Characters as are, in your opinion, qualified to fill the several Offices in one Regiment of Infantry—a Battalion, or part thereof; and who would be willing to receive these appointments, annexing to their names the respective grades and the places or Counties of their Residence.

To facilitate this selection, and to observe the proportion before mentioned, I have thought it best to follow the four Grand Divisions of the State, as laid off by the Inspector General for the purposes of recruiting, and to endeavour to select the Officers of one Regiment from each. In that case, the Division in which you reside, will comprehend the Counties of Hanover, Henrico, New Kent, Charles City, James City, Mathews, Gloucester, York, Warwick, Elizabeth City, Acomac, Northampton, Caroline, King and Queen, Essex, King William, Middlesex, Lancaster, Northumberland, Richmond, Westmoreland and King George. To these Counties then, you will be pleased more particularly to confine your attention. But if suitable Characters are known to you in other parts of the State, I will thank you for the names of them also.

As these Counties form a large district, and may comprehend more valuable Characters than the acquaintance of any one person in it may extend to, it is left with you to advice with others, or, from such Counties therein as your intimacy is greatest, to select a proportionate part. In a word, Sir, paying some attention to the policy of distribution, to select in whole or part, such characters as would do honor to the service and would be gratifying to your own feelings to command: A measure, though if it cannot be asked, is highly to be wished, and would have been gladly embraced in the arrangement of the twelve Regiments now recruiting if any thing had appeared at that time indicative of your inclination to re-enter the Military line.[2]

You will readily see that these names must be handed to the President of the United States for his approbation, and afterwards confirmed or rejected by the Senate; it is therefore proper that no assurances of *appointment* be given to the parties which will render a change impracticable without wounding their feelings too much.

Where you are not personally well acquainted with such Characters as are fit and willing to serve, you will be so good as to obtain the best recommendations, and such as you can rely upon. And every cautionary measure is necessary to guard against errors which frequently result from the ease with which recommendations are generally obtained, the partiality of friends, and a delusive hope that men of bad habits, by being transplanted into the Army, will become good men and good Officers.

I have ventured, Sir, to give you this trouble; because, from your former services in the military line, I could confide in your knowledge and judgment of proper Characters to be brought forward at this time; and beleiving that I might readily count upon your best exertions to render a service to your Country.

I will thank you for an acknowledgement of the Receipt of this letter as soon as it gets to your hands, and for your observations on the subject of it, so far as you may then be prepared to give them. With very great esteem, I have the honor to be, Sir, Your most obedt Servt

Go: Washington

LS, in Tobias Lear's hand, PWacD; Df, in Lear's hand, DLC:GW, with changes made by GW. This letter was the substitute for one dated 6 June and not sent to Cropper. See GW to John Marshall, 6 June, n.1; see also note 1 below.

At the age of about twenty-one, on 5 Feb. 1776, John Cropper, Jr. (1755–1821), of Accomac on Virginia's Eastern Shore was made captain of the first company of the 9th Virginia Regiment. He advanced rapidly, becoming a major in the 7th Virginia Regiment in January 1777 and its lieutenant colonel the following March (*Calendar of Virginia State Papers*, 1:271, 275, 317). After distinguishing himself at the Battle of Brandywine, he was made lieutenant colonel commandant of the 11th Virginia Regiment in October 1777. Cropper resigned from the army in August 1779 to return to the Virginia Eastern Shore where as county lieutenant he led the fight against British raiders in 1781 and 1782, and as a commissary he was one of the important suppliers of provisions to the army at the siege of Yorktown. Cropper since 1793 had been lieutenant colonel of the 2d Regiment of the Virginia militia, and he remained the senior military officer on the Eastern Shore until the War of 1812.

1. Heeding John Marshall's warning that Cropper might properly expect to be made a brigadier if the Provisional Army were to materialize, GW substituted the long paragraph ending here for the following sentence in the discarded letter of 6 June (see source note): "Upon this ground, Sir, may I be permitted to give in your name as one who is willing to take the Command of a Regiment in the Provisional Army, if you should be appointed thereto?" Neither the wording nor the organization of the remainder of the discarded letter of 6 June is identical to this one of 17 June, but it is written to the same purpose and conveys the same meaning.

2. GW inserted this paragraph in Lear's draft of the letter.

To James McHenry

Sir,   Mount Vernon June 17th 1799

Enclosed are two letters of application for appointments in the immediate Army. One from John Smith, for a Lieutenancy, recommended by General Posey, and Captn Presley Thornton— the other a Recommendation of Richd Robey, by Captn Garnett Peyton and others, for the appointment of Cadet.[1]

Captn George S. Washington has requested that I would mention to you the name of John Stephens, of Berkley County, who wishes to be appointed a Cadet in his Company. Captn Washington speaks of him as a person well deserving and every way fit for such an appointment, and says he will be particularly useful to him at this time in the recruiting business, as both his lieutenants have been chosen to fill offices in the Staff department of the Regiment, and he does not know that any others are yet appointed to supply their places.[2]

From the first essays in this business (in this part of the State) the prospect is not discouraging; and nothing would add more to it's progress than the receipt of the Cloathing. With due consideration I have the honor to be &c.

Df, in Tobias Lear's hand, DLC:GW.

1. None of these letters has been found. Neither Richard Robey nor John Smith received an appointment.

2. John Stephens was appointed second lieutenant in the 8th Infantry Regiment (Return of Officers, 1800, *ASP: Military Affairs*, 1:146–51).

From John C. Ogden

Sir   Wooster House—New Haven [Conn.] June 17 1799

It is with reluctance, that I trouble you, with a further detail of the outrages and unmilitary proceedings of the soldiery stationed in Litchfield. The malevo[l]ence of a party in that Town, who constantly circulate prejudices against your excellent fellow citizen Mr Jefferson and other invaluable statesmen, has given latitude to rancors and prejudices subversive of government, law, order, peace and social happiness. This party encouraged the soldiery in their insolence to me three times: On the day following my enlargement, business led me to walk to the house of Colol Stone, about four miles from Litchfield. I had not arrived an hour, before I was followed by a party of soldiers, about twenty in number, who seized me by the collar, and forced me to attend them two miles and an half amidst a well settled country, in presence of the inhabitants⟨,⟩ at eleven oclock in the forenoon.

The impertinenc[e] of the soldiers in calling me, a Democrat an Jacobin and a Frenchman, was not more odious, than their idle remarks upon the farmers, who in a very warm day, were busy in the fields. These young men made themselves merry on the occasion, and concluded, that they had rather "list"—A remark which was to be expected from those who have left their apprenticeships and parents in the hour of thoughtlesness, to embark their lives and felicity with a standing army, in a country which presents such extensive objects to allure the young to industry and enterprize, under the banners of peace.

The violence of the soldiery, was restrained by the interference, as I conclude, of General Judson of the militia, who was on a journey to Litchfield, witnessed the transaction, and received information also from the family of Colol Stone, who was not present when I was forced from his house. This outrage before the officers of the militia and inhabitants of the country, exhibits in a notable degree, what we are to expect, if further progress is made in marshaling an army and leaving detachments in the country, in the neighbourhood of our advocates for war.

You may rest assured Sir, that these events have opened the eyes of the people of Connecticut, who boldly condemn the attempts to keep them ignorant of public affairs, and the raising of an army to be supported in idleness, To place allurements to draw their sons from useful labor in order to ⟨support the⟩ party in the nation must provoke discords and end in civil wars. When civilians, who have never studied tactics, assume the military garb in old age, and abandon science for arms, the society of the learned, for the parade of a military levee in a country village, to gain a re-election, we must expect the people will consider the signs of the times to be dark and intricate, When they draw religion into the vortex of politics, the thoughtful will be alarmed.

The eyes of our fellow citizens are again placed upon you as their guardian and protector. They are weary of the broils in the national legislature, which have caused animosities in the country, & They wish to hear that the army is disbanded. To be seduced from our real happiness, from preserving the laws and constitution is contrary to our inclinations and determinations. Civil discord we abhor. Calm collected and considerate, we will be deluded no longer by fallacious pretexts of foreign invasions or domestic discontents, to butcher each other, or foster party elections.

More than twenty years residence in New England has afforded me an extensive acquaintance and every possible means for information. Determined to adhere to my duty and country, and to live under the banners of religion, benevolence and peace I shall communicate such facts to individuals, or the nation as are important. I wish to exist in this world no longer than while I enjoy my rights and may defend them against open or secret assaults, from any quarter. The exalted Senator and new re⟨cruits⟩ who would deprive me of liberty & safety, I shall ⟨in⟩ due season, present to the examination of their countrymen. Treating the inexperienced with tenderness, I shall at the same time, that I obey the powers which be, attempt to restrain the inhumanity which Mr Tracy, may wish indiscriminately to execute upon me or others.[1]

Paying great respect to the memories of those who were allied to me by various endearing ties, & fell in war, it shall be my study to avoid fixing the stigma upon them as rebels or traitors, who died as the fool dieth. This will not be the case if we permit a standing army to insult our citizens ravage the country, and trample upon the order of civil society, as is frequently done at this time.

With these motives and impressions, all good men will patiently hear, and candidly consider every address either in person or by epistle in behalf of myself or others. In presenting this, I am prompted, by a regard for the happiness and prosperity of my country family & kindred—I have seen too many of these fall by war & public convulsions to be indifferent at this time of discord— War is a scourge, while peace is a blessing and divine gift from heaven. To secure peace and prevent wars, whether foreign or domestic is the noblest pursuit of man in his social state.[2] I am Sir With great esteem & veneration Your devoted servant

John C. Ogden

ALS, DLC:GW.

1. Uriah Tracy (1755–1807) of Litchfield, after having served from 1793 to 1796 in the U.S. House of Representatives, was at this time a Federalist senator from Connecticut.

2. John C. Ogden, a retired Episcopal clergyman in New Hampshire who was thought by many to be deranged, had been writing to GW for nearly a decade without receiving a reply to any of his letters. See Ogden to GW, 20 Sept. 1798, n.1. There is a letter that Ogden wrote from his "Cell in Litchfield" on 13 May 1799 in DLC:GW which he presumably either wrote to GW or sent a copy of it to him. It reads: "The public news papers, must have detailed to you the horrid condition to which I am reduced, in this place, and the sufferings of General Woosters family. Relying upon the humanity, patriotism, and love of justice which activate General Washington, we have looked in vain for friendship ⟨for⟩ him. My miseries arise chiefly from the plunderings of the church. Ten years ago I gave notice of these nefarious proceedings. In every stage of their progress, I have not been negligent in giving information. Twelve years sufferings, amidst sacrilege is sufficient to destroy a whole order of ministers. I now live in a prison, to tell the leaders in America, that the decisions of the federal judges as to the rights of Episcopalians, have not their due effect in New Hampshire. More public ac-

counts are circulating. In this business some of our leaders in the army and revolution, have taken a wicked share. Yourself and President Adams, have not corrected it. In the most serious moments of my life, I must say, that when I first gave notice to General Washington, it was totally in his power alone, to have saved my Episcopal brethren, General Woosters family and me, from the losses and distresses we have experienced. This I write in a prison. If such a place can give any sanction to what I communicate, it comes with this corroborating circumstance of the signature of a man in real distress, from public ⟨wrongs⟩ & neglects.

"Copies of this go by the post to Bishops White & Maddison, Mr Jefferson and others. I subjoin also an extract from the last letter I ever receiv'd from the Bishop from whom I received my commission, and whom I have every obeyed, Bishop Seabury. 'You have (said that venerable succesor of the Apostles) been diligently employed in the service of the church, and have met with many and great difficulties. I heartely wish it was in my power to lighten your trouble, or to free you from any difficulties you meet with. But, I am armed with no power, and consequently my single interference would do you no good. Was it other wise, I should rejoice in adding my aid to your endeavors. Time however and your own exertions will, I hope, surmount all obstacles and bring you to a season of retribution, for all you do, and all you suffer.' It appeared to be proper to circulate this extract in my letters, As every thing relating to the distresses of the church & me, is preparing as fast & carefully as possible for the press, I wished to assure my country men, that I had taken the silent, peaceable, & manly mode of appealing to Superiors in Church & State, before I publish in letters & other writings, extensively."

To William Roberts

Mr Roberts,   Mount Vernon 17th June 1799
   I have caused some enquiries to be made, lately, respecting your present situation, & conduct; and am sorry to learn that the first is not eligable; and that the latter is far from being such as one would have hoped that experience, reflection, & I might add misfortunes, would have produced.[1]

   Had these enabled you to overcome a practice which has involved you in the most heartfelt distress, and in a manner brought you to the brink of Ruin; or, if I could entertain any well grounded hope that you would, by shifting the scene, & entering into your old walks at my Mill, refrain from drink, & the evils which it has produced, I would employ you again.

   Whether you are able to accomplish the latter, or not, none but yourself can tell—and to you only I apply. If then, you would seriously resolve, & religeously adhere to a determination to be sober, & orderly in your deportment; and would be content with such wages and allowances as I give, & beyond which I cannot go, I would receive you as a Miller after the term of the person who looks after it at present, expires which will be on the 12th of August.[2]

These terms (although in the articles of agreement which exist, are more detailed) may be seen in substance by the enclosed Paper from my Manager Mr Anderson;[3] and are as high as I have given to any Miller since you left the Mill, and as high as I can afford to give. Mr Davenport, who succeeded you, lived at the Mill until his death (about three years ago); and the one who succeeded him (and is now the Miller) Callahan, has (as I am informed) no inclination to leave it; But, though tolerably knowing as a Miller he is an indolent man, and thereby unfit for exertion, although perfectly sober, & no charge against his honesty.[4]

You will perceive from what is here written that your coming to me, as a Miller, depends absolutely upon two things; first—a solemn and fixed determination to refrain from liquor, & to be diligent in your duty & attentions to the Mill, & Cowpers; and 2dly, that you will do it upon the terms mentioned in the enclosed paper, drawn into proper form. Whether you could be here, so as to take charge of the Mill by the 12th of August is not material; a month after might answer; but it is essential that you do, without delay, say yea, or nay, to the proposal, as I must decide with Callahan by the time an answer (in the common course of the Post) can be received from you.

The Work at my Mill is by no means hard; and a Man & a boy when there is water sufficient—assists: It follows of course that a Miller cannot be more at his ease any where; and you know from experience, that no man discharges the demand of wages, or fulfils agreements with more punctuality than I do—Such a place then, to a man in the decline of life, might be more desirable than one with higher wages accompanied with infinite more trouble & uncertainty: In a word, if you could keep yourself within bounds, it might be considered as a settlement, as it were, for life. I wish you well and am Your friend

Go: Washington.

ALS (letterpress copy), DLC:GW.

1. See William Booker to GW, 15 May and 6 June.

2. Roberts accepted the offer on 21 June. For his arrival at Mount Vernon, see GW to James Anderson, 8 September.

3. The enclosed "Paper" from GW's farm manager, James Anderson, has not been identified.

4. For reference to the death of Joseph Davenport in January 1796 and the appointment of Patrick Callahan as miller at Mount Vernon, see GW to Clement Biddle, 8 April 1798, n.3.

From Edward Savage

Sir   Philadelphia June 17 1799

The print I promist to Send Mrs Washington was ready Last March I have Been So unlucky as to Miss Every oppertunity Since; till the present one; it is Shipt on board the Schooner Tryal Capt. Hand Master, Not being acquainted with any one in Alexandra I Directed the Cas to the Care of the Customhouse.[1]

This Last winter I Discovered the Method of Engraving with Acquafortis, in order to proove my Experement I Executed two prints which is my first Specimen in that Stile of Engraving, one is the Chace the other the action of the Constellation with the L'Insurgent, I have put two of those prints into the Case for you to See that Method of working on Copper. I intend as Soone as time will permit, to Execute a Set of Large prints of the Most Striking and Beautifull Views in America, in that Stile of Engraving, as it is Best Calculated for Landskips: and a very Expeditious Method of working.[2]

I hope Yourself and Mrs Washington will Excuse the Delay of the print it woud have been Sent Last Summer if the Sickness Had not Dreven me out of the City before I had time to print any in Colours. I am Sir your Much Oblidg'd Humble Sert

Edward Savage

Please to present my Most Respectfull Compliments to Mrs Washington & Family.

ALS, DLC:GW.

1. When Savage wrote GW on 3 June 1798 that he had sent to Clement Biddle, for GW, four copies of his print of his painting of the Washington family, he added: "As Soone as I have one printed in Colours I Shall take the Liberty to Send it to Mrs Washington."

2. GW wrote on 30 June: "Sir, Your letter of the 17th instant and the Print (which is exceedingly handsome, and well set) have come safe; and receives, as it highly deserves, the thanks of Mrs Washington; to whom you have had the kindness, and politeness to present it.

"I thank you also for the prints of the Chase, & action between the Constellation and the L'Insurgent; exhibiting a specimen of the art of Engraving by means of Aquafortis. The invention is curious, and if the sample of it which you have sent is the first essay, it will, no doubt, prove a valuable discovery, as, like all other discoveries⟨,⟩ it will undergo improvements.

"Mrs Washington is thankful for your kind remembrance of her, and joins in every good wish for you & yours, with Sir—Your Most Obedt & very Hble Servant Go: Washington.

"P.S. Whenever you have fixed upon your Landscapes, for Engraving by means of Aquafortis, and have executed them, be so good as to inform me thereof" (letterpress copy, DLC:GW).

From James McHenry

Dear Sir   Philad[elphia] 18 June 1799
I have recd your packet of the 6th and letter of the 7th of June inst. This is intended chiefly to acknowledge the circumstance.

Mr Frances being Purveyor I have employed him to procure the articles mentioned in your letter.[1] I have also seen Mr McAlpin, who informed me, that, tho' some Spring Ships had arrived, he has not been able to obtain the gold thread; and that he had apprehensions he should fail; but would use every endeavour to get it. I shall send the stars at least.

I beleive the trade with S. Domingo will be opened: but as carrying it on with safety, and keeping the Islanders in a situation, least likely to renew depredations, is so closely connected with a participation in it by Great Britain, it is not considered expedient to open it, till an arrangement to that effect can take place between Touissaint and Gen. Maitland.

I shall not overlook Mr Lewis. Yours affectionately
James McHenry

ALS, DLC:GW; ADf, MdAA.
1. See GW to McHenry, 7 June, n.1.

From Archibald Blair

Sir   Richmond June 19th 1799
The original letter from my departed Friend, Patrick Henry esqr., of which the enclosed is the only copy ever suffered to be taken, was intended merely to counteract some malicious reports circulating in this District, that Mr Henry was unfriendly to the

election of Mr Marshall as a Representative to the next Congress—But as it contain⟨s⟩ Sentiments which contradict the base Insinuations that he was an enemy to the opposition measures of our Government towards the French, and unfriendly to you, I feel anxious for his letter to be lodged in some place that hereafter it may stand a chance to be brought forth as a proof against such calumny; and with this view I transmit you a copy, in hopes that it will find a place in a corner of your Cabinet.[1] I would have sent the original had it not been much torn by the frequent resort to it during the canvassing for the late election. I have been often urged to publish it in the News papers, but that Source of communication being at present so polluted, where virtue is traduced & Vice supported, I have thought that posterity will be unable hereafter, from it, to decide whether their Ancestors were virtuous or vicious. It is much to be lamented that a Man of Mr Henry's merits should be so little personally known in the world—I remember at the commencement of the revolution he was dreaded as the Cromwell of America, and since, he has been counted upon by the opposition Party as a rival to you, and the Destroyer of our happy & most valuable Constitution. I had the honor of qualifying to my present office when Mr Henry commenced the Administration of our revolutionary Government, from which period to the day of his death, I have been upon the most intimate, and I believe, freindly terms with him; And I can with truth say that I never saw any thing tyrannical in his Disposition, nor otherwise ambitious than to be serviceable to Mankind. With regard to you sir, I may say as he said of Marshall—that he *loved you*—and for the same reason—*because you felt & acted as a republican—as an American*; for I have no doubt but he alludes to you when he makes the exception of "One other who was in another line" to whom he would give the preference. During the war an attempt was made by an anonymous letter to enlist Mr Henry on the side of an infamous Faction opposed to you as Commander in Chief—his letter to you on that subject and your answer, have been lost I believe during Arnolds invasion, which I lament, as his letter was a proof of his confidence in, & attachment to you, and I had a desire to preserve those documents.[2]

I have now to apologize for obtruding where I have not the honor of a personal acquaintance, and I flatter myself the Motive of rescuing the Character of my valuable friend from the imputation of being a Jacobin, & foe to you, will plead the Excuse of him who has the honor to be, with the highest respect, Yr Most obedt & very humble Servant

A. Blair

ALS, DLC:GW.

Archibald Blair (1753–1824), son of Councillor John Blair (1687–1771) and brother of associate justice of the U.S. Supreme Court John Blair (1732–1800), had been clerk of the Virginia council of state since its inception in July 1776.

1. The particular copy of Patrick Henry's letter to Blair of 8 Jan. 1799 that Blair sent to GW has not been found. The letter has been printed in Henry, *Patrick Henry*, 2:591–94. Writing from Red Hill in Charlotte County, Henry expressed his doubts about the motives of the "opposition party" and denounced "French manners and principles." He wrote: "Tell Marshall I love him because he felt and acted [in France] as a republican, as an American. The story of the Scotch merchants and old torys voting for him is too stale, childish, and foolish, and is a French *finesse*; an appeal to prejudice, not reason and good sense. . . . As to the particular words stated by you [in a letter of 28 Dec. 1798, which has not been found], and said to come from me, I do not recollect saying them. But certain I am, I never said anything derogatory to General Marshall; but on the contrary, I really should give him my vote for Congress, preferably to any citizen in the state at this juncture, one only excepted, and that one is in another line."

2. See GW to Blair, 24 June, and note 3 of that document.

To Alexander Hamilton

Dear Sir,   Mount Vernon, June 19th 1799

Your favour of the 7th instant, with its enclosures, has been duly received.

I am very glad to learn that the recruiting business, so far as it has been put in Operation, succeeds agreeably to your wishes. It has commenced in Virginia, and I am informed that, in this vicinity (and I have no intelligence from the more distant parts of the State) its progress is very flattering. A supply of Cloathing would, however, promote this service even hereabouts; and unless it be furnished soon I am apprehensive it will languish, if not stop entirely.

I understand, by a letter which I received a few days since from General Pinckney, that the selection of Officers from No. & So. Carolina and Georgia, has been transmitted to the War Office. I hope, on every account, there will be no delay in completing this arrangement.[1]

The disposition you have made of the Artillery Regiments is, I have no doubt, just and proper, and calculated to promote the good of the Service.

I thank you for the information from Mr King. I have long beleived that France owes the facility of her Conquests more to the Jealousy and want of cordial co-operation among the Powers of Europe, whose interest it is to check her desolating Ravages, than to any exertions of her own, great as they may have been. It appears from every account (altho' there is none so full & distinct as I could wish) that her Armies have not only been checked; but obliged to retreat. And her internal Affairs do not seem to be in the best situation. Should these advantages be properly improved, I think the happiest effects may result from them. With very sincere regard I am, Dear Sir, Your Affecte & Obedt Servt

Go: Washington

LS, in Tobias Lear's hand, DLC: Hamilton Papers; Df, in Lear's hand, DLC:GW.
   1. See Charles Cotesworth Pinckney to GW, 4 June.

From Francis Deakins

Sir   George Town 21st June 1799

Your favor of the 16th Inst. came Duly to Hand—& Having Sold your Tobo at 4⅓ ℀Ct now enclose you the Money $101.59 Together with the 26 Dolls. Recd for you Some time ago[1]—I have Advised Mr Veatch of your Obliging offer to permit his with holding what I Judged reasonable for his Exstra Trouble. & fixed it at 25 Dolls. Part of Reads Bond in his Hands—I have also informed him as he has been permit'd to put on Tenants to Suit himself. A future Additional Salary is not to be expected. With Great Respect Yr Mt Obedt St

Francis Deakins

ALS, DLC:GW.
   1. GW's letter to Deakins of 16 June is printed in Deakins to GW, 12 June, n.2.

From William Roberts

Dear Sir   Petersburg 21st of June 1799

Your Letter of the 17th of June is now Before Me & I Must Confess Am Much Surprised To think your Excellency woud think Me worth Notis after All the Misfortuens I have went through. To Right Me Such A Letter of Comfurt As to Once More think of Imploying Me Again in your Generous & worthe Imploy—Now Sir if you Can Place Any Confedence in Me As usel, I hope it will be in My power to Give you General Satis Faction in the Time I hope to be in your Good Imploy And Serves—As for Speretus Licquers I Am Resolvd To Renounse to the Day of My Death—And when Wather is Vary Cold A Drink of Sider & Ginger in it will be Better for Me & My helth then Any Sperets I Could Make Use of & Small Beer As Common Drink for the water about the Mill is Not Vary Good—As you Menchen Refraning from Drink in your Letter, ile Giv you My Sollom Promes before Almighte God that I Shall Detest & Despise all Sperets of Any Kind As you Obserd it has been My Ruen And the Cause of All My Aflection And Discontent— Now Sir As you Observ whether, or No I can Accomplesh the promes I have Maid Or Not is Best Known to My inward feelings—I have Determend to Liv Sober & orderly Amongst My Nabours & To be Obedent to your Commands at All Times—And Can be Content with the wages & Preveleges you have offred Me As your word was Always Sufesiant to Any Contract Ever purposed—Now Sir if I Can Git up To your Mill the Last of August, Or the Last of September you think it will Answer, but I Shall Indever to be thare the Last of August & On the Terms you have Purposed—Only this I must inform you—I have No famaly at preasant—But Must Tri And Keep house As well as I Can if Not So Well ⟨as⟩ I Could wish. From Sir your Most Obedent Hbe Servt

W:M. Roberts

ALS, DLC:GW.

To Elias Boudinot

Dear Sir, Mount Vernon, June 22d 1799

When I had the pleasure of seeing you in Philadelphia last winter, I mentioned my intention of writing to Mr Pintard for a fresh supply of wine, as my stock was getting low, and you were so good as to offer to furnish me with a pipe from some which you expected from Mr Pintard for your own use. At that time I had no doubt but I should be able to get a s[u]pply from Madeira befor this; but, having written to Mr Pintard on the 13th of January, and hearing nothing from him since, I am apprehensive that my letters

may have miscarried, and that my stock will be nearly exhausted
before he can be informed of my wants, which I have again intimated to him in a letter of this date the original & duplicate of
which I beg the favor of you to forward by the 1st convey[an]ce[1]—
If, therefore, the wine which you expected, has come to hand, and
you can, without any inconvenience to yourself, let me have a pipe
of it, I will desire Colo. Biddle (who transacts business for me in
Philada) to have it ship'd to this place, and pay you the amount,
to which I should add my best thanks.[2] Mrs Washington unites in
respects & best wishes for the health & happiness of Mrs Boudinot,
Mrs Bradford[3] & yourself with Dear Sir Yr most Obdt Servt

Df, in Tobias Lear's hand, ViMtV.

1. Neither of GW's letters to John Marsden Pintard, that of 13 Jan. 1799 or
that of this date, 22 June, has been found. John Marsden Pintard (d. 1811) was
the son of the New York merchant Lewis Pintard and a family connection of Elias
Boudinot. At this time he was U.S. consul at Madeira and had his own company
on the island. He had been supplying GW with wine since the 1780s.

2. Boudinot replied on 28 June: "Your Letter of the 22d Instt with its Enclosures for Mr Pintard came safe to hand, and which I shall be careful to forward
by the first Opportunity. I have been, and still am in daily expectation of the
arrival of my Wine from Madeira: as it was to be shipped in January, I am at a loss
to account for its nonarrival, unless our good friends the Sans culottes have
thought it necessary for their present necessities. If it should arrive & turn out as
good as I have reason to expect it will be, I will loose no time in sending a pipe as
you have directed" (DLC:GW). On 18 Oct., having had no reply to his letters of
13 Jan. and 22 June, GW had his secretary, Tobias Lear, write again to Pintard,
who it had been learned was back in the United States from Madeira. Lear explained that GW wished to determine whether or not Pintard had received either
of his letters and "if any measures have been taken to forward the wine, so that
he may expect it in a short time." "If this is not the case," Lear wrote, "and you
have any wine for sale in this Country, of the quality which you have been used
to supply the General, he will thank you to forward one or two pipes to him
without delay . . . for his stock is now so nearly exhausted that he must get a supply
from some quarter or another in a *very short time* . . . " (ViMtV). Lear sent this
letter, unsealed, to Boudinot under cover of a letter to Boudinot of the same date.
Boudinot wrote Lear on 28 Oct. that Pintard had left Madeira before either of
GW's letters could have got there but that Pintard had assured him that "his
House [in Madeira] will forward the Wines as well as if he had been present"
(DLC:GW). Pintard confirmed this in a letter to Lear from New York on 8 Nov.
and then went on to say: "In the Interim I can accomodate the General with one
or two pipes of very Superiour wine which I Sent to this Country Six years ago to
lay by for my own drinking when I Retired from Buisness which I was in hopes to
have done long ere this But the depredations of French and British Cruisers have
deprived me of most of the fruits of nine years labour and I am obliged to Return

to Madeira again perhaps for nine years Longer by which time my wine here would be older than perhaps I can afford to drink I have therefore determined to Sell it and the price will be three dollars per Gallon they are in the hands of Mr John Halsey No. 77 Broad Street of this city and If you will drop him a line he will Ship you one or Both of them . . ." (DLC:GW).

A week later, on 13 Nov., in letters to Clement Biddle and to Boudinot, GW indicated that he had received from Madeira notification of the shipment of the wine that he had ordered. The letter from Madeira was dated 20 Sept. and was written by Charles Alder. It reads: "I am emboldened to take the present liberty of addressing your Excellency by the desire of Tobias Lear Esqr. as Attorney for Mr J: M: Pintard, and in Consequence of the Honor which your Excellency has conferred on said Gentn by ordering from him a Couple of Pipes of our Wines. I have embraced the present Opportunity of Shipping them, as ℔ bill of lading transmitted to Mr Lear; and nothing could prove more gratifying to me than to learn that the Quality thereof meets the Approbation of your Excellency" (DLC: GW). In a letter of the same date to Tobias Lear informing him of the shipment of the wine to GW, Alder includes this postscript: "At the present Juncture, and on account of the scarcity of Sugar there is no good Citron for Sale your influence with his Excy may probably induce him to accept of a couple of small Boxes which Mrs Alder happened to have in the house and takes the liberty of sending" (DLC:GW). Alder's enclosed invoice dated 20 Sept. 1799 shows that Charles Alder & Co. shipped to GW "Two pipes of fine Old London particular Madeira Wine . . . on board the Lavinia James Cook Master for Philadelphia," at a charge of £84.

Even after receiving this assurance that the wine from Madeira was on its way, GW had Lear write Pintard on 20 Nov.: "The General is much obliged to you for the offer you make of letting him have some wine which you had sent to this Country six years since, for your own use, and, notwithstanding the arrival of the two pipes from Madeira, he will take one pipe of the wine you mention, provided you can insure it to be of the first quality, and that it has not undergone any change for the worse since its importation, and if the payment at ninety days (as for the other) will answer" (ViMtV). After the wine arrived from Madeira, Lear drafted for GW a letter to Charles Alder, dated 12 Dec.: "Sir, I have duly received your letter of the 20th of Septr informing me that you had ship'd two pipes of Madeira Wine for me, in consequence of an order sent to Mr J. M. Pintard for that purpose; but which did no[t] arrive till after he had left Madeira.

"Mr Lear will have informed you that the wine has arrived in good order, and that your bill for eighty four pounds sterling has been accepted and will be duly paid.

"Requesting you to accept my thanks for your polite attention to this business, I am Sir, Your most Obedt Sert" (ViMtV). The next day, the day before GW's death, Lear drafted a letter to Pintard's agent in New York, John Halsey, enclosing a copy of his letter to Pintard of 20 Nov. and asking Halsey to attend to the matter. It is not known whether GW's letter was sent to Alder or whether or not Lear sent his to Halsey, but they may have been among the letters GW franked on the day before his death (see Tobias Lear's Narrative Accounts of the Death of George Washington, printed below).

3. Mrs. Bradford was Boudinot's widowed sister, Susan Vergereau Boudinot Bradford.

To James McHenry

Sir,   Mount Vernon June 22d 1799

I have been desired by Mr Saml Love, of Loudoun County, in this State, to mention to you his wish to contract for furnishing Horses for the Army. I have informed him that I am unacquainted with the mode in which it is contemplated to obtain Horses, leaving the business of contracts & supplies to the departments to which they are assigned; but that I would mention his name to you in the way he desired. Of Mr Love's qualifications to execute a Contract of this kind I am ignorant, as I have but little personal knowledge of him. But if he comes forward in the business, it will lay with him to produce such evidence of his fitness as shall be satisfactory.[1]

While I am upon this subject, I would beg leave to suggest, whether it would not be the most eligible mode of obtaining the best Horses for *Cavalry* service, to permit the Captains to purchase them for their respective Troops, limiting them to a certain price? Two advantages would, in my opinion, evidently result from this mode. The Captains would be particularly attentive to procure the best horses that could be had for the price, knowing that their own Credit, the appearance of their Troops and the services expected of them would in a great measure depend upon their care in the choice of Horses; And their dispersed situations would give a better opportunity of obtaining them from different quarters than could be done by any Individual fixed in one place; to say nothing of the advanced prices put upon horses, from their first purchase, by contractors, and the impositions to which the public may be exposed.

I merely suggest this for your consideration, not doubting but, upon mature deliberation, such plan will be pursued as shall appear best calculated to promote the public good. With due respect I have the honor to be &c.

G. W——n

P.S. Since writing the foregoing your favor of the 18th inst. has come to hand, which I take this opportunity to acknowledge.

Df, in Tobias Lear's hand, DLC:GW.

1. Samuel Love wrote to GW from Salisbury, Md., on 17 June: "Expecting a Number of Horses will shortly be wanting for the use of the Army of the U. States; I am desirous of Contracting to supply what may be wanting for this, & the State of Maryland, or for Virginia alone; I have lately wrote the Secretary of War my desire of entering into such a Contract with Government, to him I am a Strainger in every respect; If you think me Competent to such an undertakeing, I beg leave to request the favr of you in the Course of your Correspondence with that Gentn to mention me to him, as person qualified to serve Government in the above business" (DLC:GW).

GW responded to Love on 22 June: "Sir, I have received your letter of the 17th inst. requesting that I would mention your name to the Secretary of War as a person wishing to contract for furnishing Horses for the Army of the United States.

"I do not know in what measure it is proposed to obtain Horses for the Army, as I have never entered into the detail of contracts or supplies of any kind, leaving these matters to the departments to which they are assigned. I shall, however, mention your name to the Secretary of War, in the way you have desired. I am, Sir, Your most Obedt Servt" (Df, in Tobias Lear's hand, DLC:GW). On 28 June McHenry wrote GW that his suggestions about horses for the cavalry "strike me favourable."

Letter not found: to John Marsden Pintard, 22 June 1799. On 22 June GW forwarded to Elias Boudinot the original and duplicate of "a letter of this date" addressed to Pintard.

From Jonathan Trumbull, Jr.

My Dear Sir   Lebanon [Conn.] 22d June 1799

I take much pleasure in complying with a request of my Brother Colo. John Trumbull, to communicate to you a Copy of a political Letter, which he has lately written to me from London.[1] His project you will find is a great One. But—were the moral powers of our Country, equal to her physical force, so far from starting at the magnitude of the Object, some of her Sons I presume, would not hesitate at an attempt to bring into effect the projected Union of two Countries, which nature has so nearly conjoined; and whose destinies & Interests, we may fairly conjecture, must at some future period—& that not far distant perhaps—be very intimately connected together. Would to Heaven! that the Counsels of our Country were now influenced by that Union of Sentiment & will, which you & I so ardently wish! but Providence is Wise & Good—& will accomplish its designs in the best manner—& in its own way.

You may perhaps recollect, my Dear Sir! that in some conversation of mine with you on the Event of your resignation of the Presidency, or in some Letter written to you on that subject, I expressed to you *my wish*, that no untoward Events might take place, which should once more draw you from your beloved solitude & retirement, and *force* you again to assume the Cares of Goverment[2]—The period then alluded to, and the necessity which I then contemplated might exist, I now begin to realize as fast approaching. Another Election of a President is near at hand, and I have confidence in believing, that, should your Name again be brort up, with a View to that Object, you will not disappoint the hopes & Desires of the Wise & Good in every State, by refusing to come forward once more to the relief & support of your injured Country. Need I apologize to you Sir! for this hint? Or shall I frankly tell you, that this Idea is not vaguely started by me, but is strongly prompted by the necessity of our situation, and may probably be pursued in earnest; for unless some eminently prominent Character shall be brort up to view on the Occasion, the next Election of President, I fear, will have a very illfated Issue. With my best regards to Mrs W. & the family I am Dear Sir Your constant & assured Friend & Obet hume Servant

Jona. Trumbull

ALS, DLC:GW.

1. The enclosed copy of John Trumbull's very long letter to his brother Jonathan, dated London 5 April 1799, is in DLC:GW. For references to the contents of this letter of John Trumbull to his brother, see GW to Jonathan Trumbull, Jr., 21 July 1799, and note 1 of that document. Toward the end of his letter, John Trumbull informed his brother: "I have written to Genl Washington a letter [dated 24 Mar. 1799] somewhat similar to this; and I will be obliged to you to communicate this to ⟨him, to⟩ Mr [Oliver] Ellsworth, [Jeremiah] Wadsworth, Genl J[edediah] Huntington & other friends, particularly to [Oliver] Wollcott." GW commented on John Trumbull's letter of 24 Mar. in the reply he made to that letter on 25 June.

2. On 23 Jan. 1797, shortly before GW left the presidency, Jonathan Trumbull wrote: "I most devoutly pray Heaven to grant, that no evil Demon of Discord may be suffered to arise and agitate the Peace & Happiness of our Country, so as again to dragg you from your pleasing Quiet & repose!! But of this event I am far— too far alas, from being confident." In response to this letter from Jonathan Trumbull of 22 June 1799, GW wrote on 21 July: "I remember well, the conversation which you allude to, and have not forgot the answer I gave you."

From James Anderson

Most Excellent Sir   Mount Vernon 23d June 1799

On [   ] day of June 1797 I took the liberty to Write You relative to the management of the Farms on this Estate, And on the 18th of same month I had the honor of Your Answer. In this letter it was proposed to lessen the number of hands And Abridge the quantity of Land yearly to be under the Plough.[1]

Circumstances unnecessary to mention, prevented the Execution of this Plan. And since a Scheme of Rotation has been Adopted and puting in Execution, And upon good Lands would be usefull & turn out to be profitable—But as this Estate is poor and the Soil not so much adapted to the raising of Hoed Crops, And that there are Still an equal qty of Land as formerly under the Plough It does Occur to me that there are exceptions to this Rotation Scheme And that something near to the former System may be adopted by the which Your Lands would much sooner Improve, the expence be lessened and a much greater Revenue Acrue to Your Excellency.

The following are the Outlines of what I shall humbly submit to Your consideration, And Are the result of mature deliberation—And Permit me to offer You a Statement of Union Farm, which may apply to River Farm pretty nearly. And to Doguerun with the alteration of fewer Horses & people left on this Farm.

The Scheme of Planting all muddy hole with Peach trees is without any doubt the best. And a few more hands may be usefull on this Farm on that Account, But I would incline ⟨crossing⟩ it[2] ligh[t]ly to improve the Soil.

As there are on Union Farm 7 fields besides 4 Lotts & 5 Lotts of Meadow I would propose to manage the whole thus.

No. 1 a Compleat Summer fallow, and all the Manure that can be obtained laid thereon

 2—" Wheat
 3—" Pasture
 4—" Do
 5—" Do
 6—" Do
and 7—" Do

Lotts No. 1 Corn   Meadows No. 1 Oats, fallowed after
                       & Sown in the fall

2	Oats	2	Timothy
3	Clover	3	Timothy
4	Do	4	Do
		5	Do

To Accomplish this worth 8 mules, & 3 Ox Carts will be necessary Together with 4 men & 4 women, who I suppose may have 12 Children.

The 4 ploughs are managed by one man & 3 women And three men manages the Carts, the Additional woman to do any hoeing work.

These Carts to be employed every day when not hauling of Rails to haul manure & good Soil over the Fallow field, preparing for the wheat Crop, by minute Calculation I find the Ploughs will be sufficient for all the work alloted to them. And have 30 days in the time of harvest to spare for that purpose.

I shall first State the produce that may be expected by the proposed, And that which from experience (the one puting in Practise) will afford.

the System proposed

120 Acres in wheat after being fallowed & manured after deducting seed to produce 9 Bush.

℔ acre at 6/ ℔ Bu.   £324.

Lotts No. 1   in Corn highly manured, 10 Acres at 6
                    Blls ℔ acre 15/   45.

            2d   in Oats producing besids Seed 20 Bu. ℔
                    acre 3/   30.

            3   in Clover made into Hay one Ton ℔
                    acre £5 p. Ton   50.

            4   in Clover partly fed to the Stock &
                    partly made into seed

Meadows No. 1   in Oats. fallowed after the Crop is
        taken from off the Ground. & then sown in
        Timothy 16 Acres producing after deducting the
        Seed 12 Bush. ℔ acre & at 3/   28.16.

        2, 3, 4 & 5   in Hay at half a Ton ℔ Acre £5   say
        in all 60 Acres   150.

Wool from the Sheep encreased (by such large
        pasture as 150 Sheep might have over 600 Acres
        Land) to 400 lb. at 2/   40.
                                        Carried over   £667.16.

The expence on this Scheme might be

One Overseer hire & finding who behoved to work	£ 77. 7.
8 horses or Mules fed by 8 Blls Corn each 15/	48.
20 Negroes Old & Young at one peck meal each ℔ week	37.10.
10 of do to be Cloathed 40/ each week & Young Children	20. 4.
Taxes over these Blks & Horses supposed at being the ⅓, as now it comes to	5.16.6
Smiths Bill	15.
Carpenters do	11.10.
8 Backbands & 4 lines	1.10.
10 Barrels of Herrings Yearly	10.
Whiskie & meat in Harvest	16.10.
Spades Sythes, & Cradles	6.14.
Carried over	£250. 1.6
Brought over the produce of Union Farm	£667.16.
Brought over the expence on Union Farm	£250. 1.6
Doctors Bill reduced to	3.
16 Bags every 2d Year 4/ each the half ℔ year	1.10.
Negroe hires 4 men £15 & 4 Women £8 each	92.
Incidental feeding of Oxen, &ca on Corn 40 Blls at 15/	30.
	£376.11.6
leaving a Profit of	£291. 4.6

Followeth the experimental Calculation on the Scheme at present puting in Practice

No. 1 in Corn 120 Acres at 3 Blls ℔ acre 360 at 15/	£270.
2 in wheat 120 Acres at 5 Bu. ℔ Acre after seed 6/	180.
3 in pease 60 acres at 3 Bu. ℔ do 4/6	40.10.
60 do of the worst in fallow	
4 in Oats 60 Acres following the pease & after seed 6 Bu. at 3/	54.
60 in wheat after seed 6 Bu. 6/	112.
5, 6 & 7 in Pasture	
Lotts No. 1 Potatoes 10 Acres 80 Bu. deduce Seed 10 Bu. the remaining 70 @ 1/6 ℔ Bu.	52.10.

2	in Oats, & after seed 20 Bush. at 3/	30.
3	in Clover made into Hay 1 Ton at £5	50.
4	in Do for Green feeding & Seed	

Meadows No. 1   in Oats on 16 Acres afterwards
    Sown with Timothy as in the former plan
    producing besides Seed 12 Bu. 3/   28.16.
    Nos. 2 3 4 & 5   in Timothy made into Hay at half
    a Ton ℔ acre and at 100/   150.

Carried over   967.16.

Contra A/c of expence
To Overseers hire & causuvality[3] as at present pd   £ 77. 7.
Negroe hires 9 men £15 & 12 women £8 each   231.
Dos Meal ℔ Year & familys 16½ Bushels ℔ week 3/   128.14.
Horses 16 fed with 8 Blls Corn each 15/   96.
Incidental feeding of Oxen &ca 40 Blls do   30.
Fish for the present Negroes 35 Blls ℔ year 20/   35.
Whiskie & Meat in harvest as formerly   16.10.

Carried over   £614.11.

Brought over Account of Crops   £967.16.
Brought over expence account in part   £614.11.
16 Backbands 3/ & 8 Lines for the Horses at 1/6   3.
Smiths Bill ℔ Year Amounts to   30.
Carpenters do ℔ do   23.
Taxes in commen Years are   17.10.
Cloathing for 40 Negroes 40/ each & for 6 Infants
    2/ each   80.12.
2 Spades & 8 Cradles & Sythes ℔ Year   6.14.
16 Bags ℔ Year at 4/ & half were only   1.10.
Doctors Bill   12.
                                                              ——————
                                                             788.17.
leaving a profit by this Scheme of   178.19.
                                                              ——————
                                                             £967.16.
By these Statements appears for the first Scheme   £291. 4.6
And for the latter only   £178.16.
Ballance in favor of the former   112. 8.6
                                                              ——————
                                                             £391. 4.6

And that no Partiality may appear in favor of one, or other of
these Schemes no Statement is made as to Stock, But from the
quanity of Lands in Pasture, and the encreasing improving of the

Soil, the Stock A/c must be in favor of this newly proposed Plan, And that the Land must soon improve needs little Logical reasoning as I propose to keep only 150 Sheep on 5 pasture fields—600 Acres—And in both Schemes all the Cattle to pasture in the Woods, working Horses & Oxen excepted, who I purpose feeding in the Shades all Summer on green food, And never Pasture the Meadows by which they will very much improve. It may be questioned what is to be done with the Surplus hands? To which I answer they can be hired to Advantage or perhaps more profitably employed in Settling some of Your Back Lands, which after a few Years might make a proper return. And make these Lands Sell or Lease to more Advantage, And if these Hints merit any part of Your Ex. Attention—I should think of puting the Scheme so far into Execution this fall by leaving on each farm the Number only proposed to remain (and so soon as the Crops are Secured[)] Set the others to work to make all Your Fences, Ditches, Roads & other Improvements. And with much respect & Esteem I am Most Excellent Sir Your most Obedt Humble Set

Jas Anderson

ALS, ViMtV.

1. On 18 June 1797 GW wrote Anderson: "As far as time and circumstances have enabled me to attend to the subject, I have given your Memorial a careful perusal; and what follows is the result of my reflections thereupon." Anderson's "Memorial" has not been found. Nor has any response by GW to this letter of 23 June 1799 from Anderson been found, but see GW to Anderson, 10 Sept. 1799, in which GW suggests a plan of action whereby Anderson would be relieved of the management of the farms at Mount Vernon. See also note 2 to the letter of 10 September.

2. I.e., cross-plowing.

3. A casualty, or casuality, was a casual or incidental charge or payment.

To Archibald Blair

Sir,   Mount Vernon 24th June 1799

Your favor of the 19th instt enclosing the copy of a letter from our deceased friend Patrick Henry Esqr., to you, dated the 8th of Jany last, came duly to hand: for this instance of your polite attention to me, I pray you to accept my thanks, and an assurance that the latter shall find a distinguished place in my Beaureau of Public Papers.[1]

At any time I should have recd the account of this Gentleman's death with sorrow. In the present crisis of our public affairs, I have heard it with deep regret. But the ways of Providence are inscrutable, not to be scanned by short sighted man, whose duty is submission, without repining at its decrees.

I had often heard of the Political Sentimts expressed in Mr Henry's letter to you—and as often a wish that they were promulgated through the medium of the Gazettes. The propriety, or inexpediency of which measure, none can decide more correctly than yourself. But after what you have written to me, I feel an incumbancy to inform you, that another copy of that letter has been either surreptitiously obtained, or fabricated; & more than probable is now in the Press; for I was informed on the day preceeding my receipt of your letter, that one was in the hands of a Gentleman in this County (Fairfax) and that he had been asked to, and it was supposed would, have it Printed.[2]

My breast never harboured a suspicion that Mr Henry was unfriendly to me, although I had reason to believe that the same Spirit which was at work to destroy all confidence in the Public functionaries, was not less busy in poisoning private fountains, and sowing the seeds of distrust amg men of the same Political sentiments. Mr Henry had given me the most unequivocal proof whilst I had the honor to command the Troops of the United States in their Revolutionary struggle, that he was not to be worked upon by Intriguers; and not conscious that I had furnished any cause for it, I could not suppose that without a cause, he had become my enemy since. This proof, contained in the letter to wch you allude, is deposited among my files. (but for want of a proper receptable for them, which I mean to erect), they are yet in packages. When I shall be able to open them with convenience, I will furnish you with a copy of what passed between Mr Henry & myself, in consequence of the attempt which was made by a Party in Congress, to supplant me in that command, since you think they are not to be found among his Papers, & wish to be possessed of them.[3]

Your letter to me, Sir, required no apology, but has a just claim to the thanks, and gratitude of one who has the honor to be, Your Most Obedt (and for its contents) obliged Hble Servt

Go: Washington

ALS (letterpress copy), DLC:GW; copy in Blair's hand, MHi: Pickering Papers.

1. GW's copy of Patrick Henry's letter to Archibald Blair of 8 Jan. 1799 has not been found, but for its contents, see Blair to GW, 19 June, n.1.

2. No evidence has been found that Henry's letter was printed in a newspaper.

3. Henry's letter to GW of 20 Feb. 1778 enclosing Benjamin Rush's anonymous letter of 12 Jan. 1778 calling for GW's removal begins: "You will no Doubt be surprised at seeing the inclosed Letter, in which the Encomiums bestowed on me are as undeserved, as the Censures aimed at you are unjust. I am sorry there should be one man who counts himself my Friend, who is not yours." Henry made it clear that the identity of the writer was unknown to him. After learning more about the movement to replace GW, Henry wrote GW again on 5 Mar. 1778, expressing his fervent support of the commander in chief. GW in turn wrote warm letters of appreciation to Henry on 27 and 28 Mar. 1778.

From William Booker

Sir　　　　　　　　　　　　　　Richmond 24 June 1799

When I wrote you last, I Expected to have been at Mount Vernon before this time.[1]

But it has been Impossible to Send the Mill Stones around before last Saturday, when for the first time, for a good while past, any vessel has gone from this place up the potomac that I knew of, I have shiped the Stones and Irons, on board of a Small Sloop, for Colchester, Joseph Jones Capt., who has promised to deliver them at Mount Vernon, if he Goes from Colchester to Alexandria, or to Mr William Mason, at Colchester, if he gets a freight there and returns back.[2]

I Expect it will be 10 or 12 days before he Gets to Colchester, and by that time I will Certainly be at Mount Vernon, and 4 or 5 days after that, the Mill may Easely be set agoing. I am with Greatis Respect—Your Most Obt an Humbl. Se.

Wm Booker

ALS, DLC:GW.

1. See Booker to GW, 6 June, and note 2 of that document.

2. Booker enclosed Joseph Jones's receipt, dated 22 June, for "a pair of Small Mill Stones & Spindle to be delive[re]d at Mount Vernon to Genl Washington or at Colchester to Mr William Mason also three dollars freight." William Mason (1757–1818), George Mason's son, lived across the Potomac in Charles County, Maryland. The Masons owned the ferry at Colchester in Virginia.

From James McHenry

Dear Sir.   War Dept. [Philadelphia] 24 June 1799.
    I send you by this mail, a small box containing military figures for the practice of tactics, being one of a few sets I ordered from London. Perhaps they may occasionally serve as a substitute for the chess board.[1]
    Mr McAlpin called this morning to inform me that he had procured a sufficient quantity of gold thread and a person to work it; but that he was by no means certain he could have the coat ready by next monday early enough for that days mail. I have urged it upon him to use all his industry to procure a second person to assist at the embroidery part which will be done if such a person can be found. At all events I think it will be proper you should send to Alexandria on wednesday the 3d of July, as I shall if ready send the whole by post.[2]
    I shall send you tomorrow or next day six silver stars. One is yet to be made, other wise I should have forwarded them to-day.[3] I am my dear Sir Yours Affly

                                        James McHenry

ALS, DLC:GW.
    1. GW acknowledged the receipt of the "figures" on 30 June. When the appraisers of GW's estate took an inventory of Mount Vernon in 1800, they found in the study "1 Box Military figures," which they valued at two dollars (Prussing, *Estate of Washington*, 418).
    2. See GW to McHenry, 7 June, n.3.
    3. McHenry wrote the next day: "Inclosed are six silver Stars which I have just received" (DLC:GW). He also sent a receipt from Michael Roberts and Thomas Levering for $6 in payment for "6 Silver Stars."

To Alexander Hamilton

Private
Dear Sir,   Mount Vernon 25th June 1799
    Your private letter of the 15th instant came duly to hand.
    So far as my information extends (which by the bye is very limited) the Recruiting Service in this State progresses beyond my expectation, But is retarded very considerably from the want of cloathing: the ragged appearance of the Recruits having a tendency to disgust, rather than to excite, enlistments.

I think with you, that policy dictates the expediency of promoting Brigadier Wilkinson to the Rank of Majr General, and will suggest the measure to the Secretary of War in a private communication. It would feed his ambition, sooth his vanity, and by arresting discontent, produce the good effect you contemplate. But in the appointment of this Gentleman, regard must be had to time, circumstances, and dates; otherwise by endeavouring to avoid Charibdas we might run upon Scylla.

What I mean by this is, that the President may deem it expedient to take the next Majr General from the Eastern States; again, may recur to the former appointments of that Gra⟨de in⟩ the Provisional Army; and further (if Services in the Revolutionary Army are to be regarded) to relative Rank also in dating the Commissions of the Major Generals, yet to be appointed.

If Genl Wilkinson should be promoted, it will be expected, no doubt, that the oldest Lieutt Coll Commandant should step into his Shoes as Brigadier; of course, the oldest Major of the old line, would succeed to the vacancy occasioned thereby. Who, & what the character of these Gentleman are, I know not—the measure deserves consideration.[1] I am always Yr Affecte

Go: Washington

ALS, DLC: Hamilton Papers; ALS (letterpress copy), DLC:GW.

1. On this date GW wrote a letter marked "Private" to James McHenry: "Dear Sir By Transmitting General Hamilton's letter to me of the 15th instant, respecting the expediency of promoting General [James] Wilkinson to the Rank of Major General in the Armies of the United States, and my reply thereto of the present date, I find it the easiest mode of communicating the ideas of both of us on this subject; and the necessity of enlarging thereon is superceded thereby. I have only to pray that both may be returned to Dear Sir Your Affecte Hble Servant Go: Washington" (ALS, PHi: Dreer Collection; letterpress copy, DLC:GW).

To William Herbert

Dear Sir,   Mount Vernon, June 25th, 1799

In expectation of receiving considerable sums of money for Lands sold for the express purpose of raising it, I have (being able hitherto to get along without it) forborne to apply to the Bank for aid. But out of $15,000 which ought to have been paid by the first of June 1798, and nearly the same sum this month for Lands, sold by me I have recd $1700 *only*.

This disappointment, and calls upon me which I would ⟨*illegible*⟩ to parry under ⟨*illegible*⟩ly true, induced me to accept your kind offer of endorsing my notes for the money I may have occasion to ⟨desire.⟩[1] On, or about the first of July I shall have demands to answer ⟨*illegible*⟩ (exclusive of the balance I have rem[ain]g ⟨*illegible*⟩ of about $1,500 and wish ⟨*illegible*⟩ such steps as are necessary ⟨*illegible*⟩ (as borrowing ⟨*illegible*⟩ new to me) I would thank you to point out; and to inform me of. arrangements can be made ⟨*illegible*⟩ my attendance in Alexandria whether my draughts will be honored. and if so, that you would be so good as to secure or prepare in my behalf, the needful. I have no stamps, if they be necy.

I would thank you also for information of the terms on which this accomodation at the Bank is to be obtained; for as I have observed before it is quite a new scene I am entering upon.[2] With very great esteem & regard I am—Dear Sir Your Most Obedt Hble Servt

Go: Washington

P.S. Besides the 1,500$ above, I may, from ⟨*illegible*⟩ some causes be obliged ⟨*illegible*⟩ 'ere long ⟨*illegible*⟩ desirous ⟨*illegible*⟩ taking the Land ⟨*illegible*⟩ before I do this.

ALS (letterpress copy), DLC:GW.

1. Facing the prospect of making large expenditures for the construction of his pair of houses near the Capitol in Washington, GW on 4 Oct. 1798 asked the president of the bank in Alexandria, William Herbert, about the possibility of his borrowing money. Herbert wrote GW the day following assuring him that he would have no problem in securing from the bank a loan of up to "Six to ten thousand Dollars."

2. Later in the day Herbert wrote GW: "I Am honor'd With your letter of this date, the Money you want to Borrow from the Bank of Alexandria, can be obtain'd Without Difficulty. your Presence here, is by no means Necessary. Inclosed you have a Note which you will be pleased to Sign, & return It to me, Any time before Monday Next, & the Day after you may Draw for the Proceeds which will be 1485 Dollars. Whenever a farther Sum is Wanted, you have only to Inform me of the Amount, & I will forward to you a Note for Signature, & have it Discounted" (DLC:GW).

From Charles Cotesworth Pinckney

Dear Sr   Charleston [S.C.] June 25th 1799

I am much obliged to you for your favour of the fifth instant— The Communications made you from Mulberry Grove were by no means troublesome to me. It will always give me pleasure to keep you regularly informed of the situation of the command entrusted to me; and I solemnly assure you I meant no compliment, but it is my most sincere & earnest desire to be favoured from time to time with your instructions & advice. I should indeed be very self sufficient not to wish to avail myself of your knowledge, abilities & Judgment.

Brigr Genl Washington left home this day week for the Northward so that you may expect to see him a few days after receiving this.[1]

The enclosed letter is a copy of one in Cypher sent me from the Hague by Major Mountflorence, on whose information I can depend. You may remember you had a conversation on the subject of the Gentleman mentioned in the letter with Genl Hamilton & myself at Philadelphia. I lament that he does not seem disposed to keep himself quiet at present. But it is impossible; I never knew an individual of that nation but who loved to be meddling.[2]

I have put Capn Thornton in orders, and am much obliged to you for having procured him for me. I would not have him move Southwardly at present. Mrs Pinckney who is still indisposed unites with my Daughters & myself in best respects to Mrs Washington & you & in Compts to Coll Lear & Mr Custis. When you write to Mr & Mrs Lewis pray remember us to them. I sincerely congratulate you on the late defeats of the French in Italy & Germany. There will be no solid peace for Europe or for ourselves 'till they are reduced within their antient limits. I ever am with the greatest gratitude & affection Your most devoted & obedt sert

                                        Charles Cotesworth Pinckney

ALS, DLC:GW.

1. Gen. William Washington did not reach Mount Vernon until 6 August. See GW to Pinckney, 10 August.

2. Writing from The Hague on 12 Mar., Maj. James G. Montflorence expressed his strong suspicion that Talleyrand was attempting to use Lafayette as a pawn by sending him as a French agent to America: "In my letter to the Secry of State of the 9th instant, I communicated the *positive* intelligence, I had from Paris, that the Consul there & Mr [Joel] Barlow, had individually written to the French Directory, praising their wise & prudent conduct towards the U. states, & recommending that a Minister be immediately sent to America to adjust matters, & thereby to be beforehand with the President. They recommend particularly that this person should have manifested even before the French Revolution, if possible, Republican principles & done some great service to America. I smell in this, a double intrigue of crafty Talleyrand, & I beleive you will be of my opinion, when

I inform you that La Fayette, has been in this country for some weeks, with an intention of going to America—that he has letters from Talleyrand advising him strongly to it, & buoying him up with his canting flattery; that a man of his talents, respectability &c. could be of infinite service in settling matters between the two Nations, & founding his disposition to that effect. . . . Trusting to what popularity, & influence this character may still retain in the U. states, especially among the people, Talleyrand expects that on his arrival, he would be courted, flattered & cherished by the Democrats & Anti's . . ." (DLC:GW).

From William Thornton

Dear Sir   City of Washington June 25th 1799

The Day on which I had the honor of receiving your last favour I waited on Mr Blagdin, and communicated the contents. He had not then gotten the Boxes of Glass, therefore Coll Gilpin would no doubt take the first opportunity of returning the Box which came to him by mistake.[1] I should not have delayed answering your Letter, but at the time it arrived I received one from Mr Anderson, by which I learnt that you have very kindly directed that nothing should be paid for the Asses I sent down. I lament exceedingly that he should have troubled you with any Answer I requested from him, for I find that you are disposed to lay me under a fresh obligation, when you know that I can never repay my present Debts. I cannot refuse your kindness, because it would be indecorous, but I should be glad if you could point out any mode by which I could hope to repay your goodness. In the mean time however I remain silent, hoping the Day may arrive in which I may be able to shew you my sense of your politeness to me, my gratitude, and my wish to return your favours. I am, dear Sir, with the sincerest good wishes your obedt & affection[a]te Friend

William Thornton

ALS, DLC:GW.

1. For reference to the mistake made in the shipment from Boston of glass for GW's Federal City houses, see GW to Thornton, 15 Feb. 1799, n.1.

To John Trumbull

Dear Sir   Mount Vernon 25th June 1799

Your favor of the 18th of Septr last, with the small box containing four pair of Prints, came safe to hand, but long after the date of the letter.

Immediately upon the receipt of these—having forgot the terms of the Subscription, and not knowing, as you were absent, to whom the money was to be paid—I wrote to Governor Trumbell for information on this head, without obtaining further satisfaction than that he thought it probable, Mr Anthony of Philadelphia was authorised, by you, to receive the amount. In consequence, I addressed this Gentleman; (who being absent from that City—as he said, by way of apology for the delay in answering my letter in a reasonable time) and shall, immediately, pay what is due from me, thereon.[1]

I give you the trouble of this detail because I should feel unpleasant myself if after your marked politeness and attentions to me in this, as in every other transaction, any tardiness should have appeared on my part, in return for Prints so valuable.

The two Vols. put into your hands by Mr West for transmission to me, are the product of a Mr Uvedale Price on the Picturesque; accompanied by a very polite letter of which the enclosed is an acknowledgment to that Gentleman—recommended to your care, with my best respects to Mr West.[2]

I was on the point of closing this letter with my thanks for the favorable Sentiments you have been pleased to express for me, and adding Mrs Washington's complimts and best wishes thereto, when the Mail from Philadelphia brought me your interesting letter of the 24th of March.

For the political information contained in it I feel grateful, as I always shall for the free & unreserved communication of your Sentiments upon subjects so important in their nature, and tendency. No well informed and unprejudiced man, who has viewed with attention the conduct of the French Government since the Revolution in that Country, can mistake its objects, or the tendency of the ambitious Plans it is pursuing. Yet, strange as it may seem, a party, and a powerful one too, among us, affect to believe that the measures of it are dictated by a principle of self preservation; that the outrages of which the Directory are guilty, proceeds from dire necessity; that it wishes to be upon the most friendly & amicable terms with the United States; that it will be the fault of the latter if this is not the case; that the defensive measures which this Country have adopted, are not only unnecessary & expensive, but have a tendency to produce the evil which, to deprecate, is mere pretence, because War with France they say is the wish of this Government; that on the Militia we should rest our Security; and, that it is time enough to call upon these when the danger is imminent &ca &ca &ca.

With these, and such like ideas, attempted to be inculcated upon the public mind (& prejudice not yet eradicated) with all the arts of sophistry, & no regard to truth, decency or respect to characters—public or private—who happen to differ from themselves in Politics, I leave you to decide on the probability of carrying such an extensive plan of defence as you have suggested in your last letter, into operation; and in the short period you suppose may be allowed to accomplish it in.

The public mind has changed, and is yet changing every day, with respect to French principles. The people begin to see clearly— that the words and actions of the governing powers of that Nation can not be reconciled, and that, hitherto, they have been misled by sounds; in a word that while they were in pursuit of the shadow they had lost the substance. The late changes in the Congressional Representation sufficiently evince this opinion: for of the two sent from the State of Georgia, one certain, some say both, are Federal characters; of six from South Carolina five are, decidedly so; of ten from North Carolina, seven may be counted upon; & of nineteen from this State (Virginia) eight are certain, a ninth doubtful, and, but for some egregious mismanagement, Eleven supporters of Governmental measures would have been elected.

I mention these facts, merely to shew that we are *progressing* to a better state of things; not because we are quite right yet. Time I hope will shew us the necessity, or at least the propriety of becoming so. God grant it, and soon.

It is unfortunate when men cannot, or will not, see danger at a distance; or seeing it, are restrained in the means which are necessary to avert, or keep it afar off. I question whether the evil arising from the French getting possession of Louisiana and the Floridas would be *generally* seen, until it is felt; and yet no problem in Euclid is more evident, or susceptible of clearer demonstration—Not less difficult is it to make them believe, that offensive operations, often times, is the *surest*, if not the *only* (in some cases) means of defence.

Mrs Washington is grateful for your kind remembrance of her, and with Mrs Lewis' (formerly your old acquaintance Nelly Custis) Compliments & good wishes united, I am with sentiments of the most perfect esteem & regd Dr Sir

[Go: Washington]

AL[S], CtY: U.S. Presidents Collection; ALS (letterpress copy), DLC:GW. The signature on the ALS has been clipped.

1. For GW's prolonged correspondence with Joseph Anthony regarding payment for Trumbull's prints, see GW to Anthony, 17 Mar. 1799, n.1.

2. See Uvedale Price to GW, 31 Mar. 1798.

Letter not found: to Bartholomew Dandridge, 26 June 1799. On 17 Oct. Dandridge wrote from London thanking GW for his "very Kind letter of the 26. June."

To Samuel Mickle Fox

Sir,   Mount Vernon 26th June 1799

I thank you for the prompt answer to my enquiries respecting Ritchie and Shreves Bonds, deposited in the Bank of Pennsylvania for collection.[1]

I pray you to inform me, whether the circumstances attending the deposit of the $250 to Mr Ross's credit—my Agent as he was called—were such as to enable me to transfer or rather would authorise the Bank to pay, the same to my draught, or not.[2]

If nothing since the date of your last has been heard from Shreve or the representatives of M. Ritchie to good effect—nor from Mr Ross, you would oblige me by forwarding the letter enclosed to the last named Gentleman.[3]

It would distress me to be obliged to put the judgment Bonds of the above named persons in Suit, but necessity will drive me to it if I cannot obtain payment, & shortly, without.

I thank you for the tender of the Services of the Institution over which you preside & am Sir—Yr Obedt H. Servt

Go: Washington

ALS (letterpress copy), owned (1978) by Leon H. Becker, Rancho La Costa, California.

1. See GW to Fox, 10 June, n.2.

2. In his response on 2 July, Fox refers to the "deposit which was made on the 12th of April being carried to the credit of Mr Ross as your agent"; and in his account with Shreve GW has the following entry: "By Cash lodged on my a/c in the Bank of Pennsylvania I presume by you—$250." GW dates this entry 28 July 1799 in Ledger C, 12, but he gives the same date to his entry on the same page in his account with Matthew Ritchie for the receipt of Addison's payment to the bank on 6 July (see Addison to GW, 6 July, and note 1 of that document).

3. GW's letter to James Ross is dated this day.

From Daniel Morgan

Dear Sir   Soldiers Rest 26th June 1799

I take the liberty to transmit you a list of the names and Recommendations; who have applied to me since I wrote to you *on* the 12th instant, which you will receive inclosed.[1] I have the honor to be sir Your Obt Hle Sert

                                      Danl Morgan

LS, DLC:GW. Written on the cover: "Battle town June 27th 1799."

1. Morgan's list of possible officers for the Provisional Army reads: "James Stephenson—Majr—mentioned in my last since which I have received a recommendation from Mr A. Waggener.

"John Stubblefield Battle town Frederick County—Ensign—Son to Colo. George Stubblefield of the late War, a young man of good character but has seen no Service.

"Elias Edmonds—mentioned in my last since which I have received recommendations from Mr Charles Marshall & Mr [Martin] Pickett.

"Burwell Bullitt recommended by Mr Pickett Mr Marshall, Mr [George Steptoe] Washington & Mr [Robert] Lewis—I know little of Mr Bullitt from my own knowledge, he is half Brother to Capt. Thomas Bullitt in the French War of 1755/6.

"John Campbell Ensign—I could wish Mr Campbell to be appointed, his Father Arthur Campbell being a very leading Character in Washington County Virginia.

"John Bronaugh recommended by Mr Pickett & Mr Marshall—Ensign, I am not acquainted with Mr Bronaugh from my own knowledge, but, suppose him to be a man of good character from the recommendations.

"John Dowdall Son of Colo. [James G.] Dowdall of Winchester a man of good Character has Commanded a Company of Militia some time & I think wo⟨uld⟩ make an excellent Lieutenant."

The letters of recommendation written to General Morgan referred to here include Andrew Waggener's letter of 14 June, Martin Pickett's from Fauquier County of 24 and 25 June, Charles Marshall's two of 25 June, Robert Lewis's of 24 June, and George Steptoe Washington's of 25 June. All of these letters are in DLC:GW. The writers of the letters generally refer to the good reputation of the candidate, his militia service, and to his being a "friend to the Goverment" (Waggener to Morgan, 14 June).

On the next day, 27 June, Humphrey Brooke wrote to GW from Fauquier recommending one of these men: "Mr Elias Edmonds is desirous of entering into the service of his Country in one of the 24 additional Regiments, as a Captain, I have known him from his Infancy, and beleive him to be a very worthy Man, firmly attached to the Government of the United States, and that he will be able to recruit his Men as speedily as any one" (DLC:GW).

From Leven Powell

Dear Sir, Middleburg June 26th 1799.

Mr Elias Edmonds Junr Mr Burwell Bullitt and Mr John Bronaugh all of the County of Fauquier wish to be appointed to the command of Companies in the eventual army, the two first in the infantry and the latter in the artilery.[1] I have been long acquainted with them and as I feel a confidence that they will be found to acquit themselves to the advantage of their Country and honor to themselves, it is with pleasure that I take the liberty to recommend them to your aid and attention & this I more readily do because they are decidedly friendly to the government of our Country.[2] With much respect and esteem I am Dear Sir, Yr obt Hble Servt

Leven Powell

ALS, DLC:GW. Powell wrote "Mr Bullitt" on the lower left of the letter cover. Burwell Bullitt arrived at Mount Vernon on 1 July and spent the night (*Diaries*, 6:355).

1. On this day Gen. Daniel Morgan also recommended these three men. See note 1 to Morgan's letter.

2. Powell wrote again from Middleburg the next day: "Mr Thomas Brent of the County of Fauquier is desirous of the appointment of a Lieutenant in the army which the President is authorised to raise in the event of its being wanting. Altho' I am well acquainted with this Young gentlemans family and Connexions which are respectable I have no personal Acquaintance with him. But he comes to me so strongly recommended by gentlemen on whom I can rely with the greatest confidence as well for his sobriety & propriety of conduct as for his Attachment to the government of our Country, that I can have no doubt but he will well fill the Office which he Solicits . . ." (DLC:GW).

GW replied on 9 July: "Dear Sir, Your letters of the 26th & 27th ultimo, recommending certain persons for appointments in the eventual Army, have been received, and will meet with due attention.

"Whenever the applications for offices in this Army shall be sufficiently numerous to furnish the quota alotted to this State, a selection will be made and forwarded to the Secretary of War. In the mean time it will give me pleasure to receive recommendations of suitable Characters from those on whose judgement and patriotism I can rely: And altho' it is not customary for me to answer all letters of Recommendation, as the subject does not require it, yet I cannot butt acknowledge the receipt of yours to assure you that I place a reliance upon them, being persuaded that you will recommend none but such as will do Credit to the service. With great regard I am Dear Sir Yr Mo. Ob. St" (Df, DLC:GW).

Powell wrote again on 4 Sept.: "I beg leave to recommend to you as a Candidate for an Office in the eventual Army Mr John Bayly who is a Young man that in my opinion will make a good Officer, he is a Son of Mr Peirce Bayly from whose respectability in this County I am persuaded his son who has conducted himself with propriety will meet with no difficulty in recruiting his men. Mr Bayly does not wish his son Appointed to a higher office than first or second Lieutenant. My Youngest son Alfred now in his twentieth year has expressed to me a wish for an appointment in that army. He is now engaged in the Study of the Law and it would be more Agreeable to me for him to pursue his Studies without interruption, but as it will be the duty of all to defend their Country in the Situation in which we shall stand if it shall be necessary to raise that Army. I have no hesitation to gratify him, but if Sir, you may think proper to place him on the list of Officers, I shall prefer his standing as Second Lieutenant—if he should go into Service and Merit a higher place he will soon get it" (DLC:GW).

To James Ross

Dear Sir   Mount Vernon 26th June 1799

Early in January last, in answer to a letter from Colo. Shreve in the old style of unprovidedness, and craving further indulgence, I wrote him, and transmitted the letter open under a Cover to you, that I would stay proceedings on his judgment Bond until the first of April last, and no longer; and that I should, without fail, expect to have the next Instalment paid at the appointed time (the first of the present mo.) since which I have not heard a tittle from him.[1]

Waiting 'till this Month had come in, I wrote to the President of the Bank of Pennsylvania to know if Shreve, or the Executors of Colo. Ritchie had made any deposits there on my a/c, and if not, whether any intimations had been given of such intention, and am answered No—except, that $250 had been placed there to your credit supposed to be for my use.[2]

No man can, with more reluctance than myself seek justice in a Court of Law. nor no one with more unwillingness distress another: but my situation (with respect to pecuniary matters) is really such as to require these payments, being obliged to obtain money from the Banks on discount, as substitutes therefor; which, by the difference of interest would, in time, intirely sink the Instalments I am to receive from Shreve, & the heirs of Ritchie.

I am really sorry & ashamed, to give you so much trouble in my concerns; but between being pressed myself, and an unwillingness to proceed to extremities with others, I feel the want of some person who can give me such information as I can rely on; and who, possibly, may stimulate exertions which may supersede the necessity of the latter, before the measure is adopted; which it must be, if a well grounded assurance cannot be given of my receiving my dues in time. At your leisure I would beg to hear from you, and with great & sincere esteem & regard, I am—Dear Sir Your most Obedt & Obliged Ser⟨vt⟩

Go: Washington

ALS (photocopy), NN: U.S. Presidents. Ross docketed the letter, "Ansd 25 July," but his answer, in fact, is dated 24 July.

1. Israel Shreve's letter to GW is dated 21 Dec. 1798, and GW's reply is dated 10 Jan. 1799. For a summary of GW's dealings with Shreve regarding his payments for GW's tract of land in Fayette County, Pa., called Washington's Bottom, see GW to Samuel M. Fox, 10 June 1799, n.1. See also Ross to GW, 24 July 1799. Ross had acted as GW's agent in the sale of Washington's Bottom to Shreve in 1795 and also in the sale of his Millers Run tract to Matthew Ritchie in 1796.

2. See GW to Samuel M. Fox, 10 June, n.2, and 26 June, n.2.

From James McAlpin

Sir,   Philad[elphi]a June 27th 1799

I never had the honour of writing to you upon a subject which gave me so much concern as the present! but however painful the task, it is my duty to Acquaint you with my ill success in the execution of your order for your Regimentals.[1]

Having, after considerable enquiry, found out an embroiderer, I had flattered myself that nothing was wanting to the completion of the business but the gold thread—And waited with much Anxious solicitude, the arrival of the Ships from Europe. That no dissappointment might arise on Account of the thread, I had wrote to a friend in New York—And on the same day on which a parcel was landed here, I received anoth⟨er⟩ from him. I now thought the business finished And Acquainted the Secretary at War, that he might depend on having your Regimentals to send by next mondays Mail—but how great was my dissappointment, on calling on the embroiderer, to see how he proceded, to find that he was not master of his business, And that his work was so wretchedly done, that I was convinced you would never wear it—However, not to rely intirely on my own opinion, I took the liberty of asking General McPherson, & the Secretary at war to see it, who both concurred with me, that it would be highly improper to have it finished in that manner, And put you to a great expence, when they were sure you would not wear it.[2]

Not being able to do more at the present time, I wait your Orders how to act, begging leave to suggest the propriety of sending the Coat to London, in order to have it embroidered there, which I think possible to be done, and have it out again, by one of the fall Ships. Should you approve of that or any other method, I shall be glad to receive your Commands as soon as possible. I remain, with the utmost respect Sir, your Most Obedient & much Obliged Humble Servant

James McAlpin

ALS, DLC:GW.

1. See McAlpin's letter of 24 June printed in GW to James McHenry, 7 June, n.3.

2. McHenry wrote GW on 28 June confirming what McAlpin wrote here about the embroidery on his uniform.

From Wilson Allen

Dr sir   Richm[on]d 28th June 1799.

Before your favor of date the 17th inst: came to hand, the General Court had risen—but knowing that no evil cou'd result from the recording your deed to Genl Lee, and supposing it possible that Mr B. Washington might wish it recorded in that Court for some particular reason—I presented it to the Judges on the last day of the term when they directed it to be recorded *for preservation.*

The Deed from Genl Lee to you for the land mentiond in the deed above alluded to, I find has already been recorded here— but it was done prior to the establishment of Kentucky into an independent state (1790) when it came *properly within* the jurisdiction of this Court.

So soon as your deed to Genl Lee is recorded I will (if not otherwise directed) forward it you with the usual certificate annexed. Yrs with the greatest respect

Wilson Allen

ALS, DLC:GW.

From James McHenry

Dear Sir.   Philad[elphia] 28 June 1799

After every exertion Mr McAlpin has been able to make, and after having procured the gold thread and a man who pretended to be fully competent to working it, he has been obliged to suspend the whole operation. The man was ignorant, and no person can be found more skilful. He has therefore prefered, rather than send you what I am sure you would not wear, sending the coat to England where it will be properly finished and expects to have it returned to him by one of the fall vessels. I thought it right to give you this hasty information, to prevent any disappointment which might have been felt had you depended upon receiving it, as I had given you reason to expect.[1] Yours Affly

James McHenry

P.S. I recd yesterday your letter of the 22d Inst. Your observations respecting purchasing horses for the cavalry strike me favourable. If however I should say any thing more now I must give up to days mail.[2]

ALS, DLC:GW.
    1. See James McAlpin to GW, 27 June.
    2. For GW's correspondence with Samuel Love regarding horses for the army, see GW to McHenry, 22 June, n.1.

From James McHenry

Private & confid.
My dear Sir.   Philad[elphia] 29 June 1799
    I received yesterday your private letter of the 25th inst. and its inclosures which I now return.
    The objections you suggest relative to the promotion of the officer in question are intitled to very serious consideration. Major Generals Lee & Hand may expect a station in the regular army, and certainly the Eastern quarter of the Union will not be pleased unless they have in it one Major General.[1]
    I have but one observation to make. If the promotion contemplated is to be attempted, it will be proper, that the general should be recommended by you in an official form that the subject may be laid before the President.
    I inclose a letter I received from Majr Gen. Hamilton and my answer, both of which you will be pleased to return.[2]
    Col. Howard & Gen. Lloyd have declined, on account of pretended difficulties making a selection of persons for off[i]cers for the eventual army.[3] They are affraid of what good men ought not

to be affraid, to risk a little popularity. May I venture to ask you to undertake for Maryland? Your ever affectionate

James McHenry

ALS, DLC:GW; Df, in McHenry's hand, DLC: McHenry Papers.

1. On 25 June GW sent McHenry copies of Alexander Hamilton's letter to GW of 15 June and of GW's reply of 25 June regarding the promotion of James Wilkinson to the rank of major general. GW's letter to McHenry of 25 June transmitting these letters is printed in note 1 to GW's letter to Hamilton of that date.

2. On 25 June, Hamilton wrote McHenry: "General Wilkinson is soon expected. I am strongly inclined to see him made a Major General. . . ." On 27 June McHenry wrote Hamilton: "General W. has certainly claims to promotion, and so far as it respects myself I shall not oppose it. It will be proper however, that General Washington be consulted" (Syrett, *Hamilton Papers*, 23:215, 226).

3. When McHenry wrote to GW on 2 May asking him to provide names of men in Virginia for officers in "the eventual army," he informed GW that he would ask the two senators in each state to the north of Virginia to do the same for their states. James Lloyd and John Eager Howard were the U.S. senators from Maryland.

To James McHenry

Private

Dear Sir,   Mount Vernon 30th June 1799

Your favours of the 24th & 25th instant have been received.[1]

For the Stars, enclosed in the latter, I thank you. The amount of cost, Six dollars, is herein remitted. I preferred sending a Columbia Bank note for a dollar, to one of Silver (in a letter), as it can readily be exchanged for the latter, and the other Banks issue no notes under five dollars.

For the Box which accompanied the letter of the 24th I feel much obliged. I have not had time yet to examine, and compare the figures with the Instructions; but primæ faciæ, there is something curious, and I dare say useful in the design.

I shall send up to Alexandria on Wednesday; but shall feel no disappointmt if my Uniform is not there. With very grt esteem & regard—I am—Dear Sir Your Most Obedt & Affecte Hble Ser⟨vt⟩

Go: Washington

ALS, CSmH; ALS (letterpress copy), DLC:GW.

1. McHenry's letter of 25 June is printed in note 3 to his letter of 24 June.

To James McHenry

Sir,   Mount Vernon June 30th 1799

Enclosed are letters from several persons, as mentioned at foot, applying for appointments in the actual Army. I have no personal knowledge of the Characters of the Applicants, nor do I know whether there are any vacancies to which they can be appointed, however deserving they may be.[1] With due consideration I have the honor to be Sir Yr mo. ob. St

G. W——n.

Df, in Tobias Lear's hand, DLC:GW.

1. Below "G. W——n," Lear listed the men who had been recommended for appointment in the New Army and gave the name of the man who had written in favor of each; none of these letters has been found. The list reads:

"Charles Thompson, recommended by B[ushrod] Washington Esqr. for a Lieut. in the Cavalry, or an appointt in the Infantry.

"Charles Julian—recommended by Generals [Thomas] Posey & [Alexander] Spotswood for an appointmt in the Artillery.

"William H. Powell—applies for a Captaincy in the Cavalry. Note Since Mr Powell's application came to hand I have been informed that he drinks hard. If so, he is unfit for any appointment.

"Ruben Thornton. Heretofore appointd an Ensign in Infantry, which he declined. applying for an appoint. in the Cavalry.

"John Campbell recommended by his father Auther Campbell."

From Daniel Marshal

Sir,   Chatham Street 132. Newyork June 30th 1799.

wishing to prove my Respectfulness to you, I Send you the inclosed Writings. I would be glad, if you had not read yet *all* them and most happy, if you would not send them back. I got them double.

I came, with my Boy Seven Years of Age, from Magdeburgh to the United States of America, in the last Year, intending to purchase and cultivate a small Farm; but Circumstances have engaged me in Trade here, which gives me more Money and less contentment, than I want. I am respectfully Your humble Servant

Daniel Marshal

ALS, DLC:GW. In his docket of this letter, Tobias Lear wrote: "acknowledged July 7. [17]99." GW's letter thanking Marshal for the "Writings" was offered for sale in 1962 by King V. Hostick. Marshal has not been identified.

From Bartholomew Dandridge, Jr.

My dear sir,   London July 1st 1799

Mr Charles W. Valangin who will have the honor to hand you this, is the Son of Dr de Valangin an eminent & very respectable physician of this City. I have had the pleasure of his acquaintance since my first arrival in England & with great confidence take the liberty of making him known to you as an intelligent & worthy man. Mr Valangin goes to the United States with the intention of making it his permanent residence if he finds our Country to correspond with the Expectations he has formed of it. He is a man of liberal Education & has made Law & Physic his more particular Studies. He has also been engaged in & paid much attention to Agriculture which seems to be his favorite pursuit & respecting the state of which in this Country he will be able if you permit him to give you many interesting particulars which will be useful to you & our Country generally. It is his intention to purchase a Farm & establish himself in that part of the U.S. which after viewing them all he shall most approve. I have advised him however not to be in a hurry in *purchasing*, & he will probably find it better to *rent* for a year or more. I have been induced, Sir, to give Mr V—— this letter to you as I know it is yr wish to encourage the improvement of our husbandry by the introduction of farmers of good character, & as I am certain the information wch he can & is desirous to impart will amply reward any civilities that may be shewn him. He carries with him samples of many of the best seeds from this Country, of the various kinds of wheat, potatoes, turnips &ca which I have advised him in the first instance to entrust to yr care & which he will do with pleasure.[1] With the truest respect & attachmt very sincerely Yrs

B. Dandridge

ALS, DLC:GW.

1. Charles Valangin "came to dinner" at Mount Vernon on 3 Nov. 1799, and on 14 Nov. he again "came to dinner & stayed all night" (*Diaries*, 6:373, 375).

To Benjamin Lincoln

My Dear Sir,   Mount Vernon 1st July 1799

Your favours of the 11th of May and 4th Ulto have come ⟨late⟩ to hand. The last the day before yesterday only.

The cost of the Glass therein enclosed, shall be immediately paid to Messrs Solomon Cotton & Co. Merchts in Baltimore—and for your agency in this business I pray you to accept my thanks.[1]

The mistake will, I trust, soon be rectified as the wrong box of glass was returned to Baltimore (according to desire) and the proper one expected from thence.[2] With the highest esteem and regard I remain my dear Sir Yr Most Obedt & Affece Servt

Go: Washington

ALS (letterpress copy), NN: Washington Papers.

1. GW's letter of 1 July to the Baltimore firm of Solomon Cotton & Co. led to an exchange of letters. GW wrote on 1 July: "Gentlemen, From my correspondent in Boston, I have (within these two days) received the bill of cost of Glass shipped from thence for my use—viz.—$250.43—and am advised that the amount is to be paid to your house.

"Be so good therefore as to advise me whether you have any Agent in Alexandria to whom I shall pay the money? or whether you would prefer having it remitted in a *letter*, in Bank notes? as there is no person in Baltimore to whom I give the trouble of doing business for Gentlemen Your Most Obedt Hble Servt Go: Washington" (letterpress copy, NN: Washington Papers). Solomon Cotton & Co. replied on 6 July: "we duly recd yours of the 1st Inst. in answer to your request respecting the money for Mr Kupfer as we have no agent in alexandria we will thank you to be So good as to cutt the bills in halves & Send them at 2 different times" (DLC:GW).

On 10 July GW wrote: "Gentlemen, Enclosed you will receive, I trust, the half parts of Two hundred and fifty dollars, sent in the manner requested by you. The other half parts, I shall retain until I am advised of the safe arrival of these—of which you will please to inform. Gentlemen—Your Most Obedt Servant Go: Washington" (ALS, CSmH; letterpress copy, NN: Washington Papers). On the same day GW entered in his Day Book: "By Cash (in Bank notes) sent Messrs Solomon Cotton & Co. Merchts in Bal[timore] for Glass sent me by Genl [Benjamin] Lincoln from the Glass Manufactury at Boston—Mr [Charles F.] Kupfer $250.43." Solomon Cotton & Co. then wrote on 13 July: "We have the Honor to acknowledge your favor of July 1—for which please to accept our thanks. one of our House having lately gone home to Boston informs us that the Box that was deficient is sent by a more direct way than Coming here—permit us to offer our S⟨ervi⟩ces in Balto: if at any time you may have occasion for them" (DLC:GW).

GW replied on 17 July: "In your letter of the 13th instant, you acknowledged to have recd mine of the 1st of this month, and say nothing of that of the 10th containing the half parts of $250; which by your own desire, were remitted to you therein, although, in the usual course you ought to have received them by the 11th.

"This being the case, I shall withhold the other half parts of the Bank notes until the receipt of the first parts are acknowledged. I am Gentlemen—Your Obedt Hble Servant Go: Washington" (letterpress copy, NN: Washington Papers). On 18 July Solomon Cotton & Co. wrote: "We have just recd yours of Yesterday, are very Sorry you Should have any trouble, about such a trifle. ours of the 13th was an acknowledgement of the rect of the halves of 250 ⟨D.⟩ in bank bills, the Error is in our writing *1st* instead of *10th* which we find is the Case on referring to our Letter Book—in the Hurry of business we Cannot always be free from Errors" (DLC:GW). GW responded on 21 July: "Gentlemen Enclosed are the other half parts of the two hundred and fifty dollars, remitted in my letter of the 10th instant; together with half a dollar to make the sum charged for the Glass, from the Manufactury at Boston.

"If your letter of the 13th acknowledging the receipt of that from me dated the 1st instant which had been written instead of the 10th which contained the parts of Bills, had taken the least notice of the contents of the latter, all doubt of their having reached you would have ceased, the mistake of dates notwithstanding.

"You will please to acknowledge the receipt of this money—and the purpose for which it has been remitted by—Gentlemen Your Most Obedient Servt Go: Washington" (letterpress copy, NN: Washington Papers).

2. Lincoln wrote GW on 4 June that one of the boxes of glass intended for GW had been left behind and another, mistakenly, sent in its place. Lincoln's letter is printed in Lincoln to GW, 3 April, n.1. See also GW to William Thornton, 2 July.

From Timothy Pickering

Sir   Philadelphia July 1. 1799.

This morning's mail brought me your letter of the 25th. I will forward the two letters you inclosed for John Trumbull Esqr. & Mr Dandridge, to the care of Mr King, by the Grantham packet, which is to sail this week.[1]

Governor Davie of No. Carolina is appointed, and, should the mission proceed, *will* accept the place of Envoy to the French Republic, in the room of Patrick Henry Esqr. who declined, and is since dead.[2] I have made no *publication* of this fact, nor shall I do it. Would to God it was possible to annihilate the original act—and the remembrance of it. I am most respectfully sir, your obt servt

                                          Timothy Pickering

P.S. I inclose a letter confirming the report that La Fayette has been thought of for the French Envoy to the U. States.[3]

ALS (letterpress copy), MHi: Pickering Papers.

1. Neither GW's letter to Pickering of 25 June nor one to Bartholomew Dandridge of recent date has been found. His letter to John Trumbull is dated 25 June.

2. Pickering on 1 June sent to William R. Davie his appointment as "Envoy Extraordinary and Minister Plenipotentiary to the French Republic," with the request that Davie would advise him "whether, if it should become necessary, your acceptance of it may be expected." Davie's acceptance is dated 17 June (MHi: Pickering Papers).

3. The enclosure has not been found, but on 14 July GW wrote Pickering that since receiving the enclosure Charles Cotesworth Pinckney "has given me the whole of Major [James G.] Mountf[l]orence's letter to him." See Pinckney to GW, 25 June 1799, n.2.

From Samuel Mickle Fox

Sir   Bank of Pennsylvania [Philadelphia] July 2nd 1799

I was yesterday honor'd with your letter of the 26th Ult. As no information has been rec'd at Bank of any intention on the part of Mr Shreve or of the representatives of Col. Ritchie to make the payments due to you I sent the enclosure for the Honble Mr Ross to the Post office on the same day.

Hearing accidentally that Mrs Ritchie was in town I called upon the Gentleman at whose house she resides & thro. him (as I did not see her) conveyed your desire that immediate attention should be given to the discharge of her late Husband's bond—The reply was that Mrs Ritchie would write by the next Post to her Brother in law & press him to take measures for the payment of the debt. If I should have any further information from her upon this business I will in course communicate it.[1]

The deposit which was made on the 12th of April being carried to the credit of Mr Ross as your Agent your draft at sight upon the Cashier of this Bank will be duly honored or if you should please to direct it the amount shall be forwarded to you in Southern notes.[2] With sincere Respect I am Sir Your Obt Servt

Sam M. F⟨ox⟩
P.B.P.

ALS, DLC:GW.

1. For the payments due from Matthew Ritchie's estate for the purchase of GW's Millers Run land, see GW to Fox, 10 June, n.1. See also Alexander Addison to GW, 6 July, and James Ross to GW, 24 July 1799.

2. See GW to Fox, 26 June, n.2.

To William Thornton

Dear Sir,   Mount Vernon 2d July 1799

Your favour of the 25th has been received; but you have mistaken the case entirely with respect to the Asses who were sent to my Jacks; charging you nothing for the services of the latter, was not designed to lay you under obligation, but a feeble effort to repay the kindnesses you have heaped upon me.

Colo. Gilpin has forwarded the wrong box of glass to Baltimore, and soon will, I hope, receive the proper one in return.[1]

Enclosed is a check on the Bank of Alexandria for one thousand dollars agreeably to the demand of Mr Blagden, for the purpose of defraying the expences incurred on my buildings in the Fedl City.[2] With very great esteem & regard I am—Dear [Sir] Your Obedt & obliged Humble Servant

Go: Washington

P.S. In the letter accompanying the Glass from Boston—the Makers say "The Glass must be set convex out."[3]

ALS (letterpress copy), NN: Washington Papers; copy, CSt.

1. See GW to Benjamin Lincoln, 1 July, n.2.

2. For this payment to George Blagdin, see Thornton to GW, 5–6 June, n.1. Until now, GW had been able to provide the builder the money that he required without securing a loan from the bank, his first ever (see GW to William Herbert, 25 June). GW renewed the loan in August (see GW to Herbert and Herbert to GW, both 30 August).

3. GW is quoting Benjamin Lincoln's letter of 4 June, printed in Lincoln to GW, 3 April 1799, n.1.

From William Thornton

Dear Sir   City of Washington July 3rd 1799

I have just received your Favour of the 2nd Inst: and am highly sensible of your goodness in estimating so much the little I have yet been capable of doing to serve you. I only lament that I have not had it more in my power to shew my Inclination to repay in part your manifold kindness.

The check on the Bank of Alexandria for one thousand Dollars, which you enclosed to me I immediately paid on Account of your Houses, to Mr Blagdin, who means to set out this Evening for Alexandria to direct the Glass which had before arrived, and for which he had not occasion until now, to be sent up. He told me he had been asked two Dollars pr Day by two different Painters for the sizing & painting. I observed that they thought you could afford to pay extra prices, and therefore charged unreasonably: I begged he would engage a painter through the medium of another person without letting him know what, or whose, work it was. This will be done.[1] I find the Mail-Stage is passing. Business in the Office prevented my answering your Letter till I was afraid I should not be able to reply by the present Post.

We have had some very severe Gusts. Many Trees in the Country, within the District, were blown down and shattered to pieces; and in the City Mr Robert Peter Junr had two Horses killed by Lightening. I heard that Dr Stewart had one killed at Hope Park. There was a Tree torn to pieces at the side of the Capitol Hill with Lightening. We have ordered Conductors. Adieu, dear Sir, and may you enjoy all felicity!

William Thornton

I mentioned the Directions, relative to the mode of putting in the Glass, to Mr Blagdin.

ALS, DLC:GW.

1. George Blagdin set the cost of glazing the windows and painting the houses in Washington at $840 (enclosure in GW to John Francis, 25 Aug. 1799, n.1). In late September 1799 when the time came to arrange for the painting of the houses, GW got an estimate for the job from the firm of McLeod & Lumley in Alexandria. Its estimate was close to Blagdin's price, and after consulting with Thornton GW decided to leave it to Blagdin to get the painting done. See GW to Thornton, 29 Sept., and 1, 6 Oct. 1799.

To Mason Locke Weems

Reverend Sir,   Mount Vernon, July 3, 1799

For your kind compliment—"The Immortal Mentor," I beg you to accept my best thanks. I have perused it with singular satisfaction; and I hesitate not to say that it is, *in my opinion at least*, an *invaluable* compilation. I cannot but hope that a book whose contents do such *credit* to its *title*, will meet with a very generous patronage.

Should the Patronage equal my wishes, you will have no reason to regret that you ever printed the Immortal Mentor.[1] With respect I am Reverend Sir Your most Obedient Humble Servant

George Washington

Magazine of American History (1880), 5:102.

1. Parson Weems's *The Immortal Mentor: or, Man's Unerring Guide to a Healthy, Wealthy, and Happy Life* . . . was first printed in Philadelphia in 1796.

From John Cropper, Jr.

Sir   Accomac Courthouse 4th July 1799

I received your favor of the 17th ultimo by the last mail. The opinion entertained by you of my services in the American War, and the confidence expressed of my Patriotism and Judgment are a most precious addition to the approbation of my fellow Citizens within the circle of my acquaintance. Many more marks of approbation have been bestowed upon me by my Countrymen, than my services have merited, but not more than will be gratefully remembered to the latest hour of my existance.

After serving my native Country for sixteen years, partly in a military and partly in a civil capacity, I resigned in the year 1791 all pretensions to public office, and prescribed to myself the pleasure of enjoying the remainder of my life in domestic tranquility.

But Sir, I have remained a faithful 'tho' feeble friend to the Government of the United States, and am one of those who have approved of the administration of it. I beleive this Government has been established with as much wisdom, and conducted with as much integrity as any other in the world.

Therefore, considering the critical situation of public affairs at this juncture, and the sacred obligations which bind a dutiful Citizen to his Country, I shall take upon me the duties assigned by your letter, and perform them according to my best ability.

You may name me to the President of the United States to fill such grade in the provisional Army, as I may be thought to suit and deserve.

My knowledge of the military characters of the western shore part of the Division to which I am allotted is very contracted, and as far as my reflections have gone, shall be much at a loss to asscertain a competant judgment of those wt. whom I am personally unacquainted. I am with the greatest respect & esteem, Your Obdt Humble Servant

Jno. Cropper Junr

ALS, DLC:GW; copy, ViHi.

To Jane Dennison Fairfax

Mount Vernon 4th July 1799

General Washington presents his Compliments to Mrs Fairfax, and havg received a letter from Mr Fairfax, dated the 28th of April last, in which he says that he was better at that time, than he had been for months before; he could not refrain from giving Mrs Fx the pleasing account of it (in case Mr Fairfax's letters to her self should not have got to hand)—especially too, as in another part of his letter he says, he hopes he shall be able to set off on his return to this Country in a few Weeks.

AL, PWacD.

From Alexander Addison

Sir   Philadelphia July 6th 1799

I should have sooner informed you if I could have seen or ascertained what sum of money you might expect on the last instalment of your Bond on M. Ritchie. That instalment was $3116.40 of which sum I have this day paid into the Bank of Pennsylvania one half together with interest on that half from the first of last month making together $1568.[1] The instalment due at June 1798 was $3292.80. Interest on that to 11th July 1798 was $21.95; making together $3314.75 I then paid $1700 which is more than half the principal and the whole of the interest at that time due.[2]

It may be proper to state to you (because I know not that you are acquainted with) the reason of my making these two payments in this manner. When Col. Ritchie (who was a man of integrity and property) proposed to Mr Ross the purchase of your lands on Miller's run he pressed me to be concerned in the bargain. Having no means at command to make the payments I declined but on his assuring me that if the first payment could be made, he would provide for the others I agreed and though my name appears not in the contract I have half the interest in the land. Col. Ritchie's bond was as good as his and mine together and the whole land is bound by a mortgage to you. By our joint exertions the first instalment was paid with as much punctuality as could be exacted. The quantity of land was not ascertained at the time of the contract so that a bond for the precise sum could not be taken then; nor was it known to us before the day of payment of the first instalment so that we could not remit the precise sum. But we paid before the day a sum supposed equal to the first instalment of principal and interest. The difficulty of remitting money delayed the payment of the second instalment till my coming to this city at my usual time for attendance in the Court of Errors and Appeals. It was then paid with all the interest that could be exacted. Before the third instalment became due Col. Ritchie died. Lands from a variety of causes (which you can estimate better than I) had begun to sink in value and we could not make sales nor obtain payments. From his death I considered myself bound to provide for the half; but I could not do it but in this city. Almost all the payment which I made on the third instalment and all on the last I have made by discounting notes at the Bank and however hard a way of raising money this may be I would submit to much harder than fail in any obligation.

With respect to the sum yet due I have early earnestly and frequently pressed the brother and widow of Col. Ritchie with the importance and necessity in point of both interest and honour to provide for their part of the payments. I have shewn your letters particularly the last which I had the honour of receiving from you on this subject and expectations of money being paid have been held out to me. These however have yet produced nothing. Mrs Ritchie is now in Philadelphia. I have endeavored to press on her friends here (whose advice on this head might be considered as more disinterested than mine) the danger of further delinquency. I shall continue to do so and if I receive any positive information during my stay next week in this city I shall do myself the honour of informing you.[3]

This state is greatly agitated by the approach of the election of Governor. There is good reason to believe that Mr Ross will be chosen. But the whole spirit of party will be exerted against him and they speak also with confidence. This however would be the case were any other proper person the candidate: and I know none more proper or more likely to succeed than he. His success would be of important benefit to the state & the union. The Governor's influence by appointments to office, mischievous printers, and the great importation of Irish are the bane of the political (and of course moral) character of Pennsylvania: and its influence on the Union is great.[4] With most cordial wishes for your health and happiness and with the highest respect and esteem, I have the honour to be Sir Your most obedt Servt

Alexr Addison

ALS, DLC:GW.

1. As president of the Bank of Pennsylvania Samuel M. Fox informed GW on 6 July: "a payment of fifteen hundred & sixty eight dollars has been received this morning from Alexander Addison Esqr. on account of the bond of Col. Ritchie deposited here for collection. This sum is passed to your credit in Bank & of course remains subject to your drafts" (DLC:GW). GW recorded in Ledger C, 12, under the date 28 July 1799, receiving from Judge Addison $1,568.

2. For Addison's payment of $1,700 in July 1798, which was half the payment due on 1 June 1798 for the Millers Run property purchased by Matthew Ritchie in 1796, see Timothy Pickering to GW, 1 Sept. 1798 (first letter), n.1.

3. For Ritchie's initial purchase of GW's Millers Run tract and the payments made, see GW to Samuel M. Fox, 10 June 1799, n.1.

4. Former chief justice of Pennsylvania Thomas McKean, the Republican candidate, was elected governor of Pennsylvania in the election in 1799, when the Federalists also lost control of the state assembly.

To James McHenry

Private

My dear Sir,   Mount Vernon 7th July 1799

I have duly received your private letter of the 29th Ulto with its enclosures, and return your letters to and from General Hamilton.

In my letter to Genl Hamilton, which has been before you, you find I have fully expressed my opinion on the expediency—regarding circumstances—of promoting General Wilkinson to the Rank of Major General[1] and I am always willing to give publicity to any sentiment which I have expressed in this way, if circumstances should require or render it proper. But as the appointment of other Officers of high rank has been made, not only without my recommendation, but even without my knowledge, I cannot see the necessity (much less after the intimations which appear in your letter to General Hamilton respecting this Gentleman)[2] of my writing an official letter on this subject. Permit me, moreover to say, that it would seem as if, when doubts or difficulties present themselves, I am called upon to sanction the measure, and thereby take a responsibility upon myself; and in other cases, to which no blame may be attached, my opinions & inclinations are not consulted.

In giving my ideas in this manner I do not mean, my dear Sir, to express any disgust because I have not been consulted on every military appointment; but to show that there ought, in my opinion, to be consistency and uniformity observed in these matters.

I am very sorry that Colo. Howard and General Lloyd have declined making a Selection of persons for Officering the eventual army from Maryland. If my knowledge of characters in that State, was equal to theirs, or to yours, I should not hesitate a moment in undertaking what you request; but the fact is, my acquaintance there is very limited; and I find I have already undertaken more, in this State, than I shall be able to accomplish to my own satisfaction; from the difficulties which have been suggested in my former letters. Indeed, it would be concealment, not to declare, that I see no other mode of making the selection in so expanded a State as Virga (on the principle of distribution, according to population) than by having recourse to some such expedient as was suggested in a former letter of mine (in order to make the Presidents intentions generally known, and to give to all parts thereof an opportunity of making a tender of their military services)—or, by dividing the State into as many districts as there are Regiments to be raised in it, and in each District to make choice of the most eligable character for the command thereof—authorising him, either alone, or with the aid of his field Officers to select the company officers therefrom for consideration.[3]

The first of these modes you have objected to; and the second is not free from exceptions; but the fact is, that I have been so little in this State for the last twenty five years, as to be utterly unable to accomplish your views without the aid of others; and those who could assist me most, having only a Commune interest therein, do not (for the reasons which I presume operated on Messrs Howard & Lloyd) incline to commit themselves in such delicate business, where nothing they do is conclusive.

General Marshall (one of those whose aid I solicited) is gone to Kentucky; From General Lee, who discovered no promptness in the first instance, to give any assistance, I have not since heard a Syllable;[4] and with respect to Genl Morgan, his recommendations are confined to a very narrow circle;[5] I shall, notwithstandg, continue my endeavours to carry your request into effect, in this State, but can promise no favourable result from the present plan. With sincere esteem & regard—I am—My dear Sir Your Obedt and Affecte Servt

Go: Washington

ALS, MiU-C: Schoff Collection; ALS (letterpress copy), DLC:GW.

1. See GW to Alexander Hamilton, 25 June, and note 1 of that document.

2. McHenry's letter to Hamilton of 27 June is quoted in McHenry to GW, 29 June, n.2.

3. GW in effect had already adopted the latter approach. See for instance his letter of 12 May to John Marshall, Edward Carrington, and William Heth. The "former letter of mine" in which GW suggested another "expedient" is dated 13 May 1799.

4. See Henry Lee, Jr., to GW, 22 May. Lee wrote again on 11 July.

5. See Daniel Morgan to GW, 12 and 26 June.

To James McHenry

Sir,   Mount Vernon July 7th 1799

I have considered, with attention, the Rules adopted by the President of the U.S. relative to rank & promotion in the Army, which were enclosed in your letter of the 2d inst. wherein you request me to suggest any alterations which may appear proper, to make them more perfect. These Rules meet my full approbatn, and I see no inconvenience that can arise from the establishment of them unless it be in the following clause—"Provided always that Colonels who were deranged shall take rank of Lieutenant Colonels who served to the end of the War." You will recollect, that, before the close of the Revolutionary War, the title of Colonel was abolished in the American Army, to obviate some difficulties which arose in the exchange of prisoners, and that the title of Lieutenant Colonel Commandant was substituted in its place, to which rank was attached all the command, privileges and dignity which before appertained to that of Colonel. Now, may there not have been some persons at the close of the war, ranking as Lieutenant Colonels, who before held the Rank of Colonel, and who were older officers in that Rank than some who were deranged? If this should be the case difficulties may arise. You, having the dates of Commissions &c. to refer to, are better able to judge than I am, how far this may operate in the present case, and what attention it deserves. I therefore submit it to your considerations.[1] Agreeably to your request, I return the Rules which you forwarded to me, and I have the honor to be with due consideration Sir Yr Mo. Ob. St

Df, in Tobias Lear's hand, DLC:GW.

1. McHenry wrote to GW from the War Department in Philadelphia on 2 July: "If you find any thing to alter or propose which will make the enclosed Regulations more perspicuous or perfect, I wish you mention it, and return them as soon as possible" (DLC:GW). The copy of the "enclosed Regulations" that Lear made for GW reads: "The following Rules have been adopted by the President of the United States relative to Rank and Promotion in the Army.

Rank

"The Field Officers of the twelve Regiments of Infantry raised in pursuance of the Act of the 16th of July 1798 who served in the regular Army during the late war and continued therein to the end thereof shall take Rank of all others of the same Grade who were not in service or who were deranged in pursuance of any Resolution of Congress—their relative Rank with each other to be the same as at the end of the war. Those Officers who have been deranged in pursuance of any resolution of Congress to take Rank next after those who continued to the expiration of the war—their relative Rank with each other to be agreeably to their respective Grades and dates of Commission.

"Provided always that Colonels who were deranged shall take rank of Lieutenant Colonels who served to the end of the War—Lieutenant Colonels of Majors—Majors of Captains &ca. Officers who have served in the Army or Levies since the peace and have been disbanded to take rank next after the Officers deranged during the late War. Resignations shall preclude all claim to Rank. The Rank of those Officers who have not been in service shall be determined by the Commander in Chief.

Promotions

"The Captains and Subalterns in the Cavalry, Artillery and Infantry shall rise regimentally to the Rank of Major inclusive. Promotions from the Rank of Major to that of Lieut. Colonel shall be in the line of the Army—provided however that the said promotions in the Cavalry, Artillery and Infantry shall be confined to their respective lines. On a vacancy happening, the Senior Officer of the next inferior Grade in ordinary cases shall be considered as the most proper person to fill the same. But in cases of extraordinary Merit, Officers altho' not senior in Rank may be appointed to fill vacancies" (DLC:GW). On 3 Sept. McHenry sent another copy of these regulations to take effect on that date, with one alteration in what is here the second paragraph under "Rank": Inserted after the words "Provided always that Colonels" are the words "and Lieutenant Colonels Commandants."

Letter not found: to Daniel Marshal, 7 July 1799. In the docket of Daniel Marshal's letter to GW of 30 June, Lear wrote "acknowledged July 7:99." King V. Hostick advertised the ALS for sale in 1962 under the date of 5 July.

To William Roberts

Mr Roberts   Mount Vernon 8th July 1799

As you have agreed to ⟨come⟩ upon the terms I have mentioned ⟨in the letter to⟩ you.[1] Nothing therefore ⟨*illegible* to be said on that⟩ head. But as upon consideration of the Subject, I had rather you should ⟨come⟩ before my present Miller goes away ⟨*illegible*⟩ a good deal of flour in my Mill which requires judgment to preserve; ⟨*illegible* the⟩ Mill will require to ⟨*illegible*⟩ the present scarcity of Water; it would, if you could make it convenient to yourself, be agreeable to me, that you should be here before the 10th of August, the expiration of my present Millers Se⟨rvice, or⟩ even sooner than that, might ⟨*illegible*⟩ to me. Let me hear from you immediately upon receipt of this letter, ⟨and if you⟩ cannot come as soon as it is wished and point out if you can any mode for preserving my flour which is growing musty & Sour[2] with ⟨*illegible*⟩ I can accept, I wish you would ⟨*illegible*⟩ I am Your friend & ⟨*illegible*⟩

Go: Washington

P.S. If you have any thing to bring round there are Vessels frequently coming hither from Richmond. Colo. Gilpin I believe has one. Having erected a Distillery at my Mill a Well has been sunk for the use of it wch furnishes excellent water.

ALS (letterpress copy), NN: Washington Papers.

1. GW offered Roberts the job of miller at Mount Vernon on 17 June, and Roberts accepted on 21 June.

2. See Roberts's response of 12 July.

To Benjamin Stoddert

Sir,   Mount Vernon July 10th 1799

When I quitted the Chair of Government it was my full determination not to apply to the Executive in behalf of any person for an appointment, knowing the trouble and inconvenience which I must experience myself as well as give to othe[r]s without forming this resolution. In some instances I have, however, been obliged to depart from this rule, where, from particular connexions or circumstances I am called upon to be the channel of application in a way that I cannot refuse, without being thought unkind or uncivil.

But as few instances of this kind occur, I shall not have occasion to trouble you often in this way.

Inclosed is a letter from General Spotswood, expressing a wish to have one of his sons appointed a Midshipman in the Navy of the U.S.[1]—As I am unacquainted with the regulations established in your department with respect to appointments, I am not able to judge how far the request made by Genl Spotswood for his Son can be complied with. On this you will determine; and whatever answer you may think proper to give, I will thank you to transmit to me that I may forward it accordingly.

As I have no personal knowledge of the young man, altho. a relation of mine, I cannot say how far he may be qualified for the place which is asked. I have the honor to be with due consideration Sir, Yr mo. Ob. St

G. W——n

Df, in Tobias Lear's hand, DLC:GW.

1. Alexander Spotswood's letter asking GW to help secure for his son George an appointment as a midshipman in the U.S. navy has not been found, but see GW to Spotswood, 15 July, and Spotswood to GW, 25 July. Stoddert's response of 15 July appears in note 2 of GW's letter to Spotswood of that date.

From William Roberts

Sir   Petersburgh 12th July 1799

I am Very Sorry to hare you have had the Misfortune to have your flour Damnefied As you Rite Me it is[1]—Boath Muste & Sower. then thare is but One way to preserve it, tharefore to keep it from Giting wors—Order your prasent Miller to Start it Amedeately in the Meal Loft And Take A packt Barrel of flour And have it well Cleand to Role it over all the Lumps To Mash tham fine—then Sift it thorough a Sand Siv Or A Bean Siv to Git out all the Lumps then hist Up Bran And Mix it to the Temper of Ground Meal—that will Giv it Are by Turning it Morning & Evening Twise or three Times A Day it will Gro No wors Till I Can Come Up Which will be as Soon As I Reseve your Letter And Settle My Affares before Mr Hay & Captn Mcnemara—which will be in the Beginning of August—Now if I Could Git So Far in your favour As to wright to my atturney Mr George Hay & Captn Macnemara My atturney And Agent To push on Matters & Spare Not Money in Reson So As to Recover My property out of the hands of Two Vile

Men in this Town Boath of infamaous Caracters ⟨I⟩ Would Leve the whole affare in the hands of Captn Macnemara & Mr George Hay My atturney—Sir—I think a Letter from your Excellency to those Two Gentlemen would be of Infinet Servis to Me in Giting My property out of thare hands.[2]

Sir—Maneg the flour as I have Derected & it will Gro No Wors till I Can Come Up which will be as Soon as I Receiv your Letter— For your Righting for Me has already put Me More in favour with Mr Hay & Captn Macnemara then Before—Now Sir to Acquint with My Cretekel Setuation I think it My Duty So to Doe And Should be Glad to Come at the Time your preasent Millers Time Expiers But Last fall in the month of October & Novr I was Taken Vary ill & had Like to a Lost my Life, while in My Destress a Villen who Came to Se Me And Not Sent for Nither—in pertence of frindship And has Got a frind of his to Draw a Counter fit Deed for my Place but I have a witness Now in Town that was By in all my Destress which will over set the Villens Intent—Next August Cort which Comes on the first Monday in the Month if youd by So Kind as to Rite to Loyer Hay in My behalf it would be More in My favour then all the fee I Can Be Able to Giv him—Sir I have the first Loyer in Petersburgh On My Side—And I hope Matters will Go on well after I Receiv Your Letter.[3] From Sir your Sencere frind And Humble Servt

W:M. Roberts

ALS, DLC:GW.

1. GW wrote Roberts on 8 July.

2. George Hay (1765–1830) was a successful lawyer in Petersburg. As U.S. attorney for Virginia he in 1808 prosecuted Aaron Burr for treason. Hay later became U.S. district judge for Eastern Virginia. McNamara has not been identified.

3. GW wrote Roberts on 17 July refusing to intervene in Roberts's affairs in Petersburg.

Letter not found: from Jeremiah Olney, 13 July 1799. On 4 Aug. GW wrote Olney: "Your favor of the 13th Ulto . . . has been duly received."

From William Augustine Washington

My Dr Sir   Haywood July 13th 1799

Judge Washington intending to Mount Vernon I imbrace the opportunity of acknowledging rect of your Letter of the 10th Ulto with Mr Andersons, incl⟨os⟩ing the Acct between us for Corn; which is very accurate, & satisfactory—On the 15th June I drew on you in favr of Walker Roe & Co. for £⟨*illegible*⟩ payable 60 days after sight,[1] and yesterday I d⟨rew⟩ in favr of Robt Patton for £100 pay 30 days after sight;[2] I hope it will be perfectly convenient to y⟨ou⟩ to pay these drafts at the time they become d⟨ue⟩ nothing but the strongest necessity could have compelled me to have drawn on you, after ⟨your⟩ mentioning your disappointments, & pressing ⟨*mutilated*⟩ for money—Flood has not as yet called on me for a draft for his money; its possable he may have applyed person-ally, without an order from me, if he should do so you will be pleased to settle with him, I have left in your hands after my two drafts £8.7.8 which I wish to get Whiskey for my workmen, and if I can get ⟨a⟩ Vessel to call for it will thank you to send me.

If I continue to enjoy my health its my intention, with Mrs Wash-ington to Visit you in September, if you should be at home at that time, It is a visit I have long intended and wished for, but the mis-fortunes in my family ⟨and⟩ my own indisposition has prevented it.[3] Mrs Washington unites with me in our best respects to you and Mrs Washington wishing you health and happiness, conclud⟨es⟩ Your Affectionate Nephew

Wm Augt. Washington

ALS, PWacD. The right margin of the page is frayed. On the cover: "Hond by Judge [Bushrod] Washington."

1. On 24 June the Alexandria merchant William Wilson wrote to GW: "The inclosed draft was transmitted to me from Fredericksburgh, and I take the liberty of Sending it for Acceptance. Be pleased to return it by the bearer" (DLC:GW). William Augustine Washington's draft dated at Haywood, 15 June, reads: "At Sixty days sight be pleased to pay to Messrs Walter Roe & Co. on Order Five Hundred Dollars and place the same to the Acct of sir Your Most Ob. Sert Wm Augt. Washington" (owned [1990] by Nicholas and Karlene Carolides, Clearwater, Fla.). Upon receipt of Wilson's letter GW wrote in his Day Book, dated 24 June: "Charge Colo. Wm Auge Washington with his draught on me (dated the 15th instt) in favr of Messrs Walter Roe & Co. at 60 days sight and in the hands of Willm Wilson accepted by me for $500." In a missing letter of 27 Aug. the firm of Thompson & Veitch called for the payment of William Augustine Washington's draft, and on 30 Aug. GW wrote Thompson & Veitch that he was enclosing "a check on the Bank of Alexandria, in discharge of my acceptance of William Auge Washington's draught on me for $500 in favor of Messrs Waltr Roe & Co." GW also noted this in Ledger C, 54. Thompson & Veitch acknowledged the receipt of the check on the same day. Bushrod Washington arrived at Mount Vernon on 17 July (*Diaries*, 6:357).

2. On 30 July GW wrote in his Day Book: "Accepted, this day, the Draught of

Colo. Wm Auge Washington, in favor of Mr Robt Patton, in the hands of Mr Jas
Patton, payable at 30 days sight—for—£100." On 4 Sept. James Patton, a merchant in Alexandria since 1791, wrote from Alexandria: "Inclosed you'll be
pleased to receive your acceptce of Wm Augustine Washington's dft due the 1st
instt for One Hundred pounds current money. The payment you can order by a
check on the Bank to me, or in any other manner convenient, & agreeable to
yourself. It was my intention to have taken a ride down to Mount Vernon, when
this dft became due—which would have been combining a little Business with
much pleasure. this intention could not however be fulfilled without injury to my
present engagements" (DLC:GW). Patton had dined at Mount Vernon on 30 July
(*Diaries*, 6:358). GW's entry for 5 Sept. in his Day Book reads: "By check on the
Bank of Alexa. in favr of Patton & Dykes in discharge of Wm Auge Washington's
draught in favr of Robt Patton for £100—33334/100."

3. GW does not refer in the months before his death in December to any visit
to Mount Vernon by William Augustine Washington with his bride.

To Samuel Mickle Fox

Sir,   Mount Vernon 14th July 1799

In due course of the Mails, I have been honoured by the receipt
of your favours of the 2d and 6th instant. and thank you for the
trouble you have taken in reminding Mrs Ritchie of my demand
upon her deceased husbands Estate, and for forwarding my letter
to the Honble Jas Ross.

If, from the money paid into the Bank of Pennsylvania by Judge
Addison, on my A/c, Fifteen hundred dollars could be transfered
to the Bank of Alexandria, or that of Columbia; or, if neither of
these can be done—then in a secure manner in Southern notes,
it would accomodate me, greatly.[1]

The residue of the $1568 deposited by Judge Addison, & the
$250 placed to the a/c of Mr Ross, as my Agent, may remain for
further appropriation, expecting to have a call for it in the City of
Philadelphia.[2] With respectful esteem—I am Sir Your Most Obedt
& Obliged H. Ser⟨vt⟩

                                              Go: Washington

ALS, PHi: Logan-Fisher-Fox Collection.
1. For Alexander Addison's payment, see Addison to GW, 6 July, and note 1 of
that document. For the action Fox took in response to this request, see Fox to
GW, 20 July.
2. For the deposit of two hundred and fifty dollars, see GW to Fox, 10 June,
n.2, and 26 June, n.2.

To James McAlpin

Sir,   Mount Vernon July 14th 1799

Your letters of the 24th & 27th Ulto have come duly to hand;[1] and, persuaded as I am that, you have used your best endeavours to furnish my uniform Coat, agreeably to the regulations of the War department, I thank you for your exertions; although they have failed of the desired effect.

Some years ago (while the Governmt was in New York) I had a cloke well embroidered there (at the instance of a Mr Bahr, who was then my Taylor)—possibly, the same person, or some other, might be found there still, to do it, if Mr Bahr is living & was applied to.[2]

If a failure takes place there also, and the coat is not already embarked for Europe, let it remain at present, and inform me of the state of, and what can be done with it. I am Sir Your Very Hble Servant

Go: Washington

ALS, ViMtV.

1. McAlpin's letter of 24 June is printed in note 3 to GW's letter to James McHenry of 7 June.

2. Christian Baehr made livery for GW's servants when GW was serving as president in New York. See Household Accounts, 3, 40 (CtY).

To James McHenry

Private

My dear Sir,   Mount Vernon 14th July 1799

After reading, & putting a wafer into the enclosed letter, be so kind as to send it as directed.[1]

The young Cornet (in my family) is anxious to receive his Military equipments. Daily, fruitless enquiries are made of me to know when they may be expected. Perhaps if you were to jog Mr Francis, the *Purveyor*, the sooner they might be *Purveyed*, and the young Gentleman gratified.

I wish them to be handsome, and proper for an Officer, but not expensive. In my last on this subject, I requested that the Sword might be Silver mounted—but any other Mount, such as the Officers of Cavalry use, would answer just as well.[2] With esteem and regard—I am always Your Affecte Humble Servant

Go: Washington

ALS, DLC:GW.

    1. This may be GW's letter of this date to James McAlpin.

    2. See GW to McHenry, 7 June, n.1.

To Timothy Pickering

Private

Dear Sir,   Mount Vernon July 14th 1799

I thank you for the enclosure in your letter of the 1st instant, and for forwarding my letters to England, under cover to Mr King.

Since the receipt of the above, General Pinckney has given me the whole of Major Mountf[l]orence's letter to him.[1]

Surely La Fayette will not come here on such an errand, and under such circumstances as are mentioned in that letter. And yet—I believe he will, if the thing is proposed to him! although in a very long letter written to him more than six mths ago, in answer to many of his, and before such a measure was even conjectured, I gave it as my decided opinion that a visit from him to the U. States in the present political agitation of our Affairs, would be ineligable on his *own* account, as well as for other considerations of weight. But he has a blind side, not difficult to assail. What has been done, cannot be undone. to make the best of it, is all that remains to do. Yrs always & sincerely

Go: Washington

ALS, MHi: Pickering Papers. The letter is docketed "recd & answer⟨ed the⟩ 18th."

    1. GW is referring to Charles Cotesworth Pinckney's letter of 25 June and its enclosure.

To William Thornton

Dear Sir   Mount Vernon 14th July 1799

Be so good as to learn from Mr Blagden, and inform me, at what time—and what sum, the next advance must be, that I may be making arrangements therefor.

If nothing happens more than I am aware of at present, I shall be in George Town on the first Monday in next Month (August the 5th) at the annual Meeting of the Pot[oma]c Compy and should be glad to know previously thereto, when, and what the requirement of Mr Blagden will be.[1]

The generally received opinion is, that my houses in the City are engaged by Mr Francis, and I have no objection to Mr Francis becoming the occupier of them; but the matter is quite loose yet, between us; and ought to be fixed; otherwise the idea of their being engaged, will prevent offers from others; and I may be compelled to accept of such Rent as he shall think proper to offer when their wants are supplied.

Viewing the matter in this light, it is expedient that I should fix on a certain percentage on the cost of this property, which can be ascertained to a fraction, and know, in time whether he will give it as a Rent.

I am not disposed to fix this at an unreasonable rate; on the contrary, I had rather be *under*, than *over* a just standard: but I must not lose, because I do not mean to extort. In a word, I wish to know what others, who are building in the vicinity of the Capital (on the principle which has governed me—namely—the accomodation of Congress—) mean to ask as an interest on their expenditures; and if it should fall in your way to make this enquiry I would thank you for the result, as it will enable me to speak decisively to Mr Francis.[2] with esteem & regard—I remain Dear Sir Your Most Obedt & Obliged Humble Servant

Go: Washington

ALS, DLC: Thornton Papers.

1. See Thornton to GW, 19 July.

2. For GW's preliminary negotiations with the Philadelphia tavernkeeper John Francis regarding the future rental of the pair of houses that GW was planning to erect on Capitol Hill in Washington, see Francis to GW, 15 Sept. 1798, and note 1 of that document. After Thornton advised GW on 19 July 1799 about what he should charge for rental of the houses, GW reentered negotiations with Francis on 14 Aug., but when GW spelled out his terms on 25 Aug., Francis chose to let the matter drop. See also Francis to GW, 17 Aug., and GW to John Avery, 25 Sept., and note 3 of that document. Instead of moving to Washington, Francis remained in Philadelphia, and in 1800 converted the Robert Morris house into a hotel. This was where GW had lived as president and where John Adams now resided. Francis ran the place for two years as the Union Hotel (*Pa. Mag.*, 46:169).

To Benjamin Dulany

Sir,   Mount Vernon 15th July 1799

As I grow no Tobacco, and probably never shall, I have it in contemplation to make some material changes in the œconomy of my Farms.

To accomplish this object, a reduction of the present force on them is necessary; of course, the means by which it is to be effected, must have undergone consideration.

Presuming then that it might be agreeable to Mrs French—or to you—to whom they will ultimately revert, I am induced by a sense of propriety & respect; and from a persuasion that every humane owner of that species of property would rather have it in his own keeping, than suffer it to be in the possession of others, to offer you all the Negroes I hold, belonging to that Estate.[1]

And as an evidence of my disposition to act fairly, & liberally, in the business; the whole of them, old, middle aged and young, shall be produced to three disinterested and judicious men—one to be chosen by Mrs French or yourself, one by me, and the third by those two. The judgment of whom (after comparing the old with the young—and the chances of increase and decrease) shall be conclusive as to the annuity which is to be allowed me, or mine, for and during the term for which they, at present, stand engaged.

That you may be enabled to form an opinion of their usefulness, from the kind of Negroes I am making you an offer of, I enclose a list of them, with remarks, which and their ages, I believe to be accurate; and the reason for giving them at this season of the year, is, that if either Mrs French or yourself is disposed to accede to the offer, you may have time to make arrangements accordingly.[2]

For the same reason, an answer, so soon as you can conveniently decide upon the measure, would be very agreeable.[3] Sir—Your Most Obedt Hble Servt

                                        Go: Washington

ALS (letterpress copy), NN: Washington Papers. GW changed the wording of the letterpress copy in two instances, presumably reflecting changes that he made in the original letter. In the second paragraph he substituted "it is" for one or more obliterated words, and near the end of the fourth paragraph he changed the phrase, "a fixed annuity," to read, "the annuity."

1. In October 1786, after years of negotiation, GW secured from Penelope Manley French title to two tracts on Dogue Run at Mount Vernon. He at the same

time rented from Mrs. French the slaves who worked this land, with the stipula-
tion that they not be removed from Fairfax County. See particularly Charles Lee
to GW, 13 Sept. 1786, and GW to William Triplett, 25 Sept. 1786, and notes to
both documents.

2. At about this time, presumably in June, GW made a listing of all the slaves
at Mount Vernon. The roll of slaves rented from Mrs. French which GW enclosed
in this letter is almost identical to that which he made for his complete listing,
printed at the end of this volume. In the list enclosed in this letter, however, he
has sometimes expanded the information under "Remarks." Unfortunately, a
large portion of this letterpress copy is illegible.

3. Dulany replied from Alexandria on 17 July: "I recd your Letter dated the
15 Instant—Mrs French being in George Town, it is out of my power to answer it
as I coud wish—As soon as I have an opportunity of seeing her, I will make it a
point of answering the contents" (DLC:GW).

To Alexander Spotswood

Dear Sir,   Mount Vernon 15th July 1799

Your wishes, respecting your Son George, I have communicated to the Secretary of the Navy;[1] although it is contrary to a
determination I had entered into (when I left the Chair of Government) not to be the medium through which applications for appointments should be made; and from which I have not (before)
deviated, except in the Military line, since it has been made my
duty, consequent of my own appointment, to present them.

If the Secretary of the Navy should return any answer to my letter, you will be informed of the purport of it.[2] I must question,
however, whether your proposition will comport with the rules of
the Navy Department. In a word, I should not suppose that any
persons will be received as Midshipmen, until they enter the ship,
and perform the duties. The contrary (as I know the applications
are numerous) would carry with it an appearance of favoritism
which I should think, our government ⟨would⟩ not wish to be
charged with.

If in the Military line, any characters should present themselves
to you ⟨which are right⟩ly deserving of *Regimental* appointments, I
shall be obliged to you for sending in their names to me; as the Secretary of War has requested me ⟨to be⟩ provided with these, in case
the President, ⟨in⟩ the recess of Congress, shd ⟨think it⟩ expedient
to raise the eventual ⟨Army of⟩ twenty four Regiments. Field &
⟨Artillery⟩ Officers for four Regiments, ⟨*illegible*⟩ated through this

State, as near⟨ly as⟩ may be to the population of the dif⟨ferent⟩ parts, will be required, if this measure should take place.[3]

I would thank you for asking, (when an opportunity presents itself) the Executor or person who has the keeping ⟨of the⟩ late Mr James Mercer's Papers, for ⟨a con⟩veyance from "George & James Mercer Esqrs., & Messrs Lindo [&] Cozenove to me" ⟨the⟩ land purchased of them on four Mile run in this County. Having occasion to overhaul my land Papers lately this conveyance was ⟨missing *illegible*;⟩ but the following Memo ⟨*illegible*⟩ (that is the one just mentioned was sent March 15th 1787 to ⟨*illegible*⟩ to draw a Deed of ⟨conveyance *illegible*⟩.

This confirming ⟨*illegible*⟩ properly executed & recorded ⟨*illegible*⟩ other could not have been ⟨*illegible*⟩ as it is not to be found among my Papers. It is useless to ⟨any *illegible*⟩ and is no otherwise essential ⟨*illegible*⟩ recorded) than in case of accident to the records; and for the ⟨*illegible*⟩ of having my title ⟨*illegible*⟩ possession, that reco⟨rding⟩ may ⟨*illegible*⟩ them more easily.[4]

All here are well, and unite in best regards to yourself ⟨*illegible*⟩ & the family, with Dear Sir, Your Most Obedient Affecte Hble Servt

Go: Washington

ALS (letterpress copy), NN: Washington Papers.

1. Spotswood's letter in which he asked GW's aid in securing a midshipman's appointment in the U.S. navy for his son George has not been found, but see GW to Benjamin Stoddert, 10 July.

2. Secretary of the Navy Benjamin Stoddert wrote GW from Philadelphia on this date: "The President being extremely desirous to introduce into our Navy, as many young Gentlemen of Character & Education, as possible, for the sake of insuring a sufficient number of able officers hereafter—and your mentioning his name, being a sufficient recommendation of the Son of Genl Spotswood, I do myself the honor to enclose a warrant for that Young Gentleman—and a letter complying with the terms prescribed by his Father" (DLC:GW). GW informed Spotswood of Stoddert's actions in a brief and largely illegible letter of 21 July, in which he enclosed a letter from Stoddert to young George Spotswood with his commission and the prescribed oath enclosed. See Spotswood to GW, 25 July. The postscript of GW's letter to Spotswood of 21 July, which is the only even partially legible portion of the letter, reads: "P.S. I advise your Son George to take a copy of the Oath that he may never forget what he is bound ⟨by⟩ so ⟨*illegible*⟩" (letterpress copy, NN: Washington Papers).

3. See James McHenry to GW, 2 May 1799, n.1.

4. For GW's efforts at this time to clear his title to the Four Mile Run tract, see GW to Ludwell Lee, 26 April 1799, n.2. See also Spotswood to GW, 25 July 1799.

To William Roberts

Mr Roberts   Mount Vernon 17th July 1799

Your letter of the 12th instant is received, and I am obliged to you for the advice respecting the management of the flour I had on hand; which however, is less necessary now, as I have disposed of it all.

I should be glad to render you any consistent Service in my power, but must decline writing to the Gentleman you have mentioned, on the subject proposed; first, because I am entirely unacquainted with the circumstances attending your ⟨disputed⟩ property; and secondly, because I have not the honor to be acquainted with Mr Hay or Captn McNamara, who you inform me are employed to defend that property.

Gentlemen of the character you (no doubt deservedly) give Mr Hay & Captn McNamara, can stand in no need of a stimula from me to rescue your property from a fraudulent conveyance, & thereby enable you to come to me the sooner. I wish you well & ⟨am your⟩ friend

Go: Washington

ALS (letterpress copy), NN: Washington Papers.

To Thomas Peter

Dear Sir,   Mount Vernon 18th July 1799

Enclosed are Notes for two hogsheads of Tobacco—as below—Nanjemoy Warehouse, paid me for Rent.[1] If you can sell them in George Town it would oblige me; either for Cash, or on a moderate credit. If you cannot, they may be returned, or retained until I come up to the meeting of the Potomac Company the first Monday (5th day) of next Month in George Town.

I earnestly hope that this meeting will be full, & effectual; for, in my opinion it has become indispensable. All here are well, & unite with me in best wishes for you and yours. I am—Dear Sir Yr Obedt & Affe. Servt

Go: Washington

ALS, ViMtV; ALS (letterpress copy), NN: Washington Papers. GW incorrectly endorsed the letterpress copy 17 July.

1. An entry for 30 June in GW's Ledger C reads: "Recd from George Dunning-ton thro. the hds of Doctr [Daniel] Jenifer on a/c of Rent for the place he lives on—2 Hhds Tobo as below.

Mark	No.	Gross	Tare	Net	
GD	249	1136	96	1040	
	250	1122	100	1022	dated June 21st 1799
					Will. Adams—Inspect."

GW also inserted the same chart at the end of this letter to Peter. George Dunnington was one of GW's tenants in Charles County, Maryland.

From Timothy Pickering

(private)
Sir,   Philadelphia July 18, 1799.

I am honoured with your letter of the 14th. La Fayette will not come to America *as a minister*: On the 13th instant I received a private letter from Mr Murray dated the 16th of April, inclosing one from *Pichon*, dated the 12th, written with Talleyrand's privity, and indeed by his order. Pichon is eager to be the first to an-nounce to Murray the message of the President nominating him to be the envoy to negociate with France: and expresses the "im-patience with which Talleyrand waits for the letter in which he hopes Mr Murray will not delay to demand of him the passports for Paris."

Mr Murray, apparently well pleased with the thing, says he shall write Pichon a polite answer; but wait instructions from his own government: and should he have occasion to write for passports, will address himself to Talleyrand alone.

Talleyrand also desired Pichon "to assure Mr Murray of the eagerness which he personally feels to see him at Paris." and upon the whole, Pichon "affirms his persuasion, . . . from the point of view in which he (Murray) is known to Talleyrand, of the facility with which he will be listened to on the essential points."[1]

It is on this information, that I have said La Fayette will not come to the U. States as a minister: We have *anticipated the wishes of the French Government*, by nominating an Envoy—& these Envoys, to present themselves at the Luxemburg. Or if that Government should not wait the arrival of our Envoys, it will be because disas-ters press upon them too rapidly and too heavily to hazard any delay.

(Confidential) But whether envoys go or come, I expect no treaty—unless the French Government stands ready to do us *compleat justice. We shall not again waive any of our rights, or postpone their claim and admission.* This has been *resolved.* I am very respectfully, Sir, your most obt Servt

Timothy Pickering

ALS, DLC:GW; ALS (letterpress copy), MHi: Pickering Papers.

1. A copy of the letter to William Vans Murray from Louis Amédée Pichon, Talleyrand's agent in Holland, dated 12 April 1799, is in MHi: Pickering Papers. In his covering letter to Pickering of 13 April 1799, Murray reported that he had seen an announcement in the newspaper of the nomination of himself, Oliver Ellsworth, and Patrick Henry to be U.S. envoys to France and expressed his pleasure at the news (Ford, "Murray-Adams Letters," 538).

From William Thornton

Dear Sir   City of Washington July 19th 1799.

I was honored, in due Course of post, with your Favour of the 14th to which I should have replied sooner, but was desirous of knowing, from as many quarters as I could, the probable rent of Houses to be built for the accommodation of Congress. The general Idea of renting Houses in America is, to charge 10 ℔ Ct on the Expenditures, if these are made with Economy; for Taxes are high; the abuse of Houses & the consequent Repairs demand Consideration; and the Interest on Stock of all kinds being great, little Inducement to build can be offered under that ℔ Centage; but in Cities where the Congress has been generally held there are so many Houses that accommodations have generally not been wanting, and House-rent consequently cheaper than the ratio of the value of property. If it were to be much higher here than in other places, the Causes would be less considered than the Fact, and murmurs would arise; but your Idea of not losing because you do not mean to extort, I think too just to be objected to by any one. Some, with whom I have conversed, have thought that 7½ ℔ Cent, besides Taxes & Insurance, would not be deem'd by any as unreasonable, and I should be glad if the Proprietors who are building, were to make some Agreement which they would not exceed. Thus they would not lose, and it would gratify every Tenant to find that as there were no Distinctions there would be also no Impositions. If Mr Francis were to hesitate to give such a rent (for Instance 7½ ℔ Centum, & Insurance &c. which would bring it to nearly 10) as you might conclude to be reasonable, and if I might presume to advise, I would rather preserve them unrented, & keep them for sale, fixing a price on them together or separately; and I have no Doubt you could sell them for nine or ten thousand Dollars each, and if you were inclined to lay out the proceeds again in building other Houses this might be repeated to your Advantage, without any trouble, with perfect safety from risk, & to the great improvement of the City. I am induced to think the Houses would sell very well, because their Situation is uncommonly fine, and the Exterior of the Houses is calculated to attract notice. Many Gentlemen of Fortune will visit the City and be suddenly inclined to fix here. They will find your Houses perfectly suitable, being not only commodious but elegant. Mr Francis has applied to me for the Lot adjoining yours, but finding he was disposed to erect back Buildings, to communicate with your Houses, I refused to name any price, and told him I could not be so unmindful of the Advantages with which you have so kindly favoured me, as to permit any House to be built that did not correspond with those you are erecting, and should stipulate if I did not build myself, that such Houses should be built. I presume his application to me was under an impression that he should rent your Houses, but he has observed that they want more Lodging Rooms. You have done all in your power to render them convenient for a lodging-house without absolutely injuring the Tenements, and this I observed to him.[1] I saw Mr Blagdin, and made the enquiry you desired. He says he shall have occasion for a thousand Dollars when you do us the honor of a visit. I asked if he could not wait a little longer, but he said he was four hundred Doll[ar]s now in advance, and could not possibly wait longer, but that he should not have occasion for more, for some time after this payment.[2]

As the only two Families which have the honor of your alliance are both out of the City at present, permit me to solicit the honor & happiness of your Company during your Stay in the City at the time of your intended visit, and when you bring your Lady hither we should also be rendered very happy by the honor of her Company.[3] I am, dear Sir, with the greatest respect, and affectionate regard, your much obliged & obedt Friend

William Thornton

ALS, DLC:GW.

1. For GW's negotiations with John Francis regarding the rental of his pair of houses abuilding near the new Capitol, see GW to Thornton, 14 July, n.2.

2. For the payment to George Blagdin, see GW to Thornton, 1 Aug., n.1.

3. GW declined Thornton's invitation on 1 Aug., and after attending the meeting of the Potomac River Company he spent the night of 5 Aug. at the house of Thomas Law in Washington (see *Diaries*, 6:359).

From Samuel Mickle Fox

Sir   Bank of Pennsylvania [Philadelphia] July 20th 1799

Your letter of the 14 Inst. was received in due time, but as it was not in my power to transmit you a draft upon either the Bank of Alexandria or Columbia, I have been under the necessity of delaying a compliance with your directions untill the present opportunity occurred—I now enclose fifteen hundred dollars in Southern notes & shall confide this letter to Mr Charles Jolly, one of the Directors of this Institution, who will have the honor of delivering it to you.[1]

Mrs Ritchie sent me word a few days since that she was going to Washington County in order to expedite the payment of the ballance due you from her late Husband's Estate. I have not heard from Mr Shreve.[2] With sincere respect I am Sir Your obedient Servant

Sam. M. Fox
P.B.P.

ALS, DLC:GW.

1. GW wrote Fox on 28 July: "Sir, By the hands of Mr [Charles] Jolly, I have had the honor to receive your favor of the 20th instant; and fifteen hundred dollars which you had the goodness to send, and he to bring, in Southern Notes, on account of money deposited in the Bank of Pennsylvania for my use, by Judge [Alexander] Addison—in part payment of the deceased Matthew Ritchies Bond. For your kind attention to this business, I pray you to accept the best thanks of Sir Your Most Obedt and Obliged Hble Servant Go: Washington" (ALS, PHi: Logan-Fisher-Fox Collection; letterpress copy, NN: Washington Papers).

On 30 July GW wrote Charles Jolly: "Sir I am quite ashamed of the error I committed, in passing my receipt to you for fifteen, instead of fifteen hundred dollars which you had the kindness to be the bearer of from the Bank of Pennsylvania for my use.

"The notes of Columbia (the greater part) being for small sums it required some time to get at the amount of them: this circumstance, writing to Mr Fox, and fear that I was detaining you, as you were under engagement to dine in

Alexandria occasioned hurry, and the consequent mistake. I hope I was more correct in my acknowledgment to the President of the Bank of Pennsylvania. It was my intention to be so in both cases. I am Sir—Yr most obedt Hble Ser. G. Washington" (copy, Wv-Ar).

2. See GW to James Ross, 24 July.

Letter not found: to Alexander Spotswood, 20 July 1799. On 25 July Spotswood wrote GW acknowledging receipt of a letter from GW of the "20 Inst."

To Charles Carroll (of Carrollton)

Dear Sir   Mount Vernon July 21st 1799

Having received a printed letter myself, from the President & Directors of the Potomack Company dated the 2d instant the presumption is, that it is a circular Address to the Stockholders: and much indeed is it to be wished that *all of them* would attend in *person*, rather than by *substitution*.[1]

Greatly is it to be regretted that an Undertaking productive of— or rather promising such immense advantages to the States of Virginia & Maryland particularly the latter; and of such pecuniary emoluments to the Proprietors; should be suffered to progress so limpingly, as this work has done for some years back.

If this Navigation was completed and it is susceptible of being so in a short time; and the Shenandoah opened which is a work neither difficult or expensive and will as certainly follow the other as Night follows day, being suspended only thereby, I wo[ul]d predict, without fear of having my judgment arraigned by the result, that it wd be found one of (if not) the most productive funds (with the least risk to the Stockholders) of any Legalised Institution in the United States.

I speak within bounds, when I give it as my decided opinion, that it cannot fall short of 50 prCt pr Ann. The best credence I can adduce of my thorough conviction of this fact, is, that if I had the means, and was anxious to provide for those who may step into my Shoes, when I go hence, I would not hesitate a moment to complete the work at my own expence receiving proportionate Tolls.

It might be as unjust as improper, to censure the conduct of the Directors, or any of them, but if the means can be obtained I shall declare for having the residue of the Work executed by Contract (under the Inspection of the Directors)—fixing the sum, and stipulating the time to be employed thereon.[2]

I propose to be at the Genl Meeting of the Co. at George Town the 5th of next month, & should be happy to find you there,[3] being with much esteem Dear Sir—Your Most Obedt Hble Servt

Go: Washington

ALS (letterpress copy), NN: Washington Papers.

1. The printed circular letter from the president and directors of the Potomac River Company, a copy of which is in DLC:GW, is dated 2 July, from Great Falls on the Potomac. The letter was signed by James Keith as president of the company and by John Mason, Josias Clapham, Isaac McPherson, and Daniel Carroll of Duddington as directors. It reads: "Sir ENTRUSTED as we are, with the interests of the Potomack Company, we deem it a duty incumbent on us, at this time, to give you, as a Stockholder, as general a view of those interests as the short compass of a letter will admit of. It is known to you, that the Capital of the Company, at first, consisted of five hundred shares of the value of one hundred pounds sterling each; since which an additional hundred has been created by the Stockholders, rated at one hundred and thirty pounds sterling, the whole of which, except some inconsiderable balances owing by insolvent characters, has been collected. These sums have been expended in improving the navigation of the River from George's Creek, twenty-eight miles above Fort Cumberland, and two hundred and eighteen above tide water, into tide water; which, at this time, is in such a state, that at certain seasons, boats loaded with an hundred barrels of flour and upwards, can safely navigate that whole extent, except five hundred feet at the Great Falls. The difficulty and expence have proved much greater than at first contemplated: At Shenandoah and Seneca Falls, extensive Canals have been formed, by which boats are enabled to avoid the rocks and sudden descents in the bed of the river; at the great and Little Falls, similar canals have been constructed—but at those places, it has been found that Locks were indispensable: at the Little Falls, three have been made, through which, boats from the foot of the great Falls pass with the greatest ease and safety into tide water: at the Great Falls one Lock has been formed—four more are requisite, the seat of one of those is nearly excavated; to aid the intercourse till the work is compleated, at this place, a machine is constructed to pass articles from the waters above, to the waters below, which is found to answer extremely well; but the experience of two years has convinced us, that so long as any obstacle remains to a free passage into tide water, the navigation will not prove so serviceable to the public, or beneficial to the proprietors, as has been generally expected and now certainly known it will prove to be, when those are wholly removed. Independent of those four principal Falls, comprizing altogether two hundred and twenty four feet nine inches, there is, from the head of the Shenandoah Falls, fifty five miles above tide water, to George's Creek, a continued succession of smaller Falls and Ripples, forming in the aggregate a fall of eight hundred and seventy four feet four inches, these have been so far removed and improved upon, that boats safely pass them. In the

execution of these works, the whole stock of the Company has been expended, except twenty-nine shares.

"From the best and most accurate estimates which have been formed, it is supposed that the cost of the remaining work at the Great Falls will not exceed sixty thousand dollars, and that it may be effected in the course of twelve months from the time funds are provided. Various expedients have been recommended by the stock holders to the Board of Directors to procure money by. They have all been tried without producing the effect, only the small sum of four thousand two hundred and eighty one dollars and eighty six cents has as yet been obtained, this sum was partly applied in the discharge of some debts contracted in the construction of the lock at the Great Falls, the residue in the repair of breaches made in certain parts of the extensive works. Other debts contracted in the course of the work still remain unsatisfied. The works, unless properly finished and regularly inspected, will go to decay, and may prove nearly as expensive in the repair as the first formation. Having had recourse to every measure suggested to raise money by, without effect, fully informed of the heavy advances made by the stockholders; seeing those advances wholly unproductive, and knowing that they will remain so until the work is fully executed, (the absolute necessity of doing this must be apparent to every person interested) the Board of Directors, to raise the necessary funds for that purpose, take the liberty of suggesting the only measure, which to them, seems to hold out a prospect of success, that is for the stockholders to make a further advance upon each share of the stock, subject to the same regulations the original subscriptions were, one hundred dollars upon each share will raise the sum supposed sufficient for the purpose. As this advance must be a voluntary act, the assent of each stockholder must be obtained, and acts of the legislatures procured to carry the same into effect. Should a considerable majority of the stockholders approve of the measure, and others refuse to accede to it, provision will be applied for and no doubt granted by the legislatures, to enable those stockholders, making additional advances, to draw from the tolls in proportion to those advances. This provision will be made before any of the advance agreed upon will be called for. It is requested that you will communicate your sentiments upon this proposition so as to be laid before the stockholders at their annual meeting, to be held at the Union Tavern in Georgetown, on the first Monday in August next, also that you give your personal attendance at that time, if convenient, if not, that you, without fail, appoint a proxy to represent you, with full power to act upon this proposition. Your sentiments, if not personally delivered may be communicated either by your proxy, or by yourself to Mr. William Hartshorne, treasurer of the company."

2. At its meeting in Georgetown on 5 Aug., which GW attended, the Potomac River Company "determined that for the purpose of compleating the Navigation of the Potomak River, it would be expedient that each Share held in the said Company should pay an additional Sum of at least One hundred Dollars." The stockholders were to make such payments "at such times, and by such Installments, as the President & Directors shall hereafter direct; provided that no payment shall be Compelled untill the sum of Forty Thousand Dollars be subscribed; and untill the Legislatures of Virginia & Maryland shall pass Laws to enforce the payments so agreed to be made by us the Subscribers." The list of

the subscribers is headed by GW, the largest shareholder: "Go: Washington—in his own right," twenty-three shares; Robert Peter, "by direction," seven shares; Notley Young, two shares; Gustavus Scott, eleven shares; Samuel Davidson, two shares; Alexander White, one share; Tristram Dalton, two shares; Thomas Law, four shares; "Francis Deakins Executor of Wm Deakins Junr Deceased on one Share belonging to the Estate of Wm Deakins"; Daniel Carroll of Duddington, seven shares; Wallace, Johnson & Muir (firm), nine shares; James Barry, eight shares; John Laird, five shares; Daniel Jenifer, two shares; James Keith, three shares; William H. Dorsey, one share; Thomas Beall of George, one share; Charles Worthington, one share; James Keith, "as proxy for Leven Powell," one share; James Keith, "as proxy for Charles Simms," one share; John Mason, seven shares; William Campbell, "by his proxy J. Mason," nine shares; John Barnes, "by his Proxy J. Mason," one share; Richard Barnes, "by his Proxy J. Mason," one share; Thomas Mason, one share; Charles Carroll of Carrollton, "by his proxy Danl Carroll of Dudn," eleven shares; Marsham & Henry Waring (firm), one share; Waring & Millard (firm), one share; Forrest & Stoddert (firm), three shares; Charles Phillips, "by Wm Hartshorne his Attorney," two shares; Corbin Washington, "by Wm Hartshorne his Attorney," two shares (NIC).

For the steps GW took to insure that John Fitzgerald attended the meeting of the company as the legal representative of the state of Virginia, see GW to John Fitzgerald, 27 July, and GW to William Berkeley, 29 July. For GW's plea after the meeting that the state of Virginia provide aid for the project, see GW to William Berkeley, 11 Aug. 1799. For the action taken by the state of Maryland, see John Mason to GW, 4 Dec. 1799, and President and Directors of Potomac River Company to GW, 8 Dec. 1799.

3. Carroll did not attend the meeting of the stockholders of the company on 5 Aug., but on that day he wrote to GW from "Doughoragen," his home in Maryland: "I did not receive your favor of the 21st past until yesterday. The pleasure of seeing you at George Town would have been a strong inducement to me to attend the meeting of the Company to be held there this day, even on so short a notice of yr intention of giving yr attendance, had I not learnt at the same time I got your letter, that you have been lately much indisposed. Mr Law however, from whom this disagreeable intelligence came, concluded his letter, I am told, by saying you was then on the recovery. I anxiously hope & wish you may be speedily restored to perfect health.

"I have written to my relation Mr Dan. Carroll of Duddington & authorised him to subscribe on my behalf one hundred dollars for each of the shares I hold, provided the sum of forty thousand dollars be subscribed. The circular letter of the Directors states that 60,000$ will certainly complete the navigation from above fort Cumberland to tide water; a less sum therefore than 40,000$, I conceive, if subscribed, and *paid* would be doing little or nothing; no person, who could be depended on, would undertake *by contract* a work for twenty or thirty thousand dollars, the completion of which according to accurate estimates, would require 60000$. I entirely coincide with your opinion that what remains to be done to perfect the navigation of the Potomack, should be done by contract under the inspection of the directors, or of one or two confidential & intelligent persons, to be by them appointed to superintend the contractor.

"I have, Sir, an opinion equally sanguine as yours of the eventual productiveness to the Stock[h]olders, and utility to the Publick of this great undertaking, but I fear, it will not be completed for some years from the want of funds & the inability of the stockholders to furnish them to the extent estimated & required⟨.⟩ This State, to judge from the transactions of the two last Sessions of its Legislature will advance no more money towards that object, & similar causes may produce the same effects in the Legislature of Virginia" (PHi: Sprague Collection).

To Jonathan Trumbull, Jr.

My dear Sir,   Mount Vernon 21st July 1799

Your favour of the 22d Ulto got to my hands yesterday, *only*. It came safe, and without any apparent marks of violence; but whence the length of its passage, I am unable to inform you.

To you, and to your brother Colo. Jno. Trumbull, I feel much indebted for the full, frank, and interesting communication of the political sentiments contained in both your letters.

The project of the latter is vast—and under any circumstances would require very mature consideration; but in its extent, and an eye being had to the disorganizing Party in the United States, I am sure it would be impracticable in the present order of things.[1]

Not being able to convey my ideas to you, on this subject, in more concise terms than I have already done to your brother, in answer to the letter he informs you he had written to me, I shall take the liberty of giving you an extract thereof—as follow.[2]

"For the Political information contained in it (that is his letter) I feel grateful, as I always shall for the free, & unreserved communication of your sentiments upon subjects so important in their nature, and tendency. No well informed, and unprejudiced man, who has viewed with attention the conduct of the French Government since the Revolution in that Country, can mistake its objects, or the tendency of the ambitious projects it is pursuing. Yet, strange as it may seem, a party, and a powerful one too, among us, affect to believe that the measures of it are dictated by a principle of self preservation; that the outrages of which the Directory are guilty, proceed from dire necessity; that it wishes to be upon the most friendly & amicable terms with the United States; that it will be the fault of the latter if this is not the case; that the defensive measures which this Country have adopted, are not only unnecessary & expensive, but have a tendency to produce the evil which, to deprecate, is mere pretence in the Government; because War with France they say, is its wish; that on the Militia we shd rest our security; and that it is time enough to call upon these, when the danger is imminent, & apparent.

"With these, and such like ideas, attempted to be inculcated upon the public mind (aided by prejudices not yet eradicated) and with art, and Sophistry, whi⟨ch⟩ regard neither truth nor decency; attacking every character, without respect to persons— public or Private, who happen to differ from themselves in Politics, I leave you to decide on the probability of carrying such an extensive plan of defence as you have suggested in your last letter, into operation; and in the short period which you suppose may be allowed to accomplish it in."

I come now, my dear Sir, to pay particular attention to that part of Your Letter which respects myself.

I remember well, the conversation which you allude to, and have not forgot the answer I gave you.[3] In my judgment it applies with as much force *now*, as *then*; nay more, because at that time the line between Parties was not so clearly drawn, and the views of the opposition, so clearly developed as they are at present; of course, allowing your observation (as it respects myself) to be founded, personal influence would be of no avail.

Let that party set up a broomstick, and call it a true son of Liberty, a Democrat, or give it any other epithet that will suit their purpose, and it will command their votes in toto![4] Will not the Federalists meet, or rather defend their cause, on the opposite ground? Surely they must, or they will discover a want of Policy, indicative of weakness, & pregnant of mischief; which cannot be admitted. Wherein then would lye the difference between the present Gentleman in Office, & myself?

It would be matter of sore regret to me, if I could believe that a serious thot was turned towards me as his successor; not only as it respects my ardent wishes to pass through the vale of life in retiremt, undisturbed in the remnant of the days I have to sojourn here, unless called upon to defend my Country (which every citizen is bound to do)—but on Public ground also; for although I have abundant cause to be thankful for the good health with whh I am blessed, yet I am not insensible to my declination in other respects. It would be criminal therefore in me, although it should be the wish of my Country men, and I could be elected, to accept an Office under this conviction, which another would discharge with more ability; and this too at a time when I am thoroughly convinced I should not draw a *single* vote from the Anti-federal side; and of course, should stand upon no stronger ground than any other Federal character well supported; & when I should become a mark for the shafts of envenomed malice, and the basest calumny to fire at; when I should be charged not only with irresolution, but with concealed ambition, which wants only an occasion to blaze out; and, in short, with dotage and imbicility.

All this I grant, ought to be like dust in the balance, when put in compet[it]ion with a *great* public good, when the accomplishment of it is apparent. But as no problem is better defined in my mind than that principle, not men, is now, and will be, the object of contention; and that I could not obtain a *solitary* vote from that Party; that any other respectable Federal character would receive the same suffrages that I should; that at my time of life, (verging towards three score & ten) I should expose myself without rendering any essential service to my Country, or answering the end contemplated: Prudence on my part must arrest any attempt at the well meant, but mistaken views of my friends, to introduce me again into the Chair of Government.

Lengthy as this letter is, I cannot conclude it without expressing an *earnest* wish that, some intimate & confidential friend of the Presidents would give him to understand that, his long absence from the Seat of Government in the present critical conjuncture, affords matter for severe animadversion by the friends of government; who speak of it with much disappobation; while the other Party chuckle at and set it down as a favourable omen for themselves. It has been suggested to me to make this Communication, but I have declined it, conceiving that it would be better received from a private character—m⟨ore⟩ in the habits of social intercourse and friendship. With the most sincere friendship, and Affectionate regard, I am always, Your Obedient Servant

Go: Washington

ALS, NNGL; ALS (letterpress copy), NN: Washington Papers.

1. Jonathan Trumbull enclosed in his letter to GW of 22 June a very long letter of 5 April to himself from his brother John Trumbull in London, setting out a scheme for fomenting and supporting revolutions in the Western Hemisphere so as to prevent the spread of French Jacobinism to the colonies of Spain and

Portugal in the New World. See note 1 to Jonathan Trumbull's letter of 22 June to GW.

2. John Trumbull's letter to GW is dated 24 Mar. 1799, and GW's response is dated 25 June 1799, two paragraphs of which GW quotes here.

3. See Jonathan Trumbull to GW, 22 June, n.2.

4. GW placed an asterisk here and wrote at the end of the letter: "As an analysis of this position, look to the pending Election of Governor, in Pennsylvania."

Letter not found: from Richard Kidder Meade, 22 July 1799. On 12 Aug. GW wrote Meade that he "should have acknowledged the receipt of your favor of the 22d Ultimo."

From William Roberts

General Washington   Petersburgh 22 July 1799
Sir—I Can Now inform you Captn Macnemara has had my Witness[']s affedev. gaven in to Mr Hay for fare of his Death & Mr Hay Seems Much pleasd with it & Says thare is Not the Least Danger in Recovering the property from those Base Desining Men—Our Cort Coms on the first Monday in August. & After Cort I Shal Let you know how I am Like to Come off—& what Time you May Expect Me Up to Mount Vernon Mills—God Send it was to Morrow And that I may Eand my Days in your good Imploy if I Can be Lucke a Nogh to giv Sattesfaction in My besoness And attension to the Mills & Cooper shop & Avery thing that will be Benafesial to you & the Good of the Mills[.] I hope this Cort, Mr Hay & Captn Macnemara May Git My affares in Such a fare way it may enable Me to Come to you without Delay[1]—from Sir your Real well wisher & Most Humble Servant

W:M. Roberts

ALS, DLC:GW.
1. See Roberts to GW, 12 July, and GW to Roberts, 17 July.

To James McHenry

Sir,   Mount Vernon July 24th 1799
I have received your letter of the 19th inst. enclosing recommendns of sundry persons in Kanhawa County for Military appointmts—These shall be Ret[urne]d in due time, agreeably to your desire.[1]

I forward to you a letter from Gustavus B. Wallace Junr of King

George County, requesting an appointment in the *present* Cavalry. I am entirely unacquainted with the Applicant, and have had no opportunity of making any enquiries of the Gentln to whom he refers.[2] I have the honor to be with due consideration Sir, Yr Mo. Ob. St

G. W———n

Df, in Tobias Lear's hand, DLC:GW.

1. McHenry's letter of 19 July is printed in McHenry to GW, 11 May 1799, n.2.

2. The letter from Gustavus B. Wallace, Jr., has not been found. Wallace was probably the son of Michael Wallace (b. 1753), brother of Gustavus Brown Wallace (1751–1802) of King George County who had served throughout the Revolution, ending as lieutenant colonel of the 2d Virginia Regiment. Young Wallace graduated from Princeton College in 1797 and probably used the designation "Junr" to distinguish himself from his uncle. He did not receive a commission in the New Army.

From Daniel Morgan

Sir   Soldiers Rest July 24th 1799

I take the liberty to transmit you a duplicate of a letter sent to the Honble the Secretary of War and Major Genl Hamilton.[1]
Dear Sir

I beg leave to say something in favor of Major James Stephenson who I have recommended to the commander in chief.[2] Although his conduct in the military line speaks louder in his praise than I can yet at the same time I would wish to say something. I think he would command a Regiment with as much propriety perhaps as any man who will be in the service of any country, he commanded a Company in the Army commanded by Genl St Clair in the year 1791 with great propriety and at the defeat of that Officer on the 4th of November he rendered very singular service, in addition to what has already been said he is a great disciplinarian and of Course will be a great acquis[i]tion to a new raised Army, he is also a man of good Character and education, and firmly attached to Government.

I would also beg leave to mention to you Capt. James Glenn of Berkley County Virginia who also served with Genl St Clair when he was defeated and who distinguished himself in the action and rendered great service in securing the retreat, he wishes to get into the service; I need not say more of Capt. Glenn, as a man who retains his recollection in so shocking a defeat as that was don't want fortitude; he has not mentioned to me what rank he wishes but it is my opinion he will command a Company with very great propriety[3]—Mr Bushrod Taylor of Frederick County who is a man of great cleverness wishes to join the Army, at the head of a Company if he can get it, he served with me in 1794 against the Insurgents with great propriety, is a man of good Character and Education, and firmly attached to the federal Government.[4]

Capt. Edmund Taylor in Colonel Parkers regiment and Capt. Wm K. Blue of Colo. Bentleys regt wish to be appointed Brigade Majors to the General Officers who will command the Brigade they belong to, which they expect will be General William Washington; they are both good officers and have been in the regular service, which I believe they are acquainted with; they both wish me to mention them to you which I have done.[5] I have the honor to be Sir with very great esteem your Obt Hle Sert

Danl Morgan

LS, DLC:GW.

1. GW replied to Morgan on 29 July: "Dear Sir, I have duly received and thank you for your letter of the 24th inst.—annexing a duplicate of what you had written to the Secretary of War and Majr Genl Hamilton, recommendatory of sundry persons for Military appointments, which I have no doubt will meet with due attention. With very great esteem I am Dear Sir your most obedt Serv. G. Wn" (Df, DLC:GW).

2. Morgan had recommended James Stephenson to GW on 12 June and again on 26 June.

3. For other recommendations of James Glenn, see GW to James McHenry, 12 Aug., n.1.

4. Bushrod Taylor, son of Nathaniel Taylor (d. 1804) and Mary Wright Taylor, later became a citizen of Winchester. Taylor did not receive a commission in the New Army.

5. For the identification of Edmund Taylor and William K. Blue, see GW to Alexander Hamilton, 14 Aug. 1799, nn. 2–5.

From James Ross

Dear Sir　　　　　　　　　　　　　　　Pittsburgh 24 July 1799

When your letter of the 26 Ulto reached this place, I was abroad in the Western territory, but since my return I have learned upon enquiry, that Colo. Shreve is in a very low state of health; that the Sheriff Spared him for some time in consequence of a letter from you and his own fair promises, but that as yet no money is made

on the execution issued in last Autumn. I have written to a gentleman of the law in Union Town directing him to oblige the Sheriff
to collect the money without delay, and at the same time to apprize
Colo. Shreve that an Execution will go out for the installment due
last June unless it is immediately paid.[1]

Mr Addison & John Ritchie (the brother & heir of Colo. Ritchie)
are now in Philadelphia, where I am in hopes they will pay what is
due to you⟨,⟩ but I can say nothing with certainty on that Subject
as they had left this country before the arrival of your letter. I have
left notice for them to give me information whenever they reach
home which will be in a few days. Had Colo. Ritchie lived there
would have been no want of punctuality in your payments, but his
brother has not the same means, nor the same established credit
to raise money; And Mr Addison tho' a man of property, has not
the command of cash to any considerable extent. As Soon as any
additonal information can be had, it shall be immediately transmitted & in the mean While I shall press all the parties to come
forward with all arrearages.

When I left the city of Philada in March there was a considerable
sum to my credit in the Bank of Pennsa, but no money on your
account, nor have I any advice of a payment there since I left it. If
money has been deposited there for you, the person who left it
has omitted to give me notice and my Bank Book being at this
place it is impossible that I could be apprised of such a payment
without letter. I will write to Philadelphia and direct a payment of
any Sum which may be there for your Use, but I am persuaded
that there is little probability of Your deriving any advantage from
Such an order.

I beg that you will without any hesitation let me know when &
how I can render you any service in your affairs here, as it will
always afford me the most sincere pleasure to aid you in effecting
an adjustment of your concerns in this country and to transmit
every information respecting them which may be useful. With the
highest respect I have the honour to remain Dear Sir Your Most
Obedient and Most humble Servant

James Ross

ALS, DLC:GW.
    1. See GW to Samuel M. Fox, 10 June, and notes 1 and 2 of that document.

From Alexander Spotswood

Dr Sir   July. 25. 1799

Much rain last week and some other matters prevented my Sending to the post office until last Tuseday (the 23d) when I got both your favors of the 15 & 20 Inst., which I shall proceed to Answer, begining first with your private concerns.[1]

The administrators of James Mercer decd are Mr John Brooke, and James Garnet—the former lives 13 Miles from me, the latter, 36—and you may rest assured I will take the Earliest opportunity of procureing the Conveyance you wish for.[2]

The information you want as to the laws of Kentucky, respecting the recording of Deeds there made in Other states; I can only give as I had it myself when last in that State.

A Deed made here and witnessed and a certificate on the Back Signed by two Magistrates, certifying, the Said deed was Executed, Acknowledged, and witnessed in there presence, will be proof (*Sufficient*) to Carry it to Recorded, if Offered within 18 Months.

A Deed made and recorded here, with the clerks certificate thereto, will be admitted to record in Kentucky.

Whether there be any time limitted by the laws of Kentucky for bringing forward Such last mentioned deeds, I am at a Loss to Say—but I am inclined to think Not; as the laws of every country Say that no time Shall Obliterate the Testimony of Record.

About the 20th of August a Mr Duval, a man much to be relied on, moves Forward to Kentucky with his Family, so that you have Nothing to do but to Inclose your deed in a letter to Peyton Short Esqr. near lexington, and forward the Same to me, & on its comeing to hand I will Acknowledge the rect thereof—with an assureance, that Mr Duval to whose care I shall commit it; and who Settles near lexington, shall deliver the Same to Mr Short in person.[3]

I Feel myself much obliged for your Attention to my Son Georges wishes—and had I have known, that you had determined (on quitting the chair of goverment) Not to be the Medium through which applications for appointments in the navy should come; I should have declined Soliciting you into a delicate Situation.

It was not my wish to procure George a Commission, or a permanent Appointment immediatly, but only to get him Enrolled as a Midshipman, to be called on at the end of 15 Months, should there then be a Call for Such officers—dureing this time he would be closely employed in the Studdy of Mathematicks and Geography—and being a youth of fine genious would by close Studey in 12 Months make himself clever in these two branches of education and with a Knowledge of the former—he would be able in Six weeks to Make himself acquainted with the theory of Navigation—and to perfect him as much as possible in the duties of a Seaman; I am About haveing a Vessel done up with plank Masted and Spar[r]ed, and shall employ an old Seaman to instruct him in the Art of Riging (every Saturday) which will enable him to go on Ship board with Some confidence—and he Knowing the theory of his duty well, a few cruises perhaps might qualify him for a Step higher.

There are two appointments of Midshipmen from this Neighborhood; but the persons are ignorant of the duty they are to enter on and may Remain Midshipmen, until the hair grew grey on there head and be then but very little wiser, than the day they went on board.

My wish when George goes forth, is that he may be of Service, and as he Takes pleasure in Obligeing me—if ever he gets an Appointment, I shall require him to Serve the first cruise as a foremast man—which will give him experience in his duty as a Seaman.

I shall take every opportunity of pointing out to you, Such persons as I think in my opinion fit for Regimental appointments in doing of which, I will not Abuse the confidence you place in me.

Yesterday a Mr William Hedgeman Thom, came to my house, and presented me the inclosed from general Steevens, who I believe you know as well as I do—and being a Stranger to Mr Thoms Merits, Refer you to the Generals letter for the same.[4]

In justice to the Gentleman, I must relate what Passed between us.

he observed, that being under age, when the appointments to the present army was made, and Supposeing there would for a length of time be a call for officers—he thought it would be more prudent to wait until he did come of age, then to Settle his affairs and put them in Such train, that he might not have any thing to Attend to but his duty—(Should he get an appointment.)

I then asked him if he had thought of any Particular rank; he said he wished the appointment of Captain; I told him that I was well apprized that the rank of Captain was held in but too little Estimation—but that he might rely, that it was a very important command; and a man must be well known to Obtain it in the present Service.

He modestly observed, that young men was generally ambitious; he perhaps might be so—but trusted it was no fault, when it was for a good purpose—and as he intended to make a life bussiness of the profession he wished to enter on; he pledged his honor, that he would receive and Accept any Appointment that was offered him—and that his anxiety to get into the army was Such, that if his wishes could not be gratified; he would enter as a private and depend on his good behaviour for promotion—Mr Thom is a Sensible, genteel, likely young man, and appears to have been well brought up—and if men of his Age (21) is received as Captains; had I power I should not hesitate in giveing him the Appointment. My family are well and desire the best regards to you, Mrs Washington, Mr & Mrs Lewis as well as dr Sir Yr Mt Affte Obliged Hbe St

Alexr Spotswood

P.S. Just as I concluded this letter, I recd your favr of the 21 inst.[5]—enclosing a letter from the Secretary of the Navy to My Son George; with a commission, as midshipman in the Navy and a prescribed oath for him to take; but unfortunately, I was not Sufficiently Correct in his Name to you; It being—Go. Washington Spotswood—I shall address a polite letter to the Secretary—and Make my Acknowledgements to the president—for this mark of Attention—which I attribute to you—and shall impress on Georges mind the great favor which is Shewn him—and how highly he is indebted to you for the Appointment—I shall Send in the Commission &c. by My frd Brigadr gl Wm Washington of South Carolina Who is to be at my house this Evening—on his way I presume to philadelphia, of course via Mt Vernon.[6]

& on the return of the papers I will communicate to George his great good fortune when he shall address a propper letter on the Occasion to Secretary of the Navy. as usual Dr Sir A.S.

should Mr Thom Succeed—his letter may be addressed to him at Fredricksburg—to the care of Capt. Thornton.

ALS, DLC:GW.

1. No letter of 20 July has been found. What follows here regarding James Mercer's estate is in response to GW's letter of 15 July 1799, whereas that part of the letter dealing with the laws of Kentucky must be in response to queries in the missing letter of 20 July. See note 3.

2. John Taliaferro Brooke of Spotsylvania County and James Mercer Garnett of Essex County were executors of the estate of James Mercer, who died in 1791. In January 1795 the two men were appointed guardians for James Mercer's 17-year-old son, Charles Fenton Mercer, who at the time was a student at Princeton (Crozier, *Virginia County Records*, 1:51, 81).

3. For GW's decision to have recorded in Kentucky as well as in Virginia his deed from Henry Lee to the tract of land on Rough Creek in Kentucky, see GW's letters to Spotswood and to Peyton Short of 31 July. Thomas Duvall of Fayette County, Ky., on 14 June 1799 gave Zacheus Carpenter of Spotsylvania County, Va., where Spotswood lived, power of attorney to accept his share of Jonathan Carpenter's estate in Spotsylvania (ibid., 1:508–9).

4. Edward Stevens (1745–1820) of Culpeper County became the major general of the Virginia militia during the Revolutionary War. If GW followed his usual procedure, he forwarded Stevens's letter about William Hedgeman Thom, also of Culpeper County, to Secretary of War James McHenry. Stevens's letter has not been found, and young Thom's name does not appear on the list of those who were offered commissions in the New Army (*ASP: Military Affairs*, 1:146–51).

5. For GW's letter of 21 July, see GW to Spotswood, 15 July, n.2.

6. Gen. William Washington arrived at Mount Vernon on 6 August. See GW to Charles Cotesworth Pinckney, 10 Aug. 1799, n.1.

Letter not found: from William Vans Murray, 26 July 1799. On 26 Oct. GW wrote Murray: "Within the space of a few days, I have been favoured with your letters of the 26th of July. . . ."

To John Fitzgerald

Dear Sir,   Mount Vernon 27th July 1799

Recollecting that you had some doubt, at the last General Meeting of the Potomack Company, concerning the validity of your Powers to represent the State of Virginia in its interest therein, I wish to know whether those doubts have been removed by the Treasurer *now* in Office.[1]

The Stockholders are called upon, I perceive⟨,⟩ by a Printed (and I presume circular) letter in precise terms to attend the next Genl Meeting in George Town the 5th of next month, to consider, & decide on an important measure.[2] Much is it to be regretted, that a work of such public utility and (if executed) of such immense advantage to the Undertakers, should be forcd to go limpingly on as that has done; particularly to the injury of those individuals who (in affect⟨ingly⟩ endeavo⟩red to promote the completion of it.

If you have not powers of sufficient validity to justify your voting on this occasion, I hope, to your successor they will be given before the meeting; and if they are sufficient let me pray you to attend, and in time, for it is really necessary as well for the reputation as interest of the Company that the business should be rescued from its present Sloth.

I shall make a point of it, to be at the Union Tavern in George Town on the day appointed and by 11 oclock unless prevented by sickness; and in that case shall appear by Proxy; and I shall feel much chagreen if the State of Virginia is unrepresented thereat. With great esteem and regard I am—Dear Sir Your Obedt & Affecte Servt

Go: Washington

ALS (letterpress copy), NN: Washington Papers.

1. See GW to the Virginia state treasurer, William Berkeley, 29 July 1799, and note 1 of that document.

2. For the Potomac River Company circular letter, see GW to Charles Carroll, 21 July, n.1.

To William Berkeley

Sir,   Mount Vernon 29th July 1799

On monday the fifth of August the annual, *General* Meeting of the Potomac ⟨Compy is⟩ to be held in George Town ⟨*illegible*⟩.

Recollecting that at ⟨*illegible*⟩ meeting ⟨*illegible*⟩ *last* year, Colo. Fitzgerald ⟨*mutilated* em⟩powered to represent the interests of this Commonwealth therein, had doubt of the validity of that as your late worthy Predecessor in office was then no more; I take the liberty, without expressing any opinion with respect to the propriety of this doubt, to make you acquainted with the fact. For I shall feel much regret if the ⟨State⟩ is unrepresented at a meeting which will have important matters to consider, and when it has become so essential to do ⟨some *illegible*⟩.[1]

It is indeed to be lamented that an Undertaking of such immense advantage to ⟨the Commonwealth⟩ if completed—and of such profit ⟨to the Stockhol⟩ders, should go limpingly on, as ⟨it⟩

has done for some years back. Excuse this liberty & believe me to be—Sir Your ⟨*illegible*⟩

Go: Washington

ALS (letterpress copy), NN: Washington Papers.

1. William Berkeley (Barclay), treasurer of the state, replied from Richmond on 1 August: "Your favor of the 29th ultimo arrived too late to be answered by the return post, without omitting the power of Attorney which I now enclose you. I find by reference to my rough cash book, that I paid postage on a letter to Col. Fitzgerald, on the 19th of last October enclosing a power of Attorney, which I am apprehensive miscarried. You will oblige me by communicating with him on the subject, and informing me whether he ever received it—should it have arrived safe, I will thank him to destroy whichever he may think most advisable" (DLC: GW). GW wrote Berkeley on 11 Aug.: "Sir, I thank you for your prompt answer of the 1st instant, to my letter of a preceeding date; and for the Power of Attorney enclos'd therein for Colo. Fitzgerald, as Proxy to represent the State at the General Meeting of the Potomack Company, lately held at George Town—the 5th past.

"It appearing at the meeting, that Colo. Fitzgerald was duly authorised by you, to act in behalf of the State, I return the Power you were so obliging as to send him, under cover to me. And my anxiety that the State should be duly represented on that occasion, is the best apology I can make for the trouble I have given you.

"I have only to add, as an earnest wish, that the Commonwealth of Virginia would afford its aid to the mode which was then adopted to raise money; and lend its influence to carry a Work of such utility into complete effect. I have no hesitation in giving it as my decided opinion, that in a pecuniary point of view alone—putting the policy of the measure entirely out of sight, there is no way in which it can employ its money more advantageously. To dilate on the benefits which would result from improving the great *high way* which nature has marked out as the easiest, and most direct communication with the Western World (maugre all the the endeavours of Pennsylvania & New York to divert it into other Channels) would be a mere waste of time; because every one who is disposed to investigate the subject must see them at the first glance. But it must be acknowledged at the sametime, that habits & customs are not easily overcome. consequently, if the produce of upper Ohio, & the Lakes should settle in either of the channels abovementioned, it will require time, as well as convenience, to bring it back into the course which nature has ordered, and which ultimately it will effect. Excuse these Sentimts, & believe me to be—Sir Your Most obedt Hble Servant Go: Washington" (letterpress copy, NN: Washington Papers).

To Mrs. E. Gravatt

Madam   Mount Vernon 29th July 1799

I have been honoured—but not so soon as might have been expected from the date—with your favour of the 4th of January last, and wish, sincerely, that it was in my power to give you a more satisfactory answer than follows.[1]

You will have been informed from the correspondence with Mrs Montagu, with which you seem to be acquainted, that the Mortgage of Lands, &ca given by Colo. George Mercer to Mr Gravatt & Miss Wroughton, or the Power of Attorney to sell the same was contested by the Mortgagees of the same property in this Country, under an authority vested by him, to his brother James Mercer; and that it was necessary to institute a suit in our High Court of Chancery before any ulterior measures could be pursued ⟨with res⟩pect to either of the Powers. The result of which was a Decretal order to *sell* the Estate subject to a *final* decree, with respect to the different claimants.

This was accordingly done (on twelve months credit, agreeably thereto) in November 1774, and Bonds, with security, taken for payment of the purchase money.[2] Before these became due, on Novr 1775, the dispute between this Country & Great Britain became serious. In May, I was sent by the State of Virginia as one of its delegates to Congress; and by Congress to command the Armies of the United States the June following. Clearly forseeing that this dispute was not likely to terminate shortly, I wrote to Colo. Tayloe (the other acting Attorney) & before the Bonds became due, desiring him to collect, & deposit the money agreeably to the Decree of the Court, as I cd render no further assistance, and would not be responsible for any proceedings thereafter.

The view I had taken of the dispute was confirmed by the event; and excepting the short period of the Siege of York, I was upwards of eight years absent from this State suffering material wrongs in my own private concerns, because I could bestow no attention on them, which I mention, merely as an evidence of my incapacity to attend to those of others.

The deranged state into which the War had thrown matters in this Country, and the shutting up our Courts of Justice for a while, suspended all kinds of business the first years of it; and Colo. Tayloe's death happening soon after I was much pressed by the Claimants on Colo. Mercer's Estate in this Country, but always refused, to renew my Agency in that concern. In consequence of which, Colo. John Francis Mercer, another brother of Colo. George Mercer, having a large claim on his estate, applied for, and obtained a decree of the same Court of Chancery, to receive *all* the monies due on the Sales—subject, as in the former case, to the final decision of the Chancellor.[3]

This statement is given from Memory—all the papers relative to the business having passed from me in consequence of the above decree—but I believe it may be depended upon as substantially accurate. What the present Agent has done—or how the matter now stands, is unknown to me. He has removed from Virginia into Maryland, and resides near Annapolis; and is a Gentleman of property.

With respect to the advance of Six thousand pounds on Land belonging to Colo. George Mercer, situated on the River Ohio, I can say nothing; because the subject is now, unconnected entirely with the business on which I was formerly concerned. Colo. Mercer has or had, some very valuable Lands in that Region; but in whose possession they are now, or under what predicament they may be found, I know not.

I wish it had been in my power to have answered your letter more satisfactorily but my public duties compelled me to relinquish the trust, with which I was vested at the commencement of our revolution. It was placed in the hands of the Gentleman whose name I have given you, two or three years before the close of it and my own ⟨business have⟩ been so much deranged by an absence ⟨*illegible*⟩ short intervals) of twenty five years from home, as to require all my attention to recover ⟨*illegible*⟩ I have the honor to be, Madam Your Most Obedt Hble Servt

Go: Washington

ALS (letterpress copy), NN: Washington Papers.

1. Mrs. Gravatt's letter of 4 Jan. 1799 from London reads: "An apology for presuming to address you on a Case of Justice, would be an Insult to the Greatness of your Character, whose Life is an Example of Justness of Principle, and Beneficence of Action. Permit me Sir to inform you, I am the Widow of the late Mr Richard Gravatt, Banker, in Fleetstreet; who was honored by the Friendship of that ever to be revered Character, the late Mr Edward Montagu, one of the Masters in Chancery; who introduced to Mr Gravatt near thirty years since, Colonel George Mercer, as a Gentleman who had Claims on Government, although much inconvenienced for Money: The Colonel experienced brotherly Attention from Mr Gravatt for the Space of nine Years, during which Time, he often extricated him from the most lamentable scenes of Distress; he also advanced Six Thousand Pounds upon an Estate Col. Mercer was possessed of in Virginia, upon the Ohio; Mr Montagu likewise advanced a considerable Sum of his Sister's Miss Wroughton's. The Estate was sold, the Troubles in America made it a Matter of Debate in what Manner to vest the Money. Mr Montagu was advised by you Sir,

and I think Colonel Taylo (who was concerned in the Business) to secure it by putting it in Congress Notes, which I believe was done. My Chain of Information was stopped, by the Death of a much lamented Husband, whose Executors trusted the Management of the Business wholly to Mr Montagu; his Decease prevents all Intelligence concerning it, which occasions Sir, my taking the Liberty of refering to you. The Americans have shewn a noble Wish, worthy themselves, to discharge all debts upon their Country! Surely, they cannot desire to deprive the Widow and Fatherless of their Right, especially those labouring under Penury and Imposition of the World. To you Sir, I prefer my Suit, trusting by this imperfect account, you will be able to collect Materials sufficient, for an Investigation of the Transaction, by which you will perform a benevolent Action, and confer a distinguished Obligation. I have Sir the Honour to be, with the highest Respect, your most faithful, obedient Servent, E. Gravatt P.S. My address is, at Mrs Mills's, No. 15, Devonshire Street, Queen Square, London" (DLC:GW).

2. For GW's role as an agent for George Mercer in the selling of Mercer's Virginia estate in 1774, see particularly GW to John Tayloe, 20 Aug. 1773, n.1., in *Papers, Colonial Series*, 9:309–10.

3. For a summary of the problems connected with the settlement of George Mercer's estate, see Statement concerning George Mercer's Estate, 1 Feb. 1789, in *Papers, Presidential Series*, 1:269–76.

From James McHenry

Dear Sir.   Philad[elphia] 29 July 1799

Mr Bordley left the inclosed collection of his works with me with a request that I should forward it to you. There are some useful things in the book, but I believe little of it his own.[1]

Francis has procured the Sword for our young warrior, and tells me, the helmit will soon be finished, when the whole will be forwarded.[2]

It appears by a letter from Mr Murray to the Secy of State, that he had received the Secy's letter advising the appointment of the 3 Commissioners and forwarded or was about to forward to Paris the conditions under which the appointment was made.[3] Can any good possibly come out of this business? I fear not. Yours ever & Affly

James McHenry

ALS, DLC:GW.

1. GW wrote John Beale Bordley on 4 Aug.: "Through the medium of the Secretary of War, I have been honoured with your 'Essays and Notes on Husbandry, and Rural Affairs' and offer you my sincere thanks for your kindness in sending them. . . . With best respects, in which Mrs. Washington unites, to Mrs. and Miss Bordley and yourself . . ." (quoted in item 375, Parke-Bernet Catalog, 26 Nov. 1952). A copy of *Sketches on Rotations of Crops and Other Rural Matters*,

printed in Philadelphia in 1797 and bound with other pamphlets relating to agriculture, was in GW's library at the time of his death (Griffin, *Boston Athenæum Washington Collection*, 28).

2. GW wrote McHenry on 14 July about the uniform and other military equipment for George Washington Parke Custis.

3. See the reference to William Vans Murray's letter to Timothy Pickering in Pickering to GW, 18 July, n.1.

To William Baynham

Sir,   Mount Vernon July 30th 1799

The bearer of this ⟨letter⟩ my Ploughman, has, for ⟨some months⟩ past, been afflicted with a tumour which has occasioned partial, and threatens (if relief can not be obtained) total blindness.[1]

He has been under the care of Doctor Craik & others, without receiving much, if any benefit; and being desirous of relieving him from so serious a malady, if ⟨you⟩ can accomplish it, I send him to you.

What operation it will be necessary for him to undergo; how long to stay with you; or what expence to incur, you better than I, can decide. The two first you will be the judge of, and the latter you will add to your Bill.

I would thank you for a line by the first Post (after your rect ⟨of this letter⟩) advising me of his arrival; and ⟨the time of &⟩ *medium of conveyance* of his departure.[2] I am Sir Yr Most Obedt Servt

Go: Washington

ALS (letterpress copy), NN: Washington Papers.

William Baynham (1749–1814), who studied in Scotland and London, was a noted surgeon at this time practicing in Essex County, Virginia. He dined at Mount Vernon on 20 Feb. 1799 (*Diaries*, 6:335).

1. The plowman, named Tom, was one of the slaves at Mount Vernon rented from Penelope Manley French. He was twenty-eight years old, unmarried, and, as GW noted, "getting blind" (List of Slaves, 1799, printed at the end of this volume).

2. See Baynham to GW, 10 and 21 August.

To Peyton Short

Sir,   Mount Vernon 31st July 1799

I avail myself of your obliging offer (when last in Virginia to serve me in Kentucky)[1] by requesting the favour of you to have the Deed, herewith sent admitted to Record in the County of Kentucky, in which the land may *now* be, if a division of Jefferson has been made since the granting of the Patent, originally.

This Land was conveyed to me by Genl Lee, and is of Record in the Territory of the Commonwealth before Kentucky was acknowledged as a State; but I thot it best, on account of some little informalities, (which, however, would not have affected the title) to have the business take its present shape. wch makes it necessary to be of Record in the County & State in which the land is situated.

Not knowing with precision, what time is allowed by the Laws of Kentucky for proofs of this kind, the Deed may come to your hands out of Season. Should this happen, I would thank you to advise me in order that I may be certain of its having got to your hands, you would do me a favour in acknowledging the receipt ⟨of it⟩ under any circumstances.[2]

The expence attending this business, be what it may, will, with thanks also, be most chearfully paid by Sir Your Most Obedt Very Humble Servant

Go: Washington

ALS (letterpress copy), NN: Washington Papers.

1. On 11 May GW recorded in his diary a visit from "Mr. Small" who departed on 12 May as "Mr. Short" (*Diaries*, 6:347). See also Short to GW, 1 Nov. 1798.

2. See Alexander Spotswood to GW, 25 July, and note 3 of that document. See also GW to Spotswood, this date.

To Alexander Spotswood

Dear Sir,   Mount Vernon 31st July 1799

I have been duly favoured in the receipt of your letter of the 25th instant; and thank you for the kind information given in it respecting the removal of Mr Duval to Kentucky; and your intention of embracing the earliest opportunity of enquiring after the Conveyance from the deceased James Mercer, Esqr. &ca to me.

Enclosed is the Deed from Genl Lee to me, for the Land he sold me; lying on Rough Creek in Kentucky; now sent for the purpose of transmission by Mr Duval to Peyton Short Esqr.—to whom, having received a very polite tender of his service in Kentucky, civility, (as he will be the medium through which the business is to be transacted) required I should write.

I leave my letter to him, covering the Deed, open for your perusal: requesting that, you would be so good as to inclose it in one from yourself to Mr Short; and in a particular manner recommending them to the care of Mr Duval. If eighteen months are allowed by the Laws of Kentucky for the admission of proof, there is yet sufficient time for Lee's Deed to me to be recorded in that State. If otherwise, Mr Short, I persuade myself, will advise me thereof.

I think your determination to qualify your Son for the duties he will have to perform, is highly proper. It will give him confidence in himself—and advantages in the eyes of his Superior Officers—which cannot but be serviceable to his rise in the Navy.

Mr Thom's name shall be entered on my list, and his pretensions duly considered & compared, when an arrangement of the whole is to be made.

Mrs Washington unites with me in every good wish for yourself Mrs Spotswood & family—and I am Dr Sir—Yr Obliged & Affecte

Go: Washington

ALS, PWacD.

To William Thornton

Dear Sir, Mount Vernon 1st Augt 1799

I shall be obliged to you for letting Mr Blagden know, that I forsee nothing, at present, that will prevent my being at the Union Tavern in George Town on Monday next (the 5th instant) by eleven Oclock. When & where, if he will attend I shall be provided with, & ready to pay him, a thousand Dollars in Columbia Notes.[1]

I thank you for the information, & sentiments given in your last favour of the 19th Ulto, which came duly to hand; and for your kind invitation to lodge at your House: but as the same cause which takes me up, will, at least ought to carry Mr Law there also, one, if not both the families at whose Houses I usually lodge will be there. With very great esteem & regard—I am Dr Sir Yr Most Obedt Servt

Go: Washington

ALS (letterpress copy), NN: Washington Papers; copy, DLC: Thornton Papers. The copy in the Thornton Papers was used to confirm the reading of the very faint portions of the letterpress copy.

1. An entry in GW's Day Book for 5 Aug. reads: "By Cash pd Mr Blagden through Doctr Thornton—on a/c of my building. $1000."

From Timothy Pickering

(confidential)

Sir,   Philadelphia August 2. 1799.

A letter from Mr Murray of May 17 received this week, covers a letter from Talleyrand, dated May 12th, assuring him that the Executive Directory will receive the Envoys of the U. States in their official character; and that they shall enjoy all the prerogatives attached to it by the law of nations; and that one or more ministers shall be duly authorized to treat with them.[1]

These papers I have sent to the President. The day before, I had sent to him a letter from Mr King, informing that Russia, otherwise ready to enter into a commercial treaty with us, had suspended it, *because we were about to treat with France.*[2]

Govr Davie of No. Carolina has been appointed, and consents to serve, in the room of the late Govr Henry, as one of the Envoys.

Mr Adams has agreed on the terms of a treaty with Prussia.[3]

I believe I have before mentioned, that the mission of Mr Smith to Constantinople has been suspended: It will now be more than ever necessary previously to ascertain whether he would be received. Mr King will make the inquiry.[4] I am with great respect Sir yr obt servt

                                              Timothy Pickering

ALS, DLC:GW; copy, in Pickering's hand, MHi: Pickering Papers.

1. William Vans Murray's copy of Talleyrand's letter of 12 May and Murray's covering letter of 17 May are both in MHi: Pickering Papers.

2. Rufus King wrote from London on 5 June that Count Woronzow had told him "that the success *of the negotiation must in his opinion* at least for the present depend *upon our situation with France.* If *we were* about *a negotiation with France*, it would, *in his opinion* be advisable *for us* to suspend further proceedings *with Russia* . . ." (King, *Life and Correspondence of King*, 3:29–30). The italicized words were in code. Count Semeon (Semen, Simon) Romanovich Vorontsov (Woronzow) was the Russian ambassador to Great Britain.

3. John Quincy Adams, the American minister to Prussia, wrote Pickering from Berlin on 10 May 1799: "we are fully agreed upon the tenor of the treaty" (*ASP: Foreign Relations*, 2:268); and on 13 July he sent the secretary of state copies of the text of a treaty of "amity and commerce between His Majesty the King of Prussia, and the United States" (ibid., 244–49, 269).

4. See Pickering to GW, 21 Feb. 1799, n.5.

Letter not found: from Edward Rutledge, 3 Aug. 1799. On 9 Sept. GW wrote Rutledge that he had received "your obliging favour of the 3d of Augt."

To Jeremiah Olney

Dear Sir,   Mount Vernon 4th Augt 1799

Your favor of the 13th Ulto, accompanying the oration of Mr Maxcy, has been duly received, and for your politeness in sending me the latter, I pray you to accept my thanks.[1]

The sentiments expressed by that Gentleman on Government, and tendency of such conduct as is opposed to the Public functionaries in our own, are too just not to carry conviction to every well disposed, and reflecting mind. With very great esteem—I remain Dear Sir Your Most Obedt Servt

Go: Washington

ALS (photocopy), DLC:GW.
   Jeremiah Olney (1749–1812) served in the Rhode Island forces during the Revolution and rose to the rank of lieutenant colonel in the Continental army. In 1790 GW made him collector of the customs at Providence.
   1. Letter not found. Jonathan Maxcy (1768–1820), a Baptist preacher, at this time was president of Rhode Island College (later Brown University) in Providence. In 1804 he became the first president of South Carolina College in Columbia. Maxcy's oration has not been identified.

To Timothy Pickering

Private
Dear Sir,   Mount Vernon Augt 4th 1799

Your favour of the 18th Ulto came to hand in due course of the Mail, and I thank you for the information contained in it.

Is it not time to learn, *Officially*, and *unequivocally*, the result of the Presidents message, and consequent (I presume) intimation to the French Government, respecting the appointment of Envoys to Treat with it?

Having no Church nearer than Alexandria (nine miles distant) I usually postpone writing, or answering letters that do not require immediate attention, until then; that the regular exercise I take, and the avocations which employ me, may be less interrupted.

On this principle, the present acknowledgment of your letter (abovc) has bccn dclaycd, and thcrcby a question, which I in tended to propound in it, I find solved, in the Aurora which came to hand last night.

The question I allude to, is, whether the Officers of Government intended to be quiescent under the direct charge of bribery, ex- hibited in such aggrivated terms by the Editor of the above Paper? The most dangerous consequences would, in my opinion, have flowed from such silence, & therefore could not be overlooked: and yet, I am persuaded that if a rope, a little longer had been given him, he would have hung himself in something worse; if possible: for there seems to be no bounds to his attempts to de- stroy all confidence, that the People might, and (without sufficient proof of its demerits) ought, to have in their government; thereby dissolving it, and producing a disunion of the States. That this is the object of such Publications as the Aurora and other Papers of the same complexion teem with, those who "run, may read" the motives which are ascribed to them, notwithstanding.

They dare not, at present, act less under covert; but they unfold very fast; and like untimely fruit, or flowers forced in a hot bed, will, I hope, whatever my expectation⟨s⟩ may be, soon wither, and in principle, die like them.

All of the administration, or some of the members are now to look to it, for Mr Duane I perceive, in his address to the Public, on the occasion of his arrest, has assured it "that he has not published a *fact* which he cannot prove, and that neither persecution nor any other peril to which *bad* men may expose him, can make him swerve from the cause of republicanism."[1] With very great esteem & regard I am—Dear Sir Your Most Obedt Servt

Go: Washington

ALS, MHi: Pickering Papers; ALS (letterpress copy), DLC:GW. The ALS is dock- eted "recd 8th."

1. Following the death of Benjamin Franklin Bache in September 1798, Wil- liam Duane (1760–1835) became editor of the *Aurora*, the most strident and influential of the Republican newspapers. In February 1799 Duane was acquitted of charges brought against him under the Sedition Act, but he was charged again on 30 July when his attacks on the Adams administration for corruption and un- due British influence in its moves to re-open trade with Saint Domingue culmi- nated on 24 July in an accusation of British bribery. After reading Duane's attack of 24 July, Pickering wrote on the same day to President Adams that Duane had declared that Adams "had asserted the influence of the British Government in the affairs of our own—and insinuated that it was obtained by bribery" (quoted

in Smith, *Freedom's Fetters*, 283). Pickering also sent a copy of Duane's article to the federal district attorney in Philadelphia. On 31 July, Duane reported to the readers of the *Aurora* that he "was yesterday between nine and ten o'clock arrested by John Nichols, esq. marshal of this district, upon a warrant from Judge [Richard] Peters, and on behalf of the administration, for publishing in the Aurora of the 24th instant, certain matters alledged to be defamatory, or untrue, concerning the administration." Duane's statement included the assertion that GW quotes here. Duane remained free on bail until he was brought to trial in October, when the case was postponed until 1800. For further references to the prosecution of Duane, see James McHenry to GW, 10 Nov. 1799, and note 4 of that document. See also GW to McHenry, 11 Aug., and notes.

From Alexander Spotswood

Dr Sir   Newpost August 4. 1799.

   your favour of the 31 of July, Covering your letter to Mr Short, and Lees deed to you, has come to hand, and shall be duly Attended to.

   I am about to Build a Yawl for the Convenience of my Family going by water to Fredericksburg; which mode of conveyance in the Summer is more pleasant than a Carraige; yours pleaseing me better than any I have yet Seen, will thank you to direct Mr Anderson, to send me on paper her dimensions as Follows[1]

   1. the whole length from the middle of her transom to the top of her Stern

   2. Width across her transom,

   3. Width across the middle of the boat, and depth

   4—width across the foremast Seat.

   Mrs Spotswood and family desire there best Regards to you Mrs Washington, & Mr & Mrs Lewis as well as dr sir yr aff. & Obt St

                                          Alexr Spotswood

ALS, DLC:GW.

   1. GW's response to this request has not been found.

From James McHenry

(Private)

my Dear Sir.   Philad[elphia] 5 Augt 1799.

   Mr Murray has executed his instructions and Mr Pickering has received from him the answer of Mr Talyrand ⟨so⟩ that Mr Elsworth &c. will be received according to their functions, and respected agreeably to the law of nations, and one or several persons be duly appointed to treat with them.

So far the answer would seem a compliance with the conditions announced to the Senate by the President. The Secy insisted in his letter to Mr Murray, by order of the President, that they were to have an audience of the Directory, and this condition was also communicated to Talyrand. On this condition Talyrand is silent, of course it is reserved by the Directory to omit or grant it, as the one or the other may best suit their purpose.

In this point they have not complied with the conditions. But besides this reserve, there is an insult in Talyrands communication. He thinks it strange, that so much time should have been suffered to elapse, to *repeat* an inquiry which he had before answered to Mr Gerry and ⟨also⟩ to Mr Murray.[1]

The whole has been sent to Quincy to take its fate there.

You will observe that a very great change has taken place in the affairs of Europe since the mission was thought of: That a treaty with France, cannot in point of trade and commerce, place us in so good a situation as that we are now in: That if we form a treaty with France we expose our trade to the more serious inconveniences from the other powers opposed to France: and finally, that a treaty gives us no hold upon France. With all this before us ought we to desire a treaty? I really find the dilemma extremely distressing. Yours ever & Affly

James McHenry

ALS, DLC:GW; ADf, MdAA.

1. See Timothy Pickering to GW, 2 Aug., and note 1 of that document.

From George Walker

Sir   Washington City August 5th 1799

Being informed Sometime ago, that a Copy of a letter wrote to you by Doctor Thornton in May last, respecting the division of Some Squares on my ground in this City, with your reply to it, had been read by many in Georgetown, I had the curiosity to procure copies of these letters, with Dr Thornton's protest on the Same Subject; all of which, are now before me[1]—The whole design of Dr Thorntons protest, and his letter to you, is apparently intended, to impress upon your mind, as well as all others who have read them, that I am disposed to be Singularly troublesome to the Commissioners, by making requests that no other proprietor has asked or obtained.

In order to refute this groundless Charge, I was at the trouble of procuring from the Commissioners division Books, (by their permission) a list of Squares divided and recorded, which do not appear in the Engraved plan of this City.

This list I have now inclosed you for your better information on the Subject, and when you have perused it, will thank you to give it to Mr T. Peter to be returned to me—All the Squares in the inclosed list, So far as I can learn, were laid out, platted, and presented to the respective proprietors by the Commissioners, for division, without the necessity of request, or "*Contending*"—and I never heard that any opposition was made to their division by any of the Commissioners—Thus far I can assert, that the Squares belonging to me in the inclosed list, divided on the 5th of Septr 1795, were produced to me for division at that time, along with many others, without any request from me, or oppos[it]ion to them by Dr Thornton, as you will See his name to the division of them.[2]

Doctor Thornton begins his letter to you by Saying that the Commissioners were "*exceedingly Urged*" by me to divide the Squares they divided with me on the 22d of May last. From your knowledge of Messrs Scott and Whites Characters, possessing a full recollection of their past transactions as Commissioners, you cannot believe Sir, that they would require to be "*urged*" to execute a duty to one proprietor, which for Some years past they have been in the practice of granting to all others who had Similar Claims; as you will See by the inclosed list—By what means Dr Thornton has contrived to forget, that he himself has been in the constant practice of Signing Squares not in the Engraved plan, without protest or oppos[it]ion, I am at a loss to know—In your reply to Dr Thornton, you Seem to consider the Engraved plan as a Standard—So far no doubt it ought to be considered, in regard to the places pointed out in it for the public buildings, and principal public areas—But you no doubt recalled Sir, that the Engraved plan was drawn by Mr Ellicott in Philada (I believe from Scanty Materials,) after the late Commissioners and Major L'Infant had parted— When however Mr Ellicott came to apply this plan to the ground intended for the City, he found the mensuration did not Suit a plan drawn upon So Small a Scale—hence it became necessary, in many instances, to draw the rectangular Streets, much farther from one another, than they appeared upon the Engraved plan—consequently, a great number of valuable Squares were found to intervene, which have been inserted by the concurrence of Dr Thornton, in order, to keep up the regularity of the City.[3] Had these Squares been left out, (which the proprietors would not have Submitted to,) they would have left unmeaning and irregular vacancies. For instance, while Square No. 915 in the Engraved plan, and on my ground, is only 7,500 Square feet in content, with its accute points run out to the full extent—Yet Square South of 915 (not in the Engraved plan,) contains near 50,000 Square feet—If therefore either of these Squares were to be left out, it certainly ought to be the one in the Engraved plan.

Doctor Thornton Seems to think that these intervening Squares will be occupied as Stables or greater nuisances—This proves that he is not acquanted with the occupation of property in great Cities, where at least three fourths of the front on the lower floors is occupied by Stores of all kinds, Compting houses, offices, and other places of public business; while Stables, and the nuisances alluded to, are always put upon the back part of large lots—besides, every one knows, that a corner Lot, which has no room for back buildings, is always double the value of the deep lots in the middle of the Square—Merchants generally have their Stores, Warehouses, and compting rooms, in the most public parts of a City; while their dwelling houses, are in a more retired Situation—Hence therefore, these Small Squares, will be extremely valuable, as Retail Stores, and other places of public business, which do not require much back ground—and when rounded off at the accute points, in a Semicircular manner, they will keep up the regularity of the City, and prevent disgusting triangular open Spaces—In the inclosed list, you will See that Dr Thornton has Signed Several Squares which do not contain a Standard lot, while Square North of Sqr. No. 507 Signed by him, does not contain half a Standard Lot, by 533 Sqr. feet. Dr Thornton informs you that the whole content of the Squares not in the Engraved plan, only amounts to 381,683 Sqr. feet—The content of the Squares in the inclosed list is 3,370,568 Sqr. feet, and there are 54 others, which at the Same rate, will make 1,629432 Sqr. feet more—in all *four Millions* Sqr.

feet—This Shews that he was not acquanted with the Subject—
The Squares belonging to me, divided on the 22d of May last, are
upwards of 100,000 Square feet, and while the greatest part of
them, are Sixteen and twenty thousand Sqr. feet, none of them
are less than Seven thousand. Doctr Thornton complains that I
alone, and Singularly, from all other proprietors, would not accept
of £25 per Acre, for what is now worth £1600 pr acre—For what
reason he Should expect I ought to be less attached to my own
interest than other proprietors, I am at a loss to know—He also
complains that I would not wait till the opinion of the President of
the unitted States was known on that Subject—My reason was, that
the President not having proper means of information, would
turn the matter back to the Commissioners; therefore did not
think it necessary to trouble him on the occasion.

While Dr Thornton is labouring under the apprehension of nuisances, he allots Some of these Squares for *Infirmaries* the greatest
nuisance that can be introduced into a City—What kind of *Temples*
we are to have in this City, or to what *Gods* or *Goddesses* they are to
be dedicated, I have not yet learned.

Upon the whole Sir, you must be Sensible, that it is extremely
aggravating for me, to be So obstinately opposed in procuring
what all others have peaceably obtained—and when you Shall
have compared Dr Thorntons protest and letter to you, with the
inclosed list, you will be able to Judge, whether his opposition on
this Occasion, accords with that *impartiality—knowledge of duty—
and recollection of past Actions*—expected of a Commissioner of the
City of Washington—With great respect I have the honour to be
Sir Your Most Obt and Humle Servant

George Walker

P.S. Should you have an opty will be happy if you Shew this letter
to Dr Thornton and the other Commissioners for their information.[4] G.W[alker]
N.B. The Inclosed List contains 76 Squares 73 of which are Signed
by Dr Thornton. G.W[alker]

ALS, DNA: RG 42, General Records, Letters Received, 1791–1867.

1. William Thornton's letter criticizing Walker is dated 31 May; GW wrote
Thornton in support of his position on 1 June.

2. The enclosed list of Federal City squares has not been identified.

3. For reference to the 1792 engraving of the L'Enfant plan for the Federal
City, see GW to William Thornton, 1 June 1799, n.1.

4. GW forwarded Walker's letter to the District of Columbia commissioners on 7 Aug.: "Gentlemen, The request at the foot of the enclosed letter (which I received on my return home yesterday) must be my apology for giving you the trouble of this address. The statement which it refers to, is sent to Mr Walker agreeably to his desire—With great esteem and regard I am Gentlemen Your Most Obedt Servt Go: Washington" (ALS, Gallery of History, Las Vegas; letterpress copy, NN: Washington Papers). And on the same day GW wrote Walker: "Sir Your letter of the 5th instant was presented to me yesterday, on my way home, and not read until I reached it.

"As I have no concern in public matters, unconnected with Military duties; so it is neither my *wish*, ⟨n⟩or intention, to interfere with them, if they do not relate to myself personally. Having neither Doctr Thornton's letter nor my answer to it before me, I mean to express no sentiment on either; or on the subject to which they related, further than that, a question was askd me to which I gave an answer from the best recollection I had of the case.

"Because you have requested it and for as much as I had no opportunity of complying therewith while I was in the City, I *now* enclose your letter *to me* of the above date, to the Commissioners. The list transmitted therein you will receive under this cover. I am—Sir—Your most Hble Servt Go: Washington" (letterpress copy, NN: Washington Papers). Over Thornton's continuing protest commissioners Scott and White upheld Walker's position. For references to the division of the odd parcels of land, see the editor's note in Harris, *Thornton Papers*, 1:495.

From Robert Lewis

Hond Uncle,   Spring Hill August 7th 1799

Inclosed you will receive a draught on Mr Russell Mercht of Alexandria, for the balance of Mr Ariss's rent, which you will be so kind as to get Mr Anderson to present immediately—Mr Ariss's infirmities prevents me from being as rigid as I ought to be—He is *always*, and ever will be (I am fearful) backward in discharging his rent.[1] When my execution accounts are settled with the Sheriffs of Berkley & Fauquier, I shall either remit you the money by some safe hand or come with it myself.[2]

A few days since I had the pleasure of seeing my Brother Lawrence & his Lady at Mr Carters in Culpeper. They are both well— My brother has received great benefit from the sulphur mud which he has been advised to apply to his eye, and drinking freely of the water obtain'd from Mr Voss's Springs.[3]

An intense drought from the latter end of June to the last week in July has been the means of lessening our crops of Hay, Since which we have been very seasonable—The last fall's drought and

Hessian flye combin'd, has depriv'd us completely of seed wheat—
Crops of corn & Tobacco are remarkable fine.

Mrs Lewis presents her affectionate regards to you & my Aunt—
with Your much oblig'd & very dutiful Nephew

Robt Lewis

ALS, ViMtV.

1. John Ariss, the noted housebuilder who died before the end of the year, had been renting a 700-acre tract on Bullskin Run in Berkeley County from GW for £60 per annum since 1786. See Ariss to GW, 5 Aug. 1784, and notes. GW wrote Lewis on 17 Aug. 1799 that he had received Ariss's draft on James Russell of Alexandria for £42, but see also GW to Lewis, 23 August.

2. GW does not record in existing accounts any further payments from Lewis.

3. Voss's spring may have been on the land of Robert B. Voss (died c.1811) of Mountain Prospect, Culpeper County.

Letter not found: from George Steptoe Washington, 7 Aug. 1799. On 14 Aug. Tobias Lear wrote George Steptoe Washington: "The General has received your letter of the 7th inst." (DLC:GW).

Letter not found: from William Vans Murray, 9 Aug. 1799. GW wrote Murray on 26 Oct. that he had just received a number of letters from him, including those dated the "9th and 17th of August."

From William Baynham

Sir   Essex 10th Augt 1799

I returned last evening from a visit to Gloucester, and found your servant, Tom, who had arrived on the day after I left home, waiting with your letter of the 30th July.

I have this morning operated on both Eyes, although, I must confess, with no very sanguine expectations of the boy's deriving essential relief by the operations: but I have thereby given him the only chance, which the case admits of, of seeing better with one eye, and of preventing total blindness in the other. The result will be known in the course of a fortnight; at the expiration of which time he will, I expect, be in a condition to travel with safety, and will, in that case, set out on his return to Mount Vernon; of which I will most assuredly advise you by post.[1] With great respect I have the honor to be Sir your mo. obedt Servt

Wm Baynham

ALS, DLC:GW.

    1. Baynham wrote GW again on 21 August.

From Francis Deakins

George Town post Office Augt 10th [17]99

    I have this minute Recd the inclosed Letter[1]—I Cant advise any Change in the mode of the Rents that I think may answer better then the present—the plantation is rather worn to Confind them to Grain alone—while they have to pay in Tobo they may pick out manuerd Land enought for it—Shou'd you however wish any Change whatever please to mention it & it Shall be done[2]—with great Respect

Francis Deakins

ALS, DLC:GW.

    1. As the collector of rents from the tenants on GW's Woodstock Manor property in Montgomery County, Md., Hezekiah Veatch wrote Deakins on 7 Aug.: "Dear Sir The Tenants on General Washingtons part of Woodstock have all give up their places—Mr Warring Says he Informed you when he was down with Tobo That he should not Continue on his place Another Year—And he still says the same—And that you may rent his place to any person makeing application for it—And Mr Nathan Harding Come over to me this morning And give up both his places—And says he Intends to set out on Sunday next in order to get him a place over the allegany mountains near the mouth of Buffolow—As the Tenants are now about to leave their places, If any new Arrangements are thought Necessary this would be the only time to make them—And if not the Rents I expect will continue the same Together with every other Instruction to the Succeeding Tenants—As I have no doubts but there will be many apply But I shall not Engage Any of the places untill I hear from you" (DLC:GW). For references to GW's acquisition of one-half of Woodstock Manor in 1792 from John Francis Mercer, see the note to Priscilla Beale to GW, 2 April 1797 (*Papers, Retirement Series*, 1:60).

    2. GW's reply to Deakins of 17 Aug. reads: "Dear Sir, Your favor of the 10th Inst. enclosing a letter from Mr Veatch of the 7th instant, came duly to hand. The receipt of which ought to have been sooner acknowledged as he appears to be waiting directions.

    "I am very well satisfied with the Rents of my part of Woodstock as they now stand; but if you, on consulting Mr Veatch, should be of opinion that they could be placed on a better footing now, or at any time hence, it would be equally agreeable to me that you should make the alteration and it shall be confirmed by Dear Sir Your most Obedt & obligd Servt Go: Washington" (letterpress copy, NN: Washington Papers).

From Benjamin Fendall

Dr Sir   Cedar-Hill [Charles County, Md.] Augt 10th [17]99
    Within this Day, or two, I found myself, so much relieved, from my long continued, & painful illness, though I use my left arm, with some difficulty, as to be enabled, to finish Mrs Washingtons Teeth, and you'll receive them, safe, I hope, by my Servant. They are—as nearly as I can now, recollect—like the old ones—As there are so many ways, to make, & shape Teeth—'twou'd be almost impossible, to make 'em, exactly alike—after some time, without having the old ones present. The Model I took, has, also, by accident, sustain'd some injury. I am extremely sorry, indeed, yr Lady has been obliged to wait so long—owing to my long absence from home and my Illness, after I had arriv'd at Cedar-Hill.[1] I wish you, & Mrs Washington, to have every conviction within yourselves, I ever will, with promptitude, and with pleasure, serve you both when ever you may choose to Command me—if in my power, and I fondly flatter myself, youll both deem my excuse to be sufficiently admissible—at this Time.[2] Please to present my most Respectful Compts to Mrs Washington, & believe me, Dr Sir Yrs, with due respect,

B: Fendall

ALS, DLC:GW. "By John" is written on the cover.
    1. Dr. Fendall was at Mount Vernon in December 1797, and on 6 Mar. 1798 GW wrote Fendall that Mrs. Washington had been long in "want" of the teeth that Fendall had taken away "unfinished." See *Diaries*, 6:271–72.
    2. Fendall appended a receipt dated 10 Aug., which reads: "To making 4 artificial Teeth with an Enamel for Mrs W——n Twenty Eight Dollars which, if the Genl chooses—he can enclose me by my Sert John—Then re[ceive]d the above in full. B. Fendall." An entry for 8 Aug. in GW's cash accounts, Ledger C, 53, reads: "By Doct. Fendal sent by his man John pr his order $28 gave his man $1—[$]29."

From Thomas Law

Dear Sir.   Washington Augt 10 1799.
    I hope you arrived well & that the Sun & fatigue did not encrease the bile[1]—Dr Thornton has applied to Mr Carroll who will not take less than 15d. or 15 Cents—which in truth the Lot is

worth[2] A Gentleman from Baltimore has been with me to day for a Lot to build upon, & the Stenographer (or short hand writer) to Congress is going to build on one of my Lots in the small Square above my stable & he is to pay me a Dollar rent ℔ annum & the principal in 10 Years; which is selling the Lot at the rate of 15 or 16 Cents ℔ Square foot.[3]

Mr Fenno the Printer is here & Blodget &ca.[4] Mr Humphrys has sounded all the Eastern branch & says that there are two or three places fit for the Navy Yard—he is glad to find that the bottom is so muddy & soft.[5]

Last night I heard Bernard & Darley, and spent a very pleasent Eveng there were Thornton the Architect Cliffin the Poet & Painter, Bernard the Actor & Darley the Singer in short several choice spirits the forerunners of numbers such.[6]

I have to thank Mrs Washington & to be angry at her sending snuff by Eliza—such an attention tho' it evinces her kindness yet it encourages a bad habit.

Pray do not take the trouble to acknowledge this, unless you wish to have Mr Carrolls corner Lot.[7] I remain

AL[S], DLC:GW. Part of the closing and Law's signature are missing.

1. GW returned to Mount Vernon on 6 Aug., a "Clear & warm" day, from Law's house in Washington. He had "lodged" at Law's the night before after attending a meeting of the Potomac River Company in Georgetown (*Diaries*, 6:359).

2. Perhaps GW discussed with Law and William Thornton while he was in Georgetown and Washington, 5–6 Aug., the possibility of his buying a lot on Capitol Hill from Daniel Carroll of Duddington, the man who had sold him in 1798 one of the two lots on which his double house was being built. No correspondence with Thornton about this has been found. In the partially illegible letter that GW wrote in response to Law on 13 Aug., GW expressed doubts about his being able to come to terms with Carroll and explained that it was "the situation *alone*" of the lot that accounted for his interest in it. On 21 Sept. GW identified the lot in question as "the corner lot . . . on New Jersey Avenue," which indicates that it adjoined his two lots on Capitol Hill; but by this time he had already "abandoned the idea" of trying to purchase the lot (GW to Law, 21 Sept. 1799).

3. Jonathan Williams Condy had replaced the Republican John Beckley as clerk of the House of Representatives; the "Stenographer" may have been one of Condy's assistants.

4. John Ward Fenno published the *Gazette of the United States* (Philadelphia) for two years after his father John Fenno died in the Philadelphia yellow fever epidemic of 1798. Samuel Blodget (1757–1814) became one of the largest speculators in Washington real estate in 1792.

5. Joshua Humphreys (1751–1838), noted shipbuilder, was made the first naval contracter for the United States. For further references to seeking to fix

upon a site in Washington for the navy yard, see Benjamin Stoddert to GW, 16 Sept. 1798.

6. "Cliffin" was a Scottish portrait painter Lewis Clephane. John Bernard was an English comedian who came to America in 1797. John Darley, a popular singer at Covent Garden, was recruited in 1793 by Thomas Wignell for his company of actors at the New Theater in Philadelphia, which opened in 1794. Darley brought with him his son John Darley, Jr., who became a distinguished American actor (*Columbia Hist. Soc. Recs.*, 21:263; Seilhamer, *American Theater*, 1:231, 3: 137–39).

7. See note 2.

To Charles Cotesworth Pinckney

My dear Sir,   Mount Vernon 10th Augt 1799

Daily expectation of Genl Washington's arrival, must be received as my apology for not having given your obliging favour of the 25th of June, an earlier acknowledgment. He did not (on account of the indisposition of his Son, in North Carolina) reach this place until the 6th instant. He left us yesterday, with the young Gentleman; both in good health, and Spirits.[1]

Permit me to offer you my best thanks for the Plumes you had the kindness to send me; which are, indeed, very handsome. Colo. Lear has, I presume, done the same in the enclosed letter; and the one for Captn Thornton (for the whole came hither in a general case) shall be sent to him by the first safe conveyance to Fredericksg his recruitg Station.[2]

I thank you too, my good Sir, for the transcript of Major Mountflorence's letter to you—which is an interesting one. But whether the knowledge the French Directory has of the President's appointment of three Envoys, to treat—on certain previous stipulations—in France; & their reverse of fortunes, may not have given a different complexion to the business, remains to be decided. I wish this Nomination & appointment, may not be productive of embarrassmt in the measures of this Government.

Had the Gentleman, whose name is mentioned in Montflorences letter, been actually appointed as the Negociator of Peace, little doubt remains in my mind of his acceptance thereof; notwithstanding the admonitions which had been given him of the delicate situation in which he would be involved, in a visit to the United States at this crisis of our affairs, in any capacity whatsoever.[3]

Lest Captain Thornton should not have been written to by you, or seen your orders appointing him one of your aids—and have understood that you do not re⟨quire⟩ his attendance to the Southward, I will cause him to be advised ⟨*illegible*⟩.[4]

Recruiting in so⟨me States⟩ has progressed tolerably well, ⟨*illegible*⟩ others it is at a stand; and indeed ⟨*illegible*⟩tion that can be ⟨thrown *illegible*⟩ by the enemies to our government ⟨*illegible*⟩—In a word, the Aurora, and ⟨*illegible*⟩ Gazettes which emanate from it, ⟨*illegible*⟩ which supports the same ⟨*illegible*⟩ are endeavouring by every ⟨means *illegible*⟩ and alarm, to create resistance to the Law, insubordination in ⟨the *illegible*⟩; In short, to prostrate discipline, and to introduce anarchy in the Military ⟨as they⟩ have attempted to do in the Civil government of this Country.

When—where—and how such things are to terminate, is beyond the reach of human Ken; but ⟨*illegible*⟩ they cannot progress much ⟨further with⟩out an explosion. Indeed ⟨*illegible*⟩ the Aurora (if one ⟨*illegible*⟩ publications) seems desirous ⟨*illegible*⟩ crisis. His inuendos, & charges ⟨*illegible*⟩ longer to be borne, ⟨*illegible* according⟩ to his account (and I have no doubt ⟨*illegible*⟩) there is a contest in Philadelphia for the honor of becoming his Bail. ⟨*illegible* am⟩ong other things, in language, & ⟨*illegible*⟩ impossible to be misunderstood, the ⟨Government⟩ is not only accused of being under ⟨British influence,⟩ but of bribery to a considerable amount. If the semblance of this on a fair & impartial investigation of the case shall appear, I will not only ac⟨knowledge⟩ myself to be among those who ⟨*illegible*⟩ in the Officers of it, but ⟨will pronounce⟩ him, not only a bold, but a ⟨*illegible*⟩ Printer; deserving of thanks, and high reward for bringing to light conduct so abominable. On the other hand, if it shall be found that it is all calumny—⟨calcula⟩ted to poison the minds of the People ⟨*illegible*⟩ disquietude, destroy all confidence ⟨in Public⟩ functionaries, prostrate the go⟨vernment &⟩ produce disunion of the States; ⟨*illegible* punishment⟩ ought to be inflicted on such ⟨*illegible*[5] and⟩ Mr & Mrs Lewis are from home; ⟨the⟩ rest of the family unite in every good wish ⟨*illegible*⟩ Mrs Pinckney—whose indisposition ⟨*illegible*⟩ rest of the family; and I am ⟨*illegible*⟩ affece frd &ca

Go: Washington

ALS (letterpress copy), NN: Washington Papers.

1. When GW returned home on 6 Aug. from the meeting of the Potomac River Company in Georgetown, he "found Genl. Wm. Washington of So. Carolina

& Son here" (*Diaries*, 6:359). The son, William, was born in 1785 and lived until 1830.

2. Pinckney wrote GW on 4 June that he was sending by William Washington two plumes for GW and one plume each for Tobias Lear and Presly Thornton. According to George Washington Parke Custis, GW gave "the magnificent white plumes presented to him by Major-General Pinckney" to the bride Nelly Custis, "preferring the old Continental cocked hat, with the plain black-ribbon cockade, a type of the brave old days of '76" (Custis, *Recollections*, 450).

3. For the Montflorence letter, see Pinckney to GW, 25 June, n.2.

4. GW wrote Presly Thornton on 12 Aug.: "Dear Sir, I have in my care a plume sent by General Pinckney for your acceptance, which shall be forwarded to you by the first convenient opportunity, or sent agreeably to your directions, if any mode of conveying it should occur to you.

"General Pinckney informs me that he has mentioned you as his Aid in General Orders; but that he does not think it necessary for you to make a journey to Carolina for the purpose of joining his family at present. If, in any event, your attendance should be necessary before General Pinckney comes into this State (which he expects to do in the ensuing fall) he will undoubtedly advise you thereof.

"I hope the recruiting business goes on with more spirit in your quarter than I am informed it has done of late. The arrival of Clothing &c. will, I think, give a spring to it. Mrs Washington unites with me in Compliments to Mrs Thornton. With great esteem & regard I am Dear Sir Your most obedt Sert" (Df, in Lear's hand, DLC:GW).

5. For references to the accusations of bribery of public officials, see GW to Timothy Pickering, 4 Aug., and note 1 of that document.

From Jonathan Trumbull, Jr.

My Dear Sir!   Lebanon [Conn.] 10th Augst 1799

The Delay which my last Letter experienced in reaching you, may be partly accounted for, by sending my Brothers Letter (which accompanied mine) under cover to Mr Wolcott in Phila. for his & Colo. Pickerings observation[1] —what further delay it may have met with, I cannot tell; I only know, that in too many instances, there is not that punctual attention to Duty in our Post Offices, which the Public have a right to expect.

Your reply to Colo. Trumbull, on the project suggested by him, is very similar to what I had written him on the same subject:[2] & is such, as must be given by every well informed, prudent & reflecting Mind, under present circumstances of our political situation. I feel myself much obliged to you Sir! for this communication of your sentiments.

As to the *particular* subject of my former Letter, I beg leave to observe, that my sentiments on the present State, & probable conduct of the two parties in the U. States, on the coming Event aluded to, are very coincident with yours; and I expect that the two sides will be perfectly *Pitted* on the occasion. The *Idea* which I took the liberty to *hint* to you, was not grounded in an Opinion of detatching thereby any *single* Antifederal Vote from *their* Man, whoever, or whatever he may be; but in the *necessity* of securing *every* Federal one on the other part; which is all that may be expected, under present circumstances, for any Gentleman who may be proposed. My Fears, & those of other well-wishers to our Country are, that, neither the present Gentleman in Office, nor any other who can be named, will be likely to secure with *certainty*, that decided & necessary *totality* of Votes, which are to be wished; unless it be the Gentleman *I hinted* to you before: and *his Name*, we flatter ourselves, would succeed without a *single* failure. Of the present *locum tenens*, I need say nothing to you—Your critical discernment of Characters, & general knowledge of public & private opinions, are such, as enable you to fix your own estimate, & form your own Judgment of *future contingencies* as respecting him. As to any others which might be named, I will not trouble you at present—I only beg leave to express my confidence, that *your* disposition to effect *all* the *public Good* you can, still remains; & will continue to exist, so long as Health, vigor & activity, shall be among the Blessings, which Heaven is pleased to indulge you with; & which I hope & trust, will, in Mercy to our Dear Country, be elongated beyond the Term of *Three score Years & Ten.*

I am not, my Dear Sir! among the Class of intimate & confidential Friends of the President, who might be entituled to whisper in his Ear, the Hint you suggest. I have been casting about in my mind, & making enquiries, for some one among his Massachusetts Friends, who might do this kind Office for him; but, altho many are wishing it, yet I cannot learn that any thing of the kind has yet been done to any *good* effect—nor do I learn that it is likely to be done, with any hopes of success. His own self-sufficiency, I fancy, will determine his Conduct on this, as on other subjects. Pardon my Dear Sir, the trouble I give you—& believe me to be—with high regard, & unceasing respect & Friendship—sir Your Obedient and very hume Servt

Jona. Trumbull

ALS, DLC:GW; ADfS, ViMtV.

1. On 21 July GW reported to Jonathan Trumbull, Jr., having received the day before Trumbull's letter of 22 June, in which Trumbull enclosed a lengthy "political Letter," dated 5 April, to himself from his brother John Trumbull in London.

2. GW replied on 25 June to John Trumbull's letter of 24 Mar. 1799.

To Burwell Bassett, Jr.

Dear Sir,   Mount Vernon ⟨11th Augt⟩ 1799

Sometime ⟨between *illegible*⟩ment to the walks of ⟨private *illegible*⟩ girl*, the body servant of Mrs Washington⟨,⟩ absconded without the least pr⟨ovocation⟩ and without our having ⟨*illegible* sus⟩-picion of such, her intention ⟨*illegible*⟩ whither she had gone.

At length, we learnt ⟨*illegible*⟩ got to Portsmouth in New H⟨ampshire; in⟩ consequence of this information ⟨*illegible*⟩ authentic) I wrote to the Collect⟨or of the⟩ Port, Mr Whipple requesting ⟨*illegible*⟩ use proper means to restore ⟨her to her⟩ Mistress. At first, according to ⟨*illegible*⟩ she appeared willing to return: ⟨*illegible*⟩ the Vessel in which she was to ⟨*illegible*⟩ about to sail, she concealed ⟨*illegible*⟩ one difficulty and delay ⟨*illegible*⟩ther, so as to keep her Mistress ⟨from *illegible*⟩ Services until this time.

If, under this statement of ⟨*illegible*⟩ intention (as declared when here) of ⟨*illegible*⟩ Portsmouth, you could by any easy ⟨*illegible*⟩self & proper means, be the ⟨*illegible*⟩ of recovering, & forwarding the ⟨*illegible*⟩ place, it would be a pleasing circumstance to your Aunt.

I do not however wish you to undertake anything, that may involve ⟨*illegible*⟩ unpleasant, or troublesome ⟨*illegible.*⟩ The girl, as we have been ⟨*illegible*⟩ was enticed away by a Frenchman, ⟨*illegible*⟩ her, she was willing to come back; but ⟨*illegible*⟩ other connexions, wan⟨*illegible*⟩ conditions to her return, afterwards.

This I could not *then*, nor will ⟨I⟩ agree to; further than that, if she put⟨s me⟩ to no unnecessary trouble and expence; ⟨and⟩ conduct⟨s⟩ herself well for the time ⟨*illegible*⟩ she will escape punishment for the ⟨*illegible*⟩, & be treated according to her merit⟨s *illegible*⟩. To promise *more*, would be ⟨an im⟩politic & *dangerous* precedent.[1] Your Aunt unites with me in ⟨best wishes⟩ for you; and I am—Dear Sir Your obedt & Affecte Servant

                                                        Go: Washington

*She went by the name of Oney Judge.

ALS (letterpress copy), ViMtV.

1. Most of the information that can be drawn or inferred from the partially illegible letterpress copy of this letter to Burwell Bassett can be found in GW's letter about the young runaway slave Oney Judge, written on 28 Nov. 1796 to the collector of the customs at Portsmouth, N.H., Joseph Whipple (1738–1816). GW wrote Whipple: "I regret that the attempt you made to restore the girl (Oney Judge as she called herself while with us, and who, without the least provocation absconded from her Mistress) should have been attended with so little success. . . . there is no doubt in this family, of her having been seduced and enticed off by a Frenchman . . . who getting tired of her, as is presumed left her, and that she had betaken herself to the Needle—the use of which she well understood—for a livelihood. . . . If she will return to her former Service, without obliging me to resort to compulsory means to effect it, her late conduct will be forgiven by her Mistress." If she refused to return, he should "put her on board a Vessel bound either to Alexandria or the Federal City," provided such action would not be likely to "excite a mob or riot." Oney Judge, who was 12 years old in February 1786, was the daughter of a seamstress at Mount Vernon, a dower slave named Betty (*Diaries*, 4:277–78).

To James McHenry

Private

My dear Sir,   Mount Vernon 11th August 1799

Your private letters of the 29th Ulto & 5th instant, have been duly received. Mr Bordley for presenting, and you for forwarding his Essays on Husbandry, are entitled to, and, accordingly receive, my thanks for these instances of both your kindnesses.

(Confidential)

I think you Wisemen of the East, have got yourselves into a hobble, relatively to France, Great Britain, Russia & the Porte—to which, Allow me the priviledge of adding our worthy Demos. All cannot be pleased! Whom will you offend? Here then is a severe trial for your Diplomatic skill, in which the Editor of the Aurora says you are great adepts. But to be serious, I think the nomination, & appointment of Ambassadors to treat with France would, in any event, have been liable to unpleasant reflections (after the Declarations wch have been made)—and in the present state of matters, in Europe, must be exceedingly Embarrassing. The President has a choice of difficulties before him, in this business; If he pursues the line he marked out, *all* the consequences cannot be foreseen: If he relinquishes it, it will be said to be of a piece with all the other Acts of the Administration—unmeaning if not wicked, deceptious—&ca—&ca—&ca; and will arm the opposition with fresh weapons, to commence new attacks upon the Government, be the turn given to it, and reasons assigned what they may. I come now, to the Scene of Bribery.

And pray, my good Sir, what part of the $800,000 have come to your share? As you are high in Office, I hope you did not disgrace yourself in the acceptance of a paltry bribe. A 100,000$ perhaps— But here again I become serious. There can be no medium between the reward & punishment of an Editor, who shall publish such things as Duane has been doing for sometime past— On what ground then does he *pretend* to stand, in his exhibition of the charges, or the insinuations which he has handed to the Public? Can hardihood itself be so great, as to stigmatise characters in the Public Gazettes for the most heineous offences, and when prosecuted, pledge it-self to support the alligations, unless there was something to build on? I hope & expect, that the Prosecutors will probe this matter to the bottom. It will have an unhappy effect on the public mind if it be not so.[1]

But how stands the charge—in verity & truth—with respect to the Consul General (Stephens) purchase of Coffee, and breach of trust; or in other words, taking advantage of his Official knowledge to monopolise that article at a low price? This thing makes a good deal of noize among the friends, as well as the enemies of government; and if true, proves him unworthy, altogether, of public confidence; & denominates him a mercenary ⟨wretch⟩—one who would do any thing for lucre.[2]

Is the President returned to the Seat of Government? When will he return? His absence (I mention it from the best motives) gives much discontent to the friends of government, while its enemies chuckle at it, & think it a favourable omen for them. I am always— Your Affecte

Go: Washington

ALS, NNGL; ALS (letterpress copy), DLC:GW; copy, DLC: Hamilton Papers.

1. For the *Aurora*'s charge of corruption and bribery in the dealings of the Adams administration with Saint Domingue, see GW to Timothy Pickering, 4 Aug., n.1. On 24 July the editor William Duane asserted in the *Aurora*: "*in America alone during the year 1798, Great Britain has expended Secret Service money to the amount of one hundred and eighty thousand pounds, sterling—or 800,000 dollars!*"

2. When the new American consul general to Saint Domingue, Dr. Edward Stevens, sailed from Philadelphia in March 1799, he took with him, on Secretary

of State Timothy Pickering's instructions, a load of provisions and supplies to be sold to Toussaint L'Ouverture to defray Stevens's expenses in negotiating with the rebel leader about opening trade with the island. This provoked protests from Philadelphia merchants, and the situation was exacerbated when Jacob Mayer, the American consul at Cap-Français, spread a rumor that Stevens and Toussaint L'Ouverture's agent in the negotiations, Joseph Bunel, were engaged in speculation in Saint Domingue provisions (Tansill, *U.S. and Santo Domingo*, 58; see also McHenry's description of Stevens's mission and defense of the administration's policy in his letter to GW of 10 Nov. 1799).

To Timothy Pickering

Private
Dear Sir,   Mount Vernon Augt 11th 1799
A day or two after my last letter to you was sent to the Post Office,[1] I received your obliging favor of the 2d instant.

The embarrassments occasioned by the late appointment of Envoys, begin now to shew themselves; and must place the Government—whether it advances towards or retreats from the object, for which they were appointed, in a delicate situation. Of the two evils, the least, no doubt will be chosen. Neither, can be pleasant in its operation.

The advantage taken of a confidential trust, and Monopoly of Coffee by our Agent in St Domingo—is spoken of in severe terms by friends, as well as the enemies of our Government.[2] With very great esteem & regard I am—Dear Sir Your Obedt Hble Servt
                                                    Go: Washington

ALS, MHi: Pickering Papers; ALS (letterpress copy), DLC:GW. The ALS is docketed "recd 15th."
    1. GW wrote Pickering on 4 August.
    2. See GW to James McHenry, this date, n.2.

To James McHenry

Sir   Mount Vernon Augt 12th 1799
I have duly received your letter of the 7th inst., enclosing reccommendations in favor of Mr James Glenn for a Captaincy in the Provisional Army; and shall attend to your request to return this, and similar papers, whenever the list for Virginia shall be completed.[1]

But, Sir, I must candidly acknowledge to you that I see no prospect of completing the selection of Officers from this State, for the Provisional Army, within any reasonable time, if at all, unless some other measure than that now pursued shd be adopted.

When, agreeably to your request, I assured you of my readiness to promote, so far as was in my power, the President's wish to select officers for the 24 Regiments authorized to be raised, I very candidly stated to you the circumstances which had prevented my having such personal knowledge of Characters in this State as would enable me to make a selection here without the assistance of others; and, at the same time, submitted to your consideration, whether the President's views might not be carried into effect with more facility & dispatch by having his determination to appoint Officers made known in such a manner as to give an opportunity to all who were desireous of serving to come forward with their pretensions; Or that proper Characters for the command of the Regiments should be appointed in the several Districts and power given to them, with the assistance of their Majors (who shd also be previously selected) to appoint the Company Officers of their respective Regiments. For the rejection of the first of these propositions you have given me your reasons.[2] To the second I do not recollect that I have had any reply.

I must, however, endeavour to impress you with the necessity of adopting some other mode for Officering those Regiments, at least in this State, than that which has been pursued, if it is intended that the Officers shall be appointed before the meeting of Congress; for, with all my endeavours to obtain information respecting characters who are fit and willing to serve, I find that very few indeed have been brought forward, and these only from particular places. Immediately upon receiving your request to aid in this business, I wrote to several influential and confidential Characters, requesting them to furnish me with the names of such persons within their districts or the sphere of their acquaintance as were qualified and would be willing to accept appointments. From these sources I have obtain but little information. Genl Marshall, Colo. Carrington and Colo. Heth on whom I placed great dependence for information have not furnished me with any except in two or three cases. From Genl Lee I have received only a single letter on the subject and that recommendg one person. Genl Morgan has been so good as to recommend a number of Characters; but they are confined to a particular part of the State. Colo. Cropper, of the Eastern shore, has signified to me his willingness to accept the command of a Regiment, and has promised to furnish a list of names for other offices; but his selection will be limited to a few Counties, or at most to one District[3]—I have also given eve[r]y encouragement in my power to others to come forward with recommendations or offers of service, but without effect. And, indeed, it can hardly be expected that persons would interest themselves in pointing out Characte[r]s for office unless there was a degree of certainty that they would be appointed. I shall, however, continue my endeavours to comply with your wishes in the way you desire; unless some other mode shd be adopted.

Enclosed is a letter from Captn George S. Washington with a recommendation of John Atwell, to be appointed a Cadet in his Company, vice [John] Stephens, who is promoted to a first lieutenancy.[4] So far as I am acquainted with the Subscribers to this recommendation they are respectable Characters, and may be relied upon. With due consideration I have the honor to be

Df, DLC:GW.

1. McHenry's letter from Philadelphia of 7 Aug. reads: "Enclosed, I transmit you Recommendations in favour of Mr James Glenn for a Captaincy in the Provisional Army. When you shall have completed the list for Virginia, I pray you to return these papers, with others of a like description" (DLC:GW). On 4 Oct. 1799 both James Stephenson and Andrew Waggener wrote to GW recommending Glenn for an appointment in the Provisional Army. Stephenson's letter from "Berkley Mill Creek" in Berkeley County reads: "I have taken the liberty of mentioning to you Capt. James Glenn of this County who wishes an appointment in the Provisional Army, having servd with him on the expedition in the year 1791 and afterward having acting as my Lieut. under Genl Wayne I therefore can say confidently that I consider him a good Officer and well quallified to Command a Battalion, he is popular in this Country as a Military man and in my Opinion would have as little difficulty in raising men as any other whatever he is a plain man, possesses a considerable degree of firmness and is not defficient in understanding. Not having the honour of a personal acquaintance with you difficulties have arose in my mind in what manner I ought to address you but feeling anxious for Capt. Glenns success knowing him to be a man well qu[a]llified for the Army induced me to take the liberty to address you as aforesd" (DLC:GW). Gen. Daniel Morgan on 12 June 1799 had highly recommended Stephenson to GW for appointment in the Provisional Army. The letter from Winchester of 4 Oct. written by Andrew Waggener reads: "Give me leave to recommend to you in a particular manner Capt. James Glenn of Berkeley County, as a proper person to Command a Battalion he was an Officer under Genl St Clair at the time he was defeated in

'91 in which action he behavd with great propriety and firmness, he was also an Officer under Genl Wayne and was considerd one of considerable Utillity, he is a friend to Goverment and if the Provetional Army is raised a Command in it is what he wishes. Capt. Glenn is a man of unblemishd Charactor, he is temperate and well disposd" (DLC:GW). Two days later, on 6 Oct., Maj. William Campbell of the 8th Infantry Regiment wrote from Winchester: "Capt. James Glenn of Berkely County informs me he has Solicited for a Majority in the Provisional Army. I therefore in Justice to his Charactor take the liberty *through you* to recommend him as a Gentn deserving that appointment, having observed his Conduct as Waggon Conductor to the Virga & Maryland Militia on the Expedition made by them against the Insurgents of Pensylvania in 1794. From Bentleys Farm to this Place I had the Honour to Command Genl [Thomas] Mathewss Brigade & Charge of the Military Stores when Capt. Glenn was with me as Conductor of Waggons & to that arduous & perplexing office When very little order or discipline was observed by the Troops, he discharged his duty with prudence & good conduct & I must acknowledge rendered me great assistance—his Knowledge of the Tactics is from experience in the Western army where he Served as a Subaltern two years with credit to himself & Country & Sir I have no doubt but that he will do Justice to the office he Sollicits" (DLC:GW). In DLC:GW there is also a letter from Joseph Swearingen to Daniel Morgan, dated 30 June 1799, written in support of Glenn.

2. GW is referring to his letter to McHenry of 13 May and to McHenry's of 19 May.

3. For a discussion of GW's efforts to identify men who might serve as officers in the Provisional Army, see McHenry to GW, 2 May 1799, n.1.

4. George Steptoe Washington's letter has not been found, but on 14 Aug. Tobias Lear wrote to him: "The General has received your letter of the 7th inst. inclosing a recommendation if favor of Mr John Atwell to be a Cadet in your Company. This recommendation has been forwarded to the Secretary of War, from whom you will learn the result of this application if it be successful" (DLC:GW).

To Richard Kidder Meade

Dear Sir, Mount Vernon 12th Augt 1799

I should have acknowledged the receipt of your favor of the 22d Ultimo before this, had I not been for sometime in daily expectation of seeing Genl Wm Washington, to whom I wished to communicate the contents of it. The General was here a few days since, when I put your recommendation of Captn Edmund Taylor for Brigade Inspector into his hands, and as he is gone on to Philadelphia, I presume that he will, while there, have the proper arrangements made on the subject.[1]

Can you, my dear Sir, give me any assistance in selecting proper characters from this State, to Officer four Regiments of Infantry which is the proportion allotted to Virginia of the 24 Regts authorized to be eventually raised? The Secy of War sometime since, requested ⟨me⟩ to furnish him with names of suitable characters for this purpose.

From a variety of circumstances my personal acquaintance with the ⟨inhabitants of this State has⟩ become very limited. To others then, on whom I can rely, I must look for information. But ⟨*illegible*⟩ had only a small proportion of the ⟨names *illegible*⟩ handed to me, and these confined principally to particular spots, when it is the Secretarys ⟨duty⟩ to have them dissiminated through the State. ⟨Whether⟩ this is owing to its not being generally known ⟨that⟩ he is ⟨*illegible*⟩ determined to take preparatory ⟨*illegible*⟩ to facilitate the raising of this Corps, or to ⟨*illegible*⟩ recommending characters for particular ⟨*illegible*⟩ with their own consent, when it is uncer⟨tain *illegible*⟩ appointed or not, I cannot say ⟨*illegible* un⟩able to select proper ⟨*illegible*⟩ for the command of the Regiments from ⟨*illegible*⟩ of the State, and through them to obtain the selection of the Company Officers, of their respective Regiments.[2]

If any persons occur to you as being well qualified & willing to accept appointments in the eventual Army, you will much oblige me by handing their names, with such information respecting them as you may be able to obtain, & on which I shall place great reliance.[3] Mrs Washington unites in respects, & best wishes to Mrs Meade & yourself with Dr Sir—Your Affecte & Obedt Servant

Go: Washington

ALS (letterpress copy), NN: Washington Papers.

Richard Kidder Meade (1746–1805) served as an aide to GW from March 1777 to the end of the Revolutionary War.

1. Letter not found. For other references to Capt. Edmund Taylor, see GW to Alexander Hamilton, 14 Aug., n.2. See also Meade to GW, 20 Sept., printed here in note 3.

2. For GW's efforts to identify men to be officers in the Provisional Army, see James McHenry to GW, 2 May, n.1.

3. Meade did not reply until 20 Sept., when he had more to say about Taylor and suggested to GW another name: "Your favor of the 12th Ultimo met with such delay that it only got to hand on monday last—this circumstance I hope, Sir will fully account for the date of this. Your mention of Capt. Taylor induces me to observe, that since I took the liberty of naming him to you, that he still stands high in the good opinion of Colo. Parker, & I very much wish on my own part & for my country's sake, that every commission in the army was as well filled—doubtless there are many good appointments, but I am asham'd of the present

race of youths who are passing their time, as on a former occasion, in total idleness, when their Country has certainly a claim to their services. To officer the 4 Regts you mention, I fear will be a difficult task, but you may be assur'd that no inquiry on my part shall be neglected to find out such characters. I have not the least doubt but, that if good Field Officers can be selected, that they will be the proper persons to fix on the inferior ones; for I must confess I have been astonished at the recommendations given by some Gentlemen, to persons unfit one way or another, to fill Commissions. I have in my mind only one character, that perhaps may be made known to you—he serv'd with reputation in the continental Line, & is now esteem'd in private life, but unfortunately he is, by marriage, connected with the Rutherford family, who have been uniformly opposed to Government—This Gentn, Mr Go. Hite, applied to me some time past, to aid him in getting a Majority in case the Troops you now speak of should be call'd for. It shall be my business to procure from him, in writing, his sentiments, from which I shall be enabled to determine, whether I need communicate with you on the subject or not" (DLC:GW).

George Hite was earlier considered for a commission and was rejected. See James McHenry to GW, 10 Jan. 1799, n.4. In his letter of 15 Oct. from his plantation in Frederick County, Meade wrote further about Hite and named several other men worthy of consideration: "The military characters who have been mentioned to me by letter & in person since I answer'd your favor on the subject, are Mr James Stephenson, Mr James Glenn & Mr Monroe, whose Christian name I do [not] recollect at present. The inclos'd letters should have been forwarded earlier to you but from a wish to hear from Colo. Jo. Swearingan & Mr Geo. Hite before I sent them off—The Colo. tells me in his answer to my inquiry that he is too infirm to take a military command—Mr Hite has been with me & will cheerfully accept one; I had written to him requesting answers to certain questions relative to his political opinions—these I have in writing; I will not however Sir trouble you with the perusal of it, or any of the many letters I have in my possession, but relying on the confidence you place in me, proceed in as few words as I can, (having seen all the Gentn) to give you my candid opinion of them, which might prove erroneous notwithstanding the most intimate acquaintance with them all—If Mr Hite is sincere, (& this I can by no means doubt) he stands in my judgment a Virtuous Citizen—he serv'd in the War with Britain with reputation, is of a Military turn, & is a well looking, well inform'd man—Mr James Stephenson, from whom you have a letter in favor of James Glenn, I have never seen more than three or four times, he is a person of good countenance, & is spoken of in the highest terms by Colo. [Thomas] Parker & many others in whom I concive reliance may be plac'd—Mr Stephenson has seen service—I have mention'd the names of Hite & Stephenson first from an opinion that they have had the best educations—I have no grounds to suppose they have any preference as Soldiers. Mr Glenn I never was in company with until the other day—he has a Soldierly honest go[o]d countenance—is spoken very highly of by all I met with, & is said to be a good training officer. Mr—— Monroe I have often seen (as he lives in this County, the others are of Berkley) he appears a plain honest man, of a slender education, fond of a Military life, of which he experienc'd a good deal in the line of this State, during the revolution—Our Militia officers speak well of him as an adjutant. In my interview with all the Gentn I have named, I think they only spoke of Majority's; but perhaps, I may venture, to suppose that unless your list furnishes great choice, that both Hite & Stephenson may do justice to the command of Regts. I will only add to the trouble I have given you, by observing, that I have written to one of the purest characters, of my acquaintance to know if I may mention his name to you—you may perhaps recollect, the person of Mr Carter Page who served in Baylors Regt—was the command in the Horse, I should have hopes of getting his consent, as it is, I fear he will decline. On hearing from him I will communicate with you if necessary" (DLC:GW).

James Stephenson (1764–1833) of Martinsburg in what is now West Virginia, served as a member of the Virginia house of delegates from 1800 to 1803 and in 1806 and 1807, and as a Federalist member of Congress in 1803–5, 1809–11, and 1822–25. For Stephenson's recommendation of James Glenn, see GW to McHenry, 12 Aug., n.1. Daniel Morgan had earlier recommended William Monroe in his letter to GW of 12 June. In his response of 27 Oct., GW acknowledges the receipt of the "inclos'd letters" that Meade refers to in this letter of 15 Oct., but they have not been identified. GW's letter to Meade reads: "Dear Sir, By the last Mail I had the pleasure to receive your letter of the 15th inst. with its enclosures. Whenever the appointments for the Provisional Army take place, the Characters you have recommended will be brought into view, and their respective merits duly considered and attended to. And, in the meantime, I will thank you for the names of such others as you can, with confidence, recommend, and who would be willing to serve.

"Mrs Washington unites with me in reciprocating the respects and good wishes of yourself and Mrs Meade. With very great esteem & regard I am, Dear Sir, Your affect. & obedt Servt" (Df, DLC:GW).

Meade followed up his letter of 15 Oct. with a final letter on 3 Nov.: "In my last I observ'd to you that I had written to Mr Carter Page on the subject of a command in the eventual Troops—The day before yesterday I got his very pleasing answer; avowing his attachment to his Country, & his willingness to serve it, at any time when calld on—he however laments that the service he may be call'd into, is not in the Cavalry, having been traind there, & not in the infantry, this however proceeds from his difidence. My observations on his character, were, I think ample in my former correspondence, I will therefore only add, that should we be compell'd to call an Army into the field, that I should feel the highest confidence in knowing that such men as he is, were in Commission. I have very lately rec'd a letter from Mr Abraham Shepherd, of Shepherds Town expressing a desire to command a Regt—he requests me to forward his name to you—My acquaintance with him is not intimate, but I can safely venture to present him as a warm Government man, popular, active & enterprising. By his letter to me, & one in his favor from Colo. Jo. Swearingan, I find that he serv'd in [Moses] Rawlings regt, during Captivity &ca for 5 years & that he left the army as the Senr Supernumerary Captn in the Virginia line" (DLC:GW). Carter Page (c.1758–1825) rose to the rank of captain in the 3d Continental Dragoons during the Revolutionary War and in 1781 served as an aide-de-camp to General Lafayette. He was the son of John Page of Rosewell and was a student at William and Mary at the time that he went into the army in 1776.

Abraham Shepherd, who Meade indicates in his letter of 3 Nov. desired to be given command of a regiment in the Provisional Army, had written to GW from Shepherdstown on 15 Oct.: "In a late conversation with Coll Mede I have learned that you had requested him to enquire who would be suitable persons, to be honoured with Commissions in the provisional army consious of my zeal for the good of my Country and emboldened by the expiriance which four years service had afforded during the revolution and being the Oldest Capt. in the Virginia line, when I retired as a supernumerary Officer by your permission. I beg leave to place myself on the list of those who wish to distinguish themselves only by being usefull as you are not a Stranger to my Genl Charector you can readily determine whether or not, I could hold a Col. Commission with Honour to my-self, and advantage to my Country, and therefore I shall ondly express my sincere wish, that if a more suitable person should offer himself he may be preferred" (DLC:GW). GW responded on 21 Oct.: "Your letter of the 15th inst. offering your services as Colonel in the Provisional Army, has been duly received. When-ever the Appointment of the Officers of this Army shall take place, it will be pleas-ing to find, in the list of Candidates, the names of such as were valuable officers in our Revolutionary War. They will meet with due attention, and among them your letter will not be forgotten" (DLC:GW). Shepherd (1754–1822), son of Thomas Shepherd who founded Shepherdstown (now in West Virginia), was a captain of a rifle company when he was captured at Fort Washington in New York in 1776. After his exchange, he left the army because of illness. He was a promi-nent citizen of Hampshire County.

Letter not found: from Thomas (later Robert Treat) Paine, 12 Aug. 1799. On 1 Sept. GW wrote Paine: "I have duly received your letter of the 12th of August."

From William Smith

Honoured Sir   Camberwell [England] Augst 12th 1799.

It may be justly expected that I should make some Apology for giving you this Trouble. I am embolden'd to it, from your Charac-ter in the World, & from a persuasion that the recollection of an Old Friend, & fellow Soldier, may afford you *some* Pleasure. The reason of my Application will best be explained to you by the pe-rusal of a Letter I received last March—a Copy of which I shall now transcribe.

Sir   Glasgow March 19th 1799

A Friend of mine from Virginia who as well as me, was well ac-quainted with the late Mr Robt Stobo, who on account of his ap-pointment in the Virginia Regiment was entitled to certain Lands in the back Country of that State, which are now become valuable & may *still* be recovered; & as I understand you are Son in Law to a Mrs Janet Richardson Sister to Mr Stobo who has a right to these Lands you may correspond with Mr James Lyle Mercht at Manchester on James River Virginia, in respect to them; and if you chuse to send Him a Letter of Attorney from your Mother in Law to transact the business, something considerable may be got, and you will be very safe in the Hands of that Gentleman & you may consult wt. Mr James Parker & Mr Samuel Donaldson both Merchts in London respecting the Character of that Gentleman & the writer of this Letter. I am Sir your most humble Servant

Alexr McCaul

To the Revd William Smith
Camberwell near London

In compliance with the Purport of this Letter we have sent out a full Power of Attorney, & the other Heirs with myself have bound ourselves to pay every Expense that may be incurred. From two of your Letters which I have had the privilege of reading, one I think in /71 to Capt. Stobo & the other in 1773 to my late Father in Law Mr David Richardson, I find there were certain Conditions to be fulfilled on the Part of the *Grantee*[1]—This I fear has not been done—The Sudden Death of the one, & inability of the other may have prevented it—What we have to request of you Sir is, that if these Obstacles can be removed you would be so kind as lend us a helping hand. Nat[ura]l Justice seems to say, that an Original Grant made for honorable Services, should not be vacated from the non-performance of lesser Stipulations—In your last Letter to Mr Richardson you suggested that if Capt. Stobo's Proportion of the Expenses Should not arrive some Expedient *should* be fallen upon to subject the Land to the Payment thereof. This I think both reasonable & just, as well as, that every other Person who may have been at any expense in fulfilling other Conditions should be fully re-imbursed—But after all it is to be hoped there will be a handsome overplus or remainder to my Mother in Law, & to us her natural heirs. Dear Sir I find myself again inclined to apologize for the trouble this may give you—yet I cannot persuade myself *but* that it must be a pleasing thought to you, if in any measure you can be useful to the Descendants & Relatives of one, who was a Companion wt. you in many noble Exploits, & *suffered* more perhaps than any Man for the Sake of Virginia—Should you condescend to favor me with a few Lines you may direct as above— In the Hope that something will be done—I remain Hond Sir with every good Wish & the highest Esteem your obliged humble Servant

William Smith

ALS, ViMtV. The cover is marked "pr Amiable Matilda via New York."

1. Robert Stobo (1717–1770) was a captain in the Virginia forces which were commanded by GW at the capitulation of Fort Necessity on 3 July 1754, when he was taken hostage by the French. On 22 Nov. 1771 GW wrote Stobo that the veterans of that campaign finally were to receive their proportionate shares of the 200,000 acres of land set aside for them by Gov. Robert Dinwiddie's Proclamation of 1754. On 30 Dec. 1773 GW wrote Daniel (instead of, mistakenly it would seem, David) Richardson that Stobo's heirs were entitled to 9,000 of the 200,000 acres and commented: "After acknowledging the receipt of my Letter of the 22d of Novr 1771 to Captn Stobo—declaring yourself his Representative— and promising to settle for his proportion of the expence incur'd in obtaining our Lands I little expected that I should have remaind till this time without hearing from you or receiving the needful" (see GW to Jacob Van Braam, 30 Dec. 1773, n.1, in *Papers, Colonial Series*, 9:423).

To Thomas Law

Dear Sir,   Mount Vernon Augt 13th 1799

Your letter of the 10th came to hand yesterday—and since you have desired it, the subject of this shall be confined to Mr Carrolls lot *only*.

I am not at all solicitous to purchase it; nor shall I pronounce the price he has set upon it, high, or low; The situation *alone* constitutes the value of it in my estimation, but my becoming the purchaser thereof, depends upon *three* things; two of which I have little expectation of his acceding to.

First, the quantum of Square feet in the lot; for the amount, at 15 Cents pr foot, is the criterion by which ⟨my *illegible*⟩ is to be tested. and is a matter of my own.

Second, a pretty considerable credit, paying interest; ⟨*illegible*⟩ to be desired, however, without interest, and

Third, to be under no obligation to improve the lot sooner than it shall conform with my own convenience; and that will depend upon circumstances not at present, under my controul.

You will perceive that, Mr Carroll⟨s decision⟩, with respect to the two last points is necessary for my determination on the first, and until the result is known I must be Mum—so far as it respects this subject[1] but am always Your Obedt & Affecte Servt

Go: Washington

ALS (incomplete), Czartoryski Library, Kraków, Poland; ALS (letterpress copy), NN: Washington Papers. The portions of the letter before the word "purchase" in the second paragraph and that between "pr foot" in the third paragraph and "respects" in the last are taken from the letterpress copy.

1. See note 2 to Law's letter of 10 August.

To John Francis

Sir,   Mount Vernon 14th August 1799

It is reported, & generally believed, that the Houses I am building in the Federal City are engaged to you.

To your having the houses I have no objection, nor should I have any to the prevalence of the report, if a specific agreement had ever taken place. But as this is not the case, and until it happens may, & doubtless will be injurious to me, inasmuch as they may prevent applications from others, it has become necessary that this matter should be clearly understood.[1]

It is not my intention, nor is it my wish, on the one hand, to ask an unreasonable rent; on the other hand, I am not disposed to be a loser by that building. I have made the best enquiries my opportunities have afforded, into the expectations of others with respect to Rents, & find none who are inclined to let their property in the Federal City or any where else indeed, for less than seven & an half prcent on the whole expenditure: to which they add the taxes thereon, & that of Insurance against Fire. Some, I am told, will not accept of this as an equivalent Rent, because it will give them little (if any more they say) than *common* interest for their money; when it is well known that the ware & Tare of houses require much more.[2]

Upon the terms, however, herementioned (having no pecuniary inducement to build) you may become the occupant of my lots and the Improvements thereon in the Federal City; keeping them in repair as is customary; and it rests with you to say yea, or nay, to make it a bargain, or otherwise. The whole amount of the cost can,

& shall be shewn to the minutest fraction, to whomsoever is disposed to accede to these terms; because the prices of the lots are
known, & every thing being new, ⟨*illegible*⟩ are ready, & can easily
be shewn to any one.

You may reasonably, and justly suppose that the Lots are obtained upon the best terms, because building ⟨*illegible*⟩ the condition thereof; and because the materials were procured without
credit, for I pay on demd for them, & the Workmens wages. All
parts of the Work will, I persuade myself, from the character of the
Undertaker, be well executed, and in a neat & handsome, but not
costly style.

With this explanation & information, you will be enabled to give
a definitive answer: which I shall shortly expect, that I may know
whether to consider you as a Tenant or not. One of the Houses, by
contract is to be finished in November next—the other in March
following.[3] I am Sir Yr very Hble Servt

Go: Washington

ALS (letterpress copy), NN: Washington Papers.

1. Francis first wrote GW on 15 Sept. 1798 about his renting a pair of houses
to be built for GW near the Capitol in the Federal City. For reference to their
subsequent negotiations in the summer of 1799, see GW to William Thornton,
14 July 1799, n.2.

2. In setting the rent in this way, GW was following the advice given him by
William Thornton in a letter of 19 July.

3. On 17 Aug. Francis asked GW for the precise terms of his rental and informed him that he would not be able to begin renting until August 1800. GW
replied on 25 Aug., spelling out in detail his terms and setting 1 June 1800 as the
latest date for beginning the rental. To this, Francis made no reply, bringing an
end to their negotiations.

To Alexander Hamilton

Sir,   Mount Vernon, August 14th 1799

Enclosed are sundry letters (as mentioned on the other side)
which have come to my hands, recommending Captain Edmund
Taylor and Captain William K. Blue for the Office of Brigade
Inspector.

As this Officer is to be appointed by the Inspector General I
forward these letters for your consideration; and add, that I have
not a personal knowledge of the Gentlemen recommended which

can enable me to give any further information respecting their merits or pretensions. With very great regard I am, Sir, Your most obedt Servt

Go: Washington

List of Letters enclosed.

Letter from Colo. Richd K. Meade recommendg Captn Taylor[1]

Do from Colo. Thomas Parker recommendg ditto[2]—

Do from Colo. Leven Powell recommendg Captn Blue[3]

Do from Colo. Thomas Parker recommendg ditto[4]

Do from Colo. T. Blackburn recommendg   ditto.[5]

LS, DLC: Hamilton Papers; Df, DLC:GW. Both copies are in Tobias Lear's hand.

1. Richard Kidder Meade's letter of 22 July has not been found, but see GW to Meade, 12 August.

2. Col. Thomas Parker's letter recommending Edmund Taylor was written from Winchester and dated 23 July: "It is understood that Brigadier General Washington will Command the Brigade of which my Regiment will compose a part. If this shoud be the Case Capt. Edmund Taylor Solicits for the appointment of Brigade Major. He is a young Gentleman of Excellent character of Good Talents has served with Credit in the western army & is a Nephew to the Comodore of that name [Richard Taylor] who with five or six other Brothers served with Reputation in the Revolutionary war. If from what shall be said in his favor you think him worthy of the appointment you will Greatly oblige me by droping a few lines to Genls Hamilton & Washington on the Subject" (DLC: Hamilton Papers).

3. Leven Powell wrote from Middleburg on 29 July: "Capt. William K. Blue of 7th Regt who will deliver this is desirious of being appointed Brigade Major & inspector to the Brigade to which he is annexed. I have not had any personal Acquaintance with this gentleman, but he comes to me well recommended & I have often heard him spoken highly of as an Officer in the Western Army in which it is said he acquitted himself well and particularly in the Character of an Adjutant—From you I am sure he will meet with such aid towards the accomplishment of his wishes as his Merits entitle him to" (DLC: Hamilton Papers).

4. Parker recommended William K. Blue on 26 July: "I did myself the Honor to write to you a few days Ago in favour of Capt. Edmund Taylor of the 8th Regt who wished the appointment of Brigade Major. I am now applied to by Capt. Wm K. Blue of the 7th Regt who wishes a Similar appointment & has Requested me to write to you on the Subject. I have been in the habits of Intimacy with Capt. Blue for a Considerable time & think him a Verry Valuable officer & that he woud fill the post with verry Great propriety. I wrote to you some time ago [letter not found] Stating to you more fully my Opinion of the young Gentleman" (DLC: Hamilton Papers).

5. Writing from Rippon Lodge on 31 July, Thomas Blackburn recommended Blue in these terms: "This will be handed to You by Capt. Blue of the 7th United States Regiment of Infantry; who fills the Vacancy occasioned by the Nonacceptance of Mr Thomas Turner. I have known this Gentn for some Time past—He

was, some years ago, a Lieutenant in one of our Regiments and on Service in the Western Army; where, I have been informed, by Officers attached to the same, He conducted himself like a good & brave Officer. He is the Son of an honest industrious Farmer of Berkely County, and was bred in a Counting-House, so that it is presumable, that He has a good Knowledge of Figures: this with a fair Character, which I believe him to posess, promise that He may be an usefull Officer, in more than one military Department in our Army. With Respect to his Views they will be best Known to You through himself" (DLC: Hamilton Papers).

From James McHenry

Dear Sir   War Department [Philadelphia] 14 Augt 1799

Governor Davie of N. Carolina sent me by the last mail, three copies of a little work of his intitled, "instructions to be observed for the formations and movements of Cavalry," one of which he requested me, which I now do, to present to the commander in chief.[1]

I do not recollect whether I mentioned to you, that he is one in the Commission to the Directory. The President has directed the mission to proceed. Whatever opinions may have been entertained respecting its original propriety, *now*, it having been adopted, I think, the honour and dignity of the government demand, that it should be pursued in a spirit of fairness and liberal good faith. I am my dear Sir most sincerely & Affly yours

James McHenry

ALS, DLC:GW; ADf, MdAA.

1. William R. Davie's pamphlet in GW's library, printed in Halifax, N.C., in 1799, was entitled *Instructions for the Formations and Movements of the Cavalry*.

From William Tazewell

Williamsburg Augt 14 1799

A few days ago in Norfolk, I was informed that it was contemplated by government to establish a marine hospital there. I had received similar information in Europe & mentioned the subject to Colo. Pickering, immediately on my arrival in America, who informed me that Congress had defered taking the business into consideration so late in the last cession, that it was necessarily put off till the next.[1] But in Norfolk I was told that an Hospital establishment would in all probability take place immediately, under somc old law with which you are better acquainted than myself. If the circumstance of my having attended hospitals in Edinburg, London, & Paris for five years afford me any pretensions & my application is not anticipated by some member of the faculty more worthy such a charge, it would be particularly flattering to me to be intrusted with the medical care of the hospital alluded to—I will only add that however great the afflictions of such of my Countrymen as may suffer from disease or the impending war may be they shall not exceed my zeal & exertions to relieve such as may fall to be treated by me. As the interest you may feel in appointing me to the honorable charge to which I aspire must influence my preparations for settling at the Federal City you will much oblige by letting me hear from you as soon as convenient.[2] With unfeigned attachment Your m[o]st respectful & Obt Sert

                                                    William Tazewell

ALS, DLC:GW.

    After completing his medical training in Edinburgh, Dr. William Tazewell in 1797 went to Paris to become secretary to Elbridge Gerry, one of the three U.S. envoys. He remained behind with Gerry after the other two envoys, John Marshall and Charles Cotesworth Pinckney, had left, and then, at Gerry's behest, he traveled to The Hague and London to report to William Vans Murray and Rufus King on developments in France. Tazewell had only recently returned to the United States, having been taken prisoner by a French privateer on his first attempted voyage home (Legislative Petition, 13 Mar. 1800, in Cullen, *Marshall Papers*, 4: 112–13, 126–27). On 25 Aug. 1799, the same day that GW replied (see note 2), Tazewell wrote Secretary of State Timothy Pickering asking to be made secretary to one of the three new envoys to France (Pickering to William R. Davie and to Tazewell, both 7 Sept. 1799, MHi: Pickering Papers). Tazewell in 1800 was practicing medicine in Williamsburg and later moved his practice to Richmond.

    1. On 20 Jan. 1798 the legislature of Virginia authorized the governor to convey to the United States the marine hospital built by the state at Norfolk. The handover was completed on 20 April 1801 (Holcomb, *Norfolk Naval Hospital*, 108–10).

    2. The draft of GW's reply of 25 Aug. reads: "Sir, I have duly received your letter of the 14th inst. expressing a wish to be intrusted with the medical care of the Marine Hospital, about to be established in Norfolk.

    "Whether it is determined to make such an establishment at present, or not, I am unable to say. But, in any event, if the establishment is in the *Marine* Department, it is out of the line in which I have engaged to serve the public, if called upon. And as I determined, when I quitted the Chair of Government, not to be the medium of applications for appointments, however deserving I might conceive the applicant to be, it would, therefore, be proper for you to make your wishes known to the President through some other Channel.

"Should the establishment be connected with the Military Department, I would willingly forward your application, and any testimonials you might chuse to produce, to the War Office, as I have been accustomed to do in similar cases, where they would remain to be considered and determined upon according to their merits. With esteem I am Sir, Your most Obedt Servt Go: Washington" (Df, in Tobias Lear's hand, DLC:GW).

Letter not found: from Zechariah Lewis, 15 Aug. 1799. On 30 Aug. GW wrote Lewis that he had received his "favor of the 15th instant."

From John Francis

Sir   Philadelphia August 17th 1799

I was favored this morning with your letter of the 14th instant, and hasten to reply to it in order that it may be speedily ascertained whether I am to have your two houses in the Federal City, and the terms. From what passed when I was at that place last year I counted upon them with so much certainty that I have not thought of applying elsewhere, and I am still as desirous to occupy them as I was then, provided I can have the prospect of doing it with satisfaction to you, and advantage to myself.

I entertain no doubt that the houses will be finished in a suitable manner, and that they will be sufficiently dry to live in by the first of August next, from which time I am willing the rent should begin to accrue. I cannot take possession sooner, nor will the business which I am in enable me to pay rent for houses there, and here at the same time. Should this correspond with your expectations and wishes, it will only remain for you to state the precise sum which I am to pay pr annum including insurance, taxes of all kinds, and in full of every other demand whatsoever.[1] This you will be able to do I presume without difficulty from the bills and estimates in your possession; upon receipt of which I will immediately return you a definitive answer. In this way I shall know before hand what I promise and can assure you with the more confidence that I will perform my engagements. As I expect to incur considerable expenses in removing and establishing myself at a new place it is incumbent on me to proceed with caution, that I may not improvidently run the risk of losing the character of a punctual man, which I have hitherto maintained in all my dealings. I need not urge arguments to induce you to let me have the houses upon reasonable terms. Your own sense of justice will I am sure fix the rent (as it ought to be) in an equitable, and proper manner. I have the honor to be, Sir With the greatest respect Your most Obt & humble servant

John Francis

ALS, DLC:GW.
   1. See GW to Francis, 25 August.

To Robert Lewis

Dear Sir,   Mount Vernon 17th Augt 1799
   Your letter of the 7th instant came duly to hand, but being received with many other letters, it was laid by, and entirely forgotten, until I came across it yesterday again. Mr Ariss's draught on Mr James Russell for £42 pounds shall be presented to him, but if he is indisposed to pay it, or wants time to do it, he has a good pretext for delay, as you have sent it without your Endorsement, although made payable to *you*.[1]
   Of the facts related in the enclosed letter, relative to the loss of his Crop, by the Hessian fly, I know nothing. If it should appear to you evident, that Kercheval has used his true endeavour to raise the means to discharge his Rent, & is deprived thereof by an Act of Providence, I am willing, however illy I can afford to do it, to make some reasonable abatement therefrom; of wch you, from enquiry, will be the best judge.[2]
   It is demonstratively clear, that on this Estate (Mount Vernon) I have more working Negros by a full moiety, than can be employed to any advantage in the farming System; and I shall never turn Planter thereon.
   To sell the overplus I cannot, because I am principled against this kind of traffic in the human species. To hire them out, is almost as bad, because they could not be disposed of in families to any advantage, and to disperse the families I have an aversion. What then is to be done? Something must, or I shall be ruined; for all the money (in addition to what I raise by Crops, and rents) that have been *received* for Lands, sold within the last four years, to the amount of Fifty thousand dollars, has scarcely been able to keep me a float.[3]
   Under these circumstances, and a thorough conviction that half

the workers I keep on this Estate, would render me a greater *nett* profit than I *now* derive from the whole, has made me resolve, if it can be accomplished, to settle Plantations on some of my other Lands. But where? without going to the Western Country, I am unable, as yet to decide; as the *best*, if not *all* the Lands I have on the East of the Alliganies, are under Leases, or some kind of incumbrance or an other. But as you can give me correct information relative to this matter, I now *early* apply for it.

What then is the State of Kerchevals lot, & the other adjoining? are they under Leases? If not, is the Land good? and how many hands would it work to advantage?[4] Have I any other good Land in Berkeley that could be obtained on reasonable terms?[5] Is that small tract above the Warm Springs engaged for the ensuing year?[6] How much cleared Land is there on it? and what kind of buildings? How many hands could be usefully employed thereon? Information on these points, and any others relative thereto, would be acceptable to me.

The drought has been so excessive on this Estate, that I have made no Oats—& if it continues a few days longer, shall make no Corn. I have cut little or no Grass; and my Meadows, at this time, are as bare as the pavements; of consequence no second Crop can be expected. These things will compel me, I expect, to reduce the Mouths that feed on the Hay. I have two or three young Jacks (besides young Royal Gift) and several She Asses, that I would dispose of. Would Fauquier, or where else, be a good place to dispose of them?

I am glad to hear that your bro: Lawrence is so much amended, as your letter indicates, whether it be from Sulpher application, or other causes: but if Doctr Baynham, under whose hands he was, was unable to effect a radical cure, I should not place much confidence in Voss's Springs, as the disorder must be deep rooted.

Your Aunt unites with me in best wishes for Mrs Lewis, yourself & family, and I am—Dear Sir, Your Sincere friend and Affectionate Uncle

Go: Washington

P.S. Since writing the foregoing, Mr Anderson informs me that he saw you in Alexandria yesterday; and that you told him you were to be in Winchester on Monday, or Tuesday next: being desirous that this letter should get to your hands as early as possible—and especially while you were over the Ridge, I have put it under cover to Mr Bush of Winchester, with a request that if you should not be there to send it by Post to Fauquier Court House.[7]

ALS, ViMtV; ALS (letterpress copy), NN: Washington Papers.

1. James Russell of Alexandria returned John Ariss's draft to GW. See GW to Robert Lewis, 23 August.

2. In December 1785 GW leased to William Kercheval a 172-acre tract on the Shenandoah River in Frederick County for an annual rent of £17.6, the lease to run from 1 Jan. 1786 to 1 Jan. 1799. See GW to Battaile Muse, 28 July 1785, n.1.

3. During the summer of 1799 GW made a list of all the slaves living on his farms at Mount Vernon. The Slave List is printed at the end of this volume.

4. For the land on the Shenandoah River in Frederick County that GW bought from George Mercer in 1774 and the terms on which parcels of it were leased to tenants, see GW to Battaile Muse, 28 July 1785, n.1 (*Papers, Confederation Series*, 3:160–61), and the references in that note.

5. In addition to the 700-acre tract rented by John Ariss (see Lewis to GW, 7 Aug. 1799, n.1), GW owned nine or ten smaller parcels of land in Berkeley County on or near Bullskin Run. See List of Tenants, 18 Sept. 1785, nn.1–9, (ibid., 259–61). After Ariss's death, GW wrote Lewis again, on 7 Dec. 1799, about his regaining the use of his lands in Frederick and Berkeley counties.

6. For problems with the tract near Warm, or Berkeley, Springs in Hampshire County, see GW to Isaac Weatherinton, 20 Oct., and the note to that document.

7. GW's letter of 17 Aug. to Philip Bush, a tavern keeper and merchant in Winchester whom GW had known since his own days as colonel of the Virginia Regiment in the 1750s, reads: "Sir Just Learning that Mr Robert Lewis (who manages my business in the Counties of Frederick &c.) is to be in Winchester on Monday or Tuesday next, and it being necessary that the enclosed letter should get into his hands while there, or while he is over the Ridge, you would do me a Kindness in accomplishing this.

"If he should not be in Winchester, but you should hear certainly of his being in Berkeley, I would have the letter sent to him by Express—the expence of which he will pay. If he shd be in neither be pleased to let it go by Post to Fauquier Court House. Remember me Kindly to Mrs Bush, if living—and with Esteem I am Sir Your very Hble Servt Go. Washington" (copy, sent to the Louisville [Ky.] *Courier Journal*, June 1881, ViU).

From William Vans Murray

Dear Sir,   17 August 1799

Yesterday I went to 1268. 1175. 1582. to meet Mr 913. 753⟨.⟩ I had before met him at a more distant place. Knowing from ⟨his⟩ letters to me, that he intended to go to the United States, a measure ⟨which⟩ I opposed by every argument I could think of— I since that enjoyed ⟨the⟩ pleasure of your letter to him of December last, & on his lately w⟨riting⟩ to me for passports, informing me of his intentions of going, I w⟨ent⟩ yesterday to meet him & to urge the reasons which I had scattered in my several letters to dissuade him.[1] Though I have no rights over his friendly letters, yet I may with good faith inclose to you Sir, a press copy of my last to him,[2] before my ride yesterday I found him still much bent upon going—Leaving his lady & daughter in France & his plan, if he go, is to settle for life. To buy a farm near Mount Vernon—To land in the Chesepeak & hasten to present himself to his paternal house, as he says & pass the winter, that he is sure that he can convince you that he could have no azylum elsewhere from the present & probable future State of Europe, for though war is not yet declared by or against Sweden & Denmark & though the States of Germany are not all in the war, he expects that the first will be in war & in the last he cannot live & this Country is threatened with invasion.

He seems to have no idea of being in the party which will Soon be the triumphant party, because their *principles* are not his & he avows those which he acted on in 1791. It was in vain to urge on this head the apology afforded by that tremendous NECESSITY which in those moments crushes men of all sorts together for the public good & for the great end of indeed pursuing the Independance of all other nations! He cannot join if they would let home the parties that overturned the constitutional Monarchy of 1791. Thus he is left by the storm he helped to raise, high & dry on a shore to which no ebbs & flows can reach him, to launch him again for any quiet port.

I have urged every thing to Indispose him for the voyage to U.S. He avows that he will be a federalist & Support the Govt U.S. I tell him that will be little in his power & that title will be decisive against his affairs & family in France, if she exist as a Republic (which I do not expect[)]—He answered, I care not for my affairs, I will pursue my principles, and I would be against democratizing the American Govt—I am against what France has done towards the United States. In fact he attempted to remove my arguments continually—He repeated a question which he before made at our other interview—Could I not said he be useful in uniting parties? I told him no! but this little trait will shew you Sir, that he perpetually thinks ⟨&⟩ feels in the sense of a public character, notwithstanding all that has past—The steady adherance to those

Theories which have deluged Europe with affliction, excited more of melancholy than ⟨of⟩ Admiration. Though he is I think less cheerful a little than when I saw him in March, he is fat & hearty, unbroken in mind & body, full of pleasant & interesting conversation & a most agreeable & one who will have influence go where he will, except among those who reflect & have experience enough to seperate the pleasing from the proper—I left him apparently undecided whether he will go or not—but I think rather that he will go⟨.⟩ The passport he asked for was for Emden, Hamburgh & Ame⟨rica.⟩ I had sent him a letter, the one of which a copy is inclosed which I promised him one—Though a very interesting man yet I wish him to stay here where he is quiet untill things are more tranquil among us. Long since cured of visionary speculations, I hope myself—I dread their union in a popular character in the United States—In a possible state of things in Europe—were it practicable for parties in France—to themselves restore Monarchy—it might perhaps be useful⟨.⟩ All the attractions belonging to that inducement to re⟨main⟩ in Europe, I urged as far as they occurred—Once before I had very much relyd on that line of persuasion—& then it s⟨eemed⟩ to impress him—but now he Seemed to have no idea of the probability of that project—Indeed Suwarrows late proclamation announces what is perhaps the only practicable scheme—the Restoration of L. 18[3]—& if it be accomplished, I rather believe that the chants of Philosophy will have little to do in the business & that the respective theories which have buried under bloody ruins will be in France what the Ludicrous, but bloody extravagances of puritanism, were in England after the Restoration of Charles 2d—a theme of Ridicule & dramatic exhibition!

I thought dear, Sir, that I ought to inform you upon a subject that has brought your pen into action & to shew you that I wished not only to do good but that I take a pride in pursuing what I believe to be accordant with your paternal views & vigilance towards our native land—even in cases where your personal friendship tended to another biass[4]—I am with perfect & affecte respect & attachment Dear Sir yo. mo. obdt Sert &c. &c. &c.

Df, NNPM. The draft is in Murray's letter book. As the letter from Murray to John Quincy Adams printed in note 1 indicates, the coded numbers in the first sentence of this letter to GW stand for "Leyden" and "Lafayette."

1. Murray wrote to John Quincy Adams in Berlin on 15 Aug.: "I go to Leyden tomorrow morning to meet M. La Fayette who has requested to meet me somewhere. We have lately written about his voyage to the United States—I to dissuade him. General W[ashington] wrote to him in December [1798] dissuading him *neatly*; but he writes me he will go, and be quiet at Mount Vernon" (Ford, "Murray-Adams Letters," 583–84). Murray also drafted a letter to GW on 15 Aug. (NNPM), a copy of which he may or may not have sent to him. On 26 Oct. 1799 GW acknowledged the receipt of a number of letters dating back to April 1799, including one dated 17 Aug. but not one dated 15 August. The letters of 15 and 17 Aug. are both about Lafayette and include much the same information. In both letters Murray says he is enclosing the "press copy" of his letter to Lafayette. Murray went to see Lafayette after drafting the letter of 15 Aug. and before composing the letter of 17 August. It may well be that he wrote and sent the letter of 17 Aug. in the place of the one drafted on 15 Aug., which GW had not received by 26 Oct. perhaps because it was never sent. In any case, the copy of Murray's letter of 15 Aug. reads: "The Gentleman *to whom you wrote last december* & who is actually in this Country, is I believe resolved to go to America & especially to Mount Vernon. He thinks of setting off this autumn. I have Said all I could to put him off from this ill timed visit. I have no rights over his letters to me, but I can without a breach of delicacy inclose Sir to you the press copy of my last letter to him on this subject. In answer however he says that 'any consequences of my preferring Mount Vernon to every other place on earth I would meet with pleasure & pride.' I have most Seriously & at different times combatted his intentions by every way I thought most successful. I confess Sir that his unconquered restlessness—the tough attachment to his first opinions, notwithstanding these are bury'd under those bloody ruins that demonstrate at least their prematurity & want of sound application to his own Country, his facilities in regenerating his half killed body & mind—So lately from a Dungeon—His fond hopes of *Liberty*!! European liberty—that strumpet that no Sermons—no examples can reform. These things both astonish me & execite some uneasiness when I consider him as the Citizen of the United States, possessed of a certain desire of popularity—& having had indeed great merit in our Glorious Revolution. Of course it would be best that he should be kept out of the Critical Scene, where it may be feared his Self love & ambition might be playd on—As you have long honoured him with your friendly offices it may be not unpleasing to hear more particularly of him—I had never seen him & went [in March 1799], at his request, to meet him—Thirty miles off. Instead of the grave & thoughtful countenance which his Misfortunes of all sorts justified the expectation of—I found him cheerful, & even pleasant in Anecdotes & old American war Stories, in which he delig⟨hted.⟩ With an air perfectly disengaged—in good health & of sound Consti⟨tution⟩ & of the same set of abstract & political principles which he carry'd from the U.S. to his Country & which he still adhered to—Condemning Jacobinism, but still talking about liberty (that of his own nation) and of the progress of the human mind & the yet hopeful amelioration of Europe upon the principles of liberty—He always spoke of you Sir, with great attachment—& we talked much of parties—One trait alone will give you a clue to his way of thinking & what must be expected of him. He asked if it would not be in his power to Unite parties in

U.S.! if he were there. I took the occasion which a long walk offered to shew him the uneasy Situation in which a residence there at present would place him—He told me Col. H—— had written to the same effect—I left him with the persuasion that his mind is impenetrable ⟨to⟩ perfectly defeated & scouted experiments— that he seems as if he considered his fame as bottomed on the alliance between American forms & theories & the Revolution of his own country—& I believe he knows that the American Revolution is the basis on which his statue rests. His unconquered mind excited somewhat ⟨of⟩ melancholy rather than of Admiration—& the fecundity of his resources to explain why this principle had not been fairly try⟨'d⟩ & that experiment not fairly made, accompany'd by so much Sang froid—left the same impression that the Chapter of Gil Blas always does— Sangrado had hot watered & blooded half ⟨the⟩ nobility & burghers of Valadolid to death—Twenty years constant mortality had testified to his Theory & practice—He did doubt—but he said he had when young *written a book* to support his Theory—his fame was at Stake—he could not recede! with a thousand excellent qualities he would I fear be sported with by events & by a certain party of impenetrables in the U.S.—I must add however that he seems most cordially to condemn the great injuries perpetrated by his Country against us. The French Republic has not been able, nor will she be, I think Sir, to oppose a dam against that torrent of Victories that has lately poured against her—We have it *as certain* that at last *Mantua* has surrendered—In the actual state of Europe this is a very important thing. Suwarrow has detached 20,000 men towards Swisserland—he may thus probably turn Massena's right along the Aar; though Championet has some troops, army of the alps, in Savoy. The interior of France is becoming as it was in the year 1793 So. of the Vendee. The exterior force of the enemy Stronger & Successful & opinion outside & inside different. In Holland all is in preparation against expected invasion—But the moment of actual attack—if it come, will be attended by great desertion, it is believed to the Prince hereditary of Orange, who with a Russian General & a corps of cidevant Dutch Officers is now at Lingen on the Ems, near the borders" (NNPM). For Murray's visit to Lafayette in March 1799, see also Lafayette to GW, 9 May 1799, n.4.

2. In addition to the copy in McHenry's hand of Murray's letter to GW of 15 Aug., there is at the New York State Library at Albany a copy of a letter, also in McHenry's hand, without heading or date, from Murray to Lafayette. This undoubtedly is a copy of the letter, a press copy of which Murray told GW in his letters of 15 and 17 Aug. that he was enclosing. After writing about Lafayette's passport and, at length, about the different meanings of the word *liberty*, Murray had this to say to Lafayette in conclusion: "My Dear Sir, as to your pleasing idea of being still & tranquil at Mount Vernon! It is true that you would be tranquil there—all men hold it in veneration—but that is to be ⟨with⟩ our free & glorious Govrnt & Constitution. You would there be a Monarchy man, Royalist, British, and a thousand & one wretched things against you. On the contrary if you are not there—though you cannot be a jacobin—yet the jacobins would count upon you! Neutrality is impossible! A middle man would be suspected as a spy! If our internal struggles had no relation to the interests of France & her revolutionaries & worst of principles, there you would be more quiet, as things are you would be either in a situation such as you never were in—or be obliged to be on one side or the other. The one side, the side you would take, is that which would be deci-

sive against you in France. The other side—so like the Tory side against which you broke your first spear—you *could not* take."

3. Gen. Aleksandr Vasilievich Suvorov (1729–1800), a noted Russian military commander, was conducting a campaign against the French in Italy. On 13 June 1799 Murray had written Pickering of the possibility that Louis XVIII would be "on the throne in a few months" (manuscript quoted in Hill, *William Vans Murray*, 155).

4. GW remained fearful that Lafayette was coming to the United States; as late as 24 Oct. 1799 Secretary of State Timothy Pickering wrote GW that he suspected that "la Fayette is coming to America."

Letter not found: from Auguste de Grasse, 20 Aug. 1799. On 9 Sept. GW wrote de Grasse: "I have received your letter of the 20th of August."

From William Baynham

Sir   Essex 21st Augt 1799
I did myself the honor to inform you in my last that I had operated on your Servant Tom's Eyes, that I had not very sanguine hopes of rendering him essential relief, and that the result would be ascertained in a fortnight.[1]

I am sorry that present appearances afford me no reason to alter my opinion. The tumor in the left Eye is, I am convinced, incurable; and a growing film in the right threatens to overspread the transparent Cornea and thereby deprive him of the sight of this eye, in which the vision is, at present, but imperfect—against this increasing evil I know of no remedy save that which I have applied, and which having failed I would advise that nothing more be attempted but to leave it to nature.

Having received an account today of an only brother's lying dangerously ill, in the county of Gloucester, I propose to set off to see him tomorrow:[2] and altho' it was not my intention to have discharged Tom before the expiration of the fortnight, yet being called away on so emergent an occasion, and seeing no prospect of his being benefit⟨ed⟩ by a longer stay, I shall direct him to set out on his return home as soon as the weather clears which I trust will be in a day or two. In the operations which I performed, as I was prompted rather by a wish than an expectation of relieving the poor fellow, I hope you will not take it amiss if I claim no more than a consultati⟨on⟩ fee of five dollars.[3] With the highest esteem & respect I am Sir yr mo. obedt Servt

Wm Baynham

1. See Baynham to GW, 10 August.
2. Richard Baynham was a prominent citizen of Gloucester County.
3. See GW to Baynham, 27 August.

From Alexander Hamilton

Sir   New York August 21st 1799

I was yesterday honored with your letter of the 14th instant.

The recommendations of Captains Taylor and Blue will not fail to be considered when the situation of things is mature for the appointment of Brigade Inspectors.

Inclosed you will find a General Abstract of the recruiting returns, which at its date were received at the Office of the Adjutant General.[1] Other Information induces me to estimate that the number now actually inlisted for *Eleven* of the *Twelve* additional Regiments exceeds Two thousand. The *other* is not yet in activity.

I ought to have informed you before this that General Wilkinson had arrived at this place. I have delivered to him heads of inquiry and conference, which embrace all the material points of consideration in our Western Affairs. He is busily engaged in reporting upon them; written rather than verbal Communications being by him preferred. The result of our Consultations will be transmitted to you for any direction which you may think fit to give.[2] With the truest respect & attachment I have the honor to be Sir Yr Obedt Servant

Alex. Hamilton

LS, DLC:GW; ADf, DLC: Hamilton Papers.
1. Hamilton's abstract of monthly recruiting returns, dated 17 Aug., is in DLC:GW.
2. Hamilton wrote to GW on 15 June urging the promotion of James Wilkinson to major general. On 9 Sept. Hamilton sent Wilkinson's report to GW. GW commented on the report in a letter to Hamilton of 15 September.

From Timothy Pickering

Sir,   Philadelphia Augt 22. 1799.

The inclosed I have cut from a New-York paper.[1] It reminds me of what I have repeatedly proposed to different citizens of Philadelphia—That in order to avoid the impurities of docks partly uncovered at low water, and to preserve a sufficient depth of water for vessels to enter, & even lie afloat, the wharfing of the city should be newly arranged. For this end, fixing a curve line which should embrace the most valuable of the existing wharf-improvements, the general abutment on the river should have *one regular sweep*; and in *deep water*. If from this one line there were to be no projections, it is plain that the current of the river would always keep the depth of water: But to make more room for shipping, as well as to defend the vessels from driving Ice (which in the Delaware would soon cut them through) wharfs must be run off, nearly at right angles with the general abutment. If, however, a wide passage be left, next the curve, in its whole length, the current will still sweep all clean. This crude sketch will explain my meaning, and save more words:[2]

Instead of *perfectly solid* piers, from bottom to top, they may, after a close, solid foundation is laid⟨,⟩ be built with cross-logs, so as to give a passage to the water; and be made solid only so far from the top downward, as to give firmness to the piers.

If the Delaware, at the site of Philadelphia now washed a plain shore, as when Mr Penn founded the city, there would be no question of the utility of the plan I have intimated. The city of Washington is now in such a situation; and therefore I trouble you with these hints. *Economy* as well as *utility*, recommend such an improvement: for being once made, all below the surface of the water will last forever. Otherwise, as the original docks fill up, the proprietors must extend their wharves, at fresh expences; at the same time probably injuring their neighbours' prior improvements, for want of a uniform, well concerted plan at the outset.[3] I am very respectfully sir, your most obt servt

Timothy Pickering

P.S. The Eastern Branch of Potowmack wanting a large head of water, will require extraordinary precautions to preserve its depth.

ALS (letterpress copy), MHi: Pickering Papers; copy, DNA: RG 42, General Records, Letters Received, 1791–1867. Written on the DNA copy: "The original of this letter was returned to Genl Washington."

1. A "Communication" in the New York *Daily Advertiser* on 19 Aug. 1799 from *Civis* begins: "It is contemplated, we understand, to alter totally the wharves on the East River." *Civis* goes on to set out in great detail the plan Pickering describes here.

2. The small "crude sketch" that Pickering made here shows wharves jutting out from the curving "Shore of the river Delaware" with a "Free Water course" under the wharves along the shore and another parallel one farther out in the river.

3. After receiving Pickering's letter, GW on 28 Aug. forwarded it to the District of Columbia commissioners: "Gentlemen, Monday's Mail, brought me the enclosed letter of the 22d instant from Colo. Pickering. As it is more in your line than in mine, to give it the consideration which so interesting a subject merits; and as the field (hitherto so little cultivated) is now open to the adoption of any plan which wisdom, sound policy & foresight may dictate, I take the liberty of transmitting it for your perusal; being persuaded that the thoughts of any intelligent and well disposed person on a point of such importance to the well being of a City which is designated to be the Seat of Empire, cannot be illy received by you. With great esteem and regard I am Gentlemen Your Most Obedt Servt Go: Washington" (ALS, ViMtV; letterpress copy, NN: Washington Papers). See also William Thornton to GW, 1 September. The commissioners, Gustavus Scott, William Thornton, and Alexander White, replied on 2 Sept.: "We received your favor of the 28th Ulto, enclosing a Letter from Colonel Pickering, of which we have taken a copy, and return the original. The Subject is truly deserving of consideration, and we thank you for this mark of Attention" (DLC:GW). See also GW to Pickering, 8 September.

To Robert Lewis

Dear Sir,   Mount Vernon 23d August 1799

Enclosed you have Mr Ariss's draught on James Russell Esqr., returned. It was presented to the latter for acceptance, by Mr Anderson, who received the following answer—to wit—that he had only £19 of Mr Ariss's money in his hands, and could pay no more. This sum Mr Anderson refused to receive; and thus the matter ended with Mr Russell.[1]

Enclosed also you have the Press copy of a letter I wrote to you on the day of its date, & was on the point of sending it to the Post Office in Alexandria, when Mr Anderson (just returned from that place) informing me that he saw you there, and that you proposed to be in Winchester as on Monday or Tuesday last, I put it under cover to Mr Philip Bush to be delivered to you in that Town.

As it is probable some delay, or miscarriage may have attended the Letter, I send the Press copy of it; which you will return to me, whether the original gets to your hands or not; as it is a custom with me to keep copies of lettrs on business.[2]

Not knowing with certainty where your Brother Law[renc]e is, the enclosed letter for his wife, from your aunt, is committed to your care; and she begs it may get to hand safely, & as soon as convenient—as also one from Mrs Law.

As there is a regular Post from Alexandria to Fauquier Court House, you have only to learn on what day & hour the Mail closes at the latter, for the former, to insure your letters getting into my hands in two or three days after they are written, as I never fail sending to the Post Office in Alexandria three times a week. Mine to you may lye longer in the Office at the Court House, if you are not in the habit of making frequent enquiries there, for letters.

Since my last we have had a sufficiency of fine Rain, but what effect it will have upon the poor, & miserably looking Corn, and before parched up meadows, no one can yet tell; especially if the Season should continue to be seasonable hence forward.

Your Aunt unites her best wishes to mine for Mrs Lewis, yourself & family—and I am Yr sincere friend and Affectionate Uncle

Go: Washington

ALS, PPRF.

1. Lewis sent John Ariss's draft for £42 on James Russell to GW on 7 August.

2. See GW to Lewis, 17 Aug., and note 6 of that document. The letterpress copy of GW's letter to Lewis has not been found.

From James McHenry

Dear Sir.   Philadelphia 24th Augt 1799

At length the articles for my young friend has been procurr'd and is now waiting for a conveyance. There is a vessel up for Alexandria which I am informed is to sail in a day or two. I shall send them on board to day directed to the care of Col. Fitzgerald. They are in two small boxes. The sword is well wrapped up and directed in like manner.[1]

The office will move on monday to Trenton. Yours most affly

James McHenry

ALS, DLC:GW.

1. McHenry is referring to the uniform and other military equipment that Tench Francis in June was asked to secure for young George Washington Parke Custis. See GW to McHenry, 7 June, n.1. There apparently was some problem with the shipment, for on 22 Sept. GW wrote Francis: "Sir, Much time has elapsed since I requested the favour of the Secretary of War (that they might be ⟨comport⟩able to any regulations which might have been established there) to provide

⟨*mutilated*⟩ be provided, some articles for the equipment of Mr Custis as a Cornet of Horse.

"In answer, he informed me that he had commissioned you to execute my request. To know the result, as some of those article are much needed, must be my apology for giving you the trouble of receiving this address from Sir Your most Obedt Hble Servt Go: Washington" (letterpress copy, NN: Washington Papers). Francis's reply of 27 Sept. has not been found, but GW wrote him again on 7 Oct.: "Sir, A few days after giving you the trouble of my last, two boxes came to hand with sundry articles of equipmt for Mr Custis; but no letter, invoice or account accompanying them, it is not known whether a clock, which was requested at the time the other things were has been provided, or not.

"If, as this little Commission has passed through your hands, you could give me any information respecting ⟨*illegible*⟩ would be kindly received; and might be the means of preventing a double ⟨*illegible*⟩ of this article.

"I pray you to present me respectfully, to your Lady—& neighbour Mrs ⟨*illegible*⟩ in which Mrs Washington unites. I am Sir Your Most Obedient ⟨&⟩ very Hble Servant Go: Washington P.S. Your favr of the 27th Ulto is just recd" (letterpress copy, NN: Washington Papers).

To John Francis

Sir,   Mount Vernon 25th Augt 1799

Your letter of the 17th instant in answer to mine of the 14th, has been received.

I have already given you the specific terms on which I propose to rent my houses in the Federal City, and from which I shall not depart an iota; because I fixed them as low as *any*, with whom I conversed, though⟨t⟩ I ought to ask, and much lower than *many* seem disposed to take.

It is true I did not give you the aggregate amount of the Rent, nor is it in my power (upon the principle I act) to do it at this time, with exact precision; because the cost of some parts of the Work is not, nor will not be known until the whole is completed; But as I am entirely disposed to give you all the data I possess, to enable you to form a judgment thereof, I send you enclosed the cost of all things which is conclusively fixed, and an ennumeration of ⟨them⟩ which are not; to which I shall add your information, that all the work, inside and out, is plain. Possessed of these facts you can err but little in ascertaining the ⟨*question*⟩ of Rent.[1]

My reason for informing you of the epochs at which my houses— by Contract—were to be completed, was not that I expected the

Rents of them were to commence precisely on those days. They may not, although Mr Blagden seems quite certain of being within the time stipulated, be in condition to receive ⟨a⟩ tenant—or tenants, so soon. And as they are to be papered, some little time may be required for that, although occupancy is not to be retarded on that account as that operation can be performed as well after, as before the entry of the tenant; probably must be so, to prevent injury to the Paper, which must be on Plaster uncommonly well seasoned, to avoid its ⟨ranting⟩.

After giving this explanation, I must be permitted ⟨to⟩ add as there are two views of the cas⟨e, that I conceive⟩ in naming the first of August, you ⟨*illegible*⟩ extended the time for commencing the Rent ⟨unreasonably⟩ long; for certainly, it would be as hard for me, if the houses are ready, agreeably to Contract, to keep them empty five months to accomodate you, as it would be on you to pay two Rents, when the presumption is, that such houses will be in demand. Considering the matter therefore in both points of view, I am not indisposed to share the inconvenience with you; that is—be the interval what it may—between the completion of the houses (as before mentioned) and the first of Aug. that it shall be borne between ⟨us; for exam⟩ple suppose, that instead of the 1st ⟨of March⟩, they are not ready until the end of it there will then be a vacuum of four months, in which case the Rent shd commence the 1st of June. again, if not ready until the 1st of May, then to commence the middle of ⟨July⟩.

I am thus particular, that you may, in your next—decide *positively* whether you will take the houses on the terms here mentioned, or not. If an affirmative answer is not, unconditionally given, I shall consider myself as under no further obligation to give you a preference, and will let the houses to any good tenant or tenants, who may apply, or dispose of them in any other manner.[2] I am Sir—Your most obedient Servant

Go: Washington

ALS (letterpress copy), NN: Washington Papers.

1. GW enclosed this statement: "Cost of two Lots in the Federal City, extending from North Capitol Street, to New Jersey Avenue in Square 634, together with the expence of the Buildings now erecting thereon, according to Contract; and an estimate of work not included in the said Contract—occasioned by alterations agreed on, since viz.

	Dollars
For lot No. 16, bought from the Commissioners	$535.71
Ditto No. 7, bought from Mr Danl Carroll	428.40

On the price of these lots considerable abatement was made, on condition of my building *two* brick houses *three* Stories high each.

To—Mr [George] Blagden, Undertaker of the Buildings; according to written Contract. ⟨Estimate⟩ of Glazing—Painting—And Ironmongry*   11,250.

Glazing & Painting—agreeably to this estimate handed in by Mr Blagden, but not acceded to, nor included in the Contract.   840.

Ironmongry   Ditto   Do   Do   397.20

A Well of fine Water at the back doors of both houses—30 odd feet deep—walled, & a Pump therein; the cost of which has not been ⟨exhi⟩bited, as it was procured to be done by Mr Blagden, & paid for by him, out of the monies advanced him for general purposes.

A Pediment, and Parapet, in addition to the original cost of the Buildings. No specific sum agreed on for erecting them.

⟨*illegible*⟩ for the original design of ⟨*illegible*⟩ to add to the appearance of the House⟨s⟩: also undefined in the cost.

Papering all the Rooms, except Cellars and ⟨garrets,⟩

⟨*illegible*⟩ being, by Contract to have no more Coats of Plaster than is merely sufficient for that purpose Taxes—if *any* at present, they are very trifling, and probably will remain so for ⟨a⟩ length of time. But to guard against this contingency, and to insure Seven & an half per Cent upon my expenditures, is the cause of this insert.

⟨Insurance⟩ against Fire—What this will amount to on Brick buildings, may be ⟨better ascertained⟩ in Philadelphia (where ⟨*illegible*⟩ Baltimore it will probably be made) ⟨*illegible* were.⟩ It is inserted on the princi⟨ple⟩ of the last article.

There may be some other charges which are not recollected; and expences ac⟨crued,⟩ which will, on the principle here ⟨*illegible*⟩ be to be added; but none that will be costly, or unneccessary; as plainness & simplicity will run through ⟨the whole⟩ work.

Go: Washington

*Conceiving these charges were high, in the estimate, I took them upon myself. But whether I shall ⟨*illegible*⟩ lose by so doing, remains to be decided. Mr Blagden assured me that he could not obtain them ⟨*illegible*⟩ on better terms than was specified" (letterpress copy, NN: Washington Papers).

2. GW received no answer to this letter. See GW to John Avery, 25 Sept. and GW to Alexander Hamilton, 13 Oct., printed in note 3 to his letter to Avery.

To James McHenry

Sir,   Mount Vernon 25th August 1799

Some of the Officers of Cavalry, who accepted their appointments, and were informed by you in the Public Gazettes, that their

Pay would commence therewith, have applied to me to know where, & in what manner they were to draw for it.

Not being able to supply them on these points, I take the liberty of troubling you with this Address, on the subject; that I may be enabled to answer any enquiries of the sort in future.[1] With great esteem & respect I have the honor to be, Sir, Your most Obedt Hble Servt

Go: Washington

ALS (letterpress copy), DLC:GW. GW traced over a portion of the letterpress copy with a pencil.

1. McHenry responded from Trenton on 4 Sept.: "In answer to your letter of the 25th of August ultimo, I beg you to inform such of the Officers of the Cavalry who have applied to you to know where and in what manner they are to draw for their pay; that there being no paymaster appointed to the Regiment, they may draw upon the paymaster General at the Seat of Government for their pay and Forage Money from the date of their acceptance to the 31st of August ulto inclusive, except those who have received an advance from the Accountant's Office who will draw upon him for the Balance due to them up to that period" (DLC:GW).

To William Baynham

Sir,   Mount Vernon 27th Augt 1799

By my Servant Tom, I was honored with your letter of the 21st instant.

I am persuaded that, all ⟨the⟩ benefit which the nature of his case would admit he has, or will receive from your treatment of the affliction under which he labors and if it is incurable, I must be satisfied that I have neglected nothing to restore his sight to him.

It was an *imposition* to ask you for money, (for I gave him more than sufficient to bear his expences down & up)—and *imprudent*, to say I had directed it. A liberty I never should have thought of.

Your charge is extremely moderate—and the amount is herein enclosed[1] by Sir, Your Most Obedient Humble Servant

Go: Washington

ALS (letterpress copy), NN: Washington Papers.

1. GW's entry in his Day Book for 27 Aug. reads: "By Cash sent Doctr Baynham in a letter of this date for his Services to Tom of Union Farm—[$]10."

Letter not found: from Thompson & Veitch, 27 Aug. 1799. On 30 Aug. GW apologized to Thompson & Veitch for "not acknowledging the receipt of your letter of the 27th instant sooner."

To William Thornton

Dear[1]   Mount Vernon 28th Aug. [17]99

I would thank you for requesting Mr Blagden to give me as early notice of the *time*, and *amount* of his next call upon me, as he can, that I may prepare accordingly.[2] With great esteem & regard I am—Dear Sir Yr most Obedt Servt

Go: Washington

ALS (photocopy), NjP.

1. Presumably GW intended to write "Sir."

2. GW on 30 Aug. wrote William Herbert, president of the Bank of Alexandria, that he wished to extend the sixty-day loan of $1,500 which he had taken out in June and used to make a payment of $1,000 on 2 July to the builder George Blagdin. See GW to Herbert, 25 June 1799, and notes 1 and 2 of that document. Thornton notified GW on 1 Sept. that Blagdin would need another $1,000 by 20 September. GW sent Thornton the money for Blagdin on 11 September.

To William Roberts

Mr Roberts,   Mount Vernon 29th Augt 1799

I have been much disappointed in not seeing you according to promise—and more so from your silence.

My Millers time, as I informed you would be the case, expired the 12th of this month; but rather than leave my Mill to the care of Negros, he has consented to remain until this time; & will do so until the day after tomorrow, when he has engaged a Waggon to remove him & his things, to the place to which he is going—many miles from hence.

I request to hear from you immediately, for it is better to know the worst of a thing, than to be held in suspence.[1] I remain Your friend &ca

Go: Washington

ALS (letterpress copy), NN: Washington Papers.

1. By 8 Sept. Roberts had arrived at Mount Vernon, very ill. See GW's letter to Anderson of that date.

To Mason Locke Weems

Revd Sir, Mount Vernon 29th Augt 1799
I have been duly favored with your letter of the 20th instant—accompanying "The Philanthropist." [1]

For your politeness in sending the latter, I pray you to receive my best thanks. Much indeed is it to be wished that the sentiments contained in the Pamphlet, and the doctrine it endeavours to inculcate, were more prevalent. Happy would it be for *this country at least,* if they were so. But while the passions of Mankind are under so little restraint as they are among us. and while there are so many motives, & views, to bring them into action we may wish for, but will never see the accomplishment of it. With respect—I am—Revd Sir Your most obedt Hble Servant,

Go: Washington

ALS (letterpress copy), NN: Washington Papers.
1. Weems's letter of 20 Aug. reads: "Illustrious Sir—I have taken the liberty to dedicate this little pamphlet to your Excellency, from an humble hope that the sentiments containd in it wou'd prove (in some measure at least) pleasing to yourself, and profitable to our common country. If these my fond hopes shd be realized, I shall be very thankful and happy; and shall not fail to pray that the Author of All good will grant me the honor to be farther pleasing and useful" (NIC). Weems's pamphlet *The Philanthropist, or, A Good Twenty-five Cents Worth of Political Love Powder, for Honest Adamites and Jeffersonians* (Dumfries, Va., 1799) was printed in several places with variations in its title.

To William Herbert

Dear Sir, Mount Vernon 30th Augt 1799
Although I have more than a sufficient deposit in the Bank of Alexandria to take up my note;[1] yet, as I know also that there will be calls upon me that may not be conveniently answered without that aid; I have thought it advisable (as the 60 days has, or is about to expire) to renew it: and will thank you for taking the necessary steps to effect it accordingly.[2] With very great esteem and regard—I am Dear Sir Your Most Obedt & Affecte Servant

Go: Washington

ALS (letterpress copy), NN: Washington Papers.
1. GW took out his first bank loan in June 1799. See GW to Herbert, 25 June, nn.1 and 2.

2. Herbert replied later this day: "From what passed between us, when I was Last at Mount Vernon, I Concluded, that you did not Mean to renew your Note in Bank, Consequently did Not Send you a Note to Sign for that purpose, however It is not now too late, & you have one Inclosed, which You will please to return to me to Morrow, as it must make a part of this Weeks discount & of Course, dated on Monday last" (DLC:GW). Herbert had dined at Mount Vernon as recently as 7 Aug. (*Diaries*, 6:359). See GW's response of 1 September.

To Zechariah Lewis

Sir,   Mount Vernon 30th Augt 1799.
Your favor of the 15th instant accompanying the Oration of the Honble Mr Daggett, and that delivered by yourself, have been duly received, and read with pleasure.[1]
For your polite attention in sending them to me, I pray you to accept the thanks of Revd Sir Your Most obedient Humble Servt
                                                    Go: Washington

ALS (photocopy), DLC:GW.
1. Letter not found. David Daggett (1764–1851), a staunch Connecticut Federalist, delivered a Fourth of July oration in 1799 to the citizens of New Haven. He entitled it *Sunbeams May Be Extracted from Cucumbers, But the Process Is Tedious*. On the same day, Zechariah Lewis, the former tutor of George Washington Parke Custis, gave to the Connecticut Society of the Cincinnati at New Haven *An Oration, on the Apparent, and the Real Political Situation of the United States*. Both speeches were printed in New Haven in 1799.

To Thompson & Veitch

Gentlemen   Mt Vernon 30th Augt 1799
Not sending to the Post Office every day, is the cause of my not acknowledging the receipt of your letter of the 27th instant sooner.[1]
I now enclose you a check on the Bank of Alexandria, in discharge of my acceptance of William Auge Washington's draught on me for $500 in favor of Messrs Waltr Roe & Co.[2]
If you know of any Vessel bound to Falmouth (England) I should ⟨be⟩ glad to send Mr Hambly a few Hams[3]—At all times I should be happy to see you at this place, being Gentlemen Your Obedt Hble Servant
                                                    Go: Washington

ALS (photocopy), ViMtV.

  1. Letter not found.

  2. See W.A. Washington to GW, 13 July, n.1.

  3. Thompson & Veitch replied from Alexandria later in the day: "We are favoured with yours of this date—incloseing Chk for five hundred Dollars being amount of your acceptance; At present there is no Vessel offering for Falmouth, nor doe we think there will be one soon from this Port. Should you wish to send anything to Mr Hambly you can direct it to our care, and it shall be immediately forwarded via Baltimore, Norfolk or to New York, to go on by the British packet. Be pleased to accept our Thanks for your polite invitation and we shall doe ourselves the Honour of waiting on you at Mount Vernon very soon" (DLC:GW). See William Hambly to GW, 13 April 1799.

To Jonathan Trumbull, Jr.

My dear Sir,　　　　　　　　　Mount Vernon 30th Augt 1799

Your favor of the 10th instant came duly to hand. It gave me pleasure to find by the contents of it, that your sentiments respecting the comprehensive project of Colo. Trumbull, coincided with those I had expressed to him.

A very different state of Politics must obtain in this Country, and more unanimity prevail in our Public councils than is the case at present, 'ere such a measure could be undertaken with the least prospect of success. By unanimity *alone* the plan could be accomplished: while then a party, and a strong one too, is hanging upon the wheels of Government, opposing measures calculated solely for Internal defence, and is endeavouring to defeat all the Laws which have been passed for this purpose, by rendering them obnoxious, to attempt any thing beyond this, would be to encounter *certain* disappointment.

And yet, if the Policy of this Country, or the necessity occasioned by the existing opposition to its measures, should suffer the French to Possess themselves of Louisiana and the Floridas— either by exchange or otherwise—I will venture to predict, without the gift of "*second sight*" that there will be "no peace in Israel." Or, in other words, that the restless, ambitious, & Intrieguing spirit of that People, will keep the United States in a continual state of Warfare with the numerous tribes of Indians that inhabit our Frontiers. For doing which their "Diplomatic skill" is well adapted.

With respect to the other subject of your letter, I must again express a strong, and ardent wish and desire that, no eye, no tongue, no thought, may be turned towards me for the purpose alluded to therein. For, besides the reasons which I urged against the measure in my last, and which in my judgment, and by my feelings are insurmountable, you, yourself, have furnished a cogent one.

You have conceded, what before was self-evident in my mind—namely—that not a single vote would, thereby, be drawn from the anti-federal Candidate. You add, however, that it might be a mean of uniting the federal Votes. Here then, my dear Sir, let me ask, what satisfaction—what consolation—what safety—should I find in support, which depends upon caprice?

If *Men*, not *Principles*, can influence the choice, on the part of the Federalists, what but fluctuations are to be expected? The favourite to day, may have the curtain dropped on him tomorrow, while steadiness marks the conduct of the Anti's; and whoever is not on *their* side, must expect to be loaded with all the calumny that malice can invent; in addition to which, I should be charged with inconsistency, concealed ambition, dotage—and a thousand more etceteras.

It is too interesting not to be again repeated, that if principles, instead of men, are not the steady pursuit of the Federalists, their cause will soon be at an end. If *these* are pursued, they *will not divide* at the next Election of a President; If they do divide on so *important* a point, it would be dangerous to trust them on any other; and none except those who might be solicitous to fill the Chair of Government would do it.

In a word, my dear Sir, I am too far advanced into the vale of life to bear such buffiting as I should meet with, in such an event. A mind that has been constantly on the stretch since the year 1753, with but short intervals, & little relaxation, requires rest, & composure; and I believe that nothing short of a serious Invasion of our Country (in which case I conceive it to be the duty of every citizen to step forward in its defence) will ever draw me from my present retirement. But let me be in that, or in any other situation, I shall always remain Your sincere friend and Affectionate Humble Servt

Go: Washington

ALS, CtY: U.S. Presidents Collection; ALS (letterpress copy), NN: Washington Papers.

Letter not found: from William Augustine Washington, 30 Aug. 1799. On 7 Oct. GW wrote William Augustine Washington: "Strange as it may seem, it is nevertheless true, that your letter of the 30th of August never got to my hands until the 4th instant."

To Thomas Attwood Digges

Mount Vernon 31st [August] 1799

Genl Washington presents his compliments to Mr Digges, and will, with pleasure, exchange 20 bushels of the *early white wheat* with him when he gets it out of the straw; which is not the case at present—nor can be until the latter end of next week or beginning of the week following: which would be full early for sowing *that* kind of Wheat—Indeed any time in September is in good season. The middle, better than sooner in that month.

A good journey to Mrs Digges.

AL (photocopy), *Columbia Hist. Soc. Recs.*, 7:8. The letter is dated "31st Septr 1799," but the contents of the letter make it clear that it was not written in late September but rather, probably, in August, and the "31st" suggests that GW inadvertently wrote September instead of August. After his return from England in late 1798 or early 1799, Thomas Attwood Digges (1742–1821) of Warburton in Maryland had visited Mount Vernon several times, most recently on 15 Aug. (*Diaries*, 6:333, 346, 351, 361). Mrs. Digges is probably Thomas Digges's sister-in-law Catherine Brent Digges, widow of George Digges.

To William Hambly

Sir,   Mount Vernon Septr 1st 1799

I have been duly honoured with your favour of the 13th of April from Falmouth, accompanying what I persuade myself will (when opened) be found to be, a very fine Cheese; as all which I have had from you, have proved.

For this additional evidence of your kind, and polite attention to me, I pray you to accept my gratitude and thanks.

Unsuccessful in my first attempt to get a few (Virginia) Hams to you, I am making another trial—through the medium of Messrs Thompson & Veitch—and hope they will meet a better fate than the last.[1]

For your obliging wishes respecting me I feel very sensibly. I reciprocatc thcm cordially—and am Sir Your Obliged and Most Obedt Hble Servt

Go: Washington

ALS (photocopy), Joseph Baer & Co., catalog no. 600; ALS (letterpress copy), NN: Washington Papers.

1. See GW to Hambly, 28 July 1798, and GW's exchange of letters with Thompson & Veitch, 30 Aug. 1799.

To William Herbert

Dear Sir,   Mount Vernon Septr 1st 1799

Your letter with its enclosure, was not received until after candle light last night; owing, I presume, to my not having sent to the Post Office on friday: rarely sending—oftener than every other day, for my letters & Papers.[1]

I have put my name to the enclosed note, although it ought to have been at the Bank yesterday; to be returned, or destroyed, as circu[m]stances require.

This business of borrowing & discount (as you will perceive) I am quite a novice in. What I meant by renewing my note, was no more than, instead of taking it up, by applying so much of my deposit in Bank to this purpose (in payment thereof) to let it remain—so as that, this sum might be at my command; whether I adopted proper means to effect this end, you are the best judge.

It is quite immaterial to me, whether the discount was made last week—or may be this week—or the next—provided all things are right with respect to the *old* note; which being for Sixty days I know ought to be paid at the end thereof, or renewed. With this explanation of my intentions, you will please to do, or cause to be done, what is proper on my part—that I may not be brought into any unpleasant predicament at the Bank.

It is far from my intention, or wish, to saddle you with the expence of stamps; and therefore pray to be charged with their cost, and to be told where, & in what manner I can be provided with others.[2] With very great esteem—I am—Dear Sir Yr Most Obedt & Affece Servt

Go: Washington

ALS (letterpress copy), NN: Washington Papers.

1. Herbert's letter is printed in GW to Herbert, 30 Aug., n.2.

2. Herbert responded from Alexandria the next day, 2 Sept.: "I Received your

favor by Doctr [James] Craik, Covering the Note I Sent you, Executed, as I looked for it, I had the Accounts of last Week, Kept Open, Untill it Came to hand, of Course Matters Stand, as if it was Offered at the Precise Day. Without a renual of your Note, It would be Impossible to Continue the loan, the Laws & regulations of the Bank, making such a Measure Indispensable—This Being Complyed With, your Deposit in Bank, Stands undiminished, farther, than What the Discount of the last Note Comes to, Whenever you Send up your Bank Book, your Account Shall be Settled, & the Old Note, which is, for the Present, entered up as a Check, will be returned to you. The Stamps that I furnished, I have Charged you With, & Can be Settled When we meet, a Mr Page, Who Writes in the Collectors Office, is the Vender of Stamps in this Town" (DLC:GW). Mr. Page is probably William Byrd Page, who was married to Light-Horse Harry Lee's sister Anne.

To James McHenry

Private
Dear Sir,   Mount Vernon Sepr 1st 1799

I find, by looking over my files, that your favours of the 14th & 24th of August have never been acknowledged. I now do, the receipt of them.

I thank you, and through you, Governor Davie, for his "Instructions to be observed for the formations and movements of Cavalry" and would thank you to mention this to him, when you shall see him, which I presume must be soon.

I pray you to direct Mr Francis, the Purveyor—to furnish me with the cost of the equipment of Washington Custis, as a Cavalry Officer.[1] I have had a small Sum in the Bank of Pennsylvania *locked up*,[2] being affraid to touch it, lest there might not be enough for ⟨the payment⟩ & I should find difficulty in remitting the Bal-[anc]e—I regret exceedingly the cause of your removal to Trenton and am—My dear Sir—with great esteem Your Affecte Hble Servt

                                        Go: Washington

ALS (letterpress copy), DLC:GW.

1. For the arrangements GW made with McHenry to have Tench Francis secure the military accoutrements that George Washington Parke Custis would need, see GW to McHenry, 7 June, n.1, and 14 July. See also McHenry to GW, 24 Aug., n.1.

2. In his letter of 14 July 1799 to Samuel Mickle Fox, president of the Bank of Pennsylvania, GW arranged to have a small balance left in his account with the bank.

To Thomas (Robert Treat) Paine

Sir,   Mount Vernon Septr 1st 1799
   I have duly received your letter of the 12th of August, together
with the Oration delivered by you in Boston on the 17th of July.[1]
   I thank you for the very flattering sentiments which you have
expressed in your letter respecting myself, and I consider your
sending me your Oration as a mark of polite attention which demands my best acknowledgment; and I pray you will be assured,
that I am never more gratified than when I see the effusions of
genius from some of the rising generation, which promises to secure our National rank in the liter⟨ary wor⟩ld, as I trust their firm,
manly and ⟨patriotic⟩ conduct will ever maintain ⟨it with dignity⟩
in the Political. I am Sir Very respectfully Your Most Obedt Servt
                                              Go: Washington

ALS, MWA; ALS (letterpress copy), NN: Washington Papers. The words and let-
ters in angle brackets were taken from the letterpress copy.
   Thomas Paine (1773–1811), son of one of the signers of the Declaration of
Independence from Massachusetts, in 1801 changed his name from Thomas
Paine to that of his father, Robert Treat Paine. A firebrand and a poet, Paine at
this time was reading law with Theophilus Parsons. The title page of the pamphlet, printed in Boston in 1799, reads: *An Oration, Written at the Request of the
Young Men of Boston, and Delivered, July 17th, 1799: in Commemoration of the Dissolu-
tion of the Treaties, and Consular Convention, between France and the United States of
America. By Thomas Paine.*
   1. Letter not found.

From William Thornton

Dear Sir   City of Washington Septr 1st 1799.
   As soon as I had the honor of your Favour of the 28th Ulto I
made the necessary Enquiry of Mr Blagdin, but did not receive his
Answer till yesterday Afternoon, as he had a Statement to make of
some Ironmongery wanted for the Houses. This return I enclose,
but if it should be inconvenient to you to order the Articles, either
Mr Blagdin or I will get them for you. He informs me he shall have
occasion for one thousand Dollars, on the 20th of this month.[1]
   We meant to have paid our respects to you and Mrs Washington
Yesterday, but Mr Tayloe of Mount Airy spent the Day with us, and
Mr Wm Hamilton of the Woodlands, near Philada is to be with us

tomorrow. He is returning immediately, and laments he cannot have the happiness of paying you a Visit.[2]

I was pleased to see Mr Pickering's Letter to you, which you did us the honor of transmitting, for our Perusal. It is a Subject highly interesting, and one I have urged, for three years, to the Board.[3] Our late Sales have been very productive, and purchases of great extent have been made by persons resident in Baltimore. We shall continue them as long as we find Purchasers. The Trustees, of Morris & Nicholson, are going to finish the Houses at the Point.[4]

I have lately been much engaged, and have not yet been able to notice Mr Walker's Letter.[5] The Navy-Yard will be fixed, I have reason to believe, where I recommended it—in the Space South of Square 930. The Board voted a portion of the Marine-hospital Square for that purpose. I remonstrated to them & to the Secretary of the Navy, stating the impropriety of touching Grounds already appropriated, and wished also the point of the City to be left for a Military Academy; for parade-Ground; for the Exercise of the great Guns; for Magazines, &c. &c. I am jealous of Innovations where Decisions have been made after mature Deliberation; and I yet hope that the City will be preserved from that extensive Injury contemplated by some never-to-be-contented and covetous Individuals.[6] My Family join me in most respectful Compliments & good wishes to your Lady & self. I am, dear Sir, your obedient & affectionate Friend

William Thornton

ALS, DLC:GW.

1. By the terms of his agreement with George Blagdin, GW was to supply what iron Blagdin needed in the construction of GW's houses in Washington. See District of Columbia Commissioners to GW, 27 Oct. 1798, n.3. The enclosed statement, dated "Capitol Septr 1st 1799" and signed by Blagdin, reads:

"Iron Momongery

3 Pair of 5 Inch Butt Hinges for the front doors & 1¾ Inch screws to D[itt]o

2 Pair of 14 or 16 Inch HL Hinges to the back doors & Screws 1¼ Inch long.

4 Pair of Hooks and bands to the 4 basement Doors with a screw and Nut to each.

4 12 Inch locks to the principal doors Iron rims brass Pendants &

4 Do of a plainer kind for the 4 basement doors" (DLC:GW). See GW's response of 5 September.

2. GW's acquaintance with William Hamilton (1745–1813), of the famed Woodlands estate near Philadelphia, dated back to 1774 when GW attended the First Continental Congress (*Diaries*, 3:277–78).

3. On 28 Aug. GW forwarded to the three District of Columbia commissioners

Timothy Pickering's letter of 22 Aug. suggesting a mode of building docks and wharves for the new Federal City's waterfront. See note 3 to Pickering's letter.

4. For reference to the disastrous speculation in lots in the new Federal City by John Nicholson and Robert Morris, the latter of whom was by now in prison for debt and Nicholson was soon to follow, see George Washington Parke Custis to GW, 30 July 1797, n.1. In June 1797 Morris and Nicholson reached a complicated agreement with their creditors which provided that their creditors would act as trustees of the partners' holdings and be empowered to mortgage or sell the partners' lots in the Federal City to provide security for all of their debts (Chernow, *Robert Morris*, 163–67).

5. See George Walker to GW, 5 Aug., and note 4 of that document.

6. In his answer of 26 Sept. 1798 to a query from Secretary of the Navy Benjamin Stoddert of 16 Sept. about placing the Washington navy yard in the area that in 1796 had been set aside for a marine hospital, GW offered no objections. Thornton, however, had consistently opposed the move and in the end prevailed (see Harris, *Thornton Papers*, 1:483).

Letter not found: from John Avery, 2 Sept. 1799. On 25 Sept. GW wrote Avery: "Your letter of the 2d instt came duly to hand."

From James McHenry

Sir   Trenton [N.J.] War Department 3 Septr 1799

Inclosed are the rules which have been adopted by the President of the United States relative to rank and promotion in the Army.[1]

It is requested that you will as speedily as the nature of the case and circumstances admit determine the relative rank of the field officers of the Regiment of Cavalry, and of the 12 regiments of Infantry raised in pursuance of the Act of the 16 July 1798. For your information on this subject I inclose a return extracted from the records of this office exhibiting the names and rank of the field officers in the regiments who were in service to the termination of the late war, the rank of those who were deranged and when deranged together with the names of those who have served in the army or levies since the peace and have been disbanded. I also inclose a copy of my queries to the officers and the statement made by them of their respective claims.[2]

With respect to the relative rank of the company officers. On the 21st March ultimo Major General Hamilton was authorized "in every case in which an association of company officers (or Majors) different from the Schedule (framed by the General Officers) should appear to be more conducive to harmony, and promotive of the public service, to make the same definitively or provisionally as he might determine." The Major General in consequence transmitted to me on the 25th of August ultimo an arrangement of the company officers of the 7, 10, 11 & 12th regiments. I have since requested him on the 3d instant as you will see by a copy of my letter which is inclosed to hasten to fix the relative rank of the company officers of the remaining regiments.[3]

Sensible that I have occupied much of your time in the affairs of the army, and that the duty now assigned you will require a further portion of it, I request you will permit me, to transmit to you, two months pay. It is not right that you should render services so essential without compensation.[4] I have the honor to be, with the greatest respect, Sir Your Most Obedt, & Most Hl. Servt

James McHenry

LS, DLC:GW.

1. The copy of the rules enclosed in this letter of 3 Sept. is in DLC:GW. For the rules respecting promotions in the army, see GW to McHenry (second letter), 7 July 1799, n.1.

2. See Enclosure: List of Field Officers, this date. GW wrote McHenry on 15 Sept. that he was returning the "letters written to you by the Lieutt Colonels & Majors." These letters have not been identified.

3. See McHenry to Alexander Hamilton, 21 Mar. 1799, in Syrett, *Hamilton Papers*, 22:560–66. For McHenry's letter to Hamilton of 3 Sept. 1799, see ibid., 23:374–75.

4. GW refused to accept pay (GW to McHenry, 14 September).

Enclosure
List of Field Officers

[c.3 September 1799]

As the Letters from the Colonels and Majors do not exactly agree with the records of the War department, it has been thought proper to annex to such of them as were in service during the late War, the time of their entering and quitting the service as entered in the Books and settlements of the Office.

Lieutenant Colonels

John Smith	Captain	1 April 1778	deranged 1 Jany 1783
James Read	Captain	8 July 1777	no letter from him
William Bentley	Captain	1 May 1779	deranged 1 Januy 1783

Thomas Parker	Captain	23 April 1778	ditto
Josias C. Hall	Colonel	1 January 1777	deranged 1 Jany 1781
Thomas L. Moore	Major	12 May 1779	deranged 1 Jany 1783
Aaron Ogden	Captain	2 February 1779	contind till end of War
William S. Smith	Lt Colonel	1 January 1777	contind till end of War
Timothy Taylor	Captain	17 Decemr 1781	contd till end of War
Nathan Rice	Major	1 January 1781	contd till end of War
Richard Hunnewell	Lieutenant	Decemr 1776	resigned Nov. 1778
Rufus Graves		Never before in service	
		Majors	
James Armstrong	Captain	17 Novemr 1780	contd till end of War
Henry M. Rutledge			
Alexander D. Moore			
William Brickell			
Robert Beale	Captain	June 1779	deranged 1 Jany 1783
James Baytop	Captain	11 Decr 1777	resigned 12 May 1779
William Campbell	Captain		
Lawrence Butler	Captain	14 May 1779	deranged 1 Jany 1783
William D. Beale	Major	6 Novemr 1781	deranged 1 Jany 1783
David Hopkins	Major	1 January 1781	contd till end of War
William Henderson	Captain	16 May 1778	deranged 1 Jany 1783
George Stephenson	Lieutenant	17 Jany 1777	resigned
William Shute	Ensign	17 June 1780	contd till end of War
John Adlum			no letter from him
William Willcocks			
John Ripley			
Jabez Huntington			
John Walker			
Isaac Winslow			
William Jones			
John Rowe	Ensign	15 June 1781	contd till end of War
Timothy Darling			
Cornelius Lynde			

D, DLC:GW. The comments after the names of James Read, Rufus Graves, and John Adlum are in a different hand.

To William Thornton

Dear Sir   Mount Vernon 5th Sepr 1799

Not sending to Alexandria every day, letters sometimes lye longer in the Post Office than they otherwise would do. This is the reason why your favour of the 1st instant has not been acknowledged sooner.

If Mr Blagden would be at the trouble of chusing the Iron-mongry *himself* and pay ready money for it (thereby providing it on the best terms) I had rather he should get it than I because he would be a better judge of it's quality. With the means for making such purchases, he shall always be furnished; and he may count upon the $1000 the 20th instant.

I am glad to hear that your late sales have been productive, & that the people of Baltimore are turning their attention towards the Federal City. At all times we shall be glad to see you & Mrs Thornton here—& with great esteem—I am Dr Sir Yr Obedt Servt

Go: Washington

ALS, DLC: Thornton Papers; ALS (letterpress copy), NN: Washington Papers.

Letter not found: from Landon Carter, 6 Sept. 1799. On 11 Sept. GW wrote Carter: "In answer to your favor of the 6th instant. . . ."

To Thomas Peter

Dear Sir,   [Mount Vernon, 7 September 1799]
The Carriage is sent agreeably to Mrs Peter's request; and we shall expect to see you by three 'oclock.[1]

Mrs Washington has been exceedingly unwell for more than eight days. Yesterday she was so ill as to keep her bed all day, and to occasion my sending for Doctr Craik the night before, at midnight. She is now better, and taking the Bark; but low, weak and fatiegued. Under his direction.

Her's has been a kind of Ague & fever—the latter never, entirely, intermitting until now. I sent for the Doctor to her on Sunday last, but she could not, until he came the second time—yesterday morning—be prevailed upon to take any thing to arrest them. Our best regards attend you—and I am Dr Sir Yr Obedt &ca

Go: Washington

Since writing and Sealing this letter—Mrs Washingtons fever has returned with uneasy & restless Symptoms.[2]

G. W——n

Inform Mrs Law thereof.

ALS, ViMtV. GW addressed the letter to "Mr Thos Peter if absent to Mrs Peter Federal City by Cyrus." He wrote the postscript on the cover.

1. Thomas Peter and his wife, Martha Parke Custis Peter, arrived at Mount Vernon "in the afternoon" of the seventh, and Mrs. Peter, with her children, apparently remained at Mount Vernon until 12 Oct., perhaps because of her grandmother's prolonged illness (*Diaries*, 6:364).

2. GW recorded in his diary for 1 Sept.: "Doctr. Craik dined here—sent for to Mrs. Washington who was sick," and on 6 Sept. Craik was sent for "in the Night" (*Diaries*, 6:363). Tobias Lear wrote William Thornton from Mount Vernon on 12 Sept.: "We have lately been alarmed on account of Mrs. Washington's illness; but she is now, thank God, in a state of convalescence, and I hope will shortly be restored to her usual health" (Harris, *Thornton Papers*, 1:508–9). Lear was too optimistic, however. GW reported to Lawrence Lewis on 28 Sept. that "Mrs Washington has not recovered her health; on the contrary is, at this time, weak, low, and much indisposed." Mrs. Washington had her final visit on 12 Oct. from Dr. Craik, who in his account with GW, 25 June–December 1799 (NjMoNP) records visits on 1, 4, 6, 8, 10, 13, 19 Sept. and 12 Oct. and lists the medication he prescribed; but as late as 3 Nov. GW reported that his wife continued "much indisposed" (GW to Charles Cotesworth Pinckney, 3 Nov. 1799).

To James Anderson

Mr Anderson,   Mount Vernon 8th Sep. 1799

Mrs Washington passed a good night—is clear of a fever to day—and is taking the Bark—which I hope will prevent a return of it.[1]

I am much hurried, and pressed with one thing—or another, but do what humanity requires for Roberts: who ought not to have engaged, in the situation he is in, without first informing me of it. Doctr Craik is not *now* here, nor *expected* if Mrs Washington should not relapse; but the case may be stated to him against to morrow afternoon, when I shall send up to the Post Office. If it be found that he is not *now*—nor soon *will* be, in a condition to discharge the duties of a Miller, some other *must*, undoubtedly; be got; as I cannot loose the Fall work of the Mill. He may have medicine, or any thing else from hence.[2]

I did not send to the Post Office yesterday—of course no Papers came.

I was sorry to hear of your indisposition. I fear the charge with which you are entrusted, is too much for your health, and that to execute it properly, will rather increase than diminish your complaint. I shall therefore, so soon as company—sickness—and other circumstances will allow me time to digest my thoughts on this subject—express them to you in a more full & ample manner than I can do at present.[3] I am always your friend &ca

Go: Washington

ALS, MBOS; ALS (letterpress copy), ViMtV.

1. See GW to Thomas Peter, 7 Sept., n.2.

2. William Roberts, whom GW had rehired in June as miller at Mount Vernon, had only just arrived. See GW to Roberts, 17 June and 29 August. Roberts, who was ill, was able to act as miller if at all for only a short time and was paid in "full" on 16 Nov. 1799 (Mount Vernon Ledger, 1799–1800).

3. See GW to Anderson, 10 Sept., and note 2 of that document.

To Timothy Pickering

Dear Sir,   Mount Vernon Sepr 8th 1799

Your letter of the 22d Ulto came duly to hand. The subject being of importance to the New City; and at no time more necessary than at the commencement of the water improvements thereat— I sent it to the Commissioners of the Federal City; who were contemplating on regulations to avoid the evils which are but too common, and of late sorely felt; in almost the whole of our Seaport Towns of Magnitude, from narrow alleys, & filthy Docks. They have promised to give it all the consideration in their power.[1]

Has any trial ever been made of the medicine, in the Yellow fever, which was sent to me by a Physician in Germany, and forwarded to you? As the skill of our most eminent Medical men in this Country has been baffled in that fatal disorder—I think it merits a trial.[2] ⟨With⟩ great esteem & regard—I am—Dear Sir Yr Obedt Hble Servt

Go: Washington

ALS (letterpress copy), NN: Washington Papers; copy, MHi: Pickering Papers. Attached to the copy in the Pickering Papers is this notation: "Nov. 12. 1827. I have this day received the original of the letter, of which the above is a copy. Jared Sparks." The Sparks copy has been used to confirm the reading of blurred words in the letterpress copy.

1. See Pickering to GW, 22 Aug., n.3.

2. John Frederick Ramnitz wrote GW from Spandau on 31 Oct. 1798 describing a proposed treatment for yellow fever. GW sent this to Pickering on 20 Mar. 1799, shortly after receiving it. Pickering's response to this inquiry from GW in a letter to GW of 29 Sept. 1799 is quoted in Ramnitz to GW, 31 Oct. 1798, n.1.

To Auguste de Grasse

Sir,   Mount Vernon, Septr 9th 1799.

I have received your letter of the 20th of August, requesting an Appointment in the Corps of Engineers about to be established.[1]

I have made it a point to forward all applications for military Offices, which have been made to me, to the Secretary of War, in whose Office they will be deposited for the inspection and consideration of the President of the United States; and your letter has been transmitted to him accordingly.[2] With due respect I am, Sir, Your most Obedt Servt

                                            Go: Washington

LS (photocopy), ViMtV; copy, DLC:GW. Both the signed copy and the retained copy are in the hand of Tobias Lear. Lear wrote at the bottom of the retained copy: "Monsr Augustus De Grass Charleston S.C."

Alexandre-François-Auguste de Grasse-Rouville, comte de Grasse, marquis de Tilly (1765–1845), who came to the United States in 1793, was soon to return to France.

    1. Letter not found.
    2. See GW to McHenry, this date.

From Alexander Hamilton

Private
Dr Sir   New York Sepr 9 1799

Two days since, I received from General Wilkinson a Report of which I now send you the original. You will find it intelligent and interesting. Perhaps on the score of intrinsic propriety it deserves to be adopted to a larger extent than some collateral and extraneous considerations may permit.[1]

I had previously thought of the subject but had purposely limited myself to a few very general ideas, that I might examine with the less prepossession the plan of an officer, who possessing talents to judge has for years had his mind occupied with the scene to which he refers. Since the receipt of his plan, I have assiduously contemplated it with the aid of a full personal explanation, and my judgment has formed a result, though not definitive but liable to revision. I adopt several of the leading ideas of the General but I vary in some particulars; as well because I think the change might be too strong with reference to its influence on public opinion and the feelings of the parts of the country immediately concerned as because it seems to me that motives of real weight dictate a modification of his plan.

Premising that one complete Regiment of Infantry should be left for *Tennessee* and the Frontiers of Georgia I would propose the following Disposition for the Remaining three of the old Regiments for the batalion of Artillery and the two troops of Dragoons allotted for the Western Army. It is taken for granted that the plan must contemplate only the four old Regiments of Infantry (with those portions of Artillerists and dragoons) inasmuch as these are the only infantry regarded by our system as permanent. The twelve additional Regiments will dissolve of course, as to the non commissioned officers and privates, by the simple fact of the settlement of our dispute with France.[2]

ALS, DLC:GW.

1. For Gen. James Wilkinson's detailed recommendations for the disposal of U.S. troops in the interior of the country, see Wilkinson to Hamilton, 6 Sept. 1799, in Syrett, *Hamilton Papers*, 23:377–93.

2. The remainder of Hamilton's letter, running to eight manuscript pages, sets out his recommendations for the stationing of U.S. army troops on the frontier. His letter is printed in ibid., 402–7. See also GW's response of 15 Sept., and notes.

To James McHenry

Sir,   Mount Vernon, Septr 9th 1799

Enclosed is a letter from Monsr Augustus de Grass, requesting an appointment in the Corps of Engineers; which I forward to you, as I have done all letters of a similar nature.[1]

I received, this morning, under a blank cover from the War Office, a letter for myself from Govr Rutledge of So. Carolina, and one for Brigadier Genl Washington, which I have forwarded so as to get to his hands before he leaves this State. He left Mount Vernon yesterday Morning, on his way to Carolina.[2] With due consideration I have the honor to be Sir, Yr mo. Ob. St

Go: W——n

Copy, in Tobias Lear's hand, DLC:GW.

1. See GW to Auguste de Grasse, this date.

2. See GW to Edward Rutledge, this date.

To Edward Rutledge

My dear Sir,   Mount Vernon Sepr 9th 1799

Brigadier General Washington called upon me on Saturday night and went off again on Sunday morning—His anxiety to get to Carolina as soon as possible (having been detained to the Eastward longer than he expected) prevented his passing more time with me.[1] He gave me the model of the Cannon which you was so good as to present to me, and by him I wrote a hasty line to you acknowledging the receipt of it &ca.[2]

This morning I had the pleasure to receive, under a blank cover from the War Office, your obliging favour of the 3d of Augt and a letter addressed to Brigadr General Washington, which I shall forward so as to get to his hands before he leaves this State.[3]

Permit me, my dear Sir, to repeat my thanks for the model of the Cannon,[4] and to assure you of my grateful acknowledgements for the kind and friendly sentiments contained in your letter. No man can wish more sincerely than I do, that we may not be drawn into the conflict in which the European Powers are now involved; but, at the same time, no one is more anxious that we should make every possible preparation to meet such an event, if it should be unavoidable.

In order to [do] this, we should embrace the present moment to make our Establishments as respectable as circumstances will permit, and neglect no opportunity of introducing into them every improvement in the Military Art that can be useful, let it come from what quarter so ever it may.

I am sorry to inform you that Mrs Washington has been confined by a fever for some days past; she seems at present to be a little better; but is still very low. She is thankful for Mrs Rutledge's kind regards and most sincerely reciprocates them, in which she is joined by—My dear Sir Your Affecte friend and Obedient Servant

Go: Washington

ALS, NNGL. A retained copy in Tobias Lear's hand was advertised for sale by Christie's on 14 May 1985, item 108.

1. See *Diaries*, 6:364.

2. GW's "hasty line," dated 8 Sept., reads: "My dear Sir, I have received, by the hands of Genl W. Washington, the model of an improvement made on Gun carriages which you have been so good as to present me; and I pray you will accept my sincere thanks for this token of your friendship, which will always be dear to me.

"I see many advantages in this improvement on Gun carriages, and I think every thing of this kind ought to be adopted by us, so far as they can be usefully applied; for it will be much easier to introduce valuable improvements in the commencement of our Military establishments, than after we shall have been long accustomed to certain habits & things to deviate from them. In best wishes for the health and happiness of yourself & Mrs Rutledge Mrs Washington unites with My dear Sir Yr Affecte & Obedt Servt Go: Washington" (ALS [photocopy], ScU; copy, in Tobias Lear's hand, docketed by GW, ViMtV).

3. The letter of 3 Aug. has not been found, and the letter to William Washington has not been identified; but see GW to James McHenry, 9 September.

4. Rutledge, who served for a time during the Revolutionary War as a captain in the South Carolina artillery, was particularly interested in mechanical inventions (Haw, *John and Edward Rutledge*, 262).

To James Anderson

Mr Anderson,   Mount Vernon Septr 10th 1799

In a hasty note which I wrote to you on Sunday last, I informed you, that as soon as time and circumstances would permit, I would be more full on a subject which I could then, but barely touch upon.[1]

The latter of these has not, yet, put it so fully in my power as I could wish to fulfil this promise. I shall, however, endeavour to explain my meaning without further ⟨delay⟩.

I have, for more than two years, been a witness to your zeal, industry and exertions in the discharge of your multifarious duties; and I always have, and still do believe, that they have been rendered with the strictest sobriety & integrity. But I must have been blind, if I had not discovered also, that the *whole*, taken together, more on account of the diversity, and complexity of them, than for their aggregate magnitude, was too much for you; and that by your exertions to execute the various parts, to your own satisfaction, you might bring on, what you say has already happened, ill-health.

The intimation of this by you, with the doubt accompanying it, of being unable to go through with the business; added to the earnest desire I have long had to simplify my concerns by dividing, and letting part of them out, thereby relieving myself from much trouble; and, though less profitable perhaps, place my income on more stable ground, has suggested more strongly than ever the idea of connecting my Mill and Distillery into one concern, and renting them on reasonable terms; and as you profess to understand the Management of both, to offer them to you on a Rent⟨,⟩ for any number of years not exceeding seven, and on such terms as you, yourself, under the estimates you have given me of their annual value, shall think just—between man & man—For at the sametime that I should expect a reasonable compensation for the use of the property it would be equally my wish that you should find your account in the profit, arising therefrom—Live, & let live—is, in my opinion, a maxim founded in true policy; and is one I am disposed to pursue.[2]

If the Mill & Distillery was let in this manner, there would be no difficulty in Renting the Fishery at the Ferry—(depending on that at the Mansion house to supply my Negros)—and having a project in contemplation for the disposal of one of my Farms, which (not being sufficiently matured) is ineligable to mention at this time,[3] the others would be no more than amusement *for me*, to superintend, if I should not be drawn again into public life; and if I was, you would be on the spot to resume your old occupation—if you chose to return to it, while your son John, under your advice & directions could carry on the concerns of the Distillery & Mill for your own benefit. For I can assure you with frankness, that it is not with a view to introduce a new Manager that I have made these proposals—I have not the smallest inclination to change—But have assigned, with candour, the motives which have led to it; namely, that the business in its present shape is too complicated, & diversified to be managed to advantage; and because I want to bring my income to something more specific, as well as to avoid the expenditures which are heaped upon me in a ratio I am unable to support, when it is the first wish of my heart to be (as much as possible in my situation) exempt from cares. In a word, I wish to bring the Concerns, which would be under my *immediate* management, into so narrow a compass as to make the superintendence of them a mere matter of amusement.

I might even in this case, require your advice now and then, with respect to the ordering of Meadows—management of grounds—&ca—for which I should be well disposed to make you an allowance.

The house you live in, unless some more eligable plan could be devised, would still serve you, and your family:[4] for I have said before, I should not require it for any other superintendant.

As the operations of both Mill and Distillery might require a little money to lay in Grain, until that grain would be in a condition to raise cash for the Flour & Whiskey it would produce, I should be disposed (if The means were in my power) to advance you a little, to begin with. But as my means depend upon payment from others, it would be folly in me to promise this, absolutely, as, from experience I have found, that there is no reliance on the most solemn assurances that are given of money. I wish you better health, and remain your friend &ca

Go: Washington

ALS (letterpress copy), NN: Washington Papers. In a number of the letterpress copies of GW letters, barely legible words have been traced over with a pencil, sometimes clearly by GW himself. The tracings in this letter were probably done by someone else, either at the time or later.

1. GW's letter is dated 8 September.

2. Anderson responded to GW's letter in a missing letter of 13 Sept. in which, as GW indicates in his letter to Anderson of 16 Sept., Anderson wrote that his health and his family's was deteriorating and was not likely to improve as long as they remained at Mount Vernon. Anderson at the same time offered to help GW find a tenant for the mill and distillery at Mount Vernon. On 16 Sept. GW released Anderson from any engagement to him if Anderson's health would be endangered by continuing as farm manager, and he outlined for Anderson the terms on which he would rent the mill and distillery if Anderson should turn up a suitable tenant. Within three days Anderson had decided to continue as manager, and on 19 Sept. he wrote GW that he thought GW's terms for renting the mill and distillery reasonable and would let him know "as soon as I learn of any good Man well disposed to Rent."

The next day, 20 Sept., GW wrote to his nephew Lawrence Lewis to say that he intended at his death to leave to Lewis and his bride, Martha Washington's granddaughter Eleanor Parke Custis Lewis, Dogue Run farm at Mount Vernon and the adjacent mill and distillery, and he offered to rent all of them to Lewis at once "on a just, & equitable Rent." GW enclosed this letter in a second letter to Lewis, dated 28 Sept., in which he wrote that "Mr Anderson (in Partnership with his son John) has discovered an inclination to Rent my Distillery & Mill." GW went on to say that he would like to do this so that he could ease Anderson out of his position of farm manager and take over himself the management of the farms. He assured Lewis, however, that he would "say nothing definitively to him [Anderson], on the Subject" until he had heard from Lewis, who with his wife was visiting in Culpeper County.

Not hearing promptly from Lewis, GW wrote Anderson on 1 Oct. that as it seemed unlikely to him that Lewis would wish "to plunge at once into a scene of business to which he is a stranger," if Anderson and his son were "disposed to offer me a rent, in any degree adequate to the value of the two concerns," he would be "willing to treat with you on the subject." GW then spelled out in detail the terms on which he would rent his mill and distillery to the Andersons.

After Lewis and his wife returned to Mount Vernon in mid-October, however, it was agreed that Lewis would rent the mill and distillery as well as Dogue Run farm in 1800 and that Anderson would continue at least for a time into the new year as farm manager at Mount Vernon (see GW to Anderson, 10, 13 Dec. 1799).

3. See GW to Lawrence Lewis, 20 September.

4. Anderson lived at the house at the ferry, now a part of GW's Union farm (An Account of Property at Mount Vernon, at the end of Mount Vernon Ledger, 1799–1800).

Letter not found: from Robert Lewis, 10 Sept. 1799. GW wrote Lewis on 7 Dec.: "Your letter of the 10th of Septr came duly to hand."

To Landon Carter

Dear Sir,   Mount Vernon 11th Sep: 1799

In answer to your favor of the 6th instant, which I received yesterday;[1] I inform you that I have raised no Carrots in the field these ten or twelve years; of course, have no other seed than such as are usually cultivated in Gardens.

Previous to the year 1789, when I was drawn from retirement; I cultivated both Carrots & Potatoes (in alternate rows) between drilled Corn 8 feet a part,[2] and am persuaded that the aggregate benefit from the practice would be found highly profitable to a Farmer who has it in his power to attend to his business *himself*, and will be judicious in the application of them. Without this, they turn to little account in the hands of such Overseers as are employed in common. I did not find that they yielded equal to the Potatoes, but were more nutritious as a food for Milch Cows. With esteem I am—Dear Sir Your Obedt Hble Servt

Go: Washington

ALS, MoSM.

1. Letter not found.

2. GW began his intensive experiments with raising carrots as food for livestock in 1787. See his letters of instruction from Philadelphia during the Constitutional Convention in the summer of 1787 to his farm manager at Mount Vernon, George Augustine Washington. On 17 Aug. 1788 GW wrote John Beale Bordley about a field at Mount Vernon "planted with Corn 8 feet by 2, single stalks; with Irish Potatoes or Carrots, or partly both between."

To William Thornton

Dear Sir,   Mount Vernon 11th Sep. 1799

The 20th of this month—when Mr Blagden would require an advance of a thousand dollars—being near at hand—and Mr Peter affording a good and safe opportunity to remit it—I enclose for this purpose, a check on the Bank of Alexandria, to that amount.[1]

Mr Peter informs me that his brother [   ] has Ironmongery of a good quality, which he wants to dispose of, and would sell cheap. I pray you therefore to inform Mr Blagden of this circumstance, request him to examine it, and if of the kind & quality he requires & to be had on good terms—to supply himself therefrom, and at the foot of the Invoice to draw upon me for the amount; which shall be immediately paid.[2] With great esteem & regard I am Dear Sir Your Most Obedt Servt

Go: Washington

ALS (photocopy), DLC:GW; ALS (letterpress copy), NN: Washington Papers.

1. See GW to Thornton, 28 Aug., n.1.

2. For reference to GW's acquiring the iron articles needed by George Blagdin for the houses that he was constructing for GW on Capitol Hill, see Thornton to GW, 1 Sept., n.1. Which of Thomas Peter's five or more brothers had iron for sale at this time has not been determined.

To Benjamin Dulany

Sir,   Mount Vernon ⟨12th Septr 17⟩99

If Mrs French or yourself, have come to any determination respecting the proposal I made in a letter addressed to you on the 15th of July last, it would be obliging to inform ⟨me of⟩ the result; as the season is fully ⟨arri⟩ved when my arrangements for the ensuing year must be ⟨made.⟩

Knowing that Mrs ⟨French⟩ had rented her Farm, I did ⟨not *illegible*⟩ expect that it would have suited her to take the Negros, at any rate; unless believing, as no doubt the ⟨case⟩ would be, that obtaining them in the aggregate, on the terms they were offered, she might derive ⟨a considera⟩ble profit by again hiring them ⟨out⟩ individually; whilst a number of promising boys & girls would soon ⟨be⟩ in a situation to increase her income.[1] I thought it respectful,

& proper however, to couple her name with yours, when the pro posal (alluded to before) was made.

I certainly conceived, that as they would, ultimately, descend to you, or yours, that it would be your interest to take them on the terms they were offered; as well, knowing that you had very valuable lands to settle them on, in ⟨the⟩ vicinity of the Federal City (on both Sides the River) where every thing raised would in a little time commd a ready market, as for the reason just given—namely—individual hiring; which it would always be in your power to do, as likely Negros of the description I gave you, are always in request—But the object of this letter being to learn your decision,[2] I shall only add that I am Sir—Your Obedient, & Very Hble Servant

Go: Washington

ALS (letterpress copy), NN: Washington Papers.

1. On 17 Aug. 1799 GW wrote his nephew Robert Lewis: "To sell the overplus [of slaves at Mount Vernon] I cannot, because I am principled against this kind of traffic in the human species. To hire them out, is almost as bad, because they could not be disposed of in families to any advantage, and to disperse the families I have an aversion."

2. For Dulany's response on 17 July to GW's initial inquiry of 15 July whether Penelope Manley French, or Benjamin Dulany as her son-in-law, would wish to have returned to them all of those slaves belonging to Mrs. French who were in GW's employ, see GW to Dulany, 15 July 1799, n.3. No response from Dulany or from Mrs. French to this second inquiry has been found.

Letter not found: from James Anderson, 13 Sept. 1799. In his letter to Anderson of 16 Sept. GW refers to Anderson's "letter of the 13th instant."

To James McHenry

Private
Dear Sir   Mount Vernon 14th Sepr 1799
I feel much obliged, and accordingly thank you, for your kind intention of ordering me two months pay;[1] and I shall not suffer false modesty to assert, that my finances stand in no need of it; because it is not the time, nor the attention only; which the Public duties I am engaged in require; but their bringing upon me Ap- plicants—recommenders of applicants—and seekers of infor-

mation—with their servants and horses (none of whom perhaps are of my acquaintance) to aid in the consumption of my forage, and what, to me is more valuable—My time—that I mostly regard; for a man in the Country, nine miles from any house of Entertainment, is differently situated from one in a City, where none of these inconveniencies are felt.

Yet, even under these circumstances, which may be little known to those who wd appreciate them, and would be totally disregarded by such as are always on the look out for something to cavil at, I am resolved to draw nothing from the Public but re-embursements of *actual* expenditures; unless, by being called into the Field, I shall be entitled to full pay, and the Emoluments of Office.

Without this it *would* be said by the latter description of People, that I was enjoying retirement on very easy and lucrative terms; whilst the former might remark, that I had forgot the conditions on which I accepted my Commission; opposed to these, the loss of time, and incidental expences, are not to be compared.

I thought this explanation of my motives, for declining the acceptance of your offer, was due to your attention, and kind intention, in behalf of Dear Sir, Your Most Obedient and Affecte Hble Servant

Go: Washington

ALS, PWacD; ALS (letterpress copy), DLC:GW.
    1. See McHenry to GW, 3 September.

To Alexander Hamilton

Dear Sir,   Mount Vernon, September 15th 1799.
    Mrs Washington's indisposition (being confined eight or ten days)—and other circumstances, would not allow me to give your letter of the 9th instant, and the Reports, Journals &c. &c. which accompanied it, an earlier consideration.

Having done this, however, with as much thought as I have been able to bestow, under the circumstances mentioned, I can see no cause (with the limited force which has been enumerated, and which, I presume, is all that can be calculated upon) to differ from you in the disposition of it. Although, at the same time, I shall make some observations thereupon for consideration.

It may be remembered, that, at the time the Secretary of War laid before the General Officers in Philadelphia,[1] the letters of General Wilkinson respecting the propriety (in his Judgment) of placing a considerable force at the Natches, I gave it my decided disapprobation.[2] Inasmuch as it would excite, in the Spaniards, distrust and jealousy of our pacific disposition—would cause an augmentation of force on their part; and so on with both, if our Government would go into the measure, until the *thing* which was *intended* to be *avoided* would, more than probable, be produced— i.e. hostility. Whereas, keeping that force in the upper Country, besides its looking to *all* points, and exciting no alarm in *any*, might, if occasion should require it, either for defence or Offence, descend the stream like lightening, with all its munitions and equipments; which could be accumulated with ease, and without noise, at the upper Posts, and make the surprise more complete.

Although I have said (in effect) that the Corps de reserve, or Army of Observation, should take post at the place you have mentioned—namely—in the vicinity of the Rapids of the Ohio (Louisville); Yet I can see but two reasons which entitle it to be prefered to the *present Post* above, i.e. Fort Washington, in a geographical point of view:[3] And these are—that there is no water above the former, that can float large Vessels at all seasons, And that, by being so much lower down, the passage of the Ohio would be facilitated if an Expedition should descend the Mississippi. In other respects the latter, in my opinion, has the advantage. 1st Because it is a Post *already* established, and would incur no additional expense. 2dly Because it is *more* contiguous to Fort Wayne, Detroit, Michilimacanac, and all the Indians on the Lakes, from whom, in that quarter, we have most danger to apprehend. 3dly Because communications with it (and for the most part by water) are already established. And 4thly In case of Insurrections above or below, it is equally as well, if not better situated.

Were it not that the Mouth of the Wabash empties itself into the Ohio so low down, and yet above its confluence with Cumberland and Tennessee, I should be inclined to give a position thereabouts the preference of either the Rapids or Fort Washington; because it would command a great water Inlet towards the Lakes.

But, whether the position for the Corps de reserve be chosen at the Rapids of the Ohio—above—or below, it had better, I conceive, be on the North side of the Ohio than within the State of

Kentucky. Thereby impeding more the intercourse between the Army and the Citizens, and guarding against the evils which result from that mixture, and too much familiarity.

I am so far from agreeing with General Wilkinson that Fort Wayne ought to be abolished, that, if I mistake not the place (central between the heads of the Miamis of Lake Erie and the Ohio; the St Joseph and the Wabash;) affording good water transportation, with small portages, in every direction, I would pronounce it (were it not for the expence of subsisting Troops there) the most eligible position for the Army of observation of any in that Country.[4] It would be an effectual security against all the Indians who could annoy us in that Region; it would cover our Barrier Posts, on the line between the British and us; and Troops from thence might descend rapidly into the Mississippi by the Wabash.

General Wilkinson, in speaking of Posts along our Southern Frontier, is general; and you only notice Fort Stoddart. But, on an inspection of the maps, a place presents itself, to my view, as very eligible to occupy; provided the Creek Indians would consent to it. I mean the Apalachicoli—at its confluence with Flint River, where the line of demarkation strikes it.

But, in my opinion, if we had, or could obtain an Engineer of *real* skill, and attached to the true policy and interest of the United States, he ought to devote his whole time to the investigation of our interior Country; and mark—and erect its proper defences; for these, hitherto, have been more the work of chance and local consideration, than national design.

If the harbour of Presque Isle is good, I should think a small Garrison ought to be retained there. It certainly is the *best* on the American side of Lake Erie; and one there is important; but I see very little use of a Sergeant and 8 privates at Fort Knox.[5] It is either unnecessary, or too small; and Sergeants at a distance rarely conduct well, when they have not the eye of an Officer to inspect their conduct.

There are several references in General Wilkinson's Report which were not sent. No. 1 appears to have been essential. They are all returned.[6]

By his statement of the mutilated condition of the Troops, and present disposition of them, there must have been most horrible mismanagement somewhere. A corrective is, indeed, highly necessary. The practice of furloughing Officers, and then renewing the furloughs from time to time, is extremely injurious to the Service, and ought to be discontinued on ordinary occasions.

And that of frittering the Army into small Garrisons, is, if possible, worse. It will never be respectable where these evils exist; and until it can be more concentrated, and Garrisons frequently relieved by detachments from the main body, discipline will always be lax, and impositions on the public will prevail.

If the British are resolved to keep up armed Vessels on the lakes, I presume it will be expedient for us to do the same; but in time of peace a better way, in my opinion, is, for neither to have any. In case of a rupture, or the appearance of one, with that nation, there can be no doubt of our arming on those waters much more expeditiously than they would be able to do.

I have now gone over the material points in your letter and General Wilkinson's Report; but, as I mentioned before, it has been done under circumstances unfavorable to minute investigation or mature deliberation, and my sentiments, where differing from you, given more for consideration than decision. Should anything of importance on this subject, not noticed here, occur to me, I shall not fail to communicate it to you; for the measures now taken with respect to guarding our Frontiers and interior Country ought to be such as will be permanent and respectable. With very great regard, I am, Dear Sir, Your most Obedt Servant

Go: Washington

LS, DLC: Hamilton Papers; Df, DLC:GW. Both copies are in Tobias Lear's hand.

1. GW is referring to the meeting he held in Philadelphia in November and December 1798 with Hamilton and Gen. Charles Cotesworth Pinckney.

2. In his letter to GW of 9 Sept. (see note 2 of that document), Hamilton wrote: "I do not coincide with General Wilkinson in the disposition of the Corps De Reserve. He would have it in the neighbourhood of *Fort Adams* (say Natches). I propose for it the vicinity of the rapids of the *Ohio*" (Syrett, *Hamilton Papers*, 23: 406). See note 3.

3. In his letter of 9 Sept., after giving his suggestions about the disposition of troops in various western posts (see note 2 of that document), Hamilton wrote: "There will then remain A Regiment and a batalion of Infantry half a company of Artillery and Two troops of Dragoons: Let these be stationed at some convenient point at or near the *Rapids of the Ohio* to form an army of observation and act as exigencies may require" (ibid., 404). Fort Washington was north of the Ohio at Cincinnati.

4. Hamilton wrote in his letter of 9 Sept. (see note 2 of that document): "*As to Fort Wayne*. The critical situation of this place with regard to a number of different

waters and the influence of its immediate aspect upon the most warlike of the Indians in that quarter make it in my view a post to be maintained contrary to the idea of General Wilkinson" (ibid., 405).

5. See ibid., 403.
6. See Hamilton to GW, 9 Sept., n.1.

To James McHenry

Sir,   Mount Vernon Septr 15th 1799
   Your letter of the 3d instant, with the papers accompanying it, did not get to my hands 'till the 11th—At the same time I received a long letter from Genl Hamilton, with voluminous references, to which he requested my immediate attention, and the communication of my sentiments thereon. These circumstances will account for your not having received an answer before this time.[1]
   The Rules which have been adopted by the President of the U.S. relative to Rank in the Army, point out the mode which must determine the relative Rank of those Officers who have heretofore been in service. The documents in the War Office, and the information obtained from the parties, would enable you to fix the Rank of those Officers, at least as well as I can do it. But to manifest my readiness to comply, so far as is in my power, with any request from your department, I have, in the enclosed list, noted numerically the names of the Lieutenant Colonels & Majors, who have been in service, as they should rank, agreeably to the documents from the War Office, which you forwarded to me, annexed to their names, and in conformity with the Regulations established by the President relative to Rank.[2]
   By these Rules resignation precludes all *claim* to Rank, and places the party upon a footing with those Officers who have never before been in Service; but where a resignation took place from any cause not affecting the Character of the Officer (as it is presumed is the case with all who are now appointed under this circumstance) it does not, in my opinion, deprive the party of that consideration wh. his having been in service would give, provided he stands on equal ground, in other respects, with those who have never served.
   As the Relative Rank of Officers who have not been in service, is to be determined by the Commander in Chief, I shall make the arrangement in the best manner I can, with respect to the Officers

in your list who are of this description—But in order to do this with propriety & satisfaction a personal knowledge of the several Officers, or full information of their respective qualifications, talents and merits is necessary. The former I do not possess. The latter I have, respecting most of those who have not been in service, so far as could be ascertained from the documents laid before the Genl Officers in November last from the War Office. But to proceed on this ground alone, and without any document relatively to the Characters of the Officers from Connecticut, North & South Carolina & Georgia (who, you will recollect, were selected with out any agency of mine) and fix the Rank definitively, would be very repugnant to my ideas of propriety and justice—In a word, it wd be little better than to decide their relative Rank by lot. I have tried and tried again to make an arrangement of the Majors who have been in service, and enclose a list of the Result; but it is so unsatisfactory to myself that I request no weight may be given to it farther than it accords with better information & circumstances.

In your letter you have requested that the Relative Rank of the Field officers of the Cavalry, as well as of the 12 Regts of Infantry, should be fixed; but you have not furnished the names of these Officers; and there is one Major wanting, according to your list, to complete the No. for the 12 Regts of Infantry.[3]

I feel much obliged by your intention of remitting me two months pay; but excepting in cases which may involve me in pecuniary expences, I must beg leave, on the principle I sat out with, to decline the Acceptance of it.

The letters written to you by the Lieutt Colonels & Majors, in answer to your queries, are herewith returned.[4] With due consideration I have the honor to be Sir, Yr mo. ob. st

G. W——n

Copy, in Tobias Lear's hand, DLC:GW; copy, DLC: Hamilton Papers.

1. Alexander Hamilton's letter is dated 9 September. See GW's response to it, this date.

2. The enclosure, dated 15 Sept., reads: "A List of the Lieutenant Colonels and Majors appointed for the 12 Regiments of Infantry, who have heretofore been in Service, ranked agreeably to the documents from the War Office, and in conformity with the Rules adopted by the President of the United States relative to Rank.

Lieutenant Colonels	*Majors*
No. 1 Josias C. Hall	No. 1 David Hopkins
No. 2 William S. Smith	No. 2 Wm D. Beale

No. 3 Nathan Rice
No. 4 Thomas L. Moore
No. 5 Aaron Ogden
No. 6 Timothy Taylor
No. 7 James Read
No. 8 John Smith
No. 9 Thomas Parker
No. 10 William Bentley
No. 11 Richd Hannewell
No. 12 Rufus Graves

No. 3 James Armstrong
No. 4 William Henderson
No. 5 Lau[ren]ce Butler
No. 6 Wm Campbell
No. 7 Robt Beale
No. 8 William Shute
No. 9 John Rowe
No. 10 James Baytop
No. 11 George Stephenson

"The Majors in the following list, having never before been in Service, are ranked according to the best judgement I can form, from the information of which I am possessed; and that, as I have mentioned in my letter accompanying this, is so incomplete, from the causes therein stated, that I request no weight may be given to this arrangement farther than it accords with better information and circumstances.

"Relative Rank of Majors who have never before been in service.

No. 1   William Wilcox
     2   John Adlum
     3   Jabez Huntington
     4   John Walker
     5   Isaac Winslow
     6   Cornelius Lynde
     7   John Ripley
     8   William Jones
     9   Henry M. Rutledge
     10 Alexr D. Moore
     11 Willm Brickell
     12 Timothy Darling

Signed Go. Washington"

(copy, DLC:GW).

GW wrote McHenry on 15 Oct.: "Sir In the extracts from the Books & documents in the War Office, which were sent to me when you requested that I would fix the relative rank of the Field Officers of the 12 Regiments, Colo. Parker is stated to have been an older Captain in the Revolutionary war, than Colo. Bentley—and they were accordingly marked by me in that Order—vizt Parker the 9th and Bentley the 10th Lieutt Colonel.

"I have since been informed that Colo. Parker says he was a younger Captain than Bentley, and that the error in the statement from the War Office arose from there having been another Captain from Virginia of the name of Thomas Parker, which must have been mistaken for him; and he is very desireous that the error should be rectified lest it should be thought that his taking rank of Colo. Bentley proceded from misrepresentation on his part. You will therefore be pleased to make the alteration accordingly if it should not have been discovered & rectified already. With due consideration I have the honor to be Sir Yr mo. ob. St G. Wn" (Df, DLC:GW).

3. GW received letters from two captains both in the 8th Regiment of the New Army, about their seniority in rank. Capt. Henry Piercy wrote on 7 Nov. from "Camp near Harpers Ferry": "As the Rank of the Officers of the eighth Regimt of Infantry to which I belong, has been a matter that has engaged our attention, and being informed that the Rank will in a short time be permanently fixd, I have taken the liberty of addressing you on the subject, with respect to my claim. I enterd the Army of the United States early in the revolutionary war as Second Lieutenant in march 1777 was promoted to first Lieuten. and Served as Such untill the conclusian of peace in 1783. At the close of the War I gat a Birvet of Captains Commission. I have also been inform'd that the Officers will retain the Rank they held in the late war—Under these circumstances I beg leave to refer the matter to your consideration" (DLC:GW).

Capt. Edmund H. Taylor wrote on the same day from the same place: "The Rank of the Officers of the Eighth Regiment of Infantry to which I belong, having for sometime engaged our attention, as in all probability it will shortly be fixed. From the present list of the Officers of the Regiment and their Rank (which I am informed is only a temporary arrangement) Captains Thornton and Henry are placed before me; the former of those Gentlemen never served in the American army, until he received his present appointment, and the latter only as a Lieutenant in the Revolutionary War, (and resigned as I am informed before the conclusion) and was appointed to his present command two Months after myself. I have taken the liberty to lay before you my claim to take Rank of those Gentlemen; having served in every Volunteer expedition from the State of Kentucky against the Indians from the year '90 until I obtained an appointment in the Western Army, where I served for a considerable time. From these considerations I am persuaded that you will think with me that I ought in justice to take Rank of the Gentlemen before mentioned" (DLC:GW).

Tobias Lear gave this reply from Mount Vernon on 12 Nov. to both men: "Your letter of the 7th inst. to the Commander in Chief, has been duly received; and in obedience to his orders I have to inform you that, in conformity with the resolution which he adopted when he accepted the command of the Army, he avoids entering into any details of the military arrangements, unless where particular circumstances urge his attention, in cases which require a prompt execution. He therefore, at present, declines giving any opinion on the subject of Rank mentioned in your letter; knowing that it will be established upon well grounded principles, in which due respect will be paid to former standing and services, as well as to the respective merits and qualifications of the Officers" (DLC:GW).

4. McHenry enclosed these letters, which have not been found, in his letter to GW of 3 September.

Letter not found: from William Augustine Washington, 15 Sept. 1799. On 22 Sept. GW wrote his nephew: "Your letter of the 15th instt from New Post, has been received."

To James Anderson

Mr Anderson, Mount Vernon 16th Septr 1799

The indisposition of Mrs Washington—Dispatches of a troublesome kind, which required all my attention—and the house never being clear of company—have put it out of my power to take any notice of your letter of the 13th instant, until now.[1]

Health, being amongst (if not the most) precious gift of Heaven; without which, we are but little capable of business, or enjoyment; and as you seem to be strongly impressed with a belief that the place at which you live (or any near it) will not suffer you, or family to enjoy this blessing; and moreover, as from what you have written, your views ultimately, if not immediately, are turned to some other object than the management of my business; far, very far is it from my desire that you should, in the meantime, hazard your health, or that of your family's, by remaining in your present occupation, even another year; if that is the expected consequence of your stay.

On the plain, simple, & regular system I am resolved, undeviatingly to pursue, I shall find no difficulty in superintending my Farms, myself; if not with skill, at least with œconomy: and if I can make any contrivance at the Mansion house to cure as many Fish as will suffice for the use of my People, I shall feel more disposed to Rent the Landing at the Ferry, than to be plagued with it myself.

There would then be the Distillery & Mill only to be disposed of, and these, if I could, I wd Rent; if not, they might remain on their present footing. With an honest Miller & Distiller, & frequent settlements with them, matters could not go *very wrong*. The grain from my Farms, of which an a/c would be rendered, with the purchases, would shew the receipts; and the Manufacturing accounts, would shew how it was applied.[2]

You will perceive that the object of this letter is to release you from any embarrassment which may have been occasioned by your engagement with me, on the one hand; and your apprehension of encreasing ill-health, by remaining where you are another year, on the other hand; for I repeat to you again, that I have no other person in view, as a Manager; nor should I employ one, if by Sickness, or any other accident, your occupations were to cease.

You have said in your letter of the 13th, that if the terms on which I wou'd Rent my Mill & Distillery were made known to you, that it might be in your power to help me to a Tenant.

With respect to the first, (the Mill) I shall observe, that at the time (about 4 or 5 years ago) when it was advertised to be Rented, I was frequently offered 400$ pr ann. for it, and I once refused 500$. The latter sum, although the New Race has added to the expence, I would now take. And with respect to the Distillery, and all the apparatus belonging thereto, you can judge better than I, of the sum I ought to expect for it. And whether I rent them or not, it would be very agreeable to me (after considering the thing maturely, on a just and equitable scale between Land lord & tenant) to let me know what you conceive I ought to ask, & insist upon.

To enable you to do this, I shall inform you, that I will furnish nothing but *fuel*, delivered on the spot (not from hand to mouth, but by the quantity of Cords to be laid in, at the Alexandria price of Wood, deducting the carriage of it to that place). The hands now employed at the Distillery (and Mill also) if retained there, will be charged at what they could be hired, elsewhere—So likewise of the Waggon, Scow, and Boat, when required, & can be spared.

As some ground for Pasture might be required, that which is now appropriated to Hogs—may remain for that purpose; and so much of the field by the Mill as would be included by the Fence from thence to the old Mill race by the Bars, by that to the Tumbling dam in the other Race—by that again as it runs to the Willow Pond near the Post & Rail fence leading to Pools-run, and by that fence to the Mill again—containing by *Actual* measurement, 38¼ acres.

The Manure, arising from the feedings at the Distillery, over & above what may suffice for the Gardens there, I should chuse to reserve. I repeat my wishes for the restoration of health to yourself and family—and am Your friend &ca

Go: Washington

ALS, PWacD; ALS (letterpress copy), ViMtV.

1. Letter not found.

2. For the correspondence regarding the rental of GW's mill and distillery at Mount Vernon, see GW to Anderson, 10 Sept., n.2.

Letter not found: from Burgess Ball, 16 Sept. 1799. On 22 Sept. GW wrote Ball: "Your letter of the 16th instt has been received."

From Presly Thornton

Dear Sir   Fredericksburg Septr 16th 1799

It is with inexpressible concern I communicate to you that I last Post recieved a letter from Genl Pinkney informing that the alarming state of Mrs Pinkney's health was at such heighth that her Physicians recommended a sea trip to Rhode Island, as the only probable means of saving her life, that he had consequently availed himself of leave granted him by the Secretary at War, & requests all letters may be addressed to him at Newport, till the 1st of October & after that period to the Care of the Secretary at War[1]—I am confident this event will give Mrs Washington great uneasiness, but sincerely hope we shall soon hear that the healthy air of Rhode Island has been beneficial to Mrs Pinkney's health— The letter for Brigadier Genl Washington forwarded to my Care, will be presented him, as we expect him to pass thro' this Town to day.[2]

The recruiting service on this station, I am sorry to inform you has progressed very slowly, we have only enlisted thirteen men; It is with concern that I find many respectable & influential Citizens in this part of the Country obstinately averse to, & tho' not oppenly yet I believe secretly, as much as in their power, opposing the raising of the Army, but it gives me pleasure to hear that those sentiments do not generally pervade the minds of the citizens of other parts of the state; the 8th Regt has recruited by the last accounts I recieved upwards of 400 men, all the companies except Capt. Chinn's at Charlottesville & mine have been ordered to the General rendevous,[3] & the Colo. writes his intentions of removing mine to some more favorable station, anxious as I am for promoting the recruiting service, I am at loss to determine whether I ought to move with them, as I may probably shortly expect Genl Pinkney will be coming on or to recieve Orders to join him, this place lying immediately on the Main Post road being also most favorable for recieving his correspondencies & distributing his Orders, should he have any to communicate, your opinion on this subject, will be esteemed a great favor.

I am extremely sorry to hear of the return of Mr Lear's indisposition, but hope he will recieve benefit from the trip he has taken over the mountains.[4] Please present Mrs Thornton's & my united respects & best wishes for the welfare of Mrs Washington & yourself.[5] I have the honor to be, Sir, With the greatest Esteem Your most obliged hble Servt

Presly Thornton
Capt. 8th U.S. Regt
Aid of Division

ALS, DLC:GW.

1. The Pinckneys arrived in Newport, R.I., by ship on 13 Sept. and remained until 22 Oct., when they left for Trenton and Philadelphia. Pinckney departed from Philadelphia in the middle of November and was with the troops in winter quarters when GW died on 14 Dec. (Zahniser, *Pinckney*, 211–12).

2. William Washington left Mount Vernon and headed back to South Carolina on 8 September.

3. Richard Chinn of Loudoun County, like Thornton, was a captain in the 8th Infantry Regiment in the New Army.

4. Lear wrote William Thornton on 12 Sept.: "The General has enjoyed his health tolerably well of late; but your humble servant has had an attack of the fever. It was however of short duration, and he is now about to take a trip over the mountains for a few weeks . . ." (Harris, *Thornton Papers*, 1:508–9). GW informed Presly Thornton on 22 Sept. (see note 5) that Lear had left "a few days ago to try the Air of the Mountains," and on 13 Oct. GW reported that Lear had "returned from Berkley" (*Diaries*, 6:370).

5. GW wrote Presly Thornton on 22 Sept.: "Dear Sir, Your letter of the 16th Instant came to my hands by the last Post. I learnt with regret, the cause of General Pinckney's visit to Rhode Island. From the account given of his Lady's health by Brigr Genl Washington, it is to be feared her case is dangerous.

"I am sorry to hear that the Recruiting Service, in the District to which you were assigned, progresses so slowly. It was conjectured beforehand that you would have many difficulties to encounter therein. The result therefore, is not a matter of surprise.

"Until you are requ⟨est⟩ed to join the General Officer to whose person you are attached, or directed by him to remain Stationary for the purpose of receiving, & executing his orders, I conceive it will be incumbent on you to obey the orders of your Colonel.

"Mr Lear left this a few days ago to try the Air of the Mountains. Mrs Washington has been much indisposed—but joins in ⟨love *illegible*⟩ with—Dr Sir—Yr Obedt Hle Servant Go: Washington" (letterpress copy, NN: Washington Papers).

From James Anderson

Most Ex. Sir   Ferry [Farm] 19 Septr 1799

Your favor of 16th is before me, And have duely considered the same, I will beg leave to trouble You with a very short reply—Well knowing You have but little time to Spare.

As You in the Spring on Muddyhole ground, & in the field in the which Davies House stands spoke to me respecting continuing. And that the Sickly season is nearly gone, I have made no Arrangements for the next Year. And therefore I stay, And will endeavour to make it out—If Life, & Health permit. I am very sensible of Your Ability for a much more Arduos Task than the Management of these Farms, And am also fully convinced that my Salary is a Burthen on such Property as makes such ordinary returns—As for Accounts; You may rest Assured that after this date (unless in a case of mere necessity) I will never Obey any Order, without Your Approbation, for the procuring any thing from Alexria or any Store, or Stores Whatever. Nor will I of myself order any till You approve it, And any other regulation You may please to make will be perfectly Agreable to me.

With regard to James Lawsons Scurrileous letter I think I explained the part where Complaints are made as to the other parts they give me no trouble.[1]

I also took Notice of the stupid letter of Gordon to Mr Cunningham, Of Mr C. having passed His stipulated time of payment from 2 to 3 Mos. And that as He was seldom in Alexria He would pay into the Hands of any person, where the receipts might lye, these receipts were taken from Gordon before payment was made, which now is compleated—And Gordon shall never have another Transaction in purchasing from, or selling to this Estate thro: me while I remain here.[2]

As to my Opinion, of the Rent of the Distillery, and all its apparatus & Apurtenances, with the Hog Pasture, now ⟨un⟩employed by the Hogs, I do think it worth $600 p. Year upon Your cuting & cording Wood, in the Woods at a given price—and the reservation of the Manure. What other Land You let go with it You could best fix the price.

nothing is more uncertain than the prices of Leased Property, as a person well disposed to Rent will give a full price. And those not so fully determined, will offer very poorly. as soon as I learn of any good Man well disposed to Rent the Mill & Distillery, or any one of Your Fisherys here, I will advise You. And wishing I had it in my power to render You any agreable Service I remain with the utmost respect & esteem most Ex. Sir Your most Obedt Humble Sert

Jas Anderson

ALS, DLC:GW.

1. James Lawson, a ditcher whom GW frequently employed in the 1780s, had been paid $600 two days before this, on 17 Sept., for cutting a millrace at Mount Vernon and was given an additional bonus of $77.62 by GW (Mount Vernon Ledger, 1799–1800, 22). Lawson's "Scurrileous letter" has not been found.

2. Robert Gordon, whose house was on a lot belonging to GW in Alexandria, between 1798 and August 1799 bought large amounts of whiskey from GW's distillery, 304 gallons in 1798 alone, and paid for it in goods and cash (Mount Vernon Ledger, 1797–98, 135). C. Cunningham bought barley from GW in December 1798 and on 10 May 1799, when he paid $105.75 for the two purchases and "one Bll Yeast for Distillery," which by mistake was not recorded in the ledger until 14 July 1799 (Mount Vernon Ledger, 1799–1800). On 28 Feb. 1799 "C. Cunninghame Brewer" was paid $8 for "Yeast one Ball" (Mount Vernon Ledger, 1799–1800, 30). Gordon's "stupid letter" has not been found.

To Roger West

Sir,   Mount Vernon 19th Sepr 1799

Sometime ago the Servant who waits upon me, named Christopher (calling himself Christopher Sheels) asked my permission to marry a Mulatto girl belonging to you. As he had behaved as well as servants usually do, I told him I had no objection to the union, provided your consent (which was necessary) could be obtained.

This I presume happened⟨,⟩ because I understand they are married. I was in hopes that this connexion (as ⟨I heard⟩ the ⟨Girl⟩ well spoken of) would have been some ⟨*illegible*⟩ ⟨up⟩on his future conduct; but the reverse is to be apprehended from the enclosed note, which was found in my yard; dropped it is supposed, by him. Whether the girl can write, or not; and whose writing it is, are equally unknown to me; but it undoubtedly came from her to the Husband, from the purport of it.

He is unacquainted ⟨with *illegible*⟩ my possession, as I think his wife ⟨ought to be,⟩ until proper measures can be ⟨taken *illegible*⟩ matters upon them; which, from ⟨the contents⟩ of the letter, your vicinity to Alexandria ⟨*illegible*⟩ friends in that place, you will be enabled, much better than I to do; I mean, particularly, the discovery of the Vessel, they contemplate to escape in.

I have made this communication, my good Sir, on the supposition that you, would be equally desirous to arrest their project; but if, as some say, she is free; and as others, that you are about to make her so, our cases differ; except in the example. But in either case I would thank you for any information you can ⟨give me respecting⟩ this matter, by a line left at ⟨*illegible*⟩, goes through the med⟨ium of⟩ Doctr Craik, to avoid the suspicion that might arise by sending a messenger with ⟨it to your⟩ house. The Doctr is made acquainted with the contents; but the fewer that are so, ⟨*illegible*⟩ts, in the business of detection, the better.[1]

I heard with pleasure, that you had received much benefit in your health, from your journey to the Springs; and I sincerely wish you the perfect restoration of it, being ⟨*illegible*⟩—Sir Your most Obedt Humble Servant

Go: Washington

ALS (letterpress copy), NN: Washington Papers.

1. Christopher, or Christopher Sheels as he was sometimes called, was a young dower slave about twenty-four years old at this time. GW had taken him to New York in 1789, his old body servant William Lee being crippled. In 1797 Christopher was bitten by a rabid dog at Mount Vernon and GW sent him to Dr. William Stoy in Pennsylvania for treatment (GW to Stoy, 14 Oct. 1797). Nothing further has been found regarding the young couple's escape plans, but Christopher was at Mount Vernon at GW's bedside at the General's death. See Tobias Lear's Narrative Accounts of the Death of George Washington, printed at the end of this volume.

To Lawrence Lewis

Dear Sir,   Mount Vernon 20th Septr 1799

From the moment Mrs Washington & myself adopted the two youngest children of the late Mr Custis, it became my intention (if they survived me, and conducted themselves to my satisfaction) to consider them in my Will, when I was about to make a distribution of my property. This determination has undergone no diminution, but is strengthened by the connexion which one of them has formed with my family.

The expence at which I live, and the unproductiveness of my Estate, together, will admit of no diminution of income, while I remain in my present situation; on the contrary, were it not for occasional supplies of money, in payment for Lands sold within the last four or five years, to the amount upwards of Fifty thousand dollars; I should not be able to support the former without involving myself in debt & difficulties.

But, as it has been understood from expressions occasionally dropped from (Nelly Custis, now) your Wife, that it is the wish of you both to settle in this neighbourhood (contiguous to her

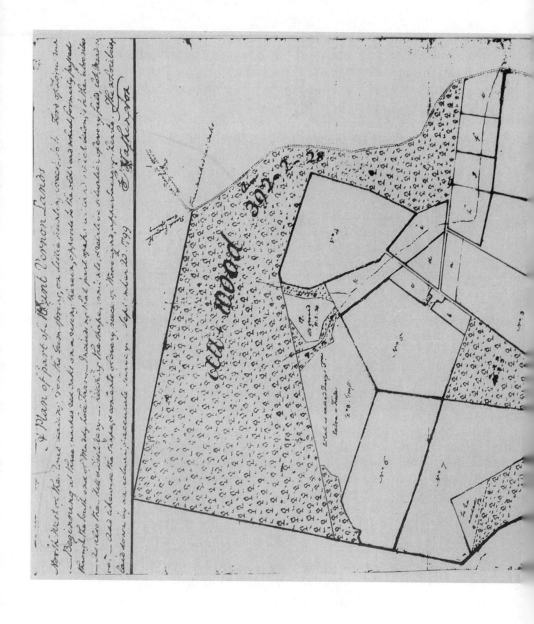

A Plan of part of Mount Vernon Lands

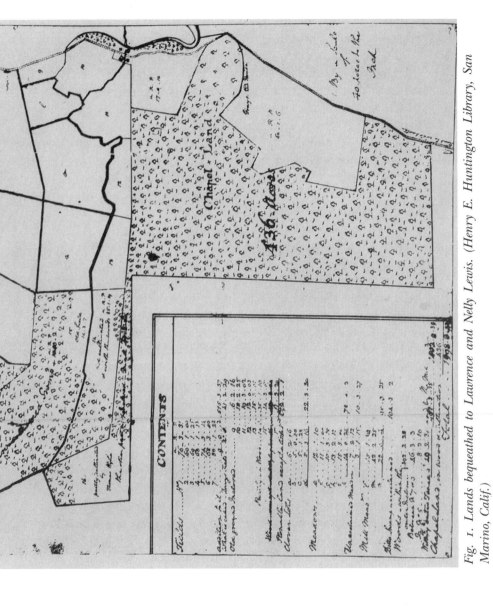

Fig. 1. Lands bequeathed to Laurence and Nelly Lewis. (Henry E. Huntington Library, San Marino, Calif.)

friends) and as it would be inexpedient, as well as expensive for you, to make a purchase of land when a measure which is in contemplation would place you on more eligable ground, I shall inform you, that in the Will which I have by me, and have no disposition to alter, that part of my Mount Vernon tract which lyes North & West of the public road leading from the Gum spring to Colchester (from a certain point which I have marked) containing about two thousand acres of Land, with the Dogue run Farm—Mill—Distillery—Grays heights—&ca is bequeathed to you and her jointly, if you incline to build on it; and few better sites for a house than Grays hill, and that range, are to be found in this County, or elsewhere.[1]

You may also have what is properly Dogue run Farm, the Mill, and Distillery, on a just, & equitable Rent;[2] as also the hands belonging thereto on a reasonable hire either next year, or the following; it being necessary, in my opinion, that a young man should have objects of employment. Idleness is dis-reputable under any circumstances; productive of no good, even when unaccompanied by vicious habits; and you might commence building as soon as you please; during the progress of which, Mount Vernon might be made your home.

You may conceive, that building, before you have an absolute title to the land, is hazardous. To obviate this, I shall only remark that, it is not likely that any occurrence will happen, or any change take place, that would alter my present intention (if the conduct of yourself & wife is such as to merit a continuance of it) but be this is it may, that you may proceed on sure ground with respect to the buildings, I will agree, and this letter shall be an evidence of it, that if, thereafter, I should find cause to make any other disposition of the property here mentioned, I will pay the actual cost of such buildings to you, or yours.

Although I have not the most distant idea that any event will happen that could effect a change in my present determination, nor any suspicion that you, or Nelly would conduct yourselves in such a manner as to incur my serious displeasure; yet, at the same-time that I am inclined to do justice to others, it behoves me to take care of myself, by keeping the staff in my own hands.

That you may have a more perfect idea of the Landed property I have bequeathed to you & Nelly in my Will, I transmit a plan of it, every part of which is correctly laid down & accurately measured. Shewing the number of Fields, Lots, Meadows, waste land,

&ca; with the contents, & relative situation of each. All of which, except the Mill swamp (wch has never been considered as part of Dogue run Farm, and is retained, merely for the purpose of putting it into a better state of improvement[)], you may have on the terms before mentioned.[3] With every kind wish for you & Nelly, in which your Aunt who has been & is, very much indisposed unites—I remain Your Affectionate Uncle

Go: Washington

I have just received an account of the death of my brother which is the oc⟨casion⟩ of my sealing with black.[4]

ALS, RPJCB; ALS (letterpress copy), DLC:GW. GW addressed the letter to "Mr Lawrence Lewis at Mr Charles Carters in Culpeper County—near Stevensburgh."

1. Lewis began building his house, Woodlawn, on Grays Hill at Dogue Run farm about 1802. He and his wife, Eleanor Parke Custis Lewis, moved into a small dependency there about 1805, while awaiting completion of the main house. After Martha Washington's death in 1802 and Bushrod Washington's move to Mount Vernon, the young Lewises lived temporarily at Betty Lewis Carter's house, Western View, in Culpeper County. The widow Ann Gray and her son John were tenants of GW near the mill.

2. For GW's negotiations at this time with his farm manager James Anderson with regard to the possibility of his renting the distillery and mill at Mount Vernon, see GW to James Anderson, 10 Sept. 1799, n.2.

3. See Figure 1 and the enclosure to this letter.

4. Burgess Ball was the first to inform GW of the death of his brother Charles Washington at Happy Retreat near Charles Town in Berkeley County. See GW to Ball, and GW to Samuel Washington, both 22 September.

Enclosure
A Plan of Part of Mount Vernon Lands

September 20th 1799

North West of the Road leading from the Gum-spring, on Little hunting Creek, to the Ford of Dogue run. Beginning at three marked red oaks on a rising therein, opposite to the old road which formerly passed through the South end of Muddy hole Farm. Including that part of Chapel land which belongs to the Subscriber. As also the Mill & Distillery. Shewing the shape, contents, & relative situation of every field, lot, meadow, &ca. And likewise the shape, & contents of every piece of Woodland, appertaining thereto. The whole being laid down by an actual, & accurate Survey.

Go: Washington

CONTENTS

	A[cres]	R[ods]	P[erches]			
Fields No. 1	76	3	31			
2	60	1	00			
3	69	1	25			
4	68	1	13			
5	74	3	14			
6	68	3	00			
7	88	1	22			
Addition to it	9	0	12	515	3	37
What is called						
Davys Field No. 8	41	2	29			
Old ground Inclosed 9	6	2	16			
10	18	2	25			
11	19	3	02			
12	12	0	03			
13	15	3	03			
Partly in Wood 14	35	1	19			
15	14	3	07			
17	11	3	20			
Plowable land except a little wd				692	2	1
Clover Lots a	6	2	16			
b	5	0	20			
c	5	1	28			
d	5	3	16	22	3	20
Meadows e	12	1	10			
f	11	1	00			
g	10	3	18			
h	13	2	13			
i	15	3	00			
k	14	0	25	78	0	3
Unreclaimed Meadow	7	2	12			
	3	1	15	10	3	27
Mill Meadws l	15	1	0			
m	42	2	25			
n	38	0	4	95	3	25
Ditto Swamp unreclaimed				104	3	2
Woods—within the outer Inclosure	392	2	23			
Between No. 7 & 3	46	3	3			
In No. 6	8	3	10			
Witht the outer Fence and by the Mill	49	2	34			
					3	
	497	3	35	1562	8	38
Chapel Land, in wood & Cultivation				436		
Total				1998	3	38

ADS, CSmH.

To Thomas Law

Dear Sir, Mount Vernon 21st Septr 1799

In acknowledging the receipt of your note—which came to hand two days since, without date—I shall only observe, that whenever it suits the convenience of yourself & Mrs Law to visit Mount Vernon, we shall be happy in seeing you.[1]

I had a desire (not a strong one) to possess the corner lot belonging to Mr Carroll on New Jersey Avenue, merely on account of its local situation; but have ⟨abandoned⟩ the idea.[2] Disappointed in every expectation of receiving money, though most solemnly assured it, I am obliged to have recourse to borrowing from the Bank of Alexandria—much against my inclination to carry on my buildings in the City. ⟨It follows,⟩ that to sell the houses I have on hand there, will comport more with my finances than to purchase & build on other lots. If then you ⟨should⟩ hear of purchasers, this circumstance ⟨should⟩ be mentioned. Mrs Washington is far from well but unites in love with Yr Obt & Affe. ⟨frd⟩

Go: Washington

ALS (letterpress copy), NN: Washington Papers.

1. Law and his wife, Eliza Parke Custis Law, had left Mount Vernon on Friday, 13 Sept., after a six-day visit. GW records visits to Mount Vernon by Law on 29 Oct. and 10 Nov. but no further visits from Mrs. Washington's granddaughter Eliza Law (*Diaries*, 6:365, 373, 375).

2. For reference to GW's interest in buying this lot on Capitol Hill belonging to Daniel Carroll of Duddington, see Law to GW, 10 Aug. 1799, n.2.

To Mary White Morris

Our dear Madam, Mount Vernon Septr 21st 1799

We never learnt with certainty, until we had the pleasure of seeing Mr White (since his return from Frederick) that you were at Winchester.[1]

We hope it is unnecessary to repeat in this place, how happy we should be to see you and Miss Morris under our roof, and for as long a stay as you shall find convenient, before you return to Philadelphia; for be assured we ever have, and still do retain, the most Affectionate regard for you Mr Morris and the family.[2] With the highest esteem & regard, and best wishes for the health & happi-

ness of the family you are in we are Dear Madam Your Most Obedt
and Very Humble Servants

Go: Washington
Martha Washington

ALS, NhD; Df[S], in GW's hand, Ia-HA. The signature, or signatures, are clipped
from the draft.

1. Alexander White, the District of Columbia commissioner and former congressman whose home was in Frederick County, had dinner at Mount Vernon on this day (see *Diaries*, 6:366).

2. Robert Morris was in debtors' prison in Philadelphia.

To Burgess Ball

Dear Sir,				Mount Vernon 22d Sepr 1799
   Your letter of the 16th instt has been received, informing me of the death of my brother.[1]
   The death of near relations, always produce awful, and affecting emotions, under whatsoever circumstances it may happen. That of my brother's, has been so long expected, and his latter days so uncomfortable to himself, must have prepared all around him for the stroke; though painful in the effect.
   I was the *first*, and am now the *last*, of my fathers Children by the second marriage who remain. when I shall be called upon to follow them, is known only to the giver of life. When the summons comes I shall endeavour to obey it with a good grace. Mrs Washington has been, and still is, very much indisposed—but unites with me in best wishes for you, Mrs Ball and family[2]—With great esteem & regard—I am—Dear Sir—Your Affecte Servt

Go: Washington

ALS, owned (1993) by Mrs. Charles Brewer, Chester, Vt.; ALS (letterpress copy), NN: Washington Papers.

1. Letter not found. Burgess Ball (1749–1800) was the son-in-law of Charles Washington whose son Samuel Washington also wrote to GW of his father's death. See GW to Samuel Washington, this date.

2. Ball's wife was Frances Washington Ball (1763–1815).

To Samuel Washington

Dear Sir,   Mount Vernon Sepr 22d 1799

Your letter, announcing the death of my Brother, came to hand last night. One from Colo. Ball, informing me of that event, arrived the evening before.[1]

I very sincerely condole with your mother and the family on this occasion. But as death, in this case, was regular in its approaches; and evident, long before it happened; she, and all of you, must have been prepared for the stroke. Of course, though painful, it must have fallen much lighter on that account.

By this event, you have become the Guardian of your mother; and as it were, the father, of your fathers family; and by care, industry & sobriety will merit the appellation of one.

Your Aunt has been, and still is⟨,⟩ much indisposed, but unites in best wishes for yr mother—self—& family with your sincere frd and—Affectionate uncle

                                        Go: Washington

ALS (letterpress copy), NN: Washington Papers.

1. Neither Samuel Washington's letter nor Burgess Ball's letter of 16 Sept. reporting Charles Washington's death has been found. See GW to Ball, this date.

To William Augustine Washington

My dear Sir,   Mount Vernon 22d Septr 1799

Your letter of the 15th instt from New Post, has been received.[1]

I am sorry to be disappointed of the visit you promised us; and regret the cause of it. In the Spring, and at all times, when your health will permit, and it suits your convenience, we shall be happy in seeing you & Mrs Washington under our Roof.

Are there any *Crops* of Wheat for Sale in your Neighbourhood? I want to keep my Mill employed in Manufacturing this Grain, & the Millers who surround me, more alert than I am, pick up all the Wheat in these parts before I am scarcely thinking of purchasing, although I am willing, and do give, as good prices as they; and (in cases of credit) pay, I believe, with more punctuallity. I would thank you for making this enquiry, & for informg me of the result.

Mrs Washington has been, & still is, very unwell; but unites her complimts to mine. I am, My dear Sir, Your Affecte frd and Uncle

Go: Washington

P.S. I received last night, an Acct of the death of my Brother in Berkeley.

ALS, MiU-C: Schoff Collection; ALS (letterpress copy), ViMtV.

1. Letter not found. New Post was the home of Alexander Spotswood in Spotsylvania County. William Augustine Washington lived at Haywood in Westmoreland County.

From Alexander Hamilton

Dear Sir   New York Sept. 23d 1799

I had the pleasure of receiving in due time your letter of the 15th instant. The Suggestions it contains will be maturely weighed. I postpone any thing definitive, till the return of General Wilkinson which is momently expected.[1] The other Documents, besides No. 8, which accompanied his letter, were not material to the consideration of its contents, or they would have been forwarded—Even Number one does nothing more than exhibit in the form of a table the propositions which are found in the letter. I was afraid of burthening you with papers, which did not necessarily require your attention, being matters of mere detail.

Inclosed is a letter of this date to Col: Parker about Winter Quarters for the Eighth Ninth and Tenth Regiments. It is late to begin, but you perceive in it the cause of the delay.[2]

It is extremely desirable that you would be pleased to take the direction of this matter, and to have the business done in such manner as you shall deem eligible. Not having a right to presume that you would choose to take the charge of it, I have adopted the expedient of addressing my self to Colonel Parker. But perhaps you may think of some preferable Agent—In which case, you will be so good as to retain the letter and give complete directions to such other Agent. Compensation and the defraying of his Expences need not be Obstacles.[3]

At any rate, I hope you will not find it inconvenient to instruct Colo. Parker to conclude a bargain for such place, as upon his reports to you, shall be, in your opinion eligible. It is very necessary that these young troops should be early covered. Collateral

Ideas with regard to Harper's Ferry as a place for Arsenals and magazines may perhaps be combined. These will more readily occur to you than to me.[4]

Scotch Plains near Bound Brook will be fixed upon for the 11th 12th & 13th Regiments. A very eligible Spot, of about Ninety Acres, is offered there at 50 Dollars per Acre, for the fee simple. It affords the advantage of a good Summer encampment also; with a prospect for a supply, for years, of fuel and Straw at cheap rates—and the convenience of a *pleasant* and *plentiful* surrounding Country.[5]

Search has been, for some time past, making for a suitable position for the three most Northern Regiments, in the vicinity of Uxbridge in Massachusetts. With true respect & attachment I have the honor to be Dr Sir yr obedt servt

Alex. Hamilton

LS, DLC:GW; LS (duplicate), DLC:GW; ADfS, DLC: Hamilton Papers.

1. James Wilkinson returned to New York on 6 Oct. (Hamilton to GW, 23 Sept., n.1, in Syrett, *Hamilton Papers*, 23:468–70).

2. See Hamilton to Thomas Parker, 23 Sept., ibid., 464–65.

3. Hamilton's letter to Col. Thomas Parker is dated 23 Sept., and GW forwarded it to Parker on 28 September. The draft of Hamilton's letter to Parker, which is printed in Syrett, *Hamilton Papers*, 23:464–65, reads: "It is contemplated to establish the Eighth Ninth and Tenth Regiments in Winter Quarters somewhere in the Vicinity of the Potowmack and near Harpurs Ferry. As this station is within the territorial limits of General Pinckneys Command, the providing of quarters there did not fall within my province. But very urgent circumstances having suddenly induced General Pinckney to proceed to Rhode Island, which has deranged the natural course of the business, The Secretary of War has just directed me [on 20 Sept.] to take the requisite measures for effecting the object. The Quarter Masters Department not being yet organised I have concluded to confide the matter to your management. The plan is to hut the troops during the present Winter which method the experience of the last war shewed to be extremely conducive to comfort as well as convenience. For this purpose a situation is to be sought, where there will be proper wood for hutting and plenty of fuel; I mean on the premises: It is scarcely necessary to add that it must be airy elevated and dry so as to secure the health of the troops and must command an ample supply of good water. About Eighty Acres will suffice. It is desireable, if practicable, to find out more than one spot, and even to extend the inquiry lower down the Potowmack towards the Fœderal City, but on the Virginia side. You will ascertain the terms upon which each spot may be purchased or hired. A purchase will probably, be found most convenient. When you have found a place, in your opinion fit, you will immediately report it with a particular description and the terms upon which it may be had to the Commander in Chief and transmit a duplicate of your report to me; and continuing your examination in the direction which I

have mentioned you will successively report in the same manner. This letter will be transmitted to him to be forwarded to you with any directions he may think fit to give. You will make arrangements for the care of the recruiting service in your absence and you will lose no time in executing this service. The late period of the season renders dispatch indispensable."

4. In his letter to Parker of 28 Sept. covering that to him from Hamilton, GW seconded Hamilton's instructions but was "more pointed" in urging Parker to build the winter encampment "at the confluence of the Potomack and Shanondoah" rivers, the site of Harpers Ferry. GW wrote to Hamilton the next day, 29 Sept., to tell him that he had forwarded his letter to Parker and had emphasized to him the desirability of building the encampment near the arsenal at Harpers Ferry. On 9 Oct. Parker wrote that the day before he had run into Tobias Lear in Charles Town (now in West Virginia) and had gone with him over to Harpers Ferry to choose sites for the camps on the banks of the Shenandoah River just above where it joined the Potomac. After informing Hamilton of this, GW received from Hamilton a letter in effect asking GW to take personal responsibility for assuring that the three regiments had suitable winter quarters (see GW to Hamilton, 15 Oct., and Hamilton to GW, 21 Oct. [second letter]). After difficulties arose about the campsites chosen by Parker and Lear, GW found himself deeply involved in searching for winter quarters for the regiments until Charles Cotesworth Pinckney returned to Virginia in November to resume his duties as commander of the forces in the South. For GW's involvement in finding winter quarters for the 8th, 9th, and 10th regiments, see Parker to GW, 24, 31 Oct., 5 Nov., GW to Hamilton, 26, 27 Oct., GW to Parker, 26, 27 Oct., GW to Benjamin Ogle, 28 Oct., Tobias Lear to GW, 30 Oct., 4 Nov., GW to Charles Cotesworth Pinckney, 3 Nov., and GW to James McHenry, 5 November. In addition Tobias Lear wrote several letters on GW's behalf to Parker and Hamilton about this and received answers from them; all of these letters to and from Lear are quoted in part in notes.

5. Scotch Plains is in Union County, New Jersey.

Letter not found: from William Thornton, 24 Sept. 1799. On 29 Sept. GW wrote Thornton: "Your letter of the 24th instant . . . came to my hands."

To John Avery

Sir,   Mount Vernon 25th Septr 1799
   Your letter of the 2d instt came duly to hand;[1] but previous thereto, I had written to Mr Jno. Francis of Philadelphia (who *report* had engaged the houses to, I was building in the Federal City) to know in explicit terms whether he meant to take them, or not, on the conditions I offered them, namely—Seven and an half percent on the whole cost; to which, taxes, if any, and Insurance against fire, were to be added. On lower terms, no person in the

Fedl City, or elsewhere that I could hear of, would Let; & but few who would rent on these, as it was but little more than legal and common interest of money, when it is well known that the wear & tare of houses required much more.

I have waited until now, to receive Mr Francis's answer, without hearing from him; which has been the cause of my not replying to your letter sooner. If his answer is detained much longer, I shall feel my self under no obligation to prefer him, because he was the first applicant, for them.[2]

Although my house, or houses (for they may be one or two as occasion requires) are, I believe, upon a larger scale than any in the vicinity of the Capital, yet they fall far short of your wishes. The largest room, and that occasionally made so, is not more than 40 feet in length. The houses are three flush stories of Brick, besides Garret rooms: and in the judgment of those better acquainted in these matters than I am, capable of accomodating between twenty & thirty boarders. The buildings are not costly, but elegantly plain. and the whole cost—at a pretty near guess—may be between fifteen & sixteen thousand dollars.[3] I am Sir Your Very Hble Servant

Go: Washington

ALS (letterpress copy), NN: Washington Papers.

1. Letter not found.

2. See GW to John Francis, 25 August.

3. After receiving Avery's missing letter of 2 Oct., GW, having heard nothing further from John Francis, wrote Avery on 13 Oct.: "Sir I have received your letter of the 2d instant.

"I never conceived myself under any legal, or even honorary agreement with Mr Jno. Francis (of Philadelphia) ⟨*illegible*⟩ did, of the Houses I am building in the Federal City. But as he was the first that applied for them, and an idea had gone forth that he was to be the occupant, it was a compliment I thought due to him, to inform him in the *first* instance of the terms on which they were to be let.

"To my last letter to him, I have received no answer; whether this is to be ascribed to his not having received it, or to his thinking an answer unnecessary, I am unable to decide. Be it either the houses *now* are equally open to the occupancy of any tenant—or tenants, of respectable character, and ablility to pay the rent, or Rents; for ⟨as I⟩ think I informed you in my last, the exterior, has the appearance of one House, and interiorly, may be so likewise; at the same time by Closing the communication between them *within*, they become perfectly seperated and distinct.

"As you have already been informed of my terms, and these are so widely apart from your proposal—it is hardly necessary to trouble you with the details, required in your letter; especially as I should be obliged to have recourse to the Undertaker to be furnished with the answer; and still more especially as I am not disposed to rent the Houses for a term of years; thereby impeding the value of them, if (as I believe will be the case) I should find it convenient to part with them.

"After this explanation of my terms; thereof, you may yet wish to have the queries contained in your last, solved; it shall be done upon notice thereof to Sir—Your Very Hble Servant Go: Washington" (letterpress copy, NN: Washington Papers).

On the same day that he wrote his second letter to Avery, GW wrote this private letter of inquiry to Alexander Hamilton: "Dear Sir, Inconvenient as it was to my finances, I have been ⟨induced *illegible*⟩ to erect convenient to the Capital, in the Federal City, two houses, to aid in the accomodation of members of Congress, which have the exterior of one, but by an arrangement of communication may, according to the desire of the occupant, or occupants—may have all the conveniencies of one, or be entirely seperate & distinct.

"For these buildings a person of the name of John Avery, wishes ⟨a boar⟩ding house in the building erected for the Governors of New York ⟨*illegible*⟩ for the occupancy of them, ⟨for that⟩ purpose. In person & character he is a stranger to me; wherefore I take the liberty to enquire of you *confidentially* ⟨*illegible*⟩ the latter is, and whether ⟨you believe⟩ Rent of about $1200 would be sure on his part. This information (especially ⟨since he seems⟩ to be too full of himself) wd very much oblige My dear Sir—Yrs always Go: Washington" (letterpress copy, NN: Washington Papers).

Hamilton wrote GW on 21 Oct. that "poor Avery is dead of the yellow fever." The Capitol Hill houses were unfinished and, apparently, unrented at the time of GW's death.

Letter not found: from Tench Francis, 27 Sept. 1799. On 7 Oct. GW wrote Francis: "Your favr of the 27th Ulto is just recd."[1]

1. See James McHenry to GW, 24 Aug. 1799, n.1.

Letter not found: from John Gill, 28 Sept. 1799. On 13 Oct. GW wrote Gill: "Your letter of the 28th Ulto came duly to hand."

To Lawrence Lewis

Dear Sir,   Mount Vernon 28th Septr 1799

The enclosed letter was written agreeably to the date, and sent up to the Post Office in Alexandria—but owing to an accident, it missed the Western Mail and was returned to me again.[1]

Since which Mr Anderson (in Partnership with his son John) has discovered an inclination to Rent my Distillery & Mill: and for reason which I shall disclose to you, but do not wish them to be made public, I am disposed to let them become the tenants; provided they will give a reasonable Rent, and matters in other respects, can be adjusted.[2]

The reasons are—that although Mr Anderson is (in my opinion) an honest, sober, & industrious man; understands the management of the Plough, the Harrow, &ca; and how to make Meadows; yet, he is not a man of arrangement, he wants system & foresight in conducting the business to advantage; is no œconomist in providing things, and takes but little care of them when provided: When to these defects in his character, are added his acting too much from the impulse of the moment (which occasions too much doing, and undoing) and his high wages and emoluments, I have no hesitation in declaring that it is my wish to place my Estate, in this County, on a new establishment; thereby bringing It into so narrow a compass, as not only to supercede the necessity of a Manager, but to make the management of what I retain in my own hands, an agreeable & healthy amusement to look after myself; if I should not be again called into the Public service of the Ctry.

As the old man is extremely obliging, and zealous in my service, I am unwilling, by any act of mine, to hurt his feelings; or (by discarding of him) to lessen his respectability in the eyes of the public. but if it should appear to be his own act (by engaging in this business) both our ends wd be answered. I should be lessened, so much, of my general concerns; and if you take the Dogue run farm (by odds the best, & most productive I possess) I can, if I remain quiet at home, with great ease attend to the other three, & the Mansion house, and thereby ease myself of the expence of a manager.

You will perceive by my letter of the 20th, herewith enclosed, that the lands therein mentioned, are given for the express purpose of accomodating you in a building seat; in which case I did not, nor do I now, see how you could do without the Farm which is part of the premises, & the hands thereon—and were it not for the reasons, which apply to Mr Anderson, the Mill & Distillery ought to accompany it, as part of the same concern. And as I shall require nothing, either for the one, or the other, that is not perfectly reasonable & just, it is not likely that we shall differ on the quantum of Rent, & hire, which will be fixed on the property, by way of annuity.

The Mules & Horses on the Farm; The Cattle (except the young

Bull I had from Mr Lloyd)[3]—The Sheep (except the Lambs which had been carried thither from *all* the Farms); and Hogs, you may have on an equitable valuation: which would ease you of the trouble of providing them elsewhere, less valuable perhaps, & not reconciled to the place.

I shall not (as by a letter from Nelly you may be expected here shortly) go more into detail, at this time. But if this yr intention should be impeded by any accident, or unforeseen event, I shall expect to hear from you by Post. Indeed, if a letter could reach this sooner than yourselves, it would be agreeable & expedient: for when Mr Anderson (after I had written my letter of the 20th) hinted his desire of Renting the Mill & Distillery, he was informed, that I had made an offer of them to you; and that, until I received your answer I could say nothing definitively to him, on the Subject. and so the matter remains.[4]

Mrs Washington has not recovered her health; on the contrary is, at this time, weak, low, and much indisposed. Mr & Mrs Peter (now here) and their Children, are well; as he says Mr & Mrs Law also are. Doctr Stuart who went from this yesterday, says Mrs Stuart was not very well—but nothing extra[ordinar]y the matter. We all unite in best wishes for you, Nelly, & Mr Carter's family; and I am—Dr Sir—Yr Affecte Uncle

Go: Washington

P.S. Mr Lear has been absent more than a fortnight in a trip to the Mountains.[5]

ALS, PWacD; ALS (letterpress copy), NN: Washington Papers. GW added the postscript to the ALS after the letterpress copy had been made.

1. See GW to Lawrence Lewis, 20 September.

2. See GW to James Anderson, 10 Sept., n.2.

3. Edward Lloyd (1779–1834) presented GW with a bull calf in the summer of 1797. See Gustavus Scott to GW, 16 June 1797, n.3.

4. See note 2.

5. For Tobias Lear's trip, see Presly Thornton to GW, 16 Sept., n.4.

To Thomas Parker

Duplicate

Sir   Mount Vernon 28th Sepr 1799

In a letter from General Hamilton, enclosing the one I now forwd to you, I am requested to change, or modulate his directions to you, in any manner which to me shall appear most conducive to the Public Service.[1]

His directions comport with my ideas; but I shall be more pointed in drawing your attention to the Site at, or as near, as one can possibly be obtained, to the Arsenal which is established at the confluence of the Potomack and Shanondoah, for your Encampment.

I view the Work at that place as important, embracing, as a place of Arms, more objects than any other in the United States; of course, possessing at the same time, all the other requisite advantages which an abounding Country, good situation—and strength, can furnish, that it ought to be the place at which the 8th 9th & 10th Regiments should be assembled: that by combining the two objects, they may mutually assist, and benifit each other.

You will readily perceive, however, that to obtain this, or any other site for your Winter Cantonment, either by purchase (which is most desirable) or hire, that address is necessary to prevent an imposing high price. It might be well therefore to hold several places up to view; such even, as from their remoteness from the *true* point as will not answer, may be talked of, and examined.

Having given a decided preference (for the reasons mentioned) to the vicinity of the Arsenal, for your Hutting; it follows, if you cannot obtain Land there, that as near thereto as possible, is next to be chosen; whether above, or below the Shanondoah; (on the Virginia side of the Potomac.) Not a moment however, that can be avoided, is to be lost in providing for the Winter quarters of the Troops; who ought to have been in their Huts 'ere this.

Upon reflexion, I am induced to believe that the United States are already possessed of Land adequate to the occasion, at, or near Harpers Ferry; if so, all difficulty is done away. Was my Secretary, Mr Lear at home, I could ascertain this matter with certainty; but he is now in Berkeley. The Land of Keep Trieste Furnace, and others belonging to General Lee, are adjoining.[2] The first is advertised for Sale; and the other I am persuaded might be had. General Lee is, I am informed, in these parts *somewhere*; if I should see him, I will sound him myself on the purchase of his Land; but this must occasion no relaxation in your exertions to have all matters fixed, as the season will admit of no delay.

In building the Huts, observe the strictest regularity: In a word, with the exactness of a well ordered Incampment. Such was the conduct & practice of the American Army to the Northward, during the Revolution in the Winter Cantonments of it. With esteem— I am Sir Your Very Hble Servant

Go: Washington

ALS, DLC: Hamilton-McLane Papers; ALS (letterpress copy), DLC:GW.

1. See Alexander Hamilton to GW, 23 Sept., and notes 3 and 4 of that document.

2. Keep Triste iron furnace was located in Virginia about two miles above the confluence of the Potomac and Shenandoah rivers.

To Alexander Hamilton

Dear Sir,   Mount Vernon 29th Sepr 1799

Your letter of the 23d instant was received the 27th; and this day will proceed in the Mail to Winchester—the nearest Post Town to Colo. Parker's residence, if he should be at his own house, the letter enclosed for him.[1]

There being no person in my view more eligable than Colo. Parker to carry your Instructions into effect: unless Colo. Carrington had been in office as Quarter Master General, I had no hesitation in forwarding your letter to him; with such sentimts as occurred to me on the subject; which differed in no essential point, from those you had given.

I confined him more pointedly than you had done, to the site near Harpers ferry for his Winter Cantonment—because very cogent reasons, in my opinion, required it; for besides possessing all the advantages enumerated in your letter to him (so far as my recollection of the spot, & information goes); being in a fertile & most abounding Country; and one of the strongest positions by nature, perhaps in America; It appeared to me, that the Encampment, and Arsenal which is established at that place, might mutually assist, & benefit each other.

If the States are wise enough to keep United, I have no doubt of this Arsenals being their principal place of Arms, and best foundary; as it is in the midst of Furnaces and Forges of the best Iron; Can receive at, & transport from it, by Inland Navigation, all its wants, & manufacture, in every direction—and is, indubitably— supposing the advantage of Water transportation out of the question altogether, the great high way to the Country on the River Ohio.

For the reasons I have assigned, I did not hesitate a moment in giving the vicinity of Harpers ferry (at the confluence of the Rivers Potomac & Shenandoah) a decided preference; but if I am not mistaken, another strong inducement is afforded, namely—that there is a sufficiency of Land, purchased for the purpose of the Arsenal, to accomodate both objects. Of this I have informed Colo. Parker; but as Mr Lear is from home (who was the Agent for the War Department in the purchase) I could not inform him with certainty. If the fact however, should be as I suspect, it will prove a most fortunate circumstance, as well in the article of expence, as in the time that will be gained in completing the Huts. If it should be otherwise, I have advised Colo. Parker to hold out to view, & examine many places, while he, by some Agent, is endeavouring to possess himself, by purchase, the Site near Harpers Ferry; without which he might be imposed on in the price of the Land. With very great esteem & regard I remain Dear Sir Your obedient and Affecte Hble Servant

Go: Washington

ALS, DLC: Hamilton Papers; ALS (letterpress copy), DLC:GW.

1. GW forwarded Hamilton's letter of 23 Sept. to Thomas Parker under cover of GW's letter to Parker of 28 September.

To Samuel Lewis, Sr.

Sir,   Mount Vernon 29th Septr 1799

I thank you for the trouble you have taken to explain the omission in the regularity of forwarding the Gazettes. I had ascribed it to the cause you have mentioned before the receipt of your letter of the 20th instant.[1]

I am not anxious to complete a file of the Aurora. If however, when Colo. Lear (my Secretary, & at present absent) returns, any of the numbers are missing, I may, probably, give you the trouble of replacing—or rather—filling them up.[2] I am Sir Your obedt Humble Servant

Go: Washington

ALS, PHi: Washington manuscripts.

1. Letter not found. Lewis was a clerk in the War Department.

2. For Tobias Lear's trip to the mountains, see Presly Thornton to GW, 16 Sept., n.4.

From Timothy Pickering

[Trenton, N.J., 29 September 1799]
⟨confidential⟩ The most ⟨satisfactory⟩ communication I have it
in my power now to make, is the probability that the mission to
France will at least be suspended. This morning I recd a letter
dated the 26th from Judge Ellsworth, in which he says—"The following is an extract of a letter I have just ⟨been⟩ honoured with
from the President—the convulsions in France, the change of the
Directory, and the prognosticks of a greater change, will certainly
induce me to postpone for a longer or shorter time the mission to
France."[1] The President has also determined to come on to Trenton to meet the Heads of Departments and the Attorney General
⟨*illegible*⟩ he finally decides on this subject. I expect Judge Ellsworth & Gov. Davie will ⟨*illegible*⟩. I have written to the Attorney
General for ⟨the purpose⟩ of calling him here by the President's
direction.

Copy, in Pickering's hand, MHi: Pickering Papers. The first two paragraphs of
this letter, commenting on a German doctor's proposed treatment for yellow
fever, is printed in John Frederick Ramnitz to GW, 31 Oct. 1798, n.1. See also
GW to Pickering, 8 September.

1. John Adams's letter to Ellsworth, dated 22 Sept., is printed in Adams, *Works
of John Adams*, 9:34–35. Adams did delay the departure of the mission, and it was
not until 3 Nov. that Ellsworth and William R. Davie sailed from Newport, R.I.,
for France.

To William Thornton

Dear Sir,   Mount Vernon 29th Septr 1799.
Your letter of the 24th instant, enclosing a note from Mr Blagden, came to my hands on thursday last; the next day I sent up to
Alexandria to see if a Painter could be had to execute the Painting
of my houses in the City, and on what terms.[1]
The principal Painters in that place, Messrs McLeod & Lumley,
promised (one or the other of them) to repair to the buildings the
next day (yesterday) and tomorrow to furnish me with an estimate
of what they will do the work for, and thereby enable me to give a
decisive answer to the proposal mentioned in your letter.
In the meantime, if no material inconvenience would result
from the measure, I hope Mr Blagden will not remove the Scaf-

fold. Particularly, as the Painting shall be (of the windows & Cornice I mean) set about immediately after receiving the expected information, by some one or other.[2] I am Dear Sir—Yr Obedt & obliged

Go: Washington

ALS, DLC: Thornton Papers; ALS (letterpress copy), NN: Washington Papers.

1. Neither Thornton's letter nor George Blagdin's note has been found.

2. By the terms of his agreement with Blagdin for the construction of the pair of houses on Capitol Hill, GW was to be responsible for "Painting & Glazing" (see GW to District of Columbia Commissioners, 27 Oct. 1798, n.2). It was decided that GW would entrust to Blagdin the task of finding painters for the houses (see GW to Thornton, 1 Oct.).

Letter not found: from Alexander Spotswood, 30 Sept. 1799. On 27 Oct. GW wrote Spotswood: "Your letter of the 30th ulto came duly to hand."

To James Anderson

Mr Anderson,   Mount Vernon Oct. 1st 1799

When you intimated to me your son's wish to Rent my Distillery & Mill next year, and your inclination to join him therein—and in that case to relinquish the management of my business; I informed you that I had made Mr Lawrence Lewis (after you had declined taking them) an offer of both; together with the Farm at Dogue-run; and that until I received his answer, I did not conceive I was at liberty to treat, with another.

But as, on re-consideration of the matter, it appears uncertain where Mr Lewis is, but very certain that he is on no Post Road. As it is uncertain when, or whether ever, my letter may reach him. As it is not probable that he would, from choice, wish to plunge at once into a scene of business to which he is a stranger. As I grow more and more anxious to form some new establishmt for my Estate in this quarter, that may lessen the expence of it, even if I should not render it more productive. and as I wish to know as soon as is convenient, whether this can be accomplished, that some preliminary arrangements may be adopted before New years day, when the new order of things would commence. I think I may venture to declare, without waiting for his answer, that if you and your son are disposed to offer me a rent, in any degree adequate to the value of the two concerns (and it is my wish that you should make money by them) that I am willing to treat with you on this subject.

And that you may have a more perfect understanding of my design in letting this property, I shall repeat what was mentioned in my former letter to you on this subject—viz.—first to reduce the income to certainty. and 2dly to bring (disposing of Dogue run Farm at the sametime) the rest of the Mount Vernon concerns into so narrow a compass as that (if I am not called from home) I may be enabled to manage them with no more than my usual exercise, by laying down rules & compelling my Overseers to abide by them strictly—and this, as I purpose to advertise the Fishery at the Ferry to be let, will give me but little trouble.

These are my primary objects, and for the accomplishment of them it is necessary I should add, that to avoid misunderstandings of every sort & kind, I propose to furnish *Nothing* but the Houses, & the apparatus's belonging thereto: an Inventory whereof is to be taken, and barring accidents, is to be returned in good order, at the expiration of the term for which they are Let.

Wood, for *Fuel only*, may be had on the terms mentioned in my former letter, if required; but even this, I have no wish to supply if it could be provided otherwise conveniently. My Scow—Boat & Waggon, when wanted, & could be spared, might be had at the rates others receive; but I would be under no previous agreement to furnish them, thereby giving a ⟨*illegible*⟩ to call for and to complain, if they were not forthcoming when required.

If the hands at present ⟨in⟩ the Distillery, the Mill, & Coopers shop are preferred, they may be had at a reasonable hire; cloathed, but not fed, or taxes paid, by me. But in case the Coopers are hired, I shall condition that when my Casks—Tubs—Pails &ca want repairing, or new ones are to be made, I shall have a right to call for any one, or all of them, at a stipulated price by the day. And I should moreover condition, that all my Grist—on the usual Toll, demandable of others, shall always be first ground in scarce times of Water, after the Distillery & your own familys wants, are suppld.

If it be required, the ground designated in my former letter, may go with these premises, at an equitable Rent. But the manure wch is made in, & about the Distillery, I must hold in reserve. And if the house in which you now live will be an accomodation, you may continue to occupy it.

You can judge better than any other, of your means to carry on these Manufactures. You know also, that the profit arising from both Mill & Distillery depend *altogether* upon the Spirit with which they are carried on—for if they are not adequately supplied with Grain and other essentials, they must prove unproductive, be the Rent what it may. On the other hand, at a reasonable one, between Man & Man—and I desire no other—a handsome profit might be made, as the old Books of my Mill will shew, if it is worked to advantage, for what has been, may be again, with equal Industry, & exertion.

I do not mean by any thing which is contained in this letter, to intimate the most distant intention of removing you from your present employment the ensuing year; or to reduce your wages or emoluments; if it is your choice to remain as you are, in preference to the New Scene which is proposed. Of this, I feel it incumbant on me to inform you; that your mind, while it is contemplating the latter measure may be perfectly at ease with respect to the former.[1] I remain your sincere well wisher, friend, and Servant

Go: Washington

P.S. I see so little prospect of receiving money to answer my own indispensable calls otherwise than by borrowing from Banks—a measure that is extremely disagreeable to me—that to hold up an idea of lending any would be idle & deceptious.

G.W.

ALS (letterpress copy), NN: Washington Papers. A number of the words in this letter have been traced over in pencil, perhaps by GW himself.

1. For GW's correspondence with Anderson and Lawrence Lewis about the rental of his mill and distillery at Mount Vernon, see GW to Anderson, 10 Sept. 1799, n.2. In the end it was decided that Lewis would rent the mill and distillery and that Anderson would remain for a time as farm manager. See also GW to Anderson, 13 Dec. 1799, and note 1 of that document, and Mount Vernon Ledger, 1799–1800.

To William Thornton

Dear Sir   Mount Vernon Octr 1st 1799
Enclosed are Messrs McLeod and Lumleys prices for painting my Houses in the City. Theirs, as you will perceive, is extended in Virginia currency; that mentioned by you, I presume, is Maryland; and if so, the prices are nearly the same.

Wherefore, if the Painter in the City will—finding *all* materials—do the Windows & Cornice, & Doors, in short all the exterior of the Buildings, the roof excepted (which must remain for future decision) upon the Terms McLeod & Lumley have offered, and there is reason to expect faithful work from him, I have no desire to resort to Alexandria, although I know the former to be capital Painters, & respectable men.

The matter now rests with Mr Blagden, with your advice, to employ whom he pleases. What is meant (in McLeods & Lumleys letter) by London measurement, I know not; and the mode of doing it ought to be ascertained beforehand, to avoid mis-conception. Every one knows that a square yard contains nine feet, in common acceptation; but how many feet by *London* measurement, I know not.[1]

Sanding, is designed to answer two purposes—durability, & representation of Stone; for the latter purpose, and in my opinion a desirable one; it is the last operation, by dashing, as long as any will stick, the Sand upon a coat of thick paint. This is the mode I pursued with the painting at this place, & wish to have pursued at my houses in the City.[2] To this, I must add, that as it is rare to meet with Sand perfectly white, & clean; all my Houses have been Sanded with the softest free stone, pounded and sifted;[3] and it is my wish to have those in the City done in the same way. If the stone cannot be thus prepared in the City, be so good as to inform me, & it shall be done here & sent up. It must be dashed hard on—& as long as any place appears bare. I am with great esteem—Dr Sir—Your Most Obedt Servt

Go: Washington

ALS, DLC: Thornton Papers; ALS (letterpress copy), NN: Washington Papers.

1. The estimate of the Alexandria firm of McLeod & Lumley of its charges for painting GW's Capitol Hill houses has not been found. See GW to Thornton, 29 Sept., and note 2 of that document. London measure derived from a former practice of London drapers of allowing something above the standard yard in their measurements.

2. In the fall of 1796, full of plans for his permanent return to Mount Vernon the following spring, GW drafted a lengthy set of instructions for his farm manager. In this memorandum, dated 5 Nov. 1796, he referred to his plans to have painting done at Mount Vernon in the summer of 1797 and wrote: "Some years ago, I had brought from Point Comfort, or some other place on the Bay of Chesapeak, a quantity of fine white Sand for the purpose of Sanding my houses anew when circumstances would enable me to give them a fresh coat of Paint."

Saunders A. Read of Alexandria did the painting at Mount Vernon that GW required, in May and June 1797 (see Read to GW, 25 April 1797, n.1). The sand was used with white paint to simulate stone.

3. GW inserted an asterisk here and wrote at the end of the letter: "the fine dust must be seperated from the Sand by a gentle breeze, & the sifter must be of the finest the sand is required."

Letter not found: from John Avery, 2 Oct. 1799. On 13 Oct. GW wrote Avery: "I have received your letter of the 2d instant." Avery's letter of 13 Oct. is printed as a note to GW's letter to Avery of 25 September.

Letter not found: from Benjamin Goodhue, 3 Oct. 1799. GW wrote Goodhue on 22 Nov.: "Your favour of the 3d of Octr never came to my hands until last night."

Letter not found: from William Thornton, 3 Oct. 1799. On 6 Oct. GW wrote Thornton: "Your letter of the 3d was recd last Night."

To Benjamin Stoddert

Sir,   Mount Vernon Octr 4th 1799.

Your polite attention to my recommendation of a Son of General Spotswood to be a Midshipman in our Navy; has opened the door for another application of a similar kind in behalf of Mr John ⟨Henley nephew⟩ to Mrs Washington.[1]

In April last, Mr Bassett, ⟨one of⟩ our Senators, and Cousin german to this young Gentleman, presented a letter from me to you respecting ⟨a younger⟩ brother of Mr Henley's.[2] The favourable reception it met with, and the appointment of young Spotswood (who is his Cousin also) to be a Midshipman, has inspired ⟨desires in⟩ John Henley to be a Midshipman ⟨on the Frigate⟩ Building at Norfolk.[3]

I have heard a ⟨*illegible*⟩ this young man, but have no ⟨personal⟩ acquaintance with him. ⟨Whatever you are⟩ pleased to say, or do, respecting ⟨*illegible*⟩ so good as to make me the ⟨medium of con⟩veyance.[4] His wish is, to enter the Service immediately. With very great esteem I am Sir Your Most Obedient and Very Humble Servant

Go: Washington

ALS (letterpress copy), NN: Washington Papers.

1. GW's letter to Secretary of the Navy Benjamin Stoddert recommending that George Spotswood be made a midshipman in the U.S. Navy is dated 10 July 1799. See also the references in note 1 of that document. Eighteen-year-old John Dandridge Henley was the son of Martha Washington's sister Elizabeth Dandridge Aylett Henley and her second husband, Leonard Henley of James City County who died in November 1798.

2. Burwell Bassett conveyed a letter from GW to Stoddert dated 31 Mar. 1799, in which GW told the secretary of the navy of Robert Henley's wish "to obtain a birth as Midshipman in one of our Frigates."

3. The keel of the ill-fated *Chesapeake*, a thirty-six-gun frigate, was laid on 10 Dec. 1798 at the Gosport navy yard at Portsmouth across from Norfolk in Virginia. The frigate, launched in December 1799, put to sea in May 1800.

4. GW forwarded to Mrs. Henley, under cover of a letter dated 20 Oct., Stoddert's letter of 14 Oct. notifying John Henley that he had been appointed a midshipman. He also sent her a draft of a letter written by himself for Henley to use as his letter of acceptance to the secretary of the navy. In the War of 1812 Robert Henley distinguished himself at the battle on Lake Champlain, and his brother John, at the Battle of New Orleans.

From John Trumbull

Sir   72 Welbeck Street London Octo. 5th 1799

I had the Honour to receive your favour of the 25th of June last, some weeks ago; I am very much obliged to you for what you have done respecting the Prints but sorry that you should have had so much trouble with them.

The wonderful Events of this Campaign in Europe have entirely contradicted my speculations of last Spring, and have at least removed to a greater distance the Danger which I then apprehended to be very near, but, wonderful as the success of the Allies has been, I cannot persuade myself that it is yet sufficiently compleat to justify us in believing ourselves to be in a State of Security from France; nor indeed does it appear to me that we should be secure, even if the Fate of France were that which her Enemies would wish, and the ancient government were reestablished: recent Events give us no reason to believe that the Human Character is changed for the better, or that the Possession of uncontroled Power, & the intoxication of Success will not produce their ancient and natural Effects in every human Bosom: and our Dangers would not perhaps be diminished, altho they would assume another form, by the complete Triumph of the Iron Systems of Russia & Germany.

The impossibility of carrying into immediate or speedy effect the Ideas which I took the Liberty of detailing to you, is made manifest by the State which you are so good as to explain to me, of Public opinions and Parties: But, if the general Idea be correct, if America & not Europe, ought, as appears to me, to become the great object of our Political attention; if neighboring Nations, numerous rich & ignorant may be converted into powerful friends, by a wise and generous Policy on our part, or become dangerous instruments of the intrigues of others, I should hope that the Influence of those who can see Danger at a Distance, would not fail to be exerted for the purpose of giving the proper direction to Public opinion; and that it would gradually make itself be felt. But these Speculations are very vain on my part: since the Affairs of our Country are in such able hands.

The Newspapers will have detailed to you the very extraordinary Series of Success which has accompanied the Armies of the Allies through this Campaign in Italy—Switzerland Syria and India. The first step in Holland was also successful; but the check which the Duke of York received before Alkmaar—on the 19th of September, has been followed by an inactivity on his part, which gives to that affair a more serious appearance than it had at first. The French by this means have acquired time to receive reinforcements, and to suppress Symptoms of Disaffection, while the position of the British Force is such that they can neither give Aid to nor receive it from those of the Dutch who are believed to be favorably disposed towards them. The Dampness of their Positions, which is encreased by the uncommon wetness and inclemency of the Season; the want of Shelter, Straw and good Water, together with the unfortunate plenty of Gin, must soon produce Sickness; and every Day's delay encreases these Evils. The Nation therefore expects with Anxiety the Issue of another Attack which is supposed to have taken place on the 29th of last Month.

It is understood that the favorable dispositions of the People of the Country were much relied upon, when this expedition was planned; and probably this reliance would have been justified by the Event, if the Force which is employed had been placed at once on the Meuse; that Position would have formed a Barrier against the French reinforcements, and would have given to the well disposed inhabitants of the Country an opportunity of affording that Aid by their cooperation, which in the present mode of attack they certainly have not. a too great eagerness to secure the Fleet at the Texel probably caused the adoption of the present Plan, which was well calculated for that purpose, but with a view to Amsterdam, may justly be compared to an Attack on Boston commenced by landing on Cape Cod.

I am much obliged to Mrs Washington and Mrs Lewis, (who I hope is as happy in her new State as She deserves) for their good wishes & remembrance of me, and beg them to accept my most respectful & cordial wishes for their continued Health & Happiness, and With Sentiments of the highest Respect & Gratitude I have the Honor to be Sir Your much obliged & obedient Servant

J. T.

LB, DLC: John Trumbull Letter Book.

To William Thornton

Dear Sir,   Mount Vernon Octr 6th 1799
Your letter of the 3d was recd last Night. I doubt not, the Painting and sanding of such parts of my houses in the City as *now* require it, will be done well, with the best materials, and on the best terms; wherefore I cannot be otherwise than pleased.[1]

As soon after this work is accomplished as I can make it convenient, I will visit the City, & take a view of my Buildings.[2] To part with which, if it could be done on terms any ways advantageous, would comport better with my finances, than to retain them for the purpose of Renting. If, therefore, you should hear of any person, or persons, disposed to buy, and who are able & willing to advance part of the purchase money, and the residue on reasonable credit, I pray you to mention mine. To aid in the accomodation of the members of the General Government, was my *only* inducement to *these* buildings. For my own convenience, another site will be chosen when, if ever, I am in circumstances to encounter the expence.

When you have occasion to write to Colo. Thomason of Tortola, let me pray you to express to him the sense I have of the politeness he has been pleased to bestow on me, through you;[3] and my thanks are due to you, for communicating it to, Dear Sir Your Most Obedt and obliged Hble Servant

Go: Washington

ALS, DLC: Thornton papers; ALS (letterpress copy), NN: Washington Papers. The cover of the ALS is marked "Favoured by Mr [Thomas] Peter." In his diary entry for 7 Oct. GW wrote: "Mr. Peter went to Geo: Town this Morng" (*Diaries*, 6:368).

1. Letter not found, but see GW to Thornton, 1 October.

2. GW went up to Washington on the "clear warm & pleasant" morning of 9 Nov. and "Viewed my building in the Fedl. City. Dined at Mr. Laws & lodged at Mr. Thos. Peter's." He was back at home by noon on the tenth (*Diaries*, 6:375).

3. Thomas Thomason (1740–c.1813), a merchant on the Caribbean island of Tortola, was the third husband of William Thornton's mother, Dorcas (Harris, *Thornton Papers*, 1:xxxv).

To William Thornton

Dear Sir   Mount Vernon Octr 7th 1799
Colo. Walker, a very respectable Gentleman of this State, will hand you this letter. He, with Mr Nelson, who married his Grand daughter, are on a visit to the Federal City, and propose to view the Canals & Falls in the Potomack before they return.

Colo. Walker is well acquainted with Mr White, but as the latter may be absent, I take the liberty of soliciting your civilities in shewing them such things as they may incline to see in the City.[1] I am—
Dear Sir Your Obedt Hble Servant

Go: Washington

ALS, CtHi.

1. GW wrote in his diary on 9 Oct.: "Colo. [John] Walker and Mr. Nelson set out for the City of Washington after breakfast." The two men had been at Mount Vernon since 4 Oct. (*Diaries*, 6:367, 369). Hugh Nelson (1768–1836), son of Gov. Thomas Nelson (1738–1789), in April 1799 married Eliza Kinloch (1781–1834), the granddaughter of Col. John Walker (1744–1809), who was the son of GW's old friend and associate Thomas Walker (1715–1794) of Albemarle County. GW is referring to District of Columbia commissioner Alexander White.

To William Augustine Washington

My dear Sir,   Mount Vernon 7th Oct. 1799
Strange as it may seem, it is nevertheless true, that your letter of the 30th of August never got to my hands until the 4th instant.[1] But it is not unusual for letters by private hands, to be thus delayed; and often to miscarry. By the Post they are certain of getting to hand, & in time.

You will not be surprised after receiving this information, that your request in favour of Mr James Digges Dishman was not complied with, nor, at your being disappointed of Whiskey, required for your own use: for whether sending it, would have placed you in my debt, or left me in yours, would have been no let to its going, *then*, or at any other time, when you want it.

Mr Dishmans Rye, and yours wd, & now will, if it is yet to be disposed of, be received, Bushel for Gallon (delivered at my landing); and with respect to Wheat, in a letter written to you about a fortnight ago, I requested you to inform me if any Crops were to be bought in your part of the Country; informing you at the sametime of my desire to purchase a quantity. Enclosed, are the present prices of this article in Alexandria. These I am willing *now* to give, or the Cash price at the time of delivery; to be ascertained by the purchasers Books, of *that* date. The Wheat to be delivered at my Landing.[2]

We shall always be glad when your health, inclination and convenience will admit of it, to see Mrs Washington and yourself at this place—to whom, Mrs Washington unites her best wishes with those of My dear Sir Your sincere friend and Affectionate Uncle

Go: Washington

ALS, NN: Liebman Collection; ALS (letterpress copy), ViMtV.

1. Letter not found. On 22 Sept. GW acknowledged the receipt of William Augustine Washington's missing letter of 15 September.

2. The enclosure, headed "Prices of Wheat in Alexandria 5th October 1799 by advice," reads: "For good *white* Wheat, weighing 58 lbs. the measured bushel, the price in Cash is 8/9d. And for red wheat, weighing the same the measured bushel, the price 8/3d. for every 60 lbs. weight; the same weight is required in white Wheat, as the weights of Wheat pr bushel, whether white or red, must be 60 lbs. And provided the Wheat is fine, and that the measured bushel weighs more than 58 lbs. then there is 2d. advance allowed for every pound above 58 lbs.—And on the other hand, if Wheats are light, & under 58 lbs. the measured bushel, then 2d. pr lb. is deducted for every lb. under 58 lbs.—and when the grain is very poor say weighing only 50, 52, or 53 lbs. pr bushel there is a greater deduction, as wheats of these Wts produce little flour & the quality not good. Rye, in common, is bought & recd by the measured bushel—Yet, notwithstanding, some purchasers this yr in Alexandria have fixed 56 lbs., as the weight of the Bushl" (AD, NN). Below this, GW wrote: "The above is an Extract of a letter just Received." The letter has not been identified. James Degges Dishman was left land in the 1778 will of his uncle James Degges of Westmoreland County (Fothergill, *Wills of Westmoreland County*, 169).

Letter not found: from Daniel Morgan, 8 Oct. 1799. In one of two letters that GW wrote Morgan on 26 Oct. he referred to Morgan's "favour of the 8th instt."

Letter not found: from William Augustine Washington, 8 Oct. 1799. On 29 Oct. GW wrote his nephew: "Your letter of the 8th instant has been duly received."

From Thomas Parker

Sir,   Charles Town Berkley 9th of October 1799
   I had the honor to Receive your letter of the 28th Ultimo on Saturday last accompanied by one from Genl Hamilton.[1]
   I fortunately met with Colo. Lear at this place yesterday morning & with him Carefully examined the different Situations in the Vicinity of the arsenal at Harper's ferry. After the most mature deliberations I have with the intire Concurrence of Colo. Lear Given a Dicided preference to the Banks of the Shanandoah, Just Above Its Confluence with the potowmack for Two of the Regiments; and about a mile above & Immediately on a Canal which Supplies a Saw Mill for the other.
   Those Situations are in my Opinion Rather too Confined But there is no other in the neighbourhood so Convenient for water & for wood—The Situations are Dry & I am Informed perfectly Healthy they are Both on Ground Belonging to the publick.
   we Shall be obliged to have Recource to Ground on the Top of the Hill About Half a mile Distant from our Camp for our field parade.
   As Timber for the purpose of making Slabs is verry Scarce in the neighbourhood I have Requested Mr [John] Mackie Superintendant of the public works to procure from The neighbouring saw mills as many Slabs as he Can for the purpose of Covering our Huts.
   It woud be pleasing to me to Receive orders to move to my winter Quarters as early as possable.[2]
   Colo. Lear who will deliver you this Letter & who has been extreamly attentive & serviceable to me in this Business will be able to Give you any further Information that you may Require.[3] with

the Highest Esteem & Respect I have the honor to be Sir your Obdt Servt

Thomas Parker

If you shoud be pleased to Give me any further orders I will thank you to direct to me at Winchester.

ALS, DLC:GW.

 1. For Alexander Hamilton's letter, see Hamilton to GW, 23 Sept., n.3.

 2. On 6 Oct. Parker wrote Hamilton: "I shall avail myself of the Aid of Colo. [Tobias] Lear who I understand is in The neighbourhood at Harpers Ferry & is perfectly acquainted with the Ground" (DLC: Hamilton Papers). After their visit to Harpers Ferry, Lear wrote to Parker from Charles Town on 10 Oct.: "The continued rain which has fallen this day has prevented my setting out for Mount Vernon as I intended. And as the Post leaves Alexandria for Winchester, on Sunday Morning, General Washington will hardly have time, after receiving yr letter to communicate his final orders to you, respecting the movement of your regiment, by the next mail. And, in that case, there will be a delay of one week, which, at this advanced season of the year, is too important to be lost. I have therefore thought it adviseable to send this letter to you by a special Messenger, and to say, that, in my opinion (founded upon the urgency experessd in the General's letter to you for providing winter quarters without delay) it would be expedient to march your Regiment to Harper's ferry as soon as you can after tuesday next, (which I presume is as early as it could be done) and, that no injury may arise from your taking this step, without final orders from the Commander in Chief, I promise you, in case he should have any reasons for delaying the movement, or making any alterations in the Arrangements for Cantoning the Troops, I will dispatch an express to you, with his orders, to meet you in Winchester on Tuesday Evening. Should you not receive any orders to the contrary at that time, you may conclude that the general arrangements made by you for providing winter quarters at Harper's Ferry meets the approbation of the Commander in chief, and his further orders (if any) will be communicated to you in the course of the Post" (DLC:GW).

 3. On 18 Oct. Lear wrote Parker from Mount Vernon: "On my arrival at this place on Sunday last, I delivered your letter to the Commander in Chief, and explained to him the Arrangements which you had made for hutting the Troops on the public Ground at Harper's Ferry; and communicated to him also a Copy of the letter which I wrote to you from Charlestown on the 10th inst.—He approves these measures, and hopes by this time that your Regiment is on the ground, and doubts not but you will make every exertion in your power to have Winter Quarters provided before the weather becomes severe. . . . I delivered to General Washington the Simlin [Cymling; i.e., summer squash] seed which you was so good as to commit to my care for him, and mentioned the extraordinary produce which you had had from this Vegitable. The General returns his best thanks for these seed, and as he is desireous of going very largely into the cultivation of every vegitable and other production, that is likely to afford good food for Stock, he will be much obliged to you for as much of this Simlin seed as you can conveniently spare. And I will thank you for an account of the quantity pro-

duced by you this season, and the dimensions of the ground upon which they grew, and the distance at which the seed were planted from each other. If you can spare the General any more seed he will thank you to have it made up in a package and put into the Post Office, by which means he will get it more readily than if it should be committed to the charge of any private hand. I shall direct this letter to Winchester, at present; but I will thank you to let me know at what place to direct in future that letters by the mail may get early to your hands" (DLC:GW).

From Timothy Pickering

(private)

Sir,   Trenton [N.J.] Oct. 9. 1799.

I received yesterday the inclosed letter from Mr Murray.[1]

The President is on his way to this place. Govr Davie has been here a week; and Mr Ellsworth writes me, in a letter recd this morning, that he will arrive himself by Friday morning. The question about the mission to France will, I expect, be then settled. The state of the President's mind, when on the 3d instant in the evening he *called* on Judge Ellsworth at Windsor (above Hartford) is thus intimated by the latter in an extract of a letter to the President written since that call, & which the Judge has communicated to me, in closing a sentence, in these words, referring to the President—"—should you *continue* inclined to such suspension of our mission, as under present aspects, universal opinion, I believe, and certainly my own, would justify." [2]

I am informed by Mr McHenry that General Hamilton & Genl Wilkinson are expected here to-day: and Mr Liston informs me that he shall be on in the course of the week from New-York. Judge Ellsworth comes on without being invited by the President; tho' on very satisfactory grounds, which he mentions in his letter. This concurrence of public characters will give rise to speculations: and if the mission to France be suspended, the *Aurora* will ascribe it to British influence—and the efforts of the British faction, as we shall in this case be called anew: altho' the arrivals of Hamilton & Wilkinson, & the passing of Mr Liston, are purely fortuitous.[3] With great respect, I am, sir, your obt servt

Timothy Pickering

ALS, DLC:GW; ALS (letterpress copy), MHi: Pickering Papers.

1. In his letter to William Vans Murray of 26 Oct., GW acknowledges the receipt of a number of letters from Murray, "Within the space of a few days."

2. In his letter to Pickering of 5 Oct. from Windsor, Conn., Oliver Ellsworth wrote: "I was the evening before last honoured with a call from the President of half an hour; but nothing passed respecting my going to Trenton. I have notwithstanding presumed to write him by this day's mail, as follows—'Since you passed on, I have concluded to meet Governor Davie at Trenton, which he probably will expect; and which, besides putting it in our power to pay you our joint respects, and to receive as fully any communication of your views as you may wish to make, may enable me to accompany him Eastward, should you continue inclined to such suspension of our Mission as, under present aspects, universal opinion I beleive, and certainly my own, would justify. It is a matter of some regret, Sir, that I did not consult you on the propriety of this visit; but if I err, experience has taught me that you can excuse.' Governor Davie will doubtless arrive before me, and I hope will be made comfortable & easy. It will be Thursday Evening or Friday morning next befor I shall have the pleasure of seeing you & him" (MHi: Pickering Papers). On 16 Oct., to Pickering's dismay, President Adams instructed him to deliver the prepared instructions to Ellsworth and William R. Davie and tell them to be ready to sail for France on the frigate *United States* by 1 November.

3. As the major general charged with the direct management of the U.S. army in the North and Northwest, Alexander Hamilton had earlier ordered Gen. James Wilkinson, who commanded the forces in the Northwest, to come east so that the two could confer (Hamilton to Wilkinson, 12 Feb. 1799, in Syrett, *Hamilton Papers*, 22:477–79). On 6 Oct. 1799 Hamilton wrote Secretary of War James McHenry from New York: "General Wilkinson has just returned to this city, and will set out together with myself for Trenton on Monday in order to settle definitively with you the requisite arrangements for the Western Army" (ibid., 23:510). Robert Liston, the British minister to the United States, wrote Pickering from New York on 8 Oct. that he would "probably pass through Trenton in the course of this week on my way southward" (MHi: Pickering Papers).

To John Gill

Sir,   Mount Vernon 13th Oct. 1799

Your letter of the 28th Ulto came duly to hand, and I have sent my Manager, Mr Anderson, twice to Alexandria to receive from you, some explanation of your meaning respecting it.[1]

If it be, to pay the Rents that are due, up to June last, according to contract, I shall consent to cancel the bargain wch you entered into for my Land on Difficult run; although it is not a usual practice with me to make, & unmake bargains; and notwithstanding I had ⟨several⟩ reasons to believe (immediately after granting you a Lease for it) that I could have obtained five guineas an Acre for it. Before it was engaged to you, I had been offered ⟨fif⟩teen hundred pounds Cash, a thousand of which down; and that, the Person who keeps the Tavern at the bridge would have given more.

That you have done nothing with the Land, and that the purchase of it has not answered your expectation, is no argument for cancelling the bargain; for with equal propriety, if by any adventitious circumstance the price had rose to ten guineas an Acre, I might have made a similar proposal to you.

The contract was of your own seeking; you, no doubt, thought you saw a profit ⟨arising to⟩ yourself from it; immediately after it was made I had (as observed before) good reason to believe I could have obtained more; *now* property of *all* kinds has declined in value; But the bargain, you must be sensible, is binding; and although there ⟨may be⟩ nothing on the Premises on which to ⟨make⟩ distress for the Rents I am not, thereby deprived of another resort, neither of which is not my wish.

If it is inconvenient for you to pay money, I will (understanding that you have brought in a Cargo of Goods) receive such articles thereof in payment, as ⟨are sui⟩table for cloathing my Negros.[2] I am Sir—Your Most Obedt Ser.

Go: Washington

ALS (letterpress copy), NN: Washington Papers.

1. Letter not found.

2. For the goods with which Gill provided GW in partial payment of what he owed for the rent of GW's Difficult Run tract, see GW to Gill, 26 Nov. 1799, n.1. See also GW to Gill, 19 Oct., n.2.

From Alexander Hamilton

Sir: Trenton [N.J.] Octor 14th [17]99

The enclosed abstract was founded on returns actually received in the office of the Adjutant General. From subsequent letters it appears that many recruits have been enlisted since the date of those returns.[1] With the Highest respect I have the honor to be Sir your obt Set

Alexander Hamilton

LS, DLC:GW; Df, DLC: Hamilton Papers.

1. Hamilton wrote GW again from Trenton on 17 Oct. before returning to New York on 19 Oct. : "I have the honor to transmit for your information An Abstract of the recruiting returns which were received at the Adjutant Generals office to the 5th of October last inclusively. From subsequent informal communications, I am authorised to say that the numbers now actually inlisted considerably exceed those which appear in the Return" (DLC:GW). The abstracts en-

closed in the two letters have not been found. Neither of these letters is listed in the Syrett edition of the *Hamilton Papers*.

To Alexander Hamilton

Sir,   Mount Vernon, October 15th 1799

Since writing to you on the 29th ultimo, I have received a letter from Colo. Parker, informing me that he had fixed upon a spot, on the public Ground, at Harper's Ferry, as the most eligable place for cantoning the 7th, 8th and 9th Regiments, agreeably to your instructions, and the ideas which I communicated to him.[1] And, I presume, measures are now taking to provide huts at that place for these Regiments.

Colo. Parker has undoubtedly written to you on this subject since fixing upon the spot;[2] and as the advanced season of the year will admit of no delay in collecting and hutting the Troops, I trust that the 7th and 9th Regiments, as well as the 8th, will receive immediate orders to march to that place.

The enclosed letter, mentioning the wish of Major Campbell to be appointed a Division Inspector, has been put into my hands, and as I have no personal knowledge of Major Campbell, and the choice of this Officer laying with the Inspector General, I have thought proper to forward it to you as I received it.[3] With very great esteem & regard I am, Sir, Your most Obedt Servt

Go: Washington

LS, DLC: Hamilton Papers; Df, DLC:GW. Both copies are in Tobias Lear's hand.

1. See Thomas Parker's letter to GW of 9 October.

2. On 21 Oct. Hamilton wrote GW about Parker's letter to him of 10 Oct. and enclosed his own letter to Parker of 21 Oct. in reply, in which he took Parker to task for implying in his letter of 10 Oct. that he intended to build barracks instead of huts for the troops that were to be quartered at Harpers Ferry. GW on 26 Oct. and Parker on 30 Oct. assured Hamilton that he had misunderstood Parker's meaning, and that Parker fully intended to build huts, not barracks, on the Shenandoah. The three letters exchanged by Parker and Hamilton are quoted at length in the notes to Hamilton's letter to GW of 21 October.

3. Maj. William Campbell of the 8th Infantry Regiment wrote Hamilton on 9 Oct. and asked to be made division inspector. In his letter to GW of 23 Oct., Hamilton had this to say about Campbell: "I find that I omitted in my official reply [of 21 Oct.] to say any thing on the subject of Major Campbell. On the appointments of this kind for the Troops South of Potowmack it is my intention particularly to consult General Pinckney with the advantage of the observations

he shall make on the spot. But I do not publish this lest I should subject the General to embarrassment & ill will" (DLC:GW). Hamilton made a noncommittal reply to Campbell on 2 November. The letter about Campbell that GW sent to Hamilton has not been identified; the two letters that Hamilton and Campbell exchanged are in DLC: Hamilton Papers. There are also in the Hamilton Papers a number of other letters recommending Campbell for the appointment, including one from Parker himself, dated 6 Oct., one from Edward Stevens, 9 Oct., and one from Henry Lee of 16 October.

Letter not found: from John Gill, 16 Oct. 1799. On 19 Oct. GW wrote Gill indicating that he had received Gill's "letter of the 16th."

Letter not found: from Benjamin Stoddert, 16 Oct. 1799. On 20 Oct. GW wrote Stoddert: "Your favor of the 16th instant was received this morning."

From Bartholomew Dandridge

Dear Sir,   London 17 Oct. 1799

I ought 'ere now to have acknowledg'd the receipt of & to have returned you my most grateful thanks for your very kind letter of the 26 June,[1] which came to my hands about the middle of Augt at Brighton (a bathing place on *the channel*) whither I had gone for a few weeks relaxation. Its coming to me at that place, a desire to examine thoroughly the path which I shd follow in consequence of it, & Mr King's absence whom I wished to consult & advise with on that part of yr letter which concerns my future walk in life, are the reasons why I have not given it an earlier reply.

After weighing all the advantages & disadvantages of a diplomatic life, I am decidedly of opinion that it wd be an ineligible pursuit *for me*, & I am the more inclined to approve my opinion as it is quite conformable to that of Mr King, than whom, as you justly say, there is no *better* judge in such a case. The leading objections to my pursuing this, are 1—that my education (if my natural abilities had) has been quite inadequate to the faithful discharge of its duties, as it requires a regular & classical education with a perfect Knowledge of Law; &c. &c. none of which I pretend to— 2d—That kind of life which a man in a public station is of necessity obliged to lead, is diametrically opposed ⟨to⟩ the Disposition which nature has implanted in me; which I conceive to be a consideration of much weight—& lastly, & perhaps the most weighty objection of all is, that *all* our diplomatic employments are so far from affording one the means of a *living*, that whoever accepts them must make considerable advances from his private funds, if he has any, or run in debt to enable him to support his station with becoming decency. This *I Know* to be the fact, & you I dare say will agree that our Govt is more disposed to lessen than to increase the pay of its diplomatic officers. I flatter myself, Dr Sir, that I need advance no further Evidence to convince you that I am right in discarding all thots of Diplomatic life.

In turning my attention towards a Commercial pursuit, I have to offer you my particular thanks for yr obliging suggestions on that subject which I trust I shall attend to & benefit by. The failure of so many of our countrymen & especially of the laudable & honest efforts of our worthy friend (for whose misfortunes no one can be more sincerely concerned than myself,) in that line is indeed somewhat discouraging, but after mature reflexion does not deter me from my resolution to ⟨follow⟩ a mercantile calling as the most probable means of obtaing pecuniary independence. You do not mention the causes of our friend's failure, & certainly if industry & fair dealing *alone* were to ensure success I shd not hope to succeed better than he has done, for I shd not aspire to possess more of either than I believe he does; but it appears to me that his want of Success must have arisen from commencing business in *too large* a scale, from contracting bad debts or from expending the *profits* in the *first instance* in property which for a long time must be unproductive. In whatever way ⟨that⟩ may have happened I truly lament it.[2]

I will now Sir, take the liberty of stating to you the precise plan which I mean to adopt, which is nearly that which you have been so good, as to point out, & which has been advised by Mr King & Mr Gore, both of whom seem to take a sincere & friendly interest in my future welfare & on all occasions since my residence here have shew'd me unbounded kindness, & it wd be ungrateful in me not to testify (& I do it with real pleasure) that Mr King's conduct towards me has been that which I coud have expected scarcely from my own brother. My plan is simply this—to procure in this country a handsome assortment of goods suitable to our Country, of the *Manufacturers themselves*, by which means I shall get them much cheaper than from a second hand. I presume that four or five thousand pounds Stg worth will be a sufficient stock to begin with; & that this amot may be sold & replacd every spring & autumn. Alexandria is the Place I fix upon for the Establishmt. I mean to get some Substantial Merchant in London, by way of Banker, to answer the Bills of the manufacturers as they become due, in case any temporary accident shd prevent my remittances from reaching this Country at the moments appointed. He will require a Commn for doing this business & a certain pr Cent upon any money he may advance for me—on the contrary if I shd be able to anticipate my remittances he will allow me the same pr centage while the money is in his hands. This mode will always secure me a character of Punctuality, desireable in a mercht. I mean to enter solely into the Dry Goods line—to sell reasonably, & for cash only. In this moderate & plain way of doing business & with attention & œconomy, I think I might hope for Success, without presumption. This is *precisely* the Track that a nephew of Mr Gore's, who is now here, pursued. He began abt six years ago in the retail way, at Boston—he had the advantages of a good character & some cash: he was content with small profits—after a few years he engaged in the whole sale line & now imports £25,000 pr ann. & has made a handsome fortune. He remains here this winter, in the course of which he has been so good as to offer to give me such information respecting my plan as will be very useful to me—& will give me Letters of introduction to his Correspondents.[3] I have explained fully & candidly my views to Mr King & am happy to say that they meet his approbation, & I hope they will do yours, as it is from the countenance of my friends joined to my own exertions that I must look for success. Mr King has been so good as to tell me to choose my own time of departure—I may stay with him as long as I please or leave him when it best suits my interest, we have agreed however that the ensuing Spring or Summer will be a good season for my leaving this country, as I am arriving at a period of life when it becomes proper to fix myself in whatever occupation I mean to pursue. In the mean time he will dispence with my services for some weeks while I visit the different manufacturers to whom he & Mr Gore will give me letters. I had a conversation with Mr K. the other day on the subject, & took the liberty of showing him that part of yr letter which contains yr opinion of the manner in wch business shd be commenced; it corresponds perfectly with his own opinions & he not only said it was his intention to furnish me with Cash to enable me to defray any expenses that might be necessary in my outfit; but with a generosity & kindness, seldom equalled, offered to become joint Security with any of my friends who wd unite with him, for the goods which I shd have occasion for, ⟨as⟩ by that means he presumed they might be had on much better terms: he authorised me to mention this to you, in particular, which I do more to show you his opinion of me & to do justice to him, than with any expectation that it will be necessary for you or him to take such a step, for I have no doubt of being able to obtain on credit whatever articles I may want. Certainly for *Cash* (or even a small proportion of it) Goods may be had much lower than without, & the nearer the Security comes to that Cash, in the same proportion will be the price of Goods.

I beg you, to pardon my giving you so much trouble, but am encouraged thereto as I think it wd be a satisfaction to you to lend any reasonable assistance to my honest efforts to obtain a comfortable independence. I shall go on & mature my plan during the winter & shall beg at your leisure any further advice or thoughts that you may think fit to bestow on it. I wd be particularly thankful for yr opinion as to the amot of the ⟨first⟩ importation ⟨*illegible*⟩ the kind of Goods most sought for & wch wd obtain the greatest sale — & whether & upon what terms, a store house & other conveniencies cou'd be had at any time on my arrival in Alexa.[4]

The public Papers will give you so much more ample Details of the present state of politics & military operations in Europe & elsewhere, than I can do, that I decline saying anything concerning them. The English continue to harrass our Commerce in all quarters & you may be assured we have nothing to expect from the *friendship* of this Country more than from that of France or any other Country. Both Engd & France want nothing but the power & an oppy to annihilate our independence & to make us subservt to their views & we ought to be equally on our guard against the open or secret attacks of either.

Mr and Mrs King desire me to present to you & Mrs W. their respectful remembrance. Be pleased to offer my affecte regards to my aunt, & to assure yourself, Dr Sir, of my continued & sincere Respect & attachmt

B. Dandridge

ADfS, owned (1977) by Mr. Patterson Branch, Sr., Richmond, Virginia.

1. GW's letter to Dandridge of 26 June, which has not been found, was probably written in response to Dandridge's letter of 12 Mar. 1799, in which Dandridge told GW of his decision not to accept a commission in the New Army but to remain in London as the secretary of U.S. minister Rufus King.

2. The "friend" is undoubtedly Tobias Lear, whose financial affairs had been worsening for several years. Lear's firm, T. Lear & Co., was organized in the mid-1790s with partners Tristram Dalton and James Greenleaf. Lear had gone to England and Holland in the fall of 1793 to make contacts among the merchants there and establish lines of credit. The company had not gotten firmly established before an economic slowdown in the District of Columbia brought a decline in business at the same time as the company's European creditors were clamoring to be paid. Lear's overextension in other areas added to the company's woes, and by 1797 Lear's finances were in a desperate condition. In October 1797 Lear attempted to borrow $3,000 from GW, but GW was able to lend him only $1,000, and in June 1798 Lear had even diverted some money he had collected for GW to his own use (see GW to Lear, 24 Oct. 1797, 25 June 1798, and 4 July 1798). For an account of Lear's financial problems, see Brighton, *Checkered Career of Tobias Lear*, 147–59.

3. Christopher Gore (1758–1827), who later was to become governor of Massachusetts and a U.S. senator from that state, was at this time in England as one of the American commissioners under article 7 of the Jay Treaty. Gore had set up his nephew John Gore, the son of his dead brother also named John, in a firm of East India traders in Boston (Pinkney, *Christopher Gore*, 18).

4. Dandridge's plans to go into business came to naught. He died in 1802 while serving as U.S. consul in Saint Domingue.

To John Gill

Sir,   Mount Vernon 19th Oct. 1799

Sending every other day *only* to the Post Office (unless something special makes it expedient to send oftener) your letter of the 16th did not reach my hands until the 17th at night.

Herewith, the Plat lent you by Mr Swift, is returned. But as my land is not laid down in connection therewith, I have derived but little information from the examination thereof; and as you remark "it does not quite join your tract" I see little or no advantage it would be to me to possess it. Especially as the whole contains but one hundred & ten acres, and that part west of Difficult run, you propose to reserve; without ⟨specification of the⟩ contents of the part which lyes ⟨on the East⟩ side. A purchase of this sort would be something like "buying a Pig in a poke." [1]

If the part *you have*, or ⟨*illegible*⟩, amounting in the whole to one hundred and ten acres, was adjoining to, and mak⟨ing the⟩ shape of mine tolerably convenient in the enlargement, I should not (as I told you, when I had the pleasure of seeing you at this place) have had any objection to receiving the Land in discharge of the Back Rents, and to the annulling our former Bargain.

Whether this can be accomplished or not, rests with you to determine, and I shall wait until I hear from you on this subject, before I shall go, or send, to examine the quality & situation of the land you would give in payment; for on these also the measure, in some degree, would rest.[2] I am Sir Your very Hble Servant

Go: Washington

ALS (letterpress copy), NN: Washington Papers.

John Gill, who was living in Alexandria until as late as 1796, had by this time moved, probably to Baltimore.

1. GW went up to Difficult Run on 5 Nov. to take a look at the tracts of land belonging to Gill and himself. While resurveying his own tract GW discovered what he believed to be an adjacent strip of unclaimed land. For the next three weeks he vigorously pursued the possibility of laying claim to it, only to learn in the end that no such vacant land existed (see GW to William Price, 7 Nov., n.1). At the same time, he worked out an agreement with John Gill whereby Gill would be released from his commitment to buy GW's Difficult Run lands and would pay GW the two years' rent that he owed on the tract with goods and a parcel of land (see note 2). Jonathan Swift was a merchant in Alexandria.

2. As GW here and hereafter makes clear, Gill proposed in his missing letters of 16 and 19 Oct. that he give GW land on Difficult Run in payment of the rent he owed on GW's 275-acre tract on Difficult Run which Gill had rented since 1795. GW acquired this piece of land from Bryan Fairfax in 1763 for £82.10, in payment of a debt (see Memorandum, List of Quitrents, 1764, n.3, in *Papers, Colonial Series*, 7:350–51; see also GW to Gill, 22 Oct. 1799). The tract was on the Loudoun County side of Difficult Run at the bridge on the main road to Leesburg, about twenty miles from Alexandria (Mitchell, *Fairfax County Patents and Grants*, 149). When he had farms on his Bullskin quarters before the Revolution, GW used the Difficult Run tract as a wagon station between Mount Vernon and Berkeley County.

In 1783 Bryan Fairfax warned GW that "the Man who lives at the Bridge" over Difficult Run, probably the tavernkeeper William Shepherd, was threatening to preempt a mill site on GW's land, but GW seems to have done nothing about his Difficult Run tract for another decade or more. In 1793 Robert Townsend Hooe wrote GW that he "was informed the other day that an attempt would be made by Shepherd, who keeps Tavern at Difficult Bridge, to Condemn part of your Land for a Mill that he is abt to erect." This was followed shortly by a letter from GW's rental agent, Robert Lewis, saying that he had "had several applications from different persons who wish to know whether you would sell your land on Difficult Run" (Bryan Fairfax to GW, 19 July and 4 Aug. 1783; Robert Townsend Hooe to GW, 23 May 1793; Robert Lewis to GW, 12 Aug. 1793). GW wrote Lewis on 26 Aug. 1793 that "Nothing short of a very high price would induce" him to sell the Difficult Run tract, "on Account of the Mill seat; quantity of Meadow land—contiguity to the Great Falls (where a town is erecting)—Georgetown, the Federal City, and Alexandria." Shortly after authorizing Lewis to rent the land, however, GW entered negotiations with John Gill in May 1794 for the sale of the tract to Gill. A year later, on 8 May 1795, Gill agreed to pay GW $433.33⅓ a year for ten years for the use of the property; for his part, GW agreed that Gill could buy the property at any time before the expiration of the ten years, and GW would convey the property to him "in fee simple" (GW to Charles Lee, 17 May 1795; see also GW to William Pearce, 1, 29 Mar. 1795, GW to George Gilpin, 29 Mar. 1795, GW to Philip R. Fendall, 29 Mar. 1795, GW to John Gill, 1, 26 April, 4, 17 May, 13 July 1795, and Gill to GW, 26 Mar., 27 April, 21 May, 17 July 1795, 18 May 1796).

When Gill first wrote GW on 16 Oct. 1799 about terminating their agreement, he had paid the rent on GW's Difficult Run land for only two of the four years he had held it. On 22 Oct. GW wrote Gill that he had received Gill's (missing) letter of 19 Oct. clarifying his proposal and that if upon examination Gill's land appeared satisfactory, he would agree to Gill's proposal that he accept the land in payment of the debt.

GW went up to Difficult Run on 5 Nov. and spent three days looking over Gill's land on either side of Difficult Run and also surveying his own tract on the run (see *Diaries*, 6:374–75). After his return to Mount Vernon on 10 Nov., GW wrote Gill telling him what he had seen at Difficult Run and specifying what land he would accept from Gill to settle their account and cancel the bargain. Gill then met with GW at Mount Vernon, and GW agreed to take a slip of land upon the upper or western side of Difficult Run along with certain specified goods in settlement of Gill's debt of $866.67 (Ledger C, 60) and release him from any further payment. See GW to Gill, 12, 26 Nov., and the notes to the latter document.

Letter not found: from John Gill, 19 Oct. 1799. On 22 Oct. GW wrote Gill: "I have been duly favoured with your letter of the 19th instant."

Letter not found: from Daniel Morgan, 19 Oct. 1799. On 26 Oct. GW wrote Morgan: "I have been duly favoured with your letter of the 19th instant."

To Elizabeth Dandridge Aylett Henley

Dear Madam,   Mount Vernon 20th Octr 1799

You will perceive by the Enclosed, which is left open for your perusal before it is forwarded, that your son John, is appointed a Mid-shipman in the Navy of the United States.[1]

You will press him to take the oath of Office, required by the Secretary of the Navy, without delay; and forward it to that Gentleman in the manner he directs—Enclosing it in a letter couched in some such terms as you will find on the other side. From the date of which letter of Acceptance, his pay will commence, according to the information given therein.

The oath may be taken before any respectable Magistrate, who must certify the same, at the bottom thereof. and I hope by his punctuality, and diligence in performing the duties which will be required of him, and his obedience to orders, he will give sufficient evidence of his deserving this first grade in the Naval Service, & thereby entitle himself to promotn.

As I expect your Sister is writing to you, I shall say nothing concerning her, or family matters;[2] only adding that with the greatest truth I remain Your most Obedient, and Affectionate Hble Servant

Go: Washington

P.S. If your Son John can write a tolerable hand, the Letter to the Secy of the Navy had better be written by himself than any other; taking care to spell his words well.[3]

ALS (photocopy), DLC:GW. This letter is addressed to "Mrs Elizabeth Henley near Williamsburgh To the care of the Postmaster at that place."

1. GW's letter to Stoddert of this date reads: "Sir, Your favor of the 16th instant was received the morning, after your letter to Mr John Henley was presented to me, & before the latter had been forwarded to that young Gentleman.

"For your politeness ⟨*illegible*⟩ for the latter's appear⟨*illegible*⟩ the former, and for this fresh instance of your kind attention to my recommendation, I feel much obliged.

"I unite most sincerely with you in wishing, that the Mission to France on the eve of embarkation, will be productive of the good the President expects, and that an honorable, permanent and happy Peace for this Country, may be the result of the measure. With very ⟨*illegible*⟩ I am—Sir Your most Obedient obliged Hble Servt Go: Washington" (letterpress copy, NN: Washington Papers).

2. Burwell Bassett wrote GW on 2 Dec. 1799 to inform him that Mrs. Henley, Martha Washington's sister and Bassett's aunt, had died in late November.

3. GW enclosed this draft of a letter to Stoddert for John Henley to use: "Sir, Through the medium of General Washington, I have been honoured with your letter of the 16th, enclosing the Presidents Warrant appointing me a Midshipman in the Navy of the United States.

"Herewith I return the Oath which I have taken, with the Magistrates certificate thereof, annexed. My thanks are due to the President for this mark of his confidence—and to you, Sir, for having had the kindness to communicate it to me.

"Your orders I shall strictly obey—and I pray you to be assured, that if zeal for the welfare of my Country, and a strict attention to the Orders of my Superior Officers can accomplish it, the President shall have no cause to regret the confidence he has been pleased to place in Sir Your Most Obedt and Very Humble Servant John Henley" (photocopy, DLC:GW).

To Timothy Pickering

Private
Dear Sir,   Mount Vernon Octr 20th 1799
Your letters of the 29th Ult. and 9th instant, have been duly received; and for the information given in them, I feel myself obliged.

In a note which I have just recd from Mr Stoddert, to whom I had occasion to write on business,[1] is added in the close thereof "The President has decided that the Mission to France shall proceed without delay. The Ministers, now here, will embark on board the Frigate United States at New Port, about the first of November."[2] This being the case, I shall take it for granted that the measure has been duly considered in all its relations; and that a favourable result is expected: than whom, no one more ardently wishes it than does Dear Sir Your most Obedient and Very Humble Servant

Go: Washington

ALS, MHi: Pickering Papers; ALS (letterpress copy), NN: Washington Papers.
1. On 20 Oct. GW acknowledged the receipt of Benjamin Stoddert's letter and forwarded it to Mrs. Henley. The letter has not been found. See GW to Elizabeth Dandridge Aylett Henley, 20 Oct., n.1.
2. For reference to Adams's decision to send the appointed envoys, William R. Davie and Oliver Ellsworth, to France in November, see Pickering to GW, 9 Oct., n.2.

To Isaac Weatherinton

Sir,   Mount Vernon ⟨20th⟩ Oct. 1799
Your letter ⟨of the 20th⟩ of August is but just come to hand. I thank you for the information contain⟨ed in it⟩ of the Tresspasses which are committed on the small piece of land which I have adjoining to yours, & Squire McCrakin's.[1]

It would, in future ⟨be⟩ friendly and obliging in you, or him (as my Land adjoins your tracts) to endeavour to prevent such invasion of private property; or if this cannot be done by admonishing the Trespassers of the injustice & impropriety ⟨of⟩ such conduct, then to furnish me with ⟨the n⟩ames, places of abode, and other circumstances of those who pay so little regard to the rights of others, that they may be prosecu⟨ted to⟩ the utmost extent of the Law; for ⟨such iniqui⟩tous practices ought to be made a common cause. If this letter should ever ⟨re⟩ach your hands be so good as to acknowledge the rect of it by the line of Posts, & yr letter will get speedily to hand; by private oppertunities there is no certainty. I am Sir Yr very Hble Servt

Go: Washington

ALS (letterpress copy), NN: Washington Papers.

1. Weatherinton wrote to GW from "Hampshire County Virginia between the Mouths of big and little Capekapon Creek August 24th [not 20 Aug.] 1799": "Sir I take this oppertunity of informing you as I think it my Duty So to do that the people have made frequaint practices of trespassing upon your Land and timber this twenty years or better and last Winter and Spring there Was A number of Walnut and poplar Sawlogs taken off the Said Land beside other timber for Cannoes and Waggon Stuff the Said Land lays in Hampshire County on the River potomak adjining Squire Virgil McCrakin and myself" (ViHi). On 8 Mar. 1753 GW secured a grant of 240 acres then in Frederick County, on the Potomac River between the Great and Little Cacapon rivers (see Land Grants, from Thomas, Lord Fairfax, in *Papers, Colonial Series*, 1:47–48). GW wrote at the bottom of Weatherinton's letter of 24 Aug.: "In acknowledging the receipt of this letter, I requested Mr Weatherinton to communicate to me the names of the persons who had committed these Tresspasses and the facts relative thereto."

From Alexander Hamilton

Dear Sir   N. York Oct. 21st 1799

On my return from Trenton, the day before yesterday, I found your private letter of the 13th as well as yr public letter of the 15th instant.

The News papers have probably informed you that poor Avery is dead of the yellow fever.[1]

The President has resolved to send the commissioners to France notwithstanding the change of affairs there. He is not understood to have consulted either of his Ministers; certainly not either the Secy of War or of Finance. All my calculations lead me to regret the measure. I hope that it may not in its consequences involve the United States in a war on the side of France with her enemies.[2] My trust in Providence which has so often interposed in our favour, is my only consolation. With great respect &c.

Copy, DLC: Hamilton Papers.

1. GW wrote Hamilton on 13 Oct. to inquire about John Avery, to whom he hoped to rent his new houses in the Federal City. See GW to Avery, 25 Sept., n.3.

2. It was on 16 Oct. that John Adams ordered Secretary of State Timothy Pickering to instruct Oliver Ellsworth and William R. Davie, who had been appointed in February 1799, to sail for France by 1 Nov. and join William Vans Murray as the three U.S. envoys to France. For John Adams's later account of Hamilton's attempt at this time to persuade him not to send the two ministers plenipotentiary to France, see Hamilton to GW, 21 Oct., n.2, in Syrett, *Hamilton Papers*, 23: 545–47.

From Alexander Hamilton

Sir   New-York Oct. 21st 1799

I have the honor to acknowledge the receipt two days since of your letter of the 15th instant, at which time I also received one from Col: Parker, informing me of the selection of ground which he had made.[1]

You will see by the enclosed letter to him the impression which his communication has made on my mind. I trust that it must be erroneous, since my supposition does not agree with the spirit of his instructions either from you or my self, nor with the manner in which you seem, by some expressions in your letter, to understand that he has executed them. But as it is possible the mode of execution may not have been sufficiently explained to you, I cannot intirely dismiss my apprehensions.

If the plan of Barracks has in fact been substituted, I must once more intreat your interposition. You will judge whether there is yet time to rectify the mistake and procure a more suitable position. Or whether making an arrangement at the place which has been fixed upon for the 8th Regiment only, it will not be best to vary the destination of the others sending the 9th to the Barracks at Frederick town in Maryland where I am very lately inform'd there are buildings sufficient for a Regiment, belonging to the State, which I presume may be borrowed, and the 10th at Carlisle in Pennsylvania where I am assured there exist buildings the property of the United States which will accommodate a Regiment.

Both these Regiments have been directed to march for their destination, the Ninth by way of Frederick-town, and the tenth to *Yorktown* there to receive further orders.[2]

Permit me to ask that you will be pleased to give these further Orders, according to your determination to which every thing is respectfully submitted.

Knowing that it is not agreeable to your general plan to take charge, at present, of military operations I am bound to apologise for the trouble I give you. But my unexpected and late agency in the affair and the advanced state of the Season leave me no alternative. With perfect respect I have the honour to be Sir Yr obdt Servt

A. Hamilton

LS, DLC:GW; ADf, DLC: Hamilton Papers; copy, DLC: Hamilton Papers.

1. In his letter to Thomas Parker of 21 Oct., Hamilton wrote: "Your letter of the 10 instant, by reason of my absence at Trenton, was not received till the 19th. Its contents are somewhat embarrassing. A leading feature of the plan for Winter Quarters which in conformity with arrangements with the Department of War was indicated by my instructions to you is that Timber for hutting and wood for fuel should be found on the premisses. The additional instruction to you from the Commander in Chief appears to me to contemplate the same thing; and yet your letter informs me that the spot fixed upon does not offer this advantage and that with the advice of Mr. Lear you had employed Mr. Mackie to procure the necessary *articles* for *building*. It would seem from this as if in your arrangement the idea of *hutts* had been exchanged for that of *barracks*. This under all the circumstances of the case would be too extensive—and being contrary to my authority from the Secretary of War cannot be ratified. Perhaps nothing more is intended than to procure rough Timber fit for hutts from some spot not distant which would not materially enhance the expence. If so—the business may proceed" (Syrett, *Hamilton Papers*, 23:542–43).

The paragraph in Parker's letter to Hamilton of 10 Oct. that led to what both GW and Parker assured Hamilton was the mistaken notion that Parker intended to build barracks instead of huts at Harpers Ferry reads: "The Ground [for the encampments] that I have described to you Belongs to the public But as there is a Scarcity of materials for Huting; that no time may be lost I have with the advice of Mr Lear employed Mr Mackie the Superintendant of the public works at Harpers [Ferry]; Immediately to procure the necessary Articles for Building" (DLC: Hamilton Papers). What Parker wrote to GW the day before, on 9 Oct., makes his meaning clear: "As Timber for the purpose of making Slabs is verry Scarce in the neighbourhood I have Requested Mr Mackie . . . to procure from The neighbouring saw mills as many Slabs as he Can for the purpose of Covering our Huts."

On 30 Oct. Parker wrote Hamilton: "I Cannot Recollect any expression in my letter which I conceived Coud induce you to Suppose that I meant to Build Barracks instead of Hutts I think I Informed you that As there was not a Sufficiency of Timber on the public ground for Huting or Covering the whole of the Troops I had employed Mr Mackie to procure by Purchase materials (meaning Rough Logs & Board or plank) for that purpose" (DLC: Hamilton Papers). See GW's assurance to Hamilton on 26 Oct. that Hamilton had misunderstood Parker's meaning.

2. For the decision eventually reached for providing winter quarters for the 9th and 10th regiments of the New Army, see Thomas Parker to GW, 24 Oct., n.1. "Yorktown" is York, Pennsylvania.

To William Herbert

Dear Sir,   Mount Vernon 21st Oct. 1799

Enclosed are Two negociable Notes, sent to the Bank of Alexandria for collection. The amount of which, when received, to be placed to my credit.[1]

I begin to feel the necessity more clearly, of renewing my note, than I do a prospect of receiving what is due to me from others. I mention it now that measures for accomplishing of it may be taken in time.[2]

Having forgot the name of the person who has the disposal of Stamps, I take the liberty of sending you enclosed a five dollar bill to be applied in the purchase of them and to pay for those you have been so good as to furnish me.[3]

There are some pecuniary matters between Mr John Gill and me in discharge of which he offers me some land on Difficult run (I think a lot No. 10) which he says is part of Land that belonged to yourself and Mr Swift. If you can give me any information respecting its situation (particularly whether it adjoins a small tract which I have leased to him at the Bridge); the quality of it; his title thereto—&ca &ca I should feel myself obliged thereby.[4] With very great esteem & regard I am Dear Sir Your Most Obedt Hble Servt

Go: Washington

ALS (letterpress copy), NN: Washington Papers.

1. GW wrote below his signature:

"Notes

Jno. G. Ladd 20th Sepr Payable 60 days	$ 80
George Gilpin 23 Augt Do Do	374
	$454"

2. GW's renewed bank note dated at Alexandria, 21 Oct. 1799, reads: "Sixty Days after Date, I promise to pay Wm Herbert or Order Negotiable in the Bank of Alexandria, fifteen Hundred Dollars Value received for the Use of Go: Washington" (ADS, ViMtV).

3. Herbert had written GW on 2 Sept. that "a Mr Page, Who Writes in the Collectors Office, is the Vender of Stamps in this Town."

4. Herbert's response to this letter has not been found. For an account of GW's dealings with John Gill, see GW to Gill, 19 Oct., n.2.

To John Gill

Sir,   Mount Vernon Octr 22d 1799

I have been duly favoured with your letter of the 19th instant.[1]

The sample of the Survey which you sent me will not answer my purpose; for which reason and because I am indisposed to throw difficulties in the way of your wish to cancel our agreement respecting my land on Difficult run, I will agree to take your small tract in discharge of the two years Rent which you are owing me; Provided it does not contain *less* than One hundred acres; and provided also, that upon examination, it shall be found to answer any useful purpose of mine. This examination shall be made as soon as it is convenient. In the meanwhile matters may remain in Statu quo.[2] I take it for granted that the Land you offer, is free from encumbrances, & a good title thereto can be made to— Sir—Your Most Obedt Hble Servt

Go: Washington

ALS (letterpress copy), NN: Washington Papers.
  1. Letter not found.
  2. See GW to Gill, 19 Oct., n.2.

From Thomas Parker

Sir,   Camp Near Harpers ferry 24th Octr [17]99

In Concecuence of the arrangements that I had previously made I arrived here on the 22nd Instant & proceeded Immediately to Cuting Timber for Huting the Troops.

on making an estimate of the Timber & Boards or plank that will be necessary for Covering the three Regiments, I find It utterly Impracticable to procure a Sufficiency, as the Rivers are Too low to Transport it by water from the upper Country & It Cannot be procured in the neighbourhood. Indeed I doubt much whether a Sufficiency of plank Can be obtained for my Regiment only by the first of December.

under these Circumstances I have thought proper to Submit to you whether It woud not be prudent to order the 9th & 10th Regiments to be provided for where they Can be Better Accomodated as I am Clearly Convinced that the Troops must Lie in their Tents the Greater part of the winter If they are Sent to this place.[1]

I am Informed that there are Barracks Sufficient for Two or three Regts at Carlisle and that this place is Surrounded by a Rich & plentifull Country.

Mr Mackee the public Agent at Harpers ferry has Used every exertion in his power to accomodate the Troops he perfectly Coincides with me in opinion and will write to you on the Subject.[2] with the Highest Esteem and Respect I have the honor to be Sir your Obdt Servt

Thomas Park⟨er⟩

ALS, DLC:GW. Noted below the date line: "recd 26 answd 27."

1. For the beginnings of GW's direct involvement in the preparation of winter quarters at Harpers Ferry for the 8th, 9th, and 10th regiments of infantry, see Alexander Hamilton to GW, 23 Sept. 1799; for references to the ensuing correspondence regarding that matter, see notes 3 and 4 of that document. Tobias Lear met with Lieutenant Colonel Parker on 8 Oct. to look over the ground at Harpers Ferry, and returned to Mount Vernon on 13 Oct. with Parker's letter to GW of 9 Oct. (*Diaries*, 6:370). On 18 Oct. Lear wrote Parker that upon reading Parker's letter and a copy of a letter that Lear had written to Parker on 10 Oct., GW had expressed satisfaction with the "measures" being adopted to prepare winter quarters at Harpers Ferry. Lear's letters of 10 and 18 Oct. to Parker are quoted in Parker to GW, 9 Oct., nn.2 and 3. After receiving Lear's letter of 18 Oct., Parker wrote Lear on 28 Oct.: "Before I Received yours of the 18th Instant I had written to General Washington Informing him that I had arrived on my Ground on the Twenty second & had proceeded Immediately to Cuting Timber for Huting my Regiment. You will see from my letter to him my opinion Relative to the Business; But to provide as far as possable for the other Regiments in Case they shoud Come on—I have left the charge of Huting my Regiment for a few days to my majors & am proceeding thrugh the Country in order to Secure & send on all the plank that can be procured. It is my most sincere wish that the Views of Government Shoud be fully Complied with. But I fear without a speedy Rise of the waters (of which there is not the Smallest prospect at present) that the winter will be far advanced Before the Troops can be Covered" (DLC:GW).

On 26 Oct., shortly before he received Parker's letter of 24 Oct., GW wrote to both Hamilton and Parker in optimistic terms about his expectations of the prompt construction of huts at Harpers Ferry for the officers and men of the three regiments. Upon reading this letter of 24 Oct. from Parker and another of the same date from John Mackey expressing a similar pessimistic view of the situation (see note 2), GW on 27 Oct. wrote two letters to Hamilton, and he sent another, by Tobias Lear, to Parker at Harpers Ferry. Lear was sent to Parker to see to it that everything possible would be done to keep the three regiments together over the winter and to keep them in an encampment at Harpers Ferry.

When Gen. Charles Cotesworth Pinckney finally arrived at Harpers Ferry in mid-November, from Rhode Island via New York and Philadelphia, to resume his duties as commander of the forces in the South, Parker's men had almost completed the building of the huts on the Shenandoah to house the soldiers of his

8th Regiment. They also had made a start on the huts for the troops of Col. Josias Carvel Hall's 9th Regiment who were expected to arrive at Harpers Ferry from Havre de Grasse, Md., early in the new year. It had been decided that the 10th Regiment would not come to Virginia but instead would winter in the barracks at Carlisle, Pennsylvania. On 9 Jan. 1800, after GW's death, Pinckney wrote Hamilton from Shepherdstown near Harpers Ferry: "The great drought has greatly retarded the hutting as the Mills could not work for want of Water, and we have been obliged to haul some of the planks the distance of forty miles. This business is however nearly finished" (Syrett, *Hamilton Papers*, 24:181–83). For other letters written about the encampment at Harpers Ferry between 28 Oct. and 16 Nov. both to and by GW, see GW to Benjamin Ogle, 28 Oct., Lear to GW, 30 Oct., 4 Nov., Thomas Parker to GW, 31 Oct., GW to Charles Cotesworth Pinckney, 3 Nov., GW to McHenry, 5 Nov., and notes to all of these documents.

2. John Mackey's letter of 24 Oct. written from Harpers Ferry reads: "At the request of Colonel Thomas Parker, I beg leave to state to you the impracticability of hutting three Regiments at this place under the present circumstances. It appears from General Hamilton's calculations, which are by no means excessive, that 84,000 feet of plank and slabs would be required to cover their huts. Having already drained for the public Buildings erected here, the principal sources from which plank could be expected, and seeing no prospect of getting any down the Potomac, which is now almost dry, I feel no hesitation in declaring that the Supply of Colonel Parker's regiment alone can hardly be effected. For this reason, and because Winter is just at hand, I am clearly of Opinion that the 9th & 10th regiments, if they should be urged forwards, must suffer by the winters cold, which is uncommonly severe between these mountains. If notice had been given last August materials for the three Regiments would have been provided" (DLC:GW).

From Timothy Pickering

(Private)
(& Confidential)
Sir,   Trenton [N.J.] Oct. 24. 1799

I am this evening honoured with your letter of the 20th. When I last wrote you, I had grounds to expect, on the President's arrival; that the mission to France would be suspended, until the fate of its government should be known.[1] This great question I supposed (& my colleagues had formed the same expectation) would be a subject of *consultation*: but we have been disappointed: the *President alone* considered and decided. Whether he has "considered it in all its relations," he only can tell: but if he has, his *conclusions* are *fatally erroneous*: and such clearly was his *reasoning* on the *consequences* of the mission, as recited by Judge Ellsworth, after he &

Govr Davie had dined with the President. He did not consult us, *because he had long deliberated on the subject, had made up his mind, & this was unchangeable.* To this effect he spoke to Mr Stoddert, who after receiving a written order to get the frigate ready, called to ask him some question.

Mr Murray (in letters mostly private, which I have laid before the President) viewing the state of France within, & in its foreign relations, from a near station, supposes the Republic will not survive *six months*:[2] the P. supposes it will last *seven years*; and desires his opinion may be remembered. The P. thinks the French Government will not accept the terms which the Envoys are instructed to propose: that they will speedily return: and that he shall have to recommend to Congress a declaration of war. Fallacious expectation! That Government will hardly hesitate about the terms; for we ask only what we have a clear right to insist on. And if we demanded any thing unreasonable—the French Government, sooner than let the envoys return & hazard immediate war, would yield every thing; with an intention of disregarding its engagements, the moment the pressure of the combined powers should cease, or that peace were made with them. *But as to the French negociation producing a war with England—if it did, England could not hurt us*!!! This last idea was part of Mr Ellsworth's recital to Mr Wolcott and me: I had not patience to hear more: but have desired Mr W. to commit the whole recital to writing; which he promised to do. And yet the P. has several times, in his letters to me from Quincy, mentioned the vast importance of keeping on good terms with England!

Among the most enlightened citizens & truest friends to our country, but one opinion prevails—all deprecate the French mission, as fraught with irreparable mischiefs. *Once* I would have relied on the good sense of the people for a remedy of the mischiefs when assailing us: but my opinion of that good sense is vastly abated: a large proportion seem more readily to embrace falsehood than truth. But I will still hope in the interposition of Providence to save our country: I have been ever fond of the motto— "Never to despair." I am most respectfully Sir, your obt servant

Timothy Pickering

P.S. I suspect la Fayette is coming to America: I saw lately a letter from an Emigrant in Germany, addressed to him in the United States.[3]

ALS, DLC:GW; ALS (letterpress copy), MHi: Pickering Papers.

1. Pickering wrote GW on 9 October. See note 2 of that document.

2. The letter to Pickering from William Vans Murray predicting the fall of the French Republic within six months is dated 28 May 1799, and in the summer of 1799 Murray was writing such things about the French government as "a scene of anarchy can not be very distant" and "It is impossible, I think, that it can last" (Murray to Pickering, 28 May, 20 July 1799, MHi: Pickering Papers; see also Murray to John Quincy Adams, 2 Aug. 1799, in Ford, "Murray-Adams Letters," 580–81).

3. For references to Lafayette's insistence, after his release from imprisonment early in 1799, that he would go to the United States without delay, see particularly Lafayette to GW, 9 May 1799, and William Vans Murray to GW, 17 Aug. 1799, and notes to both documents.

To Alexander Hamilton

Sir,   Mount Vernon, October 26th 1799.

I have duly received your letter of the 21st instant, enclosing a letter to Colo. Parker, which I have forwarded to him, and at the same time repeated my instructions for *hutting* the Troops, in conformity with the idea which you originally suggested.[1]

I presume that the impression made on your mind by Colo. Parker's letter, respecting Winter Quarters for the three Regiments, must have been erroneous.

At the time when I received and transmitted your first letter to Colo. Parker on this subject,[2] Mr Lear was in Berkley, and as he was well acquainted with the public ground at Harper's Ferry, and other situations in the vicinity of it, he informs me that Colo. Parker requested he would accompany him to that place, and give him any information and assistance in his power towards carrying into effect the orders for hutting the Troops. This was readily complied with; and upon an examination of the public ground, and making the necessary enquiries, it was determined that no situation in the vicinity of Harper's Ferry (even if it could have been obtained) was so eligable as that belonging to the United States. Colo. Parker therefore fixed upon a spot which appeared, on every account, the most convenient for hutting, and determined that the huts (which were to be built by the Soldiers) should be made of rough logs, 16 feet sqr. each (to contain 12 men) and covered with slabs, which would be much cheaper than plank or boards. As the timber which could be had from the public ground might not be sufficient for more than one half the huts wanting,

Colo. Parker requested Mr Mackie, Agent for the War Department at Harper's Ferry, to make the necessary enquiries and engagements for procuring such further quantity of logs and slabs as might be wanting. His motive for engaging Mr Mackie in the business was, that, as he had been in the habit of procuring articles for public use in that part of the Country, he could do it to more advantage than any other person, and his enquiries for them would not be so likely to raise the price as would those of another Agent. Had any other place been fixed upon for hutting the Troops, the purchase of timber, fuel &c. &c. would have been as necessary as at this; and in no situation proper for the Troops could they have been procured cheaper.

From the foregoing account, which is given to me by Mr Lear (to whom Colo. Parker refered me for particular information respecting the arrangements he had made for hutting the Troops) you will see that Barracks were not contemplated by Colo. Parker, and that the huts were to be built in as œconomical a manner as could be expected. I have, however, as I observed before, repeated my instructions to Colo. Parker, that the Troops should be hutted in the manner they were in the late war, which he must well recollect.

Presuming that the plan of Barracks has never been substituted by Colo. Parker for that of huts, it is, in my opinion, unnecessary to make any arrangements for quartering the 9th & 10th Regiments in the places which you suggest, vizt at Frederick town and Carlisle. From the view which I had of the Barracks at the latter place in the year 1794, I am convinced that the expense of repairing them, fit for the Soldiers during winter, would be much greater than that of building huts. What the situation of the Barracks at Frederick Town is, I am unable to say; but I presume they are not much, if any, better than those at Carlisle. And, at any rate, this dispersed situation of the Troops would defeat a primary and important object, I mean that of having them in one body, where they can be under the eye of a General Officer, and where the disciplining and training the Soldiers can be much better effected than if they were in detached Corps.

From the information of a Gentleman lately from Winchester, I have reason to beleive that Colo. Parker's Regiment is at Harper's Ferry before this; and I think no time should be lost in ordering the other Regiments to the same place; for there cannot be a doubt, from the circumstances mentioned in this letter, but that Colo. Parker has taken measures for hutting the Troops agreeably to our original idea; and as the Soldiers will build their own huts, it is necessary they should begin them as soon as possible.[3]

I cannot close this letter without mentioning that I have heard of repeated complaints for want of money to pay the Troops raised in this quarter, as well as for other purposes relating to them. If these complaints are well founded, you know, as well as I do, the evils which must result from such defect, and I cannot but be astonished at it, when it is well known that appropriations are made for the pay and support of the Troops, and the money is undoubtedly in the Treasury. I would wish you to inquire into this matter, and if the complaints are founded, it would be well to know from whence proceeds the inattention or deficiency. With very great esteem & regard, I am Sir, Your most obedt Servt

Go: Washington

LS, DLC: Hamilton Papers; Df, DLC:GW. Both the LS and the draft are in Tobias Lear's hand.

1. GW's letter to Thomas Parker is dated 26 October. Hamilton's letter of 21 Oct. to Parker is quoted in Hamilton to GW, 21 Oct. (second letter), n.1.

2. Hamilton's letter to Parker of 23 Sept. is quoted in Hamilton to GW, 23 Sept., n.3.

3. See the two letters that GW wrote to Hamilton the next day, 27 Oct., after receiving the letters of 24 Oct. from John Mackey and Thomas Parker with their discouraging reports about the unavailability of lumber to build the huts for the Harpers Ferry encampments. For further details about this problem, see also Parker to GW, 24 Oct., n.1.

To Daniel Morgan

Dear Sir,　　　　　　　　　　　　　　Mount Vernon Octr 26th 1799

Your favour of the 8th instt came duly to hand, and I should have given it an earlier acknowledgment, but waited to see Mr Law[renc]e Lewis, whom I expected here every day, before I did so.[1]

He is now arrived, and informs me that his brother John (as Executor of his father's Will) is determined not to pay your demand against that Estate unless he is compelled to it; and that he has requested a suit might be brought to try the merits of the case.

Under these circumstances I conceived it would be needless to write to him on the subject, and therefore return his father's letter to you, under this cover, by the Post, as the most certain means of its getting safe to your hands.[2] With great esteem & regard. I am—Dear Sir Your Most Obedient Hbl. Servant

Go: Washington

P.S. I was near forgetting to inform you, that if the *original* Deed of conveyance from me (as Attorney for Colo. George Mercer) to Colo. Fielding Lewis, is produced, that I shall have no objection to certifying before fresh evidence that I did at the time—& in the manner specified in the Instrument, put my signature thereto. But I can do no *new act* relative to this business; having invariably refused this in similar cases—the business being taken out of my hands by a Decree of the high Court of Chancery in this Commonwealth.[3]

ALS, NN: Myers Collection; ALS (letterpress copy), NN: Washington Papers.

1. Letter not found.

2. John Lewis was the eldest son of Fielding Lewis and the half brother of GW's nephew Lawrence Lewis.

3. For references to the sale conducted in November 1774 by GW as trustee of George Mercer's lands in the Bull Run Mountains in Loudoun County and on the Shenandoah River in Frederick County, see GW to John Tayloe, 30 Nov. 1774, n.2, in *Papers, Colonial Series*, 10:192. Disputes over titles to land parcels bought at the sale and other such matters had plagued GW for a quarter of a century. See, for instance, Edward Snickers to GW, 17 May 1784, and note 1 to that document, and GW to Francis Lightfoot Lee and Ralph Wormeley, Jr., 20 June 1784, and source note of that document, in *Papers, Confederation Series*, 1:392–94, 458–65. Under a decree of the Virginia General Court, dated 9 Nov. 1782, GW transferred to John Francis Mercer, half brother of George, the trusteeship of the George Mercer property sold in 1774 (see GW to John Sedwick, 8 Aug. 1785, n.1, in *Papers, Confederation Series*, 3:178).

On the day after this, 27 Oct., GW wrote to Alexander Spotswood and attached this identical postscript to that letter. GW's letter to Spotswood reads: "Dear Sir, Your letter of the 30th ulto came duly to hand, but as it appeared from the tenor of it, that I might soon expect another from you, with my Deed in the hands of Mr Jno. Brooke (one of the Administrators of Jas Mercer Esqr. deceased) I intended to have postponed the acknowledgment thereof until then; but as Mr Brooke seems to have forgot *his* promise, I shall no longer delay thanking you for the trouble you have been at, on my Account, in this business. My best wishes in wch Mrs Washington and the family at this place unite, are offered for yourself Mrs Spotswood and all at New Post. With very great esteem & regard I am—Dear Sir Your Obedt Hble Servt Go: Washington" (letterpress copy, NN: Washington Papers). Spotswood's letter of 30 Sept. 1799 has not been found, but he and GW had earlier exchanged letters about the administrators of James Mercer's estate. See Spotswood to GW, 25 July, and note 1 of that document.

To William Vans Murray

Dear Sir,   Mount Vernon Octr 26th 1799

Within the space of a few days, I have been favoured with your letters of the 26th of July, and duplicate of one of the 7th of April (the original is missing)—and of those dated the 9th and 17th of August, with their enclosures.[1]

For the information given in these, and for your kindness in sending me a sketch of the Water throwing Mill, I feel much obliged, and thank you for the trouble you have been at in making the drawing of it; being persuaded of its utility, although advanced as I am, and engaged in other pursuits, I shall not be able to avail myself of the insight it conveys. Others however may, and I shall take care to make it known on all proper occasions.

The Affairs of Europe have taken a most important, and interesting turn. What will be the final result of the uninterrupted successes of the combined Arms, (so far as the accounts which have been received in this Country, are brought down) is not for a man at the distance of 3000 miles from the great theatre of action, to predict; but he may wish, and ardently wish on principles of humanity, and for the benevolent purpose of putting a stop to the further effusion of human blood, that the successful Powers may know at what Point to give cessation to the Sword, for the purpose of negociation. It is not uncommon, however, in prosperous gales, to forget that adverse winds may blow. Such *was* the case with France. Such *may* be the case of the Coalesced Powers, against her. A by stander sees more of the game, generally, than those who are playing it; so, Neutral Nations may be better enabled to draw a line between the contending Parties, than those who are Actors in the War. My own wish is, to see every thing settled upon the best and surest foundation for the Peace & happiness of mankind, without regard to this, that, or the other Nation. A more destructive Sword never was drawn (at least in modern times) than this war has produced. It is time to sheath it, and give Peace to mankind.

A severe Electioneering contest has just closed in the state of Pennsylvania—adverse to ⟨the fortunes of⟩ the Federal Party, by a considerable majority in favour of Chief Justice McKean agt Mr Ross, Senator for that State. Great pains was taken on *both* sides, and considerable abuse of character ⟨*illegible*⟩ neither was exempt from it.[2]

You are going to be employed in an important, & delicate Negociation; for the success of which, in *all* its ⟨respects⟩, no one more ardently, and ⟨*illegible*⟩ than I do. Your Colleagues in this business will be able to give you such accurate details of the internal concerns of our Country, as not only to render any attempt of mine to do it nugatory, but injudicious; for which reason I shall refer you to them for the state of our Political ⟨Prospects⟩ &ca.

I most devoutly wish that the cogent—indeed unanswerable arguments you urged to dissuade our friend [   ] from visiting the United States in the present crisis of our Affairs may have prevailed. The measure would be injudicious in *every* point of view (so says my judgment) in which it can be placed. Embarrassing to himself—Embarrassing to his friends. and possibly embarrassing to the Government in the result.[3] ⟨His final⟩ decision however must have been made 'ere this, I shall add no more on this head—nor indeed, for the reasons already assigned, on any other subject.

Mrs Washington who has been much indisposed for sometime past—(now better) unites her best wishes with mine, for Mrs Murray & yourself; and with sincere and affectionate esteem & regard, I am always Dear Sir, Your Most Obedient, and Very Humble Servant

Go: Washington

ALS (letterpress copy), DLC:GW.

1. Only the letter of 17 Aug. has been found.

2. Thomas McKean was elected governor over James Ross by a margin of more than five thousand of the approximately seventy thousand votes cast (Tinkcom, *Republicans and Federalists in Pennsylvania*, 238). The Federalists tended to blame the Pennsylvania-German vote for the defeat. See, for example, Alexander Addison to GW, 8 November.

3. GW is referring to Lafayette. See Murray to GW, 17 Aug. 1799, and note 1 of that document.

To Thomas Parker

(Copy)

Sir,   Mount Vernon, Octr 26th 1799.

You will perceive, by the enclosed letter from General Hamilton, that he has taken up an idea, founded upon your communication to him on the subject, that you had substituted Barracks, instead of huts, for the Winter Quarters of the three Regiments ⟨at⟩ Harper's Ferry.[1]

I presume that Genl Hamilton must have had an erroneous im-

pression made on his mind by some expression in your letter
to him; for, agreeably to the instructions contained in his first
letter to you, which were confirmed by me in my letter of the
28th ultimo, nothing more was intended than that *huts* should be
built for the temporary accommodation of the Troops, in the
same manner as they were in the late War for the Winter Quarters
of the Army, and I recommended to you a regularity in building,
similar to what was observed, on like occasions, during the
Revolution.

The information which I received from Mr Lear, to whom you
refered me for particulars on this subject, was, that, upon examination of the ground, and every enquiry you could make, no
place was found more eligable than the public ground at Harper's
Ferry—that you had fixed upon a spot for that purpose, as mentioned in your letter to me—that you had determined to have the
huts built by the Soldiers, of rough logs, and covered with slabs, as
the cheapest covering, to be about 16 feet square, and to contain
12 men each—that, as the timber on the public ground would not
afford logs enough for more huts than would accommodate one,
or one and an half Regimt you had requested Mr Mackey, Agent
for the War Department at Harper's Ferry, to engage slabs and
such logs as could not be furnished from the public ground—
that, altho' it would have been desireable to have had timber and
fuel on the spot sufficient for hutting and furnishing the Troops;
yet, as this cou⟨ld⟩ not have been done in the vicinity of Harper's
Ferry without making a purchase of those Articles, it was concluded that, under all circumstances, they would come as cheap to
the public at Harper's Ferry as at any other place—And, that, as
you conceived the present accommodations would be merely temporary, you should make them as œconomical as circumstances
would permit.[2]

Under the impression made by this information, I approved the
measures you had taken for hutting the Troops, and I am persuaded that General Hamilton must have been under some mis-
apprehension when he concluded that you intended to substitute
Barracks for huts. I have therefore written to him fully on the
subject, explaining it agreeably to the information given me by
Mr Lear;[3] and have desired him to order the other Regiments to
Harper's Ferry without delay, where I presume your's is already,
and I trust that every arrangement in your power will be made to

enable the Troops to commence building their huts immediately on their arrival.

You will see the necessity of your answering General Hamilton's letter without delay, and giving him every information on the subject of it. You will also be pleased to let me know if you have seen cause to deviate from the general plan of hutting the Troops which you at first proposed, and which was communicated by Mr Lear, as stated in this letter.[4] With great esteem & regard I am &c &c

G. Washington

Copy, DLC: Hamilton Papers; Df, DLC:GW. Both copies are in Tobias Lear's hand.

1. Alexander Hamilton's letter to Parker of 21 Oct. is quoted in note 1 to Hamilton's second letter to GW of the same date.

2. See Parker to GW, 9 Oct., and notes 2 and 3 to that document.

3. GW wrote Hamilton on this date.

4. Parker wrote to Hamilton on 30 Oct. about Hamilton's misreading of Parker's letter to him of 10 October. Parker's letter to Hamilton is quoted in part in Hamilton to GW, 21 Oct. (second letter), n.1. GW wrote Parker again the next day, after receiving Parker's letter of 24 Oct., and GW sent his letter to Parker of 27 Oct. to Harpers Ferry by special messenger.

To Alexander Hamilton

Sir, Mount Vernon, Octr 27th 1799.

Since writing the enclosed letter to you yesterday, I have received a letter from Colo. Parker, and one from Mr Mackey, Agent for the War Department at Harper's Ferry; stating the impracticability of procuring plank &c. sufficient for covering the huts intended to have been built for three Regiments at Harper's Ferry.[1]

In consequence of this information I have again written to Colo. Parker, under this date, by Express, conforming my instructions, respecting Winter Quarters for the Troops, to the present state of things. I enclose a copy of my letter to him of this date, as well as that of yesterday, which will exhibit a full view of the business, and enable you to give any additional instructions you may think proper, directly to Colonel Parker.

Altho' I had determined to take no charge of any military operations, unless the Troops should be called into the field; yet, under the present circumstances, and considering that the advanced season of the year will admit of no delay in providing Winter Quarters for the Troops, I have willingly given my aid in this business, and shall never decline any assistance in my power, when necessary, to promote the good of the Service.

On the first view, I supposed that the Regiment in this State, commanded by Colo. Bentley, was included in the three to be stationed at Harper's Ferry. I find, however, that it is not. What provision is made for the Winter Quarters of that Regiment?[2]

I have not said anything to Colo. Parker respecting compensation, or reimbursement of Expences he may incur by attending to Quartering the other Regiments, if they are seperated from his. On this subject you will be pleased to write him, if necessary. With very great esteem & regard, I am, Sir, Your most obedt Servt

Go: Washington

LS, DLC: Hamilton Papers; Df, in Tobias Lear's hand, DLC:GW.

1. The letters from Thomas Parker and John Mackey are both dated 24 October.

2. William C. Bentley was the lieutenant colonel commandant of the 7th Infantry Regiment, stationed in Richmond, Virginia. Hamilton's plan was for Bentley's regiment to join the two southern regiments, the 5th and the 6th, at a winter encampment on the Savannah River near Augusta, Georgia. That encampment was never built.

To Alexander Hamilton

Private
Dear Sir,					Mount Vernon 27th Octr 1799
To my official letters I refer you for my communications with Colo. Parker. I have no conception however, that such difficulties as are ennumerated in his and Mr Mackie's letters, can exist in the erection of simple Hutts, (such as served us last War); and so I am about to inform the former.

I am averse to the seperation of the 8th 9th and 10th Regiments under any circumstances which exist at present; and still more so to the distribution of them into *three States*. If they cannot *all* be accomodated at Harpers Ferry, the Barracks at Frederick town (if sufficient to contain two Regiments) is to be preferred, vastly, to Carlisle; for as much as that it is only twenty miles from the Arsenal which is in great forwardness at the former place; and because fuel alone, at either Frederick Town or Carlisle for the Winter, would double all the expence of the establishment at Harpers ferry.[1] I have gone thus far into this business, and have given these opinions, because you desired it; and because, from the peculiar situation of things, it seemed, in a manner, almost indispensable. But I wish exceedingly, that the State of Mrs Pinckney's health, and other circumstances, would permit General Pinckney to come forward, and on his *own view* to decide on matters. To engage partially in Military arrangements is not only contrary to my original design, but unpleasant in its nature & operation; inasmuch as it incurs responsibility without proper means for decision.

With respect to Major Campbell, or any of those who are applying for appointments in the Inspectorate, I have no predeliction whatsoever towards them; handing in their names, with the testimonials of their merit & fitness as I receive them, for information *only*, is all I have in view.[2]

The purport of your (private) letter of the 21st, with respect to a late decision, has surprized me exceedingly.[3] I was surprized at the *measure*, how much more so at the manner of it? This business seems to have commenced in an evil hour, and under unfavourable auspices; and I wish mischief may not tread in all its steps, and be the final result of the measure. A wide door was open, through which a retreat might have been made from the first faux-p⟨eaux the shut⟩ting of which, to those who are not behind the Curtain, and are as little acquainted with the Secrets of the Cabinet as I am, is, from the present aspect of European Affairs, incomprehensible. But I have the same reliance on Providence which you express, and trust that matters will *end well*, however unfavourable they may appear at present. With very great esteem & regard I am, My dear Sir Your Most Obedt & Affecte

Go: Washington

ALS, DLC: Hamilton Papers; ALS (letterpress copy), DLC:GW. The cover is docketed, "Filed in a bundle private & Confidential."

1. See Thomas Parker to GW, 24 Oct., n.1.

2. For references to Maj. William Campbell's seeking to become division inspector in the army, see GW to Hamilton, 15 Oct., n.3.

3. GW refers to Hamilton's first letter of 21 October.

To James McHenry

Sir,   Mount Vernon Octr 27th 1799

The enclosed letters, from Genl Morgan and Captn G. S. Washington, recommending the Revd Mr Hill, as Chaplin to the Troops about to be stationed at Harper's Ferry, have come to my hands, and are now forwarded for your inspection.[1]

I do not observe in the "Act for the better organizing the Troops of the U.S. &c." that any provision is made for Chaplins. Whether they are provided for in any other existing law, you can best tell. Mr Hill appears to be a deserving and valuable Character; but from the tenor of General Morgan's letter, he seems rather to have it in view to officiate for a time with the Troops that may be at Harper's Ferry, than to wish a permanent appointment. Whether this is his intention or not I cannot say, neither do I know whether his services could be admitted on those terms. With your first convenience I will thank you to inform me on this subject.[2] With due consideration I have the honor to be, Sir, Your most obedt Sert

Df, DLC:GW.

1. The letters from Daniel Morgan and George Steptoe Washington have not been found, but GW wrote Morgan on 26 Oct.: "Dear Sir, I have been duly favoured with your letter of the 19th instant, recommending the Revd Mr Hill as Chaplin to the Troops to be stationed at, Harper's Ferry.

"I do not know whether any provision has been made for Chaplins, and, at any rate, I cannot tell whether or not it will be thought proper to engage a temporary Chaplin, which, from the tenor of your letter seems to be Mr Hill's object. I shall, however, transmit your letter to the Secretary of War, and will communicate to you whatever he may give me in reply on the subject.

"If provision is not already made for Chaplins I think it will be done; and it would certainly be very desireable to engage in that capacity such respectable Characters as Mr Hill appears to be. Wishing a perfect restoration of your health, I am, with very great regard, Dear Sir, Your most obedt Servt Go: Washington" (LS, PHi: Dreer Collection; Df, DLC:GW).

After receiving GW's letter Morgan wrote from Soldiers Rest in Berkeley County on 7 Nov.: "I take the liberty to inclose you a duplicate of a letter I wrote to the Secretary of War respecting the Revd William Hill, since I was honored with your answer to my letter on that occasion" (DLC:GW). The enclosed copy of Morgan's letter of 6 Nov. to McHenry reads: "I wrote to the Commander in Chief recommending the Revd William Hill as Chaplin to the three Regiments to be stationed at Harpers ferry; he writes me in answer to my letter that he does not know whether any provision has been made for Chaplins to the Army, or at any rate, cannot tell whether or not it will be thought proper to engage a temporary Chaplin. I have shewed his answer to Mr Hill who says he is willing to continue so long as his services are wanting, and to march with the Troops—in case it should be thought necessary that they move. I have only to add that Mr Hill is a man of great information and withal a very amiable character, a great Supporter of our present Government and contributed greatly to give us a federal representative in this District; if he is appointed he wishes to be annexed to the Southern Brigade, and I wish this myself, as a man of his talents and application may be of great benefit to the Southward Citizens" (DLC:GW).

2. No response from McHenry to this inquiry has been found, nor is there any further reference in GW's papers to a chaplain for the troops. On 29 Oct. Col. Thomas Parker wrote Alexander Hamilton that "the Reverend Mr Hill of Berkley offers his Services," and he then went on to say that if there was to be a chaplain at Harpers Ferry, Hill would be a good choice (DLC: Hamilton Papers).

To Thomas Parker

Sir,   Mount Vernon, Octr 27th 1799

I wrote to you very fully yesterday on the subject of hutting the Troops at Harper's Ferry, and enclosed a letter from General Hamilton on the same subject. The messenger who took that letter to the Post Office, brought from thence your letter of the 24th inst., and one of the same date from Mr Mackey.

As these letters contain information which may make it proper to countermand, in some measure, the instructions given in my letter of yesterday, I shall be obliged to send this by a special Messenger, as the Mail for Berkley County left Alexa. early this morning, and will not go into that part of the Country again 'till next week.[1]

As a primary object in quartering three Regts at Harper's Ferry, was, to collect the Troops in as large bodies as could conveniently be done, from whence many advantages would result, particularly in training and disciplining the Soldiers, I confess I am not a little mortified that the impracticability of getting plank &c. at that place, for building huts, as stated in the letters from yourself and Mr Mackey, seems likely to defeat this design. I can hardly conceive how the quantity of plank mentioned by Mr Mackey, as the calculation of Genl Hamilton, vizt 84,000 feet, could be wanting;[2] as the intention was to have the huts built in the manner they used to be for our Army in the late War, when we found no difficulty in having the logs cut and the huts built by the Soldiers, in a very short time, without the aid of large quantities of plank. They were covered in the same manner as are the common log Cabbins which are found in every part of the Country; and the principal, and indeed only use for plank, was to make floors for the Officers' huts, and doors &c. for the others.

If it be possible to have the three Regiments provided for, *in this way*, at Harper's Ferry, it is very desireable that it should be done. But if that is impracticable, then you will be pleased to hut your own Regiment there, and another, if possible; and the remainder must be quartered as near to that place as accommodations can be had; which, I presume, will be at Frederick Town; where, I am informed, there are Barracks belonging to the State of Maryland, which, I have no doubt, can be borrowed for this winter, if they can be made comfortable for the Troops at any reasonable expense.

You will, therefore, after determining as precisely as may be, what number of Troops can be quartered at Harper's Ferry, proceed to Frederick Town, examine the state of the Barracks there—make such enquiries and estimates as will enable you to determine, with certainty, how many Troops can be accommodated there—and take such measures as to enable you, if possible, to have the whole of the three Regiments, vizt the 8th 9th & 10th stationed there and at Harper's Ferry.

Altho' there are Barracks at Carlisle; yet, from the view which I had of them in the year 1794, I am persuaded the expense of making them fit for winter quarters, would be at least as much as to build huts where all the materials are to be purchased. And its distance from the central point of Rendezvous (Harper's Ferry) would make it very objectionable on that ground. My wish is, if these Regiments cannot be collected to *one* point, that they should not occupy more than two places, and these as near to each other as the nature of the thing will permit.[3]

Another disadvantage would attend their being quartered at Carlisle (which indeed applies also to Frederick town)—I mean the heavy expense of fuel in an open Country, and in the neighbourhood of a considerable town. This would be an additional motive for concertering the Troops as much as possible; for a large number in one body will not consume so much as they would if divided.

General Hamilton informs me that the 9th Regt is ordered to Frederick town, and the 10th to York town, there to receive further orders.[4] And as these will be merely halting places, until arrangements are made for Winter Quarters, you will see the necessity of a prompt execution of the instructions contained in this letter, a copy of which I shall forward to General Hamilton; to whom, as well as to myself, you will be pleased to make a Report of your proceedings.[5] I am &c.

(signed) G. Washington

Copy, DLC: Hamilton Papers; Df, DLC:GW. Both copies are in Tobias Lear's hand.

1. Tobias Lear, it would seem, was the special messenger. See Lear to GW, 30 Oct., n.1.

2. In a letter to Alexander Hamilton of 29 Oct., Parker enclosed his estimate of the planking that would be needed to build the huts at Harpers Ferry, 48,540 feet (DLC: Hamilton Papers). In his letter to GW of 24 Oct., Mackey had estimated that 84,000 feet "of plank and slabs would be required to cover their huts."

3. For reference to the correspondence regarding these matters, see Parker to GW, 24 Oct., n.1.

4. These are York in Pennsylvania and Frederick in Maryland.

5. In the draft of this letter, Lear wrote this additional closing paragraph: "As it was my declared resolution, when I accepted the command of the Army, not to take charge of any military operations unless the Army should be called into the field, I have given these instructions at the pressing desire of General Hamilton, as his distance from the part of the Country where these Regts are to be quartered, would occasion delays in his communications which at this advanced state of the Season might be very injurious to the service. With great esteem & regard, I am Sir, Your most Obet Servt."

To Benjamin Ogle

Sir,   Mount Vernon, Octr 28th 1799.

It having been determined to station three Regiments of the United States Troops at Harper's Ferry, orders were given to provide huts there for their winter Quarters; but, from the Report of Colo. Parker, the Officer to whom this business was committed, it appears impracticable to provide the materials, in due season, to build the huts at that place. It therefore becomes necessary to procure other quarters without delay: And as the Barracks near Frederick town, belonging, as I am informed, to the State of Maryland, would probably, on many accounts, be the most eligible, I have to request the favor of Your Excellency to let me know if they could be had this winter, for the use of the United States, in case they should be wanting, and should be found, on inspection, to answer the purpose without incurring an unreasonable expence to the United States.[1]

Your Excellency's answer to this, as soon as is convenient, will much oblige me. And, if there be no objection to the Barracks being occupied by the United States Troops, if wanting, it would save much time to have some person, in or near Frederick Town, empowered to communicate on the subject with Colo. Thomas Parker, of the eighth United States Regiment, to whose charge this business is committed, and who will be either at Frederick town, or with his Regiment at Harper's Ferry.

Altho' it was my determination, when I accepted the Command of the Army, not to take charge of any military operations, unless the Troops should be called into the Field; yet, on the present occasion, I am urged to give some instructions for providing Winter Quarters for three Regiments which are to be stationed at or near Harper's Ferry, as much delay, and consequently injury to the service at this advanced season, would arise from waiting for communications from Genl Hamilton, at the distance he is from that part of the Country. It is therefore owing to this cause that I address your Excellency on this subject.[2] With great Respect, I have the honor to be Your Excellency's most obedt Servt

Go: Washington

LS, MdAA; Df, DLC:GW. Both are in the hand of Tobias Lear.

1. For GW's present view on providing winter quarters for the 8th, 9th, and 10th regiments, see GW to Thomas Parker, 27 October.

2. Benjamin Ogle, governor of Maryland since 1798, wrote to GW from "In Council Annapolis" on 2 Nov.: "Sir, We have had the honour to receive your Letter of the twenty eighth ultimo, requesting the use of the Barracks at Frederick Town for the Troops of the United States. and have concluded that they may be used for that purpose. Agreeably to your desire we have appointed George Murdock, Philip Thomas and Valentine Brother Esquires who are the Agents for the State for other purposes respecting these Barracks to communicate our determination on this subject to Colonel Parker" (MdAA: Council Letter Book, 1796–1818).

On 4 Nov. Tobias Lear wrote GW that he and Col. Thomas Parker had gone into Frederick from Harpers Ferry "to examine the state of the Barracks there." Finding them "in the most ruinous condition," they had decided "that nothing could be done to render them habitable for Troops this winter." After receiving this report, GW wrote Ogle on 11 Nov.: "Sir, On my return home yesterday, after an absence of a few days, I had the honor to receive Your Excellency's letter of the 2d Instant, and am much obliged by your polite attention to my request respecting the Barracks at Frederick Town. But as they were found, upon Colo. Parker's inspecting them, to be so much out of repair as not to admit of their being put in order for the reception of Troops in due season, measures have been taken to provide other quarters. With great Respect, I have the honor to be, Your Excellency's most Obedt Servt Go: Washington" (LS, MdAA; Df, DLC:GW).

Letter not found: to Thomas Parker, 28 Oct. 1799. On 31 Oct. Parker wrote: "I last evening Received your letters of the 26th 27th & 28th Instant."

To William Augustine Washington

My dear Sir,   Mount Vernon Octr 29th 1799

Your letter of the 8th instant has been duly received,[1] and this letter will be handed to you by Mr Lawe Lewis, to whom I have rented my Mill & Distillery, and who comes into your parts to see if he can procure (on reasonable terms) grain with which to keep them employed. Your advice and aid in enabling him to obtain these would be serviceable to him, & obliging to me. Mr Lewis is a cautious man, and I persuade myself will scrupulously fulfill any Contracts he may enter into. You will be perfectly safe, I conceive, in declaring this.[2]

Two hundred gallons of Whiskey will be ready this day for your call, and the sooner it is taken the better, as the demand for this article (in these parts) is brisk. The Rye may be sent when it suits your convenience—letting me know, in the meantime, the quantity I may rely on, that my purchase of this grain may be regulated thereby.[3]

Mrs Washington has got tolerably well again, and unites with me in every good wish for you and yours. With very great esteem and friendship I remain Your Affectionate Uncle

Go: Washington

ALS (letterpress copy), NN: Washington Papers.

1. Letter not found.

2. For the recent reorganization of the Mount Vernon properties, see GW to Anderson, 10 Sept., n.2. See also GW to Lawrence Lewis, 20 September.

3. See GW to W.A. Washington, 7 Oct., and note 2 of that document.

From Tobias Lear

Dear Sir   Harper's Ferry Octr 30th 1799

I arrived at this place yesterday afternoon, and finding that Colo. Parker had gone to Winchester I dispatched a messinger for him (one of the Soldiers). He got here this afternoon, when I delivered him your letters.[1]

The huts for the 8th Regt are in a state of forwardness; 22 of them are finished to the roofs; several of which are now covering, they are 16 feet sqr. and intended for 12 men each. There are logs provided, with the huts now up, enough to quarter this Regt. About twelve thousand feet of plank are on the ground, and enough to cover the huts, now preparing, will be soon here.

A person (Mr Wilson) who has the lease of a part of the ground, adjoining the public's, has offered 150 Acres for sale at £500—Virga Currency. The lease is for fifty years, yet to come, @ 6£ pr hundred per year. On this ground there is timber sufficient for logs to hut the two Regts vizt the 9th & 10th, and a considerable quantity of fuel. This, I think, will be purchased, and the logs cut immediately. The plank, for covering, can be had by the time the huts are ready to receive it; and it will be a cheap purchase for the United States if only the logs and fuel are considered, independent of the ground. Upon the whole it will be best to cover the huts with plank, as they will be so put on as to be but little injured, and may serve the public hereafter at this place, where a quantity will be wanted.

Colo. Parker and myself go over to Frederick town tomorrow morning, to look at the Barracks &c.—not so much with a view of making use of them, as to hold up an idea that a part of the troops will be quartered there, to induce Mr Wilson to take a less price for his land, which Major Campbell, to whom he has offered it for his own use, is desired to secure.[2]

I have today been over the ground belonging to the United States, and that offered for sale, and I am convinced that there can be no doubt of getting sufficient timber therefrom to hut the three Regiments (and a Battalion of Artillery, if necessary, which is ordered to this place) and to supply them very amply with fuel for *at least* the ensuing winter. Colo. Parker seems anxious to make every preparation, and I am persuaded that the Troops destined for this place can be accommodated here this winter at as little expence to the United States as they could be in any other place: and the other advantages which arise from their being embodied must be very great.

I hope to be at Mount Vernon by Saturday next. At present I see nothing to prevent it. But I shall not return until I can give you a precise account of the Winter Quarters for the three Regiments.[3]

My best respects attend Mrs Washington and the family at Mount Vernon. With the purest respect & attachment I have the honor to be, Your most affectionate & Obedt St

Tobias Lear

ALS, DLC:GW.

1. GW had sent "to the Post Office" by messenger on 27 Oct. his letter to Thomas Parker of 26 Oct. enclosing a letter for him from Alexander Hamilton dated 21 October. He wrote Parker again on 27 Oct. and sent that letter to Harpers Ferry by Tobias Lear. Presumably the letters that Lear delivered to Parker were the one of 27 Oct. and perhaps a copy of that of 26 Oct. or a missing letter of 28 Oct. (see Parker to GW, 31 October). Lear on 28 Oct. had "set out for Harpers Ferry to make some arrangements with Colo. Parker respecting Cantoning the Troops" (*Diaries*, 6:372). On 30 Oct. Parker wrote Hamilton: "Colo. Lear is now with me by order of the Commander in Chief to assist me in Endeavouring to procure the necessary materials for Accomodating the other Troops. we are on Treaty for the purchase of a piece of Land adjoining to that Belonging to the public . . ." (DLC: Hamilton Papers). Parker was in Winchester on 29 Oct. in search of logs (Parker to Hamilton, 29 Oct., DLC: Hamilton Papers).

2. Thomas Wilson was paid $2,148.66 for a little less than two hundred acres of land at Harpers Ferry on 11 Dec. 1799 (Parker to Hamilton, 10 Oct. 1799, n.1, in Syrett, *Hamilton Papers*, 23:515).

3. For Lear's full report on his mission to Harpers Ferry and to Frederick, Md., see Lear to GW, 4 Nov., written on the day of his return to Mount Vernon.

Letter not found: from Allyn Prior, 30 Oct. 1799. On 1 Nov. GW wrote Prior: "Your letter of the 30th Ulto came to my hands yesterday afternoon."

From Thomas Parker

Sir,   Camp near Harpers ferry 31st Octr 1799

I last evening Received your letters of the 26th 27th & 28th Instant.[1]

I Cannot Recollect any expression in my letter to Genl Hamilton which I supposed Coud have Induced him to Suppose that I meant to Substitute Barracks instead of Hutts.

I merely Informed him that as there was not on the Public Ground materials Sufficient to Cover the whole of The Troops that I had Requested Mr Mackie to procure Them.[2]

I have proceeded to Huting my Regiment in the Manner practiced during the Revolutionary war with this difference that we are obliged to Cover with plank instead of the Common Cabin Slabs Timber for which Cannot be procured in this Country.

This will account for the Quantity of Plank which Genl Hamilton Calculates on & which will fall Verry short of the Quantity Requisite.

you Can Hardly Conceive how this Country has been pillaged of Timber proper for Slabs. there is not a Tree on the public Ground fit for the purpose & the few that Coud be obtained in the neighbourhood woud Come Higher than plank which may be Sold when the public have no further Use for it at Verry little loss.

we are Endeavouring to purchase a piece of woodland adjoining to the public Ground. If we Can accomplish It I hope we shall be able to provide for at least a part If not the whole of The Troops.

you may Rely on it Sir that no one has felt Greater Ansiety to have the wishes of Government Gratifed than I have & I Shall still Continue to do every thing in my power to effect it.

I Shall go to Frederick Town this day to examine into the State of The Barracks at that place in Case It shoud be found necessary to Quarter any of the Troops there. with every Sentiment of Esteem & Respect Sir your Obedient Servant

Thomas Parker

Colo. Lear who Goes with me to Frederick Town will write you by the mail I find his presence & advice extreamely Serviceable to me.[3]

ALS, DLC:GW. The letter cover is marked "Charles Town Octr 31."

1. No letter from GW to Parker dated 28 Oct. has been found. See Lear to GW, 30 Oct., n.1.

2. See GW to Alexander Hamilton, 15 Oct., n.2.

3. Lear wrote GW on 30 Oct., but see especially Lear's full report to GW of 4 November.

To Allyn Prior

Sir,   Mount Vernon Novr 1st 1799

Your letter of the 30th Ulto came to my hands yesterday afternoon.[1]

As I propose, next Spring to have my lands on the Ohio critically examined by a Person in whose integrity ⟨and⟩ judgment I can confide, I am indifferent with respect to the sale of any of them, at *this time*, especially of that tract on Mill Creek which I conceive must be particularly fine, or possessing some valuable properties, from the number of applications which have been made to me of it.[2]

If, however, it is disposed of before such examination is made, the terms will be, twelve dollars pr Acre. One third down; the other two thirds by annual Instalments, with Interest; and a Mortgage on the premises for the security of payment. I am Sir, Yr Most Obedt Servt

Go: Washington

ALS (letterpress copy), NN: Washington Papers.

Allyn Prior "by Col. Daniel Boone's delay, was appointed" contractor, or commissary, for those Virginia militia companies which were sent to the mouth of the Great Kanawha in 1793 to protect that part of the frontier. Prior was a resident of Kanawha County and a successful merchant (*Calendar of Virginia State Papers*, 6:255, 279–80).

1. Letter not found.

2. The person whom GW intended to send to examine his lands on the Ohio River was probably his farm manager, James Anderson. As early as 1797 Anderson had expressed an interest in renting some of GW's western lands, and in December 1799 GW wrote Anderson that he was expecting him "to visit my Lands in the Western Country (at my expence), so soon as the weather becomes temperate and settled in the Spring" (GW to Anderson, 25 Nov. 1797 and 10 Dec. 1799). After Tobias Lear returned from Harpers Ferry on 4 Nov. and reported that Thomas Parker was planning to take a trip "to the Western Country," GW wrote Parker on 16 Nov. describing the lands that he owned on the Ohio and Great Kanawha rivers and requesting Parker to inquire about the condition of these holdings and their possible value.

To Leven Powell

Dear Sir   Mount Vernon 2d Novr 1799

I am informed that you have in use, a cutting box upon a New Construction; which, in execution, far exceeds the common kind; and is also simple in its works. If this be the case, and you *entirely* approve of the Machine, I would thank you for procuring (as soon as may be) one of the best sort; and causing it to be forwarded to Colo. Gilpin in Alexandria, for me.

The cost, & charges, shall be paid to your order, so soon as it is presented to Dear Sir Your Most Obedt Hble Serv.

Go: Washington

ALS, ViMtV; ALS (letterpress copy), NN: Washington Papers.

To Timothy Pickering

Private

Dear Sir,   Mount Vernon Novr 3d 1799

Your private & confidential letter of the 24th Ulto came duly, and safely to hand. Its contents, I confess, surprised me. But as men will view the same things in different lights, I would *now*, fain hope that the P—— has caught the *true one*; and, that good will come from the Mission, which is about to depart.

These are my wishes, and no one is more ardent in them; but I see nothing in the *present* aspect of European Affairs on which to build them. Nor no possible evil, under the same circumstances, that could result from delay, in forwarding it.

But as the measure is resolved on, and progressing, it must be left to time, & a little will do it, to develope the consequences. I trust, as you do, that that Providence which has protected all our steps hitherto, will continue to direct them—to the consumation of our happiness & prosperity.

I have not a doubt of General La Fayettes being *now* on his passage to the United States. I have done every thing in my power to induce him to suspend this determination; by representing the delicate situation in which he would be placed here, and the embarassment it might occasion. Mr Murray has enforced my observations with all his might; in vain I believe.

He replies, Poor fellow!—with too much truth I fear!—that there is no asylum for him in Europe. That he is determined (without knowing himself, I conceive) to be perfectly neutral. That his wish is to possess a small farm where he can enjoy ease & quiet. Little believing, although he has been told, that he will be assailed by the opposition party in this Country, and that it is hardly possible for him to avoid taking *a side*, without being suspected by *both sides*. That if [he] joins the Government party, he must relinquish all hope, & expectation of countenance from his own Country, under its present form; and if he joins the opposition, he will of course be frowned upon by the Government under whose protection he is settling.

To all this he asks, what can I do? and from Mr Murray's last letter to me (an answer to which I passed through your hands a few days ago) I have no doubt of his being now on his way to the

United States.[1] With the greatest esteem and regard—I am—Dear Sir Your Most Obedt Hble Servant

Go: Washington

ALS, MHi: Pickering Papers; ALS (letter-book copy), DLC:GW.
1. See GW to William Vans Murray, 26 Oct., and notes 1 and 3 to that document.

To Charles Cotesworth Pinckney

Dear Sir,   Mount Vernon Novr 3d 1799

Your favour of the ⟨*illegible*⟩d inst. from New Port, came duly to hand, and gave Mrs Washington (who continues to be much indisposed but ⟨hopes soon to be⟩ well again) and myself much pleasure to hear of Mrs Pinckney⟨'s⟩ encreasing health. A little time ⟨*illegible* the⟩ fine settled weather we enjoy at present, will, we hope, restore it entirely.[1]

The Rout from Trenton, or Philadelphia to Harpers Ferry, is, as you have marked—Lancaster, York, Hanover (or better known by McAllisters Town) Frederick Town.[2] The Road upon the whole good.

But another and better reason will induce you to take it. By ⟨a letter⟩ lately received from Colo. Parker, who had been instructed to make arrangements for Quartering (in Huts) the ⟨*illegible*⟩ Regiments on ground belonging to the U. S. (where the Arsenal is established in the vicinity of Harpers Ferry ⟨*illegible*⟩ and does not furnish sufficient ⟨*illegible*⟩ for building them, and that the Water, in both the Potomac and Shenandoah, are now so low, ⟨owing to⟩ the great drought of the Summer ⟨*illegible*⟩ no transportation in ⟨*illegible* available⟩ for the purpose of supplying those ⟨*illegible*⟩; and as the Season was so far advanced, that part of these Regiments had better go to Frederick Town in Maryld, than winter in Pennsylvania.[3]

Seperation of the Troops, was so contrary to my expectation and wishes, that I wrote two or three letters to Colo. Parker ⟨*illegible* to keep⟩ them. I resolved to send Colo. Lear to Harpers Ferry, and on the *spot* to determine whether such a seperation was indispensable; and in *that case* to proceed to Frederick Town to see what condition, and under what circumstances the Barracks at that place were; and whether attainable or not; as I believe they belong to the State. I have written a hypothetical letter on the Subject ⟨to⟩ the Governor thereof, to avoid delay, if such neccessity is manifest. Frederick Town is not more than twenty miles from Harpers Ferry, but the distance from the latter to Carlisle is considerably ⟨*illegible*⟩tion of the Troops ought ⟨*illegible*⟩, notwithstanding ⟨*illegible*⟩ Barracks at the latter, belonging ⟨*illegible*⟩ The condition the ⟨*illegible*⟩ certain it is that ⟨*illegible*⟩ cost more than the whole ⟨*illegible*⟩ at Harpers Ferry, ⟨*illegible*⟩ Cantoned at that place.[4]

The peculiar ⟨*illegible* which⟩ you were thrown by the ill health of Mrs Pinckney, and Genl Hamilton ⟨*illegible* asking that⟩ I would Instruct Colo. Parker ⟨*illegible*⟩ than he could in this business ⟨*illegible*⟩ inducements to ⟨*illegible*⟩ therein; for to go partially into military operations, is not only ⟨*illegible*⟩ upon, but adverse to my principles.

The situation of European Affairs is interesting and ⟨*illegible*⟩ much watchfulness ⟨*illegible*⟩ information respecting the Suspension ⟨*illegible*⟩ing of our Envoys has been ⟨*illegible*⟩ is my opinion from the ⟨Envoys *illegible*⟩ may be false. I thank you for the extract of Mr Mountflorence's letter.

Mrs Washington and Mr and Mrs Lewis and Mr Custis, unite there best wishes with mine for the perfect restoration of Mrs Pinckneys health. With Compliments to yourself and the young Ladies At all times I am most sincerely dear Sir Your Most Obedt and affecte Hble Servant

Go: Washington

P.S. ⟨*illegible*⟩ I have in my last by Genl Hamilton asked what was to be the destination of the 7th Regiment for none has been mentioned in his Communication to me.

ALS (letterpress copy), DLC:GW. GW docketed this letter: "1st Novr 1799."

1. In September Pinckney took his ill wife to Newport, R.I., seeking a cure. For Pinckney's subsequent movements, see Presly Thornton to GW, 16 Sept., and note 1 of that document. For references to Martha Washington's illness, see GW to Thomas Peter, 7 Sept., n.2. Pinckney's letter to GW has not been found, but Pinckney wrote Alexander Hamilton on 12 Oct.: "Mrs: Pinckney's health has so much mended lately, that I am in hopes I shall be able in about ten days to set out with her for Elizabeth Town [N.J.]; soon after which I shall have the pleasure of waiting on you, and also on the Secretary of War; and then proceed by easy Journeys to the vicinity of Harper's Ferry" (Syrett, *Hamilton Papers*, 23:525–26). Hamilton wrote Pinckney from New York on 23 Oct.: "Your letter of the 12th inst. found me at Trenton, from which place I have recently arrived" (ibid., 553–

54). Pinckney was with Hamilton in New York on 28 Oct., before going on to Philadelphia. He left Philadelphia for Virginia probably on 15 Nov. (Hamilton to Thomas Parker, 28 Oct., DLC: Hamilton Papers; Zahniser, *Pinckney*, 212).

2. Hanover is in York County, Pa., on route 194 between York, Pa., and Frederick, Maryland.

3. Thomas Parker's letter to GW is dated 24 October. See also GW to Parker, 27 October.

4. Much of this is illegible, but GW probably only more or less repeats here what he wrote to Hamilton and Parker on 27 Oct. about the disadvantages of quartering the 9th and 10th regiments in the old barracks in Frederick, Md., and Carlisle, Pa., instead of at Harpers Ferry as originally intended.

Letter not found: from Ralph Wormeley, Jr., 3 Nov. 1799. On 18 Nov. GW wrote Wormeley: "Your favour of the 3d Instant came duly to hand."

From Tobias Lear

Sir,   Mount Vernon Nov. 4th 1799

In obedience to your orders I left Mount Vernon on Monday the 28th of Octr to communicate to Colo. Parker your instructions respecting hutting the Troops at Harper's Ferry.

I reached the Camp at Harper's Ferry on the eveng of the 29th; and finding that Colo. Parker was gone to Winchester, I sent an Express for him immediately. In the afternoon of the 30th Colo. Parker arrived in Camp, when I delivered him your letters, and made such further verbal communications as were necessary on the subject.[1]

The difficulty which appeared in getting plank &c. sufficient to cover the huts for three Regts at Harper's Ferry, and the doubt whether the public ground would afford even logs enough for the huts, determined Colo. Parker to go to Frederick town to examine the state of the Barracks there. We accordingly went over to that place on the 31st of Octr where we found the Barracks in the most ruinous condition—the naked walls standing without a roof or floors, which at once decided, that nothing could be done to render them habitable for Troops this winter. And here we learned, with certainty, that a Battalion of Artillery (Major Hoops') was ordered from New York to take up their winter quarters at Harper's Ferry (having met Captn Freeman of the Artilleriests on his way to that place, who informed us that the Battalion was on its march, and might be expected in about ten days.[2]

Under these circumstances Colo. Parker was of opinion, in which I perfectly agreed, that it would be best to dispatch a Messenger to Colo. Moore of the tenth Regt at Yorktown, informing him that his regiment could not be accommodated at Harper's Ferry, and advising him that, according to orders he had, or might receive, from Genl Hamilton, it would be best to march his Regt to Carlisle and take up their quarters in the Barracks there; which Colo. Parker had been directly informed were in readiness to receive Troops having been completely repaired in the course of last summer.[3]

To Colo. Hall of the ninth Regt another Messenger was dispatched with a letter from Colo. Parker, informing him that his Regt would be hutted at Harper's Ferry, and requesting that they should be ordered there without delay, and in the meantime that every exertion would be made to get materials on the spot ready for them to begin their huts on their arrival.

At the same time, by Colo. Parker's desire, I wrote to Genl Hamilton, giving him a full detail of what had be[en] determined upon, and assurances that the eighth & ninth Regts of Infy—and Battalion of Artille[r]y would be well accommodated at Harper's Ferry. And that Colo. Moore had been written to, advising him to quarter the tenth Regt at Carlisle, if consistent with the Orders he had, or might receive.[4]

On the 1st of Novr We returned to Harper's Ferry, and upon going over the ground belonging to the U. S. and 150 Acres adjoining, which was in train of being purchased for the U. S. as mentioned in my letter of the 30th Ulto, we found there was an ample quantity of timber to furnish logs for all the huts of two Regts and Battalion of Artillery, and to afford sufficient fuel not only for the present winter; but to supply a considerable of the future wants. And as covering for the huts was the greatest desideratum, and but very few Trees on the public ground fit to make slabs, Colo. Parker sent Captn Henry & Captn Glenn to inspect some timber on the Maryland shore opposite to Harper's Ferry.[5] Their report was, that any quantity which could possibly be wanting might be had there fit to make slabs, within a very convenient distance, and the price very low. Colo. Parker therefore determined to send a party of men from his Regt immediately, under the charge of an officer acquainted with the business, who should take their tents to the ground, and continue to work there 'till they had got slabs or Clapboards enough for all the huts to be built; which, from the Report of the Captains aforesaid, could be done by 30 men in ten or twelve days.

This provision being made for covering the huts, but little more plank will be wanting than for floors &c. for the Officers Huts, which can be procured without much difficulty. There is at present on the ground about 12,000 feet, and the saw mill on the public ground is engaged in cutting constantly at the rate of 1000 feet per day, and there are logs enough to get from her about 25,000 feet.

All the logs for the Soldiers of the eighth Regt are on the spot, and almost all the huts up, ready for covering. The logs for the Officers huts are cut, and hauling to the encampment; so that this Regt would be completely hutted by the middle of this week if the covering was ready.

Having every thing completed for hutting the 8th Regt excepting covering, Colo. Parker determines that his men shall cut the logs and get them on the encamping ground for the 9th Regt and Battalion of Artille[r]y, that they may all be able to go into quarters together.[6]

The ground which I mentioned (150 Acres) is secured for the United States at £3.5.6 Virga currency pr Acre, and if it should be thought proper to increase the quantity there is no doubt it may be done at the same rate.

In order to give a better view of the relative situation of the Troops on the public ground, I have made a rough sketch of the whole ground and marked out the encampments &c.[7]

The Orders from Genl Hamilton were, that the huts for the Soldiers should be 14 feet sqr. to contain ten men; but Colo. Parker having cut most of his logs for huts of 16 feet sqr. to contain 12 men, before he received these orders, he proceeded to build them accordingly, and intends cutting the others of the same length, as several advantages result from it. Very few trees will make two logs of 16 feet, and all will make one of 18 feet. The logs will be more valuable for future use, if they shd be wanted, and 12 men are accommodated with the same trouble that ten would be.

Colo. Parker's encampment consists of two lines of huts for the Soldiers at 12 feet distant. The front line consists of 25 huts, and the rear will be according to the number of men, providing for such as may be expected to be enlisted this winter. Twenty feet in rear of the Soldiers, are the huts for the Company Officers—and the same distance in rear of these the huts for the field Officers. The bottom on which the huts are built not being sufficiently wide to give the distance most desireable for the lines.

Colo. Parker's assiduity and attention to accommodate the Troops is great—he spares no exertions, and the officers and men appear much satisfied with their situation, and have made very good progress in building their huts.

I left the Camp on Saturday evening, after the bargain for the ground was closed, so far as could be done by obligation, until the formal writings could be drawn. The purchase was negotiated by Major Campbell, and a Credit ⟨or 3 and 6 Months⟩ given to pay the money, unless the U. S. should chuse to make immediate payment, in which case the Int. for that time will be deducted from the cost of the land.[8]

Colo. Parker did not write to you at this time as he was very much engaged, and I should be able to give you the full details of the business thus far. He will write by the next Mail, and state the progress of the arrangements.[9]

I have given this hasty Report from the minutes which I had made from time to time; but if you should think it best, I will prepare another more full before your return.[10] With the highest respect & veneration I have the honor to be, Sir, Your Obedient & faithful Servant

Tobias Lear

ALS, DLC:GW; copy, DLC: Hamilton Papers. Lear wrote Alexander Hamilton on 10 Nov.: "I had the honor of writing to you from Frederick town on the 31st ulto [letter not found] respecting quarters for the 9th & 10th Regts—and on my return to this place [Mount Vernon] I made a full report to the Commander in Chief on that subject, which was sent to the Secy of War [James McHenry], with a request that he would communicate the same to you" (DLC:GW). See also GW to McHenry, 5 November.

1. See Lear to GW, 30 Oct., n.1.

2. Adam Hoops, of New Jersey, was made a major in the army on 4 June 1798 and given command of a battalion of the 2d Regiment of Artillerists and Engineers stationed at Fort Jay on Governors Island in New York Harbor (Syrett, *Hamilton Papers*, 23:77, 120). Nehemiah Freeman of West Point, N.Y., received a captain's commission on 6 Aug. 1798 and took command of one of the companies of artillery at Fort Jay. Hoops was put on special assignment for the winter in Philadelphia and so did not go to Harpers Ferry (ibid., 77, 534, 538); but

Thomas Parker wrote Lear on 13 Nov.: "Capt. Freemans Company has arrived and are engaged in Cuting logs for their Hutts. we have the whole of our Hutts up & shoud have them Covered in less than two days" (DLC:GW). When Charles Cotesworth Pinckney wrote Alexander Hamilton a month later, on 12 Dec., a second company of artillery had arrived (ibid., 24:96–98).

3. Lt. Col. Thomas Lloyd Moore on 6 Oct. was ordered by Hamilton to march the 10th Regiment to York, Pa., and on 31 Oct. to march from York to Carlisle, Pa. (Hamilton to Moore, 6 Oct., DLC: Hamilton Papers; Moore to Hamilton, 28 Oct., DLC: Hamilton Papers). Thomas Parker wrote Lear on 13 Nov., however, that Moore was remaining in York with his regiment until he received further orders (DLC:GW). It would appear that Charles Cotesworth Pinckney ordered the 10th Regiment to Carlisle after his arrival at Harpers Ferry in November (see Hamilton to GW, 18 November).

4. Hamilton wrote Lear on 8 Nov.: "I have received your letter of the thirty first of October, and am much obliged to you for your attention to the Winter Quarters of the Troops" (DLC:GW). No letter from Lear of 31 Oct. 1799 is printed or listed in Syrett, *Hamilton Papers*, but see Hamilton to GW, 18 Nov. 1799, n.1.

5. Capt. Nathaniel Henry was an officer in Parker's 8th Regiment. "Captn Glenn" may have been Richard Chinn, also a captain in the regiment.

6. Thomas Parker wrote Lear on 5 Nov. from his camp near Harpers Ferry: "we are still favoured with the most delightfull weather & I hope by the last of the week to have my Regt comfortably Covered & some provision made for the Troops that are now on their march. I have Invariably found myself deceived with Respect to the Quantity of plank said to be at the different Sawmills. But I hope to make up The Deficiency with Slabs, having sent Twenty odd men yesterday morng under the Care of Capt. Henry for the purpose of procuring as many as possable" (DLC:GW). In a letter to Parker written on 7 Nov. before he had received on 10 Nov. Parker's letter of 5 Nov., Lear wrote in a postscript dated 9 Nov.: "On my return from Harper's Ferry, I reported fully to the Commander in Chief the steps which had been taken for ordering the tenth Regt to Carlisle, and providing for the ninth Regt of Infy an Battalion of Artillery at Harper's Ferry; all which met his Approbation, and he wrote to the Secretary of War, enclosing a Copy of my report, and requesting him to provide for the payment of 150 Acres of land bo[ugh]t from Wilson for the U.S." (DLC:GW)

7. The sketch of the public grounds was enclosed and is in DLC:GW.

8. Thomas Parker wrote GW on 5 Nov. about payment for the purchase of land: "I feel Verry great Concern in not Having it in my power to Comply fully with your wishes Relative to the Accomodation of the Troops at this place. I Trust However that from Colo. Lears Report you will be convinced that no exertion on my part has been wanting to Effect this desirable Object. A purchase of About Two hundred acres of Land has been made adjoining the public Ground without which It woud have Been Impracticable to have provided Timber for Huting the Troops. the price is 6⅚ per Acre to be paid in three & Six months with a deduction of Interest provided the money be Immediately paid. as I have been Obliged to Bind myself & my Majors to have the Contract faithfully Complied with I will thank you to write to the proper authority Requesting that the necessary pro-

vision Shall be made. I am using every Exertion in my power to have the necessary articles provided for the Troops who I Imagine are now on their march & from the favourable appearance of the weather hope to Have them covered before the winter Setts in" (DLC:GW). On the same day that Parker wrote this letter, GW wrote to Secretary of War James McHenry asking that he arrange prompt payment, which McHenry on 13 Nov. promised to do (see GW to McHenry, 5 Nov., n.2). This was not the end of the matter, however; see GW to McHenry, 3 Dec., and notes.

9. See note 8.

10. On 5 Nov. GW "Set out on a trip to Difficult-run to view some Land I had there & some belonging to Mr. Jno. Gill who had offered it to me in discharge of Rent which he was owing me" (*Diaries*, 6:374). See GW to John Gill, 19 Oct., n.2.

To James McHenry

Sir,   Mount Vernon, Nov: 5th 1799

At the earnest request of General Hamilton, that I would give instructions for having the eighth, ninth and tenth Regiments of Infantry provided with Winter Quarters, which it was very desireable should be at Harper's Ferry, I have departed from the resolution which I had formed, not to take charge of any military operations, unless the Army should be called into the Field, so far as to Order the best arrangements to be made that circumstances would permit, at this advanced season of the year, for quartering these Regiments. Knowing that no time could be lost—and that the distance of Genl Hamilton from this part of the Country would occasion considerable delay in the necessary communications, and that the situation of Genl Pinckney's family must prevent his personal attention to the business.

I therefore ordered Colo. Parker, of the eighth Regiment, to make the necessary arrangements for hutting these troops on the public ground at Harper's Ferry; but in the course of my communications with him on the subject, I found, that, without great exertion, it was probable that quarters would not be provided at that place for more than one Regiment. I therefore thought it proper, in addition to my further instructions to Colo. Parker, to send my Secretary Colo. Lear, up to Harper's Ferry, who would communicate to him my wishes more fully than could be done by writing, and who was directed to give to Colo. Parker all the assistance in his power that the business might be determined without delay.

This has been done, and I now enclose you a Copy of the report which my Secretary has made to me on his return; by which you will see the definitive arrangement which has been made, and which meets my approbation.

You will be so good as to communicate this Report to Genl Hamilton or Genl Pinckney, or both, that they may see what steps have been taken for quartering these Regiments, and make their arrangements accordingly.[1]

I think that the ground mentioned in this Report will be very useful to the United States, and is certainly valuable for the timber and fuel; and if more can be had, on the same terms, I am of opinion that it ought to be purchased for the public, as the works now preparing, as well as those which may be hereafter established at Harper's Ferry, will make it an important place to the U. S. and an extension of their ground will be desireable on many Accounts. You will be pleased to observe, however, that the present purchase of 150 Acres, is not in fee, it is but the purchase of a lease, which has upwards of fifty years to run, at an annual rent of twenty dollars per hundred Acres. There can be little doubt, however, but that the fee may be obtained on reasonable terms. At any rate you will be pleased to have the present bargain confirmed and provision ordered for the payment of the money.[2] With due consideration I have the honor to be Sir Yr mo. Ob. St

G. W——n

Df, in Tobias Lear's hand, DLC:GW.

1. See Tobias Lear to GW, 4 November.

2. McHenry replied on 13 Nov.: "I have been honored with your letter of the 5th instant inclosing the report by your Secretary relative to the hutting the three Regiments which it was contemplated to canton at Harpers ferry. I caused a copy of this report to be immediately transmitted to Major General Hamilton, and communicated its contents to Major General Pinckney on his arrival here—On the 11th instant, the latter, on my learning from Lt Colonel [Thomas Lloyd] Moore who was at York town waiting for orders from General Hamilton that he had received none, directed the Colonel to proceed with his Regiment to Carlisle, where I expect they will find comfortable quarters" (DLC:GW). See also Lear to GW, 4 Nov., n.8.

Letter not found: from Timothy Pickering, 5 Nov. 1799. GW wrote Pickering on 24 Nov.: "Your favour of the 5th instant came to hand in due course."

To William Price

Fairfax County near Difficult Bridge
Sir,   November 7th 1799

I came from Mount Vernon to this place in order to run out some land which I hold in this County, near this place.

In doing which, I have discovered—or think I have discovered—some vacant land between my lines, the lines of the late Thomas Lord Fairfax, and those commonly called Tankervilles; now in the occupation of others; to whom they were sold by his Agent.[1]

Having been but little in this State since the Revolution, I am unacquainted with the legal ⟨steps⟩ necessary & proper to be taken, to make an Entry thereof; which must be my excuse if the present application to you is wrong, or informal.

If it be proper, I pray you to make such Entry as the case requires. and the cost, so soon as it is made known to me, shall be immediatley paid by Sir Your most Obedt Hble Serv⟨t⟩

Go: Washington

P.S. I do not conceive that the Waste land herein described (if there be any) can exceed a hundred Acres.

ALS, Vi.

1. When GW resurveyed at this time the tract of land on Difficult Run that he had acquired in 1763 from Bryan Fairfax (see GW to John Gill, 19 Oct. 1799, nn.1 and 2), not only did he believe that he had discovered unclaimed land between his land and the Tankerville tract immediately above, but, as he later explained to Charles Little on 20 Nov., he also discovered that he was in fact unable to fix with any certainty the boundaries of his own tract. After receiving Price's response dated 15 Nov., which is missing, GW wrote Price again on 20 Nov. to inform him that William Shepherd, who rented land from Bryan Fairfax at the Difficult Run Bridge where he had kept until recently the tavern in which GW was staying, had come to the same conclusion about the wedge of unclaimed land and had put in his claim to it. GW asked Price to enter at the land office GW's caveat against the issuance of a grant of the land to Shepherd.

In addition to his letter to Price, GW wrote on 20 Nov. letters about this matter to Charles Little and to Fairfax County surveyor William Payne, as well as to Payne's deputy Samuel Sommers. Charles Little had been somehow involved in the sale of the Tankerville Virginia property during the years following the Revolution, and in 1791 Little had himself been the purchaser of part of it (see GW to Tankerville, 20 Jan. 1784, in *Papers, Confederation Series*, 1:64–66). GW sought and received information from Little about the relevant boundary lines of the neighboring Tankerville property at Difficult Run (see GW to Little, 28 November). GW enclosed in his letter to deputy surveyor Sommers of 20 Nov. the (missing) warrant of survey for the hypothetical unclaimed land, which he had secured from Price in Richmond, and asked that the warrant be entered in the county surveyor's office in Alexandria. GW then wrote Bryan Fairfax, on 26 Nov., to seek his aid in fixing the boundaries of the tract on Difficult Run that Fairfax had long ago carved out of the 12,000-acre Fairfax holdings, so that GW might be able to determine whether there in fact was vacant land between his property and the Tankerville tract. On 30 Nov. GW acknowledged the receipt of Fairfax's missing reply of 28 Nov. enclosing "the courses of so much of your land on Difficult, as had any relation to my small tract at the Bridge." GW now saw that his tract of 275 acres (not 300 acres as he had come to believe) was bounded on all sides by land belonging to the Fairfaxes. There was no unclaimed land. GW let the matter drop.

For the precise location of and further information about the tracts of land on or near Difficult Run referred to here, see Mitchell, *Fairfax County Patents and Grants*, particularly tracts 285 and 295B, tract 403, and tract 268, on pages 149, 165, and 181. Tract 268 is what GW refers to here as the Tankerville tract.

The sixteen letters that GW wrote in October and November 1799 about his Difficult Run property included those to John Gill, 13, 19, 22 Oct., 12, 26 Nov., to William Price, 7, 8, 20 Nov., 2 Dec., to Charles Little, 20, 28 Nov., to Samuel Sommers, 20, 28 Nov., to Bryan Fairfax, 26, 30 Nov., and to William Payne, 20 November. It should be noted that not a single letter written in response, and acknowledged by GW, has been found. For reference to the missing incoming letters of the last three months of GW's life, see note 7 to Tobias Lear's Narrative Accounts of the Death of George Washington, printed at the end of this volume.

From Alexander Addison

Sir   Pittsburgh 8th Novr 1799
The other week the disputed line of the land you sold to Matthew Ritchie was run by Mr Morgan and another surveyor and settled by consent of Mr Reid who contended. There was very little difference between it and that last marked by Mr Morgan. An old line had been run probably a line of experiment and Reid had run his lines by it. The quantity may be considered as in Morgan's survey.[1]

Some time before I left Washington to reside here Mrs Ritchie and her brother in law undertook to make the payment due you. Since I came here I have not heard whether they have done so.[2]

The event of our election for Governor by the influence of abominable lies on the Germans has been unexpectedly unfortunate.[3] I am with the greatest respect Your obedt Servt
                                                      Alexr Addison

ALS, NjMoNP. Smith Collection.

1. For the question raised by James Reid about the accuracy of a survey made by Charles Morgan fixing the line between Reid's property and the Millers Run tract that GW sold to Matthew Ritchie in 1796, see Addison to GW, 22 Aug. 1798.

2. For references to the payments for the Millers Run tract, see GW to Samuel M. Fox, 10 June 1799, n.1, and Addison to GW, 6 July 1799.

3. See GW to William Vans Murray, 26 Oct., n.2.

Letter not found: from Elias Boudinot, 8 Nov. 1799. On 13 Nov. GW wrote Boudinot: "Your favour of the 8th instt was received by the last Mail to Alexand[ri]a."

To William Price

Difficult Bridge Wylies Tav⟨ern⟩
Sir,   8th November 1799

Since writing the enclosed, I have discovered that a Mr William Shepherd who was with me on the Survey, and who has acted a very disingenuous part upon the occasion, either has made, or pretends to have made, an Entry of the Vacancy (if there be such) which I have therein requested you to enter on my behalf, of land always reputed, and believed by the Neighbours, to be mine.[1]

I therefore request to be informed, if the first is the case, whether he has complied with all the formalities of the Law? for as much as I am resolved, to contest every poin⟨t⟩ with him that justice & propriety will warran⟨t.⟩

Of course, I request the Entry may be made agreeably to the description with which I have furnished you; adding (altho' I do not know that it is essential) the lines now, or lately, of the Revd Mr Fairfax's tract, called Towlston Grange. With respect I am Sir Your Most Obedt Hble Servant

Go: Washington

P.S. The Entry of Willm Shepherd, as he gives out, was made a year or two ago. If so, has he complied with the *subsequent* requisites?[2]

ALS, NNGL.

1. See GW to Price, 7 Nov., and note 1 of that document.

2. James Wylie had taken over William Shepherd's tavern at some time during the past several years.

From James McHenry

(Confidential)

My dear Sir   Philadelphia 10th Novr 1799.

My attention, for some time past, has been so completely engrossed, that notwithstanding my earnest wish to communicate with you upon several subjects, I could not without neglecting some urgent business devote any moments to that purpose. In truth, the stone, however near I may seem to get it to the summit of the mountain, is perpetually upon the recoil, and demands constant exertion and labour to keep it from descending.

I have much to say to you; many facts to entrust to your bosom. Take them without order and as they occur, you will arrange them in your own mind, and supply the results.

The prevailing rumour has no doubt reached you of disagreements in the cabinet, or that a difference of opinion exists between the President and heads of departments relative to the mission to France. I am sorry to inform you that there is too much foundation for this report. Last session of Congress, the President made the nomination of Mr Murray, to treat with the Republic of France, without any consultation, or giving the least intimation of his intentions to any of the heads of departments. This step, admitting the measure itself, to have been wise and the dictate of profound policy, was nevertheless such a departure from established practice as could not fail to excite considerable sensibility. Independent however of this circumstance, or the new practice it seemed intended to establish, the policy and wisdom of the mission, was either doubted or condemned by most if not all of the federal members of Congress, in consequence of which the nomination recieved a modification by a second message to the Senate from the President, in which they concurred.

Nothwithstanding this modification, it was very evident that most of the federal members of both branches of Congress carried home with them a settled dislike to the measure, as ill timed, predicated upon too slight grounds, and therefore humiliating to the United States; as calculated to revive French principles, strengthen the party against government, and produce changes in the sentiments and conduct of some of the European powers, that might materially affect our interests and growing commercial prospects. Have not some of these apprehensions been already realized?

You must have perceived observations and suggestions in the News-papers of different States, tending to censure the mission, which I consider as having proceeded from these dissatisfactions.

The great and important successes of the Allies, engaged against France, the changes in the Directory, and the rapidity with which every matter and thing in France seemed hurrying to a restoration of monarchy, indicated to the heads of departments, the propriety of a suspension of the mission. We accordingly, while he was at Quincy, presented the idea to the President, as a subject for his consideration.

Without taking any notice of the subject of this letter, a few days succeeding his arrival at Trenton, he convened us, to conclude upon the instructions, and shortly after gave his final orders for the departure of the commissioners, who have accordingly sailed from Rhode Island in the Frigate United States on the 3d inst.[1]

Shall we have a treaty with France in consequence of this mission? Yes, if she finds it necessary to her situation and circumstances. Will a treaty, which shall not trench upon any rights acquired by, give umbrage to, England? It is certain no good reason can be assigned why it should. Is it not also possible that the policy of the mission may be justified by events, such as a general peace in Europe this winter, the republican form of government remaining to France?

The President believes, and with reason, that three of the heads of departments have viewed the mission as impolitic and unwise. He does not I imagine class the Secretary of the Navy among its disapprovers, altho' he joined in the letter advising its suspension. I find that he is particularly displeased with Mr Pickering and Mr Wolcott, thinking they have encouraged opposition to it, to the Eastward; seemingly a little less so with me; and not at all with Mr Stoddert and the attorney General, who appear to enjoy his confidence; and yet those he is so displeased with, are still received and treated by him with apparent cordiality.

Whether he will think it expedient to dismiss any, or how many of us, is a problem. I believe, the Attorney General and Secretary of the Navy are of opinion he ought, and would perhaps, if asked, advise to the dismission at least of one. There are however powerful personal reasons, especially at this juncture, which forbid it, and it is more than possible, as these chiefly respect the Eastern quarter of the union, they will prevail.[2]

But in my view of the subject the evil does not lay in a change of Secretaries however brought about, as these may be replaced with good and able men, but in the mission, which as far as my information extends, is become an apple of discord to the federalists, that may so operate upon the ensuing election of President as to put in jeopardy, the fruits of all their past labours, by consigning to men, devoted to French innovations and demoralizing principles, the reins of government. It is this dreaded consequence which afflicts, and calls for all the wisdom of the federalists.

It is evident, from the late election in Pennsylvania, that there is a disciplened and solid army of antifederalists ready to take the field for a President of their own principles, and equally perspicuous, from the news-papers and movements among this description of men throughout the union, that the same spirit and intention actuates the whole.

The aim of these men, or their leaders, has been, to produce a change in the public opinion, which is to overthrow present powers and perhaps institutions. In this work they have not been detered by defeats, and have certainly made considerable progress. They skilfully seize upon every circumstance, which can be made to conduce to their object. A word said by a federalist against any law or measure of the government is carefully noted and adroitly used to give a false colouring to the intentions of government. Nothing in short escapes them that can be perverted or malignantly applied to their purpose.

It is among other things to be lamented, that certain recent measures of the administration, were of such a nature as to offer an appearance of favouring individual merchants, which could not without a public injury be openly explained; and that some of the gentlemen of the administration have not by their conversations on the subject, assisted to remove the suspicions industriously propagated by the opposition. I allude particularly to the mission to Toussant to St Domingo, and the supplies sent in the vessel which carried thither the agent.

To open with St Domingo a free trade; to put an effectual stop to privateering from that Island, and to set an example which might extend to other French possessions, it was necessary to accompany the agent, with certain articles, which would prove acceptable to Toussant in the then situation of his affairs and wants of the Island. The law, which enabled the President to open trade with any part of the French possessions, did not authorise him to procure such means as appeared to be indispensible, in this case, to give success to the attempt. There was no appropriation for the purpose, and to have taken that means from existing funds, appropriated to distinct objects, would have required a communication to Congress, which would probably have occasioned an investigation into all circumstances by the opposition. Thus situated, it was determin'd to permit the owners of the vessel, which was to carry out the agent, to ship the articles wanted by Toussant, at their own risk and account, limiting their profit, to such a sum, as would pay them for the expence of the voyage only. This was procuring for Touessaint, the articles which he most wanted, at a price far below what he could have obtained them in any other way, while it relieved [him] from the embarrassments which would have attended any application of the public money for that object.

This measure has been made an instrument of against administration. It has hence been accused of granting partial favours which could not possibly have been extended. There has also been confounded with the measure, to sow dissatisfaction among the merchants, the use which the agent is said to have made of his situation to purchase on his arrival at St Domingo large quantities of its produce, thereby enhancing the price upon the adventurers when the trade was opened.

How far this allegation may be founded I cannot say, or whether, had any other person than Doctor Stevens been the agent, the same complaint would not have been made.

The merchants, I understand also complain, that the Agent is either a merchant, or connected profitably with merchants, which gives a biass to his conduct. If he discovers partialities in executing the duties he is charged with it is a reason for his removal; but you know that the practice has been to vest merchants with the consular office.

I have learned from the Secretary of State, that Doctor Stevens has the ear and confidence of Toussaint in a very high degree. To retain this is important, but should he have made an improper use of his situation, it ought not to prevent his being superseded.[3]

Another point on which opposition dwells with uncommon energy and perseverance is the charge of British influence adverted to in your letter of the 11th of August ultimo. I am informed, that Mr Dallas has in his possession, a letter from Mr Adams to Mr Tench Coxe, written at the time, and on the occasion of the appointment of Mr Pinckney to London, as Minister plenipotentiary, in which he ascribes his appointment to British influence, and adds, that were he of the administration he should think it proper to watch attentively the course of things or words to that effect. This letter I also understand is to be produced on the trial of Duane, and his defence rested upon substantiating the charge. It is also said to be intended to call upon you and the President to give information in the case.[4]

When I consider the difference in opinion, between his ministers and the President, the effects this has produced on the public mind and may particularly among federalists; the different opinions entertained by federalists relative to the policy and wisdom of the mission; the additional strength, which the calumny of British influence must derive from the letter aluded to, in the minds of the ignorant, misled and undiscerning multitude, and subjoin to all this the growth of French principles, I confess, I see more danger to the cause of order and good government at this moment, than has at any time heretofore threatened the Country.

What ought to be done? Will it produce more harmony of action among the friends of government were the President to dismiss those ministers he seems most displeased with? I think not. The Secretary of State I believe to be an upright man, who has served the United States faithfully and to the utmost of his abilities; and the Secretary of the treasury, a very able, prudent discerning and honest man, whose place could not be better filled.

Ought the President to conciliate his ministers by a conduct which does not reduce them on great occasions, to cyphers in the government, and by this means endeavour at least to restore mutual confidence and harmony of action? This I would look upon to be the wisest expedient. But will he adopt it? Will the irritation which his mind suffers from those who flatter him or badly advise him, permit his judgment to perceive and pursue this course? I really know not. I see rocks and quicksands on all sides, and administration in the attitude of a sinking ship. It will, I imagine, depend very much upon the President whether she is to weather the storm or go down. I am with the most unalterable attachment my dear Sir yours truly and affectionately

James McHenry

ALS, DLC:GW; ALS (letterpress copy), DLC: McHenry Papers; copy, DLC: Hamilton Papers.

1. The letter to John Adams is dated 24 September. For Adams's decision to dispatch to France the two envoys who were appointed in February 1799, see Alexander Hamilton to GW, 21 Oct. (first letter), n.2.

2. It was not until May 1800 that Adams forced McHenry's resignation and soon after dismissed Timothy Pickering as secretary of state. Oliver Wolcott remained in office as secretary of the treasury until his resignation at the end of 1800.

3. For references to the controversy over the sending of Dr. Edward Stevens as consul general to Saint Domingue with a shipload of provisions, see GW to McHenry, 11 Aug. 1799, n.2.

4. For the arrest on 30 July of the editor of the *Aurora*, William Duane, and the charges brought against him under the terms of the Sedition Act, see GW to Timothy Pickering, 4 Aug. 1799, n.1. Duane was brought to trial in the October term of the U.S. circuit court in Pennsylvania. Duane's lawyer, Alexander J. Dallas, appeared in court with an authenticated copy of John Adams's letter to Tench Coxe in which Adams wrote of his suspicions that there had been "much British influence" in Thomas Pinckney's appointment as minister to Britain. The court granted Dallas's request for a postponement of the trial until the next session. For a full account of the prosecution of William Duane until the proceedings were brought to an end when Thomas Jefferson became president, see Smith, *Freedom's Fetters*, ch. 13.

To Alexandria General Assemblies Managers

Gentlemen   Mount Vernon 12th Novr 1799

Mrs Washington and myself have been honoured with your polite invitation to the Assemblies in Alexandria, this Winter; and thank you for this mark of your attention. But alas! our dancing days are no more; we wish, however, all those whose relish for so agreeable, & innocent an amusement, all the pleasure the Season will afford them. and I am Gentlemen Your Most Obedient and Obliged Humble Servant

Go: Washington

ALS, ViAlL; ALS (letterpress copy), ViMtV.

In 1791 a group of men in Alexandria organized a new dancing assembly separate from the long-established Alexandria Assemblies. Before the end of the year the managers of the two organizations agreed to unite into what was to be called the "Alexandria General Assemblies." The managers of the General Assemblies' ball in November 1799 at Gadsby's Tavern, whose names GW wrote at the bottom of the page, were Jonathan Swift, Charles Alexander, Jr., George Deneale, Robert Young, James H. Hooe, and William Newton (Powell, *Old Alexandria*, 138–42).

To John Gill

Sir,   Mount Vernon 12th Nov. 1799

I am just returned from Difficult-Run, whither I went to examine your land, and to see how it was situated in connexion with mine, to ascertain the quantity in the part you had offered to me, Its quality—&c.[1]

When you proposed to reserve all that part of lot No. 10 which lyes on the East side of Difficult run,[2] I presume you were unacquainted with three circumstances attending it—1st, that you would leave only 85 acres on the West side of the said run; 2dly, that you would take all the woodland (except a very narrow slipe or two); and 3rdly, all the land of any value. For the land on the West side is not only extremely hilly & broken, but much worn and gullied. The (uninhabited) house thereon, is tumbling down; the Fence around the field is in ruins; and not a sufficiency of timber to repair it. And no part of the land within less than 80 rod of mine.

This account you may rely on as fact: for I not only examined the premises with attention, but measured with accuracy (carrying a surveyor with me), the part of lot No. 10 which lyes on the upper, or West side of the Run.[3] In doing which I was accompanied by Mr [Jesse] Wherry (your Tenant), Mr Thomas Gunnel, and Captn Wiley; who were with me the whole time, & shewed the lines & corners, which were to be found.[4] The Meanders of Difficult run from my upper corner thereon to the place where the line of lot No. 10 crosses it, were also traversed to shew, with precision, the situation of the two tracts; a sketch of which is enclosed taken from the Survey of the lands thereabouts, which you sent me, (belonging to Mr Swift), in order to give you a more distinct & perfect view of the subject than it is supposed you had obtained from a superficial view of it, before.

From this relation, which upon enquiry you will find l⟨i⟩terally correct, you must perceive, that that part of lot No. 10 *alone*, which lyes on the upper, or West side of Difficult cannot answer my purpose, nor would be an equivolent. And you must be further con vinced, that from the scarcity of money, & fall in the price of land—indeed property of all kinds, it is not for my interest to cancel the bargain which is in existence between us. Yet, as you seem to wish it, and I am not desirous of enforcing a contract (although I missed a favourable sale by making it) that would be injurious to you; I will, if it is not convenient to you to pay money for the Rents due thereon, (which would be most acceptable to me) agree to take the *whole* of lot No. 10, to release the bargain for my land; or, as it is agreed on all hands, that Difficult run is mirey, inconvenient & troublesome to cross at *most* seasons of the year, and in winter *generally impassible*, except at the bridge, I am willing to receive (altho' stripped of its wood, & part of it much worn) the slipe on the upper side, which you bought from Doctr Dick, in lieu of that part of No. 10 which is on the lower side of the run and about the same quantity; the former comes to the upper corner of my land on the run, by a narrow gore, as may be seen by the sketch enclosed, but with the addition of the grd included by the red line, in the Plat (if hereafter it could be obtained) would connect the whole tolerably well together, and all on one side of the run; which, from my own view, and the opinion of those who were with me, would be advantageous to both interests.[5]

You now have the matter fully before you, and your answer as soon as convenient, would be acceptable to Sir—Your Most Obedient Humble Servant

Go: Washington

ALS (letterpress copy), DLC:GW. The ALS was advertised for sale in August 1922 by James F. Drake, Inc.

1. See GW to Gill, 19 Oct., n.2.

2. In his letter of 19 Oct. to Gill, GW writes that Gill had indicated he was reserving for himself that part of his land lying on the west, not east, side of Difficult Run. What GW writes here on 12 Nov. is correct. Gill's land, bought from Tankerville some years before, was a very short distance below, or to the south of, GW's tract.

3. GW examined and then surveyed Gill's tract on the 6, 7, and 8 of November (*Diaries*, 6:374–75).

4. Captain Wylie may be James Wylie who kept the tavern at the Difficult Run bridge. Thomas Gunnell was one of the heirs of his father, Henry Gunnell (d. 1792), who had inherited from his father William (d. 1760) half of an 800-acre tract on the east, or south, side of Difficult Run not far upstream from GW's holdings (King, *Fairfax Wills and Inventories*, 13, 30; Fairfax County Deed Book A-1, 26–27, ViFaCt).

5. GW's sketch of his and Gill's landholdings has not been found. For the ne-

gotiations between GW and Gill regarding their Difficult Run property, see GW to Gill, 19 Oct., n.2. For the wild-goose chase that GW was set upon by his Difficult Run surveys, see GW to William Price, 7 Nov., n.1.

To Clement Biddle

Dear Sir, Mount Vernon 13th Novr 1799

You will perceive by the enclosed Invoice & Bill of Lading, that two Pipes of old Madeira Wine, & two Boxes of Citron have been Shipped by Charles Alder and Co. for my use, on Board the Ship Lavinia, James Cook Masr, bound for Philadelphia.

As the *original* letter, enclosing these papers, has been received (via Philadelphia) It is presumed that the Wine is safe in that Port. I have to request the favour of you, therefore, to receive these things; Pay the freight and Duty; and to forward them by a *safe* conveyance to me. The amount of cost shall be paid so soon as you shall advise me of it.[1]

At the sametime that you send the Wine, forward, I pray you, one hundred, or an hundred & fifty pounds of best Mokha Coffee[2]—a small chest of the finest Tea—say about 25 lbs.—and two boxes of Spirma citi candles.

Let me know at what price Clover seed sells—and whether *good* Lucern seed can be had?[3] Neither this kind of Seed, the White Clover, or Blue grass seeds with which you furnished me this Spring, was worth the freight; little or none of it came up. Add if you please, the present prices of Wheat & Flour; and continue to mention them in your letters thereafter.[4]

In September last, I enclosed Mr Jos. Anthony a check on the Bank of Pennsylvania for $56 in discharge of my subscription for Mr John Trumbulls Prints; and requested, when he received the money, to send me a receipt therefor; since which havg heard nothing from him, I take the liberty of putting the enclosed letter for Mr Anthony, under cover to you, that I may learn what has become of the former, & the check.[5] With very great esteem & regard I remain Dear Sir Your Most Obedient Servant

Go: Washington

ALS, PHi: Washington-Biddle Correspondence; ALS (letterpress copy), NN: Washington Papers.

1. For the correspondence relating to the shipment of wine to GW from Madeira, see GW to Elias Boudinot, 22 June 1799, n.2. On the back of a note drawn by Charles Alder & Co. on Tobias Lear for £84 for the value of the wine shipped

to GW, GW certificd on 14 Nov. that it had been "Presented and accepted" (advertised by Charles Hamilton, 18 Sept. 1969, item 359; see also Day Book, 14 Nov. 1799).

2. Coffee from the Red Sea city of Mokha (Mocha) was considered the best.

3. Biddle wrote above the word "Clover," "10 Ds. Bushel," and above "Lucern," "5/7½ ℔ lb. (old)."

4. See Biddle's response of 23 November.

5. For GW's letters to Joseph Anthony of 30 Sept. and 13 Nov. 1799, see GW to Anthony, 17 Mar. 1799, n.1.

To Elias Boudinot

Dear Sir,   Mount Vernon 13th Novr 1799

Your favour of the 8th instt was received by the last Mail to Alexand[ri]a.[1] At the sametime, a letter from the House of Alder & Co. came to hand, announcing his shipment of two Pipes of Old Madeira Wine, on my account, on Board the Lavinia Captn James Cook, by Direction of Mr Pintard, for Philadelphia.[2]

Presuming on the arrival of it at that Port, I have requested Colon[e]l Clem: Biddle to pay the freight & duties and to send the wine round by the first safe and good conveyance to this River (Potomac).[3]

Having just before the receipt of these letters engaged a Pipe of Madeira, I shall have no occasion for the one you kindly offer, but thank you for your kind intention to accomodate me therewith.

Mrs Washington unites with me in every good wish for Mrs Boudinot, yourself & Mrs Bradford—and I am always Dr Sir—Yr Most Obedt

Go: Washington

ALS, NHi: Vail Collection.

1. Letter not found.

2. The letter from Charles Alder of 20 Sept. 1799 is printed in GW to Boudinot, 22 June 1799, n.2.

3. See GW to Biddle, this date.

From District of Columbia Commissioners

Sir,   Washington 13th Novr 1799

Agreeably to your request, we enclose you an account of the second Instalment on your purchase of lot No. 16 in Square No.

634, which became due 25th Septr last[1]—the amount you will please to remit when Convenient to yourself.[2] We are with sentiments of the highest respect &c.

G: Scott

W: Thornton

A: White

Copy, DNA: RG 42, Records of the Commissioners for the District of Columbia, Letters Sent, 1791–1802.

1. When GW bought this lot on Capitol Hill from the commissioners on 25 Sept. 1798, he paid them $178.57, one-third of its cost, and contracted to pay the remainder in two annual installments. See Alexander White to GW, 8 Sept. 1798, n.1.

2. GW wrote to the commissioners on 18 Nov.: "Gentlemen, Your letter of the 13th instt and its enclosure, did not reach my hands until Saturday morning.

"Enclosed you will find a check on the Bank of Columbia for my dividend on Stock, in that Bank, for the last half year. Not knowing precisely, what percentage it drew, I am uncertain whether it will exceed, or fall short of your demand on me for the 2d instalment on lot No. 16, in the City. If the latter, please to inform me of the deficiency, and the amount shall be transmitted in Bank Notes. With great esteem & respect I am Gentlemen Your Most Obedt Hble Ser. Go: Washington" (ALS, PHi: Gratz Collection). The enclosed check of 18 Nov. sent to the Bank of Columbia reads: "Please to pay to the Commissioners of the City of Washington, the dividend of my Stock in Bank due in September last. Go: Washington" (AD, PWacD). Someone made this notation on GW's check:

"178.57 C. Com[mission]ers

93 43 Cash

272 00"

Letter not found: from William Thornton, 13 Nov. 1799. On 18 Nov. GW wrote Thornton: "Your favour of the 13th inst: came duly to hand."

Letter not found: from William Price, 15 Nov. 1799. On 20 Nov. GW wrote Price that his "favour of the 15th instant" had come "duly to hand."

To Thomas Parker

Sir,   Mount Vernon 16th Novr 1799

By Colo. Lear, I am informed that you have a journey to the Western Country in contemplation.[1]

In consequence, and on the presumption that you will accomplish your intention, I take the liberty of requesting (if you go by the way of Pittsburgh, especially) that you would do me the favour of making the following enquiries, & reporting the result on your return.

First, what is the supposed value (by the Acre) of three tracts of Land which I hold on the Ohio River (East side) between the mouths of the two Kanhawas; the uppermost of wch containing 2314 acres, is the first large bottom below the little Kanhawa, running upwards of five miles on the River; the second, containing 2448 acres is about Sixteen or eighteen miles lower down the River; and is bounded more than three miles by the River; the 3d tract measuring 4395 acres, is still lower down (four or 5 miles, opposite to the Great Bend in the Ohio) and all of them said to be of the first quality. What I mean by the value thereof is, what they probably would sell for, one third of the purchase money paid down—and the other two thirds in annual Instalments, with Interest.[2]

Let me further request the favour of you to make precisely the same enquiry with respect to three tracts of Land which I hold in the Northwestern Territory on the Little Miami River; one within about a mile of the Ohio River, containing 839 acres; another about Seven miles up the former of 977 acres; and the third about 10 miles up the same, measuring 1235 acres.[3]

I pray you to enquire whether the lands on the other side the Ohio are taxed, & under what predicament mine are; and if any of the tracts hereinmentioned (on either side of the River) have settlers on them; what kind; and what sort of Improvements with the number of them.

If you should pass by the Great Kanhawa—let me repeat my request with respect to my lands thereon also[4]—I wish you a pleasant tour, & safe return, being with esteem Sir—Your Most Obedt & very Humble Servt

Go: Washington

ALS (facsimile), advertised in catalog of Superior Stamp & Coin Co., Manuscript Society Sale, 13 Feb. 1991, item 3; ALS (letterpress copy), NN: Washington Papers.

1. On 5 Nov. Parker wrote Tobias Lear: "You will be pleased to forward any Commands that you may have for the western Country as soon as possable Tho I Shall not leave my Quarters untill the Troops are Comfortably provided for & not then If my further Services Shoud be Required" (DLC:GW). Lear replied promptly, on 7 Nov.: "As you had the goodness to tell me that you would make enquiries respecting the situation of the lands granted to the late Majr Geo. Augte Washington in the North Western Territory, during your intended ex-

cursion to that Country, I take the liberty to furnish you with such particulars respecting them, as are in my possession, as Administrator to Major Washington's Estate" (DLC:GW). GW's nephew George Augustine Washington was the first husband of Lear's deceased wife Frances Bassett Washington Lear. After describing the tracts, Lear wrote: "Now, my dear Sir, if you can, from this statement, gain information respecting these two tract[s] of land, and will be so good as to pay any tax or taxes which may be due upon them, the money shall be immediately reimbursed, and you will lay me under great obligations, as well as render a singular service to the Orphans to whom the land belongs" (DLC:GW).

Parker wrote Lear on 13 Nov.: "In Concequence of the lateness of the arrival of the Other Troops I find that I Cannot without some Injury to the service avail myself of the permission that General Pinckney has Given me to go to the Western Country as soon as I expected⟨.⟩ I shall therefore postpone it untill the Begining of January when my services will not be so necessary in Camp" (DLC:GW). Lear wrote Parker again on 14 Nov. and told him that GW wished Parker also to inspect his western lands (DLC:GW).

2. On 6 Nov. 1772 the Virginia council issued to GW patents for 15,000 acres of western land, on the Ohio and Great Kanawha rivers, to which GW was entitled under the terms of Gov. Robert Dinwiddie's Proclamation of 1754. GW first advertised these lands for sale on 15 July 1773 (*Papers, Colonial Series*, 9:118–23, 278–80). His most recent of many subsequent futile attempts to peddle these three tracts on the Ohio River was in September 1798 when he tried without success to persuade Daniel McCarty to take them in exchange for the Sugar Land tract in Loudoun County (see GW to McCarty, 13 Sept. 1798; see also note 9 to GW's Schedule of Property, printed as an enclosure to his will at the end of this volume).

3. In 1788 GW used the warrant for 3,000 acres assigned to him in 1774 to claim these tracts on the Little Miami River near present-day Louisville, Kentucky. In 1798 GW was assured by the secretary of the Northwest Territory that reports that GW's title to these lands was in doubt were groundless (Winthrop Sargent to GW, 16 June 1798). See also the description of these lands in GW's Schedule of Property, which is printed as an enclosure to his will at the end of this volume. See also note 9 of the Schedule of Property.

4. In a complicated transaction GW conveyed his extensive holdings on the Kanawha River to James Welch. See GW to Welch, 29 Nov. 1797, n.1; see also GW's description of his Kanawha lands in the Schedule of Property and note 10 of that document which are printed as an enclosure to his will at the end of this volume.

To James McHenry

Private

My dear Sir,   Mount Vernon 17th Novr 1799

Your confidential and interesting letter of the 10th instant, came duly, and safely to hand. With the contents of which I have been stricken dumb; and I believe it is better that I should remain mute than to express any sentiment on the important matters which are related therein.

I have, for sometime past, viewed the political concerns of the United States with an anxious, and painful eye. They appear to me, to be moving by hasty strides to some awful crisis; but in what they will result—that Being, who sees, foresees, and directs all things, alone can tell. The Vessel is afloat, or very nearly so, and considering myself as a Passenger only, I shall trust to the Mariners whose duty it is to Watch—to steer it into a safe Port.

The charge of British influence in the appointment of Major Pinckney, to be Minister at the Court of London, is a perfect enigma—my curiosity leads me to enquire on what ground it is built—and you would oblige in giving me an explanation. Was it the measure, or the Man, that gave rise to this insinuation? the first it cannot be; because an exchange of Ministers had long been invited; saught after; and the tardiness of G. Britain in not meeting the advances of the U. States in this respect, was considered, & complained of, as an Indignity. Could it be the Man? Could *he*, who had fought against that Country; had bled in defence of his own, in the conflict; of acknowledged abilities, & irreproachable character, be suspected of undue influence? If neither, I ask again, on what is the accusation founded? The whole, is a mistery to me! And *merely* to satisfy my curiosity, I wish to have it unriddled; & not, from the present view wch I have of the subject because I shall think myself bd to answer any interrogatories which may be dictated by insiduous impertinence. With the greatest esteem and regard I remain My dear Sir—Your sincere friend and Affectionate Hble Servant

Go: Washington

ALS, PWacD; ALS (letterpress copy), DLC:GW.

From Alexander Hamilton

Sir   New York Novr 18th 1799

I have been duly honored with your letters of the 26th and 27th of October.

General Pinckney happening to be at my house when they were received, I communicated them to him, together with such other letters as had come to hand relating to the same subject—and I have since furnished him with the subsequent information transmitted to me, in order that he might take the proper measures in whatever might require his interposition. This would principally be to order the tenth Regiment to Carlisle.[1]

It is my duty, in compliance with your inquiry concerning the delay of Payment of the Troops, to enter into a free explanation. The complaints, of which you have heard, have certainly existed—And they have existed in the Northern as well as in the Southern Quarter—and the painful circumstance is, that they have been well founded—There has, no doubt, been a great & a very unfortunate delay, which has been a pretext for, if not a cause of, desertion, which has made ill impressions on the minds of the troops, and has occasioned much embarrassment to the Officers.

The history of the course of the business will best unfold the causes of the delay.

Early after the recruiting service was in train, I caused to be prepared, and transmitted to the several Regiments, the forms of Muster and Pay rolls. If my information be right, Muster and Pay rolls were made out according to these forms and forwarded first to the Department of War, afterwards to the Office of the Paymaster General.[2]

It has since appeared that forms for Muster and Payrolls had been previously established by the Department of War but these forms were never sent to me, nor otherwise communicated to the additional Regiments, till some time after the arrival of the Paymaster General at Philadelphia. A compliance with them, on the part of the distant regiments, the Officers of which, for the purpose of recruiting were dispersed over extensive regions, would, of course, involve a very distressing delay, in addition to that which unavoidably attended the mustering of the troops and the preparation of the rolls on the plan which I had prescribed: Yet for some time a compliance with these new forms seems to have been expected as a preliminary to the transmission of the money.

But in consequence of very importunate representations from me, and it being admitted that the different Rolls corresponded in substantial points, I was given to understand by the Paymaster General, that as to past dues, the new forms would not be insisted upon but that the money would be sent without waiting for them.

Difficulties, however, about modes of remitting the money,

which, it is believed had before operated in producing delay, continued to occasion it—and to this moment the three most Northern and two most Southern Regiments, remain unsupplied.

To call every regimental Paymaster to the seat of Government as often as money is to be paid is inadmissible on the Score of delay as well as of Expence. To send them the money by post must involve the double risk of loss in the Post Office, and loss by a fraudulent concealment of the Receipt of it. To send it to intermediate public Agents must be attended with the same risk, though in a less degree. The Paymaster General in order to discharge himself at the Treasury is obliged to produce vouchers in certain prescribed forms, which he has been (as he states) in the habit of obtaining before he parted with any money out of his hands; and he appeared to be fearful of a deviation from this course.

The truth is, that these Difficulties being inherent in the nature of the thing, they ought, for this very reason, as I conceive, to have been overcome. Similar Ones occur in all the pecuniary operations of the Government, and it has been found indispensable to surmount them by expedients. The same expedients which are familiar in other cases would have answered in the one under consideration.

In my opinion, the Paymaster General would have done right not to have been deterred by the additional responsibility which might have attended the employment of the usual expedients. In my opinion, if peculiar caution was incumbent upon him as a subordinate Officer, it was to have been expected, that the Secretary of War, in concert with the Secy of the Treasury, would have interposed to remove the impediment by sanctioning a course which was unavoidable.

It is not my fault that the obstacles have not been surmounted— Aware, that in the first stages of the raising of the new Corps, (of which most of the Officers as well as the men were unacquainted with Service) where the Officers for the purpose of recruiting were dispersed over extensive districts—delay and Difficulty would unavoidably attend the preparation of Muster and Pay rolls in strict form. Strongly impressed with the idea that it was of great importance in the first instance to inspire the troops with favourable ideas of the justice and attention of the Government—and that it would be very inexpedient to have to assign to the Noncommissioned Officers and privates, excuses for the delay of their dues on the Score of want of formal Documents, which it did not lie with them to prepare—I pressed the Secretary of War, and the Paymaster General for advances of money to the several Regiments in anticipation of those Documents, upon Estimates of which I furnished the Data. I thought the temporary Departure from ordinary rules, and the small addition of risk from dispensing with the usual preliminary checks were less evils than those which were inseparable from any considerable procrastination of payment.[3]

But my efforts were not sucessful. Expectations, which, in consequence of my representations were given to me by the Paymaster General, and which were by me given to the commandants of Regiments were not fulfilled. Disappointment and Dissatisfaction have, of course, ensued.

It is but candour for me to mention, that while Secretary of the Treasury, I had knowledge of the forms which had been prescribed. But I had intirely forgotten the circumstance. And it is self evident that all regulations prescribed by the Department of War, for observance in an Army, ought to be communicated from that Department, either to the Military Commander or to the chief of the particular branch of service to which they relate—and that it is not incumbent upon the military Commander to make inquiry of the Department of War for them—I therefore did what was natural in the case—I prescribed forms, where I did not know that any had been previously established by superior authority.

It is very probable that the necessity of transmitting these forms did not occur to the Secy of War—Or he may have considered it as the province of the Paymaster General to do it; but this Officer being with the Western Army, a very great delay could not fail to attend the transmission of them by him. The truth is, that a want of sufficient organisation, in this particular as in others, occasioned an omission.

The only material remark in respect to it is—that the omission having happened, it was a decisive reason for not insisting upon the forms in question as a preliminary to payment.

Upon the whole, (since I have not understood that there was any deficiency of money) I am led to conclude that Unwillingness to incur extraordinary responsibility by a deviation from general rules has been a principal cause of the very inconvenient delay which has been experienced. The mode of proceeding has certainly not corresponded with my ideas of propriety and expediency; yet I do not presume to expect that my ideas should be a Standard for the conduct of others. And I am certainly very far from imagining, that any motive more exceptionable than the one I have suggested has had the least influence in the affair. The pay-master is, no Doubt, shielded by his instructions.

I trust that things are now in a train for a more satisfactory course in future. With perfect respect & attachment I have the honor to be Sir yr obedt servt

Alex. Hamilton

LS, DLC:GW; ADf, DLC: Hamilton Papers.

1. For the "other letters" Hamilton communicated to Gen. Charles Cotesworth Pinckney, see note 1 to this letter of 18 Nov. to GW in Syrett, *Hamilton Papers*, 24: 50–54. Hamilton wrote Pinckney on 8 Nov., enclosing a letter from Tobias Lear of 31 Oct. (ibid., 15–16; see also Lear to GW, 4 Nov., n.4).

2. The difficulties that Hamilton had with the army paymaster general with regard to muster and pay rolls and to the payment of the troops, which Hamilton summarized here, may be followed in the correspondence between Hamilton and Paymaster General Caleb Swan in September, October, and November 1799. These include Hamilton to Swan, 14, 22 Sept. (ibid., 23:415–16, 460–61), 1, 13 Nov. (ibid., 24:1, 35–36), and Swan to Hamilton, 25 Sept. (two letters), 5, 31 Oct. (ibid., 23:471–72, 510, 588), 14 Nov. (ibid., 24:38).

3. For reference to Hamilton's correspondence with regimental commanders regarding pay, see note 9 to this letter of 18 Nov. to GW, ibid., 24:53.

To William Thornton

Dear Sir,   Mount Vernon 18th Novr 1799

Your favour of the 13th inst: came duly to hand.[1] I am now making arrangements at the Bank of Alexandria for obtaining money. When this is accomplished, I will forward a check, on that Bank, for the $1000 required by Mr Blagden, & hope it will be in time to answer his purposes.[2]

I have no objection to Mr Blagden's frequent calls for money; but I fear the work which is not ennumerated in the Contract with him, is pretty smartly whipped up in the price of it. I had no expectation (for instance) that a Well little more than 30 feet deep, was to cost me upwards of £70. I may, however, have misconceived the matter, from ignorance of the usual rates. With great esteem & regard—I am—Dr Sir Yr Obedt Hble Servt

Go: Washington

ALS, DLC: Thornton Papers; ALS (letterpress copy), NN: Washington Papers.
  1. Letter not found.
  2. See GW to Thornton, 20 November.

To Ralph Wormeley, Jr.

Dear Sir,   Mount Vernon 18th Novr 1799
   Your favour of the 3d Instant came duly to hand.[1] Whence the
Report of my visiting Norfolk could have arisen, I know not. From
any intention of mine it did not, for nothing was ever more foreign
from them. I have never been farther from home since I left the
Chair of Government, than the Federal City except when I was
called to Philadelphia by the Secretary of War—and that distance,
I am persuaded will circumscribe my Walks; unless, which heaven
avert! I should be obliged to resume a military career.
   I am not less obliged to you, however, my good Sir, for your
polite invitation to Rosegill; and if events (at present unforeseen)
should ever call me into those parts, I certainly shall avail myself
of it. Mrs Washington feels obliged by your kind remembrance of
her; and unites with me in best respects to yourself & Lady. I am
Dear Sir Your Most Obedient Hble Servant

                                        Go: Washington

ALS (photocopy), DLC:GW; ALS (letterpress copy), ViMtV. The ALS was advertised for sale by Joseph Rubinfine in his catalog no. 96, item 24.
  1. Letter not found.

Letter not found: from Hepburn & Dundas, 19 Nov. 1799. GW wrote the
firm of Hepburn & Dundas on 23 Nov.: "Your letter of the 19th was recd
yesterday."

Letter not found: from William W. Woodward, 19 Nov. 1799. On 24 Nov.
GW wrote Woodward: "I have been favoured with your letter of the 19th
Instant."

To Charles Little

Dear Sir,   Mount Vernon 20th Novr 1799
   The week before the last, I went up to Difficult Run to Survey a
small tract of land which I hold thereon, at the Bridge; and to view
a lot (No. 10) which Mr Jno. Gill, late of Alexandria, purchased as

part of the land formerly belonging to the Earl of Tankerville, and which he (Gill) had offered to me in discharge of a demand I had upon him.[1]

I was plagued, and indeed unable to find, either the Corner trees or lines of my tract. The upper corner on Difficult was entirely gone; a place was designated by Mr Thos Gunnell, near to which, he thought it had stood. The *only* corner which seemed to be well established, was at the end of the first course from the run above, a large white Oak, by a spring, marked IC near Stone's house. From hence I run the course of my tract which is also a line of Tankerville's, until I came to the Bridge branch (sometimes called Colvills branch)[2] but could find neither line tree nor corner at the end thereof, on the branch; and was informed by Captn Wiley, Mr Wherry, Mr Yates, and others who accompanied me, and by some whom it was said had been with you, when Tankerville's land was run out, that I was too low down the Branch; for that you struck it at the lower end of a small meadow thereon.

From this place until I came to Difficult run again, I could discover neither line tree nor corner—and the only person with me (William Shepherd) who had it in his power to give correct information had views quite incompatible therewith; and to mislead & deceive, were the *sole* objects of his attendance: for when, in running the course from the Bridge branch, it was found that I was crossing the Road lower down than all present expected; and it was declared as the invariable belief of the neighbours, that Tankerville's line & mine on this course were the same, & had always been so considered, he said No! adding, that part of a tract of 12,000 Acres belonging to the late Thos Lord Fairfax had a narrow gore running up between them; and when it was observed that this could not well be, and that, if Tankerville's line *here*, and mine were not the same, that the land between must be vacant, & in that case that I shd enter it as waste; it eked out, by degrees, that he had been prying into these lines, and either had, or meant to secure this vacancy (if it be one) to himself; and that, to deceive until it could be accomplished, was all he was aiming at.[3]

I have been thus particular in my statement of this matter to you, my good Sir, because I am about to ask, if you have any recollection, or knowledge, of these lines, or the circumstances attending them, that you would be so obliging as to furnish me therewith—particularly, as it may respect the corner *on*, or *near*, the

Bridge branch; and the course from thence; and whether the understanding at the time you Survey Tankerville's was, or was not, that mine joined it on the courses just mentioned.[4] In short, if you have the Survey of Tankerville's land by you & see no impropriety in the measure, I would thank you for letting Mr Rawlins have a copy thereof; in aid of any other information you may be so good as to give; as I dislike very much the disingenuous conduct & concealment of Mr Shepherd in this business; and, as far as Justice in it will support me shall endeavour to defeat his views. With esteem & regard I am Dr Sir Your most Obedient Servt

Go: Washington

ALS (letterpress copy), DLC:GW.

1. For GW's dealings with John Gill and his surveying trip to Difficult Run between 6 and 8 Nov., see *Diaries*, 6:374–75, and GW to Gill, 19 Oct., n.2. The fourth earl of Tankerville, Charles Bennett (1743–1822), in 1791 and 1792 sold Virginia lands bequeathed to his father by his cousin John Colvill (see GW to Tankerville, 20 Jan. 1784, in *Papers, Confederation Series*, 1:64–66, and Mitchell, *Fairfax County Patents and Grants*, 149–50).

2. "Colvills branch" appears as Colvin Branch on the map of Fairfax County in Mitchell, *Fairfax County Patents and Grants*.

3. For GW's correspondence regarding the nonexistent land for which he and William Shepherd vied, see GW to William Price, 7 Nov., n.1.

4. In his letter to Lord Tankerville of 20 Jan. 1784, GW indicates that Charles Little was, or was to become, Tankerville's agent in Virginia. In 1791 Little bought the Virginia Colvill estate Cleesh (Clish) from Tankerville. On 27 Nov. 1799 Little sent GW "a map of the Land—formerly Lord Tankervilles" (GW to Little, 28 Nov. 1799).

To William Price

Sir, Mount Vernon 20th Novr 1799

Your favour of the 15th instant, in answer to my letters of the 7th & 8th, addressed to the Surveyor General of the Land Office (wch proves the necessity there was for my plea of ignorance) came duly to hand; with the Land Office Treasury Warrant; for your obliging attention to which, I pray you to accept my thanks.[1]

Perceiving by your letter that Willm Shepherd has made a Survey, & returned it to your Office, similar in *some respects* to my proposed Entry; and believing that it must have been done unknowingly to those who have lands adjoining, and comprehends Land always reputed to be mine; and so understood by all the neighbourhood thereabts; I request the favour of you to furnish me with a copy of the Survey & Plat, that I may be enabled thereby to investigate the matter more fully. Until which, I must beg that this letter may be considered as a Caveat against a Grant thereof to Wm Shepherd.

If the rules & Proceedings in your Office require a more formal protest against such issue, I must rely on your goodness to advise me; for having had very little to do with the local Laws of the State since the Revolution, & not having those passed since that period by me, I may be mistaken in this, as in my former application.

Enclosed is a five dollar Bill; if it be insufficient to cover the Expence of the Land Warrant, Copy of Shepherd's Survey, and the Protest against a Grant issuing thereon—you will please to advise.[2]

As another proof of my unacquaintedness in this business, my expectation was, that the Entry I proposed to make would have covered *all* the land within the described location; but the Warrant fixd it, I perceive, to 100 acres *only*. It may be more, or it may be less; and cannot be ascertained until the Survey is made. I should not like to be fixed to the above quantity, if the vacant land exceeds it. I am Sir—Your Most Obedient and Very Hble Servant

Go: Washington

ALS (letterpress copy), NN: Washington Papers.

1. Price's letter of 15 Nov. has not been found.

2. For GW's correspondence regarding unclaimed land adjoining his Difficult Run property, see GW to Price, 7 Nov., n.1.

To Samuel Sommers

Sir,   Mount Vernon 20th Novr 1799

In consequence of your letter, and the information of Mr Rawlins, I sent to Richmond and obtained the enclosed warrant— With which (in the absence of Colo. Payne) I pray you to do what will be necessary to give it legal and proper effect and advise me thereof by a line lodged in the Post Office as the most certain mode of getting it to hand.[1]

You will perceive that the Warrant is for 100 Acres *only*, this has proceeded from my mistake in saying, *I believed* the vacancy would not exceed this quantity; but my intention in the Entry was to cover *all* the waste land within the limits I had described—be it more or less—and if the location cannot comprehend this I shall be disappointed and ask your advice & assistance to correct it.[2]

It appears from the Registers letter, which accompanied the Warrant that Mr William Shepherd has made, and returned a Survey to that Office which bears some similitude to my Entry, I would ask the favour of you, therefore to examine the Surveyors Books to see at what time it was made and whether, in your judgment it is the identical Land I have been aiming to obtain. Mr Shepherds conduct while I was employed in Surveying my land on Difficult was so full of concealment and deception that I have not, nor shall not place any confidence in any thing he may say respecting the premises. For if he has made a Survey of this vacancy it was done unknowingly to the neighbourhood thereabouts; who, one and all (whom I saw) expressed a belief that Tankervilles Line and mine—between which the vacancy is *now* supposed to lye—were the same, and was so understood by them all.[3] And Mr Jno. Moss who formerly lived on Tankerville's land, and whom I have lately seen declares the same.[4] With esteem I am Sir Your very Hble Servant

Go: Washington

P.S. I have written to Colo. ⟨Payne⟩ also, for informatn on this subject. but request no delay on that account.[5]

ALS (letterpress copy), NN: Washington Papers.

1. Sommers's letter has not been found, but see GW to William Price, 7, 8 November. Price enclosed the warrant in his letter of 15 Nov., which has not been found.

2. See GW to Price, 8, 20 November.

3. See GW to Price, 7 Nov., n.1.

4. John Moss is probably the John Moss who before the Revolution had an ordinary at Sugar Land Run about halfway between Leesburg and Alexandria. See *Diaries*, 3:238, 239.

5. The letterpress copy of GW's letter to William Payne, the Fairfax County surveyor, is in part not legible and the rest barely so. It appears to have been dated 28 Nov., but its contents indicate it was written before that date, probably on the twentieth. The legible portion of the letter reads: "Sir, If this letter should find you at home, the intention ⟨of it⟩ is (through Mr Rawlins the bearer) to enquire into the State of my Entry, of a supposed vacancy of land, on Difficult run ⟨*illegible*⟩ and always supposed ⟨*illegible*⟩ boundaries; and to learn what ⟨*illegible*⟩ a Mr Willm Shepherd, or others for him have taken in your Office to interrupt the progress of my Entry & Warrant.

"If you have seen your Deputy Mr S. Sommers, since your return, you would from him, have received a perfect account of the whole ⟨*illegible*⟩ business. If you have not, Mr Rawlins relation, who is acquainted therewith will save me the necessity of detailing them. I have done, and am ready to do, all that has been adjudged expedient & proper. I am Sir—Your most Obedt Servt Go: Washington" (NN: Washington Papers).

To William Thornton

Dear Sir,   Mount Vernon 20th Novr 1799
When I wrote to you the other day, I expected to have settled matters with the Bk of Alexandria so as to have been enabled to have sent you, for Mr Blagdens use, a check thereon for $1000—But not being well enough acquainted with the rules of the Bank, I suffered what are called discount days, to pass over before I applied; for which reason the business *there* must remain over until after Tuesday of next week.[1]

But, if to do this will be attended with any inconvenience to Mr Blagden, and he will be at the trouble of riding, or sending any person down here, competent to receive the money—Mr Lewis, who has it by him, will lend me that sum, and it shall be paid—Of this I would thank you for informing Mr Blagden. With esteem &ca I remain Yr Obedt Servt

Go: Washington

ALS, DLC: Thornton Papers; ALS (letterpress copy), NN: Washington Papers.
1. GW wrote Thornton on 18 November.

To Benjamin Goodhue

Dear Sir   Mount Vernon 22d Novr 1799
Your favour of the 3d of Octr never came to my hands until last night.[1] ⟨On⟩ hearing that Captn Hammond had arrived at Alexandria, I shall send up for the Fish, and pay him the cost of them—nine dollars.

For your kind recollection of my want of this article, I thank you. They came very opportunely; and just as I was thinking of writing to you for a fresh supply.[2]

Without expressing any opinion with respect to the Embassy which has just Sailed from this Country; I will hope for the best: Being among those who believe, that *Providence* after its numberless favours towards us, will still continue an out stretched arm to help, & deliver us from the evils with which we have been, & continue to be, assailed. With very great esteem & regard I am—Dear Sir Your Most Obedt Hble Servt

Go: Washington

ALS, NNS; ALS (letterpress copy), NN: Washington Papers. The letter was: "Favoured by Willm Craik Esqr."

1. Letter not found.

2. Senator Goodhue of Massachusetts had sent fish to GW from Salem in 1797. See Goodhue to GW, 30 Aug. 1797, in *Papers, Retirement Series*, 1:329–30.

From Clement Biddle

Dear Sir   Philad[elphia] Nov: 23d 1799

Before I had received your favor of 13th inst. I had on information from the Custom house entered the two pipes of wine & two boxes of Citron & shipped them in the Harmony Capt. Ellwood for Alexandria by which Vessel which left this Yesterday I also forwarded two boxes of spermaceti Candles and two bags of the best Java Coffee which is what they have sold as Mocoa but I beleive there is none real in town abetter than what I have sent—I could not meet with a small Chest of imperial Tea which I liked but expect to get one by the next vessel.

I am sorry the Grass Seed turned out so bad—there is no relying on the imported seed—some Lucerne which they ask 75 Cents a pound Appears but Ordinary—I am told some person has lately had fresh imported but cannot Yet find him out—they ask 10 Drs per bushel for the red Clover seed.

Mr Anthony has wrote you in Answer to your Letter which I delivered him—My hurry since our return from the Country has prevented my Attending the pay Office for Mr Custis's pay but I will have it enquired for.

Flour is superfine 11—Ds. Common 10 Ds. ℔ bbl 16/ to 16/8 —good Wheat both in demand. I am very respectfully Yr mo. Obed. Servt

Clement Biddle

have not got the bills for the Coffee or Candles or freight of wine but enclose bill of Loading—Capt. Ellwood has the Certificates wch should accompany the wine.

ALS, DLC:GW.

To Hepburn & Dundas

Gentlemen,   Mount Vernon 23rd Novr 1799

Your letter of the 19th was recd yesterday.[1] If my attendance at Mr Heiskill's in Alexandria on the 26th could render you any *real* Service, I would do it with pleasure.

But all that I could relate would be *hearsay* whilst means exist, to obtain (I presume) positive proofs of the facts you wish to establish.[2]

With respect to the division of the tract, of (what you call) 51,302 acres, I am as ignorant as any man whom you might pick up, *by chance* in the Streets of Alexandria.

I *believe*, Mr Jno. West, deceased, was one of the Patentees in the large Survey at the Mo. of the Great Kanhawa; but to this fact I would give no positive evidence: for after being at the *whole* trouble, and the *greater* part of the expence to obtain a recognition of the original grant of 200,000 acres; and being *compelled*, very improperly I did think, and always have thought, to take it in twenty Surveys, the Governor and Council found themselves, by this act (which was protested against) under the necessity of jumbling a number of names into the same Patent, in order to give each claimant, according to his grade, & the ratio they had alloted him, the qty allowed—whereas, if the priviledge of locating that quantity, within the District which they had assigned for this purpose had been given to each Claimant, it would have prevented all the difficulties, and perplexities which have ensued; to the inconvenience of all, and entire loss of the Land, to some.

But thus the matter was ordered, by that body; after which, and the issuing of the Patents consequent thereof, my Agency ceased; and I have concerned myself with no other part of the Land than was assigned me, & such as I purchased thereafter of others.[3]

With respect to the division of the tract you alluded to, so far am I from knowing that it was made *according to law*, that I do not know it was ever made; and as to the issue of Mr Jno. West, I am entirely unacquainted, otherwise than by report; never having been in his house, that I recollect, more than once—and that 30 years ago—and 25 of which but little in this State.[4] I am Gentn Your very Hble Servant

                                        Go: Washington

ALS (letterpress copy), NN: Washington Papers.

William Hepburn and John Dundas were merchants in Alexandria.

1. Letter not found.

2. The request that GW go to Peter Heiskill's place in Alexandria may have had to do with a piece of property on King Street in Alexandria which Heiskill purchased two months later. The line that divided this parcel of land from an adjoining one owned by John Dundas had been in dispute (Munson, *Alexandria Hustings Court Deeds, 1797–1801*, 169).

3. In the first distribution of the 200,000 acres of land in the Ohio country set aside under Governor Dinwiddie's Proclamation of 1754 for participants in the Great Meadows campaign, one of the patents issued by the Virginia council on 6 Nov. 1772 was for a tract of 51,382 acres to "George Muse, Andrew Lewis, Adam Stephen, Peter Hog, John West, [John] Polson, & Andrew Wagener" (Petition to Lord Dunmore and the Virginia Council, c.4 Nov. 1772, in *Papers, Colonial Series*, 9:118–23; see also GW to Lord Dunmore and Council, c.3 Nov. 1773, ibid., 358–66).

4. John West, Jr., was the fourth lieutenant in the Virginia Regiment of 1754, resigning his commission after the 1754 campaign. He died in 1777. GW spent the night of 17 April 1769 at West's house in Alexandria (*Diaries*, 2:141).

To Alexander Addison

Sir,   Mount Vernon 24th Novr 1799

Your favour of the 8th instant came duly to hand. Whatever is found to be the contents of the Land I sold to the deceased Colo. Ritchie, by ⟨firm⟩ and actual measurement I shall abide by.

I have not heard a tittle from Mrs Ritchie nor her brother in law on the subject of the Instalment, due me, and with pain I add, that if payment of what is due thereon is not immediately made, my own want of money *must* compel me to put the Bond in Suit. The object I had in selling that, & other lands, is entirely defeated by non-payment of the purchase money, agreeably to contract—and the consequence—a necessity of borrowing from the Banks at a ruinous interest; a measure I never, in the course of my life, have practised until within the present, & last year.

The result of your late Election was painful to hear. With esteem I remain Sir Your most Obedt Hble Servant

Go: Washington

ALS (letterpress copy), NN: Washington Papers.

To Clement Biddle

Dear Sir,   Mount Vernon 24th Novr 1799

A considerable time ago, in consequence of some applications from Officers of Cavalry, to know in what manner they were to draw pay, I wrote to the Secretary of War on the Subject; & received for answer—that as no Pay master was appointed to that Corps, they were to draw on the Pay master General.

Mr Custis (cornet in the Light Dragoons) being one of those alluded to, above, drew an order, as he informs me on the Pay master General in your favour; but is yet without the money (of which he is a good deal in want). I pray you therefore to inform him, or me, wherein lays the difficulty of obtaining it from the Pay master General, that I may apprise the Secretary of War thereof.[1]

When you inform me of the prices of those seeds which were ennumerated in my last—please to add to them that of Timothy Seed also, by the Bushel.[2] With much esteem & regard—I am Dear Sir Your Obedt Hble Servt

Go: Washington

At what price could *good* German Oznabrigs be bought—taking eight hundred, or one thousand Ells?[3]

ALS, PHi: Washington-Biddle Correspondence; ALS (letterpress copy), NN: Washington Papers.

1. See GW to James McHenry, 25 Aug. 1799. See also GW to Biddle, 8 Dec. 1799.

2. GW last wrote Biddle on 13 November. See also Biddle's response of 23 Nov., which GW had not yet received.

3. The postscript to GW's letter to Biddle of 29 Jan. 1798 has been sometimes mistakenly attached to this letter of 24 Nov. 1799.

To Timothy Pickering

Dear Sir,   Mount Vernon 24th Novr 1799

Your favour of the 5th instant came to hand in due course; and the manner in which you proposed to dispose of my letter to Mr Murray, was perfectly agreeable to me.[1]

Knowing nothing of the writer of the enclosed letter, and unwilling to be hasty in encouraging proposals of this sort, without some information of the characters who are engaged in the Work;

I take the liberty of enquiring, through you, who Mr William W. Woodward is, and if you approve of his plan.[2]

In this case, be so good as to forward my letter to him—also enclosed—as directed; If not, I pray you to return it, along with his letter to me. With Doctr Witherspoon I was acquainted, & have no objection to subscribe to his works if the publication of them is by a proper hand, and on proper principles. With great esteem & regard I am—Dear Sir Your Most Obedt & very Hble Servt

Go: Washington

ALS, MHi: Pickering Papers; ALS (letterpress copy), NN: Washington Papers. The ALS is docketed by Pickering, "answd Decr 3d and sent his letter to Mr Woodward."

1. Letter not found.

2. William W. Woodward was a printer at no. 52 South Second Street in Philadelphia, who printed between 1794 and 1796, for Pierre Egron, the French-English journal *Level of Europe*. The letter to Woodward which GW enclosed, dated 24 Nov., reads: "Sir I have been favoured with your letter of the 19th Instant. Being well acquainted with Doctr Witherspoon, whilst living, and knowing to his abilities; I shall, with pleasure, as far as becoming a subscriber to his Works may contribute, promote the success of their Publication: and do authorise you accordingly, to add my name to the subscription Paper which appears to be in existence. I am Sir Your Most Hble Servant Go: Washington" (letterpress copy, NN: Washington Papers). Woodward's letter of 19 Nov. has not been found. No answer from Pickering to GW's letter has been found. Woodward printed in 1800 and 1801 a four-volume edition of the writings of John Witherspoon.

Letter not found: from Samuel Sommers, 25 Nov. 1799. On 28 Nov. GW wrote Sommers: "Colo. Little forwarded your letter of the 25th instant to me, yesterday evening."

Letter not found: from William Price, 25 Nov. 1799. GW wrote Price on 2 Dec.: "I have been duly favoured with your letter of the 25th Ulto."

To Bryan Fairfax

My Lord,   Mount Vernon 26th Novemr 1799

In the early part of this month, I went up to Difficult-run to examine with more accuracy than I had ever done before, the small tract of Land you were so obliging (many years ago) to accomodate me with, for a Stage for my Waggons whilst I had plantations in Berkeley County; to see if it would *now* (having many years since removed my people from those Lands) answer for a small Farm; those around me being overstocked with labourers.[1]

I was unable, with the assistance of several of the Neighbours thereabouts, to ⟨discover⟩ the lines, on more than one corner of the tract. There was also a corner to the Land lately belonging to the Earl of Tankerville, and at the end of the first course after leaving the run (where it was supposed the upper corner tree thereon formerly stood). From this, *well known corner* neither line tree nor corner tree could be found; the next, called for by the Deed, was a white oak on the bridge branch. In running the course of the Deed from thence, it crossed the main (Leesburgh) road much lower, than those present, conceived it ought to have done; the concurrent opinion being, that this course & Tankerville's were the same; and it was well known to them *all* that the latter crossed the Road higher up.

The person present, who had it most in his power to give correct information, attended for other purposes than to be useful to me; for when he found my line and Tankervilles did not accord, agreeably to the received opinion, he (William Shepherd) attempted to impress a belief that a very narrow-pointed gore—of a tract of 12,000 and odd acres, belonging to the late Thos Lord Fairfax, run in between; and when it was observed that this was as improbable, as unheard of, by any of them before, it eked out by degrees, that his object was to deceive, until he could enter the gore as vacant land for himself.[2]

I have troubled you with these details by way of an apology for the liberty I am about to take (if you see no impropriety in granting it) of asking, having heard that the above mentioned tract of twelve thousand & odd acres was a bequest to you, or your sons, by the late Thos Lord Fairfax, for the courses, or so many thereof, together with such of your Towlston tract on Difficult run, below & adjoining the seperate survey of 275 acres made for one Norris, as will enable me, not only to discover my own lines, but whether there is any vacancy between them and the Lands adjoining. To accomplish this, it will not escape your penetration, that there must be some corner; or line, of one or both of the tracts I have enumerated, and mine the same; otherwise the three plats (or so much of them as is essential to my purpose) could not be connected together so as to elucidate the point in question.[3]

Having had abundant proof of your readiness to oblige me on

all occasions, I will add nothing further in excuse for asking this favour. As it is very probable Mr Ferdn. Fairfax will make you a visit shortly I will be glad to be informed of his arrival, being informed that the land adjoining me, (above Ld Tankerville's) is now in his possession. Sincerely wishing you a return of good health I am with very great esteem & respect Your Lordships Most Obedt Affecte Hble Servt

Go: Washington

ALS (letterpress copy), DLC:GW.
    1. See GW to John Gill, 19 Oct., n.2.
    2. See GW to William Price, 7 Nov., n.1.
    3. For Fairfax's missing reply of 28 Nov., see GW to Fairfax, 30 November. In her *Fairfax County Patents and Grants*, Beth Mitchell notes that the tract of 275 acres acquired by GW from Fairfax is "marked William Norris on two plats 8 June 1739" (149).

To John Gill

Sir,   Mount Vernon 26th Novr 1799
    Under cover with this, you are furnished with the Invoice of such goods as I require.[1]
    As it was not so much in my power to fix the *prices*, as to designate the *quality* of the Goods, the amount of the cost of them may exceed, or fall short, of the sum due from you to me. If the first, the balance shall be paid by me; if the latter, I shall look to you for the deficiency.
    I have drawn up, and signed before evidences, a memoranda of the agreement we entered into the day you were at this place, according to my conception of it.[2] I have not, intentionally, departed either from the spirit or letter of it; and if it meets your approbation, the counterpart may be signed by you, before witnesses, and returned to me; together with the Deed from Mr Herbert to you; and against your arrival in Alexandria I will have a conveyance of that part of lot No. 10 which lays on the upper side of Difficult-run, ready for your Signature.
    It is not *always* an easy matter to make interested men, at a distance, (when they are deprived of opportunities of seeing, & judging for themselves) believe that, there can be perfect candour used in a transaction, or relation of facts by the other party, when they are differently circumstanced ⟨*mutilated*⟩ nothing more cer-

tain than that, the Woodland part of No. 10 which is on the lower side of Difficult run, would be infinitely more valuable to the proprietor of the land adjoining it, *on that side*, than that part of Lewis's tract which lays on the upper side; seperated therefrom by a deep and Mirey run which can only be passed in place⟨s⟩ and not at those in all Seasons.[3] For the same reason, the last mentioned slipe would be advantageous to me, although entirely stripped of wood and much exhausted. I am—Sir Your—very Hble Servant

Go: Washington

ALS (letterpress copy), NN: Washington Papers.

1. GW's invoice, in his hand and signed by him at Mount Vernon on 26 Nov., reads: "Invoice of Goods to be sent for by Mr John Gill of Baltimore, for and on account of George Washington of *Mount* Vernon in Virginia, according to Agreement

6 pair of the largest—finest—and best Bed Blankets.

6 pieces of the largest—thickest and best striped

Blanketing for negros. these pieces generally contain 15 or 16 blankets each.

6 pieces of Ditto 2d sort—somewhat smaller.

1 ps. of light coloured broadcloath (not quite white) for my servants liveries; to cost about 7/6 sterg pr Yard.

1 ps. of scarlet for ditto to cost abt 8/6 pr yard Twist, silk & thread proportioned to Ditto

2 dble gross of white mettal buttons best kind

180 yards (or thereabouts, according to the number of yards in a piece) of blue thickset, or Dufd for negros cloathing.

200 yards—or thereabouts—of green do for do of a quality somewhat cheaper. 6 dble gross of the cheapest kind of white mettal Buttons. Go: Washington" (ADS, NNGL; PU: Armstrong Collection; letterpress copy, NN: Washington Papers). The invoice is docketed: "N.B. received 5th Feby 1800 by us, Huddersfield To: Thos Law Atkinson & Co."

2. The "memoranda of the agreement" have not been found. For GW's negotiations with Gill regarding the payment of back rent for GW's Difficult Run tract, see GW to Gill, 19 Oct., n.2.

3. Presumably GW is referring to the tract of 337 acres (no. 164) granted to John Lewis in January 1728, most of which was on the lower or eastern side of Difficult Run and adjacent to both Gill's and GW's land (Mitchell, *Fairfax County Patents and Grants*, 204).

To William Thornton

Dear Sir,   Mount Vernon Novr 26th 1799

For, and on account of Mr Blagden, I enclose you a Post note of the Bank of Columbia, for ninety three dollars forty three cents, and a check on the Bank of Alexandria for nine hundred and six dollars and fifty seven cents. Together, amounting to one thousand dollars, requested by Mr Blagden. With esteem and regard I am Dear Sir Your Obedt Humble Servt

Go: Washington

Let me request the favour of you to desire Mr Blagden to give me the number and sizes of the Rooms in my Houses in the City. frequent enquiries are made of me concerning them without my being able to satisfy the Enquiror.[1]

ALS (letterpress copy), NN: Washington Papers. The postscript was added after the letterpress copy was made.

1. On 30 Nov. Thornton sent George Blagdin's list of the rooms in GW's Capitol Hill houses. See GW to Thornton, 1 December.

Letter not found: from Charles Little, 27 Nov. 1799. GW wrote Little on 28 Nov.: "Mr Johnston delivered me your favour of yesterday."

Letter not found: from James Piercy, 27 Nov. 1799. On 1 Dec. GW wrote Piercy "In answer to your letter of the 27th Ulto."

Letter not found: from Bryan Fairfax, 28 Nov. 1799. In a letter to Fairfax of 30 Nov., GW refers to Fairfax's "favour of the 28th Instt."

From Alexander Hamilton

Sir   New York Novr 28th 1799

Enclosed is a copy of a letter which I have written to the Secretary of War on the subject of a military Academy.[1]

Two reasons have prevented me from communicating it to you at an earlier day. My avocations rendered it impossible for me to complete the letter till very lately, and I had had opportunities of knowing your opinion on the subject generally. Any alterations in the plan which you may do me the honor to suggest will receive the most careful attention.[2] With the truest respect & attachment I have the honor to be Sir Yr Obed. sert

A. Hamilton

LS, DLC: Hamilton Papers.

1. Hamilton's letter to Secretary of War James McHenry is dated 23 Nov. and is printed in Syrett, *Hamilton Papers*, 24:69–75.

2. See GW's response of 12 December.

To Charles Little

Dear Sir,   Mount Vernon 28th Novr 1799.

Mr Johnston delivered me your favour of yesterday, and a map of the Land—formerly Lord Tankervilles;[1] but as he came late in the afternoon, and said he was obliged to return that evening, I did not incline to detain him until I could examine, & get such information from the plat as was necessary for my purpose. I therefore dispatched him, & took the liberty of detaining the latter until this morning.

I am much obliged to you for sending it to me (and have paid Mr Johnston for bringing it). It shews clearly, that Tankervilles line and mine, from the Bridge, or Colvile branch are not the same. The question then is, whether the space between is vacant, or part of the late Thos Lord Fairfaxs twelve thousand Acre tract. I have no doubt myself, as well from other circumstances, as from Shepherds conduct, of its being waste & ungranted; but until I can get the meets & bounds of the above tract of 12000 acres, & perhaps of the Towlston Land also this fact cannot be ascertained with precision.[2]

The present Lord Fairfax has promised me every aid in his power to elucidate this matter; but thinks some of the Papers necessary to effect ⟨it⟩ are in the possession of his son (he does not say which) whom he expects down between this and Christmas: but finding that Mr Shepherd, & some who abet him, are active in their endeavours to arre⟨st⟩ my Entry, it has put me more upon my mettle than I should otherwise have been, and more perhaps than the land, if obtained, is worth.

For this reason, I mean to have the line of these several tracts, so far as they relate to me investigated with as little delay as can be avoided. If therefore, while you are in Berkeley, you should by chance fall in with either Mr Thos or Mr Ferdinand Fairfax, it would add to the favours you have already confered on me in this business, by requesting whichsoever of the⟨m⟩ has the Papers in possession (if they see no impropriety in the measure) to furnish me with a copy of the cou⟨r⟩ses of such Land as adjoin mine—it would save me the trouble & expence of sending to the Land Office in Richmond for Copies thereof. Having the boundaries of the several tracts around mine and their connection with each other before me I might be enabled to discover without going on the Land, whether there be ⟨any surveyors error⟩ or not; although a Survey would be ⟨sure to con⟩tain the amount of such ⟨*illegible*⟩ and to obtain a Grant therefor.[3]

After having obtained this information, a Survey be necessary it is more than probable that I shall avail myself of your kind offer to attend it. With esteem & regard I am—Dear Sir Your Obedt Hble Serv⟨ant⟩

Go: Washington

ALS (letterpress copy), NN: Washington Papers.

1. Letter not found. Mr. Johnston has not been identified.

2. See GW to Little, 20 Nov., and note 1 of that document.

3. See GW to Bryan Fairfax, 30 November. The words in angle brackets are taken from Fitzpatrick, *Writings of Washington*, 37:446.

To Samuel Sommers

Sir,   Mount Vernon 28th Novr 1799

Colo. Little forwarded your letter of the 25th instant to me, yesterday evening;[1] & I have now to request (if it is not already done) that my Entry may be made in the County Surveyors Book of Record, and the Treasury Warrant deposited therewith.

Not having the Laws of this Commonwealth (since the Revolution) by me, I am entirely unacquainted with the regular mode of proceeding with respect to Entries; but should conceive that, no application by letter to the Surveyors Office for one, after my letter had been there (without any person authorized to receive it) & advised to be carried to you as Deputy Surveyor, *& there entered*, could defeat my right. Be this however as it may, I am persuaded you acted from your best judgment, and the matter, if contested, must rest upon a fair representation of facts. It would be proper that my letters to the Surveyor (opened by you) should be deposited along with the Treasury Warrant and Entry.[2] Being, next to my open, and candid declaration in the presence of Shepherd and all others after finding that Tankervilles course and mine did not accord, & it having always been considered as my land, that I would enter it—the origin of the business.

I should have proceeded 'ere this to the ascertainment of this vacancy (if there be any); but it is proper that the courses of the adjoining Lands should be first obtained, and the Proprietors thereof notified of my intention to give it a fair appearance—If these can be accomplished, I shall, when the Weather will permit set about this Work with the County Surveyor or yourself. With esteem—I am Sir Your Very Hble Servt

Go: Washington

ALS, PHi: Gratz Collection; ALS (letterpress copy), NN: Washington Papers.

1. Letter not found, but see GW to Sommers, 20 November.

2. For GW's letter to William Payne, see GW to Sommers, 20 Nov., n.5.

To Bryan Fairfax

My Lord,   Mount Vernon 30th Novr 1799

I thank you for the courses of so much of your land on Difficult, as had any relation to my small tract at the Bridge, over that stream, and for the communications contained in your favour of the 28th Instt.[1]

The information derived from these sources, has satisfied me that the opinion of the Borderers on my land that it extended to Tankervilles line; and my own opinion (when I found the lines seperated at the Bridge Branch) that what lay between them was vacant, is erroneous: and it has, of course, arrested all proceedings of mine to obtain it as waste land.[2]

The smallness of my tract (275 Acs. only, by Norriss's Survey) and the pillage of its timber, together with the clearing of a part thereof (where useless to me) by Muir[3] rendered the gore which had been deemed mine, of some importance to the tract; altho' the land is hilly—broken—and the soil & wood thin, especially in the article of timber; so far as I could form an opinion by running the course of my Deed. Yet, even under these circumstances, such an addition might have enabled me to have cut down more of the 275 Acres. Which, small as it is, I am told is to have part taken away by an older Patent of Lewis's; which calls for a straight line from my corner at the *old ford* of Difficult, to my upper corner thereon; & which, will take away some of the best land in the bend of the run.[4] The right to do this you, perhaps, can judge better of than I who have no knowledge of the property thereabouts.

As you hold the land on the North & East of my tract, and (according to information) Mr Ferdo Fairfax possesses that wch is on the South & W. nothing remains to be done but in the settled and temperate part of the ensuing Spring if health will permit,[5] for

Your Lordship Mr Fairfax and myself to repair to the scene—agree upon—and mark our lines of seperation to prevent encroachments on either side in future.

Mrs Washington unites in best wishes for your restored health—and in respects to your Lady and family with Your Lordships most Obedt and affectionate Hble Servant

Go: Washington

ALS, owned (1972) by Lord Fairfax of Cameron, Gays House, Holyport, Maidenhead, Berkshire, England; ALS (letterpress copy), DLC:GW.

1. The letter and its enclosures have not been found.

2. For GW's correspondence regarding what he thought to be vacant land, see GW to William Price, 7 Nov., n.1.

3. Muir may have been the Scot John Muir, who was a merchant in Alexandria from 1758 until his death in 1791.

4. For reference to the Lewis tract on Difficult Run opposite that belonging to GW, see GW to John Gill, 26 Nov., n.3.

5. GW did not live to meet Bryan and Ferdinando Fairfax at Difficult Run to mark the boundaries between his and the Fairfaxes' land, but on 7 Dec., a week before his death, GW "Dined at Lord Fairfax's" at Mount Eagle (*Diaries*, 6:378). On that day Fairfax's sister Hannah Fairfax Washington wrote to her son Fairfax Washington from Mount Eagle: "I have the pleasure of informing my dear Son that I found his Lordship greatly mended though still weak. He had paid some morning visits to Alexandria, the day we got down. He has no legs left now, and indeed his whole body is greatly emaciated. . . . His Lordship has invited sixteen gents here today, so we are to have a feast,—all these who have paid visits since his arrival [back from England, where he assumed the title of Lord Fairfax] and during his illness. It is so long since I have conversed with Noblemen that it was very awkward the first day to address either my brother or sister by their titles—indeed I have only got over the difficulty to-day" (unidentified newspaper clipping in Toner Papers, DLC:GW).

Letter not found: from William Thornton, 30 Nov. 1799. GW wrote Thornton on 1 Dec.: "Your favour of the 30th Ulto . . . came to my hands this morning."

Letter not found: from Clement Biddle, 1 Dec. 1799. GW wrote Biddle on 8 Dec.: "Your letters of the 23d Ulto and 1st instant have both been received."

To James Piercy

Sir,   Mount Vernon 1st Decr 1799

In answer to your letter of the 27th Ulto[1]—If you have no Vessel passing *below this* (from whence the Sugar could be landed with very little trouble or delay) I request that it may be deposited at Colo. Gilpin's, in Alexandria.

Let the cask in which it is packed, be well secured; the Sugars hitherto had from you, has, sometimes, fallen short in weight.[2] I am Sir—Your very Hble Servant

Go: Washington

ALS (letterpress copy), NN: Washington Papers.

1. Letter not found.

2. In January 1800 Lear wrote on behalf of Mrs. Washington to Piercy, a sugar manufacturer in Washington, about providing sugar for Mount Vernon. See Piercy to GW, 23 May 1798, n.1.

To William Thornton

Dear Sir,   Mount Vernon Decr 1st 1799.

Your favour of the 30th Ulto, enclosing Mr Blagdens dimensions of the rooms in my houses in the City, came to my hands this morning; With a list of the different kinds of Fruit trees in the Frenchmans Garden; to whom I was a subscriber.[1]

The terms on which the subscription was set on foot, have entirely escaped me; my motive for subscribing—namely—to encourage a nursery of that sort, still rests on my memory.[2]

If taking Trees from him, at this time, will go in payment of my *former* advance, I will receive them *now* to the full amount of my Subscription; (if there be danger i[n] suffering them to remain longer with him): but, if they are otherwise to be paid for, in a word, by advancing cash, I shall decline taking any. A line from you, on this subject, will decide the matter.[3]

If Mr John G. Ladd will undertake to import *good & genuine* Plaister of Paris, on moderate terms, and will engage to have it delivered before the last of March, allowing time to prepare it for spreading in April, I would take from ten to twenty tons of it. But these matters ought to be *precisely* known, before any engagement is entered into with him.

Colo. Carrington of Richmond, who was here, & went from this yesterday, informed me that some Gentleman of that place, had imported a quantity from Nova Scotia; but as the Farmers thereabouts had not been in the practice of using it, he found it an unsaleable article; and had requested *him* to enquire if it could be disposed of in these parts. His price, the Colo. believed, was $8 pr

Ton; what the freight from thence would be, neither he, nor I, knew; but this could easily be ascertained, and by comparing the *whole* cost delivered *here*, with Ladds terms, a choice might be made of that, which under all circumstances, might appear most eligable. From Richmond, there would be a certainty of getting it in time. and the quality, by some process, might be ascertained.[4]

I thank you for the Boston Glass, furnished for my buildings in the City; which I will pay for whenever the price shall be made known to me.

The true Chinese Hogs I *lately* had; but they have got so mixed, that a boar pig is desirable; & I would thank you for securing one for me, of the genuine kind, if to be had.

I am glad to hear that the Legislature of Maryland have acted favourably on the Application made to it by the Potomak Company. Your information of this event is the first I had received.[5] It is to be hoped that the Legislature of this State will "go, and do so likewise." Niether would be backward in promoting this useful undertaking if the measure was impartially investigated, and the welfare of the respective States duly considered. With very great esteem and regard I am—Dear Sir Your obliged & Obedt Hble Servt

Go: Washington

ALS, DGU; ALS (letterpress copy), NN: Washington Papers.

1. Letter and enclosures not found, but see GW to Thornton, 26 November.

2. The *Centinel of Liberty, or George-Town and Washington Advertiser* ran this notice for Francis Motter on 15 Nov.: "Those gentlemen, who subscribed and paid the money to Mr. Leflet, to be repaid in fruit trees, at his proposed nursery, near George-Town, are informed, that the fruit trees are ready to be delivered and they are desired to call at my house on Rock Creek and receive them" (quoted in Harris, *Thornton Papers*, 1:514). On 27 Oct. 1796 GW recorded in his Day Book: "By cash pd Peter Leflet my Subscription to his Nursery 25 Dollrs."

3. See Thornton to GW, 5 December.

4. See GW to Edward Carrington, 2 Dec., and Thornton to GW, 5 December. Carrington and his wife left Mount Vernon on the morning of 30 Nov. after a stay of two nights (*Diaries*, 6:377). John G. Ladd, a merchant in Alexandria, reported on 30 Nov. that plaster of paris was selling at $10 a ton (Harris, *Thornton Papers*, 1:514).

5. GW was to receive other reports of the activities of the Maryland legislature. John Mason, a director of the Potomac River Company, wrote to him on 4 Dec., and the president and directors of the Potomac River Company wrote on 8 December. Copies of the resolutions of the Maryland legislature regarding the Potomac River Company were enclosed in both letters.

From Burwell Bassett, Jr.

Dear Sir   Eltham Dec: 2d 1799

To communicate to our friends agreable incidents we are readily promptd by the pleasure it gives but it is duty alone which can lead us to be the communicators of uncomefortable tidings Tis this that impels me to inform my friends at Mount Vernon that Mrs Henley was attacked about ten days since with a severe bilious pleurisy her weak constitution was unequal to the shock and in five days she yielded to the force of her disorder. As it relates to herself perhaps the change cannot be much regreted as she had seen the best days this life could afford her but to her children the loss will be great.[1] I have not neglected to make the inquiries relative to corn and oats as you required but so various are the opinions that it is difficult to make a Judgment about it Corn sells at two dollars by the small quantity but those who have any that would be an object ask fifteen. a merchant of Hanover town some weeks since offered to deliver the quantity you wanted at the highest navigation on this river for twelve and six I would take for my crop of 5 or 600 barrels thirteen shillings at my landing the freight asked is six pence the bushel a quantity of oats not to be bought.[2] I have by the stage forwarded some honey locust seed but there was so great a proportion of them this year that were bad that the collection is but small.[3] With respectful remembrance to my Aunt and the residents at Mount Vernon believe me to be with friendship and esteem your obt Ser.

Burwell Bassett

ALS, DLC:GW.

1. GW wrote to Elizabeth Dandridge Aylett Henley on 20 October.

2. Both Bassett's house, Eltham in New Kent County, and Hanover Town in Hanover County, were on the Pamunkey River. Eltham was down river near the confluence of the Pamunkey and the Mattaponi rivers.

3. No prior correspondence in 1799 with Bassett regarding these matters has been found, but Bassett was at Mount Vernon as recently as 15 Oct. (*Diaries*, 6: 370). GW records in his diary in 1785, 1786, and 1787 collecting seed of the honey locust tree from which he hoped to raise plants to create hedges around his fields at Mount Vernon (ibid., 4:213, 295, 297, 322, 5:142, 145).

To Edward Carrington

Dear Sir   Mount Vernon 2d Decr 1799

Since you mentioned the Plaster of Paris which was for Sale in Richmond, (but after you left this) it occurred to me, that as it was not a saleable article with you, it might be my cheapest mode to purchase *there* to supply my want of this article next year on my Farms around me.

Permit me, for this reason, to ask the favour of you to learn from the Gentleman who has it for Sale, what quantity he has? the lowest price he would take for it by the ton (the whole being purchased)? there? and what, delivered at my landing? As a Merchant, acquainted with Navigation, he will be at no loss to know at what freight it could be delivered here.

A Gentleman now in Alexandria is endeavouring to obtain Subscribers for a Vessel load from Nova Scotia; the terms I have not learned; but if that in Richmond be *good*; and had as low, I should prefer it because it is already in the Country, and the risques of the Sea avoided.[1]

All, however, depends upon its being of the *true sort*—for without this, it wou'd be as useless for the purpose intended, as pebble stones. There are two colours of it—one has a greyish—the other a blewish cast; the latter I think is prefered; but both are good when perfectly free from grit, or sand; having any of the latter is a proof of its baseness. The best criterion for ascertaining its property, is, by putting the fine pow⟨der⟩ of the Plaster, into a skillet or Pot without moisture, the good will swell, or rise up; the bad will remain dead, & motionless.

I would thank you for sending me (if to be had) two glaized leather hats such as your Postilions wore, and of that size. Accompany them with the cost, and the money shall be remitted in a bank note. I am in no immediate want of them; an occasional, or water transportation (directed to the care of Colo. Gilpin in Alexa.) will do.

I hope you got down safe—Our Compts to Mrs Carrington. I am always—Dear Sir Yr Affecte & Obedt

Go: Washington

ALS, PWacD; ALS (letterpress copy), NN: Washington Papers.

1. See GW to William Thornton, 1 Dec., n.4.

To William Price

Sir,   Mount Vernon 2d Decr 1799

I have been duly favoured with your letter of the 25th Ulto, enclosing a copy of the Survey made for William Shepherd, for four & three quarter acres, and the form of a Caveate against the issuing a Patent therefor.[1]

I cannot from the survey, discover with precision where this land lays, and therefore shall give no further opposition to the Grant of it. If it be, where I *suspect*, it is within the bounds of a Patent under which I hold, of more than sixty years standing—of course, cannot effect it.[2]

I am sorry that I have given you so much trouble in this business, at the sametime that I feel obliged by the prompt and ready advice you have been so kind as to give me for the prosecution of it. From what I had heard of Shepherd's Survey, I conceived differently of its object. I am Sir—Your Obedt Hble Servt

                                    Go: Washington

ALS, Vi; ALS (letterpress copy), NN: Washington Papers. The ALS is docketed, "No Answer."

1. Letter not found.

2. For GW's dispute with William Shepherd over nonexistent vacant land at Difficult Run, see GW to Price, 7 Nov., n.1. On 8 Sept. 1800 Shepherd secured a grant for a tract of 4¾ acres (no. 514) across Difficult Run from GW's property, "Adjacent [John] Lewis and [Bryan] Fairfax, beginning corner Lewis's 337 acre tract and Fairfax['s] 5568 acres" (Mitchell, *Fairfax County Patents and Grants*, 245).

To James McHenry

Sir   Mount Vernon Decr 3d 1799

I take the liberty of enclosing a letter from Colo. Parker to Mr Lear, in which he requests that I will write to the proper department, to have arrangements made for the payment of two thousand one hundred & seventy five dollars and one third, being the amount of the purchase of one hundred and ninety six acres of land, bought, for the United States, adjoining the public ground at Harper's Ferry.[1]

You will be pleased to observe that the Money is to be paid on the 1st day of January next, and that Major Campbell, who made the purchase, has given his bond therefor; and I am persuaded there will be no delay in fulfilling the engagement which he has made for the United States.[2] With due consideration I have the honor to be Sir, Your most obedt St

Df, in Tobias Lear's hand, DLC:GW.

1. Tobias Lear wrote Thomas Parker from Mount Vernon on 6 Dec.: "I have been duly favor'd with your letter of the 28th Ultimo, which was laid before the Commander in Chief, who immediately communicated the same to the Secretary of War, requesting him to have provision made for the payment of Major [William] Campbell's bond, which was given for the land purchased by him for the United States; and which will, without doubt, be duly attended to from that Department" (DLC:GW). Parker's letter to Lear of 28 Nov. has not been found.

2. McHenry wrote GW from Philadelphia on 12 Dec.: "I have the honor to acknowledge the receipt of your letter of the 3d instant. The Quarter Master General has been directed to remit the monies for the purchase of land adjoining the public Ground at Harpers ferry, and I have understood it has been some time since forwarded" (DLC:GW). For the decision to buy additional land for the encampment at Harpers Ferry, see Lear to GW, 30 Oct., 4 Nov., and Parker to GW, 31 October. See also Lear to GW, 4 Nov., n.8.

From James McHenry

(Private)

Philad[elphia] 3 Decr 1799.

I have recd your private letter of the 17th Novr ulto, since which I have been very closely engaged in business.

The inclosed news paper contains the Presidents speech delivered to-day. You will find it nearly what it ought to be, I had feared he would have entered into reasoning upon a certain measure which had he would most assuredly have attracted to the subject a very pointed direct or indirect disapprobation from a part of the federalists.

I am utterly unable and disqualified to give you the least information as to the ground or circumstances inducing to the letter written to Coxe.[1] I can only consider it as the evidence of a preconceived theory of the author's or as a hasty though[t]less answer to an insidious insinuation. The author has never mentioned the fact to me and I have never ⟨started⟩ the idea to him.

The President perseveres in recieving and treating the gentlemen specially alluded to with every mark of exterior attention, and I think it likely will not take any step which might serve to throw from him his present ⟨ministers⟩. Yours truly & Affecty

ADf, MdAA.
1. See McHenry to GW, 10 Nov., n.4.

To Thomas Peter

Dear Sir,   Mount Vernon 3d Decr 1799
  Have you succeeded, or are you likely to succeed, in procuring the Hemp seed I required?[1]
  The fly has got into my Wheat, very generally this Fall; and I lay my account for great ravages thereon next Spring; which makes me more desirous of laying (to use a Sea term) an anchor to windward for something else.[2]
  I congratulate you and Patcy on the birth of a "Manchild"[3]— My best wishes attend the Mother & Child—and I am—Dear Sir Your Affecte Hble Servt

                                        Go: Washington

ALS (photocopy), DLC:GW.
  1. GW spent the night of 9 Nov. at Thomas Peter's house in Georgetown, at which time he and Mr. Peter may have spoken of hemp seed (*Diaries*, 6.375). No reference to hemp has been found in their correspondence.
  2. See GW's elaborate plans for cropping his Mount Vernon farms in 1800, which he gave on 13 Dec., the day before his death, to his farm manager, James Anderson.
  3. This was probably John Parke Custis Peter, the son of Thomas and Martha Peter, who is known to have been born sometime between 1798 and 1800.

Letter not found: from Timothy Pickering, 3 Dec. 1799. GW's letter of 24 Nov. to Pickering is docketed by Pickering, "answd Decr 3d."

From John Mason

Sir   Annapolis 4th Decr 1799
  Knowing the great Interest you have always taken in the promotion of the Navigation of the Potomak—I lose not a moment to inform you that I have at length suceeded to get this great Object aided by a grant of the Legislature of this State to the full amount contemplated by the Company—and it is with extreme

Pleasure I have it in my Power to enclose a Resolution to that Effect which has this day passed both Houses—you will remark Sir that this Investment is to a much larger amount than was contemplated at the last meeting but I trust I shall not be blamed in having thus exceeded my powers saved the Difficulty & Inconvenience attending individual Subscriptions—the Clause respecting Security tho' against my wish, could not be dispensed with and it ⟨was⟩ the only Terms on which it could be had.[1]

The Legislature has also this day granted a Loan of thirty thousand Dollars to the Susquehanah Company and passed an Act to incorporate a Company for cutting a Canal from the waters of the Chesepeake to the Waters of the Delaware—the three measures were carried by assisting each other and the whole was made a matter of Conciliation[2]—With great Respect I have the honor to be Sir your very Obet Sert

J. Mason

P.S. As the Shares are rated at £130 Stg the loss by the Sale of the Stock will not be greater than to reduce them to the original Sum of £100 Stg which was the best that could be done.[3]

ALS, DLC:GW.

1. To raise the $40,000 deemed necessary, the stockholders of the Potomac River Company voted at its meeting of 5 Aug. 1799 that each shareholder should pay an additional one hundred dollars for each share held once the legislatures of Maryland and Virginia had passed laws to enforce such payments. See GW to Charles Carroll, 21 July 1799, n.2. The enclosed printed copy of the resolutions of the Maryland legislature of 4 Dec. reads: "RESOLVED, That the treasurer of the western shore be and he is hereby authorised and empowered to subscribe, on behalf of this state, for one hundred and thirty shares in the augmented capital of the Patowmack company, viz. the sum of one hundred and thirty pounds sterling for each share, to be paid in six per cent. stock of the United States, at par. RESOLVED, That the trustee of this state transfer the said amount of six per cent. stock to the president and directors of the Patowmack company, or their order, on the governor and council's certifying to him that bond, with sufficient security, has been lodged with them to complete the locks and navigation of said river at the Great falls, and not before."

2. The Maryland legislature on 4 Dec. also passed "An Act to Incorporate a Company for the Purpose of Cutting and Making a Canal between the River Delaware and the Chesapeake Bay" and "A Further Supplement to the Act, entitled, An Act for Making the River Susquehanna Navigable from the Line of this State to Tide Water" (*Laws of Maryland*, chaps. 16, 17).

3. See President and Directors of the Potomac River Company to GW, 8 Dec., n.2.

From William Thornton

Dear Sir   City of Washington 5th Decr 1799
    In answer to the Letter which I had the honour of receiving
from you Yesterday[1] I have the pleasure of informing you that
there is nothing to be paid for the Fruit Trees in addition to what
you subscribed to Leflet, therefore if you will be pleased to specify
the numbers of each Sort omiting any kinds you may not be inclined to have & calculating what you take at 1s. Maryld Cury ℔
Tree to the amount of your Subscription I will attend to them; and
if I also knew when it would be convenient or agreeable to you to
send a Boat or Cart to Alexandria, I will have them conveyed
thither by the Packet of this place to whatever address you will be
pleased to direct.[2]
    I have written to Alexa. to know how much the Captns of Packets
to Richmond would charge ℔ ton to bring Plaister-of-Paris thence,
to Alexa. or this place. I believe from Trials made by Judge Peters
& others whose reports he has given ther is not much if any difference between the Nova Scotia & the French Plaister, for Grounds.[3]
Accept, dear Sir, my highest Respects & sincerest good wishes for
your Health & happiness

                                                     W. T.

ADfS, DLC: Thornton Papers.
    1. GW's letter to Thornton is dated 1 December.
    2. See GW's instructions of 7 December.
    3. GW owned a copy of Richard Peters's *Agricultural Enquiries on Plaister of Paris*
(Philadelphia, 1797), given to him by Judge Peters in January 1797 (Griffin, *Boston Athenæum Washington Collection*, 161). See GW to John Sinclair, 6 Mar. 1797,
n.2; see also GW to Thornton, 1 Dec. 1799, n.4.

From Thomas Waters Griffith

Sir,   Mount Vernon 7 Decem. 1799
    Inclosed I take the Liberty to leave you a Letter of recommen-
dation with which I was favord by Mr St John de Crœvecœur of
Normandy, who I saw well in May last, and who desired to be respectfully rememberd to you, your Lady & Family.[1]
    I also beg leave to present to you a copy of a Work on the
Commerce of the United States, which I wrote and published at

paris during the residence there of the last American Ministers[2]—please accept this same as a testimony of my own unfeigned esteem and Respect for your person and Character, and indulge me with a recollection of the Time and place it was wrote & published whenever you shall think proper to look into it. I have the honour to be Sir, yr mo. Obedient & mo. Humble Servant

Thos Waters Griffith

ALS, DLC:GW.

Thomas Waters Griffith (1767–1838), the son of Benjamin and Rachel Waters Griffith, lived as a child in Chester County, Pa., and in Baltimore. After serving briefly as a clerk in a Baltimore mercantile firm, Griffith sailed in August 1791 from Georgetown, Md., with seventeen hogsheads of tobacco to seek his fortune in France. He witnessed the main events of the Revolution in Paris in 1792, was imprisoned late in 1793, spent the winter of 1794 and 1795 in London, and returned to France in the spring of 1795 to remain until his departure for the United States in July 1799. Griffith made a valuable contribution to the study of the history of Maryland with his *Sketches of the Early History of Maryland*, published in Baltimore in 1821, and his *Annals of Baltimore*, published in 1824.

1. The letter from Hector St. John de Crèvecoeur has not been found. Griffith reported in his "Reminiscences of an American Gentleman Resident in Paris from 1791 to 1799" that before he left France in July 1799 he "took charge of some letters from Madame de Lafayette to General Washington," which have not been found either (Elizabeth Wormeley Latimer, *My Scrap-Book of the French Revolution* [Chicago, 1903], 68).

2. Griffith wrote in his "Reminiscences": "To counteract the excitement in France against the United States in 1797, I wrote an answer to a remark in the correspondence of the ambassador Fauchet [to the United States], relative to the influence of British trade in America. The title of my pamphlet was 'L'Indépendance absolue des États Unis de l'Amérique prouvée par L'État actuel de leur Commerce' [avec les nations européennes]," printed in Paris in 1798 (ibid., 64). On the day that Griffith brought the pamphlet to GW and wrote this letter at Mount Vernon, on 7 Dec., GW was dining "at Lord Fairfax's" (*Diaries*, 6: 378).

To Robert Lewis

Dear Sir,   Mount Vernon 7th of Decemr 1799

Your letter of the 10th of Septr came duly to hand, but as there was nothing contained in it that required to be acted upon immediately, I postponed acknowledging the receipt of it at an earlier period.[1]

The death of Mr Airess, of which I have been informed—and

the direct conveyance, afforded by your brother Howells return, have induced me, to write you at this time.

What prospect the death of Mr Airess may open to the attainment of the Farm which was leased for his, and life of Mrs Airess, I know not; it may, however, be the subject of a round about enquiry of yours; for I must, if Mrs Washington and myself should both survive another year, find some place to which the supernumerary hands on *this* Estate could be removed.[2] Being well convinced, that after that period, half the number employed on the Farms around me, would yield more nett profit—it behoves me therefore to make some change which may benefit myself and not render their condition worse.

For these reason, I request that you would keep a steady eye upon all my tenements in Berkeley and Frederick; and at a crisis you shall deem most favourable, learn with precision the most favourable terms on which I could repossess such *adjoining ones*, as would work eight or ten hands to advantage, regard being had at the sametime to the Improvements of different kinds—particularly, the qua⟨n⟩tity of cleared land, and the quality of it; and the number and sort of buildings; & for what purposes they wd answe⟨r.⟩

There could be no doubt of the Utility; no⟨r⟩ would there be any hesitation in attempting, to purchase leases at a Rent of Six pounds per annum, if you are founded in your hypothesis, of there letting for £60; provided I *had,* or could see how to *come at* the means to pay for them. But, on monies owing to me, I would not engage to pay a shilling, for every pound that is promised to me; So little are engagements regarded, and so remiss are our Courts of Justice to enforce them.

Under these circumstances, and statement of facts, you will readily perceive that it would be hazardous in me to direct you positively what decisive measures to take. But apprised as you are of my wishes, you may use preparatory means for carrying them into effect; without committing me, previously to the advice of them. The present state of things may change, and I may be differently circumstanced at the time you may learn, with precision what can be accomplished with the Tenants, in facilitation of my views.

You will perceive by the letter herewith enclosed, in what manner my land in Hampshire is treated. It is more than probable, if some effectual stop cannot be put to such depredation, that it will be stripped of all its valuable Timber.[3]

I have a Jack younger than the lame one which you saw here, that will be full old enough to cover next Spring. What number of Mares do you think, you could engage to come to him at your house next season, and at what price? Your answer to these queries would enable me to decide on a stand for him, in time to advertise it.

You will have heard that Nelly Lewis has a girl born.[4] She, Mrs Washington and the family unite with me in best wishes for yourself, Mrs Lewis & the Children, and—I am Dr Sir—Your sincere friend and Affecte Uncle

Go: Washington

ALS, owned by the Scriptorium, Beverly Hills, Calif.; ALS (letterpress copy), NN: Washington Papers.

1. Letter not found.

2. For reference to the land rented by John Ariss, who from 1786 until his recent death had been GW's tenant on the Bullskin in Berkeley County, see GW to Lewis, 17 Aug. 1799. Howell Lewis and his wife left Mount Vernon to return home on the morning of 9 Dec. after more than a week's visit (*Diaries*, 6: 377–78).

3. Perhaps GW is referring to a letter from Isaac Weatherinton of Hampshire County, dated 24 Aug. 1799 but not received by GW until October. It is printed in GW to Weatherinton, 20 Oct., n.1.

4. Eleanor Parke Custis Lewis gave birth to her first child, Frances Parke Lewis (d. 1875), at Mount Vernon on the morning of 27 Nov. (*Diaries*, 6:377).

To William Thornton

Dear Sir,   Mount Vernon 7th Decr 1799

Your favour of the 5th instant was received last night. Not sending up to the Post Office *every* day, is the cause of its not getting to hand in time for my answer by the Mail of this day.

Enclosed is a list of such fruit Trees as my Gardener has chosen.[1] Be so good as to have them sent to the care of Colo. Gilpin in Alexandria, who will receive—take care of—and give me notice of their arrival: when my Boat, or Waggon shall be sent up for them. Mr Leflet will, of course, label the different kinds of fruit.

I have written to Colo. Carrington to know the terms on which the Plaster of Paris may be had in Richmond, and what the owner would ask for it delivered at my landing or higher up.[2] With much esteem I am Dear Sir—Yr Obedt & Obliged

Go: Washington

ALS, DLC: Thornton Papers.
 1. The list has not been found.
 2. See GW to Edward Carrington, 2 December.

Letter not found: from William Thornton, 7 Dec. 1799. GW thanked Thornton on 8 Dec. for "the communications contained in your letter of yesterday."

Letter not found: from Alexander White, 7 Dec. 1799. GW wrote White on 8 Dec.: "Your favour of yesterday I received this morning."

To Clement Biddle

Dear Sir,   Mount Vernon 8th Decr 1799

Your letters of the 23d Ulto and 1st instant have both been received. the part which relates to Mr Custis's pay—as an Officer in the Cavalry—has been given to him, and he writes you himself on the subject.[1] I have naught therefore to add on it.

Captn Ellwood had not arrived at Alexandria yesterday, from hence I conclude he was to have touched at Norfolk; otherwise his passage will have been tedious. I have it in contemplation, but shall not decide positively on the measure until the arrival of that Vessel, to send you a hundred or two Barrels of flour, to dispose of for me, in the Philadelphia market, as it commands a better price there, than in alexandria; and some barrels of Fish also—on Commission. If this does not take place, I have about $200 in the Bank of Pennsylvania for wch I shall give you a check, to enable you to pay for the articles already sent me by Ellwood, and such as will be requested in this letter.[2]

There can be no dependance on Imported Seeds, unless they are kept in the Steerage or Cabbin; and few Masters of Vessels will do this. In the Hold, the chance is, that the heat of it, will destroy vegetation; little of it ever turning out well. Under this impression, I shall decline taking more than a very small quantity of Mr Reay Kings seeds; supposing them to be imported.[3] But request, that you would send me by the *first* conveyance (for fear of Frost) Six bushels of Clover seed—*present year's growth—saved in the Country.*

Get, if you please, in case you are not a good judge of Seeds, some person who is so, to inspect, and see that it is not mixed with another Seed, not much unlike it, which is an injurious introduction into fields.

I am particular always in my seeds, because nothing is more to be regretted in a course of rotation, than to sow Seed that does not come up; or, that which is impure, the whole system being deranged by it. To the Clover seed, please to add by way of trial, 5 lbs. of Lucerne; and as I am unacquainted with Herdgrass, one pound of that Seed also, for an experiment. With estm and regard, I am—Dear Sir Your Obedient Hble Servant

Go: Washington

ALS, owned (1977) by the National Infantry Museum, Fort Benning, Georgia; ALS (letterpress copy), NN: Washington Papers.

1. Biddle's letter of 1 Dec. has not been found, but see GW to Biddle, 24 November.

2. For the $200 in the Bank of Pennsylvania, see GW to Samuel M. Fox, 14 July 1799, and the references in note 2 to that document.

3. Reay King (died c. 1824) was a New York Quaker who in 1795 married Anna Wilson, of Philadelphia, where at this time he was in business.

To John Mason

Sir,   Mount Vernon 8th Decr 1799

I have received your letter of the 4th instant, enclosing a Resolution of the Legislature of Maryland to take, on account of the State, one hundred & thirty shares in the augmented Capital of the Potomak Company, and thank you for your politeness in forwarding of it to me.

Altho' this mode of obtaining money to complete the Navigation of the River, differs from the plan adopted at the last General Meeting of the Stock holders, and will make the original shares less valuable than they would have been by the mode proposed (if it could have been carried into effect); yet, my primary wish being, to see a completion on almost any terms, I rejoice, sincerely, that the means are likely to be obtained, to effect so desireable an object; and I trust that every exertion will now be made to complete the work with all possible expedition. I am Sir, very respectfully, Your most Obedient Servant

Go: Washington

ALS (letterpress copy), NN: Washington Papers. The ALS was listed in a 1978 catalog of J. A. Stargart, Marburg, Germany.

From the President and Directors of the Potomac River Company

Sir,   George Town 8 Decr 1799

Enclosed we have the honor to hand two Resolutions which were passed last week by the Legislature of this State;[1] by a calculation noted at foot, to which we beg to refer you, we find it will be a great Object to obtain the transfer of this Stock before the 15th of this month, at which time the Books are shut, & no transfer can be made untill after the 1st of January when a Dividend of 3½ p. Ct will be paid.[2]

In order to effect this we have thought it best, to call together as many of the Stockholders, as on so short a notice can be had, on Tuesday next, for the purpose of taking such Steps as may be necessary to get the transfer made in the course of the present week.

Your Presence Sir, on this occasion, if convenient [to] yourself, will be very gratifying to us—we have appointed the Union Tavern in this Town for the Place of meeting, because having so little time to collect the Members in, we find it is likely we shall have by this means, a greater number assembled as there are many who live in this neighbourhood[3]—With great Respect We have the Honor to be Sir Your very Ob. & Hle Servts

Jas Keith
J. Mason
Wm H. Dorsey
John Laird

LS, DLC:GW.

1. On 4 Dec. John Mason sent GW a printed copy of the resolutions of the Maryland legislature, a handwritten copy of which was enclosed here. For the resolutions, see Mason to GW, 4 Dec., n.1.

2. The attached "calculation" reads: "130 Shares at £130 Ste. each is £28166.13.4 Maryd Cury equal to Dollars—75111 ^{19}/100.

75111 ^{19}/100 Dollars of unredeemed Stock make 81367 ^{19}/100 Dollars of original or gross Stock if transferred in the last quarter of 1799.

3½ p. Ct on the gross Sum (81.367 ^{19}/100) payable on 1st Jany 1800 will produce 2847 Dollars in Cash, of which 1740 will be on account of principal.

2847$ to be recd on 1st Jany

1740 of which on account of principal

$\overline{1107}$ will be the amount of Interest then paid

435 is the difference on 1740 (the principal then redeemed) between selling price and par

1542 Dollars clear gain to the Company by receiving the transfer in Decr 1799" (DLC:GW).

3. GW replied on the same day to the president and directors of the company: "Gentln I have received your letter of this date, inform[ing] me of the Resolutions of the Legislature of Maryland to take 130 Shares in the augmented Capital of the Potomac Company, and enclosing a calculation shewing the advantages to be derived from drawing the six per Cent Stock from the Treasurer of Maryland before the 1st of January. And also requesting my attendance at a meeting of the Stockholders on Tuesday next.

"I am very much pleased to learn that the means for comp[l]eating the important work of the Navigation of the River may be obtained; and I should, with pleasure, attend the meeting on Tuesday did not an expectation of Company at that time, and other circumstances, make it inconvenient for me to leave home; and did I not also beleive that my proxy to vote on the occasion (which will be given to Mr Keith, the President) would answer every purpose that could be effected by my personal attendance, as I am persuaded there can be but one object in view with the Stock holders, which is to take such measures as will ensure the completion of the work with *certainty* and *expedition*, agreeably to the sense of the Stock holders at their meeting in Augt last. I have the honor to be with great respect Gentln Yr mo. ob. St Go: Washington" (Df, in Tobias Lear's hand, owned [1994] by Mr. Robert Batchelder, Ambler, Pa.; GW's signature appears to have been photographed and imposed on the Lear draft).

On the next day GW wrote James Keith, president of the Potomac River Company: "Dear Sir, As it will be inconvenient for me to attend a Meeting of the Stock-holders of the Potomac Company on Tuesday next, agreeably to the request of the President and Directors; I have taken the liberty to enclose you my proxy to vote and act for me on that occasion, which you will oblige me by doing. With great esteem, I am Dear Sir Your most obedt Sevt G. Washington" (typescript, DLC:GW).

To William Thornton

Dear Sir,   Mount Vernon 8th Decr 1799

For the communications contained in your letter of yesterday, I thank you.[1] As a citizen of the United States, it gives me pleasure, at all times, to hear that works of public ⟨uti⟩lity are resolved on, and in a state of progression—wheresoever adopted, and whensoever begun.

The one resolved on between the Chesapeake and Delaware is of great magnitude, and will be, I trust, the Precursor of another between the Delaware and sound, at Amboy. These, with the one now about, between the Chesapeak (for Norfolk) and Albemarle Sound, will, in a manner, open a kind of Inland Navigation (with what assuredly will be attempted in the Eastern States) from one extremety of the Union to the other.[2]

Never having read any of the late Acts of Congress relatively to the Federal City, or rather to the public buildings, and property the Public is possessed of in that place; I know not on what grd the Attorney General of the United States has founded the opinion communicated in your letter, of the insufficiency of the Presidents Powers to Authorize the Commissioners of the City to accept a loan, for the purpose of carrying on the public works, in that place. Under the original Act empowering the President to estab-lish the permanent Seat of the Government on the Potomac no doubt ever occured to my mind—nor I believe to the Minds of any of the Officers thereof, around me, of a want of this Power.[3] But, by the obstructions continually thrown in its way—by *friends* or *enemies*—⟨this⟩ City has had to pass through a firey trial—Yet, I trust will, ultimately, escape the Ordea⟨l⟩ with eclat. Instead of *a firey trial* it would have been more appropriate to have said, it has passed, or is on its passage through, the Ordea⟨l⟩ of local interests, destructive Jealousies, and inveterate prejudices; as difficult, and as dangerous I conceive, as any of the other ordeals. With very great esteem & regard, I am—Dear Sir Your Most Obedt and obliged Humble Servant

Go: Washington

ALS (letterpress copy), NN: Washington Papers.

1. Letter not found.

2. For the canal planned between the Delaware River and the Chesapeake Bay, see John Mason to GW, 4 Dec., and note 2 to that document. The states of Vir-ginia and North Carolina finally agreed in 1790 on the building of the Dismal Swamp canal, and in 1793 the digging at both ends of the canal connecting rivers flowing into the Chesapeake Bay and Albemarle Sound was begun; by 1799 con-siderable progress had been made (Brown, *Dismal Swamp Canal*, ch. 2).

3. For what Thornton probably wrote to GW concerning the problems arising out of the District of Columbia commissioners' decision to seek a loan from the state of Maryland, see Harris, *Thornton Papers*, 1:521–22.

To Alexander White

Dear Sir   Mount Vernon 8th December 1799

Your favour of yesterday I received this morning.[1] Altho' the Legislature of Maryland has taken up the business of the Potomack Company upon different ground, than on that which was adopted at the last General meeting of the Stockholders, and less advantageous for *them* if they could have carried *their* mode into effect; yet, as my primary wish, is to see the work completed, I rejoice that the means are likely to be obtained which will accomplish this desirable object—and trust that on its progress to this end, there will be no more lingering.

Percieving no object Mr Liston could have in misrepresenting the expression of Mr Stoddard, respecting a site near the Capital; the pre⟨sumption⟩ is—all other considerations apart, that he was ⟨cor⟩rect in the recital. But to the attempt of diverting the followers of the Government from engaging houses in the vicinity of the Capital, Mrs Liston was more pointed, & full than He was.[2] I trust, notwithstanding, that the event will prove that ⟨accomoda⟩tions will be found equal to the ⟨demand⟩ for them, and altho' (I believe it may be said with truth) that those whose interest it was, most to promote the welfare & growth of the City, have been its worst enemies, yet that matters will still go right.

I should, as yesterday or to day (according to your first intentions), and at all other times when it is convenient to you, be glad to see you at this place. Being—Dear Sir—with great esteem and regard Your most Obedt Humble Servant

                                                Go: Washington

ALS (letterpress copy), NN: Washington Papers.

1. Letter not found.

2. Robert Liston (1742–1836) began his tenure as British minister to the United States in May 1796 and served until his departure in December 1800. In May 1797 the District of Columbia commissioners, with the approval of President John Adams, offered Liston and other foreign envoys land in the Federal City for residences and embassies. On a trip to Mount Vernon, where the ambassador and his wife, Henrietta Marchant Liston, stayed with their entourage from 13 to 16 Nov. 1797 (*Diaries*, 6:268–69), Liston selected the site for the British embassy in Washington, "about midway between the President's House and what is termed the *Capitol*" (Harris, *Thornton Papers*, 1:436). On 17 Feb. 1798 William Thornton wrote Liston: "Soon after your departure from this place I made known to my colleagues the preference you gave to the ground on the edge of

the Capitol Park, situated between Ninth and Tenth Streets West. . . . The Board
signify through me their willingness to vest in you this property for the use of the
Ambassador of England to the United States of America. . . . If on further consideration you have any objections to that square, I shall be very happy in giving any
information in my power respecting other property" (ibid., 435–36).

What "the expression of Mr Stoddard [Secretary of the Navy Benjamin Stoddert], respecting a site near the Capitol" was, has not been determined, but it
probably was during the second visit of the Listons to Mount Vernon, from 22 to
25 Oct. 1799, that GW found Mrs. Liston's comments "more pointed, & full"
than her husband's. Doubts had arisen earlier in the year about the legality of the
grants of land the commissioners had made to foreign envoys, and it was decided
that an act of Congress would be required if the grants were to be validated. At
that point Liston decided not to proceed in the matter (ibid., 436).

Letter not found: from Robert Boggess, 9 Dec. 1799. GW wrote Boggess
on 10 Dec.: "In answer to your letter of yesterday's date. . . ."

From Gouverneur Morris

My dear Sir   Morrisania [N.Y.] 9 Decr 1799
  During a late Visit to New York, I learnt that the leading federal
Characters (even in Massachusetts) consider Mr Adams as unfit
for the Office he now holds. Without pretending to decide on the
Merits of that Opinion, which will operate alike whether well or
illfounded, it appeared necessary to name some other Person. You
will easily conceive that his Predecessor was wished for and regretted, nor will you be surpriz'd that the Doubt whether he would
again accept should have excited much Concern; for you are so
perfectly acquainted with the different Characters in America and
with the Opinions which prevail respecting them, that you must
be convinced (however painful the Conviction) that should you
decline no Man will be chosen whom you would wish to see in that
high Office.
  Beleiving then that the dearest Interests of our Country are at
Stake, I beg Leave to speak with you freely on this Subject.
  No reasonable Man can doubt that after a Life of glorious Labor
you must wish for Repose, and it would not be surprizing that a
Wish so natural should, by frequent Disappointment, have acquired the Force of Passion. But is Retirement, in the strict Sense
of the Word, a possible Thing? And is the Half-Retirement which
you may attain to more peaceful than public Life? Nay, has it not

the Disadvantage of leaving you involved in Measures you can neither direct nor control? Another Question suggests itself, from
another View of the Subject, Will you not when the Seat of Government is in your Neighbourhood, enjoy more Retirement as President of the United States than as General of the Army? And in this
same View again another Question arises, may not your Acceptance be the needful Means of fixing the Government in that Seat?

There is a more important Consideration. Shall the vast Trea-
sure of your Fame be committed to the Uncertainty of events, be
exposed to the Attempts of Envy, and subject to the Spoliation of
Slander? From Envy and Slander no Retreat is safe but the Grave,
And you must not yet hide you behind that Bulwark. As to the
Influence of Events, if there be a human Being who may look
them fairly in the Face you are the Man. Recollect Sir, that each
Occasion which has brought you back on the public Stage has
been to you the Means of new and greater Glory. If General Washington had not become Member of the Convention he would have
been considered only as the Defender and not as the Legislator of
his Country. And if the President of the Convention had not become President of the United States he would not have added the
Character of a Statesman to those of a Patriot and a Hero. Your
Modesty may repel these Titles but Europe has conferred them
and the World will set its Seal of Approbation when in these tempestuous Times your Country shall have again confided the Helm
of her Affairs to your steady Hand.

But you may perhaps say that you stand indirectly pledged to
private Life. Surely Sir you neither gave nor meant to give such
Pledge to the Extent of possible Contingencies. The Acceptance
of your present Office proves that you did not. Nay, you stand
pledged by all your former Conduct that when Circumstances
arise which may require it you will act again. Those Circumstances
seem to be now imminent, and it is meet that you consider them
on the broad Ground of your extensive Information. Ponder them
I pray: and whatever may be the Decision pardon my Freedom and
beleive me truly yours

Gouv. Morris

ALS, DLC:GW; ALB, DLC: Gouverneur Morris Papers. Someone wrote on the
ALS below the dateline: "recd—16 De[cembe]r 99." Someone else wrote on the
last page, probably at a later time, "Recd after Gen. Washington's death."

To Robert Boggess

Sir   Mount Vernon 10th Decr 1799

In answer to your letter of yesterday's date,[1] I have to observe that you, as well as others, have mistaken my real situation very much when it is supposed that I have it in my power to *lend* money.

The truth is, that my receipts of this article, for some years back, have fallen so far short of my expenditures—without having made any purchases to increase my property (excepting a lot or two in the Federal City) that I have been under the necessity of selling land, & borrowing money myself to enable me to support, ⟨*illegible*⟩ these expences.[2] I am Sir Your Hble Servant

                                                Go: Washington

ALS (letterpress copy), NN: Washington Papers.

1. Letter not found.

2. Robert Boggess, whose house was on the Cameron-Colchester stage road not far from Mount Vernon, seems not to have stood very high in GW's estimation: GW wrote his farm manager, Anthony Whitting, on 9 Dec. 1792 that he hoped "the Overseer you have got from Boggess['']s will answer your expectations" but confessed that he had "no opinion of any recommendation from that person."

To Alexander Hamilton

Sir,   Mount Vernon, December 12th 1799.

I have duly received your letter of the 28th ultimo, enclosing a Copy of what you had written to the Secretary of War, on the subject of a Military Academy.

The Establishment of an Institution of this kind, upon a respectable and extensive basis, has ever been considered by me as an Object of primary importance to this Country; and while I was in the Chair of Government, I omitted no proper opportunity of recommending it, in my public Speeches, and otherways, to the attention of the Legislature:[1] But I never undertook to go into a *detail* of the organization of such an Academy; leaving this task to others, whose pursuits in the paths of Science, and attention to the Arrangements of such Institutions, had better qualified them for the execution of it.

For the same reason I must now decline making any observations on the details of your plan; and as it has already been submitted to the Secretary of War, through whom it would naturally be laid before Congress, it might be too late for alterations, if any should be suggested.

I sincerely hope that the subject will meet with due attention, and that the reasons for its establishment, which you have so clearly pointed out in your letter to the Secretary, will prevail upon the Legislature to place it upon a permanent and respectable footing. With very great esteem & regard I am, Sir, Your most Obedt Servt

Go: Washington

LS, DLC: Hamilton Papers; Df, DLC:GW. Both copies are in Tobias Lear's hand.

1. GW, for instance, wrote in November 1793 in his notes for his fifth annual address to Congress that "the propriety of a Military Accademy for teaching the art of Gunnery & Engineering, can scarcely be doubted."

To James Anderson

Mr Anderson,   Mount Vernon 13th Decr 1799

I did not know that you were here yesterday morning until I had mounted my horse, otherwise I should have given you what I now send.[1]

As Mr Rawlins was going to the Union Farm, to lay off the Clover lots, I sent by him the Duplicate for that Farm to his brother—and as I was going to River Farm myself, I carried a copy for that Farm to Dowdal—Both of them have been directed to consider them attentively, & to be prepared to give you their ideas of the mode of arrangeing the Work when they are called upon.[2]

Such a Pen as I saw yesterday at Union Farm, would, if the Cattle were kept in it one Week, destroy the whole of them. They would be infinitely more comfortable in this, or any other weather, in the open fields—Dogue run Farm Pen may be in the same condition—It did not occur to me as I passed through the yard of the Barn to look into it. I am Your friend &ca

Go: Washington

ALS, PHi: Dreer Collection.

1. GW had written a letter to Anderson on 10 Dec., and he had prepared elaborate plans for each of the Mount Vernon farms which he intended to en-

close in that letter. For GW's plans, see the Enclosure. GW's letter of 10 Dec. to Anderson reads: "Mr Anderson From the various plans suggested by you, at different times, for Cropping the Farms which I propose to retain in my own hands—in the year 1800, and with a reduced force of the labourers on them in succeeding years, together with the operations necessary to carry them into effect; and comparing these with the best reflections I am able to bestow on the subject: Considering moreover, the exhausted state of my arable fields, and how important it is to adopt some system by which the evil may be arrested, and the fields in some measure restored, by a rotation of Crops which will not press hard upon, while Sufficient interval between them, is allowed for improv⟨e⟩ment: I have digested the following Instructions for my Manager (while it is necessary for me to employ one) and for the government of my Overseers [see Enclosure]; and request that they may be most *strictly*, and *pointedly* attended to and executed; as far however, as the measures therein required, will permit.

"A System closely pursued (altho' it may not in all its parts be the *best* that could be devised) is attended with innumerable advantages. The Conductor of the bu[si]ness in this case can never be under any dilemma in his proceedings; The Overseers, & even the Negros, know, what is to be done, and what they are capable of doing, in ordinary seasons: in short every thing would move like *clock work*⟨;⟩ and the force to be employed, may be in due proportion to the Work which is to be performed; & a reasonable and tolerably accurate estimate may be made of the produce. But when no plan is fixed, when directions flow from day to day, the business becomes a mere chaos: frequently shifting, and sometimes at a stand—for want of directions what to do, or the manner of doing it. These occasion a waste of time, which is of more importance than is generally imagined.

"Nothing can so effectually obviate the evil, as an established, & regular course of proceeding; made known to *all* who are actors in it; that *all may*, thereby, be enabled to play their parts, to advantage.

"This would give ease to the principal Conductor of the business; It would be more satisfactory to the persons who *immediately* Overlook it; and would be less harrassing to those who labour; as well as more beneficial for those who employ them.

"Under this view of the subject, & of the change which is about to take place next year, by having rented one of the Farms, the Mill, and Distillery, and havg it in contempla[tio]n to do the same with the Fishery, at the Ferry, the principal services which you can render me (after these events take place) is to explain to the Overseers, (who will be furnished with duplicates), the plan, in all its parts, which is detailed in the following sheets; hear their ideas with respect to the *order* in which the different sorts of work therein pointed out, shall succeed each other, for the purpose of carrying it on to the best advantage, correct any erroneous projects they may be disposed to adopt for the execution thereof; and then see that, they adhere strictly to whatsoever may be resolved on—and that they are always (except when otherwise permitted) on their respective Farms, & with their People.

"The work under such circumstances will go on smoothly; and that the Stock may be well fed, littered, and taken care of according to the directions which are given; it will be necessary to Inspect the conduct of the Overseers in this particular, and those also whose immediate business it is to attend upon them, with a watchful eye: otherwise, and generally in severe weather, when attention & care is most needed, they will be most neglected.

"Œconomy in all things is as commendable, in the Manager as it is beneficial and desirable by the Employer. And on a Farm, it shews itself in nothing more evidently or more essentially, than in not suffering the Provender to be wasted, but on the contrary, that every atom of it be used to the best advantage; and likewise in not suffering the Ploughs, Harrows and other implements of husbandry thereon, and the Gears belonging to them, to be unnecessarily exposed; trodden underfoot—Carts running over them; and abused in other respects.

"More good is derived from looking into the minutiæs on a Farm, than strikes people at first view; and by examining the Farm yards fences, & looking into fields—to see that *nothing* is within, but what are *allowed* to be there, produces more good, or at least avoids more evil, oftentimes, than riding from one working party, or from one Overseer to another, generally accomplishes.

"I have mentioned these things not only because they have occurred to me; and tho' apparently, trifles, but because they prove far otherwise, in the result.

"And It is hoped, and will be expected, that more effectual measures will be pursued to make butter another year; for it is almost beyond belief, that from 101 Cows actually reported on a late enumeration of the Cattle, that I am obliged to *buy butter* for the use of my family.

"To visit my Lands in the Western Country (at my expence), so soon as the weather becomes temperate and settled in the Spring, Reporting the circumstances under which they are—and what they are cap⟨able of⟩—will be expected, It being of importance for me to receive a just, & faithful acct respecting ⟨them⟩.

"After perusing the accompanying plans, *carefully*, furnish me with your opinion on the two following points. 1st what quantity of Seeds, & of what kinds, I shall have occasion to *buy*; and against what periods, for seeding the Grounds in the year 1800 in the manner therein directed: and 2d whether any & what number of hands can be withdrawn from the three Farms I retain in that year; In considering this last mentioned point, hear the opinions of the Overseers.

"The a/cts for the *present* quarter must be made final; as an entire new scene will take place afterwards; In doing this, advertise (in the Alexa. Paper) for the claims, of every kind and nature whatsoever, against me, to be brot in to you, by the 1st of Jan:, that I may wipe them off, & begin on a fresh score; All balances in my favr must either be recd; or reduced to speci⟨alties,⟩ that there may be no disputes thereafter. I am Yr sincere friend—Well wisher—and Servant Go: Washington" (ADfS, DLC:GW). The plans for the future management of the three Mount Vernon farms that GW planned to begin his personal management of in 1800 (River, Union, and Muddy Hole farms) are printed as an enclosure to this letter to Anderson. Lawrence Lewis had rented Dogue Run farm, the mill, and the distillery.

2. The somewhat more concise version of the plans for the three farms, also in DLC:GW, perhaps is the form that GW gave to the "Duplicate" plans that he prepared for the overseers of the individual farms. George Rawlins was overseer of Union Farm and Moses Dowdal of River Farm.

Enclosure
Washington's Plans for His River, Union,
and Muddy Hole Farms

[10 December 1799]

River-Farm

Crops for, & operations thereon, for the year 1800

Field No. 1—Is now partly in Wheat. Part thereof is to be sown with Oats. another part may be sown with Pease, broadcast. Part is in meadow, and will remain so. and the most broken, washed, & indifferent part, is to remain uncultivated; but to be harrowed & smoothed in the Spring, and the worst parts thereof (if practicable) to be covered with litter, straw, weeds or any kind of vegitable Rubbish to prevent them from running into gullies.

No. 2—One fourth is to be in Corn, and to be sown with wheat; another fourth is to be in Buckwheat and Pease, half of it in the one, and half of it in the other, sown in April; to be plowed in as a green dressing; and by actual experiment, to ascertain which is best. The whole of this fourth is to be sown with Wheat also; another fourth part is to be naked fallow for wheat; and the other, and last quarter, to be appropriated for Pumpkins, Simlins, Turnips[,] Yateman Pease (in hills), and such other things of this kind as may be required—and to be sown likewise with Rye after they are taken off, for Seed.

No. 3—Is now in wheat, to be harvested in the year 1800; the stubble of which, immediately after Harvest, is to be plowed in and sown thin with Rye; and such parts thereof as are low, or produces a luxurient growth of grain, is to have grass-seeds sprinkled over it. The whole for Sheep to run on, in the day, (but housed at night) during the winter and spring months. If it should be found expedient, part thereof in the spring might be reserved, for the purpose of Seed.

No. 4—Will be in Corn, and is to be sown in the Autumn of that year with Wheat, to be harvested in 1801—and to be treated in all respects as has been directed for No. 3, the preceeding year. It is to be manured, as much as the means will permit, with such aids as can be procured during the present Winter, and ensuing Spring.

Nos. 5, 6, 7 and 8—Are to remain as they are, but nothing suffered to run upon them; as ground will be allotted for the sole purpose of Pasturage, and invariably used as such.

Clover-Lots

No. 1—Counting from the Spring branch, is to be planted in Potatoes.

No. 2—That part thereof which is now in Turnips, is to be sown with Oats & clover; the other part, being *now* in clover, is to remain so until it comes into Potatoes, by rotation.

No. 3—Is also in Clover at present, and is to remain so, as just mentioned, for No. 3.

No. 4—Is partly in Clover, and partly in Timothy, & so to be, until its turn for Potatoes.

The rotation for these Lots

Invariably is to be—1st Potatoes, highly manured; 2d Oats, & clover sown therewith; 3d Clover; 4th Clover. Then to begin again with Potatoes, and proceed as before. The present Clover lots must be Plastered.

All green Sward, rough ground, or that wch is heavily covered with weeds, bottle brush grass, and such things as by being turned in will ferment, putrify, & ameliorate the Soil, should be plowed in, in Autumn, and at such times in Winter, as can be done while the ground is dry, and in condition for it.

Pasture-Grounds

The large lot adjoining the Negro houses and Orchd, is to have Oats sown on the Potatoe and Pumpkin ground; with which, and on the Rye also, in that lot and on the Mellon part, orchard-grass seeds are to be sown; and thereafter to be kept as a standing calf pasture; and for Ewes (which may require extra: care) at yeaning, or after they have yeaned.

The other large lot, North East of the Barnlan⟨e⟩ is to be appropriated, *always*, as a Pasture for the Milch Cows; and probably working Oxen, during the Summer Season.

The Woodland, and the old field, commonly called Johnstons, are designed for *Common* Pasture—and to be so applied, *always*. to which, if it should be found inadequate to the Stock of the Farm, Field No. 8 and the Woodland therein, may be added.

Meadows

Those already established, and in train, must continue; and the next to be added to them, is the Arm of the Creek which runs up to the Spring house, & forks; both prongs of which must be

References

A   Within these lines, one or two medium farms might be formed, independent of [t]he land is capable of high improvement into Meadow, being low; part of it is already [so] to be so; requiring to be drained. — There are no houses on it.

B   Great part within these lines is in Wood, but there is a sufficiency of ground clea[r] middle sized farm, with a house thereon; and a most beautiful site for a Gentlema[n]

C   Possesses the same advantage. — The whole of it is cleared of the Wood, but has [...]

D   Is cleared land, and might be added to River farm; — or if that farm should b[e] of the smaller ones — affording pleasant sites for houses on the River. —

E   The use of this farm is given to a Relation. —

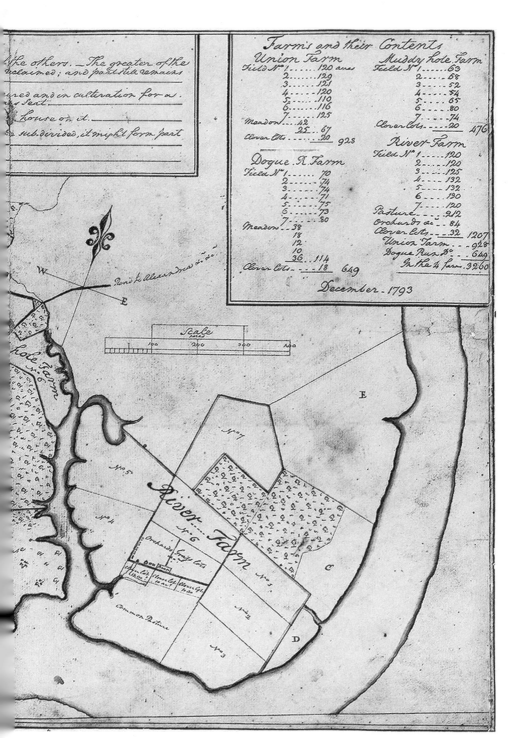

Fig. 2. Washington's drawing of his farms at Mount Vernon, 1793.
(Henry E. Huntington Library, San Marino, Calif.)

grubbed, and wrought upon at every convenient moment when the weather will permit, down to the line of the Ditch which encloses the lots for clover &ca.

And as the fields come into cultivation—or, as labour can be spared from other work, and circumstances will permit, the heads of all the Inlets in them must be reclaimed, and laid to grass—whether they be large, or small; & inasmuch as nothing will run on or can tresspass upon, or injure the Grass; no fencing being req[uire]d.

Mud—for—Compost

The season is now too far advanced, and too cold to be engaged in a work that will expose the hands to wet: but, it is of such essential importance that it should be set about seriously, and with spirit next year, for the Summers Sun, & Winters frost to prepare it for the Corn, & other Crops of 1801, that all the hands of the Farm, not indispensably engaged in the Crops, should, so soon as Corn planting is compleated in the spring, be uninterruptedly employed in raising Mud from the Pocosons, & even from the bed of the Creek, into the Scow; and the Carts, so soon as the Manure for the Corn & Potatoes in 1800 is carried out is to be incessantly drawing it to compost heaps in the field, which is to be manured by it. What number of hands can be set apart for this *all important work*, remains to be considered, and decided upon.

Penning Cattle—& folding Sheep.

On the fields intended for Wheat, from the first of May, when the former should be turned out to Pasture, until the first of November, when they ought to be Housed, must be practiced *invariably*: and to do it with regularity & propriety, the Pen for the first, & the fold for the latter, should be proportioned to the number of each kind of Stock; and both these to as much ground as they will manure sufficiently, in the space of a Week, for Wheat; beyond which they are not to remain in a place, except on the poorest spots; and even *these* had better be aided by litter or something else than to depart from an established rule of removing the Pens on a *certain* day in every week: For in this, as in everything else, system is essential to carry on business well, & with ease.

Feeding

The work horses and Mules are always to be in their Stalls—& well littered & cleaned when they are out of Harness; and they are to be plenteously fed with cut straw, and as much chopped Grain, Meal, or Bran, with a little salt mixed therewith, as will keep them *always* in good condition for work; seeing also that they are watered, as regularly as they are fed. this is their winter feed: for Spring, Summer and Autumn, it is expected that Soiling of them on green food—first with Rye, then with Lucern, and next with Clover, with very little grain, will enable them to perform their Work.

The Oxen, and other horned Cattle, are to be housed from the first of November, until the first of May; and to be fed as well as the means on the Farm will admit. The first (Oxen) must always be kept in good condition. Housed in the Stalls designed for them. and the Cows (so many of them as can find places) on the opposite side—The rest, with the other Cattle, must be in the newly erected Sheds; and the whole carefully Watered every day. The Ice, in frosen weather, being broken, so as to admit them to clean Water.

With respect to the Sheep, they must receive the best protection that can be given them *this* Winter; against the next, I hope they will be better provided for.

And with regard to the Hogs, the plan must be to raise a given number of *good ones*, instead of an indiscriminate number of *indifferent ones*—half of which die, or are stolen before the period arrives for putting them up as porkers. To accomplish this, a sufficient number of the best Sows should be appropriated to the purpose; and so many pigs raised from them as will ensure the quantity of Pork the Farm ought to furnish. Whether it will be most advisable to restrain these hogs from running at large or not, can be decided with more precision after the result of those *now* in close pens are better known. The exact quantity of Corn used by those which are now in Pens should be ascertained, and regularly reported, in order to learn the result.

Stables—and—Farm Pens

These ought to be kept well littered, and the Stalls clean; as well for the comfort of the Creatures that are contained in them, as for the purpose of manure; but as straw canot be afforded for this purpose, *Leaves*, & such spoiled Straw or weeds as will not do for food, must serve for the Stables; and the first, that is leaves and Corn Stalks, is all that can be applied to the Pens. To do this work effectually, let the Corn stalks be cut down by a *few* careful people with *sharp* hoes, so low as never to be in the way of Scythes at harvest; and whenever the Wheat will admit Carts to run on it without injury, to bring them off, & stack them near the Farm Pens. In like manner let the People, with their blankets go every evening, or as often as occasion may require, to the nearest wood and fill them with leaves for the purposes abovementioned; bottoming the beds with Corn Stalks, and covering them *thick* with leaves. A measure of this sort will be—if strictly attended to, and punctually performed, of great utility in every point of view. It will save food, Make the Cattle lay warm and comfortable, and produce much manure. The Hogs also in pens must be well bedded in leaves.

Fencing

As stock of no kind, according to this plan, will be suffered to run on the arable fields, or Clover lots (except Sheep, in the day, on the Rye field, as has been mentioned before) partition fences between the fields until they can be raised of Quicks, may be dispens'd with—But it is of great importance that all the exterior or outer fences, should be substantially good; and those also wch divide the Common, or Woodland Pasture, from the fields and Clover Lots are to be very respectable.

To accomplish this desirable object in as short a time as possible, and with the smallest expence of timber—the Post & Rail fence which runs from the Negro quarters or rather from the corner of the lot enclosing them up to the division between fields No. 7 & No. 8 may be placed on the Bank (which must be raised higher) that runs from thence (where it was burnt) to the Creek. In like manner the fence from the gate which opens into No. 2, quite down to the River, along the Cedar, hedge Row—as also those Rails which are between No. 1 & 2 and between No. 2 & 3 may all be taken away and applied to the outer fences, & the fences of the lanes from the Barn into the Woodland Pasture, and from the former (the Barn) into No. 5; for the fences of all these lanes must be *good*, as the Stock must have a free and uninterrupted passage along them, at all times, from the Barnyard to the Woodland Pasture.

One of the gates near the Fodder house, may be moved up to the range of the lane, by the gate, near that which leads into field No. 2; and the other may be placed at the other end of the lane, by the Negro quarters: and so long as Mr Mason's old field remains uninclosed the outer gate into Field No. 8 wd stand better in the Fence which runs from the division between fields No. 7 & 8 to the Creek than where it now is.

All the fen[cin]g from the last mentioned place, (between me

& Mr Mason) until it joins Mr Lears Farm, and thence with the line between him & me, until it comes to the River, will require to be substantially good; at its termination on the river, dependance must be placed in a Water fence—for, if made of common Rails, they would be carried off by boatmen for fire-wood. The fences seperating fields No. 1 and No. 8 from the woodland pasture must also be made good, to prevent depredations on the fields by my own stock.

Crops &ca—for—1801

No. 5—Is to be in Corn, and to be invariable in that article. It is to be planted (if drills are thought to be ineligable until the ground is much improved) in Rows 6 feet by 4 or 7 feet by 3½; the wide part open to the South. These hills are to be manured as highly as the means will admit; and the Corn planted every year in the middle of the Rows of the preceeding year; by doing which, and mixing the Manure and Earth by the Plow & other workings, the whole in time, will be enriched.

The washed and gullied parts of this field should be levelled, & as much improved as possible—or left uncultivated. Although it is more broken than some of the other fields, it has its advantages. 1st it has several Inlets extending into it with easy assents therefrom—2d it is convenient to the Mud in the bed of the Creek whensoever (by means of the Scow) resort is had thereto—and good landing places—and thirdly, it is as near to the Barn as any other (when a bridge and causeway is made over the Spring branch.)—To these may be added, that it is more remote from Squirrels than any other.

No. 6 & 7—Or such part thereof as is not so much washed & gullied as to render plowing ineligable, are to be fallowed for wheat—One of which, if both cannot, is to have the stubble plowed in and sown with Rye; and the low, & strong parts to have Timothy or Orchard grass-seeds—perhaps both, in different places, sprinkled over them for the purpose of raising Seed. On the Rye pasture the Sheep are to be fed in winter & Spring, and treated in all respects as directed in the case of No. 3 in 1800.

In the years 1802, 1803, & so on

The Corn ground, remaining the same, two fields in following numbers, will be fallowed for Wheat; and treated in all respects as mentioned above. And if Pumpkins—Simlins[—]Turnips—Pease—and such like growths are found beneficial to the land, or useful and profitable for Stock, ground may readily be found for them.

These are the great out lines of a Plan, and the operations of it, for the next year, and for years to come, for River Farm. The necessary arrangements, and all the preparatory measures for carrying it into effect, ought to be adopted without delay, and invariably pursued. Smaller matters may, and undoubtedly will, occur occasionally; but none, it is presumed, that can militate against it materially.

To carry it into effect advantageously, it becomes the indispensable duty of him who is employed to overlook & conduct the operations, to take a prospective, and comprehensive view of the *whole* business which is laid before him, that the several parts thereof may be so ordered and arranged, as that one sort of work may follow another sort in proper Succession, and without loss of labour, or of time; for nothing is a greater waste of the latter, and consequently of the former (time producing labour, and labour money—) than shifting from one thing to another before it is finished; as if chance, or the impulse of the moment, not judgm[en]t and foresight, directed the measure. It will be acknowledged that weather, and other circumstances may, at times, interrupt a regular course of proceedings; but if a plan is well digested beforehand, they cannot interfere long, with a man who is acquainted with the nature of the business, and the Crops he is to attend to.

Every attentive, and discerning person, who has the *whole* business of the year laid before him, and is acquainted with the nature of the work, can be at no loss to lay it out to advantage. He will know that there are many things wch can be accomplished in winter as well as in summer—others, that spring, summer and Autumn *only* are fit for. In a word, to use the Wiseman's saying "that there is a time, and a season for all things" and that, unless they are embraced, nothing will thrive; or go on smoothly. There are many sorts of *Indoors* work which can be executed in Hail, rain or Snow, as well as in sunshine; and if they are set about in fair weather (unless there be a necessity for it) there will be nothing to do in foul weather; the people therefore must be idle. The man of prudence & foresight, will always keep these things in view, and order his work accordingly; so as to suffer no waste of time, or idleness. The same observations apply with equal force to frozen ground; and grounds too wet to work in, or if worked, will be injured thereby. These observations might be spun to a greater length, but they are sufficient to produce reflexion, and reflection with Industry, and proper attention, will produce the end that is to be wished.

There is one thing however I cannot forbear to add—and in strong terms; it is, that whenever I order a thing to be done, it must be done; or a reason given at the *time*, or as soon as the impracticability is discovered, why it cannot; which will produce a countermand, or change. But it is not for the person receiving the order, to suspend or dispense with its execution; and after it has been supposed to have gone into effect, for me to be told that nothing has been done in it; that it will be done; or that it could not be done; either of these is unpleasant, and disagreeable to me having been accustomed all my life to more regularity, and punctuality, and *know* that nothing but System & method is required to accomplish all reasonable requests.

Go: Washington

Mount Vernon December 10th 1799

Union-Farm
Crops for, and operations thereon in 1800

Field No. 1—Is now sown with Wheat, to be harvested in 1800. The stubble of which is to be immediately ploughed in, and rye sowed thereon for a Sheep pasture; Grass-seeds must be sown therewith on such parts as will yield grass for seed, to supply my own wants, and the market, so far as it can be spared. This field after the Rye has been eaten off by the sheep, is to be reined up from Stock of all kinds, and nothing suffered to run thereon until it comes, in course, to be cultivated, in the regular rotine of Crops.

No. 2—Will be in Corn, and although but an indifferent field, washed in some places—gullied in others, and rich in none; is, all things considered, best to be appropriated, *constantly* for this Crop. 1st & primarily, because it is most contiguous to the Barn, and the Corn therein more easily secured, & attended to; 2nd because it is as handy to the mud from the Pocosons—and the bed of the Creek—as any other, to mix in a compost—and more convenient to the manure from the Farm yard & stables—3dly because it is entirely out of the reach of squirrels—and 4thly because it is hoped, and expected, that from the manner of treating it, that it will be so much amended as to become more & more productive every year, and the impoverished places, if not restored to some degree of fertility, prevented from getting worse, and becoming such eye sores as they now are.

The corn will be planted in Rows, 6 feet by 4—or 7 by 3½; the wide part open to the South, and must be as highly manured in the hill as the means on the Farm (respect being had to other species of Crops) will admit. The Rows of the succeeding year, will be in the middle of the last, & alternately shifted; by which, & the workings the field will yearly receive, the whole will be enrichened. and it is hoped restored.

No. 3—As No. 2 is to be appropriated as a standing field for Corn, and of course cannot be sown with Wheat in the autumn of 1800; This field—that is No. 3, ought, if it be practicable, to be fallowed, and sown with that article—otherwise the Farm will produce *no* Wheat the following year, and the Stock must suffer for want of the Straw. and is to be treated in every respect as has been directed for No. 1—that is, the stubble to be plowed in immediately after harvest and Rye sowed thereon, with grass-seeds where the soil is strong enough to rear them for the purpose of producing seed again.

No. 4—The part thereof which lyes No. E[as]t of the Meadow (commonly called Manleys field) is to remain *well* inclosed, and no stock suffered to run thereon until it comes in rotation to be fallowed for Wheat in 1801. The other part of the same No. 4, is to be equally well enclosed, and reined up from Stock; and except the part along muddy hole branch (that is to be added to No. 5 in order to supply the deficiency occasioned by taking Clover lot No. 2 from it) is to be planted with Peach trees at 16½ feet asunder, except so much of it as lays flat, by the gate on the Mill Road, which, if properly prepared, it is supposed would bring grass—and on that account to be planted at double that distance, viz.—33 feet a part. What is here meant by enclosing *this* part of No. 4 well, is, that the *outer* fence shall be secure—for it will remain as now, undivided from No. 3, otherwise than by the Branch.

No. 5—Is also to be kept from Stock; and when it comes in course to be fallowed for Wheat, is to have the addition above mentioned (along the Branch) added thereto, and sown in this Article.

No. 6—Will receive such an addition to its size from No. 7, as will make it, exclusive of the Lot for Clover, Lucern, &ca, of equal size thereto. Part of this field is now sown with, and will be in wheat in 1800; Part will be in Oats, particularly where the Pease grow; and all that part of it, and No. 7 also, which *lyes low* from the meadow fence by the Overseers house, quite up to the head springs of the branch (reclaimed in the spring) is to be planted with rare ripe Corn—and in the Fall, to be treated, in every respect as the great meadow at this Farm (but at an earlier period) has been this year. For although I am not sanguine enough to expect that it will make good *Mowing* meadow I shall be much disappointed if it does not produce grass, yielding a good deal of Seed; which (until the fields come into cultivation in regular rotation, and afterwards, if it answers expectation) will be an annual profit without any other labour than gathering of it. The other part of No. 6 which will be taken from No. 7 laying South of this low ground, between it and No. ⟨1⟩ might, if it does not involve too much Ploughing, be put in Corn also. but this is a measure which will require consideration, and probably must depend upon circumstances. The poor and washed parts of No. 6 must remain uncultivated; but ought, [if] it be practicable, to be levelled, Harrowed, and trash of some kind to be thrown thereon, as will keep them from growing worse.

No. 7—Some part of this field may be sown with Buckwheat (in no great quantity) and a part may be planted with the Yateman Pease in hills—both for a Crop; some of the other kind of Pease may be sown Broadcast and mowed at a proper season for the Stock. The rest of the ground by laying uncultivated, & nothing running thereon, will be encreasing in strength while idle.

Clover & Lots

No. 1—Next the Overseer's house—same side of the lane (excepting the ground now in, and designed for Lucern, South of the slash by the Barn, & two acres where the Turnips grew or at the other end for experiments) is to be in Oats, and to be sown with Clover Seed.

No. 2—Opposite thereto, and at present part of No. 5, is to be well manured, and planted with Potatoes; whether in Hills, or Drills, may be considered.

No. 3—May receive Pumpkins—Simlins—Turnips and Mellons, there being no sown grass remaining on it; and the manure for, and shade occasion by, these vines, together with the working the lot will get, will be of Service instead of a detriment to the Potatoe Crop wch will follow.

No. 4—Is to remain in Clover until, by rotation, it comes into Potatoes again.

The Rotation for these Lots

Are, uniformly to be—1st Potatoes, highly manured. 2d Oats, and Clover sown therewith; 3d Clover; 4th Clover. Then to begin again with Potatoes—and proceed as before.

The present Clover Lots must be plastered.

All green sward, rough ground, or that which is heavily covered with Weeds, bottle brush grass, and such things as by being turned in, will ferment, putrify and ameliorate the soil, should be plowed in, in Autumn, and at such times in Winter as can be done while the ground is dry, and in condition for working.

Pasture Ground

As Stock of all sorts, except Sheep upon the Rye, are to be excluded from the Arable fields and Clover Lots, resort must be had to the Woodland and unreclaimed swamps therein for Pasture for them (the Lane up to the Barn will serve for Calves); and they will be provided, by a Fence extending from the So. West Corner of Muddy hole field (No. 2) to the So. E[as]t corner of Dogue run field (No. 4) leaving all South of it for this Farm; as the North part will be for Muddy hole Farm—and as it will be for the mutual benefit of both Farms⟨,⟩ the fence must be erected at the joint expence of both.

Fencing.

The one just mentioned must be compleated in the course of the Winter; and every possible exertion to strength, and render substantially good, the whole of the exterior or outer fence of the Farm. To do which, and to avoid all unnecessary consumption of timber, the partition fence between the fields No. 6 & 7, as it now stands, quite up to the Woods, and thence to the fence leading from the Ferry to the Mill road (from the Mansion house) may be taken away, and applied to that fence, and to the trunnel fence on the Mill road, where they unite, until it comes to the Meadow fence at the bridge; leaving the fields No. 6 & 7, and the woodland adjoining, under one inclosure. In like manner, the fences dividing No. 1 from 2 and No. 2 from 3 may be used for a fence around the Creek, until it unites with that opposite to the Mill house; without which, neither of those fields will be secure; as Hogs have been taught, or of themselves have learnt, to cross the Creek in pursuit of food; and for strengthening effectually the fence from the Plank bridge by the Barn lane to the Branch opposite to the Mill house, new rails must be got in the nearest wood between the Mill Road & the road leading to the Gumspring. The West fence of No. 5 must, next year, or as soon as it can be accomplished, be removed across the branch, and placed in a line with the new ditch fence of the lower meadow, until it comes in range with the South line of the said field—and until a fence is run from the end thereof to the nearest part of the outer fence opposite to the Mill, and a second gate established thereat—Or that, *that* intercourse between the Barn and Mill is effectually barred (which would be the cheapest, and by odds the most convenient mode) there would be no security for any Crop growing in fields No. 1[,] 2 or 3 as leaving the gate by the Mill run open, only five minutes, might deluge the whole with the Hogs at that place; which might be in them a night or two, perhaps more, before they were discovered, and do irreparable damage. Indeed the latter mode has so much the advantage of the former, especially as my intercourse with the Mill will, in a great measure cease, that I see no cause to hesitate a moment in adopting it; and to prevent opening the fence where the gate now is, a deep ditch & high bank, would be necessary (from a distance below, to the foot of the hill above, if not quite up to the Meadow)—One, among other advantages resulting from this measure would be, that the West, and even South fence of No. 5 might, if occasion required it, be applied, instead of New rails, in making the fence from the meadow towards the Mill & around the Creek more substantial: for it must be repeated again, that as there will be few, or no inner fences, the outer ones must be unassailable to the most vicious Stock.

The fences that are already around the Meadows may remain, but there is no occasion for their being formidable—To guard them against hogs if any should, by chance get through the outer fence, is all that would be necessary.

Meadows

The large Meadow below the Barn lane—and half of that above the lane, have had every thing done for them that is requisite; except manuring, when necessary, & the means are to be had. The remaining part of the last mentioned meadow above must receive a compleat Summer fallow, to cleanse it of rubbish of *all sorts* and to be sown in proper Season with Timothy, with a protecting crop of Rye for soiling the working mules &ca in the Spring. Although I may find myself mistaken, I am inclined to put the other prong of this swamp, running through No. 6 and heading in No. 7 into meadow and have, for this reason, directed already, the mode to be pursued for accomplishing it. Next to this, let as much of the Inlet in No. 2 as can be laid dry enough for Corn, be planted therewith, in order to eradicate the wild growth; when this is effected, lay it to grass. As the fields come round, the unreclaimed Inlets may be prepared for Grass, if circumstances, & the force of the Farm will admit of it; of these, there is one besides a swamp, in No. 3, which is susceptible of being converted into good grass ground: And the flat & low ground (in West) No. 4, it is presumed, wd bring grass also. Whether the part proposed to be added to field No. 5 had better be retained for Arable uses, or laid to Meadow can be determined better after it is cleared, and cleansed of the wild growth, than now. But the Inlets at the Ferry between the dwelling & Fish houses, might, by a small change of the Fence from the gate of No. 1, be thrown into that Field, and brought into excellent meadow at very little expence, whensoever time & labour can be afforded for this purpose. To dwell on the advantages of meadow, would be a mere waste of time; as the produce is always in demand, in the Market & for my own purposes; and obtained at no other expence than that of cutting the grass and making it into Hay.

Crops—&ca for—1801

No. 2—Being the field appropriated for Corn, will be planted with this article accordingly; as already directed for 1800. The poor and washed parts continuing to receive all the aids that can be given to them.

No. 3—Supposing it to have been fallowed and sown the year before, will, *this* year, produce a crop of Wheat; the stubble of which, immediately after harvest, is to be turned in, sown with Rye for the benefit of sheep, in the day, during winter and Spring, but to be housed at Night. All the low and rich spots, capable of producing grass must be sown with Timothy or Orchard grass seeds for the purpose of supplying seeds again; And a part of the field may be reserved for a Rye Crop, or the Sheep taken off early enough for the whole to yield enough of this grain to pay for the Harvesting of it.

No. 4 & 5—That part of No. 4 which lays next to the Mill, is, as has been directed already, to be planted with Peach trees; the other part (called Manleys field[)], with all that can be added to it (not exceeding 40 Acres) of Woodland adjoining No. 6, and the upper meadow, below the plank bridge is to be fallowed for Wheat; As No. 5 also is to be, with the addition at the West end, taken from No. 4. And both of them if it can be accomplished, but one certainly, must have the Stubble when the wheat comes of sowed with Rye (for the Sheep) and with grass seeds, upon low & Rich places, for the purpose of raising seed; & to be treated in all other respects as has been directed for number 3.

The reason for preferring an addition to No. 4 from the woods East of the Meadow (although the land is of inferior quality) is, because it requires no additional fencing, for the same fence that incloses No. 6 & 7 encompasses this also; because it will be more convenient for supplying the Mansion with fire wood; and because it will give a better form, & appearance to the Farm than breaking into the Woodland on the North side of the Mill Road.

Crops for 1802. 1803. & so on

The Corn ground remaining the same *always*, two fields in following numbers will every year be fallowed for wheat; and treated in all respects as hath been mentioned before. And if Pumpkins—Simlins[—]Turnips—and such like growths are found beneficial to the land, or useful & profitable for Stock, places enough may be found to raise them in.

All unnecessary Wood is to be cut down & removed from the fields as they are cultivated in Rotation.

Mud & rich earth—for—Compost
Penning Cattle, & folding Sheep
Feeding
Stables—& Farm Pens

Are all to be managed precisely as is directed for River Farm.

Muddy hole
Farm Crops for, and operations thereon, in 1800

Field No. 1—Is to remain uncultivated; to be kept well Inclosed; and Stock of no kind be suffd to feed thereon.

No. 2—All the hollows therein, and low parts thereof, are to be sown with Oats, and the *best* part of them, with Grass-seeds; and nothing permitted to run thereon. The washed & gullied parts of it ought to be levelled, & smoothed; and as far as it can be accomplished, covered with litter, straw, weeds, Corn stalks, or any other kind of vegitable rubbish, to bind together, and to prevent the Earth from gullying.

No. 3—All the ground that can be cleared in this field, of the Wood, within the fence, is to be planted with Corn; and some of the adjacent ground, if it be thought eligable, is to be added thereto for this article also. The ground *now* in wheat in this field, is, immediately after harvest, to be plowed up, & sown with Buckwheat for a Crop: such other parts of it as will produce them, is to be planted with Pease, Pumpkins, Simlins, Turnips, and such like things as may be useful for Stock. The poor parts are to remain untouched; and such other parts as are washed & gullied, are to be treated in all respects as directed above, for No. 2. The Meadow (already in Timothy) and so much of the swamp as can be reclaimed, must be appropriated to Grass; and the wheat ground on the North of it, when sown with Buckwheat, is to receive Timothy seed also.

No. 4—This field is already in wheat, and a part near the Barn, and some of the lowest, and strongest spots in other places of it, may have orchard grass-seeds sown thereon, in March, for the purpose of raising seed; as the field will be kept from Stock.

No. 5—Will be in Corn, and sowed with Wheat or Rye, as shall be deemed most eligable, at the time.

No. 6—Ought, if it could be accomplished, to be fallowed for Wheat; if not, to be enclosed, & reined up from Stock.

No. 7—Is too much exhausted to be longer cultivated. It may, therefore, be either thrown into the great woodland Pasture designed for the Mansion house, East of the new road, or—reserved as a Sheep and calf pasture for this Farm; as there will be no Rye sown for this purpose, on Wheat Stubble, on Acct of the Peach trees which are planted in the fields, & would be injured thereby, until they are so grown as to be out of their reach.

To supply the place of this field, as much land ought to be cleared, adjoin[in]g to the present No. 3, on the south side thereof, and west of the New road, as will make it large enough to be divided into two fields to be called 3 & 4; and this, it is presumed may be accomplished by the time No. 7 would be required, according to the regular rotation, for cultivation. If it could be prepared for Corn against the year 1801, it would be still more desirable; as it would give more respite to the older field.

Clover Lots

No. 1—Will be in Potatoes. to be highly manured before they are planted; and this had better be in Hills, than in Drills.

No. 2—Is now in American Clover. From which all the seed that it will afford, must be saved.

No. 3—Is in common (red) Clover, and is to remain so, until it comes into Potatoes again.

No. 4—Will be in Oats, and is to be sown in Clover⟨—⟩all the Lots now in Clover are to be man[ure]d with Plast⟨er⟩.

The Rotation for these Lots

Invariably is to be—1st Potatoes, highly manured; 2d—Oats, and Clover sown therewith; 3d, Clover; 4⟨th⟩ Clover; and then to begin again with Potatoes, and proceed as before.

All Rough ground, ground covered with weeds, bottle brush-grass, and such like growths, is to be plowed in Autumn, and in winter when it will admit of it, without injury; as well for the purpose of turning in, and rotting such stuff, thereby ameliorating the soil; as to facilitate the operations of the Spring; which, oftentimes is wet, & unfavorable for Plowing.

Fencing

The outer fences of this Farm, like all the others, ought to be, not only repaired, but made *substantially* good; and a lane between the present fields numbered 5 & 6, to be established; or nothing growing therein will be secure. To effect this, as no stock will be suffered (after the present Winter) to run on any of the fields, the Rails of the partition fences between them, may be applied in the most convenient and beneficial manner to this purpose. For instance—the fence between No. 4 and 5 may contribute to the Lane on the Mill road and to strengthen the fence along the Gumspring road, from the Corner of No. 4, at the New Ditch; and if what is *now* No. 7, is not retained for a Pasture, as beforementioned, the fence from the gate by No. 4 to the Creek, might also be removed to the nearest fences that would need Aid. But I think it had better remain, not only for the purpose of a *distinct* pasture, but as a further security to the Woodland pasture on the Creek: for if these two were thrown into one, and the gate at the Gum Spring to remain the only bar to Ingress & Regress, there would be no security for my own Stock within, or against my Neighbours without. The rails between No. 2 & 3 might, in like manner be applied to the repairing of the outer fence of No. 2, from its junction with No. 1 until it meets the branch, where the grubbing has been. And for the outer fence of No. 6, from the *New* Post & Rail corner by the Spring, to the *old* Post & Rail fence betwn Mrs Peake & me, New rails must be got from the Wood.

And whereas it is proposed to keep Stock of *all* kinds from running on the arable fields, it becomes necessary to provide other range for them during the months they are admitted to Pasture, that is to say, from the beginning of May, until the first of November—accordingly, a Woodland Pasture must be provided: to do which, a good and substantial fence (with a Gate, on the Road) must be run from the So. West Corner of Field No. 2 at this Farm, to the So. E[as]t corner of field No. 4 at Dogue run; Giving to Muddy hole Farm, all that part which lays on the No. of the said fence; and to Union Farm, that which is to the South of it. This division of the Woods Eastward of Dogue run, will not deprive that Farm of an ample woodland Pasture, formed by the Mill Swamp and the Woods between No. 3 & No. 7; making together 200 acres, of better herbage ground, than the other two woodland Pastures united. Especially too as all the hogs of that Farm will, it is presumed, be raised at the Mill; where a place is allotted for them to run in.

For the purpose of erecting this fence, the force of Union Farm and Muddy hole, must assist each other, as it will be for the mutual convenience and benefit of both places.

Crops &ca for 1801

If the land on the new road, South of field No. 3 can be cleared of the wood, in the course of next year, and the spring of 1801, so as to make *two* fields of No. 3, all the south Moiety thereof will be appropriated to Corn, *that year*: but if this should be beyond the means of accomplishment—then, and in that case, the two parts of No. 1 (on both sides the Road) ⟨is⟩ to be planted therewith, 6 by 4, or 7 by 3½ feet, and be manured in the Hill.

Farther Directions, it would be uncertain, and unnecessary to give, at present, as fallowing for Winter grain in any of the present fields, for the year 1801 must be contingent; depending, principally, upon the progress which is made in opening of new land.

and the same observations are equally applicable to the Crops— and operations for the years 1802, 1803 and so on.

Mud & rich earth—for—Compost
Penning Cattle, & folding Sheep
Feeding
Stables—&—Farm Pens

Are all to be managed precisely as is directed for River Farm; or—as nearly so, as the different circumstances of the Farms will admit.

Mount Vernon December 10th 1799   Go: Washington

ADS, DLC:GW. GW wrote this on nineteen long manuscript pages, two pages only half and another less than one-third filled. There is in DLC:GW another, somewhat shorter version of the plans, written on twelve manuscript pages (see GW to Anderson, 13 Dec., n.2). See also Figure 2.

George Washington's Last Will and Testament

Editorial Note

[9 July 1799]

George Washington prepared his will alone, without, as he attested, any "professional character" being "consulted" or having "any Agency in the draught." He dated the will, the work of many "leisure hours," the "ninth day of July" in 1799, probably the date that he finished making the final copy. And he put his name at the bottom of all but one of its twenty-nine pages. Six months later, on the day that he died, he instructed Mrs. Washington to destroy an earlier will (see Tobias Lear's Narrative Accounts of the Death of George Washington, printed below). His executors presented the new will for probate within a month, on 10 January 1800, to the Fairfax County Court, in whose custody it remains. A few days thereafter the will was printed in Alexandria. It then circulated throughout the country in pamphlet form.

The lucid and powerful prose of the text of the will displays at its best the distinctive style of writing that Washington had developed through the years. Over a span of more than half a century he had composed thousands of letters and other documents, as a private man with extensive business interests and familial and social ties, as a military leader for more than thirteen years, and, after the Revolution, as a great public figure in his own country and abroad. The contents of the will reveal much about both Washington's character and his views as well as about his diverse and valuable property, real and chattel, acquired over a lifetime. Most notable of the will's provisions, perhaps, are the instructions that he gave for freeing his slaves and for the support thereafter of the helpless children and the old and infirm among them. The extraordinary care and precision with which he spelled out how and under what conditions his land and other possessions should be distributed among the numerous members of his extended family, among his old friends, and among various dependents, provide further insight into the workings of his mind and the impulses of his heart. The language of Washington's will and its contents combine to make it a document of particular importance among his papers.

Washington made the will at a time when he was emerging from the near despondency into which he had been cast by the spectacle of the American body politic seemingly being rent asunder by conflicting views of the ongoing revolution in France. In the early summer of 1799, he was also becoming less concerned with his responsibilities as commander in chief of the army and turning back with renewed vigor to the personal concerns on which he had been focusing since his return to Mount Vernon in March 1797. The main thrust of Washington's efforts during the time left to him after his presidency was directed to putting his house in order, to doing what needed to be done to make his beloved Mount Vernon a harmonious and fruitful enterprise. Upon his arrival home in 1797, he was faced with dilapidated buildings to be repaired, worn-out soil to be made fertile, unproductive labor to be properly utilized, cropping plans to be devised and carried out, and money for all this to be sought, and perhaps found, through the sale of his western landholdings. The writing of the will was a way of taking stock of what had been done. He was determining where he stood not so much to wind things up as to consider what lay ahead. The provision in the will leaving one of the outlying farms at Mount Vernon to the newlywed Lewis couple and another to the two orphan sons of George Augustine Washington, now the wards of Tobias Lear, plays directly into Washington's decision, confirmed a few months later, to assume the direct, personal management of the farming operations at Mount Vernon, but of four (and ultimately three) farms instead of five. The will was written by a man filled not with forebodings of death but with thoughts of the future, as Washington's letters and actions in the months following attest.

Instead of only the usual widow's portion, Mrs. Washington was to retain during her lifetime possession of virtually all of her husband's property and be the beneficiary of the profits derived from it. At her death the farms at Mount Vernon and other landed and personal property named in the will would go to the heirs in accordance with the terms of the will. Washington appended to the will a Schedule of Property, printed here as an enclosure, in which he lists and describes all of his landed property and other assets not specifically bequeathed to individual heirs. He provided that, upon his wife's death, his executors would sell all of these assets and distribute the proceeds among his heirs in the manner that he specified. Washington named as executors of his will his wife Martha, her grandson, George Washington Parke Custis, and five of his nephews: William Augustine Washington, Bushrod Washington, George Steptoe Washington, Samuel Washington, and Lawrence Lewis. It was the prerogative of the Fairfax County Court to appoint the appraisers of the estate. It named as appraisers Washington's neighbor Thomson Mason, his secretary Tobias Lear, Thomas Peter, who was married to one of Martha Washington's granddaughters, and William H. Foote, the nephew of Lund Washington's widow, Elizabeth Foote Washington. A room-by-room appraisal of the articles at Mount Vernon was made, probably in 1800. It was not until 1810 that the appraisers filed their report in the office of the clerk of the Fairfax County Court (Appendix II, in Prussing, *Estate of George Washington*, 401–48). The executors held public sales of some of the livestock at Mount Vernon before Martha Washington's death in 1802, and they began selling the remainder of the listed property at sales shortly thereafter (Appendix III, ibid., 449–59). Final settlement of the estate was not achieved until 21 June 1847. For a comprehensive analysis of George Washington's will and a full account of the settlement of his estate, see Prussing, *Estate of George Washington*; see also Fitzpatrick, *Last Will and Testament of George Washington*.

[Mount Vernon, 9 July 1799]

In the name of God amen I George Washington of Mount Vernon—a citizen of the United States, and lately Pr⟨es⟩ident of the same, do make, ordai⟨n⟩ and declare this Instrument; w⟨hic⟩h is written with my own hand ⟨an⟩d every page thereof subscribed ⟨wit⟩h my name, to be my last Will & ⟨Tes⟩tament, revoking all others.

⟨I⟩mprimus.   All my ⟨deb⟩ts, of which there are but few, and none of magnitude, are to be punctu⟨al⟩ly and speedily paid—and the Legaci⟨es he⟩reinafter bequeathed, are to be disc⟨ha⟩rged as soon as circumstances will ⟨pe⟩rmit, and in the manner directe⟨d⟩.

⟨I⟩tem.   To my dearl⟨y be⟩loved wife Martha Washington ⟨I⟩ give and bequeath the use, profit ⟨an⟩d benefit of my whole Estate, real and p⟨er⟩sonal, for the term of her natural li⟨fe⟩—except such parts thereof as are sp⟨e⟩cifically disposed of hereafter: ⟨My i⟩mproved lot in the Town of Alex⟨andria, situated on⟩ Pitt & Cameron ⟨streets, I give to her and⟩ her heirs forev⟨er;⟩ [1] as I also do my⟩ household & Kitc⟨hen⟩ furniture of every sort & kind, with the liquors and groceries which may be on hand at the time of my decease; to be used & disposed of as she may think proper.

⟨Ite⟩m   Upon the deccasc ⟨of⟩ my wife, it is my Will & desire th⟨at⟩ all the Slaves which I hold in ⟨my⟩ *own right*, shall receive their free⟨dom⟩. To emancipate them during ⟨her⟩ life, would, tho' earnestly wish⟨ed by⟩ me, be attended with such insu⟨pera⟩ble difficulties on account of thei⟨r interm⟩ixture by Marriages with the ⟨dow⟩er Negroes, as to excite the most pa⟨in⟩ful sensations, if not disagreeabl⟨e c⟩onsequences from the latter, while ⟨both⟩ descriptions are in the occupancy ⟨of⟩ the same Proprietor; it not being ⟨in⟩ my power, under the tenure by which ⟨th⟩e Dower Negroes are held, to man⟨umi⟩t them. And whereas among ⟨thos⟩e who will recieve freedom ac⟨cor⟩ding to this devise, there may b⟨e so⟩me, who from old age or bodily infi⟨rm⟩ities, and others who on account of ⟨the⟩ir infancy, that will be unable to ⟨su⟩pport themselves; it is m⟨y Will and de⟩sire that all who ⟨come under the first⟩ & second descrip⟨tion shall be comfor⟩tably cloathed & ⟨fed by my heirs while⟩ they live; and that such of the latter description as have no parents living, or if living are unable, or unwilling to provide for them, shall be bound by the Court until they shall arrive at the ag⟨e⟩ of twenty five years; and in cases where no record can be produced, whereby their ages can be ascertained, the judgment of the Court, upon its own view of the subject, shall be adequate and final. The Negros thus bound, are (by their Masters or Mistresses) to be taught to read & write; and to be brought up to some useful occupation, agreeably to the Laws of the Commonwealth of Virginia, providing for the support of Orphan and other poor Children. and I do hereby expressly forbid the Sale, or transportation out of the said Commonwealth, of any Slave I may die possessed of, under any pretence whatsoever. And I do moreover most pointedly, and most solemnly enjoin it upon my Executors hereafter named, or the Survivors of them, to see that *th⟨is* cla⟩use respecting Slaves, and every part thereof be religiously fulfilled at the Epoch at which it is directed to take place; without evasion, neglect or delay, after the Crops which may then be on the ground are harvested, particularly as it respects the aged and infirm; seeing that a regular and permanent fund be established for their support so long as there are subjects requiring it; not trusting to the ⟨u⟩ncertain provision to be made by individuals.[2] And to my Mulatto man William (calling himself William Lee) I give immediate freedom; or if he should prefer it (on account of the accidents which ha⟨v⟩e befallen him, and which have rendered him incapable of walking or of any active employment) to remain in the situation he now is, it shall be optional in him to do so: In either case however, I allow him an annuity of thirty dollars during his natural life, whic⟨h⟩ shall be independent of the victuals and cloaths he has been accustomed to receive, if he chuses the last alternative; but in full, with his freedom, if he prefers the first; & this I give him as a test⟨im⟩ony of my sense of his attachment to me, and for his faithful services during the Revolutionary War.[3]

Item. To the Trustees (⟨Go⟩vernors, or by whatsoever other name they may be designated) of the Academy in the Town of Alexandria, I give and bequeath, in Trust, four thousand dollars, or in other words twenty of the shares which I hold in the Bank of Alexandria, towards the support of a Free school established at, and annexed to, the said Academy; for the purpose of Educating such Orphan children, or the children of such other poor and indigent persons as are unable to accomplish it with their own means; and who, in the judgment of the Trustees of the said Seminary, are best entitled to the benefit of this donation. The aforesaid twenty shares I give & bequeath in perpetuity; the dividends only of which are to be drawn for, and applied by the said Trustees for the time being, for the uses above mentioned; the stock to remain entire and untouched; unless indications of a failure of the said Bank should be so apparent, or a discontinuance thereof should render a removal of this fund necessary; in either of these cases, the amount of the Stock here devised, is to be vested in some other Bank or public Institution, whereby the interest may with regularity & certainty be drawn, and applied as above. And to prevent misconception, my meaning is, and is hereby declared to be, that these twenty shares are in lieu of, and not in addition to, the thousand pounds given by a missive letter some years ago; in consequence whereof an annuity of fifty pounds has since been paid towards the support of this Institution.[4]

Item. Whereas by a Law of the Commonwealth of Virginia, enacted in the year 1785, the Legislature thereof was pleased (as an evidence of Its approbation of the services I had rendered the Public during the Revolution—and partly, I believe, in consideration of my having suggested the vast advantages which the Community would derive from the ex⟨te⟩nsions of its Inland Navigation, under Legislative patronage) to present me with one hundred shares of one hundred dollars each, in the incorporated company established for the purpose of extending the navigation of James River from tide water to the Mountains: and also with fifty shares of one hundred pounds Sterling each, in the Corporation of another company, likewise established for the similar purpose of opening the Navigation of the River Potomac from tide water to Fort Cumberland, the acceptance of which, although the offer was highly honourable, and grateful to my feelings, was refused, as inconsistent with a principle which I had adopted, and had never departed from—namely—not to receive pecuniary compensation for any services I could render my country in its arduous struggle with great Britain, for its Rights; and because I had evaded similar propositions from other States in the Union; adding to this refusal, however, an intimation that, if it should be the pleasure of the Legislature to permit me to appropriate the said shares to *public uses*, I would receive them on those terms with due sensibility; and this it having consented to, in flattering terms, as will appear by a subsequent Law, and sundry resolutions, in the most ample and honourable manner, I proceed after this recital, for the more correct understanding of the case, to declare—[5]

That as it has always been a source of serious regret with me, to see the youth of these United States sent to foreign Countries for the purpose of Education, often before their minds were formed, or they had imbibed any adequate ideas of the happiness of their own; contracting, too frequently, not only habits of dissipation & extravagence, but principles unfriendly to Republican Governmt and to the true & genuine liberties of Mankind; which, thereafter are rarely overcome. For these reasons, it has been my ardent wish to see a plan devised on a liberal scale, which would have a tendency to sprd systemactic ideas through all parts of this rising Empire, thereby to do away local attachments and State prejudices, as far as the nature of things would, or indeed ought to admit, from our National Councils. Looking anxiously forward to the accomplishment of so desirable an object as this is (in my estimation) my mind has not been able to contemplate any plan more likely to effect the measure than the establishment of a UNIVERSITY in a central part of the United States, to which the youth of fortune and talents from all parts thereof might be sent for the completion of their Education in all the branches of polite literature; in arts and Sciences, in acquiring knowledge in the principles of Politics & good Government; and (as a matter of infinite Importance in

my judgment) by associating with each other, and forming friend-
ships in Juvenile years, be enabled to free themselves in a proper
degree from those local prejudices & habitual jealousies which
have just been mentioned; and which, when carried to excess, are
never failing sources of disquietude to the Public mind, and pregnant of mischievous consequences to this Country: Under these
impressions, so fully dilated,

Item   I give and bequeath in perpetuity the fifty shares which I
hold in the Potomac Company (under the aforesaid Acts of the
Legislature of Virginia) towards the endowment of a UNIVERSITY
to be established within the limits of the District of Columbia,
under the auspices of the General Government, if that government should incline to extend a fostering hand towards it; and
until such Seminary is established, and the funds arising on these
shares shall be required for its support, my further Will & desire is
that the profit accruing therefrom shall, whenever the dividends
are made, be laid out in purchasing Stock in the Bank of Columbia, or some other Bank, at the discretion of my Executors; or by
the Treasurer of the United States for the time being under the
direction of Congress; provided that Honourable body should
Patronize the measure, and the Dividends proceeding from the
purchase of such Stock is to be vested in more stock, and so on,
until a sum adequate to the accomplishment of the object is obtained, of which I have not the smallest doubt, before many years
passes away; even if no aid or encouraged is given by Legislative
authority, or from any other source.[6]

Item   The hundred shares which I held in the James River
Company, I have given, and now confirm in perpetuity to, and for
the use & benefit of Liberty-Hall Academy, in the County of Rockbridge, in the Commonwealth of Virga.[7]

Item   I release exonerate and discharge, the Estate of my deceased brother Samuel Washington, from the payment of the
money which is due to me for the Land I sold to Philip Pendleton
(lying in the County of Berkeley) who assigned the same to him
the said Samuel; who, by agreement was to pay me therefor. And
whereas by some contract (the purport of which was never communicated to me) between the said Samuel and his son Thornton
Washington, the latter became possessed of the aforesaid Land,
without any conveyance having passed from me, either to the said
Pendleton, the said Samuel, or the said Thornton, and without

any consideration having been made, by which neglect neither the legal nor equitable title has been alienated; it rests therefore with me to declare my intentions concerning the Premises—and these are, to give & bequeath the said land to whomsoever the said Thornton Washington (who is also dead) devised the same; or to his heirs forever if he died Intestate: Exonerating the estate of the said Thornton, equally with that of the said Samuel from payment of the purchase money; which, with Interest; agreeably to the original contract with the said Pendleton, would amount to more than a thousand pounds.[8] And whereas two other Sons of my said deceased brother Samuel—namely, George Steptoe Washington and Lawrence [Charles] Augustine Washington, were, by the decease of those to whose care they were committed, brought under my protection, and in conseq[uenc]e have occasioned advances on my part for their Education at College, and other Schools, for their board—cloathing—and other incidental expences, to the amount of near five thousand dollars over and above the Sums furnished by their Estate wch Sum may be inconvenient for them, or their fathers Estate to refund. I do for these reasons acquit them, and the said estate, from the payment thereof. My intention being, that all accounts between them and me, and their fathers estate and me shall stand balanced.[9]

Item   The balance due to me from the Estate of Bartholomew Dandridge deceased (my wife's brother) and which amounted on the first day of October 1795 to four hundred and twenty five pounds (as will appear by an account rendered by his deceased son John Dandridge, who was the acting Exr of his fathers Will) I release & acquit from the payment thereof. And the Negros, then thirty three in number) formerly belonging to the said estate, who were taken in execution—sold—and purchased in on my account in the year [   ] and ever since have remained in the possession, and to the use of Mary, Widow of the said Bartholomew Dandridge, with their increase, it is my Will & desire shall continue, & be in her possession, without paying hire, or making compensation for the same for the time past or to come, during her natural life; at the expiration of which, I direct that all of them who are forty years old & upwards, shall receive their freedom; all under that age and above sixteen, shall serve seven years and no longer; and all under sixteen years, shall serve until they are twenty five years of age, and then be free. And to avoid disputes respecting the ages of any of these Negros, they are to be taken to the Court of the County in which they reside, and the judgment thereof, in this relation shall be final; and a record thereof made; which may be adduced as evidence at any time thereafter, if disputes should arise concerning the same. And I further direct, that the heirs of the said Bartholomew Dandridge shall, equally, share the benefits arising from the services of the said negros according to the tenor of this devise, upon the decease of their Mother.[10]

Item   If Charles Carter who intermarried with my niece Betty Lewis is not sufficiently secured in the title to the lots he had of me in the Town of Fredericksburgh, it is my will & desire that my Executors shall make such conveyances of them as the Law requires, to render it perfect.[11]

Item   To my Nephew William Augustine Washington and his heirs (if he should conceive them to be objects worth prosecuting) and to his heirs, a lot in the Town of Manchester (opposite to Richmond) No. 265—drawn on my sole account, and also the tenth of one or two, hundred acre lots, and two or three half acre lots in the City, and vicinity of Richmond, drawn in partnership with nine others, all in the lottery of the deceased William Byrd are given—as is also a lot which I purchased of John Hood, conveyed by William Willie and Samuel Gordon Trustees of the said John Hood, numbered 139 in the Town of Edinburgh, in the County of Prince George, State of Virginia.[12]

Item   To my Nephew Bushrod Washington, I give and bequeath all the Papers in my possession, which relate to my Civel and Military Administration of the affairs of this Country; I leave to him also, such of my private Papers as are worth preserving;[13] and at the decease of wife, and before—if she is not inclined to retain them, I give and bequeath my library of Books and Pamphlets of every kind.[14]

Item   Having sold Lands which I possessed in the State of Pennsylvania, and part of a tract held in equal right with George Clinton, late Governor of New York, in the State of New York; my share of land, & interest, in the Great Dismal Swamp, and a tract of land which I owned in the County of Gloucester; withholding the legal titles thereto, until the consideration money should be paid. And having moreover leased, & conditionally sold (as will appear by the tenor of the said leases) all my lands upon the Great Kanhawa, and a tract upon Difficult Run, in the county of Loudoun, it is my Will and direction, that whensoever the Contracts are fully, & respectively complied with, according to the spirit; true intent & meaning thereof, on the part of the purchasers, their heirs or Assigns, that then, and in that case, Conveyances are to be made, agreeably to the terms of the said Contracts; and the money arising therefrom, when paid, to be vested in Bank stock; the dividends whereof, as of that also wch is already vested therein, is to inure to my said Wife during her life—but the Stock itself is to remain, & be subject to the general distribution hereafter directed.[15]

Item   To the Earl of Buchan I recommit "the box made of the Oak that sheltered the Great Sir William Wallace after the battle of Falkirk" presented to me by his Lordship, in terms too flattering for me to repeat, with a request "to pass it, on the event of my decease, to the man in my country, who should appear to merit it best, upon the same conditions that have induced him to send it to me." Whether easy, or not, to select *the man* who might comport with his Lordships opinion in this respect, is not for me to say; but conceiving that no disposition of this valuable curiosity can be more eligable than the re-commitment of it to his own Cabinet, agreeably to the original design of the Goldsmiths Company of Edenburgh, who presented it to him, and at his request, consented that is should be transferred to me; I do give & bequeath the same to his Lordship, and in case of his decease, to his heir with my grateful thanks for the distinguished honour of present-ing it to me; and more especially for the favourable sentiments with which he accompanied it.[16]

Item   To my brother Charles Washington I give & bequeath the gold headed Cane left me by Doctr Franklin in his Will. I add nothing to it, because of the ample provision I have made for his Issue.[17] To the acquaintances and friends of my Juvenile years, Lawrence Washington & Robert Washington of Chotanck, I give my other two gold headed Canes, having my Arms engraved on them; and to each (as they will be useful where they live) I leave one of the Spy-glasses which constituted part of my equipage dur-ing the late War.[18] To my compatriot in arms, and old & intimate friend Doctr Craik, I give my Bureau (or as the Cabinet makers call it, Tambour Secretary) and the circular chair—an appendage of my Study.[19] To Doctor David Stuart I give my large shaving & dressing Table, and my Telescope.[20] To the Reverend, now Bryan,

Lord Fairfax, I give a Bible in three large folio volumes, with notes, presented to me by the Right reverend Thomas Wilson, Bishop of Sodor & Man.[21] To General de la Fayette I give a pair of finely wrought steel Pistols, taken from the enemy in the Revolutionary War.[22] To my Sisters in law Hannah Washington & Mildred Washington; to my friends Eleanor Stuart, Hannah Washington of Fairfield, and Elizabeth Washington of Hayfield, I give, each, a mourning Ring of the value of one hundred dollars. These bequests are not made for the intrinsic value of them, but as mementos of my esteem & regard.[23] To Tobias Lear, I give the use of the Farm which he now holds, in virtue of a Lease from me to him and his deceased wife (for and during their natural lives) free from Rent, during his life; at the expiration of which, it is to be disposed as is hereinafter directed.[24] To Sally B. Haynie (a distant relation of mine) I give and bequeath three hundred dollars.[25] To Sarah Green daughter of the deceased Thomas Bishop,[26] & to Ann Walker daughter of Jno. Alton, also deceased, I give, each—one hundred dollars, in consideration of the attachment of their fathers to me; each of whom having lived nearly forty years in my family.[27] To each of my Nephews, William Augustine Washington, George Lewis, George Steptoe Washington, Bushrod Washington and Samuel Washington, I give one of the Swords or Cutteaux of which I may die possessed; and they are to chuse in the order they are named. These Swords are accompanied with an injunction not to unsheath them for the purpose of shedding blood, except it be for self defence, or in defence of their Country and its rights; and in the latter case, to keep them unsheathed, and prefer falling with them in their hands, to the relinquishment thereof.[28]

And now

Having gone through these specific devises, with explanations for the more correct understanding of the meaning and design of them; I proceed to the distribution of the more important parts of my Estate, in manner following–

⟨Fi⟩rst   To my Nephew Bushrod Washington and his heirs (partly in consideration of an intimation to his deceased father while we were Bachelors, & he had kindly undertaken to superintend my Estate during my Military Services in the former War between Great Britain & France, that if I should fall therein, Mount Vernon (then less extensive in domain than at present) should become his property) I give and bequeath all that part thereof which is comprehended within the following limits— viz.—Beginning at the ford of Dogue run, near my Mill, and extending along the road, and bounded thereby as it now goes, & ever has gone since my recollection of it, to the ford of little hunting Creek at the Gum spring until it comes to a knowl, opposite to an old road which formerly passed through the lower field of Muddy hole Farm; at which, on the north side of the said road are three red, or spanish Oaks marked as a corner, and a stone placed. thence by a line of trees to be marked, rectangular to the back line, or outer boundary of the tract between Thomson Mason & myself. thence with that line Easterly (now double ditching with a Post & Rail fence thereon) to the run of little hunting Creek. thence with that run which is the boundary between the Lands of the late Humphrey Peake and me, to the tide water of the said Creek; thence by that water to Potomac River. thence with the River to the mouth of Dogue Creek. and thence with the said Dogue Creek to the place of beginning at the aforesaid ford; containing upwards of four thousand Acres, be the same more or less—together with the Mansion house and all other buildings and improvemts thereon.[29]

Second   In consideration of the consanguinity between them and my wife, being as nearly related to her as to myself, as on account of the affection I had for, and the obligation I was under to, their father when living, who from his youth had attached himself to my person, and followed my fortunes through the viscissitudes of the late Revolution—afterwards devoting his time to the Superintendence of my private concerns for many years, whilst my public employments rendered it impracticable for me to do it myself, thereby affording me essential Services, and always performing them in a manner the most felial and respectful—for these reasons I say, I give and bequeath to George Fayette Washington, and Lawrence [Charles] Augustine Washington and their heirs, my Estate East of little hunting Creek, lying on the River Potomac; including the Farm of 360 Acres, Leased to Tobias Lear as noticed before, and containing in the whole, by Deeds, Two thousand and Seventy seven acres—be it more or less. Which said Estate it is my Will & desire should be equitably, & advantegeously divided between them, according to quantity, quality & other circumstances when the youngest shall have arrived at the age of twenty one years, by three judicious and disinterested men; one to be chosen by each of the brothers, and the third by these two. In the meantime, if the termination of my wife's interest therein should have ceased, the profits arising therefrom are to be applied for th[e]ir joint uses and benefit.[30]

Third   And whereas it has always been my intention, since my expectation of having Issue has ceased, to consider the Grand children of my wife in the same light as I do my own relations, and to act a friendly part by them; more especially by the two whom we have reared from their earliest infancy—namely—Eleanor Parke Custis, & George Washington Parke Custis. And whereas the former of these hath lately intermarried with Lawrence Lewis, a son of my deceased Sister Betty Lewis, by which union the inducement to provide for them both has been increased; Wherefore, I give & bequeath to the said Lawrence Lewis & Eleanor Parke Lewis, his wife, and their heirs, the residue of my Mount Vernon Estate, not already devised to my Nephew Bushrod Washington; comprehended within the following description—viz.—All the land North of the Road leading from the ford of Dogue run to the Gum spring as described in the devise of the other part of the tract, to Bushrod Washington, until it comes to the Stone & three red or Spanish Oaks on the knowl. thence with the rectangular line to the back line (between Mr Mason & me)—thence with that line westerly, along the new double ditch to Dogue run, by the tumbling Dam of my Mill; thence with the said run to the ford aforementioned; to which I add all the Land I possess West of the said Dogue run, & Dogue Crk—bounded Easterly & Southerly thereby; together with the Mill, Distillery, and all other houses & improvements on the premises, making together about two thousand Acres—be it more or less.[31]

Fourth   Actuated by the principal already mentioned, I give and bequeath to George Washington Parke Custis, the Grandson of my wife, and my Ward, and to his heirs, the tract I hold on four mile run in the vicinity of Alexandria, containing one thousd two hundred acres, more or less, & my entire Square, number twenty one, in the City of Washington.[32]

Fifth   All the rest and residue of my Estate, real & personal— not disposed of in manner aforesaid—In whatsoever consisting— wheresoever lying—and whensoever found—a schedule of which, as far as is recollected, with a reasonable estimate of its value, is hereunto annexed—I desire may be sold by my Executors at such times—in such manner—and on such credits (if an equal, valid, and satisfactory distribution of the specific property cannot be made without) as, in their judgment shall be most conducive to the interest of the parties concerned; and the monies arising therefrom to be divided into twenty three equal parts, and applied as follow[33]—viz.

To William Augustine Washington, Elizabeth Spotswood, Jane Thornton, and the heirs of Ann Ashton; son, and daughters of my deceased brother Augustine Washington, I give and bequeath four parts; that is—one part to each of them.[34]

To Fielding Lewis, George Lewis, Robert Lewis, Howell Lewis & Betty Carter, sons and daughter of my deceased Sister Betty Lewis, I give & bequeath five other parts—one to each of them.[35]

To George Steptoe Washington, Lawrence Augustine Washington, Harriot Parks, and the heirs of Thornton Washington, sons & daughter of my deceased brother Samuel Washington, I give and bequeath other four parts, one part to each of them.[36]

To Corbin Washington, and the heirs of Jane Washington, Son & daughter of my deceased brother John Augustine Washington, I give & bequeath two parts; one part to each of them.[37]

To Samuel Washington, Francis Ball & Mildred Hammond, son & daughters of my Brother Charles Washington, I give & bequeath three parts; one part to each of them. And to George Fayette Washington[,] Charles Augustine Washington & Maria Washington, sons and daughter of my deceased Nephew Geo: Augustine Washington, I give one other part; that is—to each a third of that part.[38]

To Elizabeth Parke Law, Martha Parke Peter, and Eleanor Parke Lewis, I give and bequeath three other parts, that is a part to each of them.[39]

And to my Nephews Bushrod Washington & Lawrence Lewis, and to my ward, the grandson of My wife, I give and bequeath one other part; that is, a third thereof to each of them. And if it should so happen, that any of the persons whose names are here ennumerated (unknown to me) should now be deceased—or should die before me, that in either of these cases, the heirs of such deceased person shall, notwithstanding, derive all the benefits of the bequest; in the same manner as if he, or she, was actually living at the time.

And by way of advice, I recommend it to my Executors not to be precipitate in disposing of the landed property (herein directed to be sold) if from temporary causes the Sale thereof should be dull; experience having fully evinced, that the price of land (especially above the Falls of the Rivers, & on the Western Waters) have been progressively rising, and cannot be long checked in its increasing value. And I particularly recommend it to such of the Legatees (under this clause of my Will) as can make it convenient, to take each a share of my Stock in the Potomac Company in preference to the amount of what it might sell for; being thoroughly convinced myself, that no uses to which the money can be applied will be so productive as the Tolls arising from this navigation when in full operation (and this from the nature of things it must be 'ere long) and more especially if that of the Shanondoah is added thereto.

The family Vault at Mount Vernon requiring repairs, and being improperly situated besides, I desire that a new one of Brick, and upon a larger Scale, may be built at the foot of what is commonly called the Vineyard Inclosure, on the ground which is marked out. In which my remains, with those of my deceased relatives (now in the old Vault) and such others of my family as may chuse to be entombed there, may be deposited. And it is my express desire that my Corpse may be Interred in a private manner, without parade, or funeral Oration.[40]

Lastly   I constitute and appoint my dearly beloved wife Martha Washington, My Nephews William Augustine Washington, Bushrod Washington, George Steptoe Washington, Samuel Washington, & Lawrence Lewis, & my ward George Washington Parke Custis (when he shall have arrived at the age of twenty years) Executrix & Executors of this Will & testament,[41] In the construction of which it will readily be perceived that no professional character has been consulted, or has had any Agency in the draught—and that, although it has occupied many of my leisure hours to digest, & to through it into its present form, it may, notwithstanding, appear crude and incorrect. But having endeavoured to be plain, and explicit in all Devises—even at the expence of prolixity, perhaps of tautology, I hope, and trust, that no disputes will arise concerning them; but if, contrary to expectation, the case should be otherwise from the want of legal expression, or the usual technical terms, or because too much or too little has been said on any of the Devises to be consonant with law, My Will and direction expressly is, that all disputes (if unhappily any should arise) shall be decided by three impartial and intelligent men, known for their probity and good understanding; two to be chosen by the disputants—each having the choice of one—and the third by those two. Which three men thus chosen, shall, unfettered by Law, or legal constructions, declare their sense of the Testators intention; and such decision is, to all intents and purposes to be as binding on the Parties as if it had been given in the Supreme Court of the United States.

In witness of all, and of each of the things herein contained, I have set my hand and Seal, this ninth day of July, in the year One thousand seven hundred and ninety [nine] and of the Independence of the United States the twenty fourth.

ADS, ViFaCt; copy, Fairfax County Will Book H-1, 1–23, ViFaCt. Several pages of Washington's original will in the Fairfax County Courthouse have been damaged; our reading of mutilated words has been taken from *The Will of General George Washington: To Which Is Annexed, A Schedule of His Property, Directed to Be Sold* (Alexandria, Va., 1800).

1. Washington bought the lot in Alexandria and built the house on it before the Revolution. It was the only piece of property he left outright to his wife Martha. The Virginia Assembly in 1762 voted to extend the limits of the town of Alexandria, and on 9 May 1763 fifty-eight one-half-acre lots in the expanded town were offered for sale at public auction. Washington purchased two of the lots: in 1764 he paid John Alexander, Jr., £38 for lot no. 112, at Prince and Pitt streets, and £10.10 for lot no. 118, at Pitt and Cameron streets. In the spring of 1769 he engaged Richard Lake (Leak, Leake) and Edward Rigdon to build a house on the second of these lots. The first payment to men working on the house was made in June 1769 and the last in August 1771. Washington's accounts show that over the two years he paid £59.16.1½ to Lake, £30.19.2 to the joiner Rigdon, £5.10 to cabinetmaker James Connell, £16.11.8 to plasterer Matthew Lawson, and £9.15.4 to housepainter William Bushby, which would indicate that he was out of pocket only £131.7.7½ for house and lot. A quarter of a century later he wrote Lear that he had been told his property at the corner of Pitt and Cameron streets would bring as much as £2,000 if offered for sale.

Washington's first tenant in Alexandria, Dr. William Brown, came to Virginia from the University of Edinburgh in 1770 and lived and practiced medicine in the house for a decade or so. When Brown moved at the end of 1785 or early 1786 to another house in town, he was paying an annual rent of £60, the same amount paid by his successor, William Halley, who rented the house in 1786. In November 1788, upon learning that Bushrod Washington wished to move to Alexandria and practice law there, Washington offered the house to his nephew "Rent free till you can find a more convenient one." Shortly thereafter Washington left for New York to assume the presidency, and for a time he lost sight of what was being done about the house. In December 1792 he instructed his farm manager, Anthony Whitting, to find out whether it was occupied and, if not, to secure a renter. Six months later Washington confessed to a man named Cleon

Moore that he knew nothing of the status of his property and asked his friend John Fitzgerald of Alexandria to arrange for its rental to Moore. Upon investigation, Fitzgerald found living in the house a woman with young children, whose husband was away on a trip to Boston. It turned out that the family, "orderly though poor," had rented the house from Washington's farm manager before his death in June 1793. In October 1793 Washington talked with the young man and agreed to allow him to remain in the house with his family in return for keeping it in good repair.

Washington decided in the fall of 1793 to fix up his Alexandria house for Frances Bassett (Fanny) Washington and her three little children. Fanny Washington, Martha Washington's niece, and her husband, Washington's beloved nephew George Augustine Washington, had lived at Mount Vernon since shortly before their marriage in 1785. After George Augustine's death in January 1793, Fanny declined the pressing invitation of the Washingtons that she make Mount Vernon her permanent home with her children, declaring that she would follow the advice given by her husband before his death that she find a house in Alexandria so as to provide for the education of her children, Anna Maria and the two little boys. After receiving and accepting Washington's offer of the Alexandria house, in November 1793 Fanny Washington asked that a story be added to it, which was not done, but Washington did agree to pave the cellar of the house and to have "one end of the stable laid with plank . . . to accomodate the servants" whom she "was obliged to carry" with her. Washington also took it upon himself to acquire wallpaper in Philadelphia for the house, while Martha Washington arranged to have furniture made in Philadelphia and shipped to Alexandria for her niece. At the end of the summer of 1794 the young widow finally moved into the sand-colored house with its red roof at the corner of Pitt and Cameron streets, but she lived in it for only a little over a year. Twelve months later she married Tobias Lear, Washington's former and future secretary, and in the fall of 1795 she moved with her children across the river to Georgetown where her new husband was then in business. In December 1795 Lear reported to Washington that he had succeeded in renting the house in Alexandria "for Sixty Pounds Curr. Per Annum to Nath[anie]l Washington who will go into it immediately." The new tenant kept the house for no more than a year; at the end of 1797 Washington rented it at the same rate to his former commission agent, Philip Marsteller, a merchant in the town. The first item in Martha Washington's will reads: "I give and devise to my Nephew Bartholomew Dandridge and his Heirs, my lot in the town of Alexandria situate on Pitt and Cameron Streets devised to me by my late Husband George Washington deceased" (Fields, *Papers of Martha Washington*, 406).

See GW to Carlyle & Adams, 15 Feb. 1767, n.8, Cash Accounts, January 1770, n.6, April 1770, n.7, August 1770, n.11, January 1771, n.2, August 1771, nn.6 and 7 (*Papers, Colonial Series*, 8:290–91, 322–23, 362–64, 424–25, 511–12), Ledger A, 278, 321, 323, Agreement with William Halley, 20 Feb. 1786, and note (*Papers, Confederation Series*, 3:562–63), Ledger B, 119, 185, *Diaries*, 2:182–83, Bushrod Washington to GW, 20 Nov. 1788, John Fitzgerald to GW, 11 Oct. 1793, GW to Bushrod Washington, 25 Nov. 1788 (*Papers, Presidential Series*, 1:119–20, 126–27), GW to Anthony Whitting, 16 Dec. 1792, GW to Cleon Moore, 19 July

1793, GW to John Fitzgerald, 11 Aug. 1793, Frances Bassett Washington to Martha Washington, June 1794, and Martha Washington to Frances Bassett Washington, 2 June 1793, 10 Feb., 2 Mar., 13 April, 25 May, 30 June 1794 (Fields, *Papers of Martha Washington*, 249–50, 256–57, 259–60, 264–65, 265–66, 268, 270), Frances Bassett Washington to GW, 5, 28 Mar., 22 Nov. 1793, 17 Sept. 1794, GW to Frances Bassett Washington, 10 June, 18 Aug. 1793, and GW to William Pearce, 22 Dec. 1793, 12 Jan., 9, 16 Feb., 27 April, 4, 11, 18, 25 May, 8 June, 13 July, 3 Aug., 1794, Tobias Lear to GW, 17 Nov., 14 Dec. 1795, GW to Lear, 2, 30 Nov. 1795, and GW to John Fitzgerald, William Herbert, and George Gilpin, 22 Nov. 1797, n.2 (*Papers, Retirement Series*, 1:481).

The second lot that GW bought in Alexandria in 1764, the one on the corner of Prince and Pitt streets, remained unimproved until shortly before his death. See the references to it in Schedule of Property, printed immediately below, and in note 19 of that document.

2. At about the same time that he was drawing up his will, Washington made a list of the adult and child slaves on each of the Mount Vernon farms, usually giving ages, occupations, and other pertinent information. His list of 317 slaves, printed below, includes the names of 124 who belonged to him outright and were to be freed when Martha Washington died, 153 who were Martha Washington's dower slaves and at her death would go to the Custis heir-at-law, her grandson George Washington Parke Custis, and 40 others leased by GW from his neighbor Penelope Manley French. Of the 277 slaves belonging to Washington in his own right or by marriage, 179 were twelve years old or older, eighteen of whom were "Passed labor." The remaining ninety-eight were children under the age of twelve. Of those twelve years old and over, ninety-five were females, and eighty-four were males. Shortly after Washington's death, Bushrod Washington recommended to Martha Washington that she get "clear of her negroes" at Mount Vernon. According to Eugene Prussing, she "was made unhappy by the talk in the [slave] quarters of the good time coming to the ones to be freed as soon as she died." He reported that "many did not wait for the event" but took off at once. In any case, all the slaves that Washington owned outright were freed after Martha's death, and the accounts of the executors of Washington's will show an expenditure by 1833 of more than $10,000 to the pensioned former slaves who remained at Mount Vernon or lived nearby (Bushrod Washington to Martha Washington, 27 Dec. 1799, in Fields, *Papers of Martha Washington*, 328–31; Prussing, *Estate of George Washington*, 158–60).

3. At a sale in October 1767 Washington bought "Mulatto Will" for £61.15 from Mary Smith Ball Lee, widow of John Lee of Westmoreland County, who had recently died. The young man called himself William Lee; Washington at first called him Billy, but after the Revolution he consistently referred to him in his papers as Will or William. As early as May 1770 Will Lee began going to Williamsburg as Washington's body servant for the meeting of the Virginia House of Burgesses. For the next two decades Will was in constant attendance upon Washington as his personal servant, acting by turns as valet, waiter, butler, or huntsman. He accompanied Washington to the meeting of the First Continental Congress in Philadelphia in 1774, remained by his side "through the War" and returned with him to Mount Vernon at the end of 1783, went back with him to

Philadelphia in 1787 at the calling of the Constitutional Convention, and, even though by then badly crippled, traveled to New York when Washington became president in 1789.

During the war Will Lee took as his wife "one of his own colour a free woman" from Philadelphia, named Margaret Thomas, who was, Washington wrote Clement Biddle, "also of my family." Washington's efforts after the war to bring Will Lee's wife to Mount Vernon apparently failed. According to George Washington Parke Custis, Will was "a stout active man, and a famous horseman," until two accidents in the late 1780s deprived him of the use of his legs. While acting as a chain carrier when Washington surveyed his Four Mile Run tract near Alexandria in April 1785, Will fell and "broke the pan of his knee"; three years later, in March 1788, he fell at the post office in Alexandria and "broke the Pan of his other Knee" (*Diaries*, 4:125, 5:281). In June 1788 he was still "unable to walk" (ibid., 5:349), but when Washington left Mount Vernon for New York on 16 April 1789 to assume the presidency, Will followed him. The old servant got as far as Philadelphia before problems with his knees forced him to remain there to seek treatment from doctors. On 3 May Tobias Lear, writing from New York, asked Clement Biddle in Philadelphia to persuade Will Lee to return to Mount Vernon, "for he cannot possibly be of any service here." Will was not to be persuaded: on 22 June Lear wrote Biddle that "Billy arrived here safe & well." What services if any Washington's faithful servant was able to perform in New York is unclear, but Washington informed his secretary Tobias Lear in November 1793 that Lee's replacement was "too little acquainted with the arrangement of a Table, & too stupid for a Butler." Back at Mount Vernon, Will Lee took up residence in his house near the mansion and acted as a cobbler, becoming, according to later testimony of one of Bushrod Washington's Mount Vernon slaves, a troublesome old man before his death, probably about 1810. See Cash Accounts, May 1768, n.2 (*Papers, Colonial Series*, 8:82–83), GW to Clement Biddle, 28 July 1784 (*Papers, Confederation Series*, 2:14), Custis, *Recollections*, 157, Tobias Lear to Clement Biddle, 3 May, 22 June 1789 (ViMtV), Biddle to GW, 27 April 1789, n.1 (*Papers, Presidential Series*, 2:133–34), *Diaries*, 2:238, 278, 286–88, 3:276, 5:73, GW to Lear, 8 Nov. 1793, and Prussing, *Estate of George Washington*, 27, 159.

4. When an association was formed in Alexandria in 1785 to establish an academy in the town, Washington agreed to become one of its managers, or sponsors. At the end of that year he informed the academy's trustees that he had long intended to set aside at his death £1,000, the interest of which was to be used for establishing "a school in the Town of Alexandria for the purpose of educating orphan children" and the children of "indigent parents." He explained that he could not afford to give the £1,000 immediately; instead, he would undertake to pay the trustees each year the interest on that amount and would vest the £1,000 in them, if they could assure him that the academy would provide "that kind of education which would be most extensively useful to people of the lower class of citizens, viz.—reading, writing & arithmetic, so as to fit them for the mechanical purposes." The trustees promptly promised to do "every thing in their power to comply fully" with Washington's "benevolent intentions." In January of every year thereafter Washington made the payments of £50, the last recorded payment being made on 6 Jan. 1798. He also agreed, in June 1786, that the money

he was contributing to the academy could be used for the support of girls as well as of boys, "in a ratio not to exceed one girl for four boys." In November 1785 Washington placed his nephews George Steptoe Washington and Lawrence Augustine Washington in Alexandria Academy, where they remained until after Washington became president. See GW to Trustees of the Washington Academy, 17 Dec. 1785, and note 1 of that document (*Papers, Confederation Series*, 3:463–64), Ledger C, 42, GW to William Brown, 30 June 1786 (*Papers, Confederation Series*, 4:135), and *Diaries*, 4:241.

5. Gov. Benjamin Harrison wrote Washington from Richmond on 6 Jan. 1785 to inform him that "the assembly yesterday without a discenting voice complimented you with fifty shares in the potowmack company and one hundred in the James River company." Washington agonized long and hard about whether he should accept the shares lest this be taken as pay for his public service, which he had committed himself to forego. In the end he induced the legislature to provide that the future profit from stock should go not to him personally but instead "stand appropriated to such objects of a public nature, in such manner, and under such distributions, as the said George Washington, esq. by deed during his life, or by his last will and testament, shall direct and appoint" (12 Hening 42–44). For GW's acceptance of the stock, see the references in Benjamin Harrison to GW, 6 Jan. 1785, n.1 (*Papers, Confederation Series*, 2:257); for his bequest of the fifty shares in the Potomac River Company to "a UNIVERSITY to be established within the limits of the District of Columbia," see the two ensuing paragraphs of the will and note 6; for his gift in 1797 of the one hundred shares of stock in the James River Company to Liberty Hall Academy, see note 7 below.

6. Four years before he wrote this will, in a letter to the District of Columbia commissioners dated 28 Jan. 1795, Washington presented in very much the same terms as he does here the argument for establishing a national university in the new Federal City on the Potomac. He told the commissioners that he was prepared to "grant, in perpetuity, fifty shares in the navigation of Potomac river towards the endowment" of such a university. In 1796 he wrote the commissioners three more times about this, and in his final address to Congress on 7 Dec. 1796, he stated that he had "heretofore proposed to the consideration of Congress, the expediency of establishing a National University; and also a Military Academy. The desirableness of both these Institutions, has so constantly increased with every new view I have taken of the subject, that I cannot omit the opportunity of once for all, recalling your attention to them" (DNA:46, Fourth Congress, 1795–97, Records of Legislative Proceedings, President's Messages). For other references by GW to the creation of a national university, see GW to Thomas Jefferson, 15 Nov. 1794, 15 Mar. 1795, to Alexander Hamilton, 1 Sept. 1796, and to St. George Tucker, 30 May 1797 (*Papers, Retirement Series*, 1:163); for GW's holdings in the Potomac River Company, see his notation to the entry regarding the Potomac River Company in the Schedule of Property attached to the will, printed below, and also note 23 to that document.

7. Washington informed Gov. Robert Brooke of Virginia in September 1796 that he wished to give to Liberty Hall Academy in Rockbridge County the one hundred shares in the James River Company bestowed upon him in 1785 by the Virginia legislature. Liberty Hall Academy, founded by the Rev. William Graham

and incorporated in 1782, had been renamed Washington Academy. It was soon to become Washington College, and still later Washington and Lee University. It was not until April 1798 that the trustees of the institution acknowledged that they had received in September 1797 official notice of his gift and expressed their appreciation for it. See GW to Robert Brooke, 15 Sept. 1796, Edward Graham to GW, 9 Mar. 1798, Washington Academy Trustees to GW, 12 April 1798, and notes 1 and 2 to that document (*Papers, Retirement Series*, 2:131–32, 236–37). For GW's acquisition of the James River Company stock, see Benjamin Harrison to GW, 6 Jan. 1785, n.1 (*Papers, Confederation Series*, 2:257).

8. In 1771 Washington sold a tract of 180 acres in Frederick County to Philip Pendleton (1752–1802) for £400. The next year Washington's friend Edmund Pendleton indicated that he would pay Washington the £400 on behalf of his nephew. Before any payment was made, however, Philip Pendleton, early in 1773, transferred the land, and the debt, to Washington's brother Samuel. Washington wrote his brother from New York in 1776 that he would arrange to have the title to the land transferred to him, but he failed to do so. Before his death in 1781, Samuel Washington gave the land to his son Thornton. When Washington in 1784, shortly after his return to Mount Vernon, reminded the executors of his brother's estate that he had not received a penny for the 400 acres and still retained the deed to the tract, his nephew Thornton Washington wrote him that he had been living on the land for some time and had made many improvements. He asked his uncle for assurance that he would not be evicted. Thornton Washington was allowed to remain on the land. Two years later he wrote Washington that the Hite family were preparing to challenge Washington's title to it. His fears proved groundless. No payments on the land were made either before or after Thornton's death in 1787; five percent annual rent for twenty-nine years would have raised the amount of the debt by 1799 to more than £900. See Bond to Philip Pendleton, 7 Dec. 1771 (*Papers, Colonial Series*, 8:573), Ledger B, 22, 36, Edmund Pendleton to GW, 19 Dec. 1772, GW to Samuel Washington, 4 Feb. 1773, 5 Oct. 1776, *Diaries*, 3:37, 74, GW to James Nourse, 22 Jan. 1784, and, particularly, note 3 of that document, and Thornton Washington to GW, 1 Aug. 1784, 6 June 1786 (*Papers, Confederation Series*, 1:69–70, 2:20–21, 4:100–2).

9. When Washington returned to Mount Vernon at the end of the war, 11-year-old George Steptoe Washington and 8-year-old Lawrence Augustine Washington, sons of Washington's dead brother Samuel and his fourth wife, Anne Steptoe Washington, were living in Alexandria under the care of David Griffith, the minister at Christ Church. Washington immediately notified his nephews' guardian, James Nourse, of his willingness to keep an eye on them, and it was at Washington's suggestion that later in the year Nourse sent the boys across the river to Georgetown to attend the school of the Rev. Stephen Bloomer Balch. Upon Nourse's death in October 1784, Washington assumed responsibility for supervising the education of his two nephews and for the next eight years provided most of the funds for their support. In November 1785 he moved them back to Alexandria and put them under the tutelage of William McWhir at the new Alexandria Academy. In January 1787 the two boys were moved into the house of Samuel Hanson, where their behavior brought complaints from

Hanson requiring GW's intervention on a number of occasions. When Washington went to New York in the spring of 1789, his friend Dr. James Craik took the boys into his house. At the end of the year, with Washington's approval, Craik removed them from the Academy and placed them in the school of Gilbert Harrow in Alexandria in order to have them concentrate on the study of mathematics. On Tobias Lear's advice, Washington in the fall of 1790 had his nephews brought to Philadelphia and enrolled in the college there, where they remained until their graduation in 1792. In addition to GW's correspondence from 1787 to 1790 with Samuel Hanson and George Steptoe Washington, for GW's patronage of these two nephews see his letters to James Nourse, 22 Jan. 1784, to David Griffith, 29 Aug. 1784, to Stephen Bloomer Balch, 30 Oct. 1784, 26 June, 22 Nov. 1785, to Charles Washington, 12 April 1785, to Bushrod Washington, 17 Nov. 1788, to James Craik, 8 Sept. 1789, and to Tobias Lear 10 Oct. 1790 (*Papers, Confederation Series*, 1:69–70, 2:61–2, 113, 494–95, 3:84, 378; *Papers, Presidential Series*, 1:116–17, 4:1–3, 6:547–49). See also the letters to GW from Charles Washington, 16 Nov. 1784, 19 Feb., 23 Nov., 30 Dec. 1785, from Benjamin Stoddert, 21 June 1785, from William McWhir, 8 Mar. 1788, from James Craik, 24 Aug. 1789, 3 Feb. 1790, and from Tobias Lear, 10, 28 Oct. 1790 (*Papers, Confederation Series*, 2:137–39, 370–71, 3:68, 382, 483–84, 6:148; *Papers, Presidential Series*, 3:529–31, 5:95–98, 6:549–52, 593–95). For GW's account with George Steptoe and Lawrence Augustine Washington, see Ledger B, 206, 229, 250, 301, 328. The itemized account from 1784 to 1791 shows a running total of £406.7.6 spent by Washington for the two nephews.

10. As Daniel Parke Custis's widow, and before she married George Washington in 1759, Martha Washington lent her brother Bartholomew Dandridge £600 sterling. At the settlement of Daniel Parke Custis's estate in 1759–1761, Dandridge's bond for this debt was assigned to Martha Washington's daughter, Martha Parke (Patsy) Custis. After Patsy's death in 1773 the bond passed to Washington as Martha's husband; with unpaid interest the debt at that time came to £1,219.9.4 (Guardian Accounts, 3 Nov. 1773, printed in *Papers, Colonial Series*, 9:366–74). Bartholomew Dandridge died in 1785, and three years later his son John Dandridge as executor of his father's will persuaded Washington to seek title to the Dandridge slaves in payment of the estate's debt to him. In this way he hoped to prevent other creditors from forcing their sale. Washington agreed to seek a judgment against the estate, and he succeeded in securing title to the slaves. But he arranged for the slaves to remain in the actual possession of Bartholomew Dandridge's widow, Mary Burbidge Dandridge, in New Kent County. Washington's account with the estate of Bartholomew Dandridge has not been found, but it would appear that the value placed upon the slaves was not sufficient to settle Washington's debt, leaving by 1795 almost £425 owed (Ledger C, 9). See particularly GW to Burwell Bassett, Jr., 3 Feb. 1788, and the note to that document in which the documents referred to here are cited.

11. Washington, as he reported to Gov. Benjamin Harrison in 1781, purchased in May 1771, at his mother's request and at his own expense, "a commodious house, garden, and [two] Lotts (of her own choosing) in Fredericksburg, that she might be near my Sister [Betty] Lewis, her only daughter" (GW to Benjamin Harrison, 21 Mar. 1781). Mary Ball Washington moved from Ferry

Farm across the Rappahannock into Fredericksburg in late 1771 and lived in the house that her son had bought for her until her death in August 1789. After her death, Washington had three local men examine the house and lot and recommend what price and terms should be set for their sale. Their suggested price of £450 payable in two years found no takers, and in March 1790 Washington agreed to sell the property for £350 payable in three years to Charles Carter, Jr., who probably was already living in the house with his wife Betty Lewis Carter, Mary Washington's granddaughter. In the spring of 1794 Carter made his first payment to Washington, an order for £200 on a merchant in Alexandria. Upon the receipt of the payment, Washington wrote Carter: "The remainder of the money due me for the purchase of the lots (amounting to abo⟨ve⟩ two hundred pounds more) I give . . . to my niece Mrs Carter" (GW to Carter, 29 May 1794; see also Carter to GW, 14 May 1794). Washington probably included this provision in his will simply to confirm his gift to the Carters of the unpaid balance due on the purchase, but he also may have had in mind the question raised about the title to the property arising from the fact that Carter and Washington had proceeded under the false illusion that Washington had bought the house and lot from Washington's brother-in-law and Carter's father-in-law, Fielding Lewis. The fact was that Washington had bought them both from Michael Robinson, who had bought the lots from Lewis (ten years earlier) in 1761. For the source of this confusion, see Carter to GW, 14 May 1794. For GW's purchase of the house and lots in 1771 and 1772 and his sale of them in 1790, see GW to Harrison, 21 Mar. 1781, Ledger A, 536, Cash Accounts, 1761, n.69 (*Papers, Colonial Series,* 7 : 1–10), *Diaries,* 3 : 52, 69, GW to Betty Washington Lewis, 13 Sept. 1789, Burgess Ball and Charles Carter, Jr., to GW, 8 Oct. 1789, Burgess Ball to GW, 26 Dec. 1789, Charles Carter, Jr., to GW, 6 Feb. 1790, 14 May 1794, and GW to Charles Carter, Jr., 8 Mar. 1790, 29 May 1794 (*Papers, Presidential Series,* 4 : 32–36, 146–47, 5 : 102–3).

12. As early as July 1767 the managers of a lottery to dispose of William Byrd III's holdings at the falls of the James River advertised for sale 10,000 tickets at £5 a piece. Washington had already bought twenty of the tickets, and he later entered an agreement with nine other men, Peyton Randolph, John Wayles, George Wythe, Richard Randolph, Lewis Burwell, William Fitzhugh of Chatham, Thomson Mason, Nathaniel Harrison, Jr., and Richard Kidder Meade, to purchase jointly another one hundred tickets. When the lottery was held in Williamsburg on 2 Nov. 1768, Washington won on his own one one-half-acre lot south of the James River in what was to be laid out in 1769 as the town of Manchester. He also was entitled to a one-tenth share in those prizes drawn by his partners; these included four two-acre lots in Manchester-to-be and two one-hundred-acre lots in Henrico County north of the James. Back at Mount Vernon after the Revolution, Washington wrote his lawyer Edmund Randolph in July 1784 and asked that Randolph let him "know (if you can) what is become of this property; & of what value it is—especially the Lott No. 265 which I hold in my own right—for I faintly recollect to have heard the joint stock was disposed of to no great advantage for the company—for me, I am sure it was not, as I have never received an iota on account of these prizes." Randolph replied that the value of Washington's own lot in Manchester was unknown. He also reported that as far as he could

determine Richard Randolph had sold "the most valuable" of the four lots in Manchester and that Thomson Mason had sold the two larger tracts in Henrico County north of the James. Apparently both Edmund Randolph and Washington forgot about this exchange: about five years later, in August 1789, Randolph asked Washington whether he had any information regarding the Byrd lottery prizes that Washington and his uncle Peyton Randolph had shared with others. Washington gave this answer: "The list of associates who purchased 100 Tickets in the lottery of the deceased Colo. Byrd is all the memorandom I have of that transaction. To the best of my recollection Mr Thomson Mason (deceased) was one of the associates and was either authorised, or assumed (I do not know which) the management of the business—He did it so effectually it seems as to monopolize the whole interest." When Washington made this bequest in his will in the summer of 1799 to his nephew William Augustine Washington, it may have slipped his mind that three years before, in June 1796, he had written another of his nephews, Bushrod Washington, about the prizes to which he was entitled from the Byrd lottery and also about the "lot in some Town [Edinburgh] that was established on James River (below Richmd) by a certain John Wood [Hood]." He then told Bushrod that if "upon enquiry" he thought any returns could be got from any of this, "I give you all the Interest I have therein & you may act accordingly." Washington had bought the lot in the town of Edinburgh, which never came into existence, in October 1760. See GW to Edmund Randolph, 10 July 1784, 8 Sept. 1789, Edmund Randolph to GW, 20 July 1784, 2 Aug. 1789 (*Papers, Confederation Series*, 1:494–96, 2:4–5; *Papers, Presidential Series*, 3:371–73, 4:5–6), and GW to Bushrod Washington, 29 June 1796. For an account of the Byrd auction, see Cash Accounts, May 1769, n.10 (*Papers, Colonial Series*, 8:191–94); for the purchase of the lot from John Hood, see Cash Accounts, October 1760, ibid., 6:465–66.

13. Washington prized his papers highly and long before drafting his will had come to look upon the great mass of documents that he held at Mount Vernon as part of his legacy to the new nation. Most of the letters and other papers from the pre-Revolutionary War years preserved by him have to do with his career as colonel of the Virginia Regiment in the 1750s, or they relate to his agricultural and business affairs. During the Revolution, recognizing the particular importance of the papers of the leader of the army fighting for American independence, viewing them "as a species of Public property, sacred in my hands," Washington in 1781 gained the approval of Congress to have his correspondence, orders, and instructions properly arranged and copied into bound volumes. This was accomplished in two years by a team of clerks working at Poughkeepsie, N.Y., under the direction of Richard Varick. In the summer of 1783 Varick delivered twenty-eight fat volumes of recopied documents. At the end of the year Washington had these volumes, as well as the originals of his "public and other Papers," sent overland to Mount Vernon. These Revolutionary War documents represented the larger part of the collection of papers at Mount Vernon which Washington left to his nephew Bushrod Washington; but with his heightened sense of the significance of his role in the founding of the American Republic, Washington after the Revolution was at greater pains both to retain copies of the hundreds and hundreds of letters that he wrote and to preserve the

even larger number of letters that he received. He also at some point in the 1780s put a series of clerks to work copying his letter books from the French and Indian War, but only after he himself had gone through them, correcting the mistakes in spelling and grammar of the young Washington and rewording any infelicitous or unclear passages. At the end of his presidency in 1797, Washington had his presidential secretaries, Tobias Lear and Bartholomew Dandridge, take from his files the papers that should go to his successor, John Adams, and send the rest down to him at Mount Vernon. He also had his letter-press contraption sent to Mount Vernon and in his final two years used it to make copies of most of the letters that he himself wrote. Lear reported that Washington, after saying, six hours before his death, "*I find I am going, my breath cannot continue long,*" gave instructions to Lear to "*arrange & record all my late Military letters & papers . . . and let Mr Rawlins finish recording my other letters, which he has begun.*" The "Military letters and papers" were those relating to his role as commander in chief of the army in 1798 and 1799; "Mr Rawlins" was his clerk, Albin Rawlins.

Washington's dream of erecting a separate building for his papers at Mount Vernon never materialized, and Martha Washington, it is supposed, destroyed the letters between herself and her husband before Bushrod Washington took possession of the papers, probably after Martha's death in 1802. Judge Washington soon sent most of his uncle's papers at Mount Vernon to Richmond, beginning in 1803, for Chief Justice John Marshall to use in preparing his five-volume biography of the great man, which Marshall published between 1804 and 1807. Bushrod, through the years, also gave away some of Washington's letters and returned others to the senders. In 1815 William B. Sprague, a young tutor at Lawrence Lewis's home Woodlawn, obtained Bushrod's permission to take any letters he wanted provided he left copies in their place. Sprague took full advantage of the offer to the extent of about 1500 letters. In 1827 Bushrod gave Jared Sparks access to the papers and subsequently allowed him to take many of them to Boston where Sparks put together his twelve-volume edition of *The Writings of George Washington* (Boston, 1834–37). Sparks had barely begun his work when Bushrod Washington died, in 1829, and left the papers to his nephew George Corbin Washington. George Corbin Washington sold George Washington's public papers to the United States government in 1834 for $25,000 and his private papers in 1849 for $20,000. The papers taken from Mount Vernon were deposited in the Department of State until 1904, at which time they were transferred to the Library of Congress. For the quotations, see GW to William Gordon, 23 Oct. 1782, to Richard Varick, 1 Jan. 1784, and Tobias Lear's Narrative Accounts of the Death of George Washington, printed below. For the history of the disposition of GW's papers, see the Introduction to the Library of Congress's *Index to the George Washington Papers*; for a brief description of the papers, see W. W. Abbot, "An Uncommon Awareness of Self: The Papers of George Washington" (*Prologue: Quarterly of the National Archives*, 21, no. 1 [Spring 1989]: 7–19).

14. The books at Mount Vernon are listed in the inventory made when Washington's estate was appraised after his death. The executors of Washington's will returned the inventory and appraisal of the estate to the Fairfax County court, which ordered it to be recorded on 20 Aug. 1810. The inventory was among those papers that disappeared from the courthouse in the nineteenth century.

Early in the twentieth century William K. Bixby presented the original inventory to Mount Vernon, where it remains. It was first printed in 1927 by Eugene E. Prussing as appendix II, in his *Estate of George Washington*, 401–8. The seventeen-page list of books and maps in the inventory of nearly one thousand items includes multivolume sets of books and pamphlets bound together in single volumes, valued altogether at $1,698. The books were in Washington's library at Mount Vernon, in three bookcases and "on the Table." Years later Edward Everett procured in 1860 from John A. Washington a copy made of the original inventory and printed it in his *Life of Washington*. In 1897 Appleton P. C. Griffin included in his *Boston Athenæum Washington Collection* an appendix listing the books in the inventory as printed in Everett's biography. Although the Boston Athenæum listing, arranged by categories, is based on Everett's imperfect copy of the inventory, it is very useful because William C. Lane, the librarian of the Athenæum, provides the full and correct names and the authors and titles of most of the works listed in it and, when possible, notes how and at what time each came into Washington's possession as well as its disposition after his death. See also Carroll, *Library at Mount Vernon*.

15. In the schedule of property that Washington prepared and attached to his will, he listed all of his landholdings, including the tracts referred to here which he had already sold but had not received full payment for, and he appended an explanatory note to each. This Schedule of Property with Washington's explanatory notes is printed immediately below.

16. In June 1791 David Steuart Erskine, eleventh earl of Buchan, sent by the Scottish painter Archibald Robertson the 2"x3"x4" hinged snuffbox, "made of the Oak that sheltered our Great Sir William Wallace after the Battle of Falkirk." Buchan wrote Washington that since he felt his "own unworthiness to receive this magnificently significant present," he had secured permission of the donors, the Company of Goldsmiths, "to make it over to the Man in the World to whom I thought it was most justly due" (Buchan to GW, 28 June 1791). Beginning in 1790 and until 1798, Buchan, as president of the Agriculture Society in London, was a frequent correspondent of Washington's. After the executors of Washington's will returned the box to Buchan with a copy of the will, Buchan decreed that the box be set aside "for the University of Washington with a Golden Pen to which there may be annually offered medals by the States to the honour of such young Citizens Students therein as shall be found in comparative trial to have made not only the greatest progress in useful knowledge during the whole of their course of Education but shall at the same time have been found to be most exemplary in their conduct & most preeminently posessed of the Principles & knowledge 'most friendly to Republican Government & to the true & genuine liberties of Mankind' to use the words of the great Founder himself" (see Buchan's "Observations respecting the Will of General Washington," Papers of the Earl of Buchan, William Salt Library, Stafford, United Kingdom).

17. Charles Washington, six years younger than George Washington and his last surviving brother, lived at his house Happy Retreat near present-day Charles Town, West Virginia. He died there in September 1799, less than three months before Washington died at Mount Vernon. The cane came into the possession of the United States government in 1845 and is deposited in the Smithsonian Insti-

tution. In 1789 Benjamin Franklin included this provision in a codicil to his will: "My fine crab-tree walking-stick, with a gold head curiously wrought in the form of the cap of liberty, I give to my friend, and the friend of mankind, *General Washington*. If it were a Sceptre, he has merited it, and would become it. It was a present to me from that excellent woman, Madame de Forbach, the dowager Duchess of Deux-Ponts, connected with some verses which should go with it" (Albert H. Smyth, *The Writings of Benjamin Franklin*, 10 vols. [New York, 1907], 10:501–10).

18. Lawrence Washington (1728-c.1813) of Chotank had spent several nights at Mount Vernon as recently as March 1798. He was the son of John and Mary Massey Washington and lived on the Potomac River downstream from Mount Vernon near Chotank Creek. His first cousin Robert Washington, born in 1730, was the son of Townshend Washington of Chotank and the eldest brother of Washington's longtime estate manager at Mount Vernon, Lund Washington. Robert Washington of Chotank has been tentatively identified as the "Robin" to whom GW wrote the letter that he copied in his notebook as an adolescent in the 1740s. The appraisers of the estate found "In the Study" at Mount Vernon "11 Spye Glasses," which they valued at $110, and "4 Canes," valued at $40 (Prussing, *Estate of George Washington*, 416). See *Diaries*, 6:287, and *Papers, Colonial Series*, 1:40–41.

19. In 1796 Washington had the Philadelphia cabinetmaker John Aiken make the tambour secretary for his study at Mount Vernon. Thomas Burling of New York made the revolving chair to be used with the secretary. The appraisers in 1800 valued the "Tambour Secretary" at $80 and the "Circular Chair" at $20. Both pieces were returned to Mount Vernon in the twentieth century. James Craik had been Washington's physician and close friend since accompanying him as surgeon on the expedition to the Ohio in 1754. See Christine Meadows, "A Very Handsome Study," *Mount Vernon Annual Report*, 1980, 32–41, and Prussing, *Estate of George Washington*, 416, 418.

20. The dressing table that Washington bequeathed to his friend Dr. David Stuart was a French piece which Washington acquired from the French minister to the United States, Eléanor-François-Elie, comte de Moustier, upon the minister's departure from New York in October 1789.

In his *Recollections*, George Washington Parke Custis reported that during the Revolutionary War Washington's body servant Will Lee always carried the large telescope "in a leathern case." The inventory of the contents of Mount Vernon lists, "In the Passage," a "Spye Glass" which the appraisers valued at $5. The editor of Custis's *Recollections* noted in 1859 that the telescope had "always been a conspicuous object upon the wall of the great passage at Mount Vernon." It may well be that Stuart, who was married to Eleanor Calvert Custis Stuart, the widow of Martha Washington's son, John Parke Custis, never removed the telescope from Mount Vernon; the dressing table was brought back to Mount Vernon in 1905. See Custis, *Recollections*, 224, Prussing, *Estate of George Washington*, 412–13, and *Mount Vernon Annual Report*, 1981, 16–19.

21. On 1 May 1794 the Rev. Clement Cruttwell (1743–1808) sent to Washington from Wokingham, Berkshire, in England, *The Holy Bible . . . with Notes, by Thomas Wilson, Lord Bishop of Sodor and Man, and Various Renderings Collected from the Other Translations by the Rev. Clement Cruttwell, the Editor*, published in three volumes in 1785 in Bath. According to Cruttwell, Thomas Wilson (1703–1784),

son of the noted bishop of Sodor and Man, Thomas Wilson (1663–1755), had directed in his will that this work by his father be sent to Washington. The Wilson work is listed in the inventory taken of Washington's library after his death, and the three volumes are now in the Library of Congress (Griffin, *Boston Athenæum Washington Collection*, 498).

22. Four pairs of pistols were found "in the Study" at Mount Vernon when the inventory of its contents was taken in 1800. The appraisers set a total value of $50 on three of the pairs, and $50 on the fourth. The pair of pistols given to Lafayette was exhibited at the Chicago Exhibition in 1893 as one of the "Souvenirs Franco-Américain de La Guerre de Independance." They had been on permanent display in Lafayette's château de La Grange. It is possible that these were the pistols that were sent from Philadelphia to General Washington at West Point on 22 Sept. 1779, with these words: "General Washington: accepting of these Pistols will very much oblige Sir Your most obedient very humble Sevt George Geddes." On 30 Sept., in accepting the gift, Washington called them "a pair of very elegant Pistols." By leaving this or another of his pair of pistols to Lafayette, Washington may have been returning the compliment. In 1824 Congressman Charles Fenton Mercer presented Gen. Andrew Jackson with a pair of pistols which, he said, Washington wore during the Revolution and were the gift of Lafayette. Mercer had got the pistols from William Robinson, the son-in-law of Washington's nephew William Augustine Washington. See Prussing, *Estate of George Washington*, 417–18, Richard and Carol Simpson, "Andrew Jackson's Pistols," *Gun Report*, Jan. 1985, and Andrew Jackson to Edward George Washington Butler, 20 Jan. 1824, in Sam B. Smith, Harriet Chappell Owsley et al., eds., *The Papers of Andrew Jackson*, 5 vols. to date (Knoxville, Tenn., 1980–), 5:341–42.

23. Hannah Bushrod Washington was the widow of Washington's brother John Augustine Washington, who died in January 1787. Mildred Thornton Washington was the widow of Washington's brother Charles Washington, who died in September 1799. Eleanor Calvert Custis Stuart, the wife of Dr. David Stuart, was, in consequence of her earlier marriage in February 1774 to Martha Washington's son, John Parke Custis (d. 1781), the mother of Martha's four grandchildren. Hannah Fairfax Washington, wife of Washington's cousin and friend Warner Washington of Fairfield in Frederick County, was the daughter of Washington's mentor, William Fairfax of Belvoir. Elizabeth Foote Washington of Hayfield in Fairfax County was the widow of Lund Washington, the manager of the Mount Vernon estate for more than a decade, before, during, and after the Revolution.

24. See note 30 below.

25. Sally Ball Haynie was a child 11 or 12 years old in October 1790 when her mother, Elizabeth Haynie, wrote to Washington about their destitute condition. Mrs. Haynie was probably the daughter of Washington's mother's half sister Elizabeth Johnson. To afford his impoverished relatives some relief, Washington instructed his rental agent Battaile Muse to find a vacant tenement for them on his land in Berkeley, Frederick, Fauquier, or Loudoun county and fix up a house where they might live rent free for as long as they chose. Mrs. Haynie seems not to have taken up Washington's offer but did accept occasional gifts of money from him. She and her daughter chose to live with and work for Betty Calmes, the widow of Marquis Calmes who owned land on the Shenandoah River in Frederick

County. Mrs. Haynie's health failed, and in 1794 Washington's nephew Robert Lewis, who had taken over from Muse in late 1791 the oversight of Washington's tenant farms in Virginia, settled her and young Sally in a small house near his own residence in Fauquier County. When Mrs. Haynie died in April 1796, Lewis and his wife took Sally, a "beautiful young girl" of "great œconomy and industry," into their house, with the understanding that she would go to Mount Vernon and help Mrs. Washington with the housekeeping upon the Washingtons' return home from Philadelphia in 1797. The adolescent Sally had been a member of the Lewis household for only a very short time when Robert Lewis concluded that she was "giddy" and "extremely deficient in household Economy." He was quick to inform Washington of this and to encourage Sally to accept the invitation of the widowed Mrs. Calmes to return and live with her. In January 1798 Sally herself wrote to Washington from Mrs. Calmes's, where she had been since the summer of 1796, and Washington instructed Robert Lewis to provide her with money to buy "necessaries." At the end of the year Sally wrote again saying that "nothing givs me gratter pleasure then to wright and reseve a letter from Soo grate a friend as you have bin to me." She informed Washington that she was living in the house of Capt. George Eskridge in Frederick County. See GW to Elizabeth Haynie, 27 Dec. 1790, to Battaile Muse, 27 Dec. 1790, to Robert Lewis, 26 June 1796, to Sally Ball Haynie, 11 Feb. 1798, Robert Lewis to GW, 17 Jan. 1795, 5 May, 26 June, 27 July 1796, and Sally Ball Haynie to GW, 28 Jan., 8 Sept., 7 Dec. 1798 (*Papers, Presidential Series,* 7:119–21; *Papers, Retirement Series,* 2:83–84); and see especially the notes to the letters from GW to Elizabeth Haynie, 27 Dec. 1790, and to Sally Ball Haynie, 11 Feb. 1798.

26. Sarah Green was the daughter of Thomas Bishop, Washington's old military servant, and of Susanna Bishop, who from 1766 until her death in December 1785 delivered most of the babies born to slave mothers at Mount Vernon. An only child, Sarah Bishop was married, probably by 1787, to Thomas Green, the overseer of Washington's slave carpenters. Thomas Bishop was already nearly fifty years old in 1755 when he landed in Virginia with General Edward Braddock's forces. Three months after Braddock's defeat in July 1755, Washington as colonel of the new Virginia Regiment, hired Bishop as his personal military servant. Bishop remained with the young colonel until Washington left the Virginia Regiment at the end of 1758. Bishop then returned to the British army at Philadelphia. In the spring of 1760 Washington decided that he wished to have Bishop with him at Mount Vernon and paid £10 to secure his release from the British service. The old soldier lived at Mount Vernon for the next thirty-four years, until his death in 1795. For a time, in the late 1760s, Bishop acted as overseer of Muddy Hole farm at Mount Vernon, but even before Washington left for war in 1775, Bishop seems to have been relegated to performing occasional tasks for the estate manager, Lund Washington, who complained to Washington in December 1775 that "every thing Bishop does is wrong." Despite this, Washington never wavered in his commitment to provide his old servant with the necessities of life. Bishop's house was on the river near the mansion house at Mount Vernon. George Washington Parke Custis later recalled that the old man in good weather would go outside his house, station himself at a spot where Washington would likely pass on his daily ride about the plantation, so as to greet and be

greeted by the general. Upon learning of the death of his old servant in January 1795, Washington wrote from Philadelphia to his farm manager, William Pearce: "Altho' Bishop should never have wanted victuals or cloaths whilst he lived, yet his death cannot be cause of regret, even to his daughter; to whom, from the imbecility of age, if not when he died, he soon must have become very troublesome to her, and a burthen to all around him."

Three or four months before Bishop's death in 1795, his son-in-law, Thomas Green, went off, leaving his wife Sarah and her young children behind. Washington had come to consider Green, who had been employed at Mount Vernon since 1783, a hopelessly incompetent drunkard. He viewed Green's leaving on "his own accord" as a "lucky circumstance," even though he pitied "his helpless family." In a letter that has not been found, Sarah Green wrote Washington about her distressed circumstances and told him of her intention to move into Alexandria in order to support her children and herself by taking in washing and sewing, or perhaps she would set up a shop. Washington expressed to his farm manager William Pearce his willingness to aid her, if she should move into town, "to the amount of twenty pounds in the purchase of things or on credit but not by an advance in money." He also instructed Pearce to "give her a boat load of Wood—a little flour—and some meat at killing time." Mrs. Green seems to have decided to try to open a shop in Alexandria: in March 1796 she wrote from Alexandria to ask Washington for his help. Washington sent her, "as charity," $8 in April 1795 and $10 in July 1796 (Ledger C, 22, 25). For GW's early dealings with Thomas Bishop, see particularly *Diaries*, 1:229, 259, George Mercer to GW, 17 Feb. 1760, Robert Stewart to GW, 14 April 1760, and John Mercer to GW, 16 June 1760 (*Papers, Colonial Series*, 6:387–89, 412–14, 436–37). For other references to GW's concern for Bishop's welfare, see Lund Washington to GW, 3, 10 Dec. 1775 (*Papers, Revolutionary War Series*, 2:477–82, 526–28), and GW to Bishop, 10 April 1779. For references to Bishop's house and to his duties, see GW to Anthony Whitting, 14 Oct. 1792, Custis, *Recollections*, 376, Lund Washington's Account Book, 31, 60, 71, and Cash Accounts printed in *Papers, Colonial Series*, vols. 7 and 8. For Custis's anecdote about Bishop, see his *Recollections*, 376–81. For GW's opinion of Thomas Green, see particularly his letters to Green of 23 Dec. 1793 and to William Pearce of 21 Sept. 1794. For GW's dealings with Sarah Green, see GW to William Pearce, 21 Sept., 16, 30 Nov. 1794, 25 Jan. 1795, and Sarah Green to GW, 21 Mar. 1795.

27. John Alton accompanied Washington as his body servant when the young man left Mount Vernon in April 1755 to join General Braddock. Alton remained with Washington throughout the disastrous campaign, falling ill at "abt the same time" that Washington did, "with near the same disorder." He did not return with Washington to the frontier in September 1755 when Washington was made colonel of the Virginia Regiment but remained at Mount Vernon instead. It was to Alton that Washington wrote in April 1759, shortly before bringing his bride to Mount Vernon, with instructions to have the "House very well cleand," to have "two of the best Bedsteads put up," and to see to it that the chairs and tables were "very well rubd and Cleand." In 1762 Alton was made overseer first of Dogue Run farm and then of Muddy Hole farm. In 1765 he was moved to Mill farm and in 1770 back to Muddy Hole. At the time of his death in 1785 he was overseer of

River farm, having served without interruption, it appears, as an overseer at Mount Vernon for twenty-three years. In November 1786 Washington informed Alton's widow Elizabeth that she could "have the House used for a School by my Mill if the School should be discontinued" (*Diaries*, 5:66). Although there is some uncertainty about the marriage of the Alton's daughter, Ann, it seems clear that in 1785 she married the housekeeper, or butler, at Mount Vernon named Richard Burnet, who had been hired by Martha Washington in May 1783. Burnet left the Washingtons' employ in September 1785 upon his marriage, but in May 1786 he returned to take up his old position, this time under the name of Richard Burnet Walker. He continued as butler at Mount Vernon until 1789. For John Alton's role as Washington's body servant during Braddock's campaign, see GW to John Augustine Washington, 28 June–2 July 1755, and to William Fairfax, 23 April 1755, n.3, in *Papers, Colonial Series*, 1:259, 319–28. For his employment as overseer at Mount Vernon, see GW to Alton, 5 April 1759 (ibid., 6:200), and Washington's Cash Accounts and his list of tithables in *Papers, Colonial Series*, vols. 7–10, and Lund Washington's Account Book, 34, 80, 160 (ViMtV). For the reference to Elizabeth Alton, see *Diaries*, 5:66. For the marriage of Ann Alton and the Mount Vernon career of Richard Burnet Walker, see GW to Clement Biddle, 17 Aug. 1785, n.4 (*Papers, Confederation Series*, 3:186).

28. William Augustine Washington was the son of George Washington's half brother Augustine; George Steptoe Washington was the son of his brother Samuel; George Lewis was the son of his sister Betty Washington Lewis; Bushrod was the son of his brother John Augustine Washington; and Samuel was the son of his brother Charles Washington. In the inventory of the contents of the house at Mount Vernon in 1800, the appraisers listed "7 Swords & 1 blade," which they valued as a whole at $120. The sword chosen by Samuel Washington was presented in 1843 to the U.S. Congress by his son Samuel T. Washington. At the time of the presentation the sword was described as "a plain couteau, or hangar, with a green hilt and silver guard. On the upper ward of the scabbard is engraven 'J. Bailey, Fish Kill.' It is accompanied by a buckskin belt, which is secured by a silver buckle and clasp, whereon are engraved the letters 'G.W.' and the figures '1757.' These are all of the plainest workmanship, but substantial . . ." (Prussing, *Estate of George Washington*, 416, 481).

29. Washington left to his nephew Bushrod Washington the core of the great plantation that he had created upon the Potomac. It was that part of it lying between Little Hunting and Dogue creeks which included the original 2,126-acre Mount Vernon tract on Little Hunting Creek and a number of smaller tracts between it and Dogue Run below the Alexandria road, which he had gradually added to his holdings. Three of the five farms that Washington maintained at Mount Vernon lay between the two creeks and were referred to as Muddy Hole farm, Union (Ferry and French) farm, and Mansion House farm with its gardens and buildings, including the great house itself. Bushrod's father, John Augustine Washington, the brother closest to Washington's heart, "the intimate companion of my youth and the most affectionate friend of my ripened age," spent much of his time taking care of George Washington's affairs in the late 1750s when his brother was away commanding the Virginia Regiment on the frontier. Washington took a particular interest in the education and legal education of Bushrod,

his brother's eldest son, and he frequently conferred with the young lawyer about legal matters in the 1790s before Bushrod accepted appointment to the U.S. Supreme Court in 1798. Washington left to Bushrod not only the mansion house and three farms but also all of his books and his papers (see notes 13 and 14). For Washington's sentiments regarding John Augustine, see GW to Henry Knox, 27 April 1787 (*Papers, Confederation Series*, 6:157–59).

30. Almost to the day in 1786 that he completed piecing together the plantation of more than 7,000 acres at Mount Vernon, the work of more than thirty years, Washington began arranging for its future breakup. In October of that year his nephew Maj. George Augustine Washington, who was acting as Washington's estate manager and living at Mount Vernon, married Martha Washington's niece Frances Bassett of Eltham, who also was living at Mount Vernon. In October 1786 Washington wrote his nephew that he intended "to give you at my death, my *landed* property in the neck, containing by estimation between two & three thousand acres." The tract on Clifton's Neck was that portion of the Mount Vernon plantation that lay to the east of Little Hunting Creek on the Potomac River, 1,806 acres of which he had bought from William Clifton in 1760 and 238 acres from George Brent in the same year. Washington developed on this property what he called River farm, one of the five farms that he organized and operated at Mount Vernon. At Washington's urging George Augustine Washington took over a 360-acre section of this land on Clifton's Neck at the north east corner of River farm and established a farm there with the slaves given to him by his father-in-law, Burwell Bassett. When George Augustine died in 1793, his widow retained control of the farm, called Walnut Tree farm, and at Fanny Washington's marriage to Tobias Lear in 1795 control of the farm passed to Lear, where it remained after Fanny's death in March 1796. Lear moved to Walnut Tree farm with his own young son and with the children of George Augustine and Fanny Washington, Anna Maria and the two heirs of Clifton's Neck, George Fayette and Charles Augustine Washington. In 1797 Washington expressed a willingness to lease the whole of River farm to Lear in 1798, but this was not done, possibly because Lear became occupied with the duties of military secretary for Washington. See Washington to George Augustine Washington, 25 Oct. 1786 (*Papers, Confederation Series*, 4:307–10), *Diaries*, 1:240, Tobias Lear to GW, 8 Sept., GW to Lear (second letter), 11 Sept. 1797 (*Papers, Retirement Series*, 1:339–41, 345–47); see also note 1 above.

31. Martha Washington's granddaughter Eleanor Parke Custis, who had come to live at Mount Vernon as an infant, was married in the house on Washington's birthday in 1799 to Washington's nephew Lawrence Lewis. Lewis had in August 1797 at Washington's urging come to live at Mount Vernon so as to relieve his uncle of some of the burdens of entertaining the steady stream of visitors. In September 1799, at a time when Washington was seeking ways to reduce the scope of his farm operations at Mount Vernon so that he could assume direct control of them himself, he wrote to Lawrence Lewis about the provisions he had recently made in his will for him and his wife Nelly. The portion of the Mount Vernon holdings that he indicated was to go to the newly married couple was all that lying to the north and west of the road to Alexandria. This included Dogue Run farm, the mill tract, and a wooded tract of about four hundred acres which

Washington had got from Charles West in 1772. He urged Lewis to build soon a house on the Charles West tract for himself and Nelly and to go ahead and rent at once the farm, gristmill, and distillery, all of which Lewis could manage until they came to them at Washington's death. Lewis did begin renting, and the couple later built their house, Woodlawn, beyond the mill. For Lawrence Lewis's invitation to Mount Vernon, see *Diaries*, 6:255. For the bequest to Lewis and his wife see ibid., 1:241, and GW to Lewis, 20 Sept. 1799.

32. Washington undoubtedly would have left a great deal more land to Martha Washington's only grandson and his own ward, George Washington Parke Custis, had he not already been well provided for. Eighteen-year-old Custis, who like his sister Nelly Lewis had lived at Mount Vernon since his infancy and was still living there in 1799, was the heir-at-law of his father John Parke Custis from whom he had inherited extensive holdings in New Kent, York, and Northampton counties and elsewhere. He also would at Martha Washington's death take possession of his grandmother's dower lands and slaves. The tract of land on Four Mile Run of about 1,200 acres which Washington left him was about four miles north of Alexandria on the road to Leesburg. Washington had agreed in 1774 to pay £450 for the land to each of the brothers George and James Mercer, who had been given joint ownership by their father, John Mercer. When some questions later arose about Washington's title to the land, James Mercer in 1787 confirmed Washington's ownership and agreed to credit him with the payment of £450 to George Mercer's estate in return for Washington's crediting that amount toward the payment of their father's long-standing debt to the Custis estate. For many years Washington had been bothered by timber-stealing poachers on this land, which he had left undeveloped. As recently as April 1799, he had resurveyed the tract himself and taken steps to put an end to the depredations. See GW to James Mercer, 12 Dec. 1774, and note 3 of that document, 19 Nov. 1786, n.1 (*Papers, Colonial Series*, 10:201–5; *Papers, Confederation Series*, 4:386), and GW to Ludwell Lee, 26 April 1799.

33. Washington's Schedule of Property, in which he lists and describes the residue of his property, with instructions that it should be sold, is printed as an enclosure immediately below. What Washington is saying here is that the proceeds from the sale of the property should be apportioned among the children of his three brothers, his one sister, one half brother, and Martha Washington's grandchildren. One share of the proceeds was to go to each of his eleven nephews and eight nieces, or to their heirs, and one share to each of Martha's three granddaughters. In addition one share was to be divided between his nephews Bushrod Washington and Lawrence Lewis and Martha's grandson, George Washington Parke Custis, all three of whom were otherwise major beneficiaries under the terms of the will.

34. After his return from the presidency in 1797, Washington had regular business dealings with William Augustine Washington of Haywood, Westmoreland County, the son of his half brother Augustine Washington who died in 1762. Augustine Washington's daughter Elizabeth was married to Washington's friend Alexander Spotswood of New Post, Spotsylvania County. Another daughter, Jane, was the wife of Col. John Thornton, son of Col. Francis Thornton (d. 1784) of Society Hill, King George County. His third daughter, Ann Washington Ashton,

was at the time of her death in 1777 the wife of her cousin Burdett Ashton of Northumberland County. She had four surviving children: Charles, Burdett, Ann, and Sarah. Her daughter Sarah Ashton married in 1788 Nicholas Fitzhugh of Ravensworth, Fairfax County.

35. Washington and his brother-in-law, Fielding Lewis of Fredericksburg, were frequent business associates before Lewis's death near the end of the Revolution. Lewis left his widow, Washington's sister Betty, in somewhat reduced circumstances. When Washington became president in 1789, he took steps to give the two younger Lewis boys, Robert and Howell, a start in life. He made them clerks in his presidential household, Robert in 1789 and Howell in 1792. Upon Robert Lewis's return to Virginia in 1791, he became Washington's rental agent. In 1799 Robert Lewis was living with his wife in Fauquier County. Howell Lewis returned to Virginia in 1793 to act for a short time as Washington's agent at Mount Vernon before settling in Culpeper County. He visited Washington with his wife within a week of his uncle's death. Fielding Lewis, Jr., married very young before the Revolution and suffered many years of dire poverty with his wife and children. He seems by 1799, however, to have improved his condition and was living in Fairfax County. The second son, George, served with distinction as a cavalry officer in the Revolution. In 1799 George Lewis was living with his wife at Marmion, King George County. At the time of Washington's death Lawrence Lewis was living at Mount Vernon with his wife Nelly Custis Lewis. Betty Lewis Carter, only daughter of Fielding and Betty Lewis, was the wife of Charles Carter, Jr., son of Edward Carter of Blenheim. She lived at this time in Culpeper County with her husband and children.

36. George Steptoe Washington and Lawrence Augustine Washington, sons of Washington's brother Samuel and his fourth wife, Anne Steptoe Washington, were little boys when their father died in 1781. After his return to Mount Vernon at the end of the Revolution, Washington assumed responsibility for their schooling in Georgetown and Alexandria and, later, their attendance at college in Philadelphia (see note 9). In 1799 George Steptoe Washington was living at Harewood, his father's place in Berkeley County. His brother Lawrence Augustine was living at Federal Hill, later called Hawthorn, at Winchester on a part of the estate of the family of his wife, Dorcas Wood Washington. Their younger sister, Harriot, was married to Andrew Parks of Baltimore. Thornton Washington, whose mother was Samuel's second wife, Mildred Thornton Washington, was living at the time of his death in 1787 at Cedar Lawn on land that he had acquired from his uncle George Washington through his father (see note 8). Thornton Washington's heirs included his son, Samuel, born in 1786, the child of his second wife, Frances Townshend Washington, and sons John Thornton Augustine (b. 1783) and Thomas A. (b. 1780), both born to his first wife, Mildred Berry Washington.

37. Corbin Washington had recently moved from his farm on the family place in Westmoreland County. He was living at Selby, Fairfax County, where Washington visited him in November 1799 (*Diaries*, 6:374). Jane (Jenny) Washington was married to William Augustine Washington, the son of her father's half brother Augustine Washington. She was living with him at Haywood in Westmoreland County in 1791 when she died. Her surviving children in 1799 were George Corbin Washington, Ann Aylett Washington, and Bushrod Washington, Jr. As the

major beneficiary of Washington's will, Bushrod, John Augustine Washington's eldest son, received only one third of a share (see note 33).

38. For some time before the death of Charles Washington, his son Samuel had been struggling to rescue his father's property which was heavily burdened with debt. He was recently married and had built a house in Berkeley County. His sister Mildred was married to Thomas Hammond and also lived in Berkeley County. Charles Washington's other daughter, Frances, was married to Washington's friend Col. Burgess Ball, and they lived in Loudoun County. The orphaned children of Charles Washington's eldest son, George Augustine Washington, and of Martha Washington's niece Frances Bassett Washington Lear, were named George Fayette, Charles Augustine, and Anna Maria. The children lived with their stepfather at Walnut Tree farm, a part of the Mount Vernon Clifton's Neck land that Washington left to the two little boys (see note 30).

39. Elizabeth Parke Custis (Eliza) Law, the eldest daughter of Martha Washington's son John Parke (Jacky) Custis and his wife Eleanor Calvert Custis (now Stuart), was married to the English entrepreneur Thomas Law. The Laws lived near the Capitol in the Federal City. Her sister Martha Parke Custis (Patsy) Peter was the wife of Thomas Peter, a businessman in Georgetown. The third sister, Eleanor Parke Custis (Nelly) Lewis, was at Mount Vernon with her husband, the heir to a major part of the Mount Vernon plantation (see note 31).

40. After he inherited Mount Vernon, Washington had the old tomb built according to the instructions laid down in his half brother Lawrence's will. The tomb was built on the side of a steep hill about two hundred yards south of the mansion house. It was a plain, bricked-up excavation in the hillside. Whenever the tomb was opened for a new occupant, the bricks had to be removed and replaced again after the burial. Mrs. Washington instructed that a door be made for the vault after her husband's burial, observing "that it will soon be necessary to open it again." By 1799 the tomb was in a ruinous condition from tree roots and moisture.

After Washington's death John Adams requested and received permission from Mrs. Washington to remove Washington's body for reburial in a crypt to be built under the dome of the U.S. Capitol. This was never done, however. In 1831, after an attempt was made by vandals to steal Washington's body from the decaying tomb, Lawrence Lewis and George Washington Parke Custis built a new brick tomb west of the mansion, in the "Vinyard Inclosure" mentioned in Washington's will. The bodies of George and Martha Washington and other family members buried in the old tomb were reinterred in the new vault. For more on GW's tomb, see Paul Wilstach, *Mount Vernon: Washington's Home and the Nation's Shrine* (New York and Garden City, N.Y., 1916), 223–24, 247–50, and Prussing, *Estate of George Washington*, 239–42.

41. The executors agreed among themselves that the business of the settlement of the estate should be left largely to Bushrod Washington and Lawrence Lewis. Nearly half a century after Washington's death, with all of the executors but George Washington Parke Custis dead, no final settlement of the estate had been reached. See Custis to Lorenzo Lewis, 20 June 1846 (*Mount Vernon Annual Report*, 1952, 52).

Enclosure
Schedule of Property

Mount Vernon 9th July 1799
Schedule of property comprehended in the foregoing Will, which is directed to be Sold, and some of it, conditionally is Sold; with discriptive, and explanatory notes relative thereto.

In Virginia

	acres	price	dollars
Loudoun County			
Difficult run	300		[$]6,666 (a)

(a) This tract for the size of it is valuable, more for its situation than the quality of its soil, though that is good for Farming; with a considerable portion of grd that might, very easily, be improved into Meadow. It lyes on the great road from the City of Washington, Alexandria and George Town, to Leesburgh & Winchester; at Difficult bridge; nineteen miles from Alexandria, less from the City & George Town, and not more than three from Matildaville at the Great Falls of Potomac. There is a valuable seat on the Premises—and the whole is conditionally sold—for the sum annexed in the Schedule.[1]

Loudoun & Fauquier

	acres	price	dollars
Ashbys Bent	2481 [acres]	$10	[$]24,810
Chattins Run	885	8	7,080 (b)

(b) What the selling prices of lands in the vicinity of these two tracts are, I know not; but compared with those above the ridge, and others below them, the value annexed will appear moderate—a less one would not obtain them from me.[2]

Berkeley

	acres	price	dollars
So. fork of Bullskin	1600		
Head of Evans's [Evitt's] M[arsh]	453		
On Wormeley's line	183		
	2236 [acres]	[$]20	$44,720 (c)

(c) The surrounding land, not superior in Soil, situation or properties of any sort, sell currently at from twenty to thirty dollars an acre. The lowest price is affixed to ⟨these⟩.[3]

Frederick

| Bought from Mercer | 571 [acres] | [$]20 | [$]11,420 (d) |

(d) The observations made in the last note applies equally to this tract; being in the vicinity of them, and of similar quality, altho' it lyes in another County.[4]

Hampshire

| On Potk River above B[ath] | 240 [acres] | [$]15 | [$]3,600 (e) |

(e) This tract, though small, is extremely valuable. It lyes on Potomac River about 12 miles above the Town of Bath (or Warm springs) and is in the shape of a horse Shoe; the river running almost around it. Two hundred Acres of it is rich low grounds; with a great abundance of the largest & finest Walnut trees; which, with the produce of the Soil, might (by means of the improved Navigation of the Potomac) be brought to a shipping port with more ease, and at a smaller expence, than that which is transported 30 miles only by land.[5]

Gloucester

| On North River | 400 [acres] | abt [$]3,600 (f) |

(f) This tract is of second rate Gloucester low grounds. It has no Improvements thereon, but lyes on navigable water, abounding in Fish and Oysters. It was received in payment of a debt (carrying interest) and valued in the year 1789 by an impartial Gentleman to £800. N.B. it has lately been sold, and there is due thereon, a balance equal to what is annexed the Schedule.[6]

Nansemond

| Near Suffolk ⅓ of 1119 acres | 373 [acres] | [$]18 | [$]2,984 (g) |

(g) These 373 a⟨cres⟩ are the third part of undivided purchases made by the deceased Fielding Lewis[,] Thomas Walker and myself; on full conviction that they would become valuable. The land lyes on the Road from Suffolk to Norfolk—touches (if I am not mistaken) some part of the Navigable water of Nansemond River—borders on, and comprehends part of the rich Dismal Swamp; is capable of great improvement; and from its situation must become extremely valuable.[7]

Great Dismal Swamp

My dividend thereof   abt $20,000 (h)

(h) This is an undivided Interest wch I held in the Great Dismal Swamp Company—containing about 4000 acres, with my part of the Plantation & Stock thereon belonging to the Company in the sd Swamp.[8]

Ohio River

Round bottom	587	
Little Kanhawa	2314	
16 miles lowr down	2448	
Opposite Big Bent	4395	dol.
	9744 [acres]	10 [$]97,440 (i)

(i) These several tracts of land are of the first quality on the Ohio River, in the parts where they are situated; being almost if not altogether River bottoms. The smallest of these tracts is actually sold at ten dollars an acre but the consideration therefor not received—the rest are equally valuable & will sell as high— especially that which lyes just below the little Kanhawa and is opposite to a thick settlement on the West side the Rivr. The four tracts have an aggregate breadth upon the River of Sixteen miles and is bounded there by that distance.[9]

Great Kanhawa

Near the Mouth West	10990
East side above Mouth of Cole River	7276
	2000

Opposite thereto	2950		
Burning Spring	125		
	23341 [acres]		[$]200,000 (k)

(k) These tracts are situated on the Great Kanhawa River, and the first four are bounded thereby for more than forty miles. It is acknowledged by all who have seen them (and of the tract containing 10990 acres which I have been on myself, I can assert) that there is no richer, or more valuable land in all that Region; They are conditionally sold for the sum mentioned in the Schedule— that is $200,000 and if the terms of that Sale are not complied with they will command considerably more. The tract of which the 125 acres is a Moiety, was taken up by General Andrew Lewis and myself for, and on account of a bituminous Spring which it contains, of so inflamable a nature as to burn as freely as Spirits, and is as nearly difficult to extinguish.[10]

Maryland

| Charles County | 600 [acres] | [$]6 | [$]3,600 (l) |

(l) I am but little acquainted with this land, although I have once been on it. It was received (many years since) in discharge of a debt due to me from Daniel Jenifer Adams at the value annexed thereto—and must be worth more. It is very level, lyes near the River Potomac.[11]

[Maryland]

| Montgomery | | | |
| D[itt]o | 519 [acres] | [$]12 | [$]6,228 (m) |

(m) This tract ⟨lies⟩ about 30 miles above the City of Washington, not far from Kittoctan. It is good farming Land, and by those who are well acquainted with it I am informed that it would sell at twelve or $15 pr acre.[12]

Pennsylvania

| Great Meadows | 234 [acres] | [$]6 | [$]1,404 (n) |

(n) This land is valuable on account of its local situation, and other properties. It affords an exceeding good stand on Braddocks road from Fort Cumberland to Pittsburgh—and besides a fertile soil, possesses a large quantity of natural Meadow, fit for the scythe. It is distinguished by the appellation of the Great Meadows—where the first action with the French in the year 1754 was fought.[13]

New York

| Mohawk River | abt 1000 [acres] | [$]6 | [$]6,000 (o) |

(o) This is the moiety of about 2000 Acs. which remains unsold of 6071 Acres on the Mohawk River (Montgomery Cty) in a Patent granted to Daniel Coxe in the Township of Coxeborough & Carolana—as will appear by Deed from Marinus Willet & Wife to George Clinton (late Governor of New York) and myself. The latter sales have been at Six dollars an ac[r]e and what remains unsold will fetch that or more.[14]

North Westn Territy

On little Miami	839		
Ditto	977		
Ditto	1235		
	3051 [acres]	[$]5	[$]15,251 (p)

(p) The quality of these lands & their Situation, may be known by the Surveyors certificates—which are filed along with the Patents. They ⟨li⟩e in the vicinity of Cincinnati; one tract near the mouth of the little Miami another seven & the third ten miles up the same—I have been informed that they will readily command more than they are estimated at.[15]

Kentucky

Rough Creek	3000		
Ditto adjoing	2000		
	5000 [acres]	[$]2	[$]10,000 (q)

(q) For the description of these tracts in detail, see General Spotswoods letters filed with the other papers relating to them. Besides the General good quality of the Land there is a valuable Bank of Iron Ore thereon: which, when the settlement becomes more populous (and settlers are moving that way very fast) will be found very valuable; as the rough Creek, a branch of Green River affords ample water for Furnaces & forges.[16]

Lots—viz.
City of Washington
Two, near the Capital, Sqr. 634 cost $963—and
   with Buildgs   [$]15,000 (r)

(r) The two lots near the Capital, in square 634, cost me ⟨9⟩63$
only; but in this price I was favoured, on condition that I should
build two Brick houses three Story high each: without this reduction the selling prices of those Lots would have cost me about
$1350. These lots, with the buildings thereon, when completed
will stand me in $15000 at least.[17]

[City of Washington]
No. 5. 12. 13 & 14—the 3 last, Water lots on
   the Eastern Branch, in Sqr. 667 containing
   together 34,438 sqr. feet @ 12 Cts   [$]4,132 (s)

(s) Lots No. 5. ⟨12.⟩ 13. & 14 on the Eastn branch, are advantageously situated on the water—⟨and⟩ although many lots much
less convenient have sold a great deal higher I will rate these at
12 Cts the square foot only.[18]

Alexandria
Corner of Pitt & Prince Stts half an Acre—laid
   out into buildgs 3 or 4 of wch are let on grd
   Rent at $3 pr foot   [$]4,000 (t)

(t) For this lot, though unimproved, I have refused $35⟨0⟩0—It
has since been laid off into proper sized lots for building on—
three or 4 of which are let on ground Rent—forever—at three
dollars a foot on the Street. and this price is asked for both fronts
on Pitt & Princes Street.[19]

Winchester
A lot in the Town of half an Acr. & another in
   the Commons of about 6 Acs.—supposed   [$]400 (u)

(u) As neither the lot in the Town or Common have any improvements on them, it is not easy to fix a price, but as both are well
situated, it is presumed the price annexed to them in the Schedule, ⟨is a⟩ reasonable valu[atio]n.[20]

Bath — or Warm Springs

Two Well situated, & had buildings to the amt of

£150   [$]800 (w)

(w) The Lots in Bath (two adjoining) cost me, to the best of my recollection, betwn fifty & sixty pounds 20 years ago; and the buildings thereon £150 more. Whether property there has ⟨increased⟩ or decreasd in its value, ⟨and in wha⟩t condition the houses a⟨re, I am ignora⟩nt. but s⟨uppose they are not valued too⟩ high.[21]

Stock

United States   6 prCts   [$]3746
 Do defered   [$]1873 ⎫
 3 prCts $2946 ⎭ $2500 $6,246 (x)

(x) These are the sums which are actually funded. and though no more in the aggregate than $7,566 — stand me in at least ten thousand pounds Virginia Money. be⟨ing⟩ the amount of bonded and other debts due to me, & discharged during the War when money had depreciated in that ratio—and was so se⟨tt⟩led by public author[it]y.[22]

Potomack Company

24 Shares—cost ea. £100 Sterg   [$]10,666 (y)

(y) The value, annexed to these sha[res] is what they have actually cost me, and is the price affixed by Law: and although the present selling price is under par, my advice to the Legatees (for whose benefit they are intended, especially those who can afford to lye out of the Money is that each should take and hold one; there being a Moral certainty of a great and increasing profit arising from them in the course ⟨of a few⟩ years.[23]

James River Company

5 Shares—each cost $100   [$]500 (z)

(z) It is supposed that the Shares in the James River Company must also be productive. But of this I can give no decided opinion for want of mo⟨re accur⟩ate informatn.[24]

Bank of Columbia

170 Shares—$40 each　　　　　　　　　　　　　[$]6,800

Bank of Alexandria

beside 20 to Free School 5　　　　　　　　　　[$]1,000 (&)

Th⟨ese are the no⟩minal prices of th⟨e shares in the Banks⟩ of Alexandria & Co⟨lumbia—the selling prices⟩ vary according ⟨to circumstances.⟩ But as the Sto⟨ck usually divides from⟩ eight to ten ⟨per cent per annum, they⟩ must be w⟨orth the former, at least,⟩ so long as the ⟨Banks are conceived⟩ to be Secure, ⟨although circumstan⟩ces may, so⟨metimes make them below it⟩.[25]

Stock—living—viz.

1 Covering horse, 5 Co[ac]h Horses—4 riding do—Six brood Mares—20 working horses & mares. 2 Covering Jacks—& 3 young ones—10 she asses, 42 working Mules—15 younger ones 329 head of horned Cattle 640 head of Sheep—and a large stock of Hogs—the precise number is unknown[.] My Manager has estimated this live Stock at £7,000 but I shall set it down in order to make rd sum at

　　　　　　　　　　　　　　　　　　　[$]15,653
　　　　　　　　　Agregate amt　$530,000

The va⟨lue of the live sto⟩ck depends more up⟨on the qua⟩lity than quantity of the ⟨different⟩ species of it, and this aga⟨in upon⟩ the demand, and judgment ⟨or fanc⟩y of purchasers.

　　　　　　　　　　　　　　　　　Go: Washington

ADS, ViFaCt. Washington placed his notes at the end of the original document. For the sake of clarity and readability the editors decided to insert Washington's notes just after the entries that they refer to. In addition, Washington often used periods instead of commas when recording dollar amounts; these periods have all been silently changed to commas. Since a part of Washington's property schedule at the Fairfax County Courthouse has been damaged, our reading of the mutilated words has been taken from *The Will of General George Washington: To Which Is Annexed, A Schedule of His Property, Directed to Be Sold* (Alexandria, Va., 1800).

　　1. Washington acquired the tract on Difficult Run in Loudoun County in 1763 from Bryan Fairfax for £82.10 in payment of a debt. Nothing had been done to develop the property when Washington conveyed it in May 1795 to John Gill for $6,666.66. As Gill did not have the money to pay the purchase price immediately, Washington agreed to rent him the property for $433.33⅓ per annum for as

many as ten years. During that period Gill would, it was hoped, be able to save enough money to buy the tract outright. In October 1799, having made only two of the four annual payments due, Gill asked to be released from his bargain. To reach a settlement Gill gave Washington a slip of land on the west bank of Difficult Run and a parcel of goods in payment of the arrears. Washington then revoked the original agreement, leaving himself in sole possession of the Difficult Run tract at the time of his death. See Memorandum: List of Quitrents, 1764, n.3 (*Papers, Colonial Series*, 7:350–51), GW to Charles Lee, 17 May 1795, and, especially, GW to John Gill, 19 Oct. 1799, n.2.

2. Washington in 1767 bought from George Carter's estate a tract of 2,682 (2,481) acres at Ashby's Bent in Fauquier and Loudoun counties; and in 1772 he bought from Bryan Fairfax 600 (885) acres on Chattins Run in Fauquier County. He divided the Ashby's Bent tract into twenty parcels for rental and the Chattins Run tract into four. After the war, he engaged Battaile Muse to collect the rents from his tenants in Fauquier and Loudoun counties, and from those in Frederick and Berkeley counties as well. By the time Muse was ready to turn over the collection of rents to Washington's nephew Robert Lewis in 1791, the rental payments of these tenants had come to represent a significant part of Washington's income. Washington's last letter to Lewis about the tenants was written on 7 Dec. 1799, a few days before he died. For GW's acquisition of the Ashby's Bent and Chattins Run tracts and the initial leasing of the land parcels to tenants, see the source note in Lease to Francis Ballinger, 17 Mar. 1769, and Bryan Fairfax to GW, 20 Jan. 1772, n.1 (*Papers, Colonial Series*, 8:171–77, 9:8–9). For extended references to Battaile Muse's dealings with GW's tenants, see the note to GW to Muse, 18 Sept. 1785, Lists of Tenants, same date, and Muse to GW, 28 Nov. 1785 (*Papers, Confederation Series*, 3:253–65, 413–16).

3. Between 1750 and 1752 when young Washington was engaged in surveying, he acquired either by grant or by purchase five tracts of land on the waters of Bullskin Run in Frederick (later Berkeley) County. These included grants of 453, 93 (approximately), and 760 acres and purchases of 456 and 552 acres, for a total of 2,314 acres. Parcels of the Bullskin land were rented throughout the years by a succession of tenants. The death in November 1799 of the most important of these, John Ariss, who had begun renting 700 acres in 1786, led Washington to write his rental agent Robert Lewis on 7 Dec. 1799 about the possibility of reclaiming the use of the Ariss and other tenanted tracts so that he might give employment to the "supernumerary hands" at Mount Vernon. For GW's acquisition of his Bullskin lands, see Land Grant, from Thomas, Lord Fairfax, 20 Oct. 1750 (*Papers, Colonial Series*, 1:47–48). For the renting of the Bullskin land parcels, see the references in note 2 above; see also GW to Muse, 28 July 1785, n.2 (*Papers, Confederation Series*, 3:159–62); see also John Ariss to GW, 5 Aug. 1784 (ibid., 2:24–25).

4. In November 1774 Washington conducted the sale of the American property of his boyhood friend and former military secretary George Mercer, who had moved to England. Mercer's property included a tract of 6,500 acres on the Shenandoah River in Frederick County. At the time of the sale the tract was divided into twenty-two lots of about three hundred acres each. Washington bought two of these lots, numbers 5 and 6, near present-day Berryville, Va., later deter-

mined to total 571 acres. From the time of purchase Washington rented his two lots to tenants in four parcels. For the sale of George Mercer's Frederick County land in 1774, see GW to John Tayloe, 30 Nov. 1774, n.2, Edward Snickers to GW, 17 May 1784, n.1, GW to Francis Lightfoot Lee and Ralph Wormeley, Jr., 20 June 1784, and notes (*Papers, Colonial Series*, 10:191–92; *Papers, Confederation Series*, 1:392–94, 458–65), and Ingrid Jewell Jones, "Edward Snickers, Yeoman," *Proceedings of the Clarke County Historical Association*, 17 (1971–75): 26. For GW's Frederick County tenants, see GW to Battaile Muse, 28 July 1785, n.1 (*Papers, Confederation Series*, 3:159–62).

5. On 8 Mar. 1753 Washington secured a grant of 240 acres on the Potomac River between the Great and Little Cacapon rivers, at that part of Frederick County that became Hampshire County, Va., later West Virginia. See Land Grant, from Thomas, Lord Fairfax, 20 Oct. 1750, source note (*Papers, Colonial Series*, 1:47–48). In 1763 Washington entered an agreement with Christopher Hardwick to develop jointly a plantation on this tract, but nothing came of the venture, and Washington made no further effort to develop the property. See Agreement with Christopher Hardwick, 22 Jan. 1763 (*Papers, Colonial Series*, 7:182–85). Washington advertised the tract for rent in June 1784, without success. The following September he visited his property and found the lower end covered with "rich White oak" and the upper part "with Walnut of considerable size," but his further efforts to find a renter failed (*Diaries*, 4:14, 15–16). Ten years later, in May 1794, Washington's land agent, Robert Lewis, suggested that Washington exchange this tract for one on Bullskin Run near his other holdings. The tract on the Potomac remained in Washington's possession until his death, however. After he completed his will, Washington received a letter dated 24 Aug. 1799 from Isaac Weatherinton warning him that for twenty years poachers had been cutting trees on his property. On 20 Oct. 1799 Washington asked help from Weatherinton, who lived on adjoining property, to stop this practice.

6. Washington accepted in 1789 this tract of land on Back River, a branch of North River, in Gloucester County, at a valuation of £800 from John Dandridge in payment of a debt owed by the estate of his father, Bartholomew Dandridge, Martha Washington's brother. Washington's initial attempts to sell the 400-acre tract failed, but in April 1797 George Ball agreed to buy it for £800, to be paid in three equal installments. For GW's purchase of the tract and his unsuccessful attempts to sell it, see John Dandridge to GW, 27 Oct. 1788, and references in the source note of that document (*Papers, Presidential Series*, 1:75–77); for GW's sale of the tract to George Ball, see GW to Ball, 6 Mar. 1797, n.1 (*Papers, Retirement Series*, 1:7–9). In 1799 Washington made several efforts to get from Ball the payments due on the land, but to no avail (see GW to John Page and GW to Ball, both 17 Mar. 1799, and GW to Ball, 25 Sept. 1799).

7. In December 1764 the three managers of the Dismal Swamp Land Company, namely, Washington, his brother-in-law Fielding Lewis, and Dr. Thomas Walker, together bought, for £100, 1,119 acres of land near the swamp on the Norfolk-Suffolk road. In 1782, shortly after Fielding Lewis died, his son and the executor of his will, John Lewis, wrote to Washington about the disposing of the lands held jointly by Washington and his father. See Cash Accounts, December 1764, n.3 (*Papers, Colonial Series*, 7:342–43); see also John Lewis to GW,

24 Mar. 1782, and GW to John Lewis, 17 April 1782. At the end of the war, in January 1784, Thomas Walker consulted Washington about selling the Nansemond County tract near the Dismal Swamp, but it was decided no immediate attempt to sell the tract should be made. See Walker to GW, 24 Jan. 1784, and GW to Walker, 10 April 1784 (*Papers, Confederation Series*, 1:76–80, 281–83). In September 1797 Thomas Walker's son, Francis, as the executor of his father's will asked Washington whether he would be interested in purchasing his father's share in the Nansemond tract. Washington was not interested. See Francis Walker to GW, 28 Sept. 1797, and GW to Walker, 10 Oct. 1797 (*Papers, Retirement Series*, 1:376, 401–2).

8. When the Dismal Swamp Land Company was organized in November 1763 Washington as one of the organizers offered to help survey the 40,000 acres in the swamp granted to the company by the Virginia council. He became one of the three managers of the company and for the next few years took a leading role in its affairs. He also participated in the revival and reorganization of the company after the war in 1784. Henry Lee, Jr., in November 1795 bought Washington's interest in the Dismal Swamp Company for $20,000 to be paid in three annual payments. Despite all his efforts Lee was unable to keep up his payments, which led to the exchange of a number of letters between Lee and Washington in 1797 and 1798. See especially Dismal Swamp Land Company Articles of Agreement, 3 Nov. 1763, and notes, Thomas Walker to GW, 24 Jan. 1784, and notes, and GW to Henry Lee, Jr., 2 April 1797, n.1 (*Papers, Colonial Series*, 7:269–74; *Papers, Confederation Series*, 1:76–80; *Papers, Retirement Series*, 1:66–69).

9. In response to Washington's petition presented in December 1769 to the Virginia governor and council on behalf of the officers and men of the Virginia Regiment of 1754 asking for the distribution of the 200,000 acres promised them in Robert Dinwiddie's Proclamation of 1754, the council ordered the survey of 200,000 acres along the Great Kanawha and Ohio rivers. William Crawford made the survey in 1771, and the first distribution of the land came in November 1772. As a part of the acreage to which he was entitled, Washington secured three tracts on the Ohio, of 2,314 acres, 2,448 acres, and 4,395 acres. His fourth tract on the Ohio, the Round Bottom tract of 587 acres, he claimed in 1774 on military warrants purchased by him from veterans of the war with France, to whom the warrants were issued in 1773 under the terms of the royal Proclamation of 1763. Washington's claim to the Round Bottom tract continued to be disputed even after he finally secured the grant to it in October 1784. The documents relating to the distribution of western land under the terms of the proclamations of 1754 and 1763 are printed in *Papers, Colonial Series*, but for a summary account of Washington's acquisition of the four tracts on the Ohio River, see GW to Samuel Lewis, 1 Feb. 1784, source note, and GW to Thomas Lewis, 1 Feb. 1784, n.3 (*Papers, Confederation Series*, 1:91–100). Throughout the 1780s Washington sought to lease or sell his land on the Ohio and other western lands, without success. In March 1791 he sold both his Ohio and Great Kanawha lands to the Frenchman John Joseph de Barth. When Barth was unable to make the payments, the agreement was canceled early in 1793. In 1798 Washington leased the Round Bottom tract to Alexander McClean who was to make annual payments so as to complete the purchase of the tract for $5,870 within seven years. For references

to the attempts in the 1780s to lease or sell the Ohio and Kanawha tracts, see GW to John Witherspoon, 10 Mar. 1784, and its enclosed advertisement, GW to Thomas Freeman, 23 Sept. 1784, 16 Oct. 1785, Freeman to GW, 9 June 1785, GW to Henry L. Charton, 20 May 1786, GW to Henry Banks, 22 Nov. 1787, and GW to David Stuart, 15 Jan. 1788 (*Papers, Confederation Series,* 1:197–204, 2: 78–80, 3:43–47, 308–10, 4:63–66, 5:446–48, 6:41–45). For Washington's dealings with John de Barth, see GW to George Clendenin, 21 Mar. 1791, n.2 (*Papers, Presidential Series,* 7:609–10); for Washington's dealings with McClean, see McClean to GW, 2 July 1798, n.1, and GW to McClean, 6 Aug. 1798, n.1 (*Papers, Retirement Series,* 2:364–66, 492–94).

10. Between 1772 and 1774 Washington used military warrants to claim four tracts of land totaling 23,216 acres on either side of the Great Kanawha River up-river from near its mouth at the Ohio River. In the first distribution of land under the Proclamation of 1754 (see note 9), Washington was allotted 10,990 acres running for more than seventeen miles along the west, or north, bank of the river. In the second distribution, in November 1773, he received jointly with George Muse a patent for 7,276 acres on the river; he immediately made a trade with Muse whereby he established his claim to the entire tract. In 1774 he bought from Charles Mynn Thruston a military warrant for 2,000 acres issued to Thruston under the terms of the royal Proclamation of 1763 and used it to claim a 2,000-acre tract on the Great Kanawha at the mouth of the Coal (Cole) River. As part of the 5,000 acres that Washington was entitled to in his own right under the terms of the royal proclamation, he claimed, also in 1774, the 2,950-acre tract that ran for about six miles along the east, or south, bank of the Great Kanawha. For GW's dealings with George Muse regarding the 7,276-acre tract, see Agreement with George Muse, 3 Aug. 1770, and, especially, George Muse to GW, 3 Mar. 1784, n.1 (*Papers, Colonial Series,* 8:364; *Papers, Confederation Series,* 1:171–72). For GW's acquisition of the tracts of 10,990, 7,276, 2,010, and 2,950 acres on the Great Kanawha, see GW to Samuel Lewis, 1 Feb. 1784, source note and note 1 (ibid., 91–95). For references to GW's unsuccessful efforts to lease or sell his property on the Great Kanawha and Ohio rivers in the 1780s, see note 9. In December 1797 Washington leased his lands on the Kanawha to James Welch who agreed to make specified annual payments until the total reached $200,000 when the land would become his. See particularly GW to James Keith, 10 Dec. 1797 (*Papers, Retirement Series,* 1:512–14). Washington's most recent, and last, letter from Welch, who never paid anything, is dated 16 May 1799.

The Burning Springs tract, which is near present-day Charleston, W.Va., but is not on the Great Kanawha, Washington claimed as part of the 5,000 acres due him under the terms of the Proclamation of 1763. In 1775 Washington suggested to Gen. Andrew Lewis that he survey the tract for the two of them and that he and Lewis hold it jointly. Gov. Thomas Jefferson issued the grant to the two men on 14 July 1780. See GW to Samuel Lewis, 1 Feb. 1784, n.3 (*Papers, Confederation Series,* 1:91–95). Andrew Lewis's son Thomas sold the upper half of the tract in 1795. For reference to the litigation over this property after GW's death, see Cook, *Washington's Western Lands,* 66–68.

11. Washington acquired 600 (552½) acres of land in Charles County, Md., from Daniel Jenifer Adams in 1775 after Adams was unable to pay Washington for

the flour and herring that Washington sold or consigned to Adams in 1772 for sale in the West Indies. See GW to Daniel Jenifer Adams, 20 July 1772, and the references in note 1 of that document (*Papers, Colonial Series*, 9:69–71). George Dunnington was the tenant on the Charles County land when it came into Washington's possession and was still the tenant in 1799. For a number of years after the Revolution the owner of land adjacent to Washington's, John Stromatt, disputed the boundaries of Washington's property. See William Smallwood to GW, 6 April 1784, GW to William Craik, 19 Mar. 1789, n.1, and GW to Daniel Jenifer, Jr., 7 June 1797, n.2 (*Papers, Confederation Series*, 1:271–73; *Papers, Presidential Series*, 1:408–10; *Papers, Retirement Series*, 1:171–72).

12. In April 1794 Washington took possession of the 519-acre tract in Montgomery County, Md., which John Francis Mercer had assigned to him to complete the payment of the debt of the estate of his father, John Mercer, who died in 1768. The land was one half of Woodstock Manor which Mercer's wife, Sophia Sprigg Mercer, had inherited from her father, Richard Sprigg. The three tenants on the land continued to pay an annual rent of 1,500 pounds of tobacco. See Priscilla Beale to GW, 2 April 1797, source note (*Papers, Retirement Series*, 1: 59–60).

13. On Washington's instructions William Crawford bought in December 1770 from Lawrence Harrison for thirty guineas a tract of land of 234½ acres at Great Meadows in Pennsylvania. Harrison's son-in-law William Brooks in October 1771 confirmed the sale to Washington of "a Sartain Tract or Parsel of Land Lying and being in Bedford County in Pensilvania on Bradock's road and Known by the name of they great Medows whare Colo. Washington had a batle with the frinch and Indians in they year one thousand seven Hundred and fifty four." See William Crawford to GW, 15 April 1771, nn.2 and 3 (*Papers, Colonial Series*, 8: 445–46). It was Washington's surrender of Fort Necessity at Great Meadows to the French on 3 July 1754 that first made the name of the 22-year-old officer known outside Virginia. After the Revolution, discovering that his Great Meadows tract was unoccupied, Washington in July 1784 advertised it for lease. See GW to John Lewis, 14 Feb. 1784, and GW to Thomas Richardson, 5 July 1784 (*Papers, Confederation Series*, 1:123–24, 485–86). The tract of unimproved meadowland had a house on it in the 1780s, and Washington thought its location made it a good site for an inn. He succeeded in renting it only briefly in the 1780s, however, and his attempt to sell it in 1794 came to nothing. See Thomas Freeman to GW, 9 July 1785, n.3 (ibid., 3:43–47); see also Land Memorandum, 25 May 1794, and GW to Presley Neville, 16 June 1794 (Fitzpatrick, *Writings*, 33:376–80, 405–9).

14. In November 1784 Gov. George Clinton of New York informed Washington that he had bought from Marinus Willett for the two of them 6,071 acres of land on the Mohawk River for £1,062.5. The land was in "Coxeborough & Carolana" townships in Montgomery County, New York. Washington was not able to pay Clinton his half of the purchase price until 1787. Clinton, who was empowered to sell parcels of the land for the mutual benefit of the co-owners, had by 1793 sold more than four thousand acres for a total of £3,400.2, New York currency. See GW to George Clinton, 25 Nov. 1784, n.2 (*Papers, Confederation Series*, 2:145–49).

15. When writing Winthrop Sargent in January 1798 about a challenge to his

title to lands held by him on the Ohio River, Washington reported that he owned 3,051 acres on the Little Miami River just above the Ohio in the Northwest Territory. His holdings were composed of three tracts, of 839 acres, 977 acres, and 1,235 acres, held under a patent from Gov. Beverley Randolph of Virginia, dated 1 Dec. 1790. Washington secured by purchase in February 1774 the warrant of survey for 3,000 acres allotted under the royal Proclamation of 1763 to Capt. John Rootes who had served in 1758 in Col. William Byrd's 2d Virginia Regiment. Washington did not have the tract surveyed until 1788 and granted to him in 1790. See GW to Winthrop Sargent, 27 Jan. 1798, GW to Thomas Lewis, 1 Feb. 1784, n.5, and Thomas Marshall to GW, 19 May 1786 (*Papers, Retirement Series*, 2: 53–54; *Papers, Confederation Series*, 1:95–100, 2:61–62). It may be that a second military warrant, one for 100 acres issued to a man named Thomas Cope, was used to claim for Washington 51 acres in addition to the 3,000 acres that Washington claimed under Rootes's warrant (Prussing, *Estate of George Washington*, 312–13).

16. In December 1788 Washington agreed to give to Henry (Light-Horse Harry) Lee the noted Arabian horse Magnolio in exchange for two tracts of land totaling 5,000 acres on Rough Creek in Kentucky. Washington's friend Alexander Spotswood gave up his conflicting claim to the land in 1796. For Washington's purchase of the land and for references to his correspondence regarding it beginning in 1795, see Spotswood to GW, 22 Mar. 1797, n.1 (*Papers, Retirement Series*, 1:43–44). Washington made no attempt to develop or to rent or sell this land.

17. In September 1798 Washington bought two lots in square 634 just to the north of the new Capitol in the Federal City. He paid the District of Columbia commissioners $178.57, one-third the cost of lot no. 16, and paid Daniel Carroll of Duddington $428.40 for the adjacent lot no. 6. For a description of these lots, see Alexander White to GW, 8 Sept. 1798 (*Papers, Retirement Series*, 2:594–96). With the help of William Thornton, Washington contracted with George Blagdin to build under Thornton's general supervision two three-story connected houses on these lots. Work began on their construction in the fall of 1798, and when Washington inspected the houses in November 1799 they were near completion. In this and the preceding volume of the *Retirement Series*, there is a great deal of correspondence with Thornton and Blagdin regarding the houses. See also particularly GW to District of Columbia Commissioners, 28 Sept. 1798, n.2.

18. Washington bought the four lots, the "Water lots" numbers 5, 12, 13, and 14, in square 667 to the south of the Capitol from the District of Columbia commissioners on 18 Sept. 1793 (Ledger C, 21). The lots were initially sold in June 1803 for a total of $1,725.05. For legal reasons the sale did not go through, and they were sold again in 1817 for a total of $527.93½ (Prussing, *Estate of George Washington*, 251–59).

19. Washington bought lot no. 112 at Prince and Pitt streets in Alexandria in 1764 from John Alexander, Jr., for £38. See note 1 to Washington's will. In July 1797 Washington announced in the Alexandria *Gazette* that he was dividing his half-acre lot into "convenient building squares," nine or ten in number. In August 1798 he leased two of these building squares, or lots. See John Fitzgerald to GW, 12 June 1797, n.1 (*Papers, Retirement Series*, 1:181–82).

20. Washington obtained grants to two lots in Winchester in Frederick County

in May 1753. He seems to have paid them little or no attention until 1785 when he asked his rental agent Battaile Muse about them. He learned that Dr. Robert Mackay had enclosed the smaller lot in town and incorporated a part of it in his garden. Mackay apparently continued to make use of both lots, and on 19 Aug. 1794 Washington's new rental agent Robert Lewis reported that Mackay had agreed to pay fifty shillings a year for their use. See GW to Battaile Muse, 28 July 1785, and Muse to GW, 6, 14 Sept. 1785 (*Papers, Confederation Series*, 3:159–62, 233–35, 248–49).

21. Fielding Lewis in 1777 bought for Washington two lots in the town of Bath, also known as Warm Springs and later Berkeley Springs, for £100 Virginia currency. Washington visited Bath in September 1784 and engaged James Rumsey to build on the lots a dwelling house, kitchen, and stable. Rumsey completed building in the summer of 1786 a kitchen and stable, made of logs and measuring 17 by 19 feet, and he made a beginning on the dwelling house. Washington paid Rumsey a total of £73.1.4, making his first payment in October 1786 (Ledger B, 210). Jean Le Mayeur, Washington's French dentist, lived at Washington's place in Bath in 1786, and Washington gave Robert Hanson Harrison permission to use his houses in Bath on his visit there in July 1788. See James Rumsey to GW, 10 Mar. 1785, 24 June 1785, GW to Rumsey, 5 June 1785, George Lewis to GW, 25 Aug. 1786, and GW to Robert Hanson Harrison, 28 July 1788 (*Papers, Confederation Series*, 2:425–29, 3:82–83, 40–42, 4:228–29, 6:403–4); see also *Diaries*, 4:10–11, 13. At Washington's prompting, his rental agent Robert Lewis found a tenant in the summer of 1794 who agreed to keep up the property in return for having the use of it. See GW to Robert Lewis, 16 Mar. 1794, 18 May 1794, and Lewis to GW, 19 Aug. 1794.

22. In May 1797 Washington authorized his Philadelphia agent Clement Biddle to receive the interest on his 3 and 6 percent stock held in the Bank of the United States in Philadelphia. A year later he instructed Biddle to sell his 6 percent stock amounting to $3,494.31, which Washington intended to lend to the Potomac River Company. See GW to Biddle, 28 May 1798, and the references in note 1 of that document (*Papers, Retirement Series*, 2:301).

23. In the first subscription for the Potomac River Company, which was taken when it was established in 1784, Washington bought five shares for £100 each. Washington, who was the very active president of the company until 1789, learned in early 1796 that the new president of the company, Tobias Lear, had bought twenty shares to bolster confidence in the company. In April 1796 Washington bought three of Lear's shares, and in May 1797 he bought fifteen more from Lear, who was in bad financial condition. Washington says here in his listing of property that he owned twenty-four shares in the Potomac River Company; but only twenty-three shares, the five he subscribed to in 1784, and the eighteen he bought from Lear in 1796 and 1797, are listed in his Ledger C. See the references in William Hartshorne to GW, 24 May 1797, n.1 (*Papers, Retirement Series*, 1:153). For reference to the fifty shares in the Potomac River Company awarded to GW by the Virginia assembly, which he set aside for a national university, see note 6 to Washington's Last Will and Testament.

24. When the James River Company was established in January 1785 along with the Potomac River Company, the Virginia legislature gave Washington stock

in both companies, and both companies subsequently elected him president. Washington declined to act as president of the James River Company. For GW's disposition of the one hundred shares in the James River Company bestowed on him by the Virginia legislature, see note 5 to his will. Washington bought five shares in the James River Company for $500 in 1786. See Edmund Randolph to GW, 2 Mar. 1786, and John Hopkins to GW, 1 May 1786 (*Papers, Confederation Series*, 3:579–82, 4:31–32).

25. Washington's account with the Bank of Alexandria in his Ledger C indicates that Tobias Lear bought for Washington five shares in the bank for $200 each on 28 May 1795 and ten shares for $197 each on 10 Oct. 1795, and that his farm manager William Pearce bought for him ten shares for $200 each also on 28 May 1795. See also Lear to GW, 26–27 May 1795. On 2 June 1795 Lear bought for Washington one hundred shares in the Bank of Columbia in Georgetown for $40 a share. See GW to Samuel Hanson, 23 July 1797, n.1, and references (*Papers, Retirement Series*, 1:267–68). In February 1797 Henry Lee arranged for the transfer to Washington of seventy shares in the Bank of Columbia valued at $2,800 in partial payment of the amount due on his purchase of Washington's interest in the Dismal Swamp Land Company. See GW to Henry Lee, Jr., 2 April 1797, n.1 (ibid., 66–69), and the subsequent correspondence in 1797 with Reed & Forde and with Gustavus Scott. For GW's gift of Columbia Bank stock to the Alexandria Academy, see note 4 to Washington's Last Will and Testament.

Washington's Slave List

Editorial Note

[June 1799]

The list of Mount Vernon slaves which GW drew up, probably some time in June 1799, included those slaves owned by him outright, those who were controlled by him as part of Martha Washington's dowry, and a number who were rented by him in 1786 by contract with Mrs. Penelope French at the time he acquired her life rights to land that she owned on Dogue Run.

The slaves Washington owned in his own right came from several sources. He was left eleven slaves by his father's will; a portion of his half brother Lawrence Washington's slaves, about a dozen in all, were willed to him after the death of Lawrence's infant daughter and his widow; and Washington purchased from time to time slaves for himself, mostly before the Revolution.

Washington also hired for varying periods of time individual slaves, usually skilled artisans, from neighbors and acquaintances. These do not appear on this slave list.

Only one other complete roll of the slaves at Mount Vernon has been found. In February 1786 Washington recorded in his diary all the

Mount Vernon slaves, dower and personal, the farms on which they lived, and their jobs. The total at that time came to 216; it did not include Mrs. French's slaves, the use of whom Washington acquired later in the year.

There are also in the Washington Papers at the Library of Congress Washington's lists of his tithables in Truro and Fairfax parishes (where Mount Vernon lies) for every year from 1760 through 1774. These have been printed in the *Papers, Colonial Series*. These lists name slaves living at Mount Vernon but do not include children under the age of sixteen and a few elderly slaves who were not tithed. The lists of tithables also include the names of indentured white servants and other whites living on the farms, including GW's overseers and managers. For further information on GW's slaves, see Charles Lee to GW, 13 Sept. 1786, and especially note 4 to that document, GW to William Triplett, 25 Sept. 1786, and notes 3 and 5 (*Papers, Confederation Series*, 4:247–49, 268–74), Memorandum: Division of Slaves [1762] and note to that document (*Papers, Colonial Series*, 7:172–74), Division of Slaves, 10 Dec. 1754 (ibid., 1:227–31), and *Diaries*, 4:277–83.

Negros Belonging to George Washington in his own right and by Marriage

GW

TRADESMEN &CA

Names		ages		Remarks		
Nat	Smith		His Wife	Lucy	D[ogue] R[un]	dow[e]r
George	Ditto		Ditto	Lydia	R[iver] F[arm]	Ditto
Isaac	Carp[ente]r			Kitty	Dairy	Ditto
James	Ditto	40		Darcus	Muddy Hole	GW
Sambo	Ditto			Agnes	R.F.	dowr
Davy	Ditto			Edy	U[nion] F[arm]	GW
Joe	Ditto			Dolshy	Spin[ne]r	dowr
Tom	Coop[e]r			Nanny	Muddy Hole	GW
Moses	Ditto		No Wife			
Jacob	Ditto		Ditto			
George	Gard[ene]r		His wife	Sall	D.R.	dowr
Harry	Ditto		No wife			
Boatswain	Ditc[her]		His wife	Myrtilla	Spinr	GW
Dundee	Ditto		His wife	at Mr Lears		
Charles	Ditto		Ditto	Fanny	U.F.	dowr
Ben	Ditto		Ditto	Penny	R.F.	GW
Ben	Miller		Ditto	Sinah	Mn Ho.	dow.
Forrester	Ditto		No Wife			

GW
TRADESMEN &CA (*continued*)

Names		ages		Remarks			
Nathan	Cook	31	Wife	Peg		Muddy Hole	GW
W. Muclus	B[rick] Lay[e]r		Ditto	Captn Marshalls[1]			
Juba	Carter		No wife				
Matilda	Spinner		Boson	Ditcher			
Frank	Ho[use] Servt		Wife	Lucy—Cook			
Will	Shoem[ake]r		Lame—no wife[2]				

amount 24

MANSION HOUSE
Passed Labour

Names		ages		Remarks			
Frank		80	No Wife				
Gunner		90	Wife	Judy		R.F.	GW
Sam	Cook	40	Ditto	Alce		Muddy Hole	Ditto

amount 3

Trades &ca not engagd in Cropping 24

Total 2[7] not cultivators of the Soil[3]

DOWER
TRADESMEN &CA

Names		ages		Remarks			
Tom Davis	B: layr		Wife	at Mr Lear's			
Simms	Carpr		Ditto	Daphne—French's			
Cyrus	Post[ilio]n		Ditto	Lucy		R.F.	GW
Wilson	Ditto	15	no wife				
Godfrey	Cartr		Wife	Mima		Mn. Ho.	dowr
James	Ditto		Ditto	Alla		Ditto	ditto
Hanson	Dist[ille]r		No wife				
Peter	Ditto		Ditto				
Nat	Ditto		Ditto				
Daniel	Ditto		Ditto				
Timothy	Ditto						
Sla[min] Joe	Ditchr		Wife	Sylla		D.R.	GW
Chriss	Ho. Ser:		Ditto	Majr Wests[4]			
Marcus	Ditto		no Wife				
Lucy	Cook		Husband	Ho[use] Frank			GW
Molly			No Husband[5]				
Charlotte	Sempst[res]s		No husband				
Sall	Ho[use] M[ai]d		Ditto				
Caroline	Ditto		Husb[an]d	Peter Hardman			
Kitty	Milk Md		Ditto	Isaa.		Carpr	GW
Alce	Spinr		Charles	Freeman			

DOWER

TRADESMEN &CA (*continued*)

Names		ages	Remarks			
Betty Davis	Ditto		Mrs Washington's—Dick[6]			
Dolshy			Husbd	Joe	Carpr	GW
Anna			Ditto	liv[in]g at George Town		
Judy		21	No Husband			
Delphy			Ditto	ditto		
Peter lame	Kn[i]tt[e]r		No wife			
Alla	Ditto		Husbd	James	Cartr	dower
			amount 28			

MANSION HOUSE

Will			Wife	Aggy	D.R.	GW
Joe	Postiln		Ditto	Sall	R.F.	Ditto
Mike			No wife—son to Lucy			
Sinah			Husbd	Miller	Ben	GW
Mima			Ditto	Godfrey	Wag[one]r	dowr
Lucy			No Husband			
Grace			Husbd	Mr Lear's Juba		
Letty			No husband			
Nancy			Ditto	ditto		
Viner			Ditto	ditto		
Eve		17	Ditto	a dwarf		
Delia		14	Ditto	her sister		

Children

Phil			Son	to Lucy	
Patty			daughter	to Ditto	
Rachel		12	Daughr	to Caroline	
Jemima		9	Ditto	Ditto	
Leanthe		8	Ditto	Ditto	
Polly		6	Ditto	Ditto	
Peter—B.		4	Son	Ditto	
Emery			Son	to Alce	
Tom			Ditto	Ditto	
Charles			Ditto	Ditto	
Henriette			Daughr	Ditto	
Barbara		10	Ditto	to Kitty	
Levina		6	Ditto	Ditto	
Elvey			Ditto	to Charlotte	
Jenny			Ditto	Ditto	
Eliza			Ditto	Ditto	
Nancy		9	Ditto	to Betty D[avis]	
Oney		6	Ditto	Ditto	
Lucinda		2	Ditto	Ditto	

DOWER
MANSION HOUSE (*continued*)

Names	ages		Remarks
Daniel	6	Son	to Anna
Anna	4	daugh.	Ditto
Sandy	1½	Son	Ditto
Sucky	5	daughr	to Dolshy
Dennis	2 mo.	Son	Ditto
John		Ditto	to Mima
Randolph		Ditto	Ditto
Nancy		daughr	to Sinah
Burwell		Son	to Lucy
		Passed labour	
Doll		No husband	
Jenny		Ditto	Ditto

Old	2	
Workers	12	
Children	28	
Amount	42	Mansion House
House Serts Spinners &ca &ca	28	
Total	70	Not employed in the Crops &ca

Geo: Washington	2[7]	
Dower	70	
In all	9[7]	not employed in the Crops

GW
MUDDY HOLE F[ARM]

Names	age		Remarks		
Gabriel	30	Wife	Judy	D.R.	GW
Uriah	24				
Moses	19	Son	to Darcus		GW
Kate	old	Husbd	Will	Muddy Hole	dowr
Nanny	ditto	Ditto	Tom—Cooper		GW
Sacky	40	No Husband			
Darcus	36	Husbd	James—Carpr		GW
Peg	34	Ditto	Nathan—C[oo]k		GW
Alce	38	Ditto	Sam ditto		GW
Amie	30	No Husband			
Nancy	28	Husbd	Abram		French
Molly	26	No Husband			
Virgin	24	Husbd	Gabl		Mr Lear
Letty	19	No husband			
Kate long	18	daughr of Kate			
Kate sht	18	Ditto	Alce	Muddy Hole	

GW
MUDDY HOLE F[ARM] (*continued*)

Names	age		Remarks
Isbel	16	Ditto	Sarah—dead
Townshend	14	Son	to Darcus
			Children
Alce	8	Daughr	to Darcus
Nancy	2	Ditto	ditto
Lucy	11	Daughr	to Peg
Diana	8	Ditto	ditto
Alexander	3	Son	ditto
Darcus	1	Daughr	ditto
Oliver	11	Son	to Nancy
Siss	8	Daughr	ditto
Martin	1	Son	ditto
George	8	Ditto	to Alce
Adam	7	Ditto	ditto
Cecelia	2	Daughr	ditto
Sylvia	10	Ditto	to Molly
James	7	Son	ditto
Rainey	8	Daughr	to Amie
Urinah	2	Ditto	ditto
Billy	2	Son	to Letty
Henry	1	Ditto	ditto

Workers 18
Children 18   together 36

DOWER
MUDDY HOLE F[ARM]

Names	age		Remarks		
Davy—Ov[ersee]r	56	Wife	Molly	Muddy Hole	dowr
Will—Mink	60	Ditto	Kate	ditto	GW
Molly	76	Husband	Davy—Ovr		
Patience	14	Daughtr	Dolly	U. Farm	
Mary	11	Ditto	Betty	ditto	

Workers 3
Does nothing 1
Young 1   In all 5
Altogether at this Farm 41.

GW
RIVER FARM

Names	age	Remarks			
Robin	80	nearly passed labr			
Natt	55	Wife	Doll	R.F.	dowr

GW
RIVER FARM (*continued*)

Names	age	Remarks			
Ned	56	Ditto	Hanh	ditto	ditto
Ben—Cartr	22				
Peg	56	Husbd	old Ben	R.F.	dowr
Judy	55	Ditto	Gunna		GW
Cloe	55	No husband			
Suckey	50	Ditto	ditto		
Suckey—Bay	46	husbd	belongg to Adans[7]		
Sall	30	Ditto	Postn Joe		dowr
Rose	28	No husband			
Penny	20	Husbd	Ben Hubd		GW
Lucy	18	Ditto	Cyrus Post[ilio]n		dowr
Hannah	12	daughr	Daphne dead		
Daniel	15	Son	to Suckey	R.F.	
Henry	11	Son	to Sall	ditto	
Nancy	11	daugh.	to Bay Suke	ditto	

Children

Names	age	Remarks			
Elijah	7	Son	to Sall	R.F.	
Dennis	5	Ditto	Ditto	ditto	
Gutridge	3	Ditto	Ditto	ditto	
Polly	1	daughr	Ditto	ditto	
Hagar	6	Ditto	to Rose	ditto	
Simon	4	Son	Ditto	ditto	
Tom	2	Ditto	Ditto	ditto	
Joe	1	Ditto	Ditto	ditto	
Nancy	4	Daughr	to Bay Suke	ditto	

Passed labour

Names	age	Remarks			
Ruth	70	husbd	Breechy	dowr	

Workers	17		
Children	9		
Passed labr	1	together	27

DOWER
RIVER FARM

Names	age	Remarks			
Ben	70	Nearly done	Peg for wife		
Breechy	60	not better	Ruth his wife		
Johny	39	Wife	Esther	R.F.	dowr
Richmond	20	No Wife			
Ned	20				
Heuky	17	Son	to Agnes	R.F.	
Jack	22				
Esther	40	Husbd	Johny	Ditto	
Doll	58	Husbd	Natt	R.F.	GW

DOWER
RIVER FARM (*continued*)

Names	age		Remarks		
Lydia	50	Ditto	Smith Geo:		GW
Agnes	36	Ditto	Sambo—Car[pente]r		GW
Alce	26	Ditto	Lears John		
Fanny	30	Ditto	Alexanders[8]		
Betty	20	Ditto	Lears Reuben		
Doll	16	No husbd	Daugh. to Doll		
Cecelia	14	No husbd	Ditto to Agnes		
Jack	12	Son	to Doll		
Anderson	11	Ditto	to Agnes		
Lydia	11	Daughr	to Lydia		

Children

Names	age		Remarks		
Ralph	9	Son	to Sall	R.F.	
Charity	2	Daughr	Ditto	Ditto	
Charles	1	Son	Ditto	Ditto	
Davy	6				
Lewis	4	Cornelia's Childn dece[ase]d dow.			
Alce	2				
Suckey	4	Daughtr	to Alce	R.F.	
Jude	1	Ditto	Ditto	ditto	
Milley	1	Daughr	to Betty	ditto	
Peter	9	Son	to Doll	ditto	
Hannah	old	Cooks—Husbd Ned		ditto	

Workers 19
Children 10
Cook 1 making 30
Altogether at this Farm 57.

GW
DOGUE RUN FARM

Names	age		Remarks		
Ben	57	Wife	Peg	D.R.	Dowr
Long Jack	60	Wife	Molly	Ditto	GW
Dick	46	Ditto	Charity	Ditto	Ditto
Carter Jack	40	Ditto	Grace	Ditto	Dowr
Simon	20	No Wife			
Lawrence	14	Son	to Matilda		GW
Judy—blind	50	Husbd	Gabriel	Muddy Hole	GW
Molly—Cook	45	Ditto	long Jack	D.R.	GW
Charity	42	Ditto	Dick	Ditto	Ditto
Priscilla	36	Ditto	Slamin Joe		Dowr
Linney	27	No husband			

GW
DOGUE RUN FARM (*continued*)

Names	age		Remarks		
Agnes	25	Husbd	Will	Mann Ho.	Dowr
Sarah	20	No Husband			
Betty	16	Ditto Ditto			
Sophia	14	Ditto Ditto	Siller's daughr		
Savary	13	daughr	to Siller	D.R.	

Children

Names	age		Remarks		
Penny	11	Ditto	Ditto	ditto	
Israel	10	Son	Ditto	ditto	
Isrias	3	Ditto	ditto		
Christopher	1	Son	Ditto	ditto	
Fomison	11	Daughr	to Charity	ditto	
Dick	3	Ditto	Ditto	ditto	
Bartley	6	Ditto	to Linney	ditto	
Matilda	1	Daughr	Ditto	ditto	
Lucy	2	Ditto	to Sarah	ditto	
Guy	2	Son	to Agnes	ditto	

Passed labour

Names	age		Remarks
Hannah	60	No Husbd partly an ideot	

Workers	16	
Children	10	
Pass'd labr	1	together 27

DOWER
DOGUE RUN FARM

Names	ages		Remarks		
Lucy	50	Husbd	Smith Natt		GW
Sall Twine	38	Ditto	Gardr George		GW
Grace	35	Ditto	Cartr Jack		GW
Peg	30	Ditto	Ben	D.R.	GW
Kate	18	Ditto	a Negro of Moreton's[9]		
Ned	14	Son	to Lucy	D.R.	

Children

Names	ages		Remarks	
Teney	10	Daughr	to Lucy	D.R.
Barbary	11	Daughr	to Sall T.	D.R.
Abbay	10	Ditto	Ditto	Ditto
Hannah	4	Ditto	Ditto	Ditto
George	1	Son	Ditto	Ditto
Roger	10	Ditto	to Grace	D.R.
Molly	6	Daugr	Ditto	ditto
Jenny	3	Ditto	Ditto	ditto

DOWER
DOGUE RUN FARM (*continued*)

Names	ages		Remarks	
Billy	6	Son	to Peg	ditto
Fendal	2	Ditto	Ditto	ditto
Peg	8 Mo.	Daughr	Ditto	ditto

Passed labour

Sue	70	No Husband	

Workers 6
Children 11
Pass'd labr 1   Making 18
Whole amt at this Farm 45

GW
UNION FARM

Names	ages		Remarks		
London	64	No wife		
Joe	24			
Edy	26	Husbd	Davy—Carp[ente]r		GW

Children

Sarah	6	Daughr	to Edy
Nancy	1	Ditto	ditto

Passed labr

Flora	64	No Husband

Workers 3
Children 2
Pass'd labr 1   Making 6

DOWER
UNION FARM

Names	ages		Remarks	
Sam Kitt	78	Wife	at Danl Sto⟨n⟩es [10]	
Cæsar	50	No Wife		
Paul	36	Ditto	Ditto	
John	16	Son	to Betty	U.F.
Betty	62	No husbd	Cooks	
Lucy	50	Husbd	at Cap. Marshalls	
Fanny	36	Ditto	Charles—Ditchr	
Jenny	34	Ditto	Mrs Washns George	
Rachell	34	No Husband		
Milly	22	Ditto	Ditto	
Lucretia	20	Ditto	Ditto	
Gideon	13	Son	to Betty	

DOWER
UNION FARM (*continued*)

Names	ages		Remarks	
Jamie	11	Ditto	to Fanny	
Ephraim	11	Ditto	to Rachel	

Children

Davy	8	Ditto	Ditto	
Guss	3	Ditto	Ditto	
Beck	4	Daughr	Ditto	
Eneas	1	Son	Ditto	
Elizabeth	9	Daughr		to Doll
Suckey	11	Ditto	at Mrs W.	Ditto
Elias	2 Mo.	Son		Ditto
Daphne	5	Daughr	to Fanny	
Charles	1	Son	Ditto	
Felicia	7	Daughr	to Jenny	
Jonathan	3	Son	to Ditto	
Hellam	1	Ditto	Ditto	
Diana	1	Daughr	to Milly	
Jesse	6	Son	to Patt dead	

Passed labour

Daphne	70	No Husband
Doll	52	Lame & pretds to be so

Workers 14
Children 14
Non-Workrs 2 Making 30
Whole amount at this Farm exclusive of French's Neg[roe]s 36

RECAPITULATION

Where & how Empld	Belonging to GW							Dower							Grand Total
	Men	Womn	Workg boys	Workg girls	Childn boys	Childn girls	Total	Men	Womn	Workg boys	Workg girls	Childn boys	Childn girls	Total	
Tradesmen & others, not employed on the Farms—viz.															
Smiths	2						2								2
Bricklayers	1						1	1						1	2
Carpenters	5						5	1						1	6
Coopers	3						3								3
Shoemaker	1						1								1
Cooks	1						1		1					1	2
Gardeners	2						2								2
Millers	1		1				2								2
House-Servants	1						1	2	4					6	7
Ditchers	4						4	1						1	5
Distillery								4		1				5	5
Postilions								1		1				2	2
Waggoners & Cartrs	1						1	2						2	3

						Total							Total	Grand Total
Milk Maid													1	1
Spinners & Knitrs	1					1							8	9
Mansion-Ho.						36							46	82
Muddy-hole				8	10	26							14	40
River-Farm				6	4	24							30	54
Dogue Run F.				7	3	23							18	41
Union-Farm					2	5							27	32
	36	32	4	3	21	19 **115**		28	42	11	5	26	32 **144**	259

Passed labr or that do not Work

						Total							Total	Grand Total
Muddy hole						2							1	1
River Farm						3							2	4
Dogue Run						1							1	4
Union Farm						3							3	4
Mansion Ho.													2	5
						9							9	18
Hired fm Mrs. French	37	9	2	4	6	40	40	29	50	11	5	26	40 **153**	277 / 40
Grand Total	49	36	6	7	27	29 **164**		29	50	11	5	26	32 **153**	317

A LIST OF NEGROS HIRED FROM MRS FRENCH

Names	Ages	Remarks			
Will	Old but hearty	Looks after the Stock	Wife at Mrs French's[11]		
Abram	in his prime	Wife	at Muddy hole	Nancy	
Paschall	Ditto	No wife	lately lost	Cornelia	M.H.
Tom	Ditto 28	No wife	getting Blind		
Isaac	Ditto 29	Ditto	lives at Muddy hole Farm		
Moses	Ditto 26	Plowman & Carter			
James	24	At the Distillery			
Julius	23	Carter[12]			
Spencer	20	Ditto and Mower[13]			
Sabine	60	Husband[14]			
Lucy	55	Ditto	McCarty's George	a Knitter[15]	
Daphne	40	Ditto	Simms Carpenter	Plougher[16]	
Delia	35	No Husband		Spinner[17]	
Grace	28	Husband	Mrs Washns Davy	Plougher[18]	
Siss	25	Ditto	Ditto Jack	Ditto[19]	
Milly	18	No Husband[20]			
Nancy	16	Ditto[21]			
Hannah	14	Ditto[22]			
Daniel	16	Son	of Delia's		
Isaac	14	Ditto	of Rose	deceased	
Matilda	13	Daughr	of Daphne		
Betty	13	Ditto	Delia		
Briney	12	Ditto	Lucy		
Grace	12	Ditto	Rose	deceased	

Children

Names	Ages	Remarks	
Stately	10	Son	of Lucy's
Renney	6	Daughr	Ditto
Raison	3	Ditto	Ditto
Morgan	2	Son	Ditto
Phœnix	1	Ditto	Ditto
Polly	9	Daughr	of Daphne's
Maria	2	Ditto	Ditto
Jack	7	Son	of Delia
Julia	4	Daugh.	Ditto
Nelly	2	Ditto	Ditto
Ambrose	1	Son	Ditto
Bob	10	Ditto	of Grace
Sall	8	Daugh.	Ditto
Judy	4	Ditto	Ditto
Augusta	1	Ditto	Ditto
Nancy	10	Ditto	of Sabine

Men	9
Women	9
Workg Boy's & Girls	6
Children	16 In all 40

AD, ViMtV. The format of the document has been changed somewhat in order to fit easily on the pages. The slave list for Union farm has been moved to its proper place in the document; Washington wrote at the top of the Recapitulation page: "Union Farm ought to have been entered in this place; but by mistake, was carrd to the other side." Abbreviations and contractions have been silently expanded when necessary for sake of clarity. A somewhat different list of only Mrs. French's slaves was enclosed in Washington's letter to Benjamin Dulany of 15 July 1799 (ALS [letterpress copy], NN: Washington Papers).

1. Capt. Thomas Hanson Marshall (1731–1801) lived at Marshall Hall, just across the Potomac River from Mount Vernon, in Charles County, Maryland.

2. Will was Washington's old mulatto body servant Billy, or William Lee, who had served with him throughout the Revolution. See note 3 to Washington's Last Will and Testament, printed above.

3. Washington had a total "26" here because of a mistake in bringing a figure from the previous page. The mistake was repeated in his summing up of Mansion House and Tradesmen.

4. Christopher was Washington's current body servant who was with him at his death. His wife was either a slave or a free black woman living at Roger West's. See note 11 to Tobias Lear's Narrative Accounts of the Death of George Washington, printed below.

5. Molly, Charlotte, and Caroline—all listed here among the dower slaves—were in Washington's room when he died. See Tobias Lear's Narrative Accounts of the Death of George Washington, printed below.

6. Mrs. Washington was Elizabeth Foote Washington, widow of Washington's old manager and cousin Lund Washington, who lived at Hayfield, northwest of Mount Vernon. Several other Mount Vernon servants were married to slaves at Hayfield.

7. "Adans" was probably Abednego Adams (1721–1809), Washington's closest neighbor, who lived on Little Hunting Creek.

8. This may be one of Robert Alexander's (d. 1793) sons. Alexander had lived on a plantation upriver from Mount Vernon.

9. Moreton was probably Archibald Moreton who lived near Belvoir on the road from Washington's mill to Boggess's house.

10. This may be Daniel Stone who lived in Truro Parish on the road from Washington's mill to Robert Boggess's.

11. Penelope Manley French lived at Rose Hill, on the back road to Alexandria.

12. The slave list at NN, which was enclosed in GW's letter to Benjamin Dulany of 15 July 1799, describes Julius as "A very good Carter, and can do any other work, although defective in Shape from his Infancy."

13. The slave list at NN describes him as "A good Carter and Mower and able at any business."

14. The slave list at NN calls her "A good working woman, notwithstanding her ⟨age⟩."

15. Daniel McCarty, Jr. (1759–1801), lived at Cedar Grove on Pohick Bay. The slave list at NN describes Lucy as "Lame, or pretends to be so occasioned by rheumatic pains, but is a good knitter, & so employed."

16. The slave list at NN claims she "Ploughs very Well, and is a good hand at any work."

17. The slave list at NN describes her as "Equally good at the Spinn⟨ing Wheel⟩ or Hoe, but has been kept chiefly at the ⟨farm⟩."

18. The slave list at NN calls her "A very good Plougher—and equally so at all sorts of Work."

19. The slave list at NN claims she "Ploughs Well—and can Milk & Churn."

20. The slave list at NN describes her as "A full grown Woman, and ⟨*illegible*⟩ly; has been used to Common work only."

21. The slave list at NN describes her as "The same—in all respects."

22. The slave list at NN claims she is "nearly at her full growth and a woman in appear[anc]e."

Tobias Lear's Narrative Accounts
of the Death of George Washington

I
The Journal Account

[Mount Vernon, 15 Dec. 1799]

The following circumstantial account of the last illness and death of General Washington was noted by T. Lear, on Sunday following his death, which happened on Saturday Eveng Decr 14th 1799 between the hours of ten and eleven.

On Thursday Decr 12th the General rode out to his farms about ten o'clock, and did not return home till past 3 oclk. Soon after he went out, the weather became very bad, rain hail and snow falling alternately, with a cold wind.[1] When he came in I carried some letters to him, to frank, intending to send them to the Post Office in the evening.[2] He franked the letters; but said the weather was too bad to send a Servant up to the Office that evening. I observed to him that I was afraid he had got wet, he said no, his great coat had kept him dry; but his neck appeard to be wet, and the snow was hanging on his hair. He came to dinner without changing his dress. In the Evening he appeard as well as usual.

A heavy fall of snow took place on friday, which prevented the General from riding out as usual. He had taken cold (undoubtedly from being so much exposed the day before) and complained of having a sore throat[3]—he had a hoarseness, which increased in the evening; but he made light of it, as he would never take anything to carry off a cold; always observing, "let it go as it came." In the evening, the papers having come from the post Office, he sat in the room, with Mrs Washington and myself, reading them, 'till about nine o'clock, and, when he met with anything which he thought diverting or interesting, he would read it aloud. He desired me to read to him the debates of the Virginia Assembly, on the election of a Senator and Governor; which I did.[4] On his retiring to bed, he appeared to be in perfect health, excepting the cold before mentiond, which he considerd as triffling, and had been remarkably chearful all the evening.

About two or three o'clk Saturday Morning he awoke Mrs Washington & told her he was very unwell, and had had an ague. She observed that he could scarcely speak, and breathed with difficulty—and would have got up to call a servant; but he would not permit her lest she should take cold. As soon as the day appeared, the Woman (Caroline) went into the Room to make a fire & he desired that Mr Rawlins, one of the Overseers who was used to bleeding the people, might be sent for to bleed him before the Docter could arrive—And the Woman (Caroline) came to my room requesting I might go to the General, who was very ill.[5] I got up[,] put on my Cloths as quick as possible, and went to his Chamber. Mrs Washington was then up, and related to me his being taken ill about 2 or 3 o'clk, as before stated. I found him breathing with difficulty—and hardly able to utter a word intelligibly— I went out instantly—and wrote a line to Dr Craik, which I sent off by my Servant, ordering him to go with all the swiftness his horse could carry him, and immediately returned to the General's Chamber, where I found him in the same situation I had left him. A mixture of Molasses, Vinegar & butter was prepared, to try its effect in the throat; but he could not swallow a drop, whenever he attempted it he appeard to be distressed, convulsed, and almost suffocated. Mr Rawlins came in soon after sun rise—and prepared to bleed him. When the Arm was ready—the General, observing that Rawlins appeard to be agitated, said, as well as he could speak, "*don't be afraid*," and after the incision was made, he observed "*the oriface is not large enough*." However, the blood ran pretty freely. Mrs Washington, not knowing whether bleeding was proper or not in the Generals situation; beg'd that much might not be taken from him, lest it should be injurious, and desired me to stop it; but when I was about to untie the string, the general put up his hand to prevent it, and as soon as he could speak, he said "*more*."

Mrs W. being still uneasy lest too much blood should be taken, it was stop'd after about half a pint was taken from him. Finding that no relief was obtain from bleeding, and that nothing would go down the throat, I proposed bathing the throat externally with Salvalaltita, which was done, and in the operation, which was with the hand, and in the gentlest manner, he observed *'tis very sore*. A piece of flannel was then put round his neck His feet were also soaked in warm water. This, however, gave no relief. In the mean time, before Docter Craik arrivd, Mrs Washington requested me to send for Doctr Brown of Port Tobacco, whom Docter Craik had recommended to be called, if any case should ever occur that was seriously alarming. I dispatched a Messenger (Cyrus) to Dr Brown immediately (about nine o'clk)—Docter Craik came in soon after, and upon examining the General he put a blister of cantharides on the throat & took more blood from him, and had some Vinegar & hot water put into a Teapot, for the General to draw in the steam from the nozel—which he did, as well as he was able. He also orderd sage tea and Vinegar to be mixed for a Gargle. This the General used as often as desired; but when he held back his head to let it run down, it put him into great distress and almost produced suffocation. When the mixture came out of his mouth som[e] phlegm followed it, and he woud attempt to cough, which the Docter encouraged him to do as much as he could; but without effect, he could only make the attempt. About eleven o'clock Dr Dick was sent for. Docter Craik bled the General again about this time. No effect, however was produced by it, and he continued in the same state, unable to swallow anything. Docter Dick came in about 3 o'clk, and Dr Brown arrived soon after. Upon Dr Dick's seeing the Genl & consulting a few minutes with Dr Craik, he was bled again, the blood ran slowly—appeared very thick, and did not produce any symptoms of fainting.[6] Docter Brown came into the Chamber soon after, and upon feeling the Generals pulse &c. the Physicians went out together. Dr Craik soon after returned. The General could now swallow a little (about 4 o'clk)—Calomil & tarter em. were administered; but without any effect. About half past 4 o'clk, he desired me to ask Mrs Washington to come to his bed side—when he requested her to go down into his room & take from his desk two Wills which she would find there, and bring them to him, which she did. Upon looking at them he gave her [one] which he observed was useless, as it was superceeded by the other, and desired her to burn it, which she did, and then took the other & put it away. After this was done, I returned again to his bed side and took his hand. He said to me, "*I find I am going, my breath cannot continue long, I be-leived, from the first attack it would be fatal, do you arrange & record all my late Military letters & papers—arrange my accounts & settle my books, as you know more about them than anyone else, and let Mr Rawlins finish recording my other letters, which he has begun.*" He asked "*when Mr Lewis & Washington would return*"?[7] I told him I beleived about the 20th of the month. He made no reply to it.[8] The Physicians again came in (between 5 & 6 o'clk) and when they came to his bed side, Dr Craik asked him if he could sit up in the bed. He held out his hand to me & was raised up, when he said to the Physicians. "*I feel myself going, you had better not take any more trouble about me; but let me go off quietly; I cannot last long.*" They found what had been done was without effect—he laid down again and they retired ex-cepting Dr Craik. He then said to him, "*Docter, I die hard, but I am not afraid to go, I beleived from my first attack that I shd not survive it, my breath cannot last long.*" The Docter pressed his hand but could not utter a word. He retired from the bed side—and sat by the fire absorbed in grief. About 8 o'clk the Physicians again came into the Room, and applied blisters to his legs, but went out without a ray of hope.[9] From this time he appeared to breath with less diffi-culty than he had done; but was very restless, constantly changing his position to endeavour to get ease. I aided him all in my power, and was gratified in beleiving he felt it; for he would look upon me with his eyes speaking gratitude; but unable to utter a word with-out great distress. About ten o'clock he made several attempts to speak to me before he could effect it—at length, he said, "*I am just going, Have me decently buried, and do not let my body be put into the Vault in less than two days*[10] *after I am dead.*" I bowed assent. He looked at me again, and said "*Do you understand me*"—I replied Yes, Sir, "*Tis well,*" said he. About ten minutes before he expired his breathing became much easier—he lay quietly—he withdrew his hand from mine & felt his own pulse—I spoke to Dr Craik who sat by the fire—he came to the bed side. The Generals hand fell from his wrist—I took it in mine and laid it upon my breast— Dr Craik put his hands over his eyes and he expired without a struggle or a Sigh! While we were fixed in silent grief—Mrs Wash-ington asked, with a firm & collected Voice, "*Is he gone.*" I could not speak, but held up my hand as a signal that he was. "Tis well" said she, in a firm voice "Tis All now over. I have no more trials to pass through. I shall soon follow him! ["]

Occurences not noted in the preceding pages—

The General's servant, Christopher, attended his bed side & in the room, when he was sitting up, through his whole illness. About 8 o'clk in the Morng the General expressed a wish to get up. His clothes were put on, and he was led to a Chair, by the fire. He lay down again about two hours afterwards. A glister was administerd to him, by Dr Craik's directions, about one o'clock; but produced no effect. He was helped up again about 5 o'clock—and after sitting about an hour, he desired to be undressed and put in bed, which was done. Between the hours of 6 and nine o'clk, he several times asked what hour it was. During his whole illness, he spoke but seldom & with great difficulty and distress, and in so low & broken a voice as at times hardly to be understood. His patience, fortitude & resignation never foresook him for a moment. In all his distress he uttered not a sigh nor a complaint, always endeavoring to take what was offered him, or to do what was desired.

At the time of his decease Dr Craik & myself were in the situation before mentioned. Christopher was standing by the Bedside. Mrs Washington was sitting near the foot of the bed. Caroline, Charlotte, and some other of the servants were standing in the Room near the door. Mrs Forbes, the House-keeper, was frequently in the Room in the day & evening. In the afternoon the General observing that Christopher had been standing by his bed side for a long time—made a motion for him to sit in a chair which stood by the bedside.[11]

As soon as Dr Craik could speak, after the distressing scene was closed, he desired one of the servants to ask the Gentlemen below to come up stairs. When they came around the bed, I kissed the cold hand, which I had 'till then held, laid it down, went to the fire and was for some time lost in profound grief, until aroused by Christopher desiring me to take care of the General's keys and things which he had taken out of his pockets, and which Mrs Washington directed him to give to me. I wraped them up in the General's Handkerchief, and took them with me down stairs; About 12 o'clk the Corps was brought down and laid out in the large Room.[12]

II
The Diary Account

[Mount Vernon] Saturday Decr 14th 1799.
This day being marked by an event which will be memorable in the History of America, and perhaps of the world, I shall give a particular statement of it, to which I was an eye witness.

The last illness and Death of General Washington

On thursday Decr 12th—the General rode out to his farms about ten o'clock, and did not return home 'till past three. Soon after he went out the weather became very bad, rain, hail and snow falling alternately with a cold wind: When he came in, I carried some letters to him to frank, intending to send them to the Post Office in the Evening. He franked the letters; but said the weather was too bad to send a servant to the Office that Evening. I observed to him that I was afraid he had got wet; he said no, his great coat had kept him dry; but his neck appeared to be wet and the snow was hanging upon his hair. He came to dinner (which had been waiting for him) without changing his dress. In the evening he appeared as well as usual.

A heavy fall of snow took place on friday, which prevented the General from riding out as usual. He had taken cold (undoubtedly from being so much exposed the day before) and complained of a sore throat: he however went out in the afternoon into the ground between the House and the River to mark some trees which were to be cut down in the improvement of that spot. He had a Hoarseness, which increased in the evening; but he made light of it. In the evening the Papers were brought from the Post Office, and he sat in the parlour, with Mrs Washington & myself reading them till about nine o'clock—when Mrs W. went up into Mrs Lewis' room, who was confind in Child bed, and left the General & myself reading the papers. He was very chearful, and when he met with anything interesting or entertaini[n]g, he read it aloud as well as his hoarseness would permit him. He requested me to read to him the debates of the Virginia Assembly on the election of a Senator and a Governor; and on hearing Mr Madison's observations respecting Mr Monroe, he appeared much affected and spoke with some degree of asperity on the subject; which I endeavoured to moderate, as I always did on such occasions. On his retiring I observed to him that he had better take something to remove his cold; He answered no; "you know I never take anything for a Cold. Let it go as it came."

Between two & three o'clock on Saturday Morning, he awoke Mrs Washington, and told her he was very unwell, and had had an ague. She observed that he could scarcely speak and breathed with difficulty; and would have got up to call a Servant; but he would not permit her lest she should take cold. As soon as the day appeared, the Woman (Caroline) went into the Room to make a fire, and Mrs Washington sent her immediately to call me. I got up, put on my clothes as quickly as possible and went to his Chamber. Mrs Washington was then up, and related to me his being taken ill as before stated. I found the General breathing with difficulty, and hardly able to utter a word intelligibly. He desired that Mr Rawlins (one of the Overseers) might be sent for to bleed him before the Doctor could arrive. I dispatched a Servant instantly for Rawlins, and another for Dr Craik, and returned again to the General's Chamber, where I found him in the same situation as I had left him. A mixture of Molasses, Vinegar & butter was prepared to try its effects in the throat; but he could not swallow a drop; whenever he attempted it he appeared to be distressed, convulsed and almost suffocated. Rawlins came in soon after sun rise, and prepared to bleed him. When the Arm was ready the General observing that Rawlins appeared to be agitated—said, as well as he could speak *"Don't be afraid."* And after the incision was made, he observed *"The orifice is not large enough."* However the blood ran pretty freely. Mrs Washington not knowing whether bleeding was proper or not in the General's situation, begged that much might not be taken from him, lest it should be injurious, and desired me to stop it; but when I was about to untie the string, the General put up his hand to prevent it, and as soon as he could speak, said *"more, more"*! Mrs Washington being still very uneasy lest too much blood should be taken, it was stop'd after taking about half a pint. Finding that no relief was obtained from bleeding, and that nothing would go down the throat, I proposed bathing it externally with Salvilatila, which was done; and in the operation, which was with the hand, and in the gentlest manner, he observed *" 'tis very sore."* A pi[e]ce of flannel dip'd in salvilatila was put round his neck, and his feet bathed in warm water; but without affording any relief.

In the mean time; before Dr Craik arrived, Mrs Washington desired me to send for Dr Brown of Port Tobacco, whom Dr Craik had recommended to be called, if any case should ever occur that was seriously alarming. I dispatchd a Messenger (Cyrus) immediately for Dr Brown (between 8 & 9 o'clk). Dr Cra[i]k came in soon after, and upon examining the General, he put a blister of Cantharides on the Throat, took some more blood from him, and had a gargle of Vinegar, & sage tea, and ordered some Vinegar & hot water for him to inhale the steam, which he did; but in attempting to use the gargle he was almost suffocated. When the gargle came from his throat some ph[l]egm followed it, and he attempted to cough, which the Doctor encouraged him to do as much as possible; but he could only attempt it. About eleven o'clock Dr Craik requested that Dr Dick might be sent for, as he feared Dr Brown woud not come in time. A messenger was accordingly dispatched for him. About this time the General was bled again. No effect, however, was produced by it, and he remained in the same state, unable to swallow anything. A glister was administered about 12 o'clk, which produced an evacuation; but caused no alteration in his complaint.

Doctor Dick came in about 3 o'clk, and Dr Brown arrived soon after. Upon Dr Dick's seeing the General, and consulting a few minutes with Dr Craik, he was bled again; the blood came very slow, was thick, and did not produce any symptoms of fainting. Dr Brown came into the Chamber soon after; and upon feeling the General's pulse &c. the Physicians went out together. Dr Craik returned soon after. The Genl could now swallow a little. Calomil & tarter em. were administered; but without any effect.

About half past 4 o'clk he desired me to call Mrs Washington to his bed side, when he requested her to go down into his room, and take from his desk two Wills which she would find there, and bring them to him; which she did. Upon looking at them he gave her one, which he observed was useless, as being superseded by the other, and desired her to burn it; which she did, and took the other and put it into her closet.

After this was done, I returned to his bed side and took his hand. He said to me, "*I find I am going, my breathe cannot last long; I beleived from the first that the disorder would prove fatal. Do you arrange & record all my late military letters and papers—arrange my accounts and settle my books, as you know more about them than any one else, and let*

Mr Rawlins finish recording my other letters which he has begun." I told him this should be done. He then asked if I recollected anything which it was essential for him to do, as he had but a very short time to continue among us. I told him I could recollect nothing; but that I hoped he was not so near his end; he observed, smiling, that he certainly was, and that as it was the debt which must all pay, he looked to the event with perfect resignation.

In the course of the afternoon, he appeard to be in great pain & distress, from the difficulty of breathing, and frequently changd his posture in the bed. on these occasions I lay upon the bed & endavourd to raise him, & turn him with as much ease as possible. He appeared penetrated with gratitude for my attentions, & often said, I am afraid I shall fatigue you too much; and upon my assuring him that I could feel nothing but a wish to give him ease; he replied "*Well! it is a debt we must pay to each other, and I hope when you want aid of this kind you will find it.*"

He asked when Mr Lewis & Washington Custis would return. (they were in New Kent.) I told him about the 20th of the month.

About 5 o'clk Dr Craik came again into the Room & upon going to the bed side, the Genl said to him, *Doctor, I die hard; but I am not afraid to go, I beleived from my first attack, that I should not survive it; my breath cannot last long.*

The Doctor pressed his hand; but could not utter a word. He retired from the bed side & sat by the fire absorbed in grief.

Between 5 & 6 o'clk Dr Dick & Dr Brown came into the room, and with Dr Craik went to the bed; when Dr Craik asked him if he could sit up in the bed. He held out his hand & I raised him up. He then said to the Physicians, "*I feel myself going, I thank you for your attentions; but I pray you to take no more trouble about me, let me go off quietly; I cannot last long.*" They found that all which had been done was without effect; he laid down again, and all retired, exceptg Dr Craik. He continued in the same situation, uneasy & restless; but without complaining; frequently asking what hour it was. When I helped him to move at this time he did not speak; but looked at me with strong expressions of gratitude.

About 8 oclk the Physicians came again into the room & applied blisters and cataplasms of wheat bran to his legs & feet; after which they went out (except Dr Craik) without a ray of hope.

I went out about this time, and wrote a line to Mr Law & Mr

Peter, requesting them to come with their wives (Mrs Washingtons Granddaughters) as soon as possible to Mt Vernon.

About ten o'clk he made several attempts to speak to me before he could effect it; at length he said, "*I am just going! Have me decently buried; and do not let my body be put into the vault in less than three days after I am dead.*" I bowed assent; for I could not speak. He then looked at me again and said, "*Do you understand me?*["] I replied yes! "*Tis well*" said he.

About ten minutes before he expired (which was between ten & eleven o'clk) h[is] breathing became easier; he lay qu[i]etly; he withdrew his hand from mine, and felt his own pulse. I saw his countenance change. I spoke to Dr Craik, who sat by the fire; he came to the bed side. The General's hand fell from his wrist— I took it in mine and put it into my bosom. Dr Craik put his hands over his Eyes *and he expired without a struggle or a sigh!*

While we were fixed in silent grief, Mrs Washington (who was sitting at the foot of the bed) asked, with a firm & collected voice, *Is he gone?* I could not speak; but held up my hand as a signal that he was no more. "*Tis well,* said she in the same voice, *All is now over, I shall soon follow him! I have no more trials to pass through!*["]

Occurrances not noted in the preceding Narattive.

The General's Servant *Christopher* was in the room through the day; and in the afternoon the General, directed him to sit down, as he had been standing almost the whole day. He did so.

About 8 o'clk in the Morng he expressed a desire to get up. His Clothes were put on and he was led to a chair by the fire. He found no relief from that position, and lay down again about 10 o'clk.

About 5 P.M. he was helped up again & after sitting about half an hour desired to be undressed & put in bed; which was done.

During his whole illness he spoke but seldom, and with great difficulty and distress; and in so low & broken a voice as at times hardly to be understood. His patience, fortitude and resignation never forsook him for a moment. In all his distress he uttered not a sigh nor a complaint; always endeavouring (from a sense of duty as it appeared) to take what was offered him, and to do as he was desired by the Physicians.

At the time of his decease Dr Craik and myself were in the situation beforementioned; Mrs Washington was sitting near the foot of the bed. Christopher was standing by the bedside. Caroline, Molly & Charlotte were in the room standing near the door. Mrs Forbes, the House Keeper, was frequently in the room during the day and evening.

As soon as Dr Craik could speak, after the distressing scene was closed, he desired one of the Servants to ask the Gentln below to come up stairs. When they came to the bed side; I kissed the cold hand, which I had held to my bosom; laid it down & went to the other end of the room; where I was for some time lost in profound grief; until aroused by Christopher desiri[n]g me to take care of the General's keys and other things which were taken out of his pockets; and which Mrs Washington directed him to give to me. I wrapped them in the General's handkerchief & took them with me to my room.

About 12 oclk the Corps was brought down stairs and laid out in the large Room.

AD, MiU-C; AD, PHi. Tobias Lear wrote two accounts of the illness and death of Washington. The original account, now at the William L. Clements Library in Ann Arbor, Michigan, and printed first of the two here, Lear indicates was written on 15 Dec., the day after Washington's death. The other account, which Lear entered in his diary under the date 14 Dec., was drawn from his original account and is printed second here. The second, or diary account, which is deposited in the Pennsylvania Historical Society in Philadelphia, is in part a verbatim copy of the original account, but Lear has changed the timing and sequence of events in a number of cases, altered quotations and introduced new ones, omitted bits of information, and added a good deal of new information. James Craik endorsed the diary account on 15 Dec. as correct, "so far as I can recollect," indicating that it was written shortly after the original account and suggesting that it was essentially an amplification and corrected version of the original. But as the diary account with its embellishments was a revision of the original to be read by others, it was the editors' decision to print both versions, as one document. Jared Sparks published Lear's diary version in 1837 in his edition of the *Writings of Washington*, 1:555–62; and in 1893 Worthington Chauncey Ford printed Lear's original account of Washington's death in his *Writings of Washington*, 14:245–55, where he "inserted in brackets the additional sentences contained in Sparks' printing of the Lear manuscript."

1. Washington's diary entry for 12 Dec. reads: "Morning Cloudy—Wind at No. Et. & Mer. 33. A large circle round the Moon last Night. About 1 oclock it began to snow—soon after to Hail and then turned to a settled cold Rain. Mer. 28 at Night" (*Diaries*, 6:378).

2. Washington signed two letters dated 12 Dec. drafted by Lear, one to Charles Alder and another to Alexander Hamilton.

3. Lear records at this place in his diary account of the death that Washington went out on Friday afternoon "into the ground between the House and the River." Washington reports in his diary that it was snowing in the morning and was about "3 Inches deep," but at about 4 o'clock "it became perfectly clear" (*Diaries*, 6:378).

4. For Lear's references to Washington's negative reaction at this time to the reports of James Madison's praise of James Monroe after Madison nominated Monroe for the office of governor on 5 Dec., see Lear's diary account of the death. Madison's remarks as reported in the Richmond *Argus* are printed in Mattern, *Madison Papers*, 17:286–87.

5. Caroline, a dower slave, had been a housemaid at Mount Vernon for many years. George Rawlins, the overseer of Union farm at Mount Vernon, was the brother of Washington's clerk, Albin Rawlins.

6. Dr. James Craik, Washington's old and close friend and his physician, and Dr. Elisha Cullen Dick were both from Alexandria. Dr. Gustavus Richard Brown lived across the river at Port Tobacco, Maryland. In a letter to Dr. Craik on 2 Jan. 1800, Dr. Brown was high in his praise of Dr. Dick, and wrote: "You must remember he was averse to bleeding the General, and I have often thought that if we had acted according to his suggestion when he said, 'he needs all his strength— bleeding will diminish it,' and taken no more blood from him, our good friend might have been alive now" (quoted in a note in Ford, *Writings of Washington*, 14: 257). Lear's servant who was sent to summon Dr. Craik was named Charles. Cyrus, the messenger sent to Dr. Brown, was a 14-year-old dower slave who acted as a postilion.

7. Unless a letter book has been lost, the last letter that Albin Rawlins entered in the last of the letter books, which date back to 1754, was Washington's letter to Secretary of State Timothy Pickering of 10 Feb. 1799. It also would appear that most of the letters written to Washington after the middle of September 1799 were not filed and have been lost. About a dozen or so letters written to him about officers' commissions and winter quarters for the troops and several others, dated between 20 Sept. and 1 Dec. 1799, have survived, but at least twenty-eight other letters are known to have been received by him during this time and are missing. During the same period in the fall of the preceding year, he is known to have received more than eighty letters, seventy-six of which have been found. For reference to the disposition of Washington's papers, see note 13 to his Last Will and Testament, printed above.

8. In his diary account, Lear adds here further details about his nursing of Washington during the afternoon and quotes Washington as saying: "*Well! it is a debt we must pay to each other, and I hope when you want aid of this kind you will find it.*"

9. On 21 Dec. Dr. Craik and Dr. Dick wrote an account of Washington's death in which they described what was done during the day in the attempt to save his life: "The necessity of blood-letting suggesting itself to the General, he procured a bleeder in the neighborhood, who took from his arm in the night twelve or fourteen ounces of blood. He could not by any means be prevailed on by the family to send for the attending physician till the following morning, who arrived at Mount Vernon at about 11 o'clock on Saturday. Discovering the case to be

highly alarming, and foreseeing the fatal tendency of the disease, two consulting physicians were immediately sent for, who arrived, one at half after three, and the other at four o'clock in the afternoon: in the mean time were employed two pretty copious bleedings, a blister was applied to the part affected, two moderate doses of calomel were administered, which operated on the lower intestines, but all without any perceptible advantage, the respiration becoming still more difficult and distressing. Upon the arrival of the first of the consulting physicians, it was agreed, as there were yet no signs of accumulation in the bronchial vessels of the lungs, to try the result of another bleeding, when about thirty-two ounces of blood were drawn, without the smallest apparent alleviation of the disease. Vapours of vinegar and water were frequently inhaled, ten grains of calomel were given, succeeded by repeated doses of emetic tartar, amounting in all to five or six grains, with no other effect than a copious discharge from the bowels. The powers of life seemed now manifestly yielding to the force of the disorder; blisters were applied to the extremities, together with a cataplasm of bran and vinegar to the throat. Speaking, which was painful from the beginning, now became almost impracticable; respiration grew more and more contracted and imperfect, till half after 11 on Saturday night, retaining the full possession of his intellect— when he expired without a struggle" (Ford, *Writings of Washington*, 14:255–57).

10. As he does here, Lear in his letter to his mother of 16 Dec. quotes Washington as specifying that he not be placed in the vault for at least two days; in his diary account, he quotes him as saying three days. His body was placed in the vault on 18 Dec. (Tobias Lear to Mary Lear, 16 Dec. 1799, ViMtV).

11. Christopher (Christopher Sheels), a 24-year-old dower slave, was Washington's body servant. Charlotte was Mrs. Washington's seamstress and a dower slave. Mrs. Eleanor Forbes, about fifty years old, had come to Mount Vernon in December 1797 as housekeeper, having formerly served in the same position for Gov. Robert Brooke in Richmond. For a further identification of Christopher and for the letter relating his recent plan to escape by ship from Mount Vernon, see GW to Roger West, 19 Sept. 1799 and note 1 of that document. The dower slave Molly, a cook, is named in the diary account.

12. Lear recorded in his diary account that early Sunday morning, at Mrs. Washington's behest, he sent instructions to Alexandria for a coffin to be made for a body 6 feet 3½ inches long, 1 foot 9 inches "Across the Shoulders," and 2 feet "Across the Elbows." Upon the departure after breakfast of the two physicians, Elisha Dick and Gustavus Brown, Lear paid each $40 for his services. Lear then wrote letters to President John Adams, generals Alexander Hamilton and Charles Cotesworth Pinckney, and to Washington's nephews and several other close relatives telling them of Washington's death. During the day Martha Washington's granddaughters Patsy Peter and Eliza Law arrived with their husbands and Dr. William Thornton from Georgetown and the Federal City respectively. At the urging of Dr. Craik and Dr. Thornton, it was decided not to delay the burial until the Washington kin could arrive but instead to hold the funeral on Wednesday, the fourth day after his death.

On Monday Lear "directed the people" at Mount Vernon to open the bricked-up family vault, clear "the rubbish from about it," and build a door to replace the bricks. Upon learning that the Fairfax County militia and the freemasons and the Alexandria town officers were insistent upon "attending" Washington's "body to the Grave," Lear gave orders that provisions be prepared "for a large number of people." On Mrs. Washington's instructions, he also informed certain neighbors and close friends that the time of the funeral had been set at 12 noon and asked the Rev. Thomas Davis "to read the Service." The coffin, made of mahogany and lined with lead, arrived by coach from Alexandria at midday on Tuesday. By 11 o'clock on Wednesday people had begun to assemble, but it was not until 3 o'clock that the procession "moved out of the Gate to the left wing of the House and proceeded round in front of the lawn & down to the Vault on the right wing of the House." At the vault, before the body was placed in the tomb, "The Revd Mr Davis read the Service & pronounced a short extempore speech."

Index

NOTE: Identifications of persons, places, and things in previous volumes of the *Retirement Series* are noted within parentheses.

Abbay (dower slave; Sall Twine's daughter): at Mount Vernon, 535

Abram (slave; Nancy's husband): at Mount Vernon, 531, 540

Adam (slave; Alice's son): at Mount Vernon, 532

Adams, Abednego: slaves of, 533; id., 541

Adams, Daniel Jenifer: and GW's Charles County (Md.) tract, 515, 523–24

Adams, John, 11, 132, 202, 254; and Caleb Gibbs, 5, 6; and officers for New Army, 10, 48, 50, 52, 153, 165, 288, 301, 302; resolution in support of, 14; and organization of New Army, 33, 34, 46, 179–80, 282; and organization of Provisional Army, 39–40, 63, 64, 70, 71–72, 78–79, 161; and officers for Provisional Army, 46–47, 62, 125, 126, 127, 174, 178, 190–91, 241; and Indian policy, 98; and relations with France, 155; Philadelphia house of, 188; and naval appointments, 191, 354; and U.S. envoys to France, 193, 220, 221, 224, 233, 238–39, 253, 330, 343–44, 354, 355, 356–57, 362–63, 384, 397–99; GW criticizes, 203, 239; and allegations of government corruption, 222–23, 401, 402; and districting of Federal City, 227; criticism of, 236, 452; travels to Trenton, 343; and U.S. relations with Saint Domingue, 400; speech of, 439–40; and loan for Federal City, 450; and British embassy in Federal City, 451; and GW's papers, 501; and Mount Vernon tomb, 511;

and GW's death, 554; *letters to*: from James McHenry, 34; from Timothy Pickering, 222–23; from Tobias Lear, 554

Adams, John Quincy: and U.S. relations with Prussia, 220; *letters from*: to Timothy Pickering, 220; *letters to*: from William Vans Murray, 58–59, 261

Adams, William, 193; and GW's Four Mile Run tract, 24

Addison, Alexander (*see* 2:277–78): and Millers Run tract, 113, 159, 175–77, 185, 196, 207, 395, 423; *letters from*: to GW, 175–77, 395–96; *letters to*: from GW, 423

Adlum, John: and rank in New Army, 284, 303

Agnes (Aggy; slave; Will's wife): at Mount Vernon, 530, 535; children of, 535

Agnes (dower slave; Sambo's wife): at Mount Vernon, 528, 534; children of, 533, 534

Agriculture: in England, 31; Hessian fly, 31, 228–29, 256, 440; manures, 31, 145, 146, 230, 306, 309, 332, 458, 462, 463, 464, 465, 468, 469–70, 471, 475, 476; squirrels, 465, 467

crops: wheat, 22, 31, 102–3, 145, 146, 147, 319, 440, 458, 462, 465, 467, 468, 469, 472, 473, 474; hay, 29, 146, 148, 228, 472; barley, 31; clover, 31, 146, 148, 455, 459, 462, 463, 464, 468, 469, 470; oats, 31, 145, 146, 147, 148, 257, 458, 459, 469, 470, 473, 475; turnips, 31, 458, 459, 465, 469, 473, 474; tobacco, 75, 229; corn, 145, 146, 147, 148, 229, 257, 267, 294, 458, 462, 465, 467, 468, 469, 472, 473, 474, 475, 476;